PHILOSOPHICAL FOUNDATIONS OF EUROPEAN UNION LAW

PHILOSOPHICAL FOUNDATIONS OF EUROPEAN UNION LAW

EDITED BY

JULIE DICKSON

AND

PAVLOS ELEFTHERIADIS

OXFORD

UNIVERSITY PRESS

OXFORD
UNIVERSITY PRESS

Great Clarendon Street, Oxford, OX2 6DP,
United Kingdom

Oxford University Press is a department of the University of Oxford.
It furthers the University's objective of excellence in research, scholarship,
and education by publishing worldwide. Oxford is a registered trade mark of
Oxford University Press in the UK and in certain other countries

British Library Cataloguing in Publication Data
Data available

ISBN 978-0-19-958877-0

Printed and bound by
CPI Group (UK) Ltd, Croydon, CR0 4YY

In memory of our dear friend, Amanda Perreau-Saussine

CONTENTS

PART III: CONSTITUTIONAL VIRTUES

CONTRIBUTORS

Ari Afilalo, Professor of Law, Rutgers-Camden School of Law.

Anthony Arnull, Barber Professor of Jurisprudence, University of Birmingham.

Keith Culver, Professor and Director, Okanagan Sustainability Institute, University of British Columbia.

Geert De Baere, Assistant Professor of International Law and EU Law at the Faculty of Law and Senior Member at the Leuven Centre for Global Governance Studies, University of Leuven.

Julie Dickson, Faculty of Law, University of Oxford, and Fellow and Tutor in Law, Somerville College, Oxford.

Sionaidh Douglas-Scott, Professor of European and Human Rights Law, University of Oxford.

Pavlos Eleftheriadis, Faculty of Law, University of Oxford, and Fellow and Tutor in Law, Mansfield College, Oxford.

Michael Giudice, Associate Professor of Philosophy, York University, Toronto, Canada.

Mattias Kumm, Professor for 'Rule of Law in the Age of Globalization', Social Science Research Center & Humboldt University, Berlin, and Inge Rennert Professor of Law, New York University School of Law.

George Letsas, Reader in Philosophy of Law and Human Rights, University College London.

Kalypso Nicolaïdis, Professor of International Relations, University of Oxford.

Dennis Patterson, Chair in Legal Theory and Legal Philosophy at the European University Institute, Florence; Board of Governors Professor of Law and philosophy, Rutgers University, New Jersey, USA; Professor of International Trade and Jurisprudence, Swansea University.

Andrea Sangiovanni, Lecturer, Department of Philosophy, King's College London.

Takis Tridimas, Sir John Lubbock Professor of Banking Law, Queen Mary University of London; Professor and Nancy A Patterson Distinguished Faculty Scholar, Pennsylvania State University.

W.J. Waluchow, Professor of Philosophy and Senator William McMaster Chair in Constitutional Studies, McMaster University.

J.H.H. Weiler, NYU School of Law.

Lorenzo Zucca, Reader in Jurisprudence, King's College London.

1

Introduction: The Puzzles of European Union Law

Julie Dickson and Pavlos Eleftheriadis

This is a collection of new and original essays discussing the philosophical foundations of European Union law. They are original in two senses. First, they seek to offer novel understandings of important constitutional and institutional aspects of EU law. Second, they show that the European Union is itself a new subject matter for legal and political philosophy: one which casts old problems in a very new light.

1 The Nature of the Questions

In the not so distant past, legal and political philosophy examined the law of states. This was the primary subject matter, for example, of works by Hans Kelsen, Alf Ross, HLA Hart, Lon Fuller, Ronald Dworkin, Joseph Raz, John Finnis, and of many other authors whose writings form the canon of contemporary philosophy of law. Until recently at least, few of them ventured systematically to discuss legal phenomena and institutions beyond state law. When they did so, they sought in large part to assess the international domain by identifying differences from and similarities with the national domain, which they took to be the paradigm case. HLA Hart, for example, expressed doubts about the nature of international law as law, because it did not sufficiently resemble national law in certain relevant respects, and Hans Kelsen proposed that the best account of international law was that of a national legal system with global scope.[1]

Those days are now firmly gone. International organizations and multilateral international treaties and institutions—such as those associated with the UN, the WTO, the IMF, the World Bank and, of course, the European Union—have proliferated and are now constituted by rich and complex legal materials. They have created

---

[1] HLA Hart, *The Concept of Law*, 2nd edn, (Oxford: Oxford University Press, 1994), ch X; Hans Kelsen, *Pure Theory of Law*, Max Knight (trans) (Berkeley, CA: University of California Press, 1967), 328–44.

real and practically relevant law that is applied by pluralistic and decentralized legal communities. These non-state laws and institutions have acquired a prominent role in political negotiations and in legal practice. They strongly influence both domestic public affairs and business transactions. Such phenomena are now offering a distinct paradigm of their own, a thriving example of rich and effective non-state law.

Legal and political philosophy started considering such phenomena more seriously as the relevant changes gathered pace. There is already a great deal of new and interesting work on the subject.[2] Nevertheless, the theoretical task of adequately understanding and evaluating such phenomena has proven remarkably difficult. Our established analytical tools, designed to characterize national institutions and structures, may prove too crude to account for the complexity of these new global arrangements. At the very least, to say that the international resembles the national but that it is a less complete instance, is not good enough. What the study of international institutions has shown is that the phenomena may not be as similar to national legal phenomena as some earlier theorists thought. The international appears to be a distinct domain and may thus require distinct concepts and tools in order adequately to understand it.

The international polity which exhibits this distinctness at its clearest is the European Union. Part international organization and part federation, the EU possesses distinctive institutions with executive, legislative, and judicial functions. What is the Union? Is it a species of international organization, a federation of some kind, or does it possess a *sui generis* supra-national character that defies easy, or perhaps any, categorization? What exactly is the status and function of the Court of Justice in the jurisdictions that jointly constitute the EU? What bearing does the distinctive character of the Article 267 TFEU preliminary ruling procedure have on questions such as whether the EU possesses a single legal system, and whether any such legal system now encompasses the legal systems of the Member States?

The EU recognizes distinct sources of law and has developed its own legal doctrines regarding the far-reaching impact and enforceability of its laws, such as the doctrines of direct effect, supremacy, and Member State liability. These doctrines have, to a significant extent, been accepted by the courts and institutions of the Member States such as to create a European area of law and institutions where the international and the national merge. As a result, the Union exercises considerable political power over the Member States and has far-reaching effects on the lives of Union and Member State citizens. The Union is also increasingly eager to play a meaningful role on the international stage in addressing contemporary challenges of security and defence.

---

[2] See for example S Besson and J Tasioulas (eds), *The Philosophy of International* Law (Oxford: Oxford University Press, 2010), N Tsagourias (ed), *Transnational Constitutionalism: International and European Perspectives* (Cambridge: Cambridge University Press, 2007), F Tesón, *A Philosophy of International Law* (Boulder, CO: Westview Press, 1998), A Buchanan, *Justice, Legitimacy, and Self-Determination: Moral Foundations for International Law* (Oxford: Oxford University Press, 2004). For the political philosophy of international relations see for example CR Beitz, *Political Theory and International Relations*, 2nd edn (Princeton, NJ: Princeton University Press, 1999), Onora O'Neill, *Bounds of Justice* (Cambridge: Cambridge University Press, 2000).

Other questions arise out of the ambitious and ever-evolving interpretation of the Union's institutional framework by the Court of Justice (and other EU institutions). What does it mean to say, as the Court frequently does, that the EU and its law are 'autonomous'? How seriously are we to take the Court's claims that EU law represents a 'new legal order', and constitutes a distinct legal system? Are traditional international law distinctions between monism and dualism helpful in understanding relations between EU law and national law? And what happens to Member States' national constitutions and legal systems if we take the claims of the Court of Justice at face value? Is the Court evolving the principle of primacy as a successor to more traditional EU categories of direct effect, indirect effect, and incidental effect, as some prominent legal scholars believe? In light of the Court's sometimes ambitious interpretation of the citizenship provisions in the Treaties, and in light of the concept of citizenship more generally, what are the rights and duties inherent in EU citizenship, and what duties, if any, do citizens of one Member State owe to the citizens of other Member States? In various ways that these questions are set to reveal, the EU is special and its law defies traditional categories of legal and political analysis.

Such questions are complex, and any answers to them likely to be deeply contested. They are philosophical and legal at the same time. Although a great deal of existing EU scholarship attempts to address aspects of these challenges, much of this scholarship fails to address the deeper philosophical difficulties and does not adequately draw on and develop insights from the philosophy of law and political philosophy. Similarly, much insightful work hailing from legal and political philosophers regarding inter-national institutions has paid insufficient attention to the European Union as a distinct kind of supra-national legal project. Jeremy Waldron has recently claimed that legal philosophers' failure adequately to analyse and explain aspects of international law is 'nothing short of scandalous', and that such theorising is 'the issue of the hour'.[3] As regards EU law, it is our belief that this international polity remains particularly inadequately theorized, and that the time has come for more sustained philosophical consideration in this regard.

This book accordingly brings together a diverse group of legal and political philoso-phers, constitutional theorists, and legal scholars, and invites them to reflect on certain challenges facing the contemporary European Union. We hope that the book will be read as a whole. Its contributors bring different skills and approaches and the chapters are intended to complement one other. Some contributors would identify themselves primarily as legal scholars and bring to the project a much-needed depth of under-standing of how EU law actually works. Others would more readily self-identify as legal and political philosophers who have come to see the EU as a fascinating experi-ment and novel testing-ground for their theories. In our view, it is in virtue of this distinctive combination of rich legal understanding and analysis, and penetrating

---

[3] J Waldron, 'Hart and the Principles of Legality' in C Grant, B Colburn, A Hatzistavrou, and MH Kramer (eds), *The Legacy of H.L.A. Hart, Legal, Moral and Political Philosophy* (Oxford: Oxford University Press, 2008), 69.

theoretical insights from legal and political philosophy, that progress will be made in understanding, evaluating, and assessing the EU and its law.

The book is divided into three parts. The first part discusses whether there is an EU legal *system*, and considers what the character of any such system might be. The second part discusses the general political and political-philosophical principles according to which we should justify aspects of the European Union and its institutions. The third part concerns the constitutional virtues that underlie and inform European Union treaties and law at this particular stage in the Union's development.

2 Philosophical and Constitutional Foundations of the Contemporary EU: Some Intellectual Context

In Section 3 below, we present some main topics and points of argument from the contributions to this volume. Our view, however, is that, prior to introducing our readers to the particular essays featuring here, it is valuable to discuss in more general terms the intellectual and other background informing the questions which those chapters discuss. In the remainder of the present section, then, we take each of the three main areas which the book addresses in turn—the legal system, political foundations, and constitutional virtues—and offer some thoughts on the philosophical and constitutional issues, and on the scholarship attempting to address those issues, which we regard as particularly important in understanding and evaluating the contemporary EU.

(A) The Legal System

The first part of the book discusses whether there is an EU legal system, and, if any such system can be said to exist, the relation of that system to the legal systems of the Union's constituent Member States. These issues require us to revisit some fundamental jurisprudential questions concerning the nature of law. Many theorists believe that the nature of law and the idea of a legal system are closely connected. Others find the idea of a legal system consisting of individuated and legally validated norms an unfortunate misconception. So when we ask, 'Is there an EU legal system?', we bring these wider questions in general philosophy of law to bear upon the law of the EU.[4]

It has long been claimed in much contemporary legal philosophy that in order adequately to understand the nature of law, we must consider and explain its apparently

---

[4] The legal philosopher who examined this question with the greatest thoroughness and whose work has had most lasting effect is Neil MacCormick His major work in this regard is N MacCormick, *Questioning Sovereignty* (Oxford: Oxford University Press, 1999). See also N MacCormick (ed), *Constructing Legal Systems: 'European Union' in Legal Theory* (Springer Press, 1997).

systemic character. That is to say, we must explain law not merely by investigating what it is for something to be a single law, but by considering and seeking to explicate what it is for laws to be grouped together into and hence to be members of distinct legal *systems*. Indeed for some legal philosophers, an adequate understanding of what a law is can *only* be achieved by understanding what a legal system is.[5] Wherever we stand on this latter claim, however, it is a widely held view that we think and speak of the law both of our own and of other societies as forming distinct legal systems, and that we regard the demarcation between one legal system and another as important.

But perhaps it is only in a world where the political landscape is dominated by states, and legal norms governing a given population are primarily generated and applied within the state in which that population resides, that it seems natural to conceive of each polity as possessing a body of law with its own norms, institutions, and criteria of system membership, and which is differentiated from the legal systems of other such states. Does the idea of laws being grouped together into distinct legal systems have any role to play in the supra-national context of the contemporary European Union, and, in particular, in considering the legal space occupied by both EU law and national law, a space where legal norms and institutions may overlap, interact, and conflict in complex and evolving ways?

As was noted in Section 1 above, in his 1961 book *The Concept of Law*, HLA Hart noted that, at that time, many doubts existed as regards whether international law sufficiently resembled municipal law in relevant respects in order properly to be thought of as law. In a wide-ranging discussion, Hart considers such doubts in depth although he does not reach a definitive conclusion as regards the status of international law as it stood in 1961.[6] Arguably, however, even having such a discussion, and taking seriously the view that perhaps international law is not properly viewed as law, radically contradicts some of the deepest constitutional assumptions of EU law as interpreted by the Court of Justice from the 1960s onwards. The Court of Justice famously declared in *Costa v ENEL* that:

> By contrast with ordinary international treaties, the EEC Treaty has created its own legal system which, on the entry into force of the Treaty, became an integral part of the legal systems of the Member States and which their courts are bound to apply...
>
> By creating a Community of unlimited duration, having its own institutions, its own personality, its own legal capacity and capacity of representation on the international plane and, more particularly, real powers stemming from a limitation of sovereignty or a transfer of powers from the states to the Community, the Member States have limited their sovereign rights, albeit within limited fields, and have thus created a body of law which binds both their nationals and themselves.[7]

---

[5] J Raz, *The Concept of a Legal System*, 2nd edn (Oxford: Clarendon Press, 1980), *passim*, but see eg 2 for an explicit statement of this claim.

[6] HLA Hart, *The Concept of Law*, 2nd edn (see n 1), ch X.

[7] Case 6/64 *Flaminio Costa v ENEL* [1964] ECR 585.

This doctrine of a 'new legal order' or 'new legal system' has been the centrepiece of EU constitutional law, but poses many theoretical difficulties. What kind of system is the EU legal system? How autonomous is it from that of the Member States?

Some legal scholars have embraced the position that it is autonomous. René Barents has argued in detail for the position that the Community legal system is autonomous from those of the Member States.[8] But after offering a detailed analysis of the Court of Justice's case law, Barents noticed that the position was highly ambitious. It entailed the following:

> The autonomy of Community law means that in every respect this law exercises its legal effects in an independent manner. Of course this does not mean that it is independent from 'facts', but that it is independent from any other system or source of law. Consequently, according to this concept, the contents of Community law, i.e., its scope and legal effects (creation, validity, application and interpretation) are dependent on and governed by only itself... Because of its autonomous position (as a consequence of its 'Community' character), Community law is valid and applicable in the territory of that Member State exclusively by virtue of itself.[9]

Other commentators have offered critiques of this analysis. For example, Bruno de Witte, in the course of commenting on the 'circularity' of the doctrine of supremacy, observed that:

> the view that supremacy does not set EC law completely apart from the general body of international law finds additional support in the continuing two-dimensional character of supremacy: it is a legal reality only to the extent that national courts accept their 'mandate', and the practice shows that this acceptance, so far, is selective and generally based on the national courts' own constitutional terms.[10]

De Witte has also claimed that the arguments of the Court of Justice about the 'special nature of the European Community' may have been 'overstated', and that its arguments were 'needed more to convince the national judicial interlocutors of the Court than to justify the formulation of the principles themselves'.[11]

Neil MacCormick, too, has argued that the idea of the 'autonomy' of EU law may not be all that it seems, or that it appears to the Court of Justice. He observed that the effective legislature for the Community is the Council of Ministers, 'whose members are identifiable only by reference to the place they hold according to state-systems

---

[8] R Barents, *The Autonomy of Community Law* (The Hague: Kluwer Law International, 2004). See also R Barents, 'The Precedence of EU Law from the Perspective of Constitutional Pluralism' (2009) 5 *European Constitutional Law Review* 421. In the 2009 article, Barents endorses pluralism as the proper framework within which 'autonomy' is to be understood.

[9] Barents (2004), see n 8, 253.

[10] B De Witte, 'The Nature of the Legal Order' in P Craig and G de Búrca (eds), *The Evolution of EU Law* (Oxford: Oxford University Press, 1999), 177, 209.

[11] De Witte, 208. For some more recent complexities in this regard, see A Arnull, 'Me and My Shadow: The European Court of Justice and the Disintegration of European Union Law' (2008) 31 *Fordham International Law Journal* 1174.

of law'.[12] He similarly noted that the process of constitutional amendment for the Union, which turns on the creation and amendment of treaties of public international law by an 'intergovernmental conference', means that the most essential laws of the Union remain 'a process of treaty-making among member states', which by definition is not controlled by the European courts.[13] MacCormick therefore concluded that the position that the legal orders of the Member States are intended to 'retain validity' only through the mediation of EU law was questionable.[14]

These theoretical doubts are strengthened by the case law of the major national courts. Most national courts, including the British House of Lords (now Supreme Court), and the German Federal Constitutional Court, have claimed that EU law is not autonomous in the above sense, but is rather dependent for its national validity on its reception via constitutional principles of national law. Their reasoning varies, although it always proceeds from an interpretation of the national constitution. These courts have ruled that the effect of EU law in the United Kingdom or in Germany depends on both EU and national constitutional law as interpreted and applied by national courts.[15] If we give this national legal discourse its due, then it appears that the idea of an autonomous EU legal system faces many challenges.

Despite these challenges, however, it must be acknowledged that the EU has constitutional sources in its founding treaties where its powers and principles are demarcated. In addition, the EU has officials that both create and apply EU law in the guise of the Commission, the Council, and the European Court of Justice. So it may indeed be possible to argue that the EU has a legal system of its own. But then a new question arises. What happens to the legal systems of the Member States once this new legal system is set up alongside them or indeed above them? Do we have: (i) one overarching EU legal system, (ii) merely the twenty-seven legal systems of the Union's Member States, with EU law as an aspect of each of those, or (iii) twenty-eight systems—those of the Member States plus one, the EU legal system? Moreover, how are we to understand the many and various interactions and interrelations between such systems?

These novel questions have prompted a number of different answers. One answer on offer is that the best understanding of the EU legal system is in 'monist' terms. According to this answer the EU Treaties form a foundation of a single legal system or order which sets out standards that all other courts and legal officials are bound to follow. One sophisticated defence of this view has been offered by Armin von Bogdandy, who has been at the forefront of the theoretical project of articulating a coherent constitutional law of the EU. In his essay 'Founding Principles', von Bogdandy gives a complex analysis of EU principles of public law that determine the general framework of EU law just as ordinary constitutional principles do in the

---

[12] N MacCormick, *Questioning Sovereignty*, see n 4, 117.

[13] MacCormick, 117.

[14] MacCormick, 117.

[15] The relevant case law is discussed in several of the essays in the first section of the book. The principle that the legal validity of EU law in the UK is premised upon aspects of the UK's constitutional order is restated in the recent European Union Act 2011, s 18.

domestic case.[16] His conclusion is that the EU Treaties have a constitutional character such that: a) they organize the positive legal material;[17] b) they supply arguments for a creative application of the law;[18] and c) they maintain law as 'social infrastructure'.[19] They do this by outlining positive law:

> [They are] norms of primary law having a 'normative founding function for the whole of the Union's legal order; they determine the relevant legitimatory foundations in view of the need to justify the exercise of public authority. 'Founding' principles express an overarching normative frame of reference for all primary law, indeed for the whole of the Union's legal order'.[20]

This argument links the principles of EU law with the constitutional principles of the domestic case. In both cases, we have principles that seek to justify the exercise of public authority. In the same vein, Koen Lenaerts also seems to presuppose monism when he speaks of the Union as a possibly 'autonomous political authority'.[21]

A rival view rejects such monism in favour of what is generally referred to as pluralism. The best known defender of this view is Neil MacCormick. In the most authoritative and comprehensive statement of his argument MacCormick embraces pluralism as follows:

> A pluralistic analysis is in this instance, and on these grounds, clearly preferable to the monistic one that envisages a hierarchical relationship in the rank-order International Law–Community law–Member state law. Accordingly, the doctrine of supremacy of Community law should by no means be confused with any kind of all-purpose subordination of member state law to community law. Rather, the case is that these are interacting systems, one of which constitutes in its own context and over the relevant range of topics a source of valid law superior to other sources recognized in each of the member state systems . . . It is for the ECJ to interpret in the last resort and in a finally authoritative way the norms of Community law. But equally, it must be for the highest constitutional tribunal of each member-state to interpret its constitutional and other norms, and hence to interpret the interaction of the validity of EC law with higher level norms of validity in the give state system.[22]

---

[16] A von Bogdandy, 'Founding Principles' in A von Bogdandy and J Bast (eds), *Principles of European Constitutional Law* (Oxford: Hart Publishing; Munich: Beck Publishing, 2010), 11. This is a revised version of his earlier essay 'Constitutional Principles' in A von Bogdandy and J Bast (eds), *Principles of European Constitutional Law* (Oxford: Hart Publishing, 2007), 1. A shorter version of the 2010 essay has been published as A von Bogdandy, 'Founding Principles of EU Law: A Theoretical and Doctrinal Sketch' (2010) 16 *European Law Journal* 95.

[17] von Bogdandy (2007), see n 16, 14.

[18] von Bogdandy, 17.

[19] von Bogdandy, 17.

[20] von Bogdandy, 21.

[21] See K Lenaerts and D Gerard, 'The Structure of the Union According to the Constitution for Europe: The Emperor is Getting Dressed' (2004) 29 *European Law Review* 289. See also K Lenaerts and M Desomer, 'Bricks for a Constitutional Treaty of the European Union: Values, Objectives and Means' (2002) 27 *European Law Review* 377–407 and for some earlier reflections, K Lenaerts, 'Constitutionalism and the Many Faces of Federalism' (1990) 38 *American Journal of Comparative Law* 205.

[22] MacCormick, *Questioning Sovereignty*, see n 4, 117–18.

One of the problems of specifying the content of pluralism is the question of whether it refers to the pluralism of many legal systems or to a new self-conception of a single legal system as 'pluralist', in that it does not rest on a single constitutional architecture.

Important defences of pluralism are to be found elsewhere, too. In a well-known essay Neil Walker has argued that constitutional pluralism 'recognises that in the post-Westphalian world there exists a range of different constitutional sites and processes configured in a heterarchical rather than a hierarchical pattern'.[23] Walker concludes that in the European context constitutional law has a markedly different structure to that of a nation-state:

> Constitutional pluralism, by contrast, recognises that the European order inaugurated by the Treaty of Rome has developed beyond the traditional confines of inter-*national* law and now makes its own independent constitutional claims, and that these claims exist alongside the continuing claims of states. The relationship between the orders, that is to say, is now horizontal rather than vertical.....[24]

A third view of the EU legal system is that it is not an independent system at all, but that it is an area of international law whose relation with domestic systems is dualist, as is the case with more usual instances of international law. This view is endorsed by Joseph Weiler in a number of writings,[25] and is also defended by one of us.[26] Weiler has asked if the very idea of European constitutionalism is just a set of 'new clothes' that lack 'an emperor'.[27] He argues that the official legal doctrine of the EU claims that the EU has a constitution, but fails to meet the required social and political conditions of constitutionalism. The constitutional analogy fails to capture, he argues, Europe's 'supranational citizenship'[28] or the co-existence of multiple 'demoi'[29] or any other of the complex institutional features that he calls 'supranational'.[30] These concerns follow from the fact that the EU is an entity with strong international features. He concludes that the Union's constitutional features still lack the authority of a constitution and are at most 'a constitution without some of the classic conditions of constitutionalism'.[31]

---

[23] N Walker, 'The Idea of Constitutional Pluralism' (2002) 65 *Modern Law Review* 317–59, 317.

[24] Walker, see n 23, 337.

[25] JHH Weiler, *The Constitution of Europe: 'Do the new clothes have an emperor?' and other Essays on European Integration* (Cambridge: Cambridge University Press, 1999) and JHH Weiler, 'In Defence of the Status Quo: Europe's Constitutional *Sonderweg*' in JHH Weiler and M Wind (eds), *European Constitutionalism Beyond the State* (Cambridge: Cambridge University Press, 2003) at 10. See also JHH Weiler, 'A Constitution for Europe? Some Hard Choices' (2002) 40 *Journal of Common Market Studies* 563–80.

[26] P Eleftheriadis, 'Pluralism and Integrity' (2010) 23 *Ratio Juris* 365–89, P Eleftheriadis, 'The Structure of European Union Law' (2010) 12 *Cambridge Yearbook of European Legal Studies* 121–50.

[27] See JHH Weiler, *The Constitution of Europe: 'Do the new clothes have an emperor?' and Other Essays on European Integration*, above n 25, at 238–63. See also JHH Weiler, 'The Transformation of Europe' (1991) 100 *Yale Law Journal* 2403.

[28] Weiler, *The Constitution of Europe*, see n 25, 342.

[29] Weiler, 344.

[30] Weiler, 270ff.

[31] JHH Weiler, 'In Defence of the Status Quo: Europe's Constitutional *Sonderweg*', see n 25, 10. See also JHH Weiler, 'A Constitution for Europe? Some Hard Choices' (2002) 40 *Journal of Common Market Studies* 563–80.

(B) Political Foundations

These debates concerning the EU legal system and its relations with Member States' legal systems in terms of monism, pluralism, or dualism stand on their own as important legal philosophical puzzles. They can also, however, be studied as expressions of related philosophical questions about the political, and political-philosophical, foundations upon which the European Union rests. These latter questions, which comprise the subject matter of the second part of this book, invite us to consider which are the most appropriate political principles with which to evaluate, assess, and justify EU law and institutions.

One of the most vibrant areas in contemporary political philosophy is that of global or cosmopolitan justice. Philosophers are currently engaged in fruitful discussions about the scope of social or distributive justice and the legitimacy of international law. They remain divided as to the applicability of ordinary political principles to the international domain. Even though we have rich political philosophies for states and deep accounts of the relevant values, for example, liberty, equality, democracy, justice, we lack a clear account of the political values applicable to the international or transnational domain. The question thus presents itself: 'To what extent, and in what ways, should traditional concepts developed for the realm of the nation-state, such as democracy, equality of resources or the rule of law, be applicable to EU institutions and laws?' Leading authors in these fields include Jürgen Habermas and Larry Siedentop who, in different ways, have sought to apply ideals of democracy to the EU.

In his 2001 essay 'Why Europe Needs a Constitution', Habermas outlined an argument for a European Constitution that is partly historical and partly political.[32] The main objective, for Habermas, was to maintain the specific form of social solidarity achieved in Europe, against the pressures of globalization and 'neoliberalism'. He wrote as follows:

> The question therefore is: can any of our small or medium, entangled and accommodating nation-states preserve a separate capacity to escape enforced assimilation to the social model now imposed by the predominant global economic regime? This model is informed by an anthropological image of 'man' as rational chooser and entrepreneur, exploiting his or her labour-power; by a moral view of society that accepts growing cleavages and exclusions; and by a political doctrine that trades a shrinking scope of democracy for freedoms of the market. These are the building blocks of a neo-liberal vision that does not sit well with the kind of normative self-understanding so far prevalent across Europe as a whole.[33]

---

[32] J Habermas, 'Why Europe Needs a Constitution' (2001) 11 *New Left Review* 5–26. For further arguments in the same direction see J Habermas, *The Inclusion of the Other: Studies in Political Theory, in Political Theory*, edited by Pablo de Greiff and Ciaran Cronin (Cambridge, Mass.: MIT Press, 1998) and J Habermas, *The Divided West* (Cambridge: Polity Press, 2006).

[33] Habermas, 'Why Europe Needs a Constitution', see n 32, 12.

The argument, then, is that in order to protect their achievements against the forces of globalization and seek a 're-regulation' of global economy, European nations 'have a reason for building a stronger Union with greater international influence'.[34] Habermas concedes that any closer institutional integration in Europe needs to build on a common consciousness or a minimum of cultural and political cohesion. Without a pan-European 'civic solidarity' the project will fail, since it will not be endorsed by the public it is intended to serve. What is needed, therefore, is that European citizens share something like a public sphere of a vibrant democracy: 'There will be no remedy for the legitimation deficit, however, without a European-wide public sphere—a network that gives citizens of all member states an equal opportunity to take part in an encompassing process of focused political communication.'[35]

Other political philosophers support such a project of integration. Philippe van Parijs, for example, has argued that it is not at all clear that Europe suffers from a a 'democratic deficit'. For him, democratic accountability at the EU level can maintain the distinctness of the individual political societies as self-standing democracies.[36] In his recent work van Parijs has explored the way in which 'linguistic justice' arises as a question for European integration and has argued for the promotion of English as the 'lingua franca' of the EU.[37]

A very different argument was made by Larry Siedentop in *Democracy in Europe*.[38] Siedentop noted that the preconditions for a genuine democracy were absent fom the contemporary EU. There is no common political tradition, no common language, no particular identification with other communities, no mutual trust. His conclusion was that we should delay the federalist project, at least until we know that the conditions are closer to being met.[39] A parallel argument has been put forward by Kalypso Nicolaïdis, for whom the European Union is not a democracy, but a 'demoicracy'.[40] The key to her argument is that Europe is not supposed to be a single 'demos' but a community of different 'demoi' as follows: '...today's constitution does not call for a homogeneous community or for laws grounded on the will of a single European demos. Rather, it makes mutual respect for national identities and institutions one of its foremost principles.'[41]

---

[34] Habermas, 12.

[35] Habermas, 17.

[36] P van Parijs, 'Should the European Union Become More Democratic' in A Follesdall and P Koslowski (eds), *Democracy and the European Union* (Berlin: Springer, 1997), 287–301.

[37] P van Parijs, *Linguistic Justice for Europe and for the World* (Oxford: Oxford University Press, 2011).

[38] L Siedentop, *Democracy in Europe* (London: Penguin, 2000).

[39] For a careful and historically sensitive discussion of the difficulties surrounding the construction of a European 'demos' see D Marquand, *The End of the West: The Once and Future Europe* (Princeton: Princeton University Press, 2011). See also A Moravcsik, 'In Defence of the "Democratic Deficit": Reassessing the Legitimacy of the European Union' (2001) 40 *Journal of Common Market Studies* 603–34, and A Follesdal and S Hix, 'Why There is a Democratic Deficit in the European Union: A Reply to Majone and Moravcsik' (2006) 44 *Journal of Common Market Studies* 533–62.

[40] K Nicolaïdis, 'We, the Peoples of Europe' (2004) 83 *Foreign Affairs* 97–110, 102.

[41] K Nicolaïdis, 102.

Well before any kind of systematic political philosophy of the European Union had been formed, John Rawls had asked very similar questions in a letter to Philippe van Parijs (which was recently published):

> One question the Europeans should ask themselves, if I may hazard a suggestion, is how far-reaching they want their union to be. It seems to me that much would be lost if the European union became a federal union like the United States. Here there is a common language of political discourse and a ready willingness to move from one state to another. Isn't there a conflict between a large free and open market comprising all of Europe and the individual nation-states, each with its separate political and social institutions, histor-ical memories, and forms and traditions of social policy? Surely these are great value to the citizens of these countries and give meaning to their life. The large open market including all of Europe is the aim of the large banks and the capitalist business class whose main goal is simply larger profit. The idea of economic growth, onwards and upwards, with no specific end in sight, fits this class perfectly. If they speak about distribution, it is [al]most always in terms of trickle down. The long-term result of this—which we already have in the United States—is a civil society awash in a meaningless consumerism of some kind. I can't believe that that is what you want.[42]

The views defended by Rawls remind us perhaps of Kant's view that republics are not meant to unite in a single state but are supposed to maintain their independence in a cosmopolitan congress of states (or in Rawls's terminology a 'union of peoples').

Kant described such a congress or union of states as follows:

> By a *congress* is here understood only a voluntary coalition of different states which can be dissolved at any time, not a federation (like that of the American states) which is based on a constitution and can therefore not be dissolved.—Only by such a congress can the idea of a public right of nations be realized, one to be established for deciding their disputes in a civil way, as if by a lawsuit, rather than in a barbaric way the way of savages), namely by war.[43]

Many critics of Kant find this formulation unacceptable because they consider it less than 'cosmopolitan'. Nevertheless, Kant's formulation offers an interesting alternative for the theorists of the European Union in that it describes a union of states where statehood is maintained whereas sovereignty is shared. Critics say that the fact that a federation of peace is the result of *voluntary* action appears to them to make it optional. But for Kant it is not morally optional. The idea of a public right of nations is part of the framework of justice. Such a public right is voluntary only in the sense that any moral action is voluntary. It is part of the setting up of a complete civil condition and is therefore also a strong duty of justice. So in a way, Kant's theory is a predecessor

---

[42] J Rawls and P van Parijs, 'Three Letters on the Law of Peoples and the European Union' (2003) 7 *Revue de philosophie économique* 7–20.

[43] Immanuel Kant, *The Metaphysics of Morals* in MJ Gregor (trans) and A Wood (ed), I Kant, *Practical Philosophy* (Cambridge: Cambridge University Press, 1996), 6:311488. For an introduction to these ideas see P Kleingeld, 'Kant's Theory of Peace' in Paul Guyer, *Cambridge Companion to Kant and Modern Philosophy* (Cambridge: Cambridge University Press, 2006), 477–504, and A Perreau-Saussine, 'Immanuel Kant on International Law' in Besson and Tasioulas (eds), *The Philosophy of International Law*, see n 2, 53–78.

to that of Rawls and a predecessor to some relevant contemporary views of the European Union.

The foregoing discussion reveals an emerging contrast as regards political views of the European Union: a contrast between more or less integrative positions, defended by Habermas, and more or less internationalist positions defended by Rawls and van Parijs. Such issues demarcate the territory to be addressed by the second part of the book, 'Political Foundations'.

(C) Constitutional Virtues

The third set of questions covered by the book concerns those particular constitutional virtues which EU law and institutions do and ought to exhibit. We may refer to these as the philosophical foundations of EU law narrowly conceived and, in a certain sense, identifying those virtues can be seen as combining the challenges of Parts I and II of the book. Once we arrive at a coherent position about the nature of EU law as a legal system or jurisdiction, and once we become somewhat clearer about the political foundations and values which would justify it, we may then examine its law and institutions in more concrete detail, in order to ascertain which constitutional virtues they do and should exhibit and support. Given the broad range of topics covered by EU law, this project alone could have filled an entire new volume, with chapters on the free movement of goods, services, and capital, the arrangements for the Euro through the Growth and Stability Pact, the law of competition and state aid, environmental law, citizenship law, and, last but not least, the institutional law of the EU. For present purposes, we can focus on only some of these possibilities.

The appropriate constitutional framework of the EU is to be determined by the questions addressed in Parts I and II of the book. If, as a result of those inquiries, we consider that the EU is a single legal and constitutional order, then this may have certain implications as regards the existence and character of 'its own' constitutional principles. A certain kind of monism about the EU legal system may lead to a certain kind of constitutionalism in legal doctrine. In this way, the questions addressed in this third part of the book integrate issues of legal theory with matters of legal practice.

Monism may also lead to a distinctive account of, say, the protection of human rights, or the protection against discrimination, or the effect of the four freedoms. Pluralism may justify a different reading and dualism yet another. A monist under-standing, for example, leads to important doctrinal conclusions in the work of von Bogdandy, as was discussed on page 7–8, von Bogdandy insists that the EU's and the Member States' constitutions 'confront the same central problem', namely the 'phenomenon of one-sided public power as the heart of every constitutional order' in that 'public authorities of the Union as well as of the Member States can limit a citizen without his or her consent'.[44] As a result, both the EU's constitution and the national

---

[44] von Bogdandy, 'Founding Principles of EU Law', see n 16, 24.

constitutions '[deal] first and foremost with the constitution, organisation and limita-tion of this problematic one-sidedness', and in view of this 'identity of issues' we are justified in transferring the insights of national law to the domain of EU law.[45] Von Bogdandy then concludes that the general principles of EU law are *constitutional* principles. The inescapable thought is that Europe's constitutional principles are destined to replace those of the individual Member States' constitutions as a common constitutional language.

Von Bogdandy divides these principles into two sets: principles governing relations between the Union and its Member States, and principles governing relations between the individual and the Union. The first group includes the rule of law, effectiveness, comprehensive legal protection, principles of the order of competences, the principle of the free pursuit of interests (by the States), the principle of 'structural compatibility', and the principle of loyalty. The second group consists of the principle of equal liberty, the principle of the protection of fundamental rights, the rule of law, the principle of democracy, transparency, and participation, and the solidarity principle. The detail of this highly sophisticated argument cannot be discussed here, but it is clear that, for von Bogdandy, particular constitutional readings of the character of EU law yield strong doctrinal effects.[46]

In similar vein, a group of theories seek to understand the constitutional theory of the EU through the lens of 'federalism', conceived as a constitutional, not a political doctrine. In one of the earliest discussions of federalism in the EU, Koen Lenaerts claimed that:

> The other dimension, the *vertical* division of powers between the Community and the Member States, was equally constitutionalized when the Court had to explain in the landmark *Van Gend & Loos* ruling of 1962 that although the EEC Treaty presents itself as a compact among sovereign States, it is in reality – due to its substance – a 'constitution' of a central legal order, federally related to the legal orders of the Member States.[47]

The expression 'federally related' suggests a hierarchy of law-making institutions under the auspices of the 'new legal order'. The direct effect of the treaties follows the logic of a central legal order imposing uniformity upon the Member States. Although federalism can have both centrifugal and centripetal effects, in the EU case it appears to call for more integration, not less.[48]

By contrast a pluralist reading of the EU legal and constitutional order may lead to slightly different constructions of constitutional principles of the EU. Miguel Maduro

---

[45] von Bogdandy, 24.

[46] For a similar position see W van Gerven, *The European Union: A Polity of States and Peoples* (Oxford and Portland, OR: Hart, 2005).

[47] K Lenaerts, 'Constitutionalism and the Many Faces of Federalism' (1990) 38 *American Journal of Comparative Law* 205, 208.

[48] For discussions of federalism see for example K Nicolaïdis and R Howse (eds), *The Federal Vision: Legitimacy and Levels of Governance in the United States and the European Union* (Oxford: Oxford University Press, 2001) and S Fabbrini (ed), *Democracy and Federalism in the European Union and the United States: Exploring Post-National Governance* (London: Routledge, 2005).

proposes a pluralist reading of the EU's fundamental institutional principles. He advises us to see the EU legal order as a merger of different orders into a 'broader European legal order' under the principles of 'contrapunctual law'. The potential conflicts between constitutional doctrines and judicial decisions within this broader order are to be managed according to the four principles of contrapunctual law. For example, the principle of the universal nature of judicial decisions requires that 'any judicial body (national or European) should be obliged to reason and justify its decisions in the context of a coherent and integrated European legal order'.[49] This universal nature entails that any court must ground its decisions 'in a doctrine that could be applied by any other national court in similar situations'.[50] This entails that courts seek to secure coherence 'so long as all the participants share the same commitment to a coherent legal order and adjust their competing claims in accordance with a minimal set of discourse principles'.[51] The nature and effects of a pluralist reading of EU law are hotly contested. But pluralism is now so widespread as a constitutional theory of the EU that no discussion of EU law can be complete without it.[52]

Maduro's analysis suggests that the Court of Justice and the national courts are, for the most part, able successfully to mediate disputes within the broader constitutional order according to the appropriate principles. But not all commentators share this apparent optimism. In his study, *Individualism*, Alexander Somek offers a more alarming view. Somek argues that the case law of the Court of Justice and the work of the Commission has slowly eroded the constitutional safeguards of democracy in the Member States and promoted a radical form of authoritarian materialism.[53] Employing arguments reminiscent of Habermas' critique of 'neoliberalism', Somek argues that the interpretation of EU law has taken a very wrong turn, one which is not well supported by the treaties themselves or by the constitutional law of the Member States. Similarly, Andrew Williams, observes that 'the existing philosophy of EU law rests upon a *theory of interpretation* at the expense of a *theory of justice*', and concludes that 'a satisfactory theory of justice needs to be constructed and adopted constitutionally if EU law is to be presented as the guardian of an "ideal constitution" which possesses a coherent ethical vision for the EU'.[54]

---

[49] M Poiares Maduro, 'Contrapunctual Law: Europe's Constitutional Pluralism in Action' in N Walker (ed), *Sovereignty in Transition: Essays in European Law* (Oxford: Hart, 2003), 501, 529–30.

[50] M Poiares Maduro, 530.

[51] M Poiares Maduro, 527–8.

[52] For a sophisticated 'pluralist' reading of EU law see eg M Kumm, 'Who is the Arbiter of Constitutionality in Europe?' (1999) 36 *Common Market Law Review* 351–86; Mattias Kumm, 'Beyond Golf Clubs and the Judicialization of Politics: Why Europe has a Constitution Properly So Called' (2006) 54 *American Journal of Comparative Law* 505; M Kumm, 'How does European Union Law Fit into the World of Public Law? Costa, Kadi and Three Models of Public Law' in J Neyer and A Weiner (eds), *Political Theory of the European Union* (Oxford: Oxford University Press, 2010).

[53] A Somek, *Individualism: An Essay on the Authority of the European Union* (Oxford: Oxford University Press, 2008).

[54] AT Williams, 'Taking Values Seriously: Towards a Philosophy of EU Law' (2009) 29 *Oxford Journal of Legal Studies* 549–77, 552.

Somek's work takes a distinctive approach to the constitutional principles of the EU law, urging us to view them from the point of view of their content, not the supposed architecture of 'legal systems'. This approach follows a similar argument which has been made by other commentators in respect of the European Convention of Human Rights.[55] For such theories, the constitutional principles and virtues of the EU are to be determined not by any sense of a single or divided 'legal system' but by a division of labour between European laws and institutions and those of the Member States.[56] Certain of Joseph Weiler's views of EU law may also fit such an interpretive model.[57] Weiler appears to espouse the view that the Union should be seen as a *sui generis* entity of international relations whose aim is the 'supranational' peaceful co-existence of autonomous political communities. For Weiler, the Union embodies a 'Kantian idea' of supra-nationalism which 'diminishes the importance of the statal aspects of nationality' and allows 'the individual to rise above his or her national closet'.[58]

As the foregoing discussion reveals, scholarship regarding those constitutional principles and virtues which EU law and institutions do and should exhibit is already rich in sophisticated and original arguments. Some of this territory, and especially the role which certain constitutional virtues—such as solidarity, justice, rule of law, fundamental rights—play in the contemporary Union, is explored in more detail in the final part of this book.

3 The Contributions

These are the issues that the book addresses. What are the answers offered by the contributors? They are many and varied.

In Part I of the book, the first two contributions take very different positions on the question of the existence and character of an EU legal system. In 'Towards a Theory of European Union Legal Systems', Julie Dickson, building on her previous work in this area,[59] argues that the concept of a legal system is still of vital importance in making sense of a supranational polity such as the EU, and in adequately understanding the relationship between EU law and national law. For Dickson, the time is ripe for a revival of jurisprudential interest in a theory of legal systems, and, in particular, for the development of a theory of legal systems apt for non-state contexts, which might be appropriate to and able to deal with the distinctive challenges thrown out by the Union and its law. Exploring those challenges, and what would be required

---

[55] See eg G Letsas, *A Theory of Interpretation of the European Convention of Human Rights* (Oxford: Oxford University Press, 2009).

[56] See eg P Eleftheriadis, 'The Structure of European Union Law', see n 26.

[57] JHH Weiler, *The Constitution of Europe* (Cambridge: Cambridge University Press, 1999).

[58] Weiler, 343.

[59] See J Dickson, 'How Many Legal Systems? Some Puzzles Regarding the Identity Conditions of, and Relations Between, Legal Systems in the European Union' (2008) 2 *Problema* 9–50; J Dickson, 'Directives in European Union Legal Systems: Whose Norms Are They Anyway?' (2011) 17 *European Law Journal* 190–212.

in order for a theory of legal systems to overcome them is Dickson's self-identified task in her chapter. Although she acknowledges that these challenges raise many deep-rooted puzzles for a theory of legal systems, she holds firmly to the view that legal philosophers must try to tackle, rather than elide such puzzles, because of the centrally important role which the concept of a legal system continues to play in our self-understandings as members of law-governed polities.

By contrast, Keith Culver and Michael Giudice argue that the concept of a legal system is outdated and outmoded. In 'Not a System But an Order: An Inter-Institutional View of European Union Law', they contend that, *contra* Dickson, serious consideration should be given to the possibility that the EU's claimed 'new legal order' really is something new and different which cannot be usefully understood in terms of the concept of a legal system. Proceeding from an investigation of the rival supremacy claims frequently made by the Court of Justice and by certain national constitutional courts respectively, Culver and Giudice conclude that such claims are not always what they seem, and are not necessarily to be interpreted at face value, as providing evidence for the existence of distinct and sometimes conflicting legal systems in the EU. Instead, Culver and Giudice interpret interactions between the Court of Justice and national constitutional courts in terms of their 'inter-institutional theory of law' developed in general terms in previous work.[60] According to this inter-institutional account, interactions between EU law and national law should be understood in terms of patterns of mutual reference of varying intensity between Union and Member State institutions. Culver and Giudice claim that this account explains the dynamic and ever-evolving character of the Union better, and provides a more nuanced view of the complexity of institutional interactions within it.

In 'Harmonic Law: The Case Against Pluralism', George Letsas takes a different stance. He argues that, as a matter of law, there are no meaningful conflicts of legal orders or, more concretely, of fundamental rights, in Europe. Letsas views the issue from two points of view: that of positivist legal philosophy and that of non-positivist legal philosophy. He argues that only legal positivism makes pluralism a genuine problem for courts and a threat to the determinacy of Europeans' legal rights and duties. Dialogue is a solution to a problem that exists only if positivism is true. By contrast, non-positivism, the theory that Letsas ultimately endorses, sees no problem in the existence of multiple and overlapping normative orders, because it rejects the thesis that law is a system of rules. Ultimately, Letsas too rejects the model of a 'legal system'. Any conflicts or tensions are rather to be resolved by an account of the content of the norms in question.

To conclude this first part of the book, in 'Judicial Dialogue in the European Union', Anthony Arnull examines the character of the EU legal order, and its relations with national legal orders, through the prism of the preliminary ruling procedure (Art 267 TFEU). Proceeding from a rich understanding of the law and policy surrounding this

---

[60] See, in particular, K Culver and M Giudice, *Legality's Borders: An Essay in General Jurisprudence* (Oxford: Oxford University Press, 2010).

distinctive aspect of the Union's judicial architecture, Arnull draws on theoretical work in public law on dialogic judicial review in order to illuminate the relationship between the Court of Justice and national constitutional courts as mediated by the preliminary reference procedure. He concludes that relations of interaction and compromise rather than of hierarchy and authority best characterize the EU legal order and its relations with national legal orders, and that solutions to the challenges currently faced by the preliminary rulings procedure will be found in a dialogic interaction between the Court of Justice and national courts which may be driven as much by politics as by law.

Part II of the book is concerned with those moral, political, and political-philosophical principles that are apt to provide the political foundations of the Union. Joseph Weiler's contribution, 'Deciphering the Political and Legal DNA of European Integration: An Exploratory Essay' examines some of the recent political failings of the EU from the point of view of political theory and political history. Weiler contends that the democratic deficit and lack of accountability of EU institutions has not been remedied by the Lisbon Treaty. He considers that at the root of these problems lies a fundamental flaw in institutional design. The founders of the Union were motivated by an integrationist zeal, which Weiler calls 'political messianism'. Thinking along such lines has obscured the ways in which EU institutions have undermined political legitimacy. While not offering any concrete blueprint for new institutions, Weiler sounds an optimistic tone when he argues that principles of democracy and a particular conception of the rule of law may offer a remedy.

In 'Citizenship and Obligation', Pavlos Eleftheriadis asks if the European Union can plausibly create political obligations, the particular type of obligation normally associated with states and their citizens. Many political philosophers believe that we owe moral obligations to our political communities simply because we belong to them. Can such moral obligations be created by European Union institutions? This chapter discusses the idea of a 'natural duty of justice' to support just or nearly just political institutions as defended by Kant, John Rawls, and Jeremy Waldron. Eleftheriadis suggests that European Union institutions can be seen to create similar obligations, only if we adopt a cosmopolitan theory of political legitimacy for both domestic and international institutions. He proposes a new distinction between a 'duty of jurisdiction', owed by everyone to every legitimate state, and a 'duty of civility', owed by citizens to their own states. Although European citizenship is not replacing state citizenship, the nature of the EU entails moral obligations of similar weight to those of the states.

'Constitutionalism in the European Union: Pipe Dream or Possibility?', sees legal and political philosopher Wil Waluchow reconsider his general theory of constitutionalism—which places particular emphasis on a theory of constitutional interpretation[61]—in the particular context of the EU, and especially in light of the recently elevated status

---

[61] See W Waluchow, *A Common Law Theory of Judicial Review: The Living Tree* (Cambridge: Cambridge University Press, 2006); W Waluchow, 'Constitutional Morality and Bills of Rights' in G Huscroft (ed), *Expounding the Constitution* (Cambridge: CUP, 2008), 65–92; W Waluchow, 'The Neutrality of Charter Reasoning' in J Ferrer and JJ Moreso (eds), *Neutrality and Legal Theory* (Madrid: Marcial Pons, forthcoming).

of its Charter of Fundamental Rights. Waluchow asks whether we can identify a 'community constitutional morality' of the Union which the Charter both expresses and seeks to uphold. Arguing that such a morality does exist, Waluchow contends that we should think of judges conducting constitutional judicial review in terms of the Charter as holding the Union to its community constitutional morality, and to its own fundamental value commitments. Through consideration of some of the Court of Justice's fundamental rights case law, Waluchow probes the difficulties posed by apparent disagreements regarding and tensions in the EU's constitutional morality, and offers a subtle and nuanced vision of the way in which varying interpretations of common values are tolerated within a diverse community such as the EU.

In his chapter 'The Moral Point of Constitutional Pluralism: Defining the Domain of Legitimate Institutional Civil Disobedience and Conscientious Objection', Mattias Kumm offers a new interpretation of his well-known 'pluralist' constitutional theory of the European Union. Kumm sets out to offer a theory that does not just describe the historical reality of separate 'legal orders' but also has the ambition of explaining the normative point, structure, and limits of constitutional pluralism. For Kumm, a constitutional pluralist gives an account of legal coherence even without a hierarchical system of 'norms' or 'rules', and promotes a 'third way' of conceiving the legal world: between hierarchical integration and radical pluralism. Kumm argues that we may identify relevant moral principles akin to those justifying conscientious objection in the case of single states, according to which Member States' courts may depart from EU law. Such principles construct a middle way between what Kumm defines as 'democratic statism' and 'legalist monism'.

Kalypso Nicolaïdis' chapter 'The Idea of European Demoicracy' offers a reconsideration of her well-known theory of demoicracy defined as 'a Union of peoples, understood both as states and as citizens, who govern together but not as one'. She argues that such a third way offers an escape from the sovereignty-federalism dichotomy and calls instead for a different relationship between European peoples. Accordingly, Nicolaïdis advocates a Kantian view of the EU as a federal union (rather than a federal state) which transcends the 'sacrosanct distinction' between domestic and international law. Moreover, she argues that a normative benchmark for the EU cannot simply be inferred from actual practice nor deduced from abstractions. She proposes a 'ormative-inductive' approach according to which the EU's normative core is constituted by transnational non-domination, transnational mutual recognition, and the requirement of internal-external consistency. Such norms need to be protected and perfected if the EU is to live up to its essence.

Ari Afilalo and Dennis Patterson offer a wide-ranging discussion of the political and social philosophy of the European Union. In 'Statecraft and the Foundations of European Union Law', they argue that constitutional orders are determined by historical factors encapsulated in the idea of 'statecraft'. They therefore place the European Union into a moment of transition from the 'nation-state' to the 'market-state'. Events such as the increased harmonization of economic policies, the Single

European Act, the European Monetary Union, the creation of European citizenship, and the Schengen arrangements suggest the transition from a nation-state to a 'market-state' constitutional order. The argument moves from internal challenges to external ones and shows how the nature of the state is shaped by its international relations and choices. Ultimately, Afilalo and Patterson view the European Union as a unique experiment, but also something that teaches us important lessons about statecraft in general.

The third part of the book explores certain constitutional virtues which might prove particularly relevant for the contemporary EU. Takis Tridimas's chapter, 'Precedent and the Court of Justice: A Jurisprudence of Doubt?', offers a thorough analysis of the doctrine of precedent in the Court of Justice. Tridimas identifies and discusses three aspects of the Court's doctrine of precedent: a) the precedential value attributed by the Court itself to its previous rulings, b) their binding effect on the General Court, and c) their binding effect on national courts. Tridimas' chapter focuses on the first; namely, the way the Court of Justice perceives its own precedents. He examines the doctrine of *stare decisis* and its relevance to EU law, the Court's methodology in distinguishing precedent, express and implied overruling, and the quasi-normative effect of precedent. Tridimas also seeks to provide some comparative perspectives as regards these issues by reference to the jurisprudence of the European Court of Human Rights and the Supreme Court of the United States. The picture that emerges is that of judicial behaviour which is close in result, albeit not in methodology, to that of common law supreme courts which adhere to the doctrine of *stare decisis*.

Lorenzo Zucca argues for a restoration of the idea of monism in EU law in 'Monism and Fundamental Rights'. Like Waluchow, Zucca regards the human rights architecture of the EU as an appropriate testing ground for a constitutional theory. Zucca presents a theory of 'moralism' according to which fundamental rights act as superior moral principles in the law. He then presents a version of 'positivism' according to which fundamental rights are to be treated as any other rule, and only encapsulating very important interests by way of stipulation. Under both these monist views, jurisdictional conflicts are only apparent. Value monism suggests that institutions ought to interpret rights in a coherent and harmonious way. Legal monism, on the other hand, suggests that an appropriately broad view of legal systems would bring about doctrinal unity. Zucca argues that the legal monistic reading is preferable because it is more transparent, more predictable, and mirrors closely the reality of the developing relationship between the European Union and the Council of Europe.

Geert De Baere's 'European Integration and the Rule of Law in Foreign Policy' is concerned with a quite different area of EU law; that of the legal limitations upon the common foreign and security policy. De Baere espouses a substantive sense of the rule of law. He makes the surprisingly fertile point that the project of European integration has precisely been one of increased legalization. Foreign policy, just like many other areas of executive or regulatory action, has now been partly turned into legal obligations enforceable by the vigilance of the European Commission. De Baere shows that foreign policy is subject to rule of law constraints although not to the same extent as internal policies. He derives support from the Court of Justice's remarkable judgment in *Kadi*, the case brought against the implementation by the EU of the Security Council's measures against suspected terrorists.[62] This case showed that neither the law of the UN nor the policy against terrorism is beyond the reach of EU law, and EU constitutional judicial review. De Baere concludes that the core of the Union is the setting up of mechanisms for checking the states' potential destructive force by subjecting it to rule of law constraints. Having brought the Member States' relations with one another under the rule of law, the European Union is gradually bringing the Member States' remaining foreign policies within the constraining and enabling framework of EU law.

In 'Solidarity in the European Union: Problems and Prospects', Andrea Sangiovanni offers a thorough discussion of principles of solidarity in the Union context. The argument begins with a return to the Rawls-van Parijs debate and with what the author regards as an 'evasive' answer by the American philosopher. On the basis of this exchange, Sangiovanni turns his attention to the content of social justice and solidarity it in the EU: does the EU require principles more demanding than assistance but less demanding than the full extent of liberal justice? If so, what are they, and how would we go about constructing them? The essay then turns to a fruitful discussion of arguments offered by philosophers Thomas Nagel, Jürgen Habermas, and David Miller. Sangiovanni rejects all three approaches and concludes that the most plausible view of social justice in the EU will begin with the special character and nature of European social, political, legal, and economic *cooperation*, and the *public goods* its produces for its members.

The question of social justice in the EU is addressed by Sionaidh Douglas-Scott in her contribution, 'The Problem of Justice in the European Union: Values, Pluralism and Critical Legal Justice', but from a different point of view. Douglas-Scott identifies several challenges facing the successful realization of justice in the distinctive context of the EU. She holds firm to the view that, given the kind of polity that the Union is, justice is a virtue which is crucial to it, and to which its constitutional arrangements must aspire. She argues that the most promising way forward in this regard is to recast and reinterpret rule of law requirements in terms of 'Critical Legal Justice', a conception of justice which may be particularly apt for and needed in the EU context. Her chapter counsels adherence to the underlying values which rule of law requirements aim to protect—such as opposition to unrestrained, despotic power, and an emphasis on the accountability of power, and on the freedom and equality which are enhanced by restraining it—and can thus be understood as aspiring to and attempting to realize the spirit of the rule of law rather than its formal letter.

---

[62] Joined Cases C-402/05 P and C-415/05 P *Kadi and Al Barakaat International Foundation v Council and Commission* [2008] ECR I-6351.

4 Conclusion

This book is viewed by its editors as a first step in contributing to and engendering high quality debate regarding the European Union and the challenges it faces. In our view, progress can only be made via a combination of sound and rich understandings of the EU's law and institutional architecture, and well-founded and penetrating questions and insights from the best work in legal and political philosophy. We hope that we have offered the reader a rich diet of contributions featuring each of these essential ingredients. Legal and political philosophy, in order to keep pace with and do adequate justice to the changing legal and political landscape, must develop adequate theoretical tools with which to understand and analyse, evaluate, judge, and reform the new international phenomena with which we are now faced. Between them, the chapters in this book highlight some of the most important issues which EU law and its scholarship currently face, and open up new and fruitful avenues which future research might explore. We offer this book as one step in the right direction although certainly not as the last word. The philosophical and legal analysis of the European Union promises to remain a rich and fertile area of legal and philosophical scholarship for years to come.

Oxford, March 2012

PART I
THE LEGAL SYSTEM

PART I

2

Towards a Theory of European Union Legal Systems

Julie Dickson^*

1 Introduction

What can the philosophy of law bring to our understanding of novel and complex supra-national legal phenomena such as are to be found in the European Union, and in the Union's legal relations with its constituent Member States? My proposal in this chapter is that a reconsideration of the theory of legal systems, and of the concept of a legal system, can shed light on important aspects of EU law. I put the matter in terms of a *re*consideration for two principal reasons. The theory of legal systems is a topic familiar to legal philosophers working within the analytical jurisprudence tradition, but one which has seemingly fallen out of favour and generated little scholarly interest in recent decades. One of the questions discussed here is whether we might gain a clearer understanding of the character of EU law by understanding it in terms of the concept of a legal system, and in terms of a theory of distinct but interacting EU and national legal systems. If considering the contemporary EU in terms of the concept of a legal system can lead to an improved understanding of it, then—especially given the growing importance in our legal and political lives of intra-, trans-, supra-, and international legal phenomena—the time may have come to revive jurisprudential interest in the theory of legal systems. The second reason for speaking in terms of a reconsideration is that the distinctive challenges posed by the character of the supra-national law of the EU, and by the complexity of the Union's legal and institutional arrangements, may well raise new puzzles for the theory of legal systems, hence forcing

* Faculty of Law, University of Oxford and Somerville College, Oxford. I am grateful to Pavlos Eleftheriadis, John Gardner, Michael Giudice, Matthew Grellete, Greg Messenger, Wil Waluchow, Alison Young, and an anonymous reviewer at Oxford University Press for helping me develop my thinking on the issues discussed here.

us to revisit and revise aspects of our understanding of legal systems in light of these puzzles.

The discussion which follows stays true to this chapter's title. That is to say, I attempt to move towards an understanding of what would be required for an adequate theoretical account of legal systems in the EU, of what might motivate such an account, and of why such an account matters, rather than offering a fully fledged theory here. It is not that I regard such a theory as unattainable, but that rather its attainment might be rendered more likely by first of all having in mind a clearer picture of the issues it would need to address, and of those aspects of EU law that are likely to pose challenges for it. As the discussion progresses, my own view of what is required in order for a polity to possess its own legal system will begin to emerge.

The discussion is structured as follows. In Section 2, I outline some factors motivating theories of legal systems, before noting some contemporary doubts about understanding a supra-national polity such as the EU in terms of the concept of a legal system. Section 3 identifies and begins to confront some important challenges to an adequate theory of legal systems in the EU context which are prompted by the distinctive character of EU law and its relations with other bodies of law. The discussion seeks to reveal why the concept of a legal system is important in understanding the contemporary EU, and why a legal systems analysis is well-motivated in that context, before identifying and beginning to consider some of those challenges. The concluding section reviews the importance of an adequate theory of legal systems, and considers next steps towards such a theory in the EU and other non-state contexts. In particular, I conclude by rendering explicit a distinction between two different senses of 'legal system'—or, to speak more precisely, between two different kinds of criteria which play a role in determining the existence, identity, limits, and character of legal systems—which is implicit in much of the following discussion, and which I believe will prove vitally important in future work on this topic.

2 The Theory of Legal Systems: Motivations and Doubts

For millennia, philosophers of law have wrestled with many and various puzzles regarding aspects of law's character, and its relations with other normative phenomena, such as morality, and non-legal governance arrangements. Those of a sceptical turn of mind from outside the discipline (as well as some of those within it)[1] may well feel justified in raising some awkward questions as regards whether such inquiries are getting us anywhere. We seem collectively to have no trouble producing more theories of law, but is progress being made as regards producing more accurate and

---

[1] See eg B Leiter, 'The Demarcation Problem in Jurisprudence: a New Case for Scepticism' (2011) 31 *Oxford Journal of Legal Studies* 663.

explanatorily adequate theories? If philosophers of law have applied themselves to important questions about law's character over many centuries, shouldn't some agreed correct answers have emerged by now such that we should not still be faced with a seemingly endless proliferation of new theories and new variations on old theories? This way of thinking, however, misses something vital about the kind of enterprise upon which legal philosophers are engaged. Part of the reason why philosophizing about law appears an endless task is that in a certain sense the task has not remained constant over the time that theorists have engaged in it: those questions and puzzles about law addressed in their theories have changed over time, influenced, for example, by the political, social, and intellectual preoccupations of the time and place in which theories of law emerge.

For example, a resurgence of interest in recent decades in Wittgenstein's remarks on rule-following found its way from the general philosophical community into sections of the legal philosophical community in the 1990s. As a result, many legal theorists at that time began to address Wittgensteinian questions concerning the possibility of rule-following and the role of interpretation in grasping the meaning of rules, which were heavily influenced by this intellectual current moving from philosophy of language into philosophy of law.[2] The wider historical context of the day may also influence which issues legal philosophers focus on and find particularly important to debate. For example, the 1958 Hart–Fuller debate concerning the factors which bear upon the identification of valid law, and the normative consequences of law so identified, were prompted in part by events occurring during and after the Second World War and the Nuremberg trials.[3] A more recent example of this phenomenon may be found in the academic writing which followed the legal controversy surrounding the US Supreme Court's resolution of the 2000 US Presidential election.[4]

In my view, and as I have discussed more extensively elsewhere,[5] it is the complex and multifaceted character of law that allows for a wide variety of topics in legal philosophy to come and go, and for our sense of what is difficult or puzzling even with regard to one and the same topic to change over time. Given the complexity of the phenomena, we would seem to have no reason to suppose that law's properties are few in number, hence allowing for different subsets of those properties to be focused on as

---

[2] See eg A Marmor, *Interpretation and Legal Theory*, 1st edn (Oxford: Oxford University Press, 1992; 2nd revised edition, Oxford: Hart Publishing, 2005); B Bix, *Law, Language, and Legal Determinacy* (Oxford: Oxford University Press 1993); DM Patterson (ed), *Wittgenstein and Legal Theory* (Boulder, CO.: Westview Press, 1992); GA Smith, 'Wittgenstein and the Sceptical Fallacy' (1990) 3 *Canadian Journal of Law and Jurisprudence* 155; M Stone, 'Focusing the Law: What Legal Interpretation is Not' in A Marmor (ed), *Law and Interpretation* (Oxford: Oxford University Press, 1995).

[3] See eg HLA Hart, 'Positivism and the Separation of Law and Morals' (1958) 71 *Harvard Law Review* 593; L Fuller, 'Positivism and Fidelity to Law—a Reply to Professor Hart' (1958) 71 *Harvard Law Review* 630.

[4] See, as just one of many examples, R Dworkin (ed), *A Badly Flawed Election: Debating Bush v. Gore, the Supreme Court and American Democracy* (New York: The New Press, 2002).

[5] J Dickson, 'The Central Questions of Legal Philosophy' (2003) 56 *Current Legal Problems* 63–92. Some of the remarks above draw on this work.

important, debated, and elucidated by different lines of jurisprudential inquiry over time.

An adequate understanding of the concept of a legal system is one such topic which has drifted in and out of jurisprudential fashion. Considering just its recent history: the late 1960s and early to mid-1970s witnessed a flurry of legal philosophical interest in questions surrounding the identity of legal systems (such as which criteria determine when norms belong to one and the same legal system, how we should understand the limits of legal systems and their relations with norms from outside the system in question) and their continuity through time (such as how do we know when an existing legal system has been replaced by a new one, when one legal system has split into two, or two such systems joined into one?). For some, this interest stemmed from puzzles generated by the journey to political independence taken by certain former British colonies.[6] Others looked not beyond but within the United Kingdom, keen to explore the sense in which the Scots have their own legal system without their own state, the characteristics of such a system and its relation to the Articles and Acts of Union,[7] and the role Scots law plays in expressing and shaping national identity, including national political identity.[8] Others still seemed less concerned with solving particular post-colonial or post-Union puzzles, but, perhaps influenced by the intellectual interest which such issues generated, attempted to develop aspects of their general accounts of the nature of law specifically in relation to questions concerning the identity and continuity of legal systems.[9]

Once the kinds of issues mentioned above, and the intense spate of academic activity they generated ran their course,[10] legal philosophers' interest in the theory

---

[6] For a small sample of this voluminous literature, see AM Honoré, 'Reflections on Revolutions' (1967) *Irish Jurist* 268; JM Eekelaar, 'Rhodesia: the Abdication of Constitutionalism' (1969) 32 MLR 19; JM Eekelaar, 'Principles of Revolutionary Legality' in AWB Simpson (ed), *Oxford Essays in Jurisprudence*, 2nd series (Oxford: Clarendon Press, 1973); JW Harris, 'When and Why Does the Grundnorm Change?' (1971) 29 CLJ 103–33.

[7] I refer here to the eighteenth-century Union between Scotland and England: the Articles of Union agreed in 1706 which set the terms of these kingdoms coming together, and the Scottish and English Acts of Union of 1707 giving legal effect to the agreed Articles.

[8] eg TB Smith, 'Scottish Nationalism, Law and Self-Government', in N MacCormick (ed), *The Scottish Debate* (Oxford: Oxford University Press, 1970); G Maher, 'The Identity of the Scottish Legal System' (1977) *Juridical Review* 21–37; N MacCormick, 'Does the United Kingdom Have a Constitution? Reflections on MacCormick v. Lord Advocate (1978) 29 NILQ, 1–20.

[9] eg JM Finnis, 'Revolutions and Continuity of Law' in Simpson (ed) see n 6; J Raz, *The Concept of a Legal System* 1st edn (Oxford: Oxford University Press, 1970), 2nd edn (Oxford: Oxford University Press, 1980).

[10] Arguably, in the Scottish context they have never entirely run their course, and reappear in times of political crisis, or when issues of national identity come particularly to the fore. See eg commentary on the legality of the implementation of the poll tax in Scotland in the early 1990s: N Walker and CMG Himsworth, 'The Poll Tax and Fundamental Law' (1991) *Juridical Review* 45; DJ Edwards, 'The Treaty of Union: More hints of constitutionalism' (1992) 12 *Legal Studies* 34–41, and discussion of the challenges faced by the Scottish legal system in the post-devolution era, eg CMG Himsworth, 'Devolution and its Jurisdictional Asymmetries' (2007) 70 MLR 31–58; Neil Walker's 'Report on Final Appellate Jurisdiction in the Scottish Legal System', published on the Scottish Government's website, January 2010, available at: <http://www.scotland.gov.uk/Publications/2010/01/19154813/0>

of legal systems waned dramatically, with little writing explicitly on this topic emerging from the late 1970s onwards. However, rapid growth of and increasing interest in intra- trans-, supra-, and international governance arrangements has the potential to breathe new life into this topic. This time round, the interest is not, as in the post-colonial era, how to think about states ceding territories which then go on to become independent states with separate legal systems, but rather how to understand the legal and other consequences of the coming together of formerly more independent polities in larger regional or global units of cooperation. In the case of the European Union, issues regarding the theory of legal systems are potentially made all the more vivid by the fact that EU legal institutions have consistently claimed that EU law is much more than a series of intergovernmental agreements between states, and that it represents 'a new legal order',[11] and has 'created its own legal system'.[12] Given that these claims are long-standing and consistently made, it seems that we cannot revert to existing accounts of state-based legal systems, and see EU law merely as a series of interactions between such systems, for to do so would fail adequately to take account of persistent features of the way in which EU legal officials, and EU legal institutions, understand themselves. The time thus seems ripe for a thoroughgoing consideration of the theory of legal systems in the supra-national legal context, including a consideration of whether the concept of a legal system can improve our understanding of EU law and its relations with national and international law, and of whether the Court of Justice is correct in its persistent claims that EU law itself forms a new legal system.

However, although some have viewed the growing importance of supra-national polities such as the EU as an opportunity to revisit the theory of legal systems,[13] others contend that the *sui generis* character of the EU, and the distinctive way in which EU and national norms and institutions interact, mean that the concept of a legal system is no longer a helpful analytical tool in that context. For such theorists, in the case of the EU, recently revived interest in the theory of legal systems is best strangled at birth, for the concept of a legal system is too state-bound to help us adequately understand this new kind of supra-national polity. As an example, according to Keith Culver and Michael Giudice's 'inter-institutional theory of legality',[14] legal phenomena are not to be understood in terms of discrete legal systems and the relations of those systems with

---

[11] Case 26/62 *Van Gend en Loos* [1963] ECR 1, at 12.

[12] Case 6/64 *Costa v ENEL* [1964] ECR 585, at 593.

[13] eg ML Jones, 'The Legal Nature of the European Community: a Jurisprudential Analysis Using HLA Hart's Model of Law and a Legal System' (1984) 7 *Cornell International Law Journal* 1–59; C Richmond, 'Preserving the Identity Crisis: Autonomy, System and Sovereignty in European Law' (1997) 16 *Law and Philosophy* 377–420; I Weyland, 'The Application of Kelsen's Theory of the Legal System to European Community Law—The Supremacy Puzzle Resolved' (2002) 21 *Law and Philosophy* 1–37; J Dickson, 'How Many Legal Systems?: Some Puzzles Regarding the Identity Conditions of, and Relations between, Legal Systems in the European Union', (2008) 2 *Problema* 9–50, available online at: <http://www.juridicas.unam.mx/publica/librev/rev/filotder/cont/2/dis/dis4.pdf>.

[14] K Culver and M Giudice, *Legality's Borders: An Essay in General Jurisprudence* (New York: Oxford University Press, 2010), Introduction, at xxviii, and *passim*.

the norms of other legal and non-legal normative systems. Rather, 'legality is shorn from officials, states, and geography'[15] and is understood instead in terms of various state, intra-state, trans-state, supra-state, and super-state legal institutions and norms interacting and engaging in 'mutual reference of varying intensity',[16] and appearing in individuals' lives as 'upwellings of normative force',[17] 'clustered around particular kinds of life events'.[18] In this account, the idea of those institutions and norms having a 'home' in particular legal systems is viewed as unimportant,[19] and theoretical approaches concerned with the identity and continuity of legal systems are viewed as outmoded, distortive, and incapable of explaining the variety of intra-, trans-, supra-, and super-state phenomena encountered in the contemporary legal world.[20] Specifically in relation to the EU, Culver and Giudice claim that, as a result of certain features of this polity and its law, 'it becomes increasingly less clear what meta-theoretical value is to be gained by holding onto the idea of legal system' and that 'talk of separate legal systems only seems more and more distracting'.[21]

The theory of legal systems hence seems to stand at a crossroads. Having long lain dormant, conditions now seem ripe for its revival, but while some have begun to take that path, others view it as a retrograde step which obscures the need to develop radically new theories of contemporary legal phenomena. My own view is that we should not be too quick to abandon the concept of a legal system in our attempts to understand the character of EU law and its relations with other bodies of law. Indeed I suspect that we cannot abandon it without significant loss in the quality of our explanations of certain phenomena, given the important roles which this concept can and does play in our self-understanding as individuals living in law-governed societies. In the next section, I raise and begin to confront some challenges to a theory of legal systems in the EU context. In so doing, I explore why the concept of a legal system is no mere esoteric theoretical tool mainly of interest to legal philosophers, but is rather of vital importance in understanding law, and in understanding our experience as members of political societies living under law.

3 Some Challenges Considered

(A) The Concept of a Legal System: Who Needs It and Why?

What reasons do we have for supposing that the concept of a legal system is a helpful analytical tool in understanding novel and complex contemporary legal phenomena such

---

[15] K Culver and M Giudice, 165.

[16] K Culver and M Giudice, 112.

[17] K Culver and M Giudice, 105.

[18] K Culver and M Giudice, 105.

[19] K Culver and M Giudice, 161–4.

[20] K Culver and M Giudice, but in relation to EU law and scholarship, see especially ch 2.4.1 and ch 5.2.3. See also the chapter by Culver and Giudice in the present volume: 'Not a System but an Order: An Inter-Institutional View of European Union Law'.

[21] *Legality's Borders*, see n 14, 74.

as the supra-national law of the EU? An important starting point in answering this question is to note that those administering and living under EU law, and the law of the EU's constituent Member States, have recourse to the concept of a legal system in understanding the legal phenomena around them, and in understanding their own lives in terms of it, and that their recourse to this concept is significant in a number of ways.

As I have argued elsewhere, a theory of law, in order to be successful, must appreciate and take to heart the point that the concept of law, and other legal concepts such as the concept of a legal system or the concept of legal obligation, are concepts already used by those living in societies to understand and navigate the course of their lives under law. That is to say, it is overwhelmingly the case that people living in societies governed by law are aware of law's existence and importance in their lives, and have views about its character and purpose, whether and when they ought to obey it, which law is the law of their society and which is to be viewed as foreign law, etc. The concept of a legal system, like other legal concepts, is hence not some esoteric theoretical tool introduced anew by legal philosophers in order to further their research projects: it is already 'out there' in people's discourse and thinking about law, and is already part of the conceptual currency used by individuals living under law to understand themselves and their social and political world. This being so, a theoretical account of law, if it is successfully to advance our understanding of society, must do adequate justice to participants' attitudes towards, beliefs about, and self-understandings in terms of the concept of a legal system, because those attitudes, beliefs, and self-understandings form part of the data to be explained.[22]

Examples of those living in law-governed societies thinking of laws as forming distinct legal systems with distinct characteristics are not hard to find. We speak, for example, of something being thus and so in the French legal system but not in other legal systems, such that we can ask, 'Will France Americanize Its Legal System?';[23] we discuss whether there is a place for Sharia law in the English legal system;[24] we are confidently assured by the Scottish Government that, 'the Scottish legal system has a long history, dating back to the medieval era. Its integrity and independence were acknowledged in the 1707 Act of Union...'[25] The important point about such

---

[22] For further discussion, see J Dickson, *Evaluation and Legal Theory* (Oxford: Hart Publishing, 2001). Many legal philosophers have been committed to this view of the task of legal philosophy, eg HLA Hart, *The Concept of Law*, 2nd edn (Oxford: Clarendon Press, 1994); JM Finnis, *Natural Law and Natural Rights* (Oxford: Clarendon Press, 1980), ch 1; J Raz, 'Authority, Law and Morality', in J Raz, *Ethics in the Public Domain* (Oxford: Clarendon Press, 1994), 210–37, especially section VI.

[23] 'Will France Americanize its Legal System?', Bruce Crumley, Time magazine, online edition, available at: <http://www.time.com/time/world/article/0,8599,1870443,00.html>.

[24] See eg 'Lord Bingham: 'no reason' to exclude Sharia', Frances Gibb, Legal Editor, Times Online 3 November 2008, available at: <http://business.timesonline.co.uk/tol/business/law/article5071727.ece>.

[25] 'Legal System' Factsheet (2004) produced by the Scottish Executive, available online: <http://www.scotland.gov.uk/Resource/Doc/925/0000078.pdf> p 2. The Scottish Executive—now formally renamed in law as the Scottish Government (Scotland Act 2012, s 12(1)—is the executive branch of the devolved government for Scotland, with executive responsibility for all matters not reserved to the UK parliament and government under the terms of the Scotland Acts 1998 and 2012.

discourse is not merely that we do make use of the concept of a legal system to understand ourselves and features of our social and political world, but that we do so in the service of drawing distinctions which are of importance and which matter to us, such as where 'our own' legal system ends and another begins. In referring to 'our own' legal system, I have in mind something along the following lines. Legal systems can become the focus of attitudes of identification and attachment (as well as of alienation and disaffection), and the concept of a legal system is used to demarcate that which is the object of those attitudes, and to differentiate it from other instances of legal phenomena in the world.

In my own experience, this is frequently the case with the Scottish legal system. In the factsheet referred to above, such attitudes, and the use of the concept of a legal system in identifying their object, feature prominently. The Scottish legal system is referred to by the then Scottish Justice Minister as 'proudly independent', 'a cornerstone of Scottish life for centuries',[26] and the rest of the factsheet elaborates on that legal system's 'integrity and independence'[27] in terms of its historical roots, legal sources, and institutional structure,[28] which distinguish it from other legal systems including (and perhaps especially) the legal system of England and Wales, despite this latter co-existing in the same state (the UK) as the Scottish legal system. An appreciation of Scottish culture, including Scottish legal, political, and academic culture, readily reveals that such views concerning the existence and distinctive character of the Scottish legal system are a distillation of themes which echo loudly through the media, political debate, legal academic thinking, and teaching in law schools in Scotland, and which have done so for many years, not merely in the post-devolution era.[29] Those administering and living under law can come to hold such attitudes of attachment to, identification with, and even pride in their own law, and in order to be able to say which law is 'their law', and to begin identifying its distinctive characteristics they need to, and do, make use of the concept of a legal system. This being so, the concept of a legal system is not merely something that we happen to have recourse to in navigating our way around our societies and their law, it is a concept used to draw

---

[26] Legal System Factsheet, see n 25, 1.

[27] Legal System Factsheet, see n 25, 2.

[28] Legal System Factsheet, see n 25, 2.

[29] See eg 'MPs warn UK reform must protect Scottish legal tradition', Edinburgh Evening News, online edition, 10th February 2004, <http://edinburghnews.scotsman.com/uksupremecourt/MPs-warn-UK-reform-must.2502230.jp>; 'Scotland is proud of, and jealously guards, its separate legal system', from Opinion piece, 'Fighting Fraud' in The Herald newspaper, online edition 20th February 2009, <http://www.theherald.co.uk/features/editorial/display.var.2487857.0.fighting_fraud.php>; the existence and proceedings of The Stair Society, instituted in 1934 to encourage the study and to advance the knowledge of the history of Scots law, <http://www.stairsociety.org/home.htm>. Legal and academic discourse on the topic is voluminous: for but a tiny sample, see the litigation and academic commentary mentioned in notes 8 and 10, and also HL MacQueen (ed), *Scots Law into the 21st Century: Essays in Honour of WA Wilson* (Edinburgh: W Green, 1996), E Attwooll, *The Tapestry of Law: Scotland, Legal Culture and Legal Theory* (London: Kluwer, 1997); and P Maharg, 'Imagined Communities, Imaginary Conversations: Failure and the Construction of Legal Identities' and L Farmer, 'Under the Shadow of Parliament House: The Strange Case of Legal Nationalism', both in L Farmer and S Veitch (eds), *The State of Scots Law* (London: LexisNexis, 2001).

distinctions which are of vital importance to us in terms of the way we think about those societies, their boundaries, distinctiveness, our relation to them, and the values to which they aspire.[30]

But what of the European Union? Important institutional actors within the EU clearly think of themselves as administering and developing a new legal system, and regard certain doctrines of EU law as mandated because the EU has instituted a new legal system. In *Costa v ENEL* the doctrine of the primacy of EU law—that it prevails over inconsistent national law in cases of conflict—is justified by the Court of Justice on the grounds that the then European Economic Community, 'has created its own legal system',[31] and because there has been a 'transfer by the states from their domestic legal system to the community legal system of the rights and obligations arising under the Treaty...'.[32] In this judgment, the Court of Justice uses the concept of a legal system to refer both to EU law and to the domestic law of the EU's constituent Member States. Moreover the central point of this judgment, that EU law prevails over domestic law in cases of conflict, is expressed by the Court of Justice in terms of the relation between legal systems, and is justified in terms of the distinctive kind of political and legal entity that the EU is, namely one which has, 'its own institutions, its own personality, its own legal capacity, and capacity of representation on the international plane and, more particularly, real powers stemming from a limitation of sovereignty or a transfer of powers from the States to the Community...'.[33]

Much more recently, in *Kadi and Al Barakaat v Council*, the need for and justification of thoroughgoing and robust EU judicial review, including of EU measures enacted to give effect to a norm of a distinct body of international law (a UN Security Council resolution) rests in significant part on the Court's view that, 'an international agreement cannot affect... the autonomy of the Community legal system, observance of which is ensured by the Court',[34] and that 'the review by the Court of the validity of any Community measure in the light of fundamental rights must be considered to be the expression, in a community based on the rule of law, of a constitutional guarantee stemming from the EC Treaty as an autonomous legal system which is not to be prejudiced by an international agreement'.[35] Once again, the concept of a legal system is not merely being used, but is being used to draw important distinctions which matter greatly to the actors involved. In asserting that EU law forms an autonomous legal system distinct from other international legal orders, and hence on this basis must itself take responsibility for the robustness of judicial review of its norms, the

---

[30] Admittedly, not all polities hold and express attitudes of identification with and attachment to their legal systems in the manner that Scotland does. I hope to explore this point by comparing the attitudes of various polities to their legal orders in future work on the elements necessary for a polity to possess its own legal system.

[31] Case 6/64 *Costa v ENEL* [1964] ECR 585 at 593.

[32] Case 6/64 *Costa v ENEL* [1964] ECR 585 at 594.

[33] Case 6/64 *Costa v ENEL* [1964] ECR 585 at 594. This claim is repeated in many other cases.

[34] Joined Cases C-402/05P & C-415/05P *Kadi and Al Barakaat v Council* [2008] ECR I-6351, para. 282.

[35] Joined Cases C-402/05P & C-415/05P *Kadi and Al Barakaat v Council* [2008] ECR I-6351, para. 316.

Court of Justice is using the concept of a legal system to demarcate something distinctive: that which is 'its' law, which EU institutions have certain responsibilities in respect of, which ought to realize certain values, and play certain important and distinctive roles in the international arena.

Further reference to EU institutions' view that they are administering an EU legal system can be found in statements of the European Judicial Network (set up by the Council of the EU in May 2001 to simplify judicial cooperation between Member States and to facilitate relations between Member States' and EU courts), eg: 'Community law is a legal system in its own right that generates rights and obligations for all of us in Europe'[36] and, following the Lisbon Treaty's amendments to the EU's constitutive treaties, we find primary law affirming the Union's commitment to the continued existence and distinctive characteristics of *Member State* legal systems as well.[37]

Moreover, it is not only within EU institutions that such issues arise. In recent years, the EU has faced significant challenges regarding its future direction and whether individuals affected by its law identify with or feel alienated from EU institutions and norms; whether, for example, EU citizens view EU law as 'their law', or as the law of a 'foreign' polity being imposed on them and in respect of which they have insufficient democratic input. Such attitudes have surely played and will continue to play an important role in influencing the political and legal direction to be taken by the Union in times to come. The concept of a legal system, used in demarcating bodies of law from one another, in picking out legal units with distinctive features, and in expressing attitudes of identification and alienation, frustration and pride, towards them, hence seems vitally important, and worthy of continued study, in the EU context. The challenge of investigating changing conceptions of European identity, including EU identity, held by those living within the EU is one which has more enthusiastically been taken up by sociologists than by legal scholars to date.[38] While this is not a challenge which I can take up within the confines of this chapter, the foregoing discussion indicates that there are important connections between the concept of a legal system and issues of national and EU identity, which might fruitfully be explored by legal scholars.

The present discussion is more modest in aim. I have argued that the role played by the concept of a legal system in demarcating that which is viewed by some relevant 'we' as 'our' law, and in delineating the existence and distinctive characteristics of a legal and political unit in respect of which we can hold and express a variety of practical

---

[36] <http://ec.europa.eu/civiljustice/legal_order/legal_order_ec_en.htm>.

[37] Treaty on the Functioning of the European Union (TFEU), Art 67(1): 'The Union shall constitute an area of freedom, security and justice with respect for fundamental rights and the different legal systems and traditions of the Member States.'

[38] See eg the work of sociologist Gerard Delanty, including *Inventing Europe: Idea, Identity, Reality* (London: MacMillan Press, 1995) and 'The EU and the Question of European Identity', in E Eriksen (ed), *Making the Euro-Polity: Reflexive Integration in Europe* (London: Routledge, 2005) or the 'EuroIdentities' project being coordinated at the School of Sociology, Social Policy & Social Work, and the School of History and Anthropology at the Queen's University, Belfast, <http://www.qub.ac.uk/sites/Euroidentities/>.

(such as the conditions, if any, under which we ought to obey the law) and affective (such as pride in, identification with, or indeed alienation from, the law) attitudes gives this concept an importance which goes far beyond being some esoteric theoretical tool employed by legal philosophers to further their research projects. The concept of a legal system matters, and cannot so easily be swept away by revisionist accounts of legal phenomena as some contemporary legal philosophers would have us believe. It matters simply because citizens and legal officials do try to make sense of our social and political world in terms of units or bodies of law, their distinctive characteristics, those values to which they aspire, whether we identify with or feel alienation from them, and their relation to other bodies of law. Legal philosophers are not free to downplay or ignore these aspects of law: to do so is to fail to understand vital aspects of the role which law plays in our societies and in our lives.

(B) The Challenge From Non-State Legal Phenomena

In recent times, several academic commentators have contended that legal philosophy has been overly focused on the nature of state law, and of state legal systems.[39] This, it is argued, is distortive and unsustainable given the variety of intra-, trans-, supra-, and international legal arrangements in contemporary political societies. The challenge which arises particularly in relation to EU law from this state of affairs might be rendered as follows: as the concept of a legal system as investigated by legal philosophers is in reality the concept of a state legal system, and as the EU is not a state and lacks certain features associated with states, thus we should abandon the concept of a legal system in our attempts to understand EU law and its relations with other bodies of law, as that concept lacks the explanatory resources needed to account for distinctive aspects of this novel form of legal order.[40]

This conclusion, however, need not follow. If we accept that legal theory has hitherto been overly focused on state law and state legal systems,[41] and if we regard contemporary legal phenomena as being far more diverse than that, then why isn't the

---

[39] See eg N MacCormick, 'Democracy, Subsidiarity and Citizenship in the 'European Commonwealth' (1997) 16 *Law and Philosophy* 331–56, p. 331; N MacCormick, *Questioning Sovereignty* (Oxford: Oxford University Press, 1999), *passim*; D von Daniels, *The Concept of Law From a Transnational Perspective* (Farnham, Surrey: Ashgate Press, 2010); J Waldron, 'Hart and the Principles of Legality', in M Kramer, C Grant, B Colburn, A Hatzistavrou (eds), *The Legacy of H.L.A. Hart: Legal, Political, and Moral Philosophy* (Oxford: Oxford University Press, 2008), 68–9; Culver and Giudice, *Legality's Borders*, see n 14). See also Culver and Giudice's chapter in the present volume: 'Not a System but an Order: An Inter-Institutional View of European Union Law.'

[40] Culver and Giudice seem to offer a version of this challenge in contending that, 'Prima facie legal phenomena give reasons to doubt the adequacy of at least extant analytical explanations of the nature of legal system…', and in speaking of, 'an underlying inability of dominant analytical approaches [including legal system approaches] to capture legal phenomena outside the model of the law-state', *Legality's Borders*, see n 14, both at xvi.

[41] Some leading legal philosophical works tend to confirm this view, eg J Raz, 'The Identity of Legal Systems' and 'The Institutional Nature of Law' in J Raz, *The Authority of Law*, 2nd edn (Oxford: Oxford University Press, 2009), HLA Hart, *The Concept of Law*, 2nd edn, see n 22, chs. I, V, VI, and X.

lesson to be drawn that the time is ripe to reconsider the theory of legal systems in non-state contexts, and to develop a theory of legal systems able adequately to account for and explain non-state as well as state legal phenomena? In their chapter in this volume, Culver and Giudice make the valid point that we should not assume or presume that a legal systems analysis can properly account for all such phenomena:

> Why would we expect a theory of law developed in and for the context of the municipal state legal system to serve us at all well in making sense of what so many believe is not an instance of a municipal legal system – EU law?[42]

But no such presumption is proposed here. Rather, I am advocating that we should not be too quick to move from the novel character of certain legal phenomena to a dismissal of the concept of a legal system as a useful tool in understanding it, and that we should at least pause to consider the possibility of developing a legal systems analysis apt to characterize the variety of non-state legal phenomena which we find in contemporary governance arrangements.

One reason why we might think that this is the more promising route to take emerges from the discussion in Section A: the examples adduced from both Scotland and the EU demonstrate that those administering and/or living under the law of certain non-state entities strongly regard those entities as having a distinct legal system, and employ the concept of a legal system in drawing important distinctions and boundaries regarding 'their' law and its relation with other bodies of law. The view that the concept of a legal system can only properly be applied at the unit level of the state is further undermined in the case of Scotland by the fact that the existence of a distinct Scottish legal system is recognized by the very state of which Scotland forms one constituent part. The Articles of Union, which set the terms for the founding of the then state of Great Britain, contain guarantees regarding the continued existence of Scots law and of distinctive institutions of the Scottish legal system such as the Court of Session and High Court of Justiciary.[43] More recently, the UK's Constitutional Reform Act provides that, in the transfer of jurisdiction from the Appellate Committee of the House of Lords to the new UK Supreme Court:

> S 41 (1) Nothing in this Part is to affect the distinctions between the separate legal systems of the parts of the United Kingdom.[44]

Such examples cast doubt on the challenge from non-state legal phenomena as outlined above, and indicate a possible rejoinder to it, namely that the boot should be on the other foot as regards where the real challenge lies. Given the existence of non-state entities (and, at least in some cases, the states of which they are a constituent

---

[42] 'Not a System but an Order: An Inter-Institutional View of European Union Law', in this volume, at p 60.

[43] Articles VXIII and XIX, Articles of Union 1706 (given legal effect in the Scottish and English Acts of Union of 1707), and accessible online at: <http://www.parliament.uk/actofunion/lib/visuals/pdf/articlesofunion.pdf>.

[44] Constitutional Reform Act 2005, s 41(1).

part) espousing long-standing, pervasively held, and institutionally recognized views that they have a distinct legal system, then those who contend that the concept of a legal system can only be properly applied at state level, and is only of use in understanding state-based legal phenomena, will have to explain how these institutions administering law and individuals living under it have fallen into such widespread and sustained error as regards the existence of non-state legal systems.

All this indicates that we should not accept the challenge from non-state legal phenomena in the form outlined above, and should not take the fact that much legal theory has been overly focused on state law and state legal systems as justifying abandoning the concept of a legal system in our attempts to understand EU law and its relations with national law. Rather, we should take seriously the possibility of trying to develop a theory of legal systems which is able to explain non-state as well as state legal phenomena.

But if something need not be a state in order to have a distinct legal system, this raises the question of what *does* need to be the case in this regard. In my view, the beginnings of an answer lie with some legal philosophical lessons learned from failures in Hans Kelsen's account of the identity of legal systems. For Kelsen, the key to understanding both the normativity of law, and its systemic unity, lay in the idea of norms forming chains of validity culminating in a basic norm. A particular norm, such as that one ought not to park on a certain double-yellow line, is legally valid if its creation has been authorized by a higher norm such as the relevant road traffic legislation of the jurisdiction in question. This norm's validity in turn rests on its authorization by another norm higher up the chain, and so on, until we reach the constitution, then some historically prior constitution out of which the present constitution developed, until we face the question of what authorized the creation of the historically first constitution, and all the norms created according to it. According to Kelsen, the answer is the basic norm or *grundnorm*, which, he contends, is not a norm of the positive law, but is a presupposition which must be made by anyone interpreting the norms of a given legal order as valid.[45] The basic norm hence unifies the legal system and yields its criterion of identity: a group of norms belong to one and the same legal system if they can all be traced back to the same basic norm.

Several legal philosophers writing during that period in the 1970s when questions of the identity and continuity of legal systems were in vogue noted that there are serious problems with this analysis. Kelsen's account of the identity of legal systems cannot account for certain relatively common legal phenomena, such as the peaceful and constitutionally authorized granting of independence by a state to a former colony which had hitherto been governed by the same legal system as that state. If such an event occurs without a break in constitutional continuity, for example, via a statute enacted in the state in question to grant independence to the former colony, then, according to Kelsen's analysis, all the norms of the legal system of the newly

---

[45] H Kelsen, *The Pure Theory of Law*, 2nd edn trans M Knight (Berkeley: University of California Press, 1967), especially 193–205.

independent polity can be traced back to the basic norm of the polity and legal system granting independence, hence we do not really have two separate legal systems, only one. This seems counter-intuitive as (i) it would seem to make the constitutionally authorized granting of independence to political entities which were formerly part of other political entities impossible, and (ii) it does not begin to do justice to the self-understandings of those polities, and of individuals within them: in such a situation the courts, other legal and political institutions, and the population of both polities would regard themselves as separate political entities with separate legal systems. The conclusion reached by several theorists was that it is impossible to have an adequate theory of the identity of legal systems by looking only to what we might refer to as purely legal criteria, such as the relations between norms and their traceability back to the same basic norm. Social facts, such as the attitudes and self-understandings espoused by institutions and individuals, and other sociological, historical, and, for some, ethical phenomena were all relevant to determining the identity of legal systems and their relations *inter se*.[46]

The lesson to be drawn from all this is clear. Legal systems cannot be studied in isolation from the political and societal organizations of which they are a part. A legal system is not some self-sufficient free-floating normative entity: it is a legal system *of* something, and part of the key to its identity lies in the character of that something, and in the relation of the legal system to it. This being so, in order to understand the identity of legal systems, and other aspects of their character, we must look to the political entities or units of societal governance that they are legal systems of. As I have argued in Section 3A, legal systems as distinct units matter, and they do so because in devising, administering, and participating in societal governance arrangements, we think of what we are doing in terms of the activities of some relevant unit, its claims, boundaries, relations with other such units, and our own attitudes towards it. Where they exist, legal systems are one important aspect of the political entities that they are legal systems of, and which they serve. But when we consider whether only political entities or units of societal governance in the form of states are capable of having their own distinct legal system, then the self-understandings of certain political entities, such as Scotland, or the European Union, would seem to give us strong reason to think not.

This is not to say, however, that just anything which we may be able to demarcate as in some sense a political unit—for example, Cherwell District Council local govern-ment district in Oxfordshire—will be properly described as having its own distinct legal system. Legal theorists have tackled this point in a variety of ways. For example, one way of attempting to demarcate the normative systems of such entities from, say, the legal system of England and Wales, is in terms of the comprehensiveness of the claims made by the latter—the legal system claims to be able to regulate any area of conduct, whereas Cherwell District Council is set up for particular local government

---

[46] This line of criticism can be found in JM Finnis, 'Revolutions and Continuity of Law', see n 9; J Raz, *The Concept of a Legal System*, 2nd edn, see n 9, ch 5; J Raz, *The Authority of Law*, see n 41, ch 7; G Maher, 'The Identity of the Scottish Legal System' see n 8.

purposes only, and can only regulate matters pursuant to those purposes—and in terms of a claim to supremacy, that is, a claim by the legal system that it is entitled to set up, regulate, and impose conditions on the operation of other normative systems, and is entitled to determine the relation between its own norms and the norms of those other systems—the legal system of England and Wales would make such claims in respect of Cherwell District Council, but not vice versa.[47]

Here we reach the nub of the issue as regards the work that remains to be done in order to develop a theory of legal systems apt for non-state as well as state legal phenomena: what exactly *are* the features which a political entity or unit of societal governance must possess in order for it to have its own distinct legal system? The EU is not a state, but in many respects it has a highly developed and institutionally supported political system that marks it out as a political entity in its own right. Does the EU's possession of legislative, executive, and judicial institutions; legal officials, distinctive political norms and processes for negotiating the direction of its own future development, a large civil service, legal personality, soon-to-be status as Member of the Council of Europe, means of representing itself and of acting on the international stage, etc. clearly qualify it as the kind of political unit capable of possessing a legal system, or do some of, things it is famously accused of lacking— genuinely European political parties which inform common European political debate amongst the EU's citizens, appropriately democratic institutions, and a demos who politically conceive of themselves as such and act accordingly[48]—mean that, all things considered, and despite its self-conception, we should conclude that the EU is not the kind of political entity able to possess a distinct legal system?

In my view, the answers lie with a given political entity's degree of independence (in some sense which stands in need of further investigation) from, and the character of its relations with, other political entities, and not in whether the polity concerned does or does not exhibit the features of a state. Thus we find, for example, in *Kadi*, the Court of Justice linking its claim that the EU possesses an autonomous legal system to its claims that no other body of law besides EU law itself can determine the validity of its own norms, and that only EU law can determine the relations between EU norms and norms emanating from other international bodies.[49]

All of this raises many further questions. My proposal here is that three clusters of issues stand particularly in need of investigation in moving towards a theory of legal

---

[47] For this approach, see eg J Raz, *The Authority of Law*, 2nd edn, see n 41, 115–20. The supremacy claims made by the EU, and by Member States' legal systems are discussed in Section 3D.

[48] For discussion of some of the relevant issues, see eg JHH Weiler, U Haltern, and F Mayer, 'European Democracy and its Critique' in J Hayward (ed), *The Crisis of Representation in Europe* (London: Routledge, 1995); JHH Weiler, 'Demos, Telos, Ethos and the Maastricht Decision' (1995) 1 *European Law Journal* 219; N MacCormick, 'Democracy and Subsidiarity in the European Commonwealth' in MacCormick, *Questioning Sovereignty*, see n 39.

[49] Joined Cases C-402/05P & C-415/05P *Kadi and Al Barakaat v Council* [2008] ECR I-6351, paras 282, 316.

systems apt to characterize non-state legal phenomena such as is to be found in the contemporary EU:

(1) What features must a political entity or unit of societal governance possess in order for that entity to have a distinct legal system? (and, more broadly, what other social sub-systems—educational?, cultural? economic?—need to exist in such a society to support its distinct political and legal systems?)

(2) What institutions must legal systems possess, and what role do they, and the norms they interact with, play in determining the identity of and relations between legal systems?

(3) What claims must legal systems make as regards the relations between their own norms, and norms of other bodies of law with which they come into contact, in order to qualify as legal systems? In particular, must they make supremacy claims in respect of other normative systems?

I have touched on some issues relevant to (1) at various points so far in this chapter, but clearly much work remains to be done in this regard. Some of the issues raised in (2) and (3) above, and some specific puzzles generated by the EU and its law in terms of them, are discussed further in Sections C and D below.

(C) The Identity of Legal Systems: Which Institutions? Whose Institutions?

One way in which law differs from certain other normative phenomena—such as morality, or etiquette—is in virtue of its institutional character. Legal systems are *institutionalized* normative systems—the practices and activities of human social institutions are necessary in order for law to exist and to be in force in a given jurisdiction, and play a role in determining what is required according to law in that jurisdiction. For example, that the Court of Appeal has so decided, or that the Westminster Parliament has so enacted bears a constitutive relation to what is required according to the current law of England and Wales.[50]

Some legal philosophers also regard the existence and practices of certain kinds of institutions as providing the key to questions regarding the identity of legal systems, such as how to determine where one legal system leaves off and another begins, and which norms are properly regarded as belonging to which systems. Amongst such theorists, there has historically been a division between those who regard law-creating institutions, such as sovereigns or legislatures, as being most important in this

---

[50] Stated at this level of generality, this point would be accepted by legal theorists from across the jurisprudential spectrum, including HLA Hart, John Finnis, Neil MacCormick, Joseph Raz, and Ronald Dworkin. These theorists differ in their views of the character of and reasons for the constitutive relation between the activities of certain social institutions and what the law requires.

regard,[51] and those who focus to a greater extent on law-applying institutions, such as courts and tribunals.[52]

If we take the emphasis to be on law-creating institutions, holding, for example, that legal systems must possess such institutions in order to exist, and that the key to their identity lies in identifying all those norms which can be traced back to the law-creating institutions of that system, then the EU may seem to pose few distinctive challenges for a theory of legal systems. The EU has, in the Council, the European Council, the Commission, and the Parliament, a well-developed, if complex, schema of EU legislative institutions and procedures for creating norms of various types,[53] and if we were to identify all such institutions, and the norms created by them, then this would seem to take us some distance in ascertaining the identity and limits of the EU legal system.

Some legal philosophers, however, claim that we must look not to law-*creating* institutions, but to law-*applying* institutions in order to ascertain the existence and identity of legal systems. Amongst the reasons adduced in support of this view are: (i) modern complex legal systems recognize diverse sources as capable of creating law for that system, hence the only way to ascertain all those norms properly regarded as belonging to one and the same system is to find out which norms its courts would recognise as norms for that system, and (ii) not all law in a given legal system is created by law-creating organs such as legislatures.[54] These points can be illustrated in the case of the contemporary EU, and appear sound when considered in that context. Regarding (i): the EU recognizes as (in some sense) forming part of the EU legal system not only norms created by the Council, European Council, Commission, and Parliament of the EU, but also norms hailing from other sources; for example, international agreements of various kinds and the international law created according to them.[55] Given the existence of multiple institutional sources creating law for the EU, some of which are outwith the EU itself,[56] then in order to bring unity to the EU legal order, and to ascertain all those norms properly regarded as forming part of EU law, we must look not to the array of law-creating entities from which they hail, but to those EU institutions that recognize and apply all such norms, and which determine

---

[51] eg J Austin, *The Province of Jurisprudence Determined*, WE Rumble (ed), (Cambridge: Cambridge University Press, 1995).

[52] eg J Raz, *The Concept of a Legal System*, see n 9, ch VIII.

[53] Treaty on European Union (TEU), Arts 13–18; Treaty on the Functioning of the European Union (TFEU), Arts 223–250 and 288–299.

[54] See eg JW Salmond, *Salmond on Jurisprudence*, G Williams (ed), (London: Sweet & Maxwell, 1957) at 41; Raz, *The Concept of a Legal System*, 2nd edn, see n 9, 190–2; J Raz, *Practical Reason and Norms*, 2nd edn (Princeton: Princeton University Press, 1990), 129–31.

[55] Case 181/73 *R and V Haegeman v Belgian State* [1974] ECR 449; Case C-61/94 *Germany v Commission* [1996] ECR I-3989. Of course, the exact effect which various such sources of law can have within the EU legal order and in Member States' national courts is a complex matter, and varies according to the character of the international agreement in question.

[56] As Advocate General Tesauro stated in Case C-53/96 *Hermès International v FHT Marketing Choice* [1998] ECR I-3603: 'The Community legal system is characterized by the simultaneous application of provisions of various origins, international, Community and national; but it nevertheless seeks to function and to represent itself to the outside world as a unified system.'

that they are all norms of EU law, and what their effect will be, that is, the courts of the EU legal order. Moreover, regarding (ii), it is clearly the case that not all EU law emanates from law-creating institutions such as legislative bodies, because of the central role which the Court of Justice has played and continues to play in breathing constitutional life into the provisions of the Treaties and the law made according to them, and in spelling out the precise legal effect that EU norms are to have vis-à-vis the norms of other bodies of law, such as international law or the domestic law of the EU's Member States.

This being so, the character of EU law provides support for the view that it is the activities of law-recognizing and law-applying institutions such as courts and tribunals which unify legal systems, and that the identity of legal systems is to be ascertained by reference to those norms those systems' law-applying institutions recognize and use in determining the normative situations of those subject to the law. On this view, the distinctive character of the EU generates some interesting challenges regarding whether EU law can truly be regarded as a legal system, which norms are properly regarded as belonging to any such system, and how to understand the relation between any EU legal system and other bodies of law; for example, the domestic law of EU Member States.

At first sight, these puzzles may not be apparent. The EU has, in the form of the Court of Justice and the General Court, its own distinctive judicial institutions which recognize which norms are regarded as part of the EU legal order, and which determine how those norms are to be interpreted, and what effect they are to have vis-à-vis other legal norms; for example, norms of Member States' domestic law.[57] However, although the Court of Justice claims to itself an interpretive monopoly as regards the meaning and application of EU law,[58] and although there are actions in EU law which take place specifically in the Court of Justice or in the General Court,[59] it is, famously, the *national* courts of the EU's constituent Member States which do the lion's share of the actual application and enforcement of EU law, given the terms of operation of the Treaty on the Functioning of the European Union (TFEU) Art 267 preliminary ruling procedure, and the creation by the Court of Justice of doctrines such as primacy, direct effect, the duty of consistent interpretation, and the principle of Member State liability. If we regard those national courts as law-applying institutions solely of the domestic legal system of which they seem prima facie to be a part, then this may appear to leave the EU somewhat lacking as regards possessing 'its own' law-applying institutions, and may create difficulties as regards ascertaining the content and extent of those norms which are properly regarded as norms of the EU legal system. On this view, the EU legal system will still have some of 'its own' law-applying institutions in the form the Court of Justice and the General Court, and as regards

---

[57] TEU, Art 19; TFEU, Arts 251–281.
[58] TEU, Art 19.
[59] eg the jurisdictions under TFEU Arts 263, 268, and 340, 258–260.

certain kinds of actions, for example Commission enforcement actions under TFEU Art 258 and judicial review actions under TFEU Art 263, those law-applying institutions will recognize EU law, apply it, and fully determine the normative situation of those subject to the law in terms of it. However, as regards individuals seeking access to EU rights and protections within their Member States, the EU will appear on this view not to have law-applying institutions operating at the 'sharp end' of using EU (and other) norms to decide cases, and to determine in concrete terms the normative situations of those subject to the law. The reason for this is, of course, that under the terms of the TFEU Art 267 preliminary ruling procedure, the Court is supposed to restrict itself to giving an authoritative view on the interpretation (and/or validity) of EU norms. It is not supposed to apply its interpretation to the facts or to decide the case,[60] and so does not itself fully determine the normative situations of those subject to the law in terms of EU norms. In preliminary ruling cases the Court of Justice will thus only partly determine the normative situation of those subject to EU law, as a result of the interpretation of EU norms it gives, and will thus only be part-responsible for law application as regards a given case. The puzzle here is whether we can properly speak of something being a legal system when, on this view, it possesses relatively few law-applying institutions, and when, in many cases involving EU law, those institutions do not fully decide applied legal outcomes, or fully determine the normative situation of those subject to EU law.

Some may wonder, however, whether this indicates that we should *not* take the view that national courts are only to be regarded as law-applying institutions of Member States' domestic legal systems, at least when a point of EU law is in play. Perhaps we should consider whether the correct way to understand the situation is that, when a point of EU law is in play and must be adjudicated on by national courts, those national courts are acting as, or just are, EU courts, and are hence properly regarded as part of the EU legal system. On this view, the EU will not exhibit a relative lack of law-applying institutions able fully to determine the normative situations of those subject to its law. Academic commentators frequently talk this way, contending that in recognizing and applying EU law, national courts are acting as EU courts, or simply are EU courts,[61] but how seriously should we take this talk, and how, exactly, should we understand it? Even if we take it at face value, and regard national courts as law-applying institutions of the EU legal system insofar as points of EU law are in play, several puzzles will remain. To mention but a few: it may be difficult to get adequate purchase on the 'when a point of EU law is in play' condition (if indeed it is a condition) of regarding national courts as courts of the EU legal system, because of

---

[60] Whether the Court of Justice always remains strictly within these limits is, of course, another matter.

[61] See eg A Stone Sweet and T Brunell, 'Constructing a Supranational Constitution' in A Stone Sweet, *The Judicial Construction of Europe* (Oxford: Oxford University Press, 2004), 97; N Barber, 'Legal Pluralism and The European Union' (2006) 12 *European Law Journal* 306–29 at 326–7 and note 94; M Poiares Maduro, in his contribution to M Avbelj and J Komárek (eds), 'Four Visions of Constitutional Pluralism' <http://cadmus.eui.eu/dspace/bitstream/1814/9372/1/LAW_2008_21.pdf at pp 20–1>.

the extensive and sometimes indeterminate reach of EU law;[62] national courts sometimes recognize and apply EU law without going through the preliminary ruling
procedure,[63] and so would they still properly be regarded as law-applying institutions
of the EU legal system in such cases where there is no direct input from the Court of
Justice as regards recognizing EU norms and determining norm-subjects' situations in
line with them?[64] Even in cases where preliminary rulings are made, our understanding of what it is to be a law-applying institution of a given legal system, and of the
process of norm-recognition and application in that system, may need to be revised to
accommodate the sense in which the recognition and application of norms of the EU
legal system will be a joint business, with the Court of Justice and national courts
engaging in a division of judicial labour in this regard.

The view that national courts are properly regarded as law-applying institutions of
the EU legal system, also raises issues regarding the EU legal system's relation to
Member States' domestic legal systems. If a given Member State's domestic law is
taken to constitute that Member State's own legal system, and not merely a sub-part of
some larger EU legal system,[65] then national courts will also be law-applying institutions of that domestic legal system. Are we then to understand such courts as the
law-applying institutions of two distinct legal systems—EU and Member State—
simultaneously?

Moreover, what could settle or at least help us to make progress as regards whether
courts in Member States are properly regarded as courts of the EU legal system? Might
some of the points discussed in Section 3A above, concerning attitudes of identification with and alienation from bodies of law be relevant here? If we find evidence that
courts in Member States identify with EU law, view it as 'their' law, and that such
attitudes form part of the reasons why they recognize and apply it, does this militate in
favour of regarding them as institutions of the EU legal system? If such institutions
rather view EU law as consisting of 'foreign' norms, or as norms which are applied
only in virtue of reasons grounded in the national legal order, does this give us less
reason to conclude that courts in Member States can be regarded as institutions of the
EU legal system?

For some, the complexity of the EU's institutional arrangements is more grist to
their mill that the concept of a legal system is of dubious explanatory value in the
context of supra-national legal orders.[66] For my own part, however, I do not view these
puzzles as ones which will drive us inevitably down that road. Rather, the puzzles help
to focus our minds on aspects of the theory of legal systems which need particular

---

[62] For discussion of particular examples, see eg S Peers, 'The EC's Criminal Law Competence: The plot
thickens' (2008) 33 ELRev 399.

[63] eg under the CILFIT criteria, Case 283/81 *CILFIT* [1982] ECR 3415.

[64] According to Maduro in 'Four Visions of Constitutional Pluralism', see n 61, the CILFIT criteria are
precisely concerned with trying to encourage national courts to think and act in their own right as courts of the
EU legal system.

[65] This issue is discussed further in Section 3D.

[66] See eg Culver and Giudice, *Legality's Borders*, see n 14, 72–4.

attention in the context of the EU, and are an invitation to rise to the challenge of providing an account apt to characterize such non-state legal phenomena. As has been discussed in previous sections, I regard this effort as well-motivated in part because of the persistent and pervasive self-understandings of the EU, and of various of its Member States, as possessing distinct legal systems, and because of the importance that those entities attach to possessing legal systems, and the legal consequences which their courts have taken to flow from that understanding. Moreover, the EU is not the only example of a purported legal system featuring complex institutional arrangements, including the possibility that some of its judicial institutions are shared with other legal systems. In the case of Scotland, which I also regard as possessing its own legal system, we find that a distinct Scottish court system not only exists, but that key institutions of it are constitutionally guaranteed to exist in all time coming.[67] However, we also find, albeit only in civil cases, that there is a right of final appeal from the Scottish Court of Session to the UK's Supreme Court.[68] Does the fact that this latter institution is hence shared with regard to such cases with the legal systems of England and Wales, and of Northern Ireland, threaten the distinctiveness of the Scottish legal system? In my view it does not, so long as we can find reasons to understand the Supreme Court as still forming part of a distinct Scottish legal system. Evidence in favour of this view is readily available; for example, the Constitutional Reform Act 2005 tells us that, in hearing civil appeals, 'A decision of the Supreme Court on appeal from a court of any part of the United Kingdom ... is to be regarded as the decision of a court of that part of the United Kingdom',[69] such that the Supreme Court is to be understood as sitting as a Scottish court for those purposes. Moreover, and as was also noted in Section 3B above the same section of that Act explicitly confirms the continued existence of the separate legal systems of the parts of the United Kingdom.[70]

Institutional complexity, including the possibility of distinct legal systems sharing certain institutions, is not a reason to throw the concept of a legal system 'baby' out with the hitherto overly state-based theory of legal systems 'bathwater'. Instead, certain features of contemporary intra- and supra-state legal orders highlight some puzzles which a theory of legal systems apt to characterize non-state legal phenomena will have to address. Such a theory must take seriously, and adequately explain this institutional complexity, but must also take seriously and adequately explain pervasive and consistently held views that certain non-state political units possess distinct legal systems.

---

[67] Articles of Union (see n 43), Art XIX.

[68] Constitutional Reform Act 2005, s 40(3).

[69] Constitutional Reform Act 2005, s 41(2).

[70] Constitutional Reform Act 2005, s 41(1). These issues, and the distinctness of the Scottish legal system more generally, are discussed further in J Dickson, 'The Idea of a Legal System: Between the Real and the Ideal', in N Walker (ed), *MacCormick's Scotland* (Edinburgh: Edinburgh University Press, 2012). NB I do not regard the distinctness of the Scottish Legal System to lie solely with the institutional autonomy of its courts. See further, Dickson, 'The Idea of a Legal System', and the conclusion to this chapter.

(D) The Identity of Legal Systems: Relations Between Norms and Between Systems

Further such puzzles emerge when we consider another issue highlighted during the discussion in Section 3B, namely, what claims must legal systems make as regards the relations between their own norms, and the norms of other bodies of law, in order to qualify as distinct legal systems? In particular, must they make supremacy claims of some sort in respect of other normative systems?

My proposal here is that in order to differentiate genuinely distinct legal systems from normative sub-systems, such as Cherwell District Council and its by-laws, then the system concerned must claim authority to determine the existence, force, and effect of its norms, and must claim authority to determine the relation between its own norms and the norms of other normative systems. If either of these matters is not determined by the system itself, but by some other normative system, then it should be regarded not as a distinct legal system, but rather as a normative sub-system operating under the auspices of a legal system.

Many facets of EU law provide evidence that this polity claims authority to determine the existence and effect of its own norms, that it 'calls its own shots' as regards the relation between its norms and the norms of other normative systems, and that it regards these claims as necessary to its possessing its own legal system. That EU norms exist, and which EU norms exist, are matters which are determined by the principle of conferral,[71] by the requirements of the Union's various law-making procedures,[72] and by the Court of Justice's powers of judicial review in respect of such norms.[73] All of these determinants are contained within the EU Treaties themselves. Moreover, the Court of Justice claims sole authority to determine the force and effect of EU norms, the relation between EU norms and the norms of other bodies of law, and views these claims as justified because the EU possesses its own legal system.[74] We see evidence of this vis-à-vis Member States' law in the Court's creation and continued shaping of the doctrines of primacy and of direct effect, and in claims such as that:

> ...the EEC Treaty has created its own legal system...the law stemming from the treaty, an independent source of law, could not, because of its special and original nature, be overridden by domestic legal provisions...[75]

The Court makes such claims as regards the EU's 'external' face, too, for example, in respect of relations between EU law and the law of other international organizations:

> ...an international agreement cannot affect...the autonomy of the Community legal system, observance of which is ensured by the Court...[76]

---

[71] TEU, Art 5(1) and (2).   [72] TFEU, Arts 288–299.
[73] TFEU, Art 263.   [74] See also TEU, Art 19(1).
[75] Case 6/64 *Costa v ENEL* [1964] ECR 585 at 594.
[76] Joined Cases C-402/05P & C-415/05P *Kadi and Al Barakaat v Council* [2008] ECR I-6351, para 282.

It is important to note, however, that these 'distinct legal system' claims—claims that EU law determines for itself the existence and effect of its norms, and their relations with the norms of other bodies of law—are not claims to possess some kind of absolutist political sovereignty rendering it able to regulate any matters whatsoever in any manner whatsoever. Clearly such a claim would be out of place in case of the EU, a non-state body which is a creature of Treaties concluded between states, and which only has those powers conferred on it by those Treaties, the rest remaining with the Member States.[77] The claims which I regard as necessary to something being a legal system are not claims to possess some absolutist political sovereignty, they are claims that the system 'calls its own shots' as regards the existence and effect of its norms, and the relation of those norms to the norms of other normative systems. Legal systems can be and often are limited in their legislative and other competence, and, as will be discussed further below, can permit other normative systems to operate within their domain, but they remain distinct legal systems so long as those limits and permissions are determined by, and regulated according to, that system itself.

The focus so far has largely been on EU law as a body of law, and on considering whether it is correct to think of it as forming a distinct legal system. But what of some of those other bodies of law with which EU law comes into contact? Do any or all such bodies of law also form distinct legal systems, and how should we understand the relations between the EU legal system, and other legal systems? In previous work I have postulated three possible models of relations between EU law and the domestic law of the EU's constituent Member States:[78]

(1) The 'Distinct but Interacting Legal Systems' model (or the '27 plus 1' model):[79] European Union law forms a distinct legal system, in addition to the distinct legal systems of the EU's constituent Member States, and interacts with each of those Member State legal systems;

(2) The 'Part of Member States' Legal Systems' model: EU law is to be understood merely as an aspect of each of the legal systems of the Member States, and not as a distinct legal system in addition to those domestic legal systems;

(3) The 'One Big Legal System' model: there is but one EU legal system, of which the constituent Member States' 'legal systems' are to be understood as (in some sense) sub-systems.[80]

---

[77] TEU, Arts 4(1), and 5(1) and 5(2).

[78] In the present discussion, space precludes discussion of how best to understand the relations between EU law and the law stemming from various international organizations, such as the UN or WTO.

[79] '27 plus 1' is a terminological simplification. As should be clear from the discussion so far, I believe that at least one Member State (the UK) is multi-legal system state, and I suspect that several others should also be understood in such terms. I hope to address this issue further in future work on non-state legal systems.

[80] I first introduced these models in J Dickson, 'How Many Legal Systems? Some Puzzles Regarding the Identity Conditions of, and Relations Between, Legal Systems in the European Union' (2008) 2 *Problema* 9–50, available online at: <http://www.juridicas.unam.mx/publica/librev/rev/filotder/cont/2/dis/dis4.pdf>.

The discussion thus far would seem to rule out model (2) if we are to do adequate justice to important features of EU law, and to the self-understandings of EU institutions. Some might consider model (3) to be a possibility, due to the fact that the EU legal system does not merely claim that it has the authority to determine the relationship between EU norms and norms of national law, but that it also claims that the terms of that relationship are set by the primacy doctrine: that EU law prevails over national law in cases of conflict. In this vein, Neil MacCormick once asked, (in somewhat devil's advocate mode):

> Once we have established this doctrine of the supremacy of Community law, however, the question inevitably to be posed is whether there is any need at all for an elaborate theory about interaction of distinct systems. If system X enjoys supremacy over system Y, why trouble to have a theory about separate systems, rather than a theory which acknowledges the fact that Y belongs to X as sub-system of it?[81]

As MacCormick himself went on to argue, however, to adopt this model would be to fail to do justice to important features of the national law of EU Member States, and, in particular, to fail to do justice to the self-understandings of Member States' legal institutions. This is, of course, a very familiar point to EU legal scholars; that is, that while the Court of Justice takes one view as regards the primacy of EU law over national law—that EU legal norms have such a status, and that they do so in virtue of the distinctive characteristics of the EU legal system itself[82]—national legal orders, and, in particular, national constitutional or supreme courts on behalf of those orders, frequently take a different view. Although out and out conflict is usually avoided, national constitutional courts have frequently made counter-claims placing limits or conditions on the Court of Justice's primacy doctrine, and, more importantly, have made it clear that, in their view, if and when EU law is allowed to prevail over national law in cases of conflict is a matter for the national constitutional order to determine. This latter point is clear from case law emanating from various Member States on this issue, such as the views of the House of Lords (now Supreme Court) in the UK or the *Bundesverfassungsgericht* (the Federal Constitutional Court) in Germany. The UK has, in the end, allowed EU law to prevail over conflicting national law by suspending and disapplying the latter, but has made it clear that this is by reason of and subject to features of the UK's constitutional order.[83] Germany has taken the view (expressed at various times in more or less subtle terms) that it is the German constitutional order, and the *Bundesverfassungsgericht* as guardian of it, which retain the duty to ensure that EU law is compatible with Germany's constitutional order, and the rights and duties of

---

[81] N MacCormick, 'Juridical Pluralism and the Risk of Constitutional Conflict' in MacCormick, *Questioning Sovereignty*, see n 39, 116.

[82] Case 6/64 *Costa v ENEL* [1964] ECR 585 at 594; Case 11/70 *Internationale Handelsgesellschaft* [1970] ECR 1125; Declaration #17 concerning primacy, including the Opinion of the Council Legal Service of 22nd June 2007, annexed to the final act of the intergovernmental conference which adopted the Treaty of Lisbon, OJ 2008, C115/344.

[83] See eg *Factortame Ltd v Secretary of State for Transport (No 2)* [1991] AC 603, especially per Lord Bridge. More recently see the re-statement of this understanding of the constitutional basis for EU law being operative in the UK in the European Union Act 2011, s 18.

the German people thereunder, and that hence any primacy granted to EU law is conditional on that law staying within its proper limits and properly respecting the identity of the German constitutional order.[84]

It would thus be problematic to adopt model (3) above, the 'One Big Legal System' model, because this would fail to do justice to the way in which EU Member States understand their own law, and the relation of that law with EU law. Those national legal orders are, like the EU legal order, making claims which I have contended are 'distinct legal system' claims, that is, claims to determine for themselves the existence, force, and effect of their norms, and to determine for themselves the relation between their own norms and the norms of other normative systems with which they come into contact. The fact that such claims are consistently made by national legal orders is one piece of evidence supporting the view that they remain distinct legal systems. Granting a permission to another normative system to operate within the bounds of a national legal system, and even a permission for the norms of that other system to prevail over national law in cases of conflict is still a distinct legal system claim, because the authority to grant that permission is grounded in the national legal system, which hence still 'calls the shots' as regards the relations between itself and other normative systems. This being so, it seems that model (1) outlined above, the 'Distinct but Interacting Legal Systems' model or the '27 plus 1' model, best captures the current state of affairs as regards legal systems in the EU.

Are these 'distinct legal system' claims—claims by EU and national legal orders to determine the existence and effect of their norms, and to determine the relation between their own norms and the norms of other normative systems—best understood and/or termed as claims to *supremacy*?[85] My view is that the term 'supremacy' may be misleading here. As we have seen in the preceding discussion , these 'distinct legal system'—claims, we might say, to *normative self-determination*—are not claims to possess some kind of absolutist political sovereignty, and are not necessarily claims that 'in cases of conflict between them, the legal norms of my system always trump the legal norms of your system' either. Rather, claims to normative self-determination can be claims that it lies within the grant of a given legal system to permit the operation of other legal systems within their normative domain, and can have as their content that the norms of those other systems prevail over the norms of the system granting the permission in cases of conflict.

---

[84] See *Solange I* decision of the Bundesverfassungsgericht (BVerfG) [1974] 2 CMLR 540; *Solange II* decision of the BVerfG of 22 October 1986, *Re Wünsche Handelsgesellschaft* [1987] 3 CMLR 225; Bundesverfassungsgericht Decision of 7th June 2000, 2 BvL 1/97; *Brunner v The European Union Treaty* [1994] 1 CMLR 57; Judgment on the constitutionality of the Lisbon Treaty, BVerfG, 2 BvE/08, 30th June 2009, available at: <http://www.bverfg.de/entscheidungen/es20090630_2bve000208en.html>.

[85] Several legal theorists regard a claim to supremacy in respect of other normative systems as a necessary feature of legal systems, eg J Raz, *Practical Reason and Norms*, see n 54, 151–2; J Raz, *The Authority of Law*, see n 41, 118–19; J Finnis, *Natural Law and Natural Rights*, see n 22, 148–9 and 267. Recently, however, Andrei Marmor has questioned whether a claim to supremacy is a necessary feature of legal systems, in A Marmor, *Positive Law and Objective Values* (Oxford: Clarendon Press, 2001), 39–42.

In order to be a legal system, then, I propose that something has to make a claim to normative self-determination. This claim, however, can come in many forms, including granting a permission to another normative system to operate within the normative realm of the system making the grant, and even granting a permission for that second system's norms to prevail over the legal norms of the granting system under certain conditions. So long as the permissions so granted remain within the normative determination of the granting system, which hence still 'calls the shots' as regards the relations between itself and other normative systems, then this remains a claim to normative self-determination, and the system claiming it remains a distinct legal system. Such claims to normative self-determination are persistently made by both the EU and its Member States, and are made in the context of those entities claiming to possess distinct legal systems. In my view, all this further underscores that we have reason to persist with the project of developing a theory of legal systems apt to characterize novel legal phenomena such as EU law and its relations with the national law of the EU's Member States.[86]

4 Conclusion and Next Steps

Although it is a topic which has long lain dormant, the time is ripe to revive work on the theory of legal systems, in order to develop an account of legal systems capable of characterizing and improving our understanding of non-state legal phenomena, such as that which is found in the contemporary EU. I have claimed that we should resist challenges which contend that the concept of a legal system has had its day and is no longer of use in understanding such phenomena, and have defended this claim in part

---

[86] In both *Legality's Borders*, and 'Not a System but an Order: An Inter-Institutional View of European Union Law' in this volume, Culver and Giudice contend that these claims to normative self-determination (as I have termed them) made by the EU and by its Member States do not contribute to the case for understanding these entities as possessing distinct legal systems. Their view is that, although apparently sincerely made, such claims are not to be taken at face value ('Not a System but an Order', in this volume at pp 62–8), and, in *Legality's Borders*, are to be explained away, as 'fictions' (72). It is not entirely clear to me why they so strongly wish to explain away this persistent and pervasive aspect of the self-understandings of both the EU legal order and national legal orders, especially given their declared methodological aim in *Legality's Borders* to '…test conceptual explanations of legal governance against observationally-available evidence' (in the Introduction, at xvii). In their chapter in this volume, they seem to contend that understanding the EU and national legal orders in terms of distinct legal systems cannot explain interactions between institutions and between legal norms in those orders, and cannot explain coordination and shared law in those orders, such that a legal system's analysis must hold EU and national legal orders to be doing nothing more than 'talking past each other' (see pp 66–8 in this volume). This, however, does not ring true. There are innumerable different forms of interaction between institutions and between norms in the EU and in Member States, and many EU norms are fully accepted and applied by Member States' courts in national legal systems in a way which results in co-ordination and 'shared law'. EU law and national law, EU institutions and national institutions, are hence frequently talking *to* each other, in many, various, and changing ways. My analysis above claims only that views of the *legal basis* upon which such extensive acceptance and sharing rest differ as between the EU legal system and national legal systems. That there is extensive (though not complete) such sharing, acceptance, and coordination is not seriously in doubt in a Union of more than fifty years' standing.

by reference to the existence and importance of the self-understandings of those administering and living under various bodies of law. Those administering and living under law regard it as the law *of something*, of some political entity or unit of societal governance. That we think of aspects of our social and political lives in terms of such units and their law is a pervasive feature of our self-understanding and cannot be dispensed with as lightly as some contemporary legal philosophers might have us believe. The concept of a legal system is hence no mere technical device invented by legal philosophers in order to further their research projects. It is a concept which is used by political entities, and by those living within them, in order to demarcate something important: that which is distinctively 'their law', with its own means of normative self-determination, which aims to realize certain values, and which can become the focus of attitudes of identification and attachment.

Much remains to be done in developing a fully fledged theory of legal systems able to characterize the growing range of state, intra-state, trans-state, supra-state, and other legal phenomena with which we are faced today. In concluding the present discussion, I would like to draw attention to and render explicit a distinction which has been implicit throughout much of the above analysis, and which I believe has an important place in future work on this topic.

In my view, the discussion in this chapter highlights the fact that criteria used to determine the existence, identity, limits, and character of legal systems fall into two broad categories which we might term 'legal criteria' and 'politico-social criteria' respectively. The legal criteria include matters such as those discussed in Sections 3C and 3D of this chapter, that is, regarding those legal institutions which something must possess in order to be a distinct legal system, and what claims legal systems must make regarding the relation between the legal norms of that system, and the norms of other normative systems.

However, as the preceding discussion should readily reveal, I am of the view that such legal criteria are not the only factors which legal philosophers must take into account in trying to move towards a theory of legal systems able to characterize non-state as well as state phenomena. Especially in Sections 3A and 3B above, I discussed the role which legal systems can play in shaping and expressing aspects of polities' identities. In my view, the self-understandings of those subject to and administering law, and their beliefs about and attitudes towards the legal systems in which those laws find a home—including attitudes of identification with and alienation from the law— are important in justifying the theory of legal systems as a topic worthy of continued jurisprudential attention, and also play a role in determining what counts as a distinct legal system, and in ascertaining the distinctive character of legal systems. In those sections, I also drew attention to the fact that determining the identity of a distinct legal system is bound up with the question of the identity and character of the political entity or unit of societal governance which that legal system is a legal system *of*. Questions such as which features must a political entity or unit of societal governance possess in order to have a distinct legal system, and how should we understand the relationship between that legal system, and the political entity which it is a legal system of? (and, more broadly, what other social sub-systems—educational? cultural? economic?—need to exist in a given society to support the existence of its political and legal systems?), are hence important matters to investigate in moving forward with a theory of legal systems apt to characterize contemporary governance arrangements. This second set of issues, which I have termed 'politico-social criteria', are thus, I believe, also relevant to determining the existence, identity, limits, and character of legal systems.

It should be noted that as regards this second group of criteria, and, in particular, as regards the self-understandings, attitudes, and beliefs regarding legal systems of those subject to and administering law, I am not claiming that those sometimes somewhat hazy self-understandings can alone determine the existence, identity, limits, and character of legal systems. Nor am I claiming that the job of the legal philosopher is merely to record and slavishly follow the self-understandings of those subject to and administering law. As I have argued elsewhere,[87] legal philosophy is not a kind of market research or dictation exercise wherein the legal theorist merely passively records wholesale the self-understandings of those living under law. Rather, the legal theorist has to be able to discriminate between and make evaluative judgments about the self-understandings of those living under and administering law in order to pick out which are most relevant in understanding law's important and significant features. Moreover, some self-understandings of the participants may be confused, mistaken, insufficiently focused, or vague. Some self-understandings will be more important and significant than others in explaining the concept of a legal system. There is thus no denying that legal philosophers have significant work to do in extrapolating coherent and cogent theoretical accounts from such self-understandings, and that it falls to those theorists to sort out what is central and significant in legal phenomena and in our understanding of it. All of this requires the legal theorist in constructing her theories not merely to record and reproduce but to evaluate and make judgments as regards the self-understandings of those living under and administering the law.

All that said, however, I do regard the self-understandings, attitudes, and beliefs of those living under and subject to law as vitally important to the project of developing a theory of legal systems apt to characterize non-state legal phenomena. The concept of a legal system features in the self-understandings of those living in law-governed polities. This being so, if we wish to understand ourselves and understand the polities in which we live, then part of what we must seek to understand is how we think about and navigate the course of our lives, given those self-understandings. People's attitudes towards, beliefs about, and self-understandings in terms of the concept of a legal system hence partly constitute that which we wish to explain, and must play an important role

---

[87] See eg J Dickson, *Evaluation and Legal Theory*, see n 22, *passim*; J Dickson, 'Methodology in Jurisprudence: A critical survey', (2004) 10 *Legal Theory* 117–56, especially sections IIB and IIC; J Dickson, 'On Naturalizing Jurisprudence: Some Comments on Brian Leiter's View of What Jurisprudence Should Become' (July 2011) 30 *Law and Philosophy* 477–97, section III.

in any such explanation.[88] Whether the EU or Scotland has a distinct legal system is not entirely independent of whether the citizenry, and the legal institutional actors in those polities, regard them as possessing distinct legal systems, think of them as possessing distinct legal systems, and identify, interpret, recognize, and apply law based on their view regarding whether they possess distinct legal systems.[89]

Future work on the theory of legal systems, then, must consider both legal and politico-social criteria in determining the existence, identity, limits, and character of legal systems. Moreover, such work must also consider the relation between these sets of criteria with regard to those same issues.[90] These and other matters discussed in this chapter are ripe for future attention in working towards a theory of legal systems able to improve our understanding of contemporary governance arrangements including supra-national legal regulation of the kind found in the European Union. The present discussion is both a contribution to such work, and a call to arms in respect of it.

[88] For a fuller statement of my views on these issues, see *Evaluation and Legal Theory*, see n 22, especially ch 2.

[89] In the EU context, cases such as *Costa* (Case 6/64 *Costa v ENEL* [1964] ECR 585) and *Kadi* (Joined Cases C-402/05P and C-415/05P *Kadi and Al Barakaat v Council* [2008] ECR I-6351) discussed above stand as examples of the Court's view that the EU possesses a distinct legal system, and of this view having a decisive bearing on the Court's interpretation of the strength and enforceability of EU law. I discuss some examples in relation to Scotland in Dickson, 'The Idea of a Legal System', see n 70.

[90] I hope to engage further with these issues in a book-length project considering the theory of legal systems in non-state contexts including the EU and Scotland.

3

Not a System but an Order

An Inter-Institutional View of European Union Law

Keith Culver and Michael Giudice*

The historic foundations of the European Union (EU) lie in treaty-based voluntary agreement of a sort reasonably well understood by legal theorists. Yet from early on in its existence the EU has claimed to be something else: a new legal order, neither a super-state nor an intergovernmental association.[1] But what is that legal order? And what kind of philosophical tools are needed to best explain it? In a recent article, Julie Dickson suggests that the puzzle at the heart of the EU can be usefully explored by asking the following question: how many legal systems are there in the EU?[2] Dickson explores several possible answers: one legal system for every Member State; one legal system for every Member State plus one additional EU legal system; or perhaps only one, super-EU legal system. If there is more than one system—ie more than just one super-EU legal system—how are legal theorists to characterize the relations among the systems? In particular, since many Member State courts and the Court of Justice of the EU[3] have claimed supremacy of final authority to interpret and apply EU law, can we view either Member State legal systems or an EU legal system as in some meaningful sense derivative, subordinate, or part of the other(s)? Or does this puzzle point us back to giving more serious consideration to the possibility that the EU's claimed 'new legal

* Professor and Director, Okanagan Sustainability Institute, University of British Columbia, and Associate Professor of Philosophy, York University, Toronto, Canada, respectively. For helpful comments we owe thanks to Neil MacCormick, Craig Scott, Francois Tanguay-Renaud, Wil Waluchow, and especially Julie Dickson. We also thank the audience who took part in the seminar series 'Legal Philosophy Between State and Transnationalism', co-organized by the Jack and Mae Nathanson Centre on Transnational Human Rights, Crime, and Security, Osgoode Hall Law School, and the Department of Philosophy, York University, Toronto, at which a version of this chapter was presented in November 2009. Finally, we are grateful to Oxford University Press for permission to re-use material from our book, *Legality's Borders* (New York: Oxford University Press, 2010).

[1] Case 26/62 *Van Gend en Loos v Nederlandse administratie der belastingen* [1963] ECR 1, 12.

[2] J Dickson, 'How Many Legal Systems?: Some Puzzles Regarding the Identity Conditions of, and Relations Between, Legal Systems in the European Union' (2008) 2 *Problema: Annuario de Filosophia y Teoria del Derecho* 9.

[3] Hereinafter 'the Court of Justice'.

order' really is something new and different, not usefully reduced to familiar, perhaps too familiar, talk of legal system?

While it is this last possibility that we intend to pursue, it is beyond the scope of this chapter to offer a comprehensive account of the foundations and nature of EU law and its relations with Member States' law, nor is it possible to develop in full detail the elements of a theory which would be suitable for such a task. Instead we propose to focus on one of the most philosophically puzzling aspects of EU law and its relations with Member States' law: the various rival supremacy claims made by the legal institutions of Member States and the legal institutions of the EU. We will suggest that, if taken at face value, the rival supremacy claims are indeed best explained by a clash between Member State legal systems and an EU legal system. That is, if each rival supremacy claim is taken as true or justified, the foundations of EU law and its relations with Member States' law are best explained in terms of the familiar idea of legal system and the inherent conflict which arises when legal systems attempt to combine. Yet we will argue that this view is ultimately misleading, as there are good reasons not to take such claims at face value. Our approach, which tracks law and legal orders in the interactions between institutions of law, understands EU law and its interaction with Member State law in terms of inter-institutional interaction, capturing tension and cohesion in relations between EU law and Member States' law, but setting aside as insufficiently nuanced the view which sees that interaction in terms of conflicts between adjacent legal systems.

Our analysis will proceed in the following steps. In the first section we present and distinguish the various supremacy claims made by the legal institutions of Member States and of the EU. In the second section we explain how the various supremacy claims are not only facts to be observed in the EU; they also reflect a distinct philosophical way of understanding law, in which law's foundational unit or home is taken to be the comprehensive, supreme, and open legal system. In the third section we attempt to demonstrate the limits of viewing EU law through the lens of a legal system, and suggest that its limits are sufficiently significant to warrant exploration of an alternative approach. In the fourth section we lay out in a general way the core elements of our alternative account, what we call an inter-institutional view of law, developed in greater detail elsewhere.[4] In the fifth and final section we apply our account to EU law and its relations with Member States' law.

1 Rival Supremacy Claims

One of the more remarkable features of EU law and its relations with Member States' law is the near universal agreement among EU and Member State institutions that EU law has priority over Member States' law. No other regional or international organization has achieved coordination of norms and enforcement mechanisms, including a

---

[4] See K Culver and M Giudice, *Legality's Borders* (New York: Oxford University Press, 2010).

doctrine of direct effect, understood as the direct enforceability or 'invoke-ability' in Member States' courts of legal rights derived from EU law, to the extent of the EU. Yet despite such agreement on the primacy of EU law, there exists ongoing and fundamental disagreement on two other issues: the ultimate validity of EU law in relation to Member States law and the final authority to interpret the relation in particular instances of dispute.

On the first issue, there is so far enduring disagreement between EU institutions and many Member States on the ultimate validity or legal foundation of EU law; in other words, on what authorizes the primacy of EU law over Member States' law. In several cases the Court of Justice has maintained that the ultimate validity of the doctrine of primacy of EU law rests with EU law itself. In their chapter on the supremacy of EU law, Paul Craig and Gráinne de Búrca outline five arguments presented by the Court of Justice in *Costa*, the first case in which the supremacy of EU law was explicitly asserted:

> *First* is the statement that the Treaty created its own legal order which immediately became 'an integral part' of the legal systems of the Member States . . . *Second*, and perhaps more contentious, is the Court's statement of how, in constitutional terms, the Member States created this legal order. This was done, said the Court, by the States transferring to the new Community institutions 'real powers stemming from a limitation of sovereignty' . . . In its *third* argument, the Court drew on the spirit and the aims of the Treaty to conclude that it was 'impossible' for the Member States to accord primacy to domestic laws. The 'spirit' of the Treaty required that they all act with equal diligence to give full effect to Community laws which they had accepted on the basis of 'reciprocity' . . . The *fourth* argument was that the obligations undertaken by the Member States in the Treaty would be 'merely contingent' rather than unconditional if they were to be subject to later legislative acts on the part of the States . . . The only genuinely textual evidence used by the Court was in its *final* argument: that the language of direct applicability in what is now Article 249 would be meaningless if States could negate the effect of Community law by passing subsequent inconsistent legislation . . . [5]

As Craig and de Búrca observe, while the conceptual foundations for the supremacy of EU law according to the Court of Justice are first articulated in *Costa*, it is only in subsequent cases that the scope of the supremacy doctrine emerges. The Court of Justice has maintained (i) that Member State laws, in cases of conflict with EU law, are to be disapplied, though they are in no sense repealed or deemed unconstitutional;[6] and (ii) Member State courts, as well as relevant administrative agencies,[7] are responsible for applying EU laws where these conflict with Member State laws.[8] In other words, while the Court of Justice's role is to interpret EU law and its relation with Member States' law, and to rule on the validity of EU law, responsibility for applying

---

[5] P Craig and G de Búrca (eds), *EU Law: Text, Cases, and Materials,* 4th edn (Oxford: Oxford University Press, 2008), 346.
[6] Case 11/70 *Internationale Handelsgesellschaft* [1970] ECR; Case 106/77 *Simmenthal* [1978] ECR 629; and Cases C-10–22/97 *Ministero delle Finanze v IN.CO.GE* [1998] ECR I-6307.
[7] ibid 350, referring to Case C-118/00 *Larsy v INASTI* [2001] ECR I-5063, paras 52–53.
[8] Case 106/77 *Simmenthal* [1978] ECR 629.

and enforcing the supremacy of EU laws within Member States rests with Member States. Yet, from the perspective of the Court of Justice and EU law, this does not mean that Member State courts and institutions have final authority to determine the relation between EU law and Member State law. On the second issue identified above, the Court of Justice maintains that it has final authority to interpret the meaning, scope, and application of EU law, as well as its relations with Member States' law.[9]

From the perspective of Member States and their institutions, things are very different. While Member State institutions maintain that EU law enjoys primacy, it is only because EU law is authorized by the law of Member States, especially their constitutional law. So, for example, the highest courts in Germany and France recognize that while their respective constitutions permit certain sovereignty-limiting international agreements, such agreements only have validity because authorized by domestic constitutional law.[10] On the second issue, of who holds final authority to interpret the meaning and force of EU law within Member States, several Member States have made it clear that such authority lies with their domestic courts.[11]

As we stated at the outset, the various supremacy claims made by Member State legal institutions and EU legal institutions are not simply facts to be observed, as they also exhibit a certain theoretical presumption about the nature and foundation of law. In particular, the various supremacy claims reflect a particular philosophical way of understanding law, one whose allegiance to certain assumptions regarding the nature of law tends, we argue, to hamper rather than advance understanding of supra-state legal phenomena such as EU law. Let us explain that way of understanding law, and the misleading assumptions it embodies.

2 Legal Systems as Comprehensive, Supreme, and Open Normative Systems

The vast majority of philosophers of law who have attempted to describe and explain the nature of law—what law is and what it means for a society to have law,

---

[9] See Article 19 of the Treaty on European Union (TEU). See also 11/70 *Internationale Handelsgesellschaft* [1970] ECR; Case 106/77 *Simmenthal* [1978] ECR 629; and Case 314/85 *Firma Foto-Frost v Hauptzollamt Lübeck-Ost* [1987] ECR 4199, paras 15, 17–18. For discussion see Craig and de Búrca, see n 5, 467–74, and S Weatherill (ed) *Cases and Materials on EU Law*, 9th edn (Oxford: Oxford University Press, 2010), 79–89.

[10] In Germany: *Internationale Handelsgesellschaft mbH v Einfuhr- und Vorratstelle für Getreide und Futtermittel* [1974 2 CMLR 540; *Re Wünsche Handelsgesellschaft* [1987] 3 CMLR 225; *Brunner w The European Union Treaty* [1994] 1 CMLR 57, and most recently the Judgment on 30 June 2009, *Bundesverfassungsgericht*, BVerfG, 2 BvE 2/08, available at: <http://www.bundesverfassungsgericht.de/entscheidungen/es20090630_2bve000208en.html>. In France: *Administration des Douanes v Société 'Cafés Jacques Vabre' et Sàrl Weigel et Cie* [1975] 2 CMLR 336, and *Raoul Georges Nicolo* [1990] 1 CMLR 173.

[11] eg in Germany: *Brunner v The European Union Treaty* [1994] 1 CMLR 57, and *Bundesverfassungsgericht*, BVerfG, 2 BvE 2/08, available at: <http://www.bundesverfassungsgericht.de/entscheidungen/es20090630_2bve000208en.html>. In the UK: *Factortame Ltd v Secretary of the State for Transport (No. 2)* [1991] 1 AC 603. In Italy: *Frontini v Ministero delle Finanze* [1974] 2 CMLR 372. In Poland: *Polish Membership of the European Union* (Accession Treaty) K18/04, 11 May 2005.

to live under law, etc—have taken the law of the modern sovereign state as the primary example of law and developed their theories of the nature of law on the basis of reflection about law in the context of the sovereign state. While the forms and degrees of sovereignty are many,[12] the typical existence conditions of a sovereign state are these: there is a defined territory, a permanent population, and an effective government whose institutions together (i) enjoy a monopoly of the use of force and the associated exclusive authority to create, apply, and enforce law, and (ii) have the capacity to enter into relations with other sovereign states.[13] Perhaps the best statement of the importance of theorizing the nature of state law is offered by Joseph Raz,[14] who identifies what he calls the 'assumption of the importance of municipal law', which 'reflects our, or at least my, intuitive perception that municipal legal systems are sufficiently important and sufficiently different from most other normative systems to deserve being studied for their own sake'.[15] Raz is certainly not alone in having such an 'intuitive perception', as the assumption of the importance of municipal law has been shared by nearly all philosophers of law working in the analytical tradition,[16] leading us to take for present purposes the views of Raz as generally representative of analytical theorists' approach to our topic in this chapter.[17]

What then is the nature of law within such states?[18] It is systemic, and state legal systems can be characterized, following Raz, in terms of three characteristic claims they exhibit: *comprehensiveness*, *supremacy*, and *openness*.[19] In exhibiting a claim of *comprehensiveness* a legal system embodies the assertion that there is no sphere of conduct which is immune to the system's claim to authority to regulate in some way, either by prohibition, requirement, or permission. In this way legal systems differ from other sorts of normative systems, such as sports associations and universities, which have limited purposes and so limited spheres of regulation. Legal systems claim to regulate sports associations and universities, as well as all other organizations and relations in society. A claim to *supremacy* can be seen in a legal system's self-understanding that its standards provide the ultimate foundation or authority for all other normative standards recognized by the system. In states with a written constitution, the hierarchy of rules and procedures which embodies a legal system's claim to

---

[12] See HLA Hart, *The Concept of Law*, 2nd edn (Oxford: Clarendon Press, 1994), ch 10.

[13] See A Buchanan, *Justice, Legitimacy, and Self-Determination* (Oxford: Oxford University Press, 2003), referring to the Montevideo Convention, 1933.

[14] For an account of how Raz's view modifies and develops Hart's influential account of state law, see Culver and Giudice, see n 4, 42–4.

[15] J Raz, *The Authority of Law*, 2nd edn (Oxford: Oxford University Press, 2009), 105.

[16] In addition to Hart and Raz, see R Dworkin, *Law's Empire* (Cambridge, MA: Harvard University Press, 1986), W Waluchow, *Inclusive Legal Positivism* (Oxford: Clarendon Press, 1994), J Coleman, *The Practice of Principle* (Oxford: Oxford University Press, 2001).

[17] The notable exception is Hans Kelsen. See H Kelsen, *Principles of International Law*, 2nd edn (Toronto: Holt, Rinehart & Winston of Canada, 1966).

[18] 'State legal system' and 'municipal legal system' will be used interchangeably.

[19] Raz, see n 15, 116–20.

supremacy is readily transparent: constitutions typically claim to be the supreme law of the state, and authorize the power of government officials and institutions (which might be either centrally or federally structured) to create laws and regulations. A claim to supremacy can also be detected in the way a legal system views conflicts between its legal norms and other types of normative standards; eg, where legal norms conflict with religious norms or moral norms, the legal norms will be given priority, unless the legal system itself provides otherwise (which thereby preserves its claim to supremacy). Finally, a legal system is *open*: the norms of other systems—eg, sports leagues, trade unions, universities, etc—can be supported by legal systems and 'adopted' or certified by legal systems for special purposes. Legal systems support other systems most often by providing for their creation by means of statute, as, eg, universities are typically established by legislation, and the norms of other systems are adopted when they are applied by courts to resolve disputes arising within those other systems (Raz also views conflict of laws cases in terms of the relation of adoption, in which domestic courts apply the norms of a foreign system to resolve a dispute without the foreign norms thereby becoming part of the domestic system).[20] As Raz claims, the features of comprehensiveness, supremacy, and openness serve well to explain the way in which '...we feel that legal systems not only happen to be the most important institutionalized system governing human society, but that that is part of their nature'.[21]

With these elements of Raz's account in hand, how well does such a view of law, as fundamentally systemic in the way Raz explains, make sense of EU law and its relations with Member States' law? Before answering this question we first need to raise an issue regarding its appropriateness. The question of the appropriateness of an explanation is a methodological issue, and Raz's stance with respect to that issue is expressed in the following two observations. Raz's first observation concerns the nature of 'legal system' as a conceptual tool. He writes:

> The term 'a legal system' is not a technical legal term...Therefore, when trying to clarify the notion of a legal system, the legal theorist does not aim at defining clearly the sense in which the term is employed by legislators, judges, or lawyers. He is, rather, attempting to forge a useful conceptual tool, one which will help him to a better understanding of the nature of law.[22]

Raz's creative 'forging' of a 'tool' for the specific purpose of philosophical explanation of law may seem at first glance to be at odds with the goal of presenting an explanation of law which is more than a merely subjectively satisfying set of generalizations or impressions. This tool-based, perspectival approach is, however, far from unique to Raz,[23] and once demonstrated, the meta-theoretical merits of this creative approach can be seen to outweigh concerns regarding its narrowness or subjectivity. None of the

---

[20] Raz, see n 15, 120.   [21] Raz, see n 15, 116.   [22] Raz, see n 15, 78.

[23] For Raz's most sustained work on the methodology of legal theory, see J Raz, *Between Authority and Interpretation* (Oxford: Oxford University Press, 2009), chs 2, 3.

ideas of 'grundnorm',[24] 'rule of recognition',[25] 'internal point view',[26] 'integrity',[27] and 'practical reasonableness',[28] are technical legal terms, but each figures centrally in the philosophical theories of law of Kelsen, Hart, Dworkin, and Finnis respectively, who are among the most influential legal philosophers of the twentieth century, and who each try to make sense of the nature of law as it is, in more than a limitedly subjective way. The element of creativity in these approaches to philosophical explanation should not be alarming, as in each instance creative explanation is constrained by what law really is. Each idea is meant to be philosophically illuminating—by identifying core, central, or otherwise salient elements of the nature of law—but is ultimately and for the same reason subject to assessment against the facts of law's role in social life (which is not to say that philosophers of law always agree on the facts and their relevance).

Raz's second observation in relation to the methodological issue has already been identified. This is the assumption that a theory of law is complete or minimally adequate so long as it captures salient examples of municipal legal systems. Raz is careful, however, to show that this limitation to his theory is not a matter of wilful blindness to the existence of other normative systems and the relation of municipal legal systems to those other systems:

> Obviously, in part the investigation of municipal systems is designed to compare and contrast them with other normative systems. Indeed it is to this part that the present essay is dedicated. In pursuing such investigations it may turn out that municipal systems are not unique, that all their essential features are shared by, say, international law or church law. If this is indeed so, well and good. But it is not a requirement of the adequacy of a legal theory that it should be so or indeed that it should not be so. It is, however a criterion of adequacy that the theory will successfully illuminate the nature of municipal legal systems.[29]

So it is not a requirement for the adequacy of a legal theory, according to Raz, that it illuminate or explain other non-municipal forms of normative system which may be called law, such as international law or religious law. This observation regarding the methodological purpose and limits of Raz's theory, combined with his view that the idea of legal system ought to be judged according to its usefulness in helping us to understand the nature of law, naturally invites scepticism regarding the relevance of Raz's theory of a legal system to the EU and its relations with Member States' law. Why would we expect a theory of law developed in and for the context of the municipal state legal system to serve us at all well in making sense of what so many believe is not an instance of a municipal legal system—EU law? Should we instead explore the possibility that a theoretical approach detached from presumption of the centrality

---

[24] See H Kelsen, *Pure Theory of Law*, 2nd edn, trans Max Knight (Berkeley: University of California Press, 1967).

[25] See Hart, see n 12.

[26] Hart.

[27] See R Dworkin, see n 16.

[28] See J Finnis, *Natural Law and Natural Rights* (Oxford: Clarendon Press, 1980).

[29] Raz, see n 15, 105.

of municipal law to a general theory of law might offer a better account of EU law, free of potential distortions which might be induced by the municipal assumption?

We should note that there is even some evidence which suggests that Raz would support the view that existing accounts of legal systems, including his own, may be ill-suited or unable to explain the nature of novel phenomena such as EU law. In an article on the methodology of legal theory, Raz announces in rather stark terms that the EU poses a special—as yet unmet—challenge to explaining the identity and continuity of legal systems:

> John Austin thought that, necessarily, the legal institutions of every legal system are not subject to—that is, do not recognize—the jurisdiction of legal institutions outside their system over them . . . Kelsen believed that necessarily constitutional continuity is both necessary and sufficient for the identity of a legal system. We know that both claims are false. The countries of the European Union recognize, and for a time the independent countries of the British Empire recognized, the jurisdiction of outside legal institutions over them, thus refuting Austin's theory. And the law of most countries provides counter-examples to Kelsen's claim . . . So far as I know, Austin's and Kelsen's failures were not made good. That is, no successful alternative explanations were offered. In spite of this there is no great flurry of philosophical activity to plug the gap. Rather, the problem that their mistaken doctrines were meant to explain, namely the problem of the identity and continuity of legal systems, lost its appeal to legal philosophers, who do not mind leaving it unsolved. Interest has shifted elsewhere.[30]

Raz's observation about the lack of philosophical attention to problems of identity and continuity was made in 1998, and quite clearly no longer holds, given the active interest displayed in recent philosophical work in explaining the nature of the EU.[31] But more importantly, we should not fall foul of a version of the genetic fallacy: it does not follow from the fact that an idea was developed for use in explaining a particular type of phenomenon that it will be of no use in explaining other types of phenomena. Indeed, at least in the context of the EU, the opposite seems to be true as 'legal system' may still be put to work with useful results.

In Section 1, we observed the various rival supremacy claims evident in the relations between EU law and the law of Member States. According to Raz's view of law, these various rival supremacy claims signal the presence of various rival legal systems. Indeed this is what some suggest we might have in the EU:[32] various Member State legal systems, a distinct EU legal system which is separate but connected to Member State legal systems, and possibly a super-EU legal system in which Member State legal systems are sub-systems and thus subordinate. We might also have, more importantly, a solution to the puzzle about EU law that Dickson identifies, as we appear to have a philosophical theory of law—law as fundamentally systemic in Raz's sense—which fits the facts, key facts even,

---

[30] Raz, see n 23, 58.

[31] See eg N MacCormick, *Questioning Sovereignty* (Oxford: Oxford University Press, 1999), N Walker (ed), *Sovereignty in Transition* (Oxford: Hart Publishing, 2003), and Dickson, see n 2; and of course, see the various contributions to the present volume.

[32] Dickson, see n 2.

of rival supremacy claims which characterize EU law.[33] But is our work really done? We certainly have in hand a philosophical explanation of rival supremacy claims surrounding EU law and its institutions, but is the explanation the best available?

In what follows we accept the plausibility of explaining of EU law and its relations with Member States in terms of Raz's notion of a comprehensive, supreme, and open normative system, yet we argue that this approach has limits which become especially prominent in attempting to make sense of novel legal orders such as the EU.[34] In later sections we aim to supply a theoretical approach which provides a better explanation of the phenomena. Our argument begins with critical analysis of the truth or justifiability of rival supremacy claims.

3 Can Rival Supremacy Claims All Be True?

How and why should we be critical of the view which understands rival supremacy claims as indicators of the presence of competing legal systems? After all, we have accepted that rival supremacy claims are in fact sincerely made, and we have further accepted that these rival claims are phenomena which must be explained by any satisfactory philosophical theory of the foundations of EU law and its relations with the law of Member States. Our engagement with these claims begins from observation that the making of a justified claim is very different from the mere making of a claim. Indeed, many of the central figures of analytical jurisprudence have taken pains to emphasize the importance of the task of distinguishing justified from unjustified claims. Bentham was especially colourful in expression of his contempt for what he calls 'legal fictions', warning that, '. . . above all the pestilential breath of Fiction poisons the sense of every instrument it comes near'.[35] Bentham identified several fictions as he saw them, frequently taking Blackstone's *Commentaries* to task. Here is a useful example, which illustrates Bentham's distinction between 'judgments of law' and 'judgments of common sense':

> Speaking of an Act of Parliament, 'There needs', [Blackstone] says, 'no formal promulgation to give it the force of a Law, as was necessary by the Civil Law with regard to the Emperor's Edicts: *because* every man in England is, *in judgment of Law*, party to the making of an Act of Parliament, being present threat by his representatives.' This for aught I know, may be a good *judgment of Law*; because any thing may be called judgment of Law, that comes from a Lawyer, who has got a name: it seems, however, not much like any thing that can be called *judgment of common sense*.[36]

[33] For discussion, see Chapter 2.

[34] We have also argued elsewhere that Raz's view has limits in explaining state legal systems, considered individually and in isolation. See Culver and Giudice, see n 4, ch 2.

[35] J Bentham, *A Fragment on Government* (JH Burns and HLA Hart (eds), Cambridge: Cambridge University Press, 1988), 21.

[36] Bentham, see n 35, 17.

In his typically trenchant terms, Bentham offers a useful dose of clarification. Law, through its legal institutions, might claim all sorts of things: that judges never make law, that rules of law which are grossly immoral are not rules of law at all, that a constitution will survive even the most successful and enduring revolutions, to name just a few. But as any philosopher of law knows, the making and even sincere belief in such claims does not make them true or justified.

Our sensitivity to Bentham's warning should not be read as a commitment to regarding supremacy claims as fictions in the sense that they are necessarily false or nonsensical. We do claim, however, that supremacy claims ought to be assessed wherever and whenever they are made, as they might not be true in certain contexts. We have particularly good reason to be suspicious of supremacy claims made in the context of the EU, precisely because it is a context in which several claims—rival claims—are made. Here our key question arrives: *can rival claims all be true or justified?*

As we have demonstrated in our exegesis of Raz's views, the dominant analytical approach to viewing the relations between legal systems is to presume a supreme legal system which authorizes or provides the validity for subordinate systems, much like a legal system provides support for the creation and enforcement of private contracts. This long-dominant view is thus committed to viewing the EU and its integration activities in terms of state-system interactions. Yet the relation between EU law and the law of Member States seems best characterized on this view not as integration of legal systems at all, but instead as a kind of systems clash.[37] If Member State legal systems claim to be comprehensive, supreme, and open, it seems impossible for them, as Raz suggests, to recognize the authority of external legal orders as supreme and still remain independent legal systems.[38] Yet such a self-understanding and set of claims clashes with the observation of the Court of Justice that the norms of EU law are supreme,[39] which in turn means, taking a Razian view, that the EU's legal system, to be a legal system, must claim supremacy, comprehensiveness, and openness to support the legal-normative practices of Member States. It should be noted, however, that this is not the only analytical approach to phenomena of the sort exhibited by the EU. According to a view which has its roots in Kelsen's work on the unity of law, there is no systems-clash problem generated by explaining a legal order in terms of rival supremacy claims of legal systems.[40] Kelsen's view contains his famous epistemological postulate of unity, which

[37] HP Glenn, 'Doin' the Transsystemic: Legal Systems and Legal Traditions' (2005) 50 *McGill Law Journal* 863, 896.

[38] Raz states: 'Since all legal systems claim to be supreme with respect to their subject-community, none can acknowledge any claim to supremacy over the same community which may be made by another legal system.' Raz, see n 15, 119.

[39] Case 6/64 *Costa v ENEL* [1964] ECR 585.

[40] Some of the literature on Kelsen's theory applied to the EU includes: I Weyland, 'The Application of Kelsen's Theory of the Legal System to European Community Law: The Supremacy Puzzle Resolved' (2002) 21 *Law and Philosophy* 1; C Richmond, 'Preserving the Identity Crisis: Autonomy, System and Sovereignty in European Law' (1997) 16 *Law and Philosophy* 377; N MacCormick, 'Beyond the Sovereign State' (1993) 56 *The Modern Law Review* 1; N Barber, 'Legal Pluralism and the European Union' (2006) 12 *European Law Journal* 306.

presumes that all valid legal norms must be viewed as a unitary system. Applied to the relation between state and international law, Kelsen's monistic view always reached the same conclusion: if one begins from the presumption of state law, international law must be viewed as deriving its validity from state law and completing the norms of state law.[41] From this perspective, state law is superior and international law is subordinate. Alternatively, if one begins from the presumption of international law, each state's law is to be viewed as deriving its validity from international law and the norms of each state's law are understood to complete the international legal norms. According to this view, international law is superior and state law is subordinate. Whether one begins from the presumption of state law or international law is entirely a matter of choice from the perspective of legal theory: both views can show equally well how state law and international law form one system, in a way in which the contents of state law and international law remain the same and do not conflict.[42]

A choice of explanatory stance or perspective certainly seems inevitable if one shares Kelsen's monistic view of the world of legal norms, driven by his epistemological postulate of unity. Some further grounds, then, must be sought and justified as the theorist adopts a state-law-first or international-law-first perspective.[43] Yet as Hart has shown, Kelsen's monistic view of the relation between state law and international law suffers from a decisive flaw, noticeable when one attempts to apply it in descriptive-explanation of the phenomena.[44] As Hart observes, for norms to form part of the same legal system, there must be actual practices of recognition of those norms by system-ically connected law-applying institutions such as courts. Otherwise, a theoretical presumption of unity will distort rather than illuminate the nature of relations between legal orders, and that distortion may be amplified by the necessary choice of explanatory perspectives generated by Kelsen's approach.

In the context of the EU, Neil MacCormick offers a rather different criticism of Kelsen's monistic view. MacCormick supposes that it is not an option to argue that in fact the legal systems of Member States and the EU are unconnected. Evidence of mutual recognition is easily gathered from the practices of Member State courts and the Court of Justice, and the union-constituting treaties currently in force.[45] Instead,

---

[41] Indeed, on this view, one must begin from the presumption of a particular state's law, in which case not only international law but also the law of every other state derives its validity from and completes the norms of the first state's law.

[42] H Kelsen, *General Theory of Law and State* (Anders Wedberg trans, reprint edn, New Jersey: Lawbook Exchange, 2009), 388. See also eg H Kelsen, see n 17, 587, and H Kelsen, 'Sovereignty', in SL Paulson and BL Paulson (eds), *Normativity and Norms: Critical Perspectives on Kelsenian Themes* (Oxford: Oxford University Press, 1998), 535–6. Kelsen always noted, however, that the choice is nonetheless very important from a political perspective.

[43] However, Kelsen hedges his bets on this. He writes: '[t]he two monistic theories may be accepted or rejected in the face of any empirically given stipulations of positive national or international law—just because they are epistemological hypotheses that do not carry any implications in that respect.' *General Theory of Law and State,* see n 42, 388.

[44] HLA Hart, *Essays in Jurisprudence and Philosophy of Law* (Oxford: Clarendon Press, 1983), 309.

[45] These are the Treaty on European Union (TEU) and the Treaty on the Functioning of the European Union (TFEU).

MacCormick advises that we give up the commitment to monism and hierarchy in thinking about the relations between legal systems, and adopt instead a view of juridical pluralism:

> No state's constitution is as such validated by that of any other, nor is it validated by Community law. For each state, the internal validity of Community law in the sense mandated by the 'supremacy' doctrine results from the state's amendment of constitutional and sub-constitutional law to the extent required to give effect and applicability to Community law. On the other hand, the Community's legal order is neither conditional upon the validity of any particular state's constitution, nor upon the sum of the conditions that the states might impose, for that would be no Community law at all. It would amount to no more than a bundle of overlapping laws to the extent that each state chose to acknowledge 'Community' laws and obligations. So relations between states *inter se* and between states and community are interactive rather than hierarchical. The legal systems of member-states and their common legal system of EC law are distinct but interacting systems of law, and hierarchical relationships of validity within criteria of validity proper to distinct systems do not add up to any sort of all-purpose superiority of one system over another.[46]

In MacCormick's view it is nothing less than a failure of imagination to suppose that legal systems must always interact with each other by trying to subordinate the other. There is no logical or sociological necessity for a hierarchical relation between systems. MacCormick writes:

> The key question becomes whether there can be a loss of sovereignty at one level without its inevitable and resultant re-creation at another. Is sovereignty like property, which can be given up only when another person gains it? Or should we think of it more like virginity, something that can be lost by one without another's gaining it – and whose loss in apt circumstances can even be a matter for celebration? This book is dedicated to the latter view.[47]

This is a compelling approach to the question, deserving further attention to its merits. Two observations are particularly important. First, MacCormick does not question the truth or justifiability of the rival claims of supremacy made by Member State legal institutions and EU legal institutions. Yet this is fundamentally troublesome. Consider the perspective of Member States first. With the possible exceptions of the Netherlands[48] and Estonia,[49] none suppose that the validity or foundations of EU law rest ultimately with EU law itself or with EU institutions. So while the EU might claim that its law is supreme and that its institutions have final authority to interpret EU law, such a claim is not accepted or recognized by the very legal systems and institutions of those whose acceptance and recognition matter—the legal systems and institutions of the Member States. Member States tend to view supremacy claims made by the EU as

---

[46] MacCormick, see n 31, 117–18.   [47] MacCormick, see n 31, 126.

[48] See B de Witte, 'Do Not Mention the Word: Sovereignty in Two Europhile Countries: Belgium and the Netherlands', in Walker (ed), see n 31, 351–66.

[49] D Chalmers, G Davis, and G. Monti (eds), *European Union Law: Cases and Materials*, 2nd edn (Cambridge: Cambridge University Press, 2010), 190–1.

the kind of mistake to be expected from an organization whose current prominence and relative independence have led it to forget the conditions of its origin. Yet from the perspective of the EU, the claims of supremacy made by Member State institutions for their constitutions and institutions' final authority to interpret EU law and its relation with their laws, are also rejected, and again, by the legal system and institutions which matter most for the truth or justifiability of such claims—the EU and its institutions. No matter how the EU originated and how EU law has developed, EU law on this view is separable from its history and now forms a distinct legal system with new subordinate systems and so on. Such observations show, at the very least, that it is far from safe to take any of the rival supremacy claims as clearly true or justified.

The second observation regarding MacCormick's account is that the 'interactive' nature of the relations between Member State legal systems and an EU legal system needs careful elucidation. Yet here it appears that MacCormick's own statement of juridical pluralism risks being unable to explain the interaction at all. MacCormick notes that:

> It follows also that the interpretative power of the highest decision-making authorities of the different systems must be, as to each system, ultimate. It is for the ECJ to interpret in the last resort and in a finally authoritative way the norms of Community law. But equally, it must be for the highest constitutional tribunal of each member-state to interpret its constitutional and other norms, and hence to interpret the interaction of the validity of EC law with higher level norms of validity in the given state system.[50]

This account certainly reproduces the competing views from EU and Member State institutions, but it raises two rather odd explanatory puzzles. First, if the highest decision-making authorities are each claiming supremacy to interpret the relation between Member State law and EU law, what MacCormick claims are interacting systems look more like two hierarchical systems talking past one another. Both systems include both the norms of Member States and the EU but they differ in their view of which norms are supreme and who has supreme authority to interpret the norms. So where is the interaction? Second, if one can begin from either the perspective of the Court of Justice, in which case EU law is supreme, or the perspective of a Member State court, in which case that Member State's law is supreme, we are left with a choice not unlike the choice identified by Kelsen between the primacy of state law or the primacy of international law. Indeed, what MacCormick identifies as juridical pluralism in which distinct legal systems sit in an interactive rather than hierarchical relation in fact looks no different from Kelsen's monism, a view MacCormick is attempting to escape. Kelsen's view is, after all,

---

[50] MacCormick, see n 31, 118. MacCormick also writes: 'A pluralistic analysis ... shows the systems of law operative on the European level to be distinct and partially independent of each other, though also partially overlapping and interacting. It must then follow that the constitutional court of a member-state is committed to denying that its competence to interpret the constitution by which it was established can be restricted by decisions of a tribunal external to the system. This applies even to a tribunal whose interpretative advice on points of EC law the constitutional court is obligated to accept under Article 177. Conversely, the ECJ is by the same logic committed to denying that its competence to interpret its own constitutive treaties can be restricted by decisions of member-state tribunals.' MacCormick, see n 31, 119.

pluralist in precisely the same way. Epistemologically, there are several ways in which to view the unity of the world of legal norms. These norms can be viewed by presuming the primacy of state law (with a further presumption in the choice of a particular state's law), or by presuming the primacy of international law. In the context of the EU, one can begin from the presumption of Member State law or from the presumption of EU law.[51] How, then, is MacCormick's pluralist view different from Kelsen's monism? And more importantly, has MacCormick's view successfully freed legal theory from hierarchical ways of thinking about law, especially since it appears that his view amounts to a plurality of hierarchies?

Here we need to consider an objection to our line of argument thus far. What is the precise problem with an explanation which states that legal systems, all supreme in their own right, fundamentally disagree about the ultimate authority over the relation between their laws and laws of some other order or system? What, in other words, is wrong with the possibility of hierarchical or supreme systems talking past each other? The problem, we take it, is that such a picture would suggest, even encourage, the view that there is a debilitating lack of coordination, certainty, and indeed shared law between the systems; in other words, a *lack of legal order*. No doubt such a picture might make sense of the relation between different systems—perhaps the relation between the US legal system and the UN legal system are good examples, in particular on the issue of international authorization of the use of force, where the UN Security Council claims primary responsibility over such decisions but such a claim is routinely ignored by the US which in practice authorizes itself to make such decisions.[52] But things are surely different with the EU, where there are thick membership rights of mobility and employment, a shared currency and shared markets for effective trade and commerce, and a shared (albeit imperfect) European demos.

So, while we remain sympathetic to MacCormick's approach, we reluctantly conclude that it is best taken as a demonstration of the limits of the meta-theoretical value of legal system as a tool for explanation of the nature of EU law. Where the dominant analytical understanding of law, developed by Raz, sees the EU as a set of conflicting supremacy claims, MacCormick's pluralist view advances explanation by at least attempting to incorporate explanation of the interaction of those claims. Yet both approaches offer relatively blunt pictures of these interactions. As we shall argue in the next section, presumption of the importance of legal system to explanation of EU law has inadvertently distracted theorists' attention from a more promising approach, one which takes supremacy claims seriously while explaining their interaction in terms of and at the level of diverse interactions between legal institutions. We suspect that what is more interesting in thinking about supra-national law such as EU law is the nature

---

[51] Catherine Richmond nicely explains the pluralism in Kelsen's view applied to the context of the EU. Richmond, see n 40, 408–19. Also Barber, see n 40, 326.

[52] In Korea, Iraq, etc. Also, note that the US's permanent membership in the Security Council should not be presumed to show unity or coordination. If anything, it might contribute more to the disunity and disorganization of international law on the use of force.

and force of emerging interaction between the various EU and Member State institutions. Once law is seen to depend upon both hierarchical and non-hierarchical practices of institutions interacting with each other across old state boundaries, talk of separate, supreme legal systems only seems more and more out of place.[53]

4 An Inter-Institutional View of the Foundations of Law

What would an alternative to the dominant legal system approach in explaining the foundations of supra-state law such as EU law look like? In our view, supra-state law is not best explained by tracing its existence up some chain of validity or authority ultimately resting with a Member State's constitution and its assertion of supremacy. Nor is the existence or nature of supra-state law best explained in terms of some independent supra-state, which itself exhibits the characteristic claims of state legal systems of supremacy, comprehensiveness, and openness. In this sense, our view is somewhat revisionist as it does not take at face value the various rival supremacy claims made by Member States and the EU. Instead, on our view the existence and nature of supra-state law is to be found in the interactions, or what we will call relations, of mutual reference, between EU institutions and Member State institutions which share and exchange norms and normative powers to create, apply, and enforce norms. To the extent that our inter-institutional account is not state-based, it avoids the explanatory distortions of the approach to legal theory which sees all claims of law as claims in some way parasitic upon a foundational explanation of law rooted in the central case experience of the state legal system and its typical uses of law. Escape from the historically dominant yet only contingently central experience of the state legal system opens the way to explanatory separation of the state from law. This separation enables better characterization of such blends of law and political models as devolved governments, shared governance, associations of international institutions, and especially regional supra-state organizations such as the EU. In this section we describe in general terms the elements of our inter-institutional view.[54] In the next and final section we apply our view to EU law and its relations with Member States law.

(A) Legal Norms and Legal-Normative Powers

Our criticisms of previous theories of law do not extend to their accounts of individual norms, but only their near-exclusive focus on how individual norms form part of

---

[53] Weyland, see n 40. Weyland writes: 'It does not seem plausible to maintain the separateness of an order which, like that of the Community, depends for the operation of basic functions, like law making, application and enforcement, on the institutions of another legal order.' Weyland, 35.

[54] Also Culver and Giudice, see n 4, ch 4.

state legal systems. In this way, we intend to keep a central place for Hart's notion of a legal norm as a special kind of reason for action.[55] In addition to the idea of legal norms we also retain the familiar idea of legal-normative powers, which differ in type and force. Within the dimension of type and focusing on familiar legal-normative powers, we follow Raz in asserting three overlapping but conceptually distinct categories of normative power:[56] (i) *Powers to determine legal-normative situations.* These powers enable authoritative findings of law and legally relevant facts, and enable resolution of disputes. Powers of this kind include the powers of courts, tribunals, arbitration (both voluntary and mandatory) and mediation boards, police officers, and university petitions committees. (ii) *Powers to alter legal-normative situations.* These are powers to introduce, repeal, modify, debate, etc, legal norms or legal arrangements which form part of a legal situation. Powers of this kind include the powers wielded by legislatures, public servants, courts, and citizens in, for example, assertion of constitutional rights *contra* infringing legislation. (iii) *Powers to enforce legal-normative situations.* These are powers to compel compliance with laws or alert others to the need to enforce laws. Powers of this kind are exercised by, among others, state security services, private security services, police officers, and citizens.

Legal-normative powers also exhibit a second dimension—that of force—usefully analysed in terms of three categories: (i) *Scope.* Powers differ in their scope to the extent that they extend variably over different ranges of persons. (ii) *Duration.* Powers to affect the legal-normative situations of persons also differ in terms of their period of exercise. Powers of police officers, for example, exist so long as the officers remain in standing, while powers of elected officials exist in definite durations. (iii) *Assertion of Institutional Force.* Analytical legal theorists have long recognized that legal norms are not, contrary to Ronald Dworkin's claims in *Taking Rights Seriously*, necessarily understood as simply applying or failing to apply to a given situation.[57] Rather, legal norms have some degree or amplitude of institutional force. In systemic law-states, institutional force is often evident in hierarchies of norms and officials: a university petitions committee's decision, for example, neither asserts nor enjoys the same institutional force as a lower court judge's opinion, whose decision in turn neither asserts nor enjoys the same institutional force as an appellate court judge's decision. In other words, the authority of one's decision is relative to one's place as it is determined in the hierarchical practice of legal norms and institutions.[58] Yet varying institutional force of particular norms or indeed institutions is not found uniquely in hierarchical chains of validity or hierarchies of officials. Even where hierarchies are absent, legal institutions may make reference to the institutional force of one another's operations. For

---

[55] See HLA Hart, *Essays on Bentham* (Oxford: Clarendon Press, 1982), 243–68. For developments of Hart's view, see J Raz, *Practical Reason and Norms*, 2nd edn (Oxford: Clarendon Press, 1999) and Raz, *Ethics in the Public Domain*, rev edn (Oxford: Clarendon Press, 1995), 210–37.

[56] Raz, see n 15, 103–21.

[57] R Dworkin, *Taking Rights Seriously* (Cambridge, MA: Harvard University Press, 1979), 14–45.

[58] On the idea of 'institutional force', WJ Waluchow, see n 16, ch 3.

example, the powers of a department of health are typically neither higher nor lower on a hierarchy than the powers of a department of transportation in a government.

Legal-normative powers, just like legal norms, typically do not exist in isolation, but are found in clusters within institutional contexts such as courts, legislatures, and hospitals. Let us turn now to exploration of that institutional context.

(B) Institutions of Law and Legal Institutions

The first step toward development of a useful understanding of law's institutional nature is to clarify the sense of 'institution' we use, distinguishing it from its general sense in ordinary language and multiple senses in law and legal theory. Neil MacCormick has made sustained use of the idea of institution in explaining practices characterized as *institutions of law*, such as contract, declaratory judgment, and criminal law.[59] An institution of law, in MacCormick's view, may be viewed as encapsulating a legal doctrine comprising a cluster of related norms which united serve a single or limited number of purposes. This institutional cluster of norms may be used in various areas of life under law, often within organizations confusingly labeled 'legal institutions', which persist over time while operating some range of social functions recognized as 'institutions of law'. Both quite different uses of 'institution' rely for their intelligibility on reference to wider social notions of institutions. For example, the 'institution' of contract and the 'institution' of queuing at bus stops share reliance on shared conceptions of a desirable social function performed by coordinated practices with generally recognized prompts and responses enabling operation of the function. Similarly, the idea of institution as a normative, function-oriented organization incorporating a cluster of complex normative practices, such as contract or queuing, transfers readily to the legal context from additional social contexts. Courts are readily understood as normative, function-oriented institutions, as are primary schools, the Red Cross, and the Scouting movement. On this understanding, a legal institution represents topic-specific deployment of institutions of law peculiar to its legal-institutional focus, together with supporting institutions of law capable of use in various legal contexts yet given specific content and distinctive practice in application to the legal institution's topic-specific purposes.

(C) Mutual Reference and Intensity

So far the elements of law identified should be unobjectionable: legal norms, legal-normative powers, institutions of law and legal institutions are well-established explanatory tools. The final step in our inter-institutional theory is, however, both

---

[59] N MacCormick and O Weinberger, *An Institutional Theory of Law* (Dordrecht: Kluwer, 1986) and N MacCormick, *Institutions of Law* (Oxford: Oxford University Press, 2007).

novel and crucial, as it enables explanation of how various legal institutions relate to one another in a legal order and across legal orders.

For our purpose in providing a contribution to the general part of a theory of law, it is useful to choose, as law-tracking characteristics of legal institutions interacting over time, the fact that those institutions are typically part of a composition of inter-dependent institutions related by *mutual reference* occurring at some level of *intensity*. Mutual reference is here understood to cover a wide range of types of interaction amongst legal institutions. Instances of intense mutual reference familiar from the context of the state legal system include 'vertical' reference in chains of validity such as lower courts' deference to the opinions of higher courts, expressed with intensity measured by those lower courts' regular citation of and deferral to higher courts. Less familiar yet still prominent instances of intense mutual reference may be found in divisions of power or authority, shared claims to issue binding directives, communi-cation of standards and expectations, exchange of personnel, information, and tech-niques, and adoption of norms. Our account is deliberately broad, and meant to cover well-known relations such as constitutional or statutory requirement and authoriza-tion, deference to binding authority, and inclusion of guiding authority in the balance of reasons for action, as well as less well-known relations such as legal transplantation, transnational norm-sharing, and recognition of joint or divided sovereignty.

The pattern of continued mutual reference with the normative intensity delivered by assertion and regular observation of norms supplies law over time and with the character of a particular order achieving a particular set of social outcomes. Notice that the particular pattern of law evident from legal institutions' operation of the matrix of powers available to them will constitute a pattern of inter-institutional interaction that may vary significantly over time, leaving each legal order with a uniquely variegated pattern and record of relations of mutual reference occurring at some level of intensity. In those variegations retaining a particular inter-institutional variegation over time we find the phenomenal basis for identification and distinction of legal orders. This picture of law is admittedly a reflection of institutional facts visible only after particular variegated arrangements of legal institutions have in fact interacted in mutually referential ways with varying intensity, but this ought to be expected from a philosophical approach which aims at responsiveness to phenomena, and seeks to avoid presumption of the centrality of any particular systemic or other arrangements of legal institutions.

In the next section we will apply our account to the EU, so here it might be helpful to offer a non-EU example of an arrangement of legal institutions to illustrate what we have so far described in abstract terms. Consider an example drawn from intellectual property law. The European Patent Office issues patents effective in all European Patent Convention Member States, yet enforcement is national, within individual Member States. So while the European Patent Convention provisions on validity are substantively identical to the United Kingdom's Patents Act, interpretation of those provisions is a complex matter raising the possibility of a conflict between the European Patent Office Technical Board of Appeal and courts in the United Kingdom in the event that a defendant in the United Kingdom responds to a claim of infringement by asserting the invalidity of the patent. In *Symbian Ltd v Comptroller General of Patents*, a defendant did just that, and the England and Wales Court of Appeal exhibited very clearly both the danger of the conflict, and how institutional force may operate in the absence of a hierarchy of binding authority. Writing in the context of the exclusion of programs for computers from the category of patentable subject matter, the Court of Appeal held that:

> Given that there are decisions of this court and of the Board which relate to the ambit of the computer program exclusion in art 52 [of the European Patent Convention], the right basis for assessing that ambit in this court should be as follows. If the judgments in the Court of Appeal cases give tolerably clear guidance which would resolve the issue on this appeal, then we should follow that guidance, unless it is inconsistent with clear guidance from the Board, in which case we should follow the latter guidance unless satisfied that it is wrong.[60]

Notice that while the Court of Appeal recognizes and aims to find a way around conflict between its decisions and those of the Board, it does not grasp a chain of validity to determine the 'right basis' for decisions required to apply article 52 provisions. Rather than looking up a chain, the Court looks both to its precedent decisions, *and* those of the Board, and with a further twist insofar as the Board's clear guidance normally regarded as binding may be disregarded if evaluated by the Court of Appeal as false. Not hierarchy, but truth seems to be at issue here in assessing the relative institutional force of the Court of Appeal and the Board. In this particular case, identification of the greatest institutional force bearing on interpretation of article 52 is somewhat complicated by the presence of an only partially relevant European Patent Office precedent, and the fact that the Board of appeal has not yet heard a case bearing directly on the issue in the *Symbian* case. In facing this particular circumstance the Court nonetheless takes the opportunity to engage the more general question of the relation between the institutional force of the two adjudicative bodies, reinforcing and extending the non-hierarchical nature of that relation:

> It is, of course, inevitable that there will be cases where the EPO will grant patents in this field when UKIPO should not, at least so long as the view in *Pension Benefit* and *Hitachi* is applied by the Board and is not applied here. The fact that the two offices and their supervisory courts have their own responsibilities means that discrepancies, even in approach or principle, are occasionally inevitable. However, the fact that such discrepancies have been characterised as 'absurd' by Nicholls LJ, and the reasoning in [3] of *Conor* emphasise the strong desirability of the approaches and principles in the two offices marching together as far as possible. This means that there is a need for a two-way dialogue between national tribunals and the EPO, coupled with a degree of mutual compromise. More directly relevant to the present appeal, it means that, where there may be a difference of approach or of principle, one must try to minimise the consequent differences in terms of the outcome in particular patent cases.[61]

---

[60] *Symbian Ltd v Comptroller General of Patents* [2008] EWCA Civ 1066 at para 36.
[61] *Symbian Ltd v Comptroller General of Patents* [2008] EWCA Civ 1066 at para 61.

The court's desire to avoid 'absurd' discrepancies drives not an appeal to an extant hierarchy of officials or norms, nor to a programme of building such hierarchies, but instead to practices of 'two-way dialogue' and 'mutual compromise' intended to minimize outcome variations between the two bodies. Institutional force, then, may vary within hierarchical arrangements *or* within less precisely delineated overlaps, intersections, and points of integration, and in these non-hierarchical situations the relations of intense, mutual inter-institutional reference are very plainly evident.

More of course remains to be said about how the above elements of law can combine in different ways and be brought to bear on explanation of various kinds of legal phenomena. This we cannot do here.[62] We can, however, demonstrate how our view offers an improved explanation of the rival supremacy claims of EU and Member State institutions.

5 An Inter-Institutional View of EU Law

The legal order of the EU embodies a remarkable transformation in the nature of law-states' borders. Once primarily physical edges of the geo-centric state, borders are now both physical and notional points of translation and exchange. Evidence of such transformation, translation, and exchange can be found in the relations between the EU and each Member State. The situation of the United Kingdom provides a representative example. The UK is one such Member State where the primacy of EU law is accepted by UK courts and institutions, albeit primarily on the ground of UK constitutional authorization, via the European Communities Act 1972 and case law since the UK's membership in the EU, and not on the claims of the Court of Justice. Yet despite the rival supremacy claims regarding the ultimate foundation of EU law, there are extensive relations of mutual reference which demonstrate law-constituting interaction between UK institutions and EU institutions. UK courts enforce EU law on many key issues, and the UK Parliament regularly implements EU directives in many areas. Writing about the relation of EU law and Member State courts more generally, Miguel Maduro observes that there are even 'cases where national courts have gone further than the ECJ in extending the protection granted by EU law in cases of horizontal direct effect and discrimination against a State's own nationals'.[63] As Maduro also notes, however, the emergence of EU law has depended not only on the receptiveness of Member State courts, but further on specific invocation of mutual reference at varying levels of normative force or intensity. As he puts it:

> ...the success of this process of creation of a European legal order was only possible because the [Court of Justice] looked for and found the cooperation of different national

---

[62] But see Culver and Giudice, n 4.

[63] M Maduro, 'Contrapunctual Law: Europe's Constitutional Pluralism in Action', in Walker (ed), see n 31, 518–19.

actors. For this, it also had to 'negotiate' with those actors, in particular, but not only, with national courts... The [Court of Justice] developed doctrines promoting the participation of a variety of national actors. Notably, it promoted the 'subjectivation' of the Treaties. The Treaties are not simply to be interpreted as an agreement between States, but as having been created for the 'peoples of Europe': Community rules are directed towards individuals and can be invoked by them.[64]

On the specific form of the Court of Justice's reference to and engagement with Member State legal institutions, Maduro continues:

The [Court of Justice] was also quite open to the questions posed by national courts and often relied on them to come up with original interpretations of Community rules. At the same time, the role played by national courts in requesting rulings from the ECJ and in applying these rulings provided ECJ decisions with the same authority as national judicial decisions....The relationship established between national courts and individuals on the one hand and the European Court of Justice on the other thus becomes one of dialogue rather than dictation.[65]

Two aspects of Maduro's observations are particularly important to our argument. First, where there is interaction between Member States and the EU—understood in terms of mutual relations of 'dialogue', 'cooperation', or 'subjectivation'—it occurs not between legal systems, but instead between legal institutions: between the Court of Justice and Member State courts, or between the Court of Justice and 'other national actors'. Second, the law-constituting interaction takes place notwithstanding accompanying rival supremacy claims made respectively by the Court of Justice and Member State courts. Maduro's account is again particularly instructive:

Though the grammar used by EU lawyers in describing the process of constitutionalisation may assume a top-down approach, the reality, as we have seen, is that the legitimacy of European constitutionalism has developed in close co-operation with national courts and national legal communities. That, in turn, has had an increasingly bottom-up effect on the nature of the European legal order. We have also seen that, in spite of their claims to ultimate authority and legal sovereignty, both the EU and national legal orders make more or less explicit concessions towards the claim of authority of the other legal order.[66]

Examples of mutual reference show quite clearly that the EU is best understood as an order of interaction, exchange, and translation of legal norms implemented by Member State institutions. What is perhaps most noteworthy in this situation, for our purposes in elaborating an inter-institutional theory of law, is the diminishing importance of the state legal system to an account of law, as the EU legal order is visibly and conceptually apart from phenomena and concepts of legal systems and states. More specifically, at issue and in demand of explanation is no longer the question of how a group of states forms a supra-state legal order, but instead a more basic question about particular versus universal legal orders—what it is that

---

[64] Maduro, see n 63, 512–13.   [65] Maduro, see n 63, 513.   [66] Maduro, see n 63, 522.

distinguishes particular relatively local variegations of legal orders from claims to super-state legal order found in international law. Once we are oriented toward this more basic question, we are freed from a number of preoccupations associated with the assumption that the state legal system carries the mark and measure of law. Instead we are focused on understanding a variety of contingencies associated with institutions of law and legal institutions: law may but need not be state-based, may but need not be geocentric, and need not have any particular content, as there are a variety of ways of achieving the various goals we have in life under law, using overlapping legal orders, and overlaps between state and non-state legal-normative orders.

As we ask this refocused jurisprudential question about varieties of legal orders and their interaction, a static time-slice view of a momentary hierarchy of legal institutions has very little probative value, and is inapt given the dynamic nature of the phenomena. An apt explanation takes seriously the dynamic nature of the EU, from its roots in the original treaties founding the European Coal and Steel Community (ECSC) and then the European Economic Community (EEC), to its ongoing enlargement process and diversification into more policy areas over its history. Unsurprisingly, given the historical origin of the EU, it contains elements of law identical in structure to those found in state legal systems, albeit varying in content and patterns of intense mutual reference. Institutions of law are evident in the EU in the form of, for example, directives, regulations, decisions, directly effective as well as non-directly effective treaty articles, and particular national implementation of EU legal norms. Legal institutions are also evident in the EU, from the four central institutions (Court of Justice, European Parliament, Council of the European Union, European Commission), all exercising specified legal-normative powers. Unlike state law of the kind amenable to hierarchical, system-based approaches, the EU appears to lack the sort of systematic unity visible in the state legal system via identification of core institutions responsible for maintenance of comprehensive and supreme authority of the system. Instead this responsibility seems to be distributed amongst Member States, whose authority and institutional force is subject to interplay with EU institutions such as the Court of Justice. What gives the EU its particular character is, then, both the patterns of intense mutual reference amongst its legal institutions and those of Member States, and the particular distribution amongst those institutions of functions familiar from the systemic-law state, yet not present in the same systematic fashion in the EU, since distribution and horizontal interrelation and interdependence are as prominent as state legal system hierarchy. Viewed against the state legal system, the EU amounts to a *sui generis* form of legal order *qua* variegation of legal institutions, whose origins in overlapping and intersecting institutions might over time be gradually displaced by pan-European legal norms and legal institutions, much as in common law systems, customary law has been gradually displaced by statute and precedent. Here sensitivity to law's temporally dynamic nature becomes important to adequate explanation of the EU legal order. It is a relatively recent product, developed over nearly sixty years, and by its own reckoning is far from complete in both integration of legal institutions already in relations of intense mutual reference, and in inclusion of other legal institutions via enlargement.

One obvious objection to this view is that it fails to capture and reproduce what makes the EU a distinct legal order—it fails to settle on one of the three options identified by Dickson. Yet from our stance, this apparent failure is in fact a distinctive feature of our inter-institutional view: on our view the EU can amount to a distinct non-systemic legal order whose special quality relative to the systemic law-state is evident in the union's particular kind of institutional agglomeration which is historically continuous with the state legal systems whose nature is gradually transformed through their membership in the EU. Rather than seeking to draw hard lines where deliberate practice aims to avoid the presumption or creation of hard lines, the inter-institutional view tracks and records the intensity of inter-institutional mutual reference characteristic of the EU legal order, from Member States, to enlargement process categories of 'candidate' and 'potential candidate' countries. We might of course be faulted on various grounds for having failed to provide here a comprehensive descriptive-explanatory account of the EU legal order; but since our goal is to explain why an inter-institutional *approach* ought to be preferred to prior analytical approaches, we may safely leave for future work the task of specifying more precisely the relation between the various kinds of members of the EU. For now it is sufficient that we have supplied a method and the beginning of its application, sufficient to contrast the general merits of our approach with prior analytical approaches.

4

Harmonic Law

The Case Against Pluralism

*George Letsas**

1 The Problem

If a mother orders her child to eat breakfast, the father instructs the child that he must keep an empty stomach for lunch, and the grandfather pronounces that the child is free to take his meals when he pleases, the child is bound to be confused. Even more so, if each of his family elders, having heard the others' directives, tells the child: 'you listen to *me!*' Each directive requires the child to take an action that makes it impossible for him to comply with the rest of the directives. If the child has breakfast because the mother said so, he will be disregarding both his father's instruction not to eat before lunch and his grandfather's directive to do as he pleases in matters dietary. If he skips breakfast because the father commanded so, the child will be disregarding both his mother's instruction to the contrary and his grandfather's granting of a liberty to do as he pleases. And if he decides to reflect on whether he fancies breakfast and act accordingly, following his grandfather's pronouncement, he would be defying the authority of both his parents. What should the child do?

The situation described seems to be far from ideal; nobody likes to be confronted with contradictory advice, let alone contradictory orders, particularly when one accepts prima facie the authority of each adviser or commander. The child accepts that he should do what his parents tell him to do—indeed it is in his interest to do so—but he cannot obey one parent without disobeying another; it appears that the child

* University College London (UCL), Faculty of Laws. Many thanks to Nick Barber, Pavlos Eleftheriadis, Nicholas Hatzis, Mattias Kumm, Dimitris Kyritsis, Stuart Lakin, Ioannis Lianos, Andrea Sangiovanni, Prince Saprai, Joanne Scott, Nicos Stavropoulos, Virginia Mantouvalou, and Lorenzo Zucca, for their very helpful comments on earlier drafts of this chapter. I am also grateful for comments from audience members at the University College London (UCL) Staff Seminar Series, the New York University (NYU) Colloquium on Global and Comparative Law and the UCL Institute for Human Rights Symposium on Interpretivism in International Law.

would be at a loss about what he should do. Call this the *problem of normative conflicts*. The problem is said to be the result of a kind of normative pluralism, and it consists in having to obey a plurality of authorities each of which claims to be superior to the other, each of which issues directives that may contradict those of others. The twenty-seven European Union Member States are often said to face a variant of this problem: national constitutional law is considered to be the supreme law of each Member State, yet EU law is claimed to trump national law, the constitution included. What if European Union law requires a citizen to do X (for example, submit his business premises to a search by state officials without a judicial warrant), yet national constitutional law or ECHR law entitles him not to do X? That citizen would find himself in a situation similar to that experienced by the child in our story. What if, moreover, a national constitutional court reviews and sets aside an EU measure that has been upheld by the European Court of Justice? Later courts deciding whether to apply this measure would also find themselves in the situation of the child. Whom should they obey?

Many philosophers and lawyers have taken pluralism to be a genuine problem, not specific to law, and some of them have given an account of what would count as a solution to it. One of the most popular ones in the literature is the idea of judicial dialogue. In this chapter I disagree with the relevant philosophers and lawyers: I believe that the problem of normative conflicts is not a genuine one and that this teaches us a great deal about European law, and fundamental rights in Europe. In particular, I am interested in challenging an argument whose structure goes like this: legal pluralism is an empirical fact, which generates problems of normative conflicts that in turn can be solved through some process of judicial dialogue. This argument should be familiar to EU lawyers as it permeates the relevant literature.[1] My main contention, one that contradicts views widely held by judges and theorists alike, is that as a matter of law, there are no normative conflicts of fundamental rights in Europe. My aim is not to offer a solution to the problem of pluralism, say via some harmonization or dialogue theory, nor to make conflicts disappear by stipulation. Rather, my aim is to debunk it. The paper offers an account of law and fundamental rights that both explains why such conflicts do not exist and offers some normative guidance to how European judges should decide cases. Legal philosophy should seek to contribute not only to the understanding of European law but also to its sound development.

2 Legal Pluralism: A Problem for Legal Theory or a Problem for People?

The topic of legal pluralism has attracted much interest in the last forty years and has risen to prominence in the fields of socio-legal studies and legal anthropology. As with

---

[1] See eg Miguel Maduro, 'Contrapunctual Law: Europe's Constitutional Pluralism in Action' in Walker (ed), *Sovereignty in Transition* (2003); Aida Torres Perez, *Fundamental Rights in the European Union* (2009).

any term used to describe a diverse set of ideas, not all jurists understand it in the same way, nor do they all use it in the course of addressing the same question. In the most common understanding, legal pluralism is a descriptive term that refers to a situation in which two or more distinct legal systems exist within the same political community.[2] Legal pluralists use the term to describe a number of actual societies in which a state-ordained system of norms overlaps with normative orders emanating outside state institutions (such as pre-colonial law, religious law, *lex mercatoria*, transnational law, tribal law, etc). Early legal pluralists were mainly interested in legal anthropology and sociology and less in legal philosophy. They were empiricists who studied societies in which various normative systems co-exist and are practised alongside state law, often resulting in incidents of social tension, conflict, and confusion. What was original and innovative about this empirical work was that it studied important social phenomena that were much neglected partly because they did not fit the traditional category of a legal system.

Pluralists lamented legal philosophers' preoccupation with state law as diverting attention away from these other normative practices that are often more efficacious in guiding people's conduct and hence more worthy of being studied. They also found the focus on state law too parochial and historically contingent, limited to the study of the emergence of nation states in the northern hemisphere during the last two centuries and ignoring much of the rest of world as well as Western history before the Treaty of Westphalia. It is for these reasons by and large that legal pluralists championed the importance of non-state normative systems *qua legal* systems and started pressing the claim that mainstream legal philosophy had misunderstood the concept of a legal system, unduly restricting its scope to state law. They hoped that by pushing the conceptual boundaries of 'law' to accommodate non-state normative systems, they would draw attention to important but under-studied social phenomena as well as legitimize their discipline as a universal field of scholarly inquiry.

Although pluralists' interest in how to conceptualize law was derivative from their interest in the phenomena they were seeking to describe, they gradually developed the view that the existence of legal pluralism can make trouble not only for the society that exhibits it, but also for mainstream jurisprudence. Most theories in mainstream analytic jurisprudence were developed to capture features that only state-ordained normative systems possess—such as sovereignty (Bentham and Austin), the vertical, 'top-down' structure of a legal system (Kelsen), the existence of secondary rules unifying all legal norms (Hart), state coercion (Dworkin)—and for pluralists these theories are ill-suited to capture these other normative practices that lack some or all of these features. Legal pluralism began to be presented as a potential problem not only for societies that experience it but also for jurisprudence: a case of a counter-example that embarrasses orthodox theories about the nature of law and hence calls for their modification.

---

[2] John Griffiths, 'What is Legal Pluralism?' (1986) 24 *Journal of Legal Pluralism* 1–47; Sally Engle Merry, 'Legal Pluralism' (1988) 22 *Law and Society Review* 869–96.

The following sections explore whether legal pluralism, both in general and as it is exhibited in the EU in the form of constitutional pluralism, is a problem for mainstream jurisprudence. This might seem to some too scholastic a concern. Why should we care about schools of thought and how they would conceptualize political events such as European integration? After all, it is not as if these schools of thought, and the people who represent them at academic conferences, have a direct impact on legal and political practice. It might be objected, in other words, that it matters little whether legal pluralism in the EU is a problem for jurisprudence, while it matters hugely whether it is a problem for the people of Europe.

While I am sympathetic to the spirit of this objection, it is important not to let it stand it in the way of theoretical engagement with EU law. This is because we must allow for the possibility that something appears to be a real problem for us only because our theoretical presuppositions are flawed. Let me cite an analogy. Consider the discovery that determinism is true and that all human actions are determined by prior physical events. The discovery raised concerns about the very idea of free will and whether we can hold people responsible for their actions in the absence of it. Yet such concerns are legitimate only if we are right to think that determinism is incompatible with moral responsibility and free will. If free will and moral responsibility are actually compatible with determinism, the discovery that our actions are determined causally by prior events, poses no trouble at all. Similarly, the fact of legal pluralism may appear to be a problem for us only because we accept certain questionable presuppositions at the level of legal theory, namely that legal pluralism entails legal conflict. For this reason, it is wise to sort out the theory first, before we ask whether some factual discovery or development, like determinism or European integration, is a problem for *us*. In later sections it will emerge that pluralism in the EU is a problem for *us* only if we understand it in the light of certain questionable theoretical presuppositions about the nature of law.[3]

3 Talking Past Each Other

So is legal pluralism really a problem for analytic jurisprudence? Is there really a disagreement between pluralists and analytic legal philosophers about the nature of law? At first glance, there is no reason why pluralism should embarrass theories that focus on state law, at least not while both pluralists and legal philosophers agree that state law is a species that belongs to a broader genus or family. Consider an analogy. If an ornithologist focuses on swans as an object of his study, it is no objection to point out that there are other birds that belong to the same biological family (the *Anatidae*

---

[3] One could object that I am here providing an alternative account of pluralism, as opposed to a case *against* pluralism. The difference is terminological and nothing hangs on it. Given how widespread the understanding of pluralism that I am attacking is, I have opted to frame the argument as one against pluralism. I have no quarrel with people who want to rescue the term pluralism.

family), such as ducks and geese. He needn't deny either the existence or the importance of these other similar yet different types of birds. Likewise, it is no objection against philosophers of law that focus on normative orders operating through state institutions to point out that there are normative orders outside the state. These philosophers needn't deny either the existence or the importance of other normative orders.

The pluralists' claim that there is more law than state law and that legal philosophers are wrong to deny that these other normative orders are *legal* systems is ambiguous. Understood as the claim that both state-ordained and non-state normative orders are instances of the same social practice, namely that of a normative order, the claim is trivially true. Everybody accepts it, just like everybody accepts that swans and ducks are instances of the same biological family of birds, namely the *Anatidae* family. Most analytic legal philosophers use the words 'legal system' to refer to a subcategory of normative systems, in which state institutions and officials play an important role, and to give an account of its distinctive characteristics (for example, its institutional character, its claim to supremacy, its coercive nature etc). Pluralists should happily agree with legal philosophers that, thus defined, all legal systems are normative orders but not all normative orders are legal systems. If on the other hand we understand the pluralists' claim that all normative systems are legal systems, then their claim is manifestly false. It is analogous to saying that all birds of the *Anatidae* family, like ducks and geese, are swans. Yet ducks and geese are not swans, just as non-state normative orders are not state-ordained. Legal pluralists who chide philosophers for focusing on state-ordained normative orders are either asserting a trivially true proposition (that not all normative systems are state-ordained) or are committing a manifest error (claiming that non-state normative orders are state-ordained). In either case, there is no substantive disagreement between legal pluralists and legal philosophers, only the appearance of a disagreement akin to the familiar example of two people disagreeing about whether banks are beautiful, one referring to river banks and the other to financial banks.

A substantive disagreement however would arise if legal pluralists can embarrass legal philosophers about the way the latter identify that of which they do seek to give an account, namely *state*-ordained normative practices. The fact of legal pluralism can mean trouble for a philosophical theory about the nature of law, in the same way that black swans were trouble for the ornithologists who first visited Australia: if a theory is shown to be either over-inclusive or under-inclusive, it means that it has got the essential features of what it seeks to describe wrong. If legal pluralism can show that there is either more state-ordained law (over-inclusive) or less state-ordained law (under-inclusive) than philosophical theories about the nature of law allow, then legal philosophers would have to modify their theories, just like ornithologists who first visited Australia had to abandon their view that all swans are white. The next section looks at Europe's constitutional pluralism, which is often presented as the legal philosopher's black swan, challenging what legal philosophers take to be essential features of a legal system.

4 Europe's Constitutional Pluralism

What is pluralistic about the EU? Most scholars converge in treating the EU legal order as distinct from the legal order of each of the Member States, the former overlapping and interacting with the latter. They present the situation as one of *constitutional* pluralism in that the EU legal order makes claims to constitutional supremacy that contradict claims to constitutional supremacy made by the national legal order. Most of these conflicting claims were initially not made in the text of the EU Treaty or the text of national constitutions—the majority of the latter predating the former—but by the European Court of Justice and several national constitutional courts in the course of deciding particular cases. This fact in itself should raise some doubt about how seriously these claims should be taken, given that all lawyers know that a court's dictum may be *obiter,* bearing little or no normative significance either to the case at hand, or to future cases. Be that as it may, most EU lawyers accept that claims to constitutional supremacy made by the respective courts are to be taken seriously and that they may amount to a genuine case of normative conflict.[4]

The European Court of Justice has made three claims to supremacy: first, that within its area of competence, European law has supremacy over all conflicting rules of national law, including the constitution; second, that the European Court of Justice has exclusive competence to decide what counts as a matter of European law, that is, what falls within its competence (what is called *kompetenz-kompetenz*); third, that it has ultimate authority to decide all matters of European law. On the national side of the judicial divide, both the first and second of these claims have been challenged. In a well-known exchange between the German Constitutional Court and the ECJ, the former initially questioned the supremacy of European law that violated fundamental constitutional rights, given the lack of a bill of rights in the EU, and asserted its jurisdiction to review EU law for compatibility with the rights enshrined in the Grundgezetz.[5] When, in response to this challenge, the ECJ developed a jurisprudence of fundamental rights drawing on principles found in the constitutional traditions of members states, the German Constitutional Court pulled back, saying that it will not review EU law for compatibility with constitutional rights 'so long as' the institutions of the EU provide protection of rights that is equivalent to that afforded by the German Constitution.[6] As to the issue of 'kompetenz-kompetenz', the German Con-stitutional Court has asserted that it has jurisdiction to review whether European Union organs have acted *utlra vires*, that is, whether they have acted outside the competences conferred to them by the EU Treaty, challenging the ECJ's claim to have the final say on what falls within the competence of the EU.[7]

---

[4] See eg Mattias Kumm, 'Who is the arbiter of Constitutionality in Europe?' (1999) 36 *Common Market Law Review* 351–86.

[5] (1974) 37 BVerfGE 271 ('*Solange I*').

[6] (1986) 73 BVerfGE 339 ('*Solange II*').

[7] 89 BVerGE 155 ('the Maastricht decision').

Since the early stages of the development of European law, scholars took interest in the absence of higher-order criteria of hierarchy between the overlapping legal orders and the possibility of inconsistent rules or rulings between bodies, each of which claims to be non-subordinate to the other. What if a national legislature of a Member State enacts a law, inconsistent with an EU norm, to which it explicitly gives primacy over EU law? What if a national constitutional court reviews and disapplies an EU norm which was previously upheld by the ECJ, or interprets constitutional rights in a way that contradicts the interpretation of the same rights by the ECJ? So far such conflicts have been restricted to hypothetical scenarios found in every other public-law and EU-law textbook. But the abundance and persistence of such concerns suggest that for most constitutional theorists, the lack of hierarchy and the possibility of conflicting rules of constitutional supremacy are not only constitutive of a pluralistic legal order, but also rather uncommon—perhaps even impossible—within a state-based legal system. State constitutions typically arrange the powers of legislative and judicial bodies and the relations between the various valid norms of the system in a hierarchical fashion, using ranking rules[8] in order to avoid conflicts and inconsistencies.

A related but distinct feature of the project of European integration that has attracted constitutional scholars' attention since the early years of the ECJ's jurisprudence, is the effect of European integration on the sovereignty of Member States. The project of European integration was seen as part of a wider process of chipping away at state sovereignty. Understood in a descriptive sense, as the fact of being habitually obeyed by a certain group, the transfer of legislative powers to the institutions of the EU and the subsequent efficacious enforcement of EU rules, meant that European Member States no longer enjoyed exclusive sovereignty over their people. Europeans continue to obey norms enacted by the institutions of their state but now they also obey norms enacted by the supra-national institutions of the EU and intended to apply to them. This fact sat uneasily with conceptions of national constitutionalism that were wedded to the idea of indivisible and illimitable sovereignty as the attribute of states and that informed much of the history and the text of the constitutional traditions of Member States. For most of these traditions, the constitution not only reports the fact that nationals of the state whose constitution it is form a distinct political community that is independent from others; it also expresses the normative ideal of *popular* sovereignty, namely the claim that the people of that state, often forming a single nation, are entitled to self-government, including not to be subjected to the power of any outside authority.[9] The reluctance of national constitutional courts to accept that EU law is the supreme law of the land, over and above the constitution, is the upshot of this understanding of state sovereignty, as an essential, not just fundamental, constitutional principle.

---

[8] Eg that later rules prevail over earlier rules, or that ratified international treaties prevail over ordinary legislation, etc.

[9] Kumm calls this view democratic statism and its counterpart in constitutional theory 'national constitutional supremacy'. See Mattias Kumm, 'The Jurisprudence of Constitutional Conflict: Constitutional Supremacy in Europe before and after the Constitutional Treaty' (2005) 11 *European Law Journal* 262–307.

5 European Pluralism and Legal Positivism

We are—recall—at this stage exploring whether the project of European integration is a problem for legal theory, not yet whether it is a problem for Europeans and their rights. And although European integration contradicted the way in which the constitutional traditions of Member States conceptualized state sovereignty, things are very different when we move to the way in which analytic legal philosophers understand sovereignty. For within the hall of fame of analytic jurisprudence, it is only John Austin who has argued that in every society there is one body or person whose sovereignty is unique (that is, he is the *only* sovereign on *all* matters) and whose sovereignty is united (that is, not divided between different bodies having power over separate matters).[10] The Austinian sovereign is he who is habitually obeyed by the bulk of the population and who habitually obeys no-one. Austin coupled this understanding of sovereignty with the claim that all norms belonging to a legal system have a *common origin*, namely the sovereign who either enacted them or who conferred powers for their enactment to subordinate bodies. The European Union would pose a clear counter-example to Austin's theory if, plausibly, there is more than one supreme legislative authority in Europe (for example, national parliaments and the EU institutions), and the authority of each does not derive from the authority of the other. As we saw, surpra-national institutions enact European law while national institutions enact national laws, each claiming that their respective authority is neither subordinate to, nor derivative from, the authority of the other. The Austinian would be hardpressed to explain the validity of EU laws given that their source cannot be traced back to a unique sovereign whose will is the common origin of all valid laws.

Before we turn to radically different theories of law that struggle less with the example of the EU, it should be noted that, as it happens with counter-examples, the Austinian can bite the bullet and defend his theory. He can first argue that there is one big sovereign body in Europe, comprising all the national and supranational legislative bodies, forming a single unity and having authority over all Europeans. Alternatively, he can argue that the authority of European law is ultimately derived from the authority of state constitutions. The first option would rescue the Austinian idea of a unique and united sovereignty existing in Europe, but at the cost of asserting the existence of a pan-European federal state and denying that Member States are sovereign. The second option would rescue the idea of a unique *state* sovereignty at the cost of rejecting the claims to supremacy made by the European Court of Justice and upholding as true the national courts' claims to constitutional supremacy. Both manoeuvres seem rather implausible. The fact however that the debate on constitutional conflicts in Europe is so often polarized between national

---

[10] See J Austin, *The Province of Jurisprudence Determined*, 246: 'In every society political and independent the sovereign is one individual or one body of individuals.' On the notion of united and unique sovereignty see Joseph Raz, *The Concept of a Legal System*. Bentham did not think that sovereignty is united.

constitutional supremacy on one hand and European federalism on the other, reveals how embedded the Austinian paradigm is amongst constitutional scholars.

Yet the Austinian picture of a unique and united sovereign as the common origin of all valid laws has been discredited within the jurisprudential school of legal positivism, of which Austin is taken to be amongst the founding fathers. HLA Hart was the first to point out the many shortcomings of Austin's imperative theory, but it is Joseph Raz's critique that is most pertinent to the question of sovereignty. As early as 1970, Raz explained how, given that sovereignty can be divided (that is, split between bodies that have non-subordinate legislative power over separate subject matters) as well as shared (that is, enjoyed by two bodies each of which has non-subordinate legislative power over all subject matters), one cannot use the origin of laws as a criterion of identifying all the valid laws of a legal system.[11] If it is possible that valid laws within a legal system are made by separate bodies, each of which is a supreme legislator, then there must be some criterion *other than the identity of the lawmaker* which accounts for the unity of a legal system. Austin hoped that the notion of sovereignty, defined as a legislator who is habitually obeyed and is legally illimitable, would supply such a criterion: the laws of a legislative body are valid if that body is sovereign or part of a sovereign. Among the many failures of this criterion is that it is both over-inclusive and under-inclusive: not all those whom the population habitually obeys are supreme legislators (for example, religious leaders, party leaders, public intellectuals, etc), and not all that a supreme legislator commands are valid laws (for example, commands not issued under a prescribed legislative process). Austin made the criterion of identity of a legal system dependent upon the unity of sovereignty but he had no independent way of identifying what unites a group of persons or bodies as one sovereign: he just assumed that these bodies are sovereign *because* they all make valid laws. Applied to the EU, Austin's theory has no non-circular way of establishing that both European legislators and national legislators are part of one big sovereign body who is the supreme legislator (the first manoeuvre above available to the Austinian). Political power, defined as a social fact, is not the key to explaining the identity of a legal system. In common jurisprudential parlance, Austin conflated legal and political sovereignty.[12]

With Hart's and Raz's theories legal positivism moved away from seeking to explain the nature of law by reference to norm-*creating* institutions and towards the thesis that the key to the nature of law lies in the existence of norm-*applying* institutions.[13] According to this type of positivism, the nature of a legal system lies not in the origin of legal rules, but in the workings of law-applying institutions, and in the way these institutions relate to a distinct political community or a state.[14] Hart argued that in

[11] Raz, *The Concept of a Legal System*, 35–8.

[12] On the long-lasting and distorting effect of Austinian positivism on UK public law and its doctrine of parliamentary sovereignty, see Stuart Lakin, 'Debunking the Idea Parliamentary Sovereignty: The Controlling Factor of Legality in the British Constitution' (2008) 28(4) *Oxford Journal of Legal Studies* 709–34. On law and sovereignty in general see Pavlos Eleftheriadis, 'Law and Sovereignty' (2010) 29 *Law and Philosophy* 535–69.

[13] See Raz, *Practical Reasons and Norms*, 129–31.

[14] On this account, the existence of law-applying institutions and of the state is not purely a legal creation but can be identified and explained independently of law. Otherwise the theory becomes circular. Raz for instance argues

every legal system there is a rule of recognition, accepted and practised by state officials, which identifies criteria of validity for all the rules of the system. What unites all rules of the legal system is not the fact that they were made by some supreme legislator (common origin), but the fact that they are applied by courts under criteria of validity that they accept, against those that are subject to them. The rule of recognition is a secondary rule addressed to officials that 'specifies features possession of which by a suggested rule is taken as conclusive affirmative indication that it a rule of the group to be supported by the social pressure it exerts'.[15] A corollary of this view is that the origin of a valid legal rule can lie *anywhere*: custom, religious practices, foreign legislatures, supranational authorities, international bodies, and so on and so forth. The source of all valid law needn't take the form of one supreme legislator, let alone the form of a sovereign national parliament or constitutional assembly. Legal pluralism, understood as the fact that non-state authorities can create legally valid rules, appears to pose no challenge to the type of legal positivism that Hart defended. The key aspect of this school of thought is the emphasis on the practice of those who apply rules, not on the practice of those who make them.

Yet the EU still poses a puzzle for certain aspects of Hart's theory. Hart suggested that in a developed legal system the different criteria of validity of a legal system will be multiple and that they will be ranked to prevent conflicts, making for instance custom or precedent subordinate to statute.[16] In this, he joined company with Kelsen, who thought that a normative system cannot ultimately make contradictory require-ments.[17] In the *Concept of Law,* Hart presented the ranking of different criteria of validity as a likely possibility, not a necessity.[18] He assumed moreover that each legal system has one, and no more than one, rule of recognition,[19] even where, as in a modern legal system, the sources of law are multiple. For Hart, the content of such complex rules of recognition is not necessarily stated anywhere, let alone contained in one authoritative text, like a constitution; its existence is manifested in the practice of officials when they identify and apply norms. Later however, in his review of Lon Fuller's book, Hart explained that the reason why he held that developed legal systems with multiple sources of law nevertheless have one rule of recognition is that criteria of legal validity are hierarchically structured.[20] The rule of recognition unifies all the

---

that every state has one legal system and criticizes Kelsen for claiming that the concept of a state can be explained only in legal terms. See Raz, 'The Identity of Legal Systems' (1971) *California Law Review* 812.

[15] Hart, *The Concept of Law,* 94.

[16] Hart, 95, 101.

[17] Kelsen, *General Theory of Law and the State,* (Harvard University Press, 1945), 407–8. H Kelsen, *The Pure Theory of Law* (University of California Press), 205–8.

[18] The text is clear about this. On p 95, Hart says that provision *may* be made for possible conflicts of rules by arranging them in order of superiority, and on p 101 he says that '*in most cases*' provision is made for possible conflicts by ranking these criteria in an order of relative subordination and primacy.

[19] This is the standard interpretation followed in the literature. See Raz, *PRN,* 146. Some passages in the CL however do refer to 'rules of recognition' (eg 95, 102).

[20] HLA Hart, Review of Lon Fuller's *The Morality of Law, Harvard Law Review* (1964), 1293: 'The reason for still speaking of a rule at this point is that, notwithstanding their multiplicity, these distinct criteria are unified by their hierarchical arrangement.'

norms of the system by containing both the criteria of validity of the norms of the system and rules that arrange those criteria in a hierarchical order. Hart in other words insisted that there is only one rule of recognition because he assumed that criteria of validity in a developed legal system will necessarily be ranked. And he took the existence of ranking rules to be an element that unifies the different sources of law. If one adds the fact that ranking rules solve conflicts, it is clear that for Hart the rule of recognition is meant to bring about not only unity of the law but also the *harmony* of its norms, understood as the resolution of conflicts between rules through their formal, content-independent, ranking. Now this is where the difficulty lies for Hartian positivism. The pluralist character of European law challenges Hart's aspiration that the existence of a rule of recognition will secure harmony and not just unity. Member States' courts apply both EU rules and national constitutional rules but the two sets of rules are not taken to be hierarchically ordered and conflicts arise between EU rules and national constitutional rules.

Is there a way out for the Hartian? He, like the Austinian, could defend his theory by making either of the following two arguments; he could argue either that there is one complex rule of recognition in each member (or perhaps in the whole of the EU), part of which ranks EU norms in relation to national constitutional norms; alternatively, he could argue that EU rules and national constitutional rules belong to different legal systems, with separate rules of recognition, and hence no issue of conflict ever arises.

The difficulty with the first option is that there does not seem to be any agreement amongst officials that national constitutional rules trump EU rules or vice versa. It is precisely the fact of disagreement amongst officials about which of the two is supreme that is causing trouble for jurisprudential theories. The Hartian cannot stipulate that ranking rules exist where there is no agreement amongst officials to that effect. Further difficulties compound this problem, including the counter-intuitive suggestion that there is one big legal system in Europe, identified by a single rule of recognition, containing domestic legal orders its sub-systems, each of which is ranked hierarchically in relation to the others.[21] Even if we agree, *arguendo*, that all conflicts within the domestic and EU order respectively are solved by internal ranking rules, there does not seem to be any master rule ranking conflicts between EU rules and national constitutional rules.

The alternative suggestion that no conflicts can arise between EU norms and national constitutional rules because they belong to separate legal systems, each possessing one single rule of recognition, is worth exploring in more detail. This suggestion seeks to rescue the idea of harmony (understood as the formal ranking or rules) within each legal system. According to it, the EU forms a distinct legal system that contains its own rule of recognition. When national courts apply EU rules, they

---

[21] For a discussion of how many legal systems can be said to exist in Europe see Julie Dickson, 'How Many Legal Systems? Some Puzzles Regarding the Identity Conditions of, and the Relations between, Legal Systems in the European Union' (2008) 2 *Problema* 9–50.

act as EU courts, following a single rule of recognition that ranks all rules of the EU legal system. And when they apply domestic rules they act as courts of the national legal system, applying that system's single rule of recognition. No conflicts arise, because at each given time courts follow one and only rule of recognition, applying rules of a distinct legal system that are ranked hierarchically. The idea here is that when national courts apply EU law, they wear a different hat, which transforms them into courts of the EU legal system. It is worth noting that this picture is familiar in the relevant academic literature.[22]

The problem however with this second suggestion is that it contradicts a key element of Hartian positivism; namely, that the unity of a legal system is to be found in the practice of courts, not in the origin of the rules they apply. On this view, it is not possible for the same court to belong to more than one legal system, given that courts are used as a criterion for individuating legal systems. Assuming that each Member State has its own legal system, then it follows that when domestic courts apply rules of the EU (or any other legal system for that matter), they never become courts of the EU. At best, they apply a domestic rule, identified by the domestic rule of recognition, directing them to apply rules of another system. And there is no guarantee that such a domestic rule will co-exist with, or contain, a further rule ranking the foreign rules vis-à-vis the domestic ones in case of conflict. For this second manoeuvre to work, the Hartian would have to abandon either the claim that the practice of courts unifies a legal system or the claim that all rules that a court is legally bound to apply are hierarchically ranked.

The above difficulties are the upshot of the fact that, *contra* Hart, the existence of one rule of recognition within a legal system (for example, that whatever parliament enacts is law) does not necessarily entail the existence of ranking rules. For example, it is contingent whether a system contains a ranking rule to the effect that a supreme (and unique) legislator's later rules prevail over inconsistent earlier rules.[23] A rule identifying sources of valid legal rules may, but need not, also rank them in a hierarchical fashion.

Hart's ambition to square the unity of a legal system with the idea of harmony of its rules led to difficulties that were spotted early on by his followers. Joseph Raz was the first to argue that legal systems may have more than one rule of recognition *and* that equally valid rules belonging to the same system may conflict, without the conflict being necessarily resolved.[24] First, Raz distinguished between rules of recognition and criteria of validity, arguing that though all rules of recognition set criteria of validity,

---

[22] See eg Paul Craig and Gràinne de Bùrca, *EU Law*, 4th edn (Oxford: Oxford University Press, 2008), 479: 'The relationship between national courts and the ECJ has been transformed by the development of precedent, acte clair, and sectoral delegation of responsibility. These developments have made national courts Community Courts in their own right'. See also Imelda Maher, 'National Courts as European Community Courts' (1994) 12 *Legal Studies* 226.

[23] Nick Barber makes the same point in 'Legal Pluralism and the European Union' (May 2006) 12(3) *European Law Journal*.

[24] *The Concept of a Legal System* and *PRN*.

not all criteria of validity are set in a rule of recognition: norms legally valid according to a system's rule of recognition, such as laws conferring legislative powers, may themselves contain further criteria of validity.[25] It is therefore a mistake to suppose, as Hart did, that the rule of recognition contains *all* the criteria of validity of a legal system. Second, Raz argued, *contra* Hart, that a legal system need not contain rules ranking the criteria of validity in a hierarchical order. The existence of ranking rules is *contingent* in a legal system and it is not entailed by the existence of a rule of recognition. 'There is no reason', Raz says, 'to believe that valid norms belonging to one system cannot conflict.'[26] Third, and relatedly, Raz offered two arguments in support of the claim that the existence of multiple sources of law entails the existence of multiple rules of recognition. The first is negative: given that multiple sources of law within a legal system need not be ranked, contrary to what Hart thought, there is no reason to speak of a single rule of recognition; a legal system may contain multiple rules of recognition. Raz's positive argument relates to the individuation of norms: norms regulate (prohibit, permit, or empower) specific acts, such that the regulation of two different acts entails the existence of two different norms. It follows that no *one* norm can make two different things a source of law or confer legislative powers on two different bodies.[27] The rule of recognition that makes precedent a source of law is separate from the rule of recognition that makes statute a source of law. It is precisely because rules of recognition can be multiple that they can come into conflict.

Does European pluralism embarrass this type of legal positivism, as elaborated by Raz, which is committed neither to the existence of conflict rules nor to the idea that all norms stem from a common origin? Nick Barber has offered an analysis of European pluralism that purports to be compatible with this type of legal positivism.[28] He argues that EU law forms a distinct legal system and that there are multiple and inconsistent rules of recognition operating within each EU Member State. On this Razian account, national courts follow at least two rules of recognition: one which directs them to apply norms enacted by European institutions according to criteria of validity found in EU norms, and one which directs them to apply norms enacted by national institutions according to criteria of validity found in national laws (most importantly in the constitution). There is no reason to assume that the criteria of validity found in norms identified by these two separate rules of recognition will not conflict. With respect to conflicts between EU norms and ordinary national statutes, the two rules of recognition just happen to contain conflict rules that converge in giving priority to EU norms. There is here a case of mutual recognition and accommodation, through the convergence of conflict rules: the law of most Member States makes ordinary statutes subordinate to EU law and so does EU law. But precisely because the existence of conflict rules in each legal system, as well as their convergence, is accidental, it need

---

[25] Joseph Raz, 'The Identity of Legal Systems', *California Law Review*, 809.
[26] *PRN*, 147.   [27] *PRN*, 130.
[28] NW Barber, 'Legal Pluralism and the European Union' (May 2006) 12(3) *European Law Journal*, 306–29.

not be found with respect to conflicts between EU norms and constitutional norms. And in fact no such convergence exists there. As we saw, the criteria of validity of EU law make EU law supreme whereas the criteria of validity of national constitutional law make the constitution supreme. And according to the criteria of validity of EU law, the ECJ has ultimate authority to decide both all matters of European law and what counts as matter of European law, whereas according to the law of some Member States, national constitutional courts have ultimate authority to decide all legal questions. In case of conflict between EU law and national constitutional law, the conflict rules contained in EU law and national do not converge. It follows that no legal rule governs how this conflict is to be resolved.

Nor does the fact that norm-applying institutions make for the unity of a legal system necessarily entail the existence of rules ranking the criteria of validity contained in multiple rules of recognition. First, national courts[29] may be split, some (say, lower courts) giving priority to EU law over the constitution, while others (say, constitutional courts) give priority to the constitution over EU law. As Barber notes, 'if the conduct of judges, as shown in their decision and reasoning, at a given point in time, is divided between inconsistent rules of recognition, then there is no "true" rule of recognition to be found'.[30] Second, even if all national courts converge in treating the constitution as supreme, it does not necessarily follow that their practice amounts to the creation of a ranking rule. According to the type of positivism under consideration, whether or not judicial precedent is a source of law, as well as its scope and who is bound by it, is a contingent matter which itself depends on the criteria of validity of each legal system. It is not necessary—nor is it in fact the case—that the law of Member States empowers constitutional courts to create conflict rules that are binding on the ECJ, nor that it empowers them to strike down EU measures or overturn judgments of the ECJ that violate the constitution. At best, national courts can avoid a political crisis by following a practice of giving priority to one set of rules in case of conflict, but without it being the case either that they have a legal duty to do so or that they create a legally binding rule of conflict by so doing.

Far from being a counter-example, European pluralism seems to support the positivist view that a legal system may contain more than one rule of recognition and that criteria of validity within the same legal system may conflict. National courts have chosen to give priority to EU norms when they conflict with constitutional norms but in doing so they were not applying a legal rule of conflict nor did they create one. Given that both EU rules and national constitutional rules are valid and that no legal rule of conflict between them exists, national courts can choose to give priority to EU

---

[29] I assume that on the Razian account presented here, national courts are not part of the EU legal system, nor is the ECJ part of the Member States' legal system. The reasons for this assumption is that the theory does not seem to allow that the same court belongs to more than one legal system, given that courts constitute a criterion of identity of a legal system. Barber, by contrast, takes national courts to be part of both the EU legal system and the national legal system and concludes that the EU legal system too, contains multiple and inconsistent rules of recognition.

[30] Barber, 322.

norms without it being the case either that the constitution is subordinate to EU law or that the constitution is supreme over EU law. As a matter of law, it is neither true nor false that the constitution is supreme over EU law and it will remain so until such time as national constitutions are amended, making EU law supreme in its area of competence. In the meantime, courts are legally free to choose whether to give priority to EU rules or national constitutional rules.

To sum up, European constitutional pluralism need not make any trouble for legal positivism. Thanks to important modifications introduced first by Hart and subsequently by Raz, legal positivism can coherently account for all the features of European pluralism. This is in my view no surprise, as the theoretical presuppositions of legal pluralists are shared by legal positivists. First, pluralists assume that whether or not a state-ordained legal system is the only system of norms practised in a given society is a *contingent* matter, not a necessary truth. They assume in other words, that there is no necessary connection between law and other normative systems. Second, pluralists assume that whether in a given society there are multiple normative systems practised alongside state law is a matter of *social* fact, not a matter of moral evaluation. These assumptions are not only compatible with legal positivism, they also parallel some of its central tenets. Legal positivism holds that the validity of a legal rule does not depend on its moral merits but that it is exclusively a matter of social facts.[31] It is no surprise then that legal positivism can account for the fact of legal pluralism. And if the type of legal positivism I presented here cannot, then no doubt, some modified version of it can.

6 European Constitutional Pluralism as a Problem for Courts and Dialogue as the Solution

We have taken a detour to visit mainstream theories of legal positivism and to assess whether Europe's constitutional pluralism challenges them in any way. We concluded that the most advanced and elaborate forms of legal positivism can rise to the challenge. It is now time to return to the question of whether the way in which positivism accounts for pluralism makes it a problem for people rather than just for jurisprudential theories.

Courts turn out to be the first victims of constitutional pluralism, if legal positivism holds true. For the picture of European law with which legal positivism leaves us is one that puts courts in an unenviable situation. The existence of multiple rules of recognition and the absence of convergent conflict rules means that courts cannot solve conflicts by applying a legal norm. Should national constitutional courts review the ECJ's judgments about the boundaries of EU competence? Should they review EU

---

[31] These claims are (and are known to be) too coarse. For a full elaboration of which of the different versions of these tenets legal positivism is committed to, see John Gardner, 'Legal Positivism: 5½ Myths' (2001) 46 *American Journal of Jurisprudence* 199.

measures that manifestly violate constitutional rights? Should the ECJ defer to national constitutional law in developing a jurisprudence of fundamental rights? Should the European Court of Human Rights review state measures that implement EU law? As a matter of law, there is no right answer to these questions, at least not in the legal positivist's eyes. Courts have to look elsewhere for normative guidance in order to carry out their judicial function. They have to balance a number of non-legal considerations: their constitutional loyalty, the likelihood of a constitutional crisis, the interests of the litigant parties, the goals of European integration, and many others. Pluralism, as understood by legal positivism, is no small challenge for courts.

It may here be objected that the existence of gaps and conflicts in the law and the idea that judges often have to exercise extra-legal discretion is not an anathema to many people, and certainly not to legal positivists.[32] Positivists are happy to accept that in many cases there is no law governing a particular dispute and that, when this is the case, judges should exercise good moral judgment in order to settle it. Be that as it may, surviving the challenge of constitutional pluralism has left positivism with some serious wounds. This is because the character and magnitude of normative conflicts in a pluralistic constitutional order are nothing like those that exist in the standard case of a municipal legal system that is hierarchically ordered. It is one thing to say that there may be conflicts between two rules contained in the same statute and a completely different thing to say that there are normative conflicts about which source of law is supreme, and who is the ultimate guardian of constitutionality within a legal system. Such conflicts run at the deepest level of our pre-theoretical understanding of law and shake widely held intuitions about the nature of law and the role of judges. For almost everything that the highest courts have to decide is subject to potential contradiction by another court: if the ECJ interprets a fundamental right in a way that contradicts the German constitution then it risks conflict with the German Constitutional Court. If the German Constitutional Court polices the boundaries of the competence of the EU then it risks conflict with the ECJ. If the ECtHR reviews a state measure that implements EU law and finds a human-rights violation, then it risks conflict with the ECJ. The potential of such conflicts means that there is very little law when it comes to matters that raise issues about the relationship between EU law and constitutional law. If a court's judgment may be contradicted by that of an equally supreme court, it follows that neither court can authoritatively determine what legal rights and duties litigants have. It follows in other words that it is indeterminate what legal rights and duties litigants have.[33] Pluralism affects a large, if not the largest, part of what the highest courts in Europe do. Whereas in the pre-pluralistic era, gaps and

---

[32] See Joseph Raz, 'Legal Principles and the Limits of Law' (1972) 81 *Yale Law Review* 823. Nick Barber goes further arguing that pluralism and absence of conflict rules have normative advantages in 'Legal Pluralism and the European Union'.

[33] Note that the positivist cannot argue that convergence (or agreement) between equally supreme courts entails the determinacy of the legal rights and duties that have been decided. Given that the judgments of each supreme court are not binding on the other and in the absence of a legal rule making convergent judicial outcomes legally binding, convergence cannot form a criterion of authoritativeness.

conflicts in law were at the periphery of judicial practice, positivism must now accept that they occupy centrestage. If we believe in legal positivism, we must accept that most of what EU judges do is politics, not law.

In the forty or so years of Europe's constitutional pluralism, courts have indeed struggled to develop doctrines that avoid a constitutional crisis without surrendering the claim to constitutional supremacy made on behalf of each legal order. The story of all the judicial sagas between the ECJ and national courts is well known and I will not repeat it here. Both the ECJ and national courts muddled through decades of institutional tension and legal uncertainty, averting a major constitutional crisis and securing the efficacious implementation of EU law within the national legal order. Despite the pluralism and all the potential for normative conflicts that it should entail according to positivism, the project of European integration has so far been a successful experiment in constitutional alchemy. Courts have opted for judicial outcomes that take into account what other courts and actors are doing, seeking to achieve harmony in the face of conflicting claims to constitutional supremacy. On the issue of fundamental rights for instance, the German Constitutional Court adopted the position that it will not review EU measures so long as there is equivalent protection of rights in the EU.[34] A slightly different test has been adopted by the European Court of Human Rights, which accords state measures that directly implement EU law a presumption of compatibility with the ECHR, which is however rebuttable in each case pending before it.[35] The ECJ on the other hand has often upheld national restrictions to EU fundamental freedoms that were imposed in the name of a constitutional principle, such as dignity.[36]

It is no accident that the process of developing doctrines that take into account what other courts do in the context of a pluralistic legal order, has been described by many EU scholars as one of dialogue and negotiation. The former Advocate General, Miguel Maduro, for instance has argued that the creation of a European legal order was possible because the ECJ entered into a dialogue with national legal actors and negotiated the various constitutional issues, thus legitimizing its role. He writes:

> The relationship established between national courts and individuals on one hand and the European Court of Justice on the other thus becomes one of dialogue rather than dictation. Legal discourse concerns a two-way relationship that is established between a court on the one side, and other actors with independent jurisdictions and similar or competing interpretations of the law on the other. Sometimes, this legal discourse may be subject to a final authority but ... it is arguable that in the European legal order there is no such hierarchy in legal discourse.[37]

The choice of the concept of dialogue and negotiation as the organizing idea is the direct result of the positivist assumption that what courts within a pluralistic legal order should

---

[34] *Solange II*.

[35] ECtHR, *Bosphorus v Ireland* Appl No 45036/98, Judgment of 30 May 2005.

[36] Cf the *Omega* case of the Court of Justice of the European Communities, Judgment of 14 October 2004, C-36/02 *Omega Spielhallen- und Automatenaufstellungs GmbH v Oberbürgermeisterin der Bundesstadt Bonn*.

[37] Miguel Maduro, 'Contrapunctual Law', 513.

decide is ultimately not governed by law. For on the positivist picture, the existence of a norm signifies the end of political deliberation and bargaining. In a parliamentary democracy, elected legislators have already debated the balance of reasons for taking a certain measure and expressed the outcome of their political bargaining in a legal norm. Courts that apply this norm are not meant to re-open arguments for and against having it, nor to engage in dialogue with relevant actors about its merits unless the norm itself directs them so to do.[38] It is only in the absence of a legal norm which they are under a legal duty to apply, that courts may assume the role of a political negotiator who, like parliament, must engage in dialogue with other relevant actors. The image of judicial dialogue in the EU presupposes, indeed it is premised upon, the understanding of constitutional pluralism that legal positivism offers us. It is seen as the cure to the problem of multiple and inconsistent rules of recognition and the absence of any law governing what courts should decide. Judicial dialogue stands and falls with positivism's assumptions about the nature of law. This is not only because judicial dialogue presupposes positivism, but also because it sits uncomfortably with a non-positivist account of constitutional pluralism to which I now turn.

7 Pluralism and Non-positivist Theories of Law[39]

A helpful way to describe the history of legal positivism is as the struggle to reconcile the following four elements within a single theory of law.

(i) Laws are man-made rules.
(ii) Laws form a system comprised of a fixed number of rules.
(iii) What unifies certain rules and turns them into a legal system is something other than law itself (for example, a social fact).
(iv) Law cannot, all things considered, contain contradictory requirements.[40]

Kelsen endorsed (ii) and (iv). Raz endorses (i), (ii), and (iii). Hart endorsed all four propositions. But as we saw, it is difficult to see how one can consistently hold all four of them. If both the content and the validity of laws are contingent on social facts, then there is no guarantee that valid laws will not conflict, making it possible that many or most laws conflict. If, on the other hand, valid laws cannot conflict then either their validity or their content must be independent of contingent social facts. Kelsen found the principle of non-contradiction a more appealing truth about law than the idea that certain contingent social facts about courts unify a legal system. Raz saw no great appeal in the claim that

---

[38] On the idea of norms as exclusionary reasons see Raz, *PRN*.

[39] Various authors, including myself, have used the term 'interpretivism' to refer to non-positivist theories of law. I here prefer the unimaginative term 'non-positivism' to avoid certain misleading connotations that interpretivism has in the relevant literature.

[40] I use 'requirements' broadly, to refer to duties, liabilities, rights, powers, etc. The same applies to the phrase 'legal rights and duties', as used throughout the paper.

valid laws cannot conflict, and kept Hart's emphasis on the practice of courts as the social fact that unifies the norms of a legal system. Though Raz has got the most coherent view, his theory sacrifices intuitions that many positivists and non-positivists alike have found powerful. Kelsen, Hart, Fuller, and Dworkin have all in different ways been attracted to the view that the principle of non-contradiction forms an essential truth about law; that it cannot ultimately be the case for example both that the law prohibits the search of business premises without a warrant and that it permits it.

Legal positivists who were attracted to the principle of non-contradiction had to reconcile it with their fundamental view that laws are a set of finite, man-made norms that form a system. Given that the content of man-made rules is contingent on the will of imperfect legislators who need not strive for consistency, conflicts are entirely possible. And the only way that they can be eliminated is by assigning priority to certain rules on the basis of structural features that rules possess, such as their mode of origin, time of creation, subject matter, etc. Since conflict rules (such as that later laws prevail over inconsistent earlier ones, or that *lex specialis derogat lex generalis*) is the only way that conflicts between valid man-made norms can be prevented, positivists like Hart and Kelsen came to see them as necessary in a legal system. But, as we saw, the existence of such conflict rules is itself dependent upon the will of imperfect legislators and hence contingent. A legal system may lack conflict rules in which case equally valid rules can contradict each other and the principle of non-contradiction emerges as a contingent feature of law.

If one is genuinely attracted to the principle of non-contradiction as an essential truth about law, then one's best bet is to abandon the view that laws are a set of finite, man-made norms that form a system. For as long as one holds this view, he is hostage to contingencies that make it impossible to eliminate legal conflicts. Rather than trying to choose between (iii) and (iv), some legal philosophers have disputed whether (i) and (ii) are true. Ronald Dworkin was the first to question, in 1967, whether law is a system of rules.[41] He did so by pressing the claim that moral principles are part of the law even when there is no social fact (like legislative enactment or judicial endorsement) that validates them as legal standards. Many critics misunderstood Dworkin's argument to be that law contains moral principles *as well as* man-made rules.[42] Dworkin's own view, as clarified in 1972, was that law does not contain any fixed number of standards, let alone a set of standards that comprises both rules and principles.[43] On the non-positivist picture that Dworkin first introduced, law refers to a value of political morality that normatively constrains the ways in which a political community treats

---

[41] Ronald Dworkin, 'Is Law a System of Rules?' *Chicago Law Review* (1967), reprinted as chapter 2 in *Taking Rights Seriously*.

[42] For the history of this misunderstanding and Dworkin's response see his *Justice in Robes*, ch 8.

[43] Ronald Dworkin, 'Social Rules and Legal Theory' (1972) 81 *Yale Law Journal* 855–90, Reprinted as chapter 3 (Model of Rules II) in *Taking Rights Seriously*. It is a crucial difference between Dworkin's view and legal positivism, that for the former the problem of how to individuate norms is not a genuine one. See p 74 of *Taking Rights Seriously*.

its members, in the sense that it can licence coercive force against them.[44] It is a picture in which man-made edicts, pronouncements, rules, directives, practices, etc, do not by themselves amount to any legal standard. Rather, they constitute morally relevant facts of a practice that is governed by a moral value. This moral value determines both why these social facts (for example, legislative enactments, judicial decisions, etc) are morally relevant for identifying and enforcing legal rights and *how* they are relevant; that is, how they affect the content of legal rights and duties. This value is not new: philosophers and constitutional lawyers have long referred to it by the names of *legality* or the *rule of law*, but the account they offered of it has, more often than not, assumed that law is made up of a fixed number of man-made norms.[45] This positivist assumption however makes the idea of the rule of law elusive: given that man-made enactments can be and often are morally heinous, it cannot be the case that the enforcement of law is always morally justified.

The attempt to show that law always provides a morally coherent basis for institutional action must begin by abandoning the claim that the content of the law is the content of some authoritative pronouncement. If one abandons (i) and (ii), then the principle of non-contradiction (iv) starts to gain traction. For understood as a moral value, it is hardly absurd to argue that the demands of law cannot be contradictory. It is as absurd as the claim that the demands of values like justice, equality, or friendship cannot be contradictory. Although philosophers debate whether moral values are commensurable and whether the demands of different moral values can conflict, it is far less controversial that the same value cannot ground contradictory moral requirements. We should presume, unless shown otherwise, that in the standard case the requirements of the same value are consistent. If 'law' refers to a moral value that normatively controls the effect of a community's political history on collectively enforced rights, then its demands—properly understood—should cohere.

Many critics who have no difficulty accepting that the requirements of a single value cannot be contradictory, found the thesis that law is necessarily coherent absurd, only because they sought to find coherence between norms enacted or practised by different institutions. Their mistake was to seek normative coherence in all the contingent norms enacted by a competent legislature or found in a source of law. But that is the wrong place to look: the thesis that the demands of law cannot be contradictory assumes that norms enacted by legal institutions and actors may be conflicting, contradicting, arbitrary, incomplete, etc. It assumes that politics, as expressed in norms made by institutions, is—from a moral point of view—patchy, messy, and

---

[44] See Dworkin *Law's Empire* and *Justice in Robes*. The non-positivist picture that I sketch in this section also draws on the work of Nicos Stavropoulos and Mark Greenberg but I do not mean to attribute it to any author in particular. I have benefited enormously from and draw heavily on Nicos Stavropoulos's piece 'Why Principles?', available at: <http://papers.ssrn.com/sol3/papers.cfm?abstract_id=1023758>, and Mark Greenberg's 'The Standard Picture and its Discontents', available at: <http://papers.ssrn.com/sol3/papers.cfm?abstract_id=1103569>.

[45] The best example is Lon Fuller, whose positivist assumptions made his defence of the ideal of the rule of law inconsistent.

contradictory. What it insists on is that there is always a right answer to whether, in virtue of the history of a political community (part of which includes relevant enactments), individuals have acquired certain moral rights or duties. Unlike legal positivism, it treats the question of what legal rights individuals have as a moral one from the start. Unlike legal positivism, it does not ask what moral reason is there to enforce man-made, descriptively identified, enactments. Rather, it asks whether certain enactments are morally relevant for determining the content of the moral rights individuals have against their community and, if so, whether they are relevant in the way that those who issued them intended.

Understood as the normative effect of politics on collectively enforceable entitlements, non-positivism entails a claim about law that appears at first glance counter-intuitive. It is the claim that there is a sense in which *nobody* decides what 'the law' is: not legislators, nor constitutional assemblies, nor judges, nobody. This claim will appear counter-intuitive so long as we still operate under the assumption that the word 'law' refers to some man-made norm. But if we allow ourselves to consider that it refers instead to a value of political morality (like justice, or equality), then the claim does not jar so much. As with any value, law's demands are mind-independent. They do not depend on what you and I, or anybody for that matter, think. Although what the law requires may often be close or even identical to what some institution (for example, an elected legislature) has decided, this is so in virtue of moral principles which make it the case that the content of that institution's decision contributes the whole of the content of a legal duty. But the mere social fact that some institution (be it a court or a legislature) made a decision is not sufficient for the existence of a legal right or duty. Although legislative or other decisions are typically relevant for discovering what legal rights exist (say in virtue of democratic principles), there is never a direct entailment from the content of a decision to the content of the legal right. Knowing what some institution decided never suffices to discover what legal rights or duties individuals have.[46]

What does non-positivism have to say about constitutional pluralism? The first thing to note is that non-positivism is more comfortable than positivism with the existence of conflicting claims to constitutional pluralism and the absence of conflict rules. This is because non-positivism never infers that the demands of law are contradictory from the mere existence of conflicting rules or claims and the absence of any rules ranking them. Just because there is some dictum or edict in national legal sources making the constitution supreme and another, conflicting, dictum in EU sources making it subordinate, it does not mean that we are inevitably faced with a legal conflict. That is not to say of course that conflicts are never possible for the non-positivist. However, several stringent conditions would have to be jointly met in order

---

[46] It might be worth adding that on a narrow understanding of decisions as intentional actions, they are not even a necessary condition for the existence of legal rights and duties. What matters for the purposes of the value of legality (which normatively grounds these rights) is the existence of past institutional practice enforcing (or failing to enforce) claims that individuals make against each other.

for two provisions that impose contradictory requirements to result in a genuine legal conflict. Consider the following three:

(i) Relevant moral principles make both provisions relevant for identifying a legal right and duty (the condition of relevance).

(ii) Relevant moral principles assign to both provisions equal weight (the condition of weight).

(iii) Relevant moral principles make the content of each provision conclusive of the content of the relevant legal right and duty (the condition of conclusiveness).

Take first the condition of *relevance*. There is no reason to think that each and every provision of the constitution is relevant for identifying related legal rights and duties. Take for example the question of whether an individual has a right not to be tortured or enslaved by foreign states, or whether an individual whose ship is attacked in the high seas by a foreign state has a legal right to self-defence. We do not think that the answer to such questions is controlled by whatever is written in the constitution of those states, such that if these constitutions permitted the killing or torturing of non-nationals then these individuals would prima facie have no such legal rights. Nor would it be correct to say that, were the constitution of a state to permit such wrongful acts, national law would conflict with international law: whether a state ought not to mistreat aliens does not depend at all on what its constitution says. Constitutions have moral relevance mainly insofar as they regulate the institutional design of a political community and the way in which its institutions exercise political power against its members. But they have no moral relevance to a whole set of other questions such as those regarding certain legal obligations states have towards non-nationals or other states. It follows that the claim that the constitution is the supreme law in *all* matters of law is inaccurate and that certain claims to constitutional supremacy made by national courts may be irrelevant and hence they do not compete with respective EU claims.

Consider next the condition of *weight*. Suppose that moral principles do make relevant what the constitution says on a particular issue but that the rules contained therein conflict. Suppose for instance that a constitution prohibits gender discrimination but excludes women from the army. There is no reason to suppose that the moral weight assigned to a state's decision to maintain an army for defensive purposes is equal to its duty not to discriminate on the basis of gender. Since the latter is far more weighty than the former, it is false to say that, all things considered, women have no constitutional right to be admitted to the army. This is why constitutional lawyers often speak of certain provisions of the constitution being unconstitutional: they assume that these provisions receive little or no moral support by the principles that underlie the constitution as a whole.

Finally consider the criterion of *conclusiveness*. Suppose that two moral principles of equal weight assign relevance to provisions stipulating two separate fundamental rights. For example, suppose for the sake of the argument that the political decision of the EU to create freedom of establishment is of equal moral weight to the national decision to grant workers the right to strike. Does it follow that when I go on strike to prevent you from hiring cheaper EU workers, your EU right necessarily clashes with my constitutional right?[47] One reason why it does not is that the underlying moral principles support only an *abstract* legal right to freedom of establishment or strike. The content of these abstract rights is not determined conclusively by the moral principles that justify them, but is also sensitive to further moral considerations such as the principle of proportionality, legitimate expectations, fairness, market efficiency, and many others. It would for instance be unfair if a trade union could use the right to strike as a means of depriving a group of EU workers of a freedom that everybody else in the EU—including the trade union—enjoys. Even if, other things being equal, the right to strike is of equal moral weight to freedom of establishment, it need not follow that, all things considered, the trade union had a right to strike. Hence it may be wrong to say that there was an unresolvable clash between national constitutional law and EU law. More than two moral principles may be pertinent to a case, qualifying and sharpening one's abstract legal rights.

The nature and stringency of the above three conditions suggest that on the non-positivist picture, it is unlikely that conflicts between provisions enacted by competent legal institutions will translate into conflicts in law, *all things considered*. In most cases, the requirements of the value of legality will be non-contradictory because the recalcitrant provisions that appear to generate conflict (wherever they may be found) will either be irrelevant, devoid of moral weight, or inconclusive. Law, on the non-positivist account, will turn out to be essentially *harmonic*.

It is now worth revisiting the three claims to constitutional supremacy made by the ECJ and challenged by national courts in the light of this conclusion, for it is difficult to see how these claims would meet all three conditions.

First, national constitutions cannot have any normative relevance in controlling how each Member State treats nationals of another state once a joint scheme of cooperation is in place. Consider a helpful analogy. The ground rules of my household regarding when to take the garbage out have no normative significance once a joint scheme of garbage collection is in place in the neighborhood. It would be wrong to say for instance that the in-house rule not to take the garbage out at night conflicts with the neighborhood's rule to take the garbage out only in the morning. If everybody else follows a practice of taking their garbage out in the morning, then it is not fair for my household to take the benefits of others' coordinated actions without sharing any burden. It is *that* fact that makes my in-house rule irrelevant, not some alleged fact that the neighborhood rules are supreme over my in-house rules in some constructed pyramid of validity of rules. Likewise, the fact that there is in the European Union a joint scheme of cooperation regarding the free movement of goods, services, capital, and persons makes national constitutional provisions irrelevant as far as this scheme is

---

[47] Cf the cases of Viking and Laval. Case C-438/05 *International Transport Workers' Federation and. Finnish Seamen's Union v Viking Line ABP*, Judgment of 11 December 2007; Case of C-341/05 *Laval un Partneri Ltd v Svenska Byggnadsarbetareförbundet and Others* [2007] ECR I-11767.

concerned. Again, it is the political fact that there is an ongoing scheme of common market that makes national constitutional norms *irrelevant*, not some alleged fact that EU norms are—or must be presumed to be—supreme over national constitutions.

Second, it is misleading to ask who, the ECJ or national courts, has the ultimate authority to determine the competence of the EU (kompetenz-kompetenz). If the relevance and normative weight of EU norms is partly premised on the moral significance of there being an ongoing scheme of cooperation between Member States, then *nobody* is to decide what falls within the competence of the EU because this question is objectively determined by moral facts to do with principles of social cooperation. Courts have to try to get these moral facts right, by taking EU norms as relevant only when this is justified by moral principles that apply to the scheme of cooperation in play. It might be objected here, that some institution has to decide authoritatively what the area of EU competence is, otherwise different courts will assign different boundaries, jeopardizing the efficacy and harmonious application of EU law. This objection is half right: it is right that the efficacy of the joint scheme of co-operation, and the public goods it produces for its members, is jeopardized if different courts assign different boundaries to the domain of cooperation. But that is only an argument for courts to follow the *same* boundaries, not an argument that only one court (the ECJ or the national constitutional court) should have ultimate authority to set them. As far as efficacy is concerned, it is irrelevant which courts first set which boundary. What matters is that all courts converge in following the same boundaries, *regardless of who set them*. Once some or most courts have set a boundary, then later courts have a reason to follow it, not because the former courts had ultimate authority to set boundaries, but because moral reasons of coordination and efficacy require so.

This leads me to the third question of whether the ECJ has ultimate authority to decide all matters of European law, including whether EU law violates human or fundamental rights. As in the issue of competence, it is misleading to ask who has the ultimate authority to decide what human rights European have, but for a different reason. The core human rights express moral requirements that make it impermissible for any political community to make certain individual liberties or choices the subject of a collective (majoritarian) decision. Which books one chooses to read, whether to have a family or not, what religion to practise, are not matters to be decided collect-ively.[48] It begs the question against this view of human rights to ask, as Waldron keeps insisting,[49] which institution should decide which matters should not be institutionally decided. The whole point is that it is not up to anybody to decide these matters, other than the individual whose right it is. Political morality puts these matters beyond the reach of the political process, allowing individuals to make their own choices. It is impermissible for governments to violate fundamental human rights thus understood and no institutional decision (be it by a legislature, a court, or a constitutional

---

[48] I have defended a non-teleological theory of rights as underlying the ECHR in G Letsas, *A Theory of Interpretation of the European Convention on Human Rights* (2009), ch 5.

[49] Jeremy Waldron, 'The Core of the Case Against Judicial Review' (2006) *Yale Law Journal* 115.

assembly) can change this moral fact. Courts have a duty to discover what political morality requires, because their role is to license state coercion only when it falls within the matters that we can collectively decide. To be sure, not all issues labelled as 'human rights' in the relevant legal sources, fall within the core of inviolable personal rights,[50] as sketched above. But most issues that courts adjudicate under substantive civil rights (such as freedom of expression, right to life, right not to be tortured, freedom of association, freedom of religion) recognized in fundamental sources of law in Europe and elsewhere, clearly belong to that category.

There is moreover a crucial difference between fundamental human rights, as defined above, and other issues arising within ordinary EU law.[51] Although divergent interpretations of the latter by the ECJ and national courts may jeopardize the efficacy of EU law, this is not the case with fundamental rights. Most EU measures seek to advance goals (such as a common market) that work to the mutual advantage of Member States and their citizens. EU and national institutions have to coordinate in the choice of means (such as free movement of goods, or common currency) for pursuing those goals, otherwise the joint venture will fail. But the means employed must be morally permissible: coordination creates reasons only when there was, to begin with, a choice between equally *permissible* means. It is morally indifferent, for example, whether to drive on the left or on the right side of the road. In designing a new traffic code, either option is morally permissible. Once there is an established practice of driving on a particular side, then drivers acquire reasons of coordination to drive on it. Likewise, when there is an established practice in most Member States of implementing EU measures that advance a common goal, courts deciding cases have reasons to take into account what other courts have done and coordinate their action accordingly. But reasons of coordination do not apply when the means employed are morally impermissible, say, because they violate fundamental human rights. To continue the analogy: an established practice of running over pedestrians who step on the left side of the road, violating their right to life, would not create reasons of coordination for other drivers to do the same. Likewise, means of pursuing EU goals that violate human rights and are upheld by the court that first rules on their lawfulness, do not create reasons of coordination for other courts. For example, if the ECJ has upheld an EU measure that violates human rights, this fact creates no reason for the European Court of Human Rights or national constitutional courts to do the same. Although courts in Europe should look at each other's reasoning in order to enrich their own view about what amounts to a human rights violation, each court must

---

[50] For an extensive discussion of human rights as inviolable personal rights, see Thomas Nagel, 'Personal Rights and Public Space' (1995) 24(2) *Philosophy & Public Affairs* 83–107.

[51] It should be stressed that, on the non-positivist picture, the distinction between the two is not based on the formal legal source (eg a Treaty provision vs a Directive) or the subject matter (eg individual rights vs common market) of the legal dispute in question. Fundamental human rights issues may arise in the context of litigating 'low-level' EU legislation (eg Directives); and vice versa, some issues arising in the context of the interpretation of 'fundamental rights' provisions (eg the EU Charter or the Grundgezetz) may not raise any issues to do with the morality of fundamental human rights. What the distinction turns on is the moral principles that are *in fact* engaged by the case at hand.

ultimately consider for itself whether, in the case pending before it, the litigant's human rights have been violated.[52] In so doing, each court aims at discovering whether state institutions have acted wrongly and that is a question whose answer does *not* depend on what other courts have said and held. When it comes to fundamental human rights issues, no court is the ultimate guardian of constitutionality in Europe because, strictly speaking, no court can decide which human rights people have.[53]

8 Constitutional Conflicts, Supremacy, and Kumm's Legal Positivism

It is now time to take stock of the non-positivist picture of European constitutional pluralism, before we turn to whether the idea of dialogue makes any sense within it. I hope it has become apparent by now that on the non-positivist account presented in the previous section, there are no dramatic constitutional conflicts between the Europe Union and its Member States. The claim of some national constitutional courts that the constitution is the ultimate law of the land is inaccurate, carrying no normative weight when it comes to identifying legal rights and duties born out of the process of European integration. It is to be taken as seriously as the claim that the German constitution is the ultimate law of the land in China or of the United Nations. The claim by both the ECJ and some national courts, that they have the ultimate authority to determine what falls within the area of competence of EU law, is equally inaccurate: what falls within the competence of the EU is an objective matter, to be determined by the moral principles that apply to joint projects undertaken by states. Although courts, through their judgments, influence the scope of the joint project, they are all equal actors in a typical coordination problem, each acquiring reasons partly in virtue of what other courts do, none having the ultimate authority to decide what the scope of the obligations arising out of the project is. Finally, the claim that some court should have the ultimate authority to decide what human rights Europeans have is misleading: each court must always apply itself to the question of whether the litigant's fundamental human rights have been violated, without being bound by reasons of coordination to follow what other courts have said on the same issue. They are bound only by the need to develop, as far as it is possible, a coherent vision of human rights across Europe.[54]

---

[52] This is why Strasbourg's test developed in the *Bosphorus* judgment, according to which the presumption that state-implemented EU measures is rebuttable in *each* case is the correct approach to take on a non-positivist theory. See *Bosphorus v Ireland*, Appl No 45036/98, Judgment of 30 May 2005.

[53] On the idea that fundamental rights in the EU reflect cosmopolitan moral requirements, see Pavlos Eleftheriadis, 'Cosmopolitan Law' (2003) 9(2) *European Law Journal* 241–63.

[54] For a non-positivist account of the principle of *stare decisis* see Scott Hershovitz, 'Stare Decisis' in Hershovitz (ed), *Exploring Law's Empire* (2006). It is worth noting that non-positivism offers a radically different account of how the doctrine of binding precedent works.

The absence of constitutional conflicts under the non-positivist picture is not accidental. It is borne out of the fact that questions of supremacy only make sense within a positivist framework. In that framework, the content of the law is fixed by the content of norms enacted or practised by an institution and the issue of conflicts is inevitably the issue of *whose* norms are supreme. By contrast, on the non-positivist picture, no legal requirement is individuated by direct reference to a norm. Relevant moral principles play a role not only by determining whether and which provisions or dicta matter but also, crucially, by telling us how such provisions contribute to the content of the law, all things considered. On the non-positivist picture it need not be the case, and in fact it often is not, that the content of the law is the content of any particular enactment. Given that non-positivism is not committed to the view that law is a system of rules and given that it takes moral principles as the ultimate determinants of the content of legal rights and duties, it makes no sense to talk of constitutional supremacy either; talk of supremacy is wedded to the all-or-nothing positivist view that the content of the law is the content of a rule and, in the case of conflict, either the rule prevails or it does not.

Non-positivism debunks the problem of constitutional conflicts in Europe. It refuses to accept that the mere existence of multiple and conflicting rules and claims to supremacy amounts to a normative problem *in law*. Unlike positivism, it offers a picture of European legal practice that poses no trouble for courts or individuals, because it is in essence no different to the practice of a municipal legal order. It insists that the question whether national constitutional law or European law is supreme is a pseudo dilemma, a non-issue.

Within the vast literature on European constitutional pluralism, Mattias Kumm's work[55] offers the most elaborate defence of the view that it is unhelpful to focus on who should have the ultimate say; European or national constitutionalism. It is therefore worth addressing the differences between his position and the non-positivist thesis that this chapter puts forward.

Starting from non-positivist premises that he borrows from Dworkin's work, Kumm advances a theory that he calls 'Constitutionalism Beyond the State'. The theory seeks to transcend the constitutional dilemma of choosing between European and national constitutional supremacy, by turning our attention to principles that best fit and justify existing legal practices. 'Constitutionalism Beyond the State' asks: 'What is the best understanding of the relationship between national and European constitutions, given the normative commitments underlying legal practice in Europe, seen as a whole?'[56] This question is certainly the same type of question as the one that a non-positivist, as defined above, would also want to ask about the European Union. Yet my sense is that Kumm's answer ultimately fails to escape the positivist assumptions that underlie the dilemma between European and national constitutional supremacy. To begin with, Kumm assumes throughout his work that constitutional conflicts in

---

[55] Kumm, 'Constitutional Supremacy'.   [56] Kumm, see n 55, 287.

Europe are real and genuine. He presents his theory as a solution to a real problem caused by constitutional pluralism rather than as a debunking of the problem. Second, although Kumm emphasizes the importance of looking at the principles that underlie national and European legal practices, he takes the role of such principles to be the ranking of positivistic norms. He writes:

> The task of national courts is to construct an adequate relationship between the national and the European legal order on the basis of the best interpretation of the principles underlying both. The right conflict rule or set of conflict rules for a national judge to adopt is the one that is best calculated to realize the ideals underlying legal practice in the European Union and its Member States.[57]

Kumm in other words sees principles as conflict rules, whose role is to tell us in each case *whose* norms should prevail. In the absence of a single rule of recognition that would rank criteria of validity, Kumm turns to principles as a substitute. Like Kelsen and Hart, he is attracted to the view that law's demands cannot be contradictory, yet he does not let go of the view that law is a system of *rules*. Kumm assumes that the content of legal rights and duties is the content of some enacted norm and, in the face of conflict, he uses moral principles to determine which norm should prevail. But this picture of European law is still hostage to legal positivism: it assumes that law is a system of norms that may conflict and that it is contingent whether the system contains conflict rules. When it does not, or when conflict rules contained in multiple rules of recognition do not converge, no legal norm settles how conflicts between legal norms are to be resolved, so we must look somewhere else, at morality. As we saw, this is exactly the view that the more sophisticated version of legal positivism takes of the European constitutional pluralism. Positivists would have no quarrel with the view that, in the face of multiple and inconsistent rules of recognition, courts should turn to moral principles for deciding which norms to apply. What Kumm's view leaves no space for, is the idea that the content of legal rights and duties is not co-extensive with the content of an enacted norm as well as the idea that some enacted norms (say domestic constitutional provisions), and judicial claims may be legally irrelevant for determining European law.

Perhaps Kumm has no axe to grind in the debate between positivism and non-positivism and is happy with the view that principles operate as conflict rules, ranking other rules in case of conflict. But so long as one conceives of pluralism as the problem of conflicting rules, one is still under the spell of positivism, committed to the view that nothing can be a legal right or duty unless its content is determined exclusively by the content of some enacted norm. The legal rights and duties that Europeans have under Kumm's theory would be very different to the ones entailed by a non-positivist account of European law.

---

[57] Kumm, see n 55, 286. The nuances of Kumm's theory are more sophisticated than I can do justice to here.

9 Non-positivism and Judicial Dialogue

When I took my driving licence test, the theory exam took the form of multiple-choice diagrams of unmarked junctions in which two or more cars were portrayed approaching each other from different directions. The test would list all the pictured cars, one by one, as possible answers to the question of who should give way at the junction. As if this was not hard enough, the test would often offer an additional choice to candidates: 'No car is to give way. Drivers should engage in dialogue.' In preparation for the test, my instructor gave me a useful piece of advice: 'if you are in doubt about which car should give way,' he said, 'never go for the dialogue option: it is always the wrong answer'.

Non-positivism extends my instructor's advice to European law. It argues that dialogue, no matter how generously we understand it, is an ill-suited metaphor to capture the relevance that the actions of other courts have to what a particular court should decide. Here is why. EU scholars cannot use the concept of dialogue in a literal sense: it is not that the ECJ, for instance, adjourns a case pending before it until its judges have met, discussed, and exchanged views with the judges of national constitutional courts. Nor is the request for preliminary ruling by national courts an instance of actual dialogue: the court requesting a ruling is not asking the judges of the ECJ to give their opinion on the case; it asks the ECJ to decide a question of law. Nor is the ECJ asking the requesting court what it thinks about the question of law that the latter is referring. Dialogue is a metaphor aimed at capturing the fact that what a court has said and done has normative significance for what another court should decide. And the reason why it fails to do so is that dialogue is a process-based method for determining outcomes, whereas the determinants of legal rights and duties are substance-based. The normative ideal of dialogue implies that there is no correct decision *in advance of* a dialogue between the relevant actors and that dialogue is a necessary condition for the legitimacy of the decision. But on the non-positivist account, this is never the case in law. What legal rights and duties individuals have before a court, is independent of any process of dialogue between the deciding court and other actors. According to non-positivists, what determines the content of legal rights and duties are objective, mind-independent moral principles that calculate the normative effect of past political practice on collectively enforced legal rights and duties. Two reasons make this non-positivist claim impossible to square with the idea that the ECJ and national courts should engage in a dialogue.

First, it is not necessary that the outcome (and the reasoning) of a judgment of the ECJ has normative significance for national constitutional courts and vice versa. We saw already that in the case of fundamental rights, each deciding court has one substantive question to answer: have state institutions acted wrongly by interfering impermissibly with individual choices that are outside the realm of collective decision-making? The answer to this question does not depend on what other courts have said and done. Although national courts should strive to give an account of fundamental rights that coheres with what the ECJ and the ECtHR have done and vice versa, any one judgment of any court may be mistaken and hence devoid of any normative weight.[58]

Second, even when moral principles make a past judicial outcome relevant for what a court should now decide, as is the case when coordination is required to secure efficacy, what is normatively relevant is not what the other court has *said* but had it has *done*. Consider the driving analogy again: when I am fast approaching a junction thinking that you should give way, what matters in relation to what you ought to do is not what I think but what I do. If for example the only way to avoid collision, given my location and speed, is for you to accelerate and go through the junction first then you should ignore what I think about who should give way, and you should step on the accelerator. What you ought to take into account in other words is the normative *effect* of my actions, not my *beliefs* about what that normative effect is. Who should give way is not something we are going to have to talk about. In normative accounts of dialogue, by contrast, what matters normatively is a degree of respect for, or deference to, the normative beliefs of one's interlocutor. The justifiability of an outcome depends on there being a process in which interested parties express their beliefs and due consideration is given to them. Dialogue targets the beliefs of institutional actors. Legality, by contrast, targets the normative effect of institutional action.

In summary, no matter how far one stretches the conceptual boundaries of dialogue, it is an idea that is incompatible with the fundamental tenets of non-positivism. EU scholars who are attracted to the image of judicial dialogue must either defend its normative appeal against non-positivism,[59] or alternatively, stop using the idea of dialogue in order to account for the fact that what some courts in Europe do may have normative significance for what another European court should decide. The idea that judicial dialogue is an inherent feature of Europe's constitutional dialogue is overly simplistic.

10 Conclusion

I hope to have shown that pluralism, understood as the existence of multiple and conflicting normative orders, poses no major challenge to mainstream theories of analytic jurisprudence. But the major divide in analytic jurisprudence between legal positivism and non-positivism corresponds to two radically different views about Europe's constitutional pluralism, with different practical implications.

On the positivist picture, the existence of multiple and inconsistent rules of recognition entails that the content of a large number of Europeans' rights and duties is, as a

---

[58] See Hershovitz, 'Stare Decisis'.

[59] I should stress that although the image of dialogue presupposes the account of law that legal positivism offers, legal positivism does not entail support for a dialogue model of decision making. All dialogue theorists are positivists, but not all positivists are dialogue theorists. Some positivists may wish to offer a different account of how courts should decide cases in a 'pluralistic' legal order.

matter of law, indeterminate. Positivism argues *from* pluralism *to* constitutional conflict and legal indeterminacy. It makes pluralism a genuine problem for courts and a threat to the determinacy of Europeans' legal rights and duties. Moreover, conceptualizing what the ECJ and national constitutional courts have been doing in the last forty years or so, as a process of dialogue, assumes legal positivism's picture of law. Dialogue is a solution to a problem that only exists if positivism is true of law.

Non-positivism by contrast sees no problem in the existence of multiple and overlapping normative orders, containing conflicting rules, because it rejects the thesis that law is a system of rules. It accepts that politics and the norms it generates are far from harmonious, and that is why it does not seek to find harmony and coherence therein. Non-positivism posits that law refers to a value of political morality that determines what the effect of past political practice is on collectively enforceable rights and duties. That value, often called legality or the rule of law, determines not only whether someone's edicts matter but also how they matter. The dimensions of normative relevance and weight under which the value operates to identify legal rights and duties, make questions of constitutional supremacy *irrelevant*. Nobody is to have the ultimate say on the constitutional issues that divide the ECJ and national courts because nobody *can* decide these issues: they are determined by objective moral principles. Non-positivism debunks the problem of constitutional conflicts by offering us an account of European law that is no different in character to the account it gives of municipal law. Within this non-positivist framework, describing the practice of the ECJ and national courts as one of judicial dialogue makes no sense. What legal rights and duties Europeans have is not to be determined by any process of dialogue. The image of dialogue is too crude to capture the normative significance (or lack thereof) of what courts in the EU have decided, for what other courts now have to decide. And capturing this normative significance is at the heart of what courts in 'pluralistic' Europe ought to do.

I should like to end this long chapter with a disclaimer and a plea. I have not here defended the non-positivist account of European law against its rival nor mounted a critique against legal positivism. My aim has been to present and contrast the two schools and to show how one's views or assumptions about the nature of law make a difference not only to how one sees European constitutional pluralism but also to how one identifies Europeans' legal rights and duties. But in my view, it is no accident that the theory of legal positivism has had to undergo constant modifications in order to account for the radical changes in the way political power is exercised in the last sixty years or so. And the picture it now offers us, although internally coherent, is one that puts conflicts at the centrestage of legal practices and presents pluralism as a real problem for both courts and citizens. The experience of European integration and its success as a constitutional experiment suggest that pluralism was a problem that never was. Non-positivism by contrast, instead of running after political changes, trying to account for the new ways in which political institutions interact, changed radically the old paradigm by rejecting altogether the view that law is a system of rules. The growing realization in Europe that issues of constitutional supremacy and conflict are pseudo-problems may provide further indication that positivism's intellectual days are counted. If this is the case, as I believe it is, it would be regrettable to see ideas of 'pluralism' and 'dialogue' replacing the tired image of law as a system of rules. The non-positivist's picture that puts objective principles of political morality at the heart of European law is the only real alternative to legal positivism. If you find the quest for ultimate rules of recognition, or rules of conflict resolution, *futile,* then give the idea of harmonic law a chance.

5

Judicial Dialogue in the European Union

*Anthony Arnull**

1 Introduction

The central theme of this chapter is the relationship between the European Court of Justice ('ECJ') and the national courts of the Member States. Drawing on public law scholarship on dialogic judicial review, it explores the way in which that relationship has developed and the challenges it now faces. It finds support in the dialogue metaphor for the suggestion, in the work of some theorists, that the tension between national constitutional courts and the ECJ created by the latter's claims about the nature of the European Union legal order can best be analysed in terms, not of hierarchy and authority, but of interaction and compromise.

2 Authority versus Compromise

The ECJ's case law 'constitutionalizing' the European Union Treaties and affirming the distinctiveness of the legal order they created began with *Van Gend en Loos* in 1963[1] and *Costa v ENEL* in 1964.[2] As the ECJ explained in Opinion 1/09:[3]

> ... the founding treaties of the European Union, unlike ordinary international treaties, established a new legal order, possessing its own institutions, for the benefit of which the [Member] States have limited their sovereign rights, in ever wider fields, and the subjects of which comprise not only Member States but also their nationals ... The essential

---

* Barber Professor of Jurisprudence, University of Birmingham, UK. I am very grateful to the editors, Julie Dickson and Pavlos Eleftheriadis, and an anonymous reviewer for their comments on a draft of this chapter. The usual disclaimer applies.

[1] Case 26/62 [1963] ECR 1.

[2] Case 6/64 [1964] ECR 585.

[3] On the proposed agreement creating a unified patent litigation system [2011] 3 CMLR 4, para 65.

characteristics of the European Union legal order thus constituted are in particular its primacy over the laws of the Member States and the direct effect of a whole series of provisions which are applicable to their nationals and the Member States themselves....

It was for the ECJ to 'ensure respect for the autonomy of the European Union legal order thus created by the Treaties...'.[4] The guardians of the Union's legal order and judicial system were not just the ECJ but also the courts and tribunals of the Member States, who were collectively responsible for ensuring the full application of Union law in the Member States and judicial protection of the rights conferred on individuals by that law. The national courts and the ECJ all had a duty to ensure that the law was observed in the interpretation and application of the Treaties.[5]

This view of the European Union's legal order has been pregnant with theoretical and practical questions and implications since it first took shape. It was one which departed from the international law presumption that treaties were addressed to states and that it was for them to decide whether, and if so to what extent, enforceable rights were to be conferred on individuals.[6] If Union law granted an individual a directly effective right, that right would prevail over competing provisions of national law, regardless of their internal status or the date of their adoption. Perhaps surprisingly, it is a view that encountered little overt political resistance from the Member States.[7] National courts were less sanguine, some of them rejecting the ECJ's conception of the Union as an autonomous legal order which always took precedence over national law. The most prominent judicial critic of that conception has been the German *Bundesverfassungsgericht*, which has asserted an independent power to police the protection of fundamental rights in the Union,[8] ensure respect by the Union institutions for the limits of their powers,[9] and uphold Germany's 'constitutional identity'.[10] Other supreme national courts have followed its example.

The approach of such courts forces us to confront the question of how these apparently competing claims to hierarchical supremacy can be reconciled. In other words, what is the theoretical relationship between Union law and the national laws of the Member States? To find an answer to that question, we might begin by asking whether Union law is really law. Hart maintained essentially that what gave a rule a legal quality was the fact that it was created by a legal system.[11] The emphasis he placed on state law might suggest that he thought that only states could have legal systems.[12] Since the European Union is

---

[4] [2011] 3 CMLR 4, para 67; Joined Cases C-402/05 P and C-415/05 P *Kadi and Al Barakaat v Council* [2008] ECR I-6351, paras 282 and 316.

[5] Cf Art 19(1) TEU.

[6] J Weiler, *The Constitution of Europe* (Cambridge: Cambridge University Press, 1999), 19; B de Witte, 'Direct Effect, Primacy, and the Nature of the Legal Order' in P Craig and G de Búrca (eds), *The Evolution of EU Law,* 2nd edn (Oxford: Oxford University Press, 2011), 323, 324–5.

[7] de Witte, see n 6, 347.

[8] *Internationale Handelsgesellschaft mbH v Einfuhr- und Vorratsstelle für Getreide und Futtermittel* ('*Solange I*') [1974] 2 CMLR 540; *Wünsche* ('*Solange II*') [1987] 3 CMLR 225.

[9] *Brunner v European Union Treaty* [1994] 1 CMLR 57.

[10] *Re Ratification of the Treaty of Lisbon* [2010] 3 CMLR 13.

[11] HLA Hart, *The Concept of Law,* 2nd edn (Oxford: Clarendon Press, 1994), ch V.

[12] Cf J Raz, *The Authority of Law: Essays on Law and Morality,* 2nd edn (Oxford: Oxford University Press, 2009), ch 5.

not a state, it would follow that the rules emanating from it are not law. If that were true, it would be difficult to gainsay the right of the Bundesverfassungsgericht and other like-minded national courts to contradict the ECJ when exercising the jurisdiction conferred on them by national law. But Union law is routinely treated as law, not just by national governments and the institutions of the Union but also by courts, lawyers, civil servants, businesses, and individuals in the Member States. Indeed, the view that the state should be the primary focus of analytical legal theory is now coming under increasing strain.[13]

If law needs to be the product of a legal system, perhaps the European Union is a legal system of a novel kind. This seems to be what the ECJ has in mind when it describes the Union as a 'new legal order'. That description raises questions about how many legal systems there are in the Union and what the relationship between them might be.[14] The ECJ does not suggest that the Union legal order entirely supplants the national systems[15] for the simple reason that the Union is an organization of limited powers and does not have universal jurisdiction. It also relies heavily on the national systems to implement and enforce its own rules. However, in the event of a conflict between a rule of national law and a rule of Union law, the ECJ is clear that the latter must be given precedence. Moreover, the ECJ uses its powers to circumvent or penalize failures by Member States to give effect to Union law properly. These are aspects of the so-called autonomy of Union law. As Barents explains in his monograph on the subject:

> Because of its autonomy, Community law is self-referential: a system of law which with respect to its normative character exclusively refers to itself. In practical terms this means that once Community law exists . . ., its contents (scope and legal effects) are exclusively governed by its own rules and principles. As a consequence, Community law can be described as a normatively closed system.[16]

From this perspective, Union law is valid and applicable in the territory of the Member States 'exclusively by virtue of itself'.[17] However, it is a perspective that is not universally shared. Writing about the primacy principle, de Witte observes: 'it is a legal reality only to the extent that national courts accept the role allocated to them by the ECJ, and the practice shows that this acceptance, so far, is selective and generally based on the national courts' own constitutional terms'.[18]

---

[13] Eg K Culver and M Giudice, *Legality's Borders: An Essay in General Jurisprudence* (Oxford: Oxford University Press, 2010); P Eleftheriadis, 'The Law of Laws' (2010) 1 Transnational Legal Theory 597.

[14] See J Dickson, 'How Many Legal Systems? Some Puzzles Regarding the Identity Conditions of, and Relations Between, Legal Systems in the European Union' (2008) 2 *Problema* 9; J Dickson, 'Towards a Theory of European Union Legal Systems', Chapter 2 in this volume.

[15] Cf Case 106/77 *Simmenthal* [1978] ECR 629; Joined Cases C–10/97 to C–22/97 *IN. CO. GE.'90* [1998] ECR I–6307.

[16] R Barents, *The Autonomy of Community Law* (The Hague: Kluwer, 2004), 259. See also P Eleftheriadis, 'The Structure of European Union Law' (2009–10) 12 *Cambridge Ybk of Eur Legal Studies* 121.

[17] Barents, see n 16, 253.

[18] de Witte, see n 6, 361–2. See J Schwarze (ed), *The Birth of a European Constitutional Order: The Interaction of National and European Constitutional Law* (Baden-Baden: Nomos, 2001).

How can this clash be resolved? Who has authority to resolve it? For the ECJ, if a national court declared a Union act invalid on the grounds that it infringed national principles or its own view of the limits of the adopting institution's powers, it would be acting in breach of its obligations under Union law. The result would be that the legal position in the Member State concerned would not be compatible with the requirements of the Treaties. As the ECJ made clear in Opinion 1/09,[19] it would be open to any individual who thereby suffered loss to seek damages from that state in its national courts. Moreover, the Commission would be able to institute infringement proceedings against the state concerned, which might lead to the imposition on it of a financial penalty. Because some national courts find the origin of their duty to apply Union law, not in Union law but in national law, however, they may feel unable to disregard the obligations imposed on them by norms of national law, particularly those contained in a national constitution, 'the ultimate exercise of popular sovereignty'.[20]

If neither side were willing to give way, the Union would face a constitutional crisis (whose gravity might be expected to correspond to the political weight of the state concerned). Theorists have therefore sought ways of describing the relationship between the Union and the national legal orders in ways which do not appear to condemn the Union to perch forever on the edge of an abyss. MacCormick advocates what he calls a 'pluralistic analysis', by which he means that

> the doctrine of supremacy of Community law should by no means be confused with any kind of all-purpose subordination of member-state-law to Community law. Rather the case is that these are interacting systems, one of which constitutes in its own context and over the relevant range of topics a source of valid law superior to other sources recognized in each of the member-state-systems.[21]

Therefore, he maintains,

> [i]t is for the ECJ to interpret in the last resort and in a finally authoritative way the norms of Community law. But equally, it must be for the highest constitutional tribunal of each member-state to interpret its constitutional and other norms, and hence to interpret the interaction of the validity of EC law with higher level norms of validity in the given state system.[22]

For MacCormick, the avoidance of conflict

> is a matter for circumspection and for political as much as legal judgment. The ECJ ought not to reach its interpretative judgments without regard to their potential impact on national constitutions. National courts ought not to interpret laws or constitutions without regard to the resolution of their compatriots to take full part in European Union and European Community.[23]

---

[19] Art 19(1) TEU, see n 3, paras 86 and 87.

[20] N MacCormick, *Questioning Sovereignty: Law, State, and Nation in the European Commonwealth* (Oxford: Oxford University Press, 1999), 110.

[21] MacCormick, see n 20, 110.

[22] MacCormick, see n 20, 118.

[23] MacCormick, see n 20, 119–20.

Is this a theoretical explanation of how the stance of the ECJ might be reconciled with that of the *Bundesverfassungsgericht* or just a description of the existing position? After all, they would each have no difficulty in agreeing that they should be circumspect when considering the impact of their rulings on the Union or the national legal order, as the case may be. Such circumspection has indeed characterized the case law of both courts to date, for the ECJ has made concessions to the views of the *Bundesverfassungsgericht*, while the *Bundesverfassungsgericht* has declined so far to exercise the power it has reserved to itself to declare Union law inapplicable in Germany.[24] This may well promote 'constructive negotiation over constitutional conflicts',[25] but does it explain how a clash might be resolved if one were to occur?

Culver and Giudice suggest that 'what MacCormick claims are interacting systems look more like two hierarchical systems talking past one another'.[26] They emphasize the importance of interaction between institutions rather than systems and argue that 'there is no need to suppose that the institutions are hierarchically ordered'.[27] They add that, 'when interaction fails, it fails between institutions'. So conflicting decisions 'would show failure of interaction between the German federal constitutional court and the ECJ, but not necessarily between German and European legal orders, which are comprised of several other institutions besides their respective courts'.[28] But Culver and Giudice acknowledge that 'the interactions between law-applying legal institutions in the European Union seem to involve "dialogue" and "compromise" between similarly situated, potentially conflicting legal institutions, not reference to a chain of authority to determine which legal institution holds greater authority'.[29]

The reluctance of modern writers to seek to explain the Union legal order in terms of hierarchy, and their emphasis on interaction, dialogue, and circumspection or compromise find an echo in the literature on judicial review as a form of dialogue between courts and legislatures. The underlying idea gained momentum in Canada following the adoption in 1982 of the Canadian Charter of Rights and Freedoms,[30] but is now spreading to other parts of the common law world.[31] One of its leading exponents is Roach, who identifies three types of what he calls 'dialogic judicial

---

[24] Eg *Re Honeywell* [2011] 1 CMLR 33; M Payandeh, 'Constitutional Review of EU Law After *Honeywell*: Contextualising the Relationship Between the German Constitutional Court and the EU Court of Justice' (2011) 48 CML Rev 9.

[25] M Kumm and V Ferreres Comella, 'The Future of Constitutional Conflict in the European Union: Constitutional Supremacy after the Constitutional Treaty' in *Altneuland: The EU Constitution in a Contextual Perspective* (Jean Monnet Working Paper 5/04) at 26.

[26] See n 13, 70.

[27] See n 13, 73.

[28] See n 13, 73.

[29] See n 13, 161.

[30] K Roach, 'Constitutional, Remedial, and International Dialogues About Rights: The Canadian Experience' (2004–05) 40 *Texas Intl LJ* 537.

[31] Roach, see n 30, 537–8.

review'.[32] Under the first type, courts and legislatures are taken to have an equal right to interpret rules of the constitution; the second type emphasizes the ultimate accountability of the courts to legislatures and society; while the third type sees the courts and legislatures 'playing distinctive yet complementary roles in resolving questions that involve rights and freedoms'. Roach makes it clear that his preference is for the third type. His reasons encapsulate the advantages which are claimed for a dialogic model of judicial review. According to Roach, the third type of such review is preferable[33]

> ...because it can produce the most constructive partnership between courts and legislatures...It allows courts to educate legislatures and society by providing principled and robust articulations of the values of the [Canadian] Charter [of Rights and Freedoms] and the common law constitution while allowing legislatures to educate courts and society about their regulatory and majoritarian objectives and the practical difficulties in implementing those objectives.

In order for constructive dialogue to take place, each participant must show 'an openness to outside influence and a focus on the persuasive force of law rather than its pedigree or its binding nature'.[34] These habits of mind may be encouraged by the very process of dialogic judicial review. Waldron goes so far as to suggest that dialogue is promoted by weak forms of judicial review, because judges are unlikely to listen to legislators 'when they know they can prevail in the constitutional system without having to listen, and without having to defer'.[35] Dialogic judicial review is not without drawbacks. As Roach admits, where a court's decisions can be revised or rejected by political actors, judges may 'hedge their bets' and be unwilling to 'commit themselves to absolute rules'.[36] This may make them reluctant to enforce even the most basic rights as absolute and unqualified.[37] But where it works, a dialogic approach can enable each participant to 'help the other see its potential blind spots'.[38] This, it is said, 'can produce critical self-reflection and advance the cause of justice'.[39]

3 Judicial Dialogue and the European Court of Justice

(A) Dialogue with Political Interlocutors

The case law of the ECJ contains several instances where dialogue conducted within the context of the exercise of its judicial powers has helped refine the rules applicable in particular areas. The political interlocutors of the ECJ may converse directly with it

---

[32] K Roach, 'Constitutional and Common Law Dialogues Between the Supreme Court and Canadian Legislatures' (2001) 80 *Canadian Bar Rev* 481, 485. See also J Waldron, 'Some Models of Dialogue Between Judges and Legislators' (2004) 23 *Supreme Court L Rev* (2d) 7.

[33] Roach, see n 32, 485.   [34] Roach, see n 30, 539.   [35] Waldron, see n 32, 47.

[36] Roach, see n 32, 576.   [37] Roach, see n 30, 565.

[38] Roach, see n 32, 512.   [39] Roach, see n 30, 575.

through taking part in legal proceedings, whether as a party or an intervener or by submitting observations. Dialogue may also occur when they take the case law of the ECJ into account in exercising their own decision-making powers. It is worth considering some examples, arranged broadly in order of the explicitness of their dialogic quality.

(B) Standing in Annulment Proceedings

In *Unión de Pequeños Agricultores v Council*,[40] Advocate General Jacobs invited the ECJ to adopt a radically more liberal test for determining whether a private applicant had standing to bring annulment proceedings. His view was endorsed by the General Court (then the Court of First Instance).[41] However, the ECJ's judgment, given while the Convention on the Future of Europe was sitting, reaffirmed the strict existing test. It acknowledged that it was possible to envisage alternative systems of judicial review, but declared that it was for the Member States to make any changes they considered necessary by amending the Treaty. The ECJ's failure to seize the initiative may be said to exemplify a drawback of dialogic judicial review. Be that as it may, the case led to the inclusion in the Constitutional Treaty, and subsequently the Treaty on the Function-ing of the European Union, of a provision relaxing slightly the standing rules which private applicants must satisfy.[42] The next stage in the dialogue involves the interpret-ation and application of the new provision by the Union Courts. It may be argued that the eventual outcome will enjoy enhanced legitimacy because of the dialogue that took place between the parties involved in framing it.

(C) International Agreements

In cases where the ECJ is asked to pronounce on the compatibility with the Treaties of an international agreement envisaged by the Union, the dialogic quality of the procedure is clear, because the Treaty provides that, if the ECJ's opinion is negative, 'the agreement envisaged may not enter into force unless it is amended or the Treaties are revised'.[43] In Opinion 1/91,[44] the ECJ held that the system of judicial supervision envisaged by the draft agreement creating the European Economic Area was incompatible with the EEC Treaty. That ruling led to further negotiations between the parties to the agreement and a number of amendments. The ECJ found the amended provisions compatible with the EEC Treaty in Opinion 1/92[45] and the agreement took effect at the beginning of 1994.

Opinion 2/94[46] involved a three-way conversation or 'trialogue'. The issue was whether the so-called flexibility clause of Article 235 EC (now 352 TFEU) could

---

[40] Case C-50/00 P [2002] ECR I-6677.

[41] Case T-177/01 *Jégo-Quéré v Commission* [2002] ECR II-2365 (reversed on appeal: Case C-263/02 *Commission v Jégo-Quéré* [2004] ECR I-3425).

[42] Art 263 TFEU, para 4.

[43] Art 218(11) TFEU. This was the procedure used in Opinion 1/09, see n 3.

[44] [1991] ECR I-6079.

[45] [1992] ECR I-2821.

[46] [1996] ECR I-1759.

provide a legal basis for the accession of the European Community to the European
Convention on Human Rights. In the course of answering 'no' to that question, the
ECJ remarked that Article 235 EC could not be used 'as a basis for the adoption of
provisions whose effect would, in substance, be to amend the Treaty...'.[47] That
remark appeared to be a response to the *Brunner* decision of the *Bundesverfassungsgericht*, where it had warned that Article 235 'may not have effects that are equivalent
to an extension of the Treaty'.[48] The ruling of the ECJ was also addressed to the
Member States and led to a number of responses. The most notable were the
proclamation of the Charter of Fundamental Rights in 2000 and agreement at Lisbon
on a new provision, Article 6(2) TEU, expressly authorizing (indeed requiring) the
Union to accede to the European Convention on Human Rights. Although Opinion
2/94 disappointed many observers, it may ultimately have proved beneficial to the
health of the Union legal order by reinforcing the principle of conferral and postpon-
ing attempts by the Community/Union to accede to the Convention until there was a
greater degree of consensus on the matter among the Member States.

i The Area of Freedom, Security, and Justice

The provisions introduced at Amsterdam on the so-called area of freedom, security,
and justice (AFSJ) were split between a new Title IV of Part Three of the EC Treaty and
Title VI of the TEU (the so-called third pillar). The Member States did not wish to
subject the new provisions to the classic powers of the ECJ because of fears about how
they might be interpreted and applied. Its jurisdiction over them was therefore severely
limited. However, the ECJ managed to circumvent some of those limits.[49] At Lisbon,
the AFSJ was brought fully within the scope of the classic powers of the ECJ, subject to
certain minor restrictions in cases involving law and order and internal security.[50]
However, for a period of five years from the entry into force of the Treaty of Lisbon,
the powers of the ECJ in respect of existing third-pillar measures were to remain
the same as they were under Title VI of the TEU pre-Lisbon.[51] Any post-Lisbon
amendment of a pre-existing act would bring it fully within the enlarged jurisdiction
of the ECJ.

Here we see continuing dialogue between the ECJ and the Member States. The
initial restriction of the ECJ's jurisdiction over the AFSJ was a response to the
reputation the ECJ had acquired through its case law. The ECJ had concerns about
the extent to which the new provisions were subject to judicial oversight. These it
sought to address through highly flexible interpretations of its own powers. This in
turn led the Member States to accept that the ECJ needed, in due course, to be more

---

[47] Para 30 of the ECJ's Opinion. That passage was cited by the Danish Constitutional Court in *Carlsen*: see
[1999] 3 CMLR 854, 860. See also Case C-376/98 *Germany v Parliament and Council* [2000] ECR I-8419.

[48] [1994] 1 CMLR 57, 105.

[49] Case C-354/04 P *Gestoras Pro Amnistía* [2007] ECR I-1579; Case C-355/04 P *Segi* [2007] ECR I-1657. Cf
Case C-105/03 *Pupino* [2005] ECR I-5285.

[50] Art 276 TFEU.

[51] Protocol No 36 on Transitional Provisions, Title VII.

intimately involved in scrutiny of the AFSJ. Of course, this is to over-simplify matters, for some Member States may have supported the full involvement of the ECJ from the outset and some may over time have come to support it. The UK continues to harbour reservations and has a complex opt-out.[52] But these complications do not detract from the sense of ongoing dialogue. Although one may regret the delay involved, the process may again be seen as a healthy way of forging a consensus about the best way of subjecting the AFSJ to judicial oversight.

ii The Content of Legislative Acts

There are many situations in which the case law of the ECJ has affected the substantive content of legislative acts, which may in turn be the subject of further case law. Examples are European Parliament and Council Directive 2004/38 on the right of citizens of the Union and their family members to move and reside freely within the territory of the Member States[53] and European Parliament and Council Directive 2006/123 on services in the internal market,[54] parts of which codify pre-existing case law of the ECJ.[55] Conversely, the ECJ is sometimes influenced by acts that have not yet entered into force in ruling on the effect of Treaty provisions.[56] Here the effect can be to extend an approach enshrined in legislation to cases it was not designed to cover.

(D) Inter-court dialogue

The above examples provide support for the view that the dialogue metaphor can help us to understand the nature of the interactions that take place between the ECJ and its political interlocutors. While there is interest in the details of such interactions, from a theoretical point of view they do not seem qualitatively different from those typically conducted by top national courts. In terms of the categories of dialogic judicial review identified by Roach, the examples given above seem to represent a hybrid form of all three. The Member States are the masters of the Treaties, so the ECJ is ultimately accountable to them. In this sense, the examples may all be said to have involved weak forms of judicial review. However, the need for Treaty amendments to enjoy the unanimous support of all national governments[57] can make some ECJ decisions difficult to reverse. For practical purposes this can sometimes elevate the ECJ to a status equal to or even higher than that of the Member States.

---

[52] Protocol No 21 on the Position of the UK and Ireland in Respect of the AFSJ. See S Peers, *EU Justice and Home Affairs Law*, 3rd edn (Oxford: Oxford University Press, 2011), 17–18, 73–85.

[53] [2004] OJ L158/77.

[54] [2006] OJ L376/36.

[55] In matters of judicial organization, the ECJ may be given a direct role in the decision-making process: see eg Arts 257 and 281 TFEU. This too will involve dialogue between the ECJ and the institutions, but any relationship between that dialogue and the substantive law will generally be no more than indirect.

[56] Case C–340/89 *Vlassopoulou* [1991] ECR I–2357; Case C–357/89 *Raulin* [1992] ECR I–1027; A Arnull, *The European Union and its Court of Justice*, 2nd edn (Oxford: Oxford University Press, 2006), 474–5, 507.

[57] Art 48 TEU. The ECJ sometimes plays an informal part in this process: see eg the discussion paper on the future of the EU judicial system it issued prior to the IGC which led to the Treaty of Nice.

The ECJ has yet another set of interlocutors and it is through its ongoing conversations with them that it has been able to have a particularly profound influence on the Union's development. Those interlocutors are the national courts of the Member States, identified in Opinion 1/09 as joint guardians of the Union legal order alongside the ECJ, with which they conduct a formalized dialogue under the preliminary rulings procedure established by Article 267 TFEU (ex 234 EC/177 EEC). Although that dialogue is not conducted with legislatures—indeed, it may have the effect of marginalizing legislatures, especially those of the Member States—in other respects it seems to fall into Roach's third category. The preliminary rulings procedure is a cooperative one in which the two courts involved have distinct but complementary roles to play in finding a solution to the case in hand which is in harmony with the requirements of Union law.[58] The national court is responsible for deciding questions of fact and of national law, for selecting the questions which need to be referred and for applying the ruling of the ECJ. The task of the ECJ is to decide the questions of Union law which need to be resolved before the national court can give judgment. The dialogue which takes place between the ECJ and the national courts under the preliminary rulings procedure is perhaps less variegated than that which it enjoys with the institutions and Member States. However, it is supplemented by the indirect dialogue it conducts through its case law with national courts which decline to refer and contact between past and present members of the ECJ and national judiciaries.

The importance of the preliminary rulings procedure is hard to exaggerate. Once embraced by the national courts, it enabled the ECJ to influence directly the way they applied Union law and offered it an opportunity to rule on myriads of issues on which it might otherwise have been unable to pronounce. They included the questions we have been considering about the relationship between Union law and the national laws of the Member States and the nature of the legal order created by the Treaties. The procedure thereby helped the ECJ to promote the uniform application of Union law throughout the Member States and gave it a detailed insight into the practical and legal problems it posed at the national level. In the 1970s, the ECJ used the preliminary rulings procedure with great panache to give a series of groundbreaking judgments on fundamental planks of the common market when it seemed that the integration process might stall under the baleful influence of the Luxembourg Compromise.[59] The procedure became a vehicle by which the ECJ and the national courts educated each other about the rules, principles, and methodologies of their respective systems. Because it enabled the ECJ to borrow and adapt principles and concepts of national law, it helped to bolster the legitimacy of Union law by ensuring that it was firmly rooted in the values underlying the legal systems of the Member States.

---

[58] ECJ Information Note on References from National Courts for a Preliminary Ruling, [2009] OJ C297/1, paras 7 and 8. Cf AG Poiares Maduro in Case C-127/07 *Arcelor Atlantique et Lorraine and Others* [2008] ECR I-9895, para 17.

[59] Eg Case 2/74 *Reyners v Belgium* [1974] ECR 631; Case 8/74 *Procureur du Roi v Dassonville* [1974] ECR 837; Case 33/74 *Van Binsbergen v Bedrijfsvereniging Metaalnijverheid* [1974] ECR 1299; Case 43/75 *Defrenne v SABENA* [1976] ECR 455.

It was not a foregone conclusion that the preliminary rulings procedure would develop in this way, nor can it be assumed that it will continue to play the same role in the future. In what follows, an attempt will be made to explain its evolution to date (Parts 4 and 5) and the main challenges it now faces (Parts 6 and 7). Reference will be made to the work of political scientists, who have made a particular contribution to the literature on the ECJ since the revival of European integration following the Single European Act. Indeed, the ECJ became a pawn in the ongoing debate between the intergovernmentalists, who see the integration process as driven by the outcomes of bargaining between the Member States, and the neofunctionalists, who emphasize the part played by supra-national and sub-national actors independent of national governments.[60] The ECJ was even described as 'the poster child for a revival of neofunctionalism'.[61] If, however, the ECJ's approach is based on interaction, dialogue, and compromise, as suggested by some of the writers considered above, it would be too crude for either neofunctionalists or intergovernmentalists to claim it as an ally.

4 The Reception of the Preliminary Rulings Procedure by National Courts

Because most national courts enjoy discretion in deciding whether to refer a case to the ECJ, the preliminary rulings procedure depends for its effectiveness on the willingness of national courts to make use of it. If they routinely resolve questions of Union law for themselves (as all except top national courts are entitled to do), the ECJ will be deprived of the oxygen of national cases it needs if it is to engage in a productive dialogue with its national counterparts. After a slow start,[62] the volume of references reached 123 in 1978 and continued to follow an upwards trajectory thereafter, with a notable leap to 204 in the year after the 1992 deadline for completing the internal market. By 2010 (the latest year for which statistics were available at the time of writing), the number of references had reached 385.

Why did so many national courts embrace the preliminary rulings procedure with such apparent enthusiasm? The standard lawyer's response to that question, sometimes described as 'legalist',[63] emphasizes the quality of the ECJ's reasoning. Weiler,

---

[60] P Craig, 'Integration, Democracy, and Legitimacy' in P Craig and G de Búrca (eds), *The Evolution of EU Law*, 2nd edn (Oxford: Oxford University Press, 2011), 13; L Hooghe and G Marks, 'A Postfunctionalist Theory of European Integration: From Permissive Consensus to Constraining Dissensus' (2008) 39 *British J of Political Science* 1, 3–6.

[61] W Mattli and A-M Slaughter, 'The Role of National Courts in the Process of European Integration: Accounting for Judicial Preferences and Constraints' in A-M Slaughter, A Stone Sweet, and J Weiler (eds), *The European Court and National Courts—Doctrine and Jurisprudence* (Oxford: Hart Publishing, 1997), 253, 254; A-M Burley and W Mattli, 'Europe Before the Court: A Political Theory of Legal Integration' (1993) 47 *International Organization* 41.

[62] The first reference, made under Art 177 EEC in July 1961, was Case 13/61 *Bosch v van Rijn* [1962] ECR 45.

[63] Eg Burley and Mattli (see n 61), 45–6; K Alter, 'Explaining National Court Acceptance of European Court Jurisprudence: A Critical Evaluation of Theories of Legal Integration' in Slaughter, Stone Sweet, and Weiler, see n 61, 227, 230–4.

for example, refers to 'the per se compliance pull of a dialogue conducted between courts in "legalese"' and observes: '...the overall content of the European Court jurisprudence seemed (or must have seemed) to reflect a plausible reading of the purposes of the Treaty to which the Member States had solemnly adhered'.[64] In the seminal *Jacques Vabre* case before the French Cour de Cassation in 1975, Procureur Général Touffait (a Judge at the ECJ from 1976–82) described the judgment in *Costa v ENEL* as based on 'so coherent a reasoning that its conclusion appears unavoidable'.[65] His conclusions were instrumental in persuading the Cour de Cassation to accept the doctrine of primacy. Burley and Mattli point out that convincing and apparently neutral legal reasoning was important in preserving the ECJ's freedom of action, for overtly political judgments would have been more likely to attract a political response.[66]

This though is only part of the explanation. The key to a fuller understanding of why the national courts embraced the procedure with such alacrity lies in identifying the incentives this offered them.[67] Common sense might suggest that the typical judge wishes to deliver appeal-proof rulings as quickly as possible and with the minimum of effort. If confronted with a system of law of which he has no previous experience and a mechanism for shifting to others the task of answering the questions it raises, he is likely to exploit it unless it would be quicker and equally likely to produce the right answer for him to do it himself. The confidence of national judges in the ECJ was strengthened by its extensive programme of outreach activities, which enabled them to visit the ECJ and learn about its work, and a growing body of specialist practitioners and academics, many of whom contributed to the burgeoning scholarly literature on Union law. Most such literature was initially supportive of the ECJ[68] and would undoubtedly have had an influence in Member States where judges accord importance to academic writing about the law.[69]

Weiler adds two further suggestions. One is the development of what might be termed a herd mentality among national judges. Once enough national courts had started to use the procedure, courts elsewhere were encouraged to follow suit in order to avoid damage to their professional pride and prestige. Moreover, growing acceptance of the discipline of Union law allayed the fears of particular courts that to do so themselves would weaken their governments when dealing with other Member States.[70] The second suggestion is judicial empowerment and the potential this

---

[64] J Weiler, *The Constitution of Europe* (Cambridge: Cambridge University Press, 1999), 195 (and 33).

[65] *Directeur Général des Douanes v Société Vabre* [1975] 2 CMLR 336, 363; G Mancini, 'The Making of a Constitution for Europe' (1989) 24 CML Rev 595, 605.

[66] See nn 61, 57, 73. They argue that this confirms 'the core insight of neofunctionalism—that integration is most likely to occur within a domain shielded from the interplay of direct political interests...'.

[67] Burley and Mattli, see n 61, 42.

[68] Burley and Mattli, see n 61, 70.

[69] Cf Weiler, see n 64, 203.

[70] Weiler, 196; J Weiler, 'A Quiet Revolution: The European Court of Justice and its Interlocutors' (1994) 26 *Comparative Political Studies* 510, 521–3.

brought to subvert established relationships between national courts and their domestic interlocutors. Weiler observes:[71]

> Lower courts and their judges were given the facility to engage with the highest jurisdiction in the Community and, even more remarkable, to gain the power of judicial review over the executive and legislative branches even in those jurisdictions where such judicial power was weak or non-existent ... Institutionally, for courts at all levels in all Member States, the constitutional architecture with the Court's signature meant an overall strengthening of the judicial branch vis-à-vis the other branches of government ... [N]ational courts did not feel that the empowerment of the Court was at their expense ...

Building on Weiler's work, Alter, a political scientist, developed a thesis she called 'inter-court competition'. One of the effects of Union law, she argues, is that it 'creates opportunities for some courts to escape national hierarchies and thus to bolster their independence, influence, and authority vis-à-vis other courts and political bodies'. Importantly, Union law 'can also be a threat to the independence, influence, and authority of a court because it disrupts national hierarchies ...'.[72] Since lower national courts could use the preliminary rulings procedure to circumvent the decisions of higher courts, it had the effect of undermining the finality of the latter's decisions: 'How could high courts not see this as a threat to their independence, authority, and influence?'[73] Such courts therefore 'have an interest in thwarting the expansion and penetration of EC law into the national legal order'.[74] They 'refer relatively few questions of interpretation to the European Court, and virtually no questions which could allow the European Court to expand the reach of European law into their own sphere of jurisdictional authority'.[75]

The inter-court competition thesis might seem to be borne out by the judicial statistics published each year by the ECJ.[76] These show that some top national courts are indeed extremely reluctant to make references to the ECJ. As of the end of 2010, the French Conseil Constitutionnel, the German *Bundesverfassungsgericht*, and the Spanish Tribunal Constitucional had not made any references; the Italian Corte Costituzionale had made only one.[77] The Corte Costituzionale,[78] the French Conseil Constitutionnel,[79] and the Danish Supreme Court[80] had joined the *Bundesverfassungsgericht* in purporting to

---

[71] Weiler, see n 64, 197 (and 33).

[72] K Alter, *Establishing the Supremacy of European Law: The Making of an International Rule of Law in Europe* (Oxford: Oxford University Press, 2001), 47.

[73] Alter, 48. See also Alter, see n 63, 241–2.

[74] Alter, see n 63, 242.

[75] Alter, see n 63, 242.

[76] <http://curia.europa.eu/jcms/jcms/Jo2_7032/>.

[77] The Corte Costituzionale made its first reference in 2008: F Fontanelli and G Martinico, 'Between Procedural Impermeability and Constitutional Openness: The Italian Constitutional Court and Preliminary References to the European Court of Justice' (2010) 16 *European Law Journal* 345; F Laffaille, 'Il y a toujours une première fois. A propos de l'application de l'article 234 TCE par la Cour constitutionnelle italienne' (2009) 45 *Revue Trimestrielle de Droit Européen* 459.

[78] *Frontini v Ministero delle Finanze* [1974] 2 CMLR 372. Cf *Granital*, 8 June 1984.

[79] Dec No 2004-498 DC, 29 July 2004.

[80] *Carlsen v Prime Minister Rasmussen* [1999] 3 CMLR 854.

limit the effect of the primacy doctrine in their internal legal orders, while the French Conseil d'Etat and the German *Bundesfinanzhof* had rejected the direct effect of direct- ives.[81] It has also been argued[82] that the acceptance by the French Cour de Cassation of the primacy of Community law in 1975 enabled it to gain an advantage over the Conseil d'Etat, which did not do so until 1989.[83] But this does not tell the full story. Even higher courts which have never or only rarely made a reference operate in the shadow of the ECJ, which undoubtedly takes note of their decisions on matters of Union law. In any event, the judicial statistics reveal that higher courts in some Member States are in fact regular users of the preliminary rulings procedure. Indeed, it seems that in some Member States references are more likely to be made by higher courts than by lower courts.[84] Moreover, Germany and Italy show that a single Member State may include among its higher courts both enthusiastic and reluctant referrers. Nor can it be said that higher courts do not refer constitutionally significant questions to the ECJ.[85]

Alter later made it clear that she did 'not mean to imply that lower courts always support, and supreme courts oppose, ECJ authority',[86] and recognized 'that national courts do not always have strategic calculations in mind in deciding whether to refer a case or to apply ECJ jurisprudence'.[87] Her description of the judiciary as a bureaucracy which is subject, like all bureaucracies, to 'bureaucratic rivalries based on the insti- tutional position of the actors involved',[88] offered an important insight into the factors that influence judges in their decision making. But the neofunctionalist account (to which the inter-court competition thesis seems to belong)[89] lacks the predictive power to which it aspires. Burley and Mattli argue that, 'just as neofunctionalism predicts', the process of legal integration in Europe is driven by 'supranational and subnational actors pursuing their own self-interests within a politically insulated sphere'. But

---

[81] J Plötner, 'Report on France' in Slaughter, Stone Sweet, and Weiler (see n 61), 41, 48–50, referring to the decision of the French Conseil d'Etat of 22 December 1978 in *Minister of the Interior v Cohn-Bendit* [1980] 1 CMLR 543; J Kokott, 'Report on Germany' in Slaughter, Stone Sweet, and Weiler, 77, 116.

[82] Plötner, see n 81, 60.

[83] *Directeur Général des Douanes v Société Vabre* [1975] 2 CMLR 336 and *Nicolo* [1990] 1 CMLR 173, respectively.

[84] M Wind, 'The Nordics, the EU and the Reluctance Towards Supranational Judicial Review' (2010) 48 *J of Common Market Studies* 1039, referring to Denmark and Sweden. The judicial statistics indicate that the same is true of Finland.

[85] Eg Case C-213/89 *The Queen v Secretary of State for Transport, ex parte Factortame* [1990] ECR I-2433 (referred by the House of Lords); Joined Cases C-46/93 and C-48/93 *Brasserie du Pêcheur and Factortame* [1996] ECR I-1029 (referred by the *Bundesgerichtshof* and the House of Lords respectively). The references in *Van Gend en Loos* and *Costa v ENEL* (see nn 1 and 2) were both made by courts against whose decisions there would be no judicial remedy.

[86] Alter, see n 72, 50.

[87] Alter, 51. She later confessed that she might have 'overemphasized' her argument: 'competition between courts is at best only one of many factors that lead to the emergence of new legal doctrines, and probably not the largest factor at play': K Alter, *The European Court's Political Power* (Oxford: Oxford University Press, 2009), 12.

[88] Alter, see n 72, 47.

[89] K Alter, 'Explaining National Court Acceptance of European Court Jurisprudence: A Critical Evaluation of Theories of Legal Integration' in Slaughter, Stone Sweet, and Weiler (see n 61), 227, 238–41.

neofunctionalism did not 'predict' the role the ECJ might play. Indeed, as Burley and Mattli acknowledge,[90] political scientists paid little attention to the ECJ in the 1960s and 1970s even though the dramatic developments in its case law during that period might have helped to counter the 'crescendo of criticism'[91] attracted by neofunctionalism in the wake of the Luxembourg Compromise. When Burley and Mattli claim that 'the distinctive characteristics of the ECJ and its jurisprudence correspond to neofunctionalist prediction',[92] they are writing after the fact. Paradoxically, the legalist approach, dismissed by Alter as 'clearly inadequate'[93] because it ignores politics, seems more likely to predict whether a reference to the ECJ will be made in any particular case. Indeed, analysis of cases is often striking by its absence in the political science literature on the preliminary rulings procedure. While that literature should not be dismissed because it ignores law, understanding what prompts national judges to refer clearly requires legal as well as political and other considerations to be taken into account.

To what extent, if at all, has the failure of some top national courts such as the *Bundesverfassungsgericht* to enter into a direct dialogue with the ECJ through the preliminary rulings procedure impeded the search for a mutually acceptable solution to the constitutional problems adumbrated above? It is certainly possible to argue that the present state of 'mutually assured destruction',[94] in which national courts sometimes parade their missiles but never actually press the button, is a useful brake on the more activist tendencies of the ECJ. However, regular direct dialogue over specific questions might have encouraged those involved to listen to and learn from each other in a more constructive atmosphere than periodic episodes of megaphone diplomacy, often conducted at a high level of generality. It might even have produced an accommodation that posed fewer theoretical dilemmas.

5 National Reference Rates

Whatever general factors we might identify as liable to affect the willingness of national courts to make references, the statistics show that there is a wide variation in national reference rates which cannot be explained by population size. In other words, the likelihood that a reference will be made in any particular case may depend on the Member State in which it has been brought.[95] This means that the potential of the preliminary rulings procedure to educate the ECJ and the national courts about their respective systems and approaches is not being felt uniformly across the Union.

---

[90] Burley and Mattli. see n 61, 42–3.   [91] Burley and Mattli, see n 61, 57.
[92] Burley and Mattli, see n 61, 57.   [93] See n 72, 41.
[94] Or 'MAD.' This piece of Cold War terminology is deployed in the present context by J Weiler, U Haltern, and F Mayer, 'European Democracy and its Critique' (1995) 18 *West European Politics* 4, 37.
[95] M Broberg and N Fenger, *Preliminary References to the European Court of Justice* (Oxford: Oxford University Press, 2010), ch 2.

Political scientists have made valiant attempts to explain this phenomenon through the use of quantitative research techniques. Stone Sweet and Brunell[96] argued from a neofunctionalist perspective that national variations in reference rates could be explained by levels of cross-national activity: 'The linear relationship between intra-EC trade and references is nearly perfect ... with countries that trade more with their partners in the EC generating higher levels of Article 177 references.'[97] They suggested that references would target disproportionately (a) 'national barriers to transnational activity that hinder access to larger markets relative to smaller markets' and (b) 'national rules and practices that operate to downgrade the effect and application of European secondary rules'.[98] When they examined the number of references concerning the free movement of goods, they found that 40 per cent of them concerned the legality of German rules, concluding 'that the German market ... is the prize of free traders'.[99] In the field of social policy, 24 per cent of references concerned British rules and practices. This was because litigation focused on national law 'that represented the lowest common denominator position on EC secondary legislation adopted by the council'.[100]

The suggestion that national variations in reference rates were attributable to patterns of inter-State trade was disputed by Wind, who argued that courts in 'majoritarian democracies' with little tradition of the judicial review of national legislation would be less willing to make use of the preliminary rulings procedure to test the compatibility of national law with Union law.[101] This, she claimed, explained the relative reluctance to make references to the ECJ of courts in the Nordic Member States, where judicial review was considered hard to reconcile with democracy, itself often conflated with majoritarian parliamentarianism. When references were made, it was usually by higher courts. Disputes were generally resolved without recourse to litigation. So although weak judicial review may be conducive to dialogue between courts and legislatures, it can be inimical to inter-court dialogue under the preliminary rulings procedure. Stone Sweet and Brunell's hypothesis was also criticized by Alter,[102] this time on the basis that the social policy cases had nothing to do with transnational activity. In his book *The Judicial Construction of Europe*, Stone Sweet acknowledged

[96] A Stone Sweet and T Brunell, 'Constructing a Supranational Constitution: Dispute Resolution and Governance in the European Community' (1998) 92 *American Political Science Rev* 63.

[97] Stone Sweet and Brunell, 67–8. A similar conclusion had been reached by J Golub, 'Modelling Judicial Dialogue in the European Community: The Quantitative Basis of Preliminary References to the ECJ', EUI Working Paper RSC No 96/58.

[98] Stone Sweet and Brunell, 74.

[99] Stone Sweet and Brunell, 75.

[100] Stone Sweet and Brunell, 76. They claimed that the integration process was being driven by a 'self-sustaining and expansionary dynamic', (Stone Sweet and Brunell, 65) in which inter-state trade resulted in litigation, which in turn generated a need for regulation, which produced further litigation. See also N Fligstein and A Stone Sweet, 'Constructing Polities and Markets: An Institutionalist Account of European Integration' (2002) 107 *American J of Sociology* 1206.

[101] Wind, see n 84. See also M Wind, D Martinsen, and G Rotger, 'The Uneven Legal Push for Europe: Questioning Variation when National Courts go to Europe' (2009) 10 *European Union Politics* 63.

[102] K Alter, *The European Court's Political Power* (Oxford: Oxford University Press, 2009), 182.

that the growing scope of Union law had given rise to litigation by private actors 'not engaged in cross-border economic exchange or in market integration, per se'.[103]

Stone Sweet and Brunell were, however, right to single out references from British courts in the 1980s and 1990s in the field of social policy, for they illustrated strikingly how dialogue between the ECJ and national courts could subvert the policy preferences of national governments. Many of the cases concerned were supported by the Equal Opportunities Commission (EOC), a publicly funded but independent body set up to promote equality of opportunity between men and women.[104] It was specifically empowered[105] to grant assistance to individuals claiming to have been subjected to discrimination on the ground of their sex. The year 1979 saw the election in the United Kingdom of a Conservative Government unsympathetic to the Union's developing social policy. Finding it increasingly difficult to achieve its policy objectives through the national political process, the EOC began to fund references to the ECJ to test the limits of the Union rules on equal treatment for men and women.[106] It also brought cases before the national courts itself to exploit the developing case law of the ECJ.[107] The EOC's litigation strategy assisted it to pursue its objectives notwithstanding the hostility of the government of the day. It was particularly effective at shifting government policy because the EOC was more likely than individual litigants to ensure that the benefits of victory were felt by the population at large.[108] The success of the strategy underlined the capacity of the constitutional principles laid down by the ECJ to reinforce the obligations imposed on Member States by Union law. That capacity was reinforced in 1990 when the ECJ laid down the principle of State liability.[109] This had a direct bearing on the willingness of the British Government to change the law to bring it into line with Union requirements.[110]

But litigation strategies cannot be adopted by groups which are prevented by national law from taking part in court proceedings.[111] In any event,[112] such strategies are expensive and risky, because if a case is lost the cause of the promoter might be set back. A group which thinks it can secure its policy objectives through the political process is therefore likely to prefer that route. Even if it only meets with partial success,

---

[103] Oxford: Oxford University Press, 2004, 75.

[104] See the Sex Discrimination Act 1975. The EOC was replaced in 2007 by the Equality and Human Rights Commission established under the Equality Act 2006.

[105] Sex Discrimination Act 1975, s 75.

[106] For details, see C Barnard, 'A European Litigation Strategy: The Case of the Equal Opportunities Commission' in J Shaw and G More (eds), *New Legal Dynamics of European Union* (Oxford: Oxford University Press, 1995), 253, 264.

[107] One of the most notable was *R v Secretary of State for Employment, ex parte Equal Opportunities Commission* [1995] 1 AC 1.

[108] K Alter and J Vargas, 'Explaining Variation in the Use of European Litigation Strategies: European Community Law and British Gender Equality Policy', in Alter (see n 102), 159, 180.

[109] Joined Cases C–6/90 and C–9/90 *Francovich* [1991] ECR I–5357.

[110] Alter and Vargas, see n 108, 169.

[111] K Alter, 'The European Union's Legal System and Domestic Policy: Spillover or Backlash?' in Alter, see n 102, 184, 192.

[112] Alter and Vargas, see n 108, 176–80.

it may consider that preferable to litigation and the danger of antagonizing permanently its political interlocutors. Moreover, a group which is committed to taking advantage of the political process may have had a hand in formulating the rules in force. Such a group is unlikely to back a challenge to those rules. These factors did not apply to the EOC due to the antagonism of the British Government. Moreover, the EOC's statutory duty to keep under review the domestic legislation on equality of opportunity between men and women[113] and its specialist staff made it uniquely well placed to identify emerging trends and problems. A group with a broader remit might at least occasionally have decided to give priority to other issues.

Cichowski found similar processes at work in the field of environmental law, which she compared with that of equal treatment.[114] She maintained[115] that the control of national governments over the formation of policy could be weakened by litigation and the mobilization of civil society, that is, 'the strategic action of individuals and groups to promote or resist change in a given policy arena...'.[116] Reiterating the observation of Stone Sweet and Brunell[117] that cross-national variations in reference rates were policy specific, Cichowski claimed that the extent to which a Member State generated references to the ECJ was affected by the presence of mobilized interests and the availability of legal expertise and resources, as well as national standing rules.[118] Conant drew a broader conclusion: 'judicial influence over major processes of reform relies on... the activism of organized societal actors and the responsiveness of public institutions that support legal claims'.[119] National administrations tended to adopt a policy of 'contained compliance', obeying the letter of rulings of the ECJ but ignoring their wider implications.[120] Only the presence of actors able to sue independently and institutional support for legal challenges would increase the costs of contained compliance sufficiently to prompt a more active response on the part of government. Conant found that, in the telecommunications sector, '[t]he vast majority of corporate users and aspiring entrants have been loathe to pursue their goals through legal means...'.[121] Legal challenges were viewed as a 'risky and inefficient strategy' which threatened to 'poison mutually beneficial relations' with bureaucrats and politicians:[122] 'actors affected by policy change pursued their aims overwhelmingly in political arenas'.[123]

---

[113] Sex Discrimination Act 1975, s 53(1)(c).

[114] R Cichowski, *The European Court and Civil Society: Litigation, Mobilization and Governance* (Cambridge: Cambridge University Press, 2007), 166–7.

[115] Cichowski, see n 114, 2.

[116] Cichowski, see n 114, 7.

[117] See also Mattli and Slaughter, see n 61, 276.

[118] Mattli and Slaughter, see n 61, 245.

[119] L Conant, *Justice Contained: Law and Politics in the European Union* (Ithaca and London: Cornell University Press, 2002), 3.

[120] Conant, see n 119, 3.

[121] Conant, see n 119, 116.

[122] Conant, see n 119, 118.

[123] Conant, see n 119, 116.

Talk of constitutionalization, self-sustaining dynamics, and litigation strategies should not therefore mislead us into exaggerating the role of the ECJ. Through the dialogue it has cultivated with national courts, the ECJ has been able to craft the normative framework within which Union policy is implemented, but the policy itself is laid down elsewhere. Even the normative framework may not be effective in Member States where there is no constituency with an interest in attacking national rules that do not comply with Union law and the means to do so. Moreover, in Member States where such constituencies are often absent, courts may not acquire the habit of making references. This may make them disinclined to do so even when confronted with a dispute over the effect of Union law. The result may be to impoverish the dialogue with the ECJ enjoyed by the courts of that state and damage the uniform application of Union law. One way of addressing this problem would be for the ECJ to redouble its efforts to engage with the judiciary and legal profession in Member States where the reference rate is low in order to increase familiarity with the preliminary rulings procedure and its own working methods. But judicial dialogue is not a panacea for the immense difficulties associated with ensuring the correct application of Union law throughout the Member States. It can only deliver its potential where those who are intended to benefit from Union law are aware of their rights and able to enforce them through litigation.

6 Pressure on the Preliminary Rulings Procedure

From the mid 1980s, the ECJ came under increasing strain. The renaissance of qualified majority voting triggered by the Single Market Programme 'drove home the radicalism of the constitutionalization'[124] in which the ECJ had engaged. The switch from negative to positive integration meant that Union law began to intrude increasingly into the 'nooks and crannies of national life'. The integration process began to be noticed by the general public. The signature of the Maastricht Treaty in 1992 brought the process into 'the contentious world of party competition, elections and referendums'.[125] The glare of publicity revealed a gap between the general public and the élites by whom the process had previously been steered, a gap that was forcefully exposed by the Danish and French referendums on the Maastricht Treaty in 1992. Europe's élites were slow to respond and the gap was hammered home in subsequent referendums, most crushingly those held in France and the Netherlands in 2005, which killed off the Constitutional Treaty. Swept along by the current of its own case law, the ECJ found itself having to decide cases which would attract intense outside scrutiny.[126] To what extent did the

---

[124] J Weiler, *The Constitution of Europe* (Cambridge: Cambridge University Press, 1999), 203.

[125] L Hooghe and G Marks, 'A Postfunctionalist Theory of European Integration: From Permissive Consensus to Constraining Dissensus' (2008) 39 *British J of Political Science* 1, 7.

[126] Weiler, see n 124, 214.

Treaty apply to the provision of abortions?[127] Could a national of one Member State rely on the Treaty to seek health care in another Member State at the expense of the first state?[128] What effect did the rules on establishment and services have on the right of trade unions to take collective action?[129] Criticism of the ECJ for the answers it gave to questions such as these did not just come from the media. Informed commentary on the ECJ's case law was no longer the preserve of zealots anxious to explain and proselytize.[130] The growing scope of Union law had forced lawyers specialized in areas of national law affected by it to familiarize themselves with its underlying principles. They did not see a noble project creatively supported by bold case law, but an intruder which disrupted carefully crafted national solutions to legal problems.[131] They were joined by a new generation of legal scholars, familiar with the growing body of political science literature on the Union and less convinced than their predecessors of the legitimacy of the ECJ's approach. At the same time, the frequent intergovernmental conferences which punctuated the two decades or so which followed the Single European Act gave the Member States many opportunities to respond to the ECJ's case law by amending the Treaties. They exploited those opportunities more often than is sometimes appreciated, both to contain the effect of particular decisions and to limit the ECJ's involvement in new areas of activity.[132]

The ECJ faced additional pressures due to the seemingly inexorable growth in its workload and the delay this causes. In 1975, it took six months on average to deal with a reference for a preliminary ruling, but by 2003 the figure had reached 25.5 months. Given that the time taken by the ECJ has to be added to that which has elapsed in the domestic forum, delays of that magnitude will inevitably cause national judges to hesitate before referring. In 2004, the figures began to improve (although there was a blip in 2009). Among the factors contributing to the improvement were the arrival of judges from each of the twelve Member States which acceded to the Union in 2004 and 2007 (references from those States not yet having started to arrive in significant numbers) and the introduction of procedural reforms for dealing with urgent cases. However, the improvement may not endure. References from the states which acceded in 2004 and 2007 can be expected to grow[133] and the Treaty of Lisbon is likely to generate additional references.[134] Moreover, the procedural reforms have given rise to new problems, as we shall see.

---

[127] Case C–159/90 *Society for the Protection of the Unborn Child Ireland v Grogan* [1991] ECR I–4685.

[128] Eg Case C–368/98 *Vanbraekel* [2001] ECR I–5363; Case C–157/99 *Geraets-Smits and Peerbooms* [2001] ECR I–5473.

[129] Case C–438/05 *International Transport Workers' Federation and Finnish Seamen's Union* [2007] ECR I–10779; Case C–341/05 *Laval un Partneri* [2007] ECR I–11767.

[130] Weiler, see n 124, 216–17.

[131] R Dehousse, *The European Court of Justice: The Politics of Judicial Integration* (Basingstoke: Macmillan, 1998), 173.

[132] A Arnull, 'Me and My Shadow: The European Court of Justice and the Disintegration of EU Law' (2008) 31 *Fordham Intl LJ* 1174.

[133] The year 2009 was the first in which references were made by courts in all twelve of the states concerned.

[134] A particular source of new references is likely to be the AFSJ: House of Lords EU Committee, *The Workload of the Court of Justice of the European Union* (14th Report of Session 2010–11, HL Paper 128), 17–18.

Another challenge to the ECJ was the damage to the Union's legal homogeneity caused by successive enlargements.[135] The ECJ found itself having to satisfy the expectations of national judges from the common law and Nordic traditions as well as the civil law tradition. This placed strain on the style of judgment, which will seem more familiar to judges from some backgrounds than others. The result is that the quality of the dialogue national judges feel they enjoy with the ECJ may vary according to their national background. In the United Kingdom, for example, judges have commented on how 'invisible' the thinking of the ECJ can be.[136] The ECJ has attracted unfavourable comparison with the European Court of Human Rights, whose judgments sometimes engage more directly with the concerns of national courts.[137] The House of Lords had started to follow the practice of courts in some other Member States of expressing its own view on how questions it referred should be answered,[138] a practice which has been continued by the UK Supreme Court.[139] It may be that this will result in an improved dialogue with the ECJ. But there is a broader question about the quality of the ECJ's judgments that such devices cannot resolve. Although it may once have been true that national judges accepted what the ECJ said because of the intellectual force of its judgments, that no longer seems to be the case. Even when a reference is made, the answers given by the ECJ may leave the referring court feeling that it is none the wiser.[140]

The quality of the dialogue risks being further impaired where use is made of the accelerated procedure under Article 104a of the ECJ's Rules of Procedure or the urgent procedure[141] under Article 104b, the latter applicable only to references relating to the AFSJ. Those procedures place additional strain on the quality of the ECJ's decision making. They work[142] essentially by requiring written observations to be submitted within exceptionally short deadlines and limiting the involvement of the Advocate General, who is heard but does not deliver a formal Opinion.[143] In addition, the urgent

---

[135] E Sharpston, 'Transparency and Clear Legal Language in the European Union: Ambiguous Legislative Texts, Laconic Pronouncements and the Credibility of the Judicial System' (2009–10) 12 *Cambridge Ybk of Eur Legal Studies* 409, 415–16.

[136] A Le Sueur, *A Report on Six Seminars About the UK Supreme Court*, Legal Studies Research Paper No 1/2008, Queen Mary University of London, available at: <http://ssrn.com/abstract=1324749>, 51; D Anderson, 'The Law Lords and the European Courts' in A Le Sueur (ed), *Building the UK's New Supreme Court: National and Comparative Perspectives* (Oxford: Oxford University Press, 2004), 199, 214–15.

[137] Eg *Pretty v UK* ECHR 2002-III, (2002) 35 EHRR 1; *McCann v UK* (2008) 47 EHRR 40.

[138] Eg *West Tankers Inc v RAS Riunione Adriatica di Sicurta SpA ('The Front Comor')* [2007] 1 Lloyd's Rep 391; *R (on the application of M) v HM Treasury* [2008] 2 All ER 1097.

[139] Eg *British Airways v Williams* [2010] 2 All ER 1053; *Office of Communications v Information Commissioner* [2010] UKSC 3.

[140] An egregious example is Case C-127/04 *O'Byrne* [2006] ECR I-1313; *OB v Aventis Pasteur SA* [2008] 4 All ER 881; Case C-358/08 *Aventis Pasteur* [2009] ECR I-11305; *O'Byrne v Aventis Pasteur SA* [2010] 3 CMLR 35.

[141] Known in French as the *procédure préjudicielle d'urgence*, or PPU.

[142] Statute of the ECJ, Art 23a.

[143] This attracted criticism: C Barnard, 'The PPU: "Is It Worth the Candle?" An Early Assessment' (2009) 34 ELR 281, 292–5; C Naômé, 'La procedure accélérée et la procedure préjudicielle d'urgence devant la Cour de justice des Communautés européennes' (2009) 162 *Journal de Droit Européen* 237, 246; A Rosas, 'Justice in Haste, Justice Denied? The European Court of Justice and the Area of Freedom, Security and Justice' (2008–09)

procedure reduces the class of those who are entitled to submit written observations and provides for the written part of the procedure to be omitted entirely 'in cases of extreme urgency'. These features are doubtless necessary to achieve the necessary speed of decision making, but there is a concomitant risk that judgments will be given without the issues and arguments having been fully ventilated.[144] This would be particularly unfortunate in the case of the urgent procedure, which applies in a relatively undeveloped area of Union law of direct interest to individuals. The risk is only partly attenuated by the opportunity these procedures offer the ECJ to deal with a case from start to finish while they are at the forefront of the minds of the judges involved.[145]

7 The Future of Judicial Dialogue in the European Union

The ECJ has a relationship with several interlocutors, including Union institutions and Member States, which may usefully be described as at least partly dialogic. The most distinctive and important of those relationships is that which it enjoys with the national courts of the Member States under the preliminary rulings procedure. That procedure has enabled the ECJ to constitutionalize the Union and immerse itself in the detailed business of applying Union law at the national level. The ECJ and its national counterparts have thereby been given an opportunity to explore each others' systems. The procedure exemplifies the emerging global community of courts, in which judges across the world come to recognize that they are engaged in a common enterprise based on shared values and principles that transcend national borders.[146]

However, as the Union enters the post-Lisbon era, the preliminary rulings procedure is coming under increasing pressure and the ECJ risks being caught in a pincer movement. On one side, the pressure from national constitutional courts who never or rarely make references and who are unwilling to accept the full implications of the doctrine of primacy seems likely to continue. The *Bundesverfassungsgericht* acquired a new band of potential supporters among its counterparts in the new Member States from central and eastern Europe, anxious to defend their newly recovered independence.[147] On the

---

11 *Cambridge Ybk of Eur Legal Studies* 1, 13; E Sharpston, 'The Changing Role of the Advocate General' in A Arnull, P Eeckhout, and T Tridimas (eds), *Continuity and Change in EU Law: Essays in Honour of Sir Francis Jacobs* (Oxford: Oxford University Press, 2008), 20, 29–30.

[144] S Currie, 'Accelerated Justice or a Step Too Far? Residence Rights of Non-EU Family Members and the Court's Ruling in *Metock*' (2009) 34 ELR 310, 318.

[145] Barnard, see n 143, 295–6; Naômé, see n 143, 246; Rosas, see n 143, 12.

[146] A-M Slaughter, 'Judicial Globalization' (1999–2000) 40 *Virginia Journal of International Law* 1103, 1124; A-M Slaughter, 'A Global Community of Courts' (2003) 44 *Harvard International Law Journal* 191, 215–16.

[147] Eg Polish Constitutional Tribunal, judgment of 11 May 2005, K 18/04; Constitutional Court of the Czech Republic, judgment of 31 January 2012, Pl. ÚS 5/12, 'Slovak Pensions' (where a decision of the ECJ was described as 'ultra vires'). Other such courts have been more '*Europarechtsfreundlichkeit*' (to borrow a term

other side, the ECJ may be losing the confidence of courts like the UK Supreme Court, not this time over fundamental constitutional principles but doubts about its technical competence. Unlike previous generations of judges, many of the members of such courts now feel at home with Union law and are more willing to work out the answer for themselves. Although they may sometimes be mistaken[148] or fail to accord sufficient weight to competing answers,[149] declining confidence in the ECJ's capacity to deal promptly and convincingly with references may mean that they will be made less frequently than in the past.

It may be said that greater willingness among national judges to deal with issues of Union law for themselves should be welcomed. It is in a sense a tribute to the educational role the ECJ has played over the past half-century or so. A reduction in the number of references would enable the ECJ to devote more time to the cases it did have to decide, which might in turn help to improve the quality of its judgments and the dialogue it is able to conduct with national courts.[150] But if a fall in the number of references is caused by a decline of confidence in the ECJ, it may be some time before a rise in the quality of its judgments is noticed. In the meantime, there would be a serious threat to the uniform application of Union law. Moreover, widespread disregard of the obligation to refer imposed on national courts of last resort would jeopardize the continued viability of the procedure. Although in theory such failures may be the subject of infringement proceedings[151] or actions for damages,[152] in practice the obligation of top national courts to refer is virtually unenforceable.[153] So even if in the long term national courts are to be encouraged to decide more questions of Union law for themselves, the ECJ needs to retain their confidence and maintain the quality of the dialogue it enjoys with them.

The entry into force of the Treaty of Lisbon offers the ECJ an opportunity to make concessions to the 'Bundesverfassungsgericht tendency' without departing from the spirit of the Union Treaties. Those Treaties explicitly recognize the constitutional identity and essential functions of the Member States[154] and emphasize the importance of the principles of conferral, subsidiarity, and proportionality to the exercise of the Union's powers.[155] They expressly contemplate the possibility that the powers conferred on the Union might be reduced[156] and that the Union may decide to cease exercising some of them.[157] The ECJ has effectively been reminded of the need to take

---

coined by the *Bundesverfassungsgericht* in its *Lisbon* decision [2010] 3 CMLR 13, 333), eg Supreme Court of Estonia, judgment of 11 May 2006, Case 3-4-1-3-06, [2010] CMLR 34; Constitutional Court of Latvia, judgment of 7 April 2009, Case 2008-35-01, [2010] 1 CMLR 42.

[148] Compare eg the views of Lord Hoffmann in *West Tankers*, see n 138, with Case C-185/07 *Allianz and Generali Assicurazioni Generali* [2009] ECR I-663.

[149] Cf *Office of Fair Trading v Abbey National plc* [2010] 1 AC 696.

[150] Cf Weiler, see n 124, 214–15.

[151] Case C-129/00 *Commission v Italy* [2003] ECR I-14637.

[152] Case C-224/01 *Köbler* [2003] ECR I-10239; Case C-173/03 *Traghetti del Mediterraneo* [2006] ECR I-5177.

[153] F Mayer, 'Multilevel Constitutional Jurisdiction' in A von Bogdandy and J Bast (eds), *Principles of European Constitutional Law*, 2nd edn (Oxford: Hart Publishing/Munich: Verlag CH Beck, 2010), 399, 402–3.

[154] Art 4(2) TEU.   [155] Art 5 TEU.   [156] Art 48(2) TEU.   [157] Art 2(2) TFEU.

seriously the fundamental interests of the Member States and invited to police more strictly than it has perhaps done in the past the limits of the powers conferred on the Union's institutions (and particularly their respect for the principle of subsidiarity).[158] Moreover, the ECJ cannot be oblivious to the failure of the attempt to re-establish the Union on a new, explicitly constitutional, footing.[159]

The 'UK Supreme Court tendency' is more nebulous and for that reason more difficult to address. It is often suggested that the quality of the ECJ's judgments would improve if dissenting opinions were permitted.[160] The idea is that these would reduce the pressure on the ECJ to accommodate within its judgments points of view which are essentially irreconcilable.[161] But dissenting opinions would destroy the secrecy of the ECJ's deliberations[162] and might encourage judges to dissent for political reasons. In references for preliminary rulings, dissenting opinions might debase the dialogue with national courts by impairing the clarity of the ECJ's answers to the questions referred to it.[163]

Part of the solution may lie in changing the style in which judgments of the ECJ are written.[164] The ECJ's judgments were originally modelled on those of the French Conseil d'Etat and Cour de Cassation. Although their form has since evolved, the ECJ continues to lack sureness of touch when dealing with its previous decisions[165] and rarely engages in 'serious interpretive or policy analysis'.[166] Its judgments are impenetrable to non-specialists and often make no real attempt to persuade a sceptical reader of the correctness of the result. In that sense, they provide support for Waldron's claim[167] that judicial dialogue may be damaged where a court is confident that its view will ultimately prevail in any event. This approach has become unsuitable in a context where the Union is highly contested and national courts are growing restive. The ECJ might instead consider adopting a less formal and more discursive style,[168] such as that

---

[158] Protocol No 2 on the Application of the Principles of Subsidiarity and Proportionality.

[159] H Rasmussen, 'Present and Future European Judicial Problems After Enlargement and the Post-2005 Ideological Revolt' (2007) 44 CML Rev 1661.

[160] A Arnull, *The European Union and its Court of Justice,* 2nd edn (Oxford: Oxford University Press, 2006), 9–14.

[161] Is this part of the explanation for the *O'Byrne* judgment (see n 140)?

[162] Statute of the ECJ, Art 35.

[163] Sharpston, see n 135, 416–17.

[164] Arnull, see n 160, ch 17.

[165] L Coutron, 'Style des arrêts de la Cour de justice et normativité de la jurisprudence communautaire' (2009) 45 *Revue Trimestrielle de Droit Européen* 643, 672–3. An illustration is Case C-268/91 *Keck and Mithouard* [1993] ECR I-6097, cf Case C-127/08 *Metock* [2008] ECR I-6241.

[166] See the description of French judicial decisions given by M Lasser, *Judicial Deliberations: A Comparative Analysis of Judicial Transparency and Legitimacy* (Oxford: Oxford University Press, 2004), 30–1.

[167] J Waldron, 'Some Models of Dialogue Between Judges and Legislators' (2004) 23 *Supreme Court L Rev* (2d) 7, 47.

[168] J Weiler, 'Epilogue: The Judicial Après Nice' in G de Búrca and J Weiler (eds), *The European Court of Justice* (Oxford: Oxford University Press, 2001), 215, 225; A Fritzsche, 'Discretion, Scope of Judicial Review and Institutional Balance in European Law' (2010) 47 CML Rev 361, 390, 402–3.

of the European Court of Human Rights (minus any separate opinions).[169] This would allow it to explore issues and set out its reasoning in greater depth. It might help if the ECJ replaced French as its working language with English, the language of the common law, which seems to encourage a more discursive judicial style (although the cultural and practical repercussions of such a step should not be underestimated).[170]

8 Conclusion

MacCormick and Culver and Giudice are surely right in suggesting that the Union is ultimately based, not on hierarchy and authority, but on interaction, dialogue, and compromise. The qualitative problems besetting the preliminary rulings procedure will not be solved through insistence on the authority of the ECJ's pronouncements but through improvements in the dialogue it conducts, directly or indirectly, with national courts.[171] Similarly, should a breakdown in that relationship lead to head-on conflict between the ECJ and a national constitutional court, the best chance of a solution would lie, not through law (though the law would frame the debate), but through dialogic interaction between Union and national political institutions, whose attitudes would be shaped by the media and the general public. It is true that the Union is also based on acceptance of common principles and values,[172] which may limit the room for compromise. If interaction revealed that the dissonance was not merely institutional but systemic, the state concerned might be left with little choice but to withdraw from the Union under Article 50 TEU. There is some theoretical ambiguity about that option: would such withdrawal be a vindication of national sovereignty or the autonomy of Union law?[173] The process itself, however, would be a dialogic one driven as much by politics as by law.

---

[169] Art 45(2) ECHR.

[170] The legal implications of changing the ECJ's working language from French to English have been recognized in French political circles: see the minutes of the meeting of 11 June 2003 of the Délégation pour l'Union Européenne of the French Assemblée Nationale, <http://www.assemblee-nat.fr/europe/>.

[171] See further Sharpston, see n 135, 421–3. For possible solutions to the quantitative problems, see House of Lords EU Committee, see n 134.

[172] Art 2 TEU.

[173] Cf R Barents, *The Autonomy of Community Law* (The Hague: Kluwer, 2004), 257–9.

PART II

POLITICAL
FOUNDATIONS

6

Deciphering the Political and Legal DNA of European Integration

An Exploratory Essay

*J.H.H. Weiler**

1 Exploring Political and Legal Culture

In exploring the systemic aspects of the Union in our attempts both to reach conceptual understanding as well as, instrumentally, to explain its success and failures, we reach out to the political and the legal. As regards the former, our systemic approach is to focus on institutional structure and the decision-making process. As regards the latter, our systemic approach focuses not on the substantive and material, primary rules of Union law but on what we commonly call the 'legal order' and its own operating system—the systemic, secondary rules and principles that hold together the substantive content, the law of laws.[1] The interaction between the political and legal has for a long time been a mainstay of the field, a rich and productive seam, the mining of which has enabled us to give a broader and deeper understanding of both the conceptual and the operational.[2]

In this exploratory chapter, I consider prior questions as regards both the political and the legal, questions concerning the culture which undergirds political structure and process as well as legal order.[3] That is why I use the DNA metaphor. DNA is the

* NYU School of Law.

[1] Cf Eleftheriadis, 'The Law of Laws' (2010) 1 Transnational Legal Theory 597.

[2] H Rasmussen, *On Law and Policy in the European Court of Jusice: A Comparative Study in Judicial Policymaking* (Dortrecht: M Nijhoff, 1986); A-M Burley and W Mattli, 'Europe before the Court: A Political Theory of Legal Integration' (Winter 1993) 47 *International Organization* 41–76; G Garrett, 'The Politics of Legal Integration in the European Union' (1995) 49(1) *International Organization* 171–81; A Stone Sweet, *The Judicial Construction of Europe* (Oxford: Oxford University Press, 2004); J Shaw and G More, *New Legal Dynamics of European Union* (Oxford: Clarendon Press, 1995).

[3] J Bell, 'Comparative Law and Legal Theory', in W Krawietz, N MacCormick, and GH von Wright (ed), *Prescriptive Formality and Normative Rationality in Modern Legal Systems, Festschrift for R. S. Summers,*

code which determines in advance important features of the evolving person. Political and legal culture are 'prior' in a similar ontological sense: they inform and even determine specific institutional arrangements, and at times give them meaning. Culture, including political and legal culture, is never static. It may inform the specific institutional arrangements, but in turn it is itself informed, shaped, and modified by the arrangements in a continuous cycle of interaction.[4] This poses a formidable methodological Gordian knot which may explain why, despite our long-held understanding of the importance of culture in any systematic analysis of polity, it has received somewhat less attention in European Union studies.

My way of cutting through the knot, rather than unravelling it, has been to examine the temporally 'prior', the prior-in-time, through what I hope is a fresh look at some of the most noted foundational instruments (texts) of European integration. This is inevitably a limiting methodology since it cuts out the dynamic, that continuous interaction between political institutions and processes and political culture. But even this static methodology has yielded some results which I found both unexpected and illuminating as regards the political, the legal, and their interaction. Notably, as regards legal culture, it enabled me to understand the justly much vaunted rule of law informing European integration as, counter-intuitively, tracking back to the most formal rule of law traditions typical of some of the darkest regimes in contemporary European history.[5] Likewise, as regards politics, the political DNA will help explain why the Union, as it evolved, has been, in my view of course, singularly unsuccessful in closing its democratic and political deficits, which after all manner of Treaty revision seem genetically determined in the European body politic. All in all, I believe these results contribute both to our conceptual understanding as well as, instrumentally, to the extant explanatory apparatus of the successes and failures of the integration narrative.

(Berlin 1994), 25; PS Atiyah and RS Summers, *Form and Substance in Anglo-American Law: A comparative study of legal reasoning, legal theory, and legal institutions* (Oxford: Clarendon Press, 1987); P Legrand, *Le droit comparé* (Paris: Presses Universitaires de France, 1999); C Varga, *Comparative Legal Cultures* (Budapest, 2010); D Nelken (ed), *Comparative Legal Cultures* (Dartmouth, 1997).

[4] M Crozier and E Friedberg, *L'acteur et le système* (Paris: Ed. du Seuil, 1977), 206; AL Kroeber and C Kluckhohn, 'Culture: A Critical Review of Concepts and Definitions, Papers of the Peabody Museum of American Archeology and Ethnology', 47, 1 (1952) 181 cited in FJ Gould, *A Dictionary of the Social Sciences* (Tavistock Publications, 1964) 165, 'Culture', 1.A; S Falk Moore, *Social Facts and Fabrication, 'Customary' Law on Kilimanjaro, 1880–1980*, (Cambridge, 1986) cited in E Leroy, *Le jeu des lois, une anthropologie 'dynamique' du Droit* (Paris: LGDJ, 1999), 124; M Krygier, 'Law as tradition' 5 (1986) *Law and Philosophy* 237, at 251. Generally, on understanding the nexus of law and culture I am most indebted to the writings of Menachem Mautner, eg *Law and Culture* (Ramat Gan. Bar Ilan Univ. Press, 2008) (Hebrew) and *Law and Culture in Israel* (Oxford: Oxford University Press, 2011).

[5] This jibes well with Christian Joerges and Navraj Singh Ghaleigh (eds) *Darker Legacies of Law in Europe: The Shadow of National Socialism and Fascism over Europe and its Legal Traditions* (Hart Publishing, 2003) though, as will be seen, coming to this conclusion from a different angle. NB: It is not my intention to suggest even obliquely that the project of European integration borrows from, or in anyway resembles, the substantive values of those dark regimes.

2 Europe, the Current Circumstances

Looking for the political and legal DNA, the cultural underpinning of the process of European integration has also produced a payoff in understanding one of the most remarkable features of the current political crisis. The surface manifestations of crisis are with us every day on the front pages of the press in the Euro crisis[6] and, as emblematic of the European posture in the area of defence and security, the discord over Libya. Beneath this surface at the structural level, lurk more profound and long-term signs of enduring challenge and even dysfunction and malaise.

The Euro crisis is said by many to pose the greatest challenge to the Union since its inception. And yet, strikingly, the process of seeking a solution completely abandoned the 'Union Method'. The Parliament has been *de facto* irrelevant, not part of the discourse surrounding a possible solution, and sadly irrelevant as the public place of broad popular sentiment. The Commission for the most part was neither the source of decisive thinking and certainly not the originator of policy. Most striking has been the relative silence of the Council in its various derivatives. What Europe has witnessed was a new form of extreme 'governmentalism'—with decisional power *de facto* held in the hands of two heads of state and government, with the Council playing the role of rubber stamp. Any solution will have to be a European solution. But the road to the solution was firmly in the hands of the governments of the Member States. My claim is that even though the solution has to be European, the Union lacks the reservoir of legitimacy to lead towards this. In this context I will be re-examining some understanding of legitimacy and arguing that an examination of the political and cultural DNA leads at the theoretical level to a re-adjustment of some received knowledge as regards legitimation of European integration, and at the practical political level to a better understanding of the failures of Europe in dealing with the crisis with Union tools.

But the current circumstance is not limited to the Euro Crisis. There are in addition longer-term persistent issues which simply will not go away.

First, internally, there is the persistent, chronic, troubling democratic deficit, which cannot be ignored. Then there is a deeper legitimacy crisis, whereby the citizens' growing indifference is turning to hostility and the ability of Europe to act as a political mobilizing force seems not only to be spent, but sometimes even reversed. Finally, on the world arena, Lisbon notwithstanding, there is the equally persistent, chronic, and troubling failure of Europe to translate its economic might into hard political power and the enduring (and in my view irresponsible) abdication of a serious commitment to security, leaving the field as it has for decades to a less and less engaged America.[7]

---

[6] D Dinan, 'Governance and Institutions: Implementing the Lisbon Treaty in the Shadow of the Euro Crisis' (2011) 49 SI *Journal of Common Market Studies* 103.

[7] See R Kagan, *Of Paradise and Power: America and Europe in the New World Order* (New York: Alfred A. Knopf, 2003); I Manners, 'Global Europa: Mythology of the European Union in World Politics' (2010) 48 *Journal of Common Market Studies* 67, '*The Gender Myth*', at 77ff; JJ Sheehan, *Where Have all the Soldiers gone?: The transformation of modern Europe* (Boston and New York: Houghton Mifflin, 2008).

At some level the same could have been said ten and even twenty years ago.[8] What is of interest is the trajectory which on all three issues seems to be negative, things getting worse rather than better.

What I hope is somewhat novel in this chapter is an attempt, first, to link these enduring problems to political and legal culture of the integration process and, in turn, to link that culture to some of the founding moments of the Union reflected in foundational documents. In what follows I will first elaborate somewhat on the three aspects of the European situation identified above, and then turn to an exploration of those early moments.

The manifestations of the so-called democracy deficit are persistent and no endless recitation of the powers of the European Parliament will remove them. In essence it is the inability of the Union to develop structures and processes which adequately replicate or, 'translate',[9] at the Union level even the imperfect habits of governmental control, parliamentary accountability, and administrative responsibility that are practised with different modalities in the various Member States. In essence, the two primordial features of any functioning democracy are missing—the grand principles of accountability and representation.[10,11]

As regards accountability,[12] even the basic condition of representative democracy that at election time the citizens 'can throw the scoundrels out'[13] does not operate in Europe.[14] The form of European governance,[15] governance without Government is, and will remain for a considerable time and perhaps forever such that there is no 'Government' to throw out. Dismissing the Commission by Parliament (or approving the appointment of the Commission President) is not quite the same, not even remotely so. Startlingly, political accountability of Europe is surprisingly weak. There have been some spectacular political failures of European governance. The

---

[8] See for example, European Commission, 'European Governance: A White Paper', COM(2001) 428 final, Brussels; V Bogdanor and G Woodcock, 'The European Community and Sovereignty' (1991) *Parliamentary Affairs* 492: '*The shortcomings of the Community lie in the feelings of remoteness and lack of influence and involvement on the part of many of its citizens*'; D Grimm, 'Does Europe Need a Constitution?' (1995) 1(3) *European Law Journal* 282, at 291ff; C Hill, 'European Foreign Policy: Power Bloc, Civilian Power—or Flop?' in R Rummel (ed), *The Evolution of an International Actor—Western Europe's New Assertiveness* (Boulder: Westview, 1990), 35.

[9] N Walker, 'Postnational Constitutionalism and the Problem of Translation' in JHH Weiler and M Wind (eds), *European Constitutionalism Beyond the State* (Cambridge: Cambridge University Press, 2003), 29.

[10] A Przeworski, SC Stokes, and B Manin (eds), *Democracy, Accountability and Representation* (Cambridge: Cambridge University Press, 1999); PC Schmitter and TL Karl, 'What democracy is...and is not' (Summer 1991) *Journal of Democracy* 67.

[11] P Mair, 'Popular Democracy and the European Union Policy', *European Governance Papers* (EUROGOV), no C-05-03, 4.

[12] C Harlow, *Accountability in the European Union* (Oxford: Oxford University Press, 2003).

[13] I Shapiro, *Democracy's Place* (Ithaca: Cornell University Press, 1996), 96; JHH Weiler, 'To be a European Citizen: Eros and civilization' in *The Constitution of Europe 'Do the New Clothes Have an Emperor?' and Other Essays on European Integration* (Massachussetts: Harvard University, 1999), 329.

[14] R Dehousse, 'Constitutional Reform in the EC' in J Hayward (ed), *The Crisis of Representation in Europe*, (Abigdon: Frank Cass, 1995), 118, at 123.

[15] P Allott, 'European Governance and the Re-branding of Democracy' (2002) 27(2) *European Law Review* 60.

embarrassing Copenhagen climate fiasco,[16] the weak (at best) realization of the much-touted Lisbon agenda (also known as the Lisbon strategy or Lisbon process),[17] the story of the defunct 'Constitution',[18] to mention but three. It is hard to point in these instances to any measure of political accountability, of someone paying a political price for their failure, as would be the case in national politics. In fact it is difficult to point to a single instance of accountability for political failure as distinct from personal accountability for misconduct in the annals of European integration. This is not, decidedly not, a story of corruption or malfeasance.[19] My argument is that this failure is rooted in the very structure of European governance. It is simply not designed for political accountability. In similar vein, it is impossible to link in any meaningful way the results of elections to the European Parliament to the performance of the political groups within the preceding parliamentary session, in the way that is part of the mainstay of political accountability within the Member States.[20] Structurally, dissatisfaction with 'Europe' when it exists has no channel to affect at the European level the agents of European governance.

Likewise, at the most primitive level of democracy, there is simply no moment in the civic calendar of Europe where the citizen can influence directly the outcome of any policy choice facing the Community and Union in the way that citizens can when choosing between parties which offer distinct programmes at the national level.[21] The political colour of the European Parliament only very weakly gets translated into the legislative and administrative output of the Union.[22] The political deficit, to use the felicitous phrase of Renaud Dehousse,[23] is at the core of the democracy deficit. The Commission, by its self-understanding linked to its very ontology, cannot be 'partisan' in the ideological sense of left-wing or right-wing, neither can the Council, by virtue of the haphazard political nature of its composition. Democracy normally must have

---

[16] See European Parliament resolution of 10 February 2010 on the outcome of the Copenhagen Conference on Climate Change (COP 15), P78TA(2010)0019, Wednesday, 10 February 2010, especially points 5–6.

[17] I Begg, 'Is there a Convincing Rationale for the Lisbon Strategy' (2008) 46(2) *Journal of Common Market Studies* 427; 'Facing the challenge. The Lisbon strategy for growth and employment'—Report from the High Level Group chaired by Wim Kok, November 2004,.

[18] I Ward, 'Bill and the Fall of the Constitutional Treaty' (2007) 13(3) *European Public Law* 461; Editorial Comments, 'What should replace the Constitutional Treaty?' (2007) 44 *Common Market Law Review* 561.

[19] On this aspect, see V Mehde, 'Responsibility and Accountability in the European Commission' (2003) 40 *Common Market Law Review* 423.

[20] J Priestley, 'European political parties: the missing link', *Notre Europe*, Policy Paper 41, 2010; F. Roa Bastos, 'Des partis politiques au niveau européen? Etat des lieux à la veille des élections européennes de juin 2009' (2009) 71 *Etudes et Recherches*; O. Audeoud, 'Les partis politiques au niveau européen. Fédérations de partis nationaux', Les cahiers du GERSE, Nancy, 3 février 1999.

[21] R Dehousse, 'Constitutional Reform in the EC' in J Hayward (ed), *The Crisis of Representation in Europe*, 123ff; A Follesdal and S Hix, 'Why There is a Democratic Deficit in the EU: A Response to Majone and Moravcsik' (2006) 44(3) *Journal of Common Market Studies* 533, at 536.

[22] V Bogdanor, 'Legitimacy, Accountability and Democracy in the European Union', *A Federal Trust Report* (2007), 7–8; A Follesdal and S Hix, 'Why There is a Democratic Deficit in the EU: A Response to Majone and Moravcsik', 545.

[23] R Dehousse, 'Constitutional Reform in the EC' in J Hayward (ed), *The Crisis of Representation in Europe*, 124. See also, J-M Ferry and P Thibaud, *Discussion sur l'Europe* (Paris: Calmann-Lévy, 1992).

some meaningful mechanism for expression of voter preference predicated on choice among options, typically informed by stronger or weaker ideological orientation.[24] That is an indispensable component of politics. Democracy without politics is an oxymoron.[25]

Thus the two most primordial norms of democracy, the principle of accountability and the principle of representation, are compromised in the very structure and process of the Union.

The second manifestation of the current European situation is evident in a continued slide in the legitimacy and mobilizing force of the European construct and its institutions. I pass over some of the uglier manifestations of European 'solidarity' both at governmental and popular level as regards the Euro-crisis, or the near abandonment of Italy to deal with the influx of migrants from North Africa as if this was an Italian problem and not a problem for Europe as a whole. I look instead at two deeper and longer-term trends. The first is the extraordinary decline in voter participation in elections for the European Parliament. In Europe as a whole the rate of participation is below 45 per cent, with several countries, notably in the East, with a rate below 30 per cent. The correct comparison is, of course, with political elections to national parliaments where the numbers are considerably higher.[26] What is striking about these figures is that the decline coincides with a continuous shift in powers to the European Parliament, which today is a veritable co-legislator with the Council. The more powers the European Parliament, supposedly the *vox populi*, has gained, the greater popular indifference to it seems to have developed.[27]

No less consequential is a seemingly contagious spread of 'anti-Europeanism' in national politics.[28] What was once in the province of fringe parties on the far right and left has inched its way to more central political forces. The 'question of Europe' as a central issue in political discourse was for long regarded as an 'English disease'. There is a growing contagion in Member States in north and south, east and west, where political capital is to be made among non-fringe parties by anti-European advocacy.[29] The spillover effect of this phenomenon is the shift of mainstream parties in this direction as a way of countering the gains at their flanks. If we are surprised by this it is only because we seem to have air-brushed out of our historical consciousness the rejection of the so-called European Constitution, an understandable amnesia since it represented a defeat of

---

[24] S Hix, 'Why There is a Democratic Deficit in the EU: A Response to Majone and Moravcsik', 545.

[25] See P Manent, *La raison des nations, réflexions sur la démocratie en Europe* (Paris: Gallimard, 2006), 59.

[26] A Menon and J Peet, 'Beyond the European Parliament: Rethinking the EU's democratic legitimacy', *Center for European Reform Essays* (2010); P. Magnette, 'European Governance and Civic Participation: Can the European Union be politicised?', *Jean Monnet Working Paper* 6/01.

[27] J Buzek, 'State of the Union: Three Cheers for the Lisbon Treaty and Two Warnings for Political Parties' (2011) 49(7) *Journal of Common Market Studies* 15; see also, JHH Weiler, *The Constitution of Europe 'Do the New Clothes Have an Emperor?' and Other Essays on European Integration*, 266.

[28] C Leconte, *Understanding Euroscepticism* (Palgrave Macmillan, 2010).

[29] R Harmsen and M Spiering (eds), *Euroscepticism: Party Politics, National Identity and European Integration* (Amsterdam: Rodopi, 2005), 13; A Szczerbiak and PA Taggart, *Opposing Europe?* Vols I and II (Oxford: Oxford University Press, 2008).

the collective political class in Europe by the *vox populi*,[30] albeit not speaking through, but instead giving a slap in the face to, the European institutions.[31]

The final feature of the current situation is a manifestation of an equally persistent and at times embarrassing European lack of both capacity and resolve (and a lack of resolve to have capacity) to defend and protect the values it professes to hold most dear.[32] It is only the same propensity for amnesia which enables us to avoid this problem—to look in our collective mirror without at least some measure of shame. In the 1990s, in the heart of Europe, not even 500 kms from Rome, for the third time in the same century, Europe allowed that which it had vowed would never be allowed to happen again, something that the European construct was meant to guarantee would never happen again: the genocide (qualified as such by the International Court of Justice) of a non-Christian religious minority in Bosnia. When finally the endless talking came to an end and the resolve was found to prevent the Bosnian humanitarian catastrophe from repeating itself in Kosovo, Europe discovered that it did not possess the capacity to realize its resolve.[33] Once again, the 'cavalry' from across the Atlantic had to be called in. Europe alone could not plan, target, let alone execute, this relatively simple operation.

Bosnia points, in my eyes, to a deeper facet of the political failure: the Srebrenica incident where Dutch soldiers allowed the worst atrocity of that war to take place without any attempt to intervene and put a stop to it.[34] The nationality of the soldiers is irrelevant; they could have been Italian or British soldiers or soldiers from any other of our Member States. And these immobile soldiers were, like all of us, firm believers in human rights, solidarity, and all the other values we profess. Their values might well have been in place but evidently they lacked the virtues necessary to enact them. They lacked the courage that is born from a conviction that some things, like preventing a mass slaughter of the innocent for the simple reason that they do not share your faith, is worth both killing for and dying for. They were the product of a culture in which it would appear that nothing is worth dying for or killing for, and if it is, it should be others who do the dying and killing. If anyone wants to entertain the illusion that Kosovo was an aberration, we now have Libya with a repetition of at least part of the Kosovar pathology: without massive

---

[30] N Fligstein, *Euroclash. The EU, European Identity, and the Future of Europe* (Oxford: Oxford University Press, 2008).

[31] For former examples, see JHH Weiler, UR Haltern and FC Mayer, 'European Democracy and Its Critique' in J Hayward (ed), *The Crisis of Representation in Europe* (Abingdon: Frank Cass, 1995), 4.

[32] J Richardson, 'The European Union in the World—A Community of Values' (2002) 26(1) *Fordham Journal of International Law* 12; P Boniface (ed), *Quelles valeurs pour l'Union européenne?* (Paris: IRIS-PUF, 2004); M Dony, 'Les valeurs, objectifs et principes de l'Union' in *Commentaire de la Constitution de l'Union européenne* (Brussels: Editions de l'Université de Bruxelles, 2005), 33; F Benoît-Rhomer, 'Valeurs et droits fondamentaux dans la Constitution' (2005) 41(2) *Revue Trimestrielle de Droit Européen* 261; 'Editorial', 'L'Union, une communuté de valeurs?' (2008) 44(1) *Revue Trimestrielle de Droit Européen* 1; A Euzéby, 'La Constitution—Constitution de l'Union européenne: des valeurs à défendre!' (2004) 482 *Revue du Marché Commun et de l'Union Européenne* 566.

[33] See JJ Sheehan, *Where Have all the Soldiers Gone?: The transformation of modern Europe* (Boston and New York: Houghton Mifflin, 2008), (2008) 44(1) 199 204ff.

[34] Sheehan, 206.

American military involvement, Europe, let us be clear, would have simply been unable to undertake any action in the so-called *mare nostrum*.

It is not only a question of arms. All the Lisbon efforts to strengthen and give coherence to the international manifestation of European Union were revealed to be fruitless. Not only was it the expected absenteeism from the Libyan crisis management of the European President and the EU's 'Foreign Minister', with the usual Member State leaders taking front and back seats, but even at this intergovernmental level, Europe was seen to be fragmented and fractured when at the UN, different Member States failed to vote in unison at the Security Council.[35]

3 Europe as Political 'Messianism'

The critique of the democracy deficit of the Union has itself been subjected to two types of critique itself. The first has simply contested the reality of the democracy deficit by essentially claiming that wrong criteria have been applied to the Union.[36] The lines of debate are well known.[37] For what it is worth, I have staked my position above. But I am more interested in the second type of critique which implicitly is based on the distinction between democracy and legitimacy. Since the Union, not being a state, cannot replicate or adequately translate the habits and practices of state demo-cratic governance, its legitimacy may be found elsewhere.[38]

In analysing the legitimacy (and mobilizing force) of the European Union, in particular against the background of its persistent democracy deficit, political and social science has long used the distinction between process legitimacy and outcome legitimacy (also known as input/output, process/result, etc).[39] The legitimacy of the Union more generally and the Commission more specifically, even if suffering from deficiencies in the state democratic sense, are said to rest on the results achieved—in the economic, social and, ultimately, political realms.[40] The idea hearkens back to the most classic functionalist and neo-functionalist theories.[41]

---

[35] See J Dempsey, 'Libya Crisis Reveals Splits on EU Goals', *The New York Times*, 18 April 2011; 'Extraodinary European Council, Declaration,'11 March 2011, Brussels, 20 April 2011, EUCO 7/1/11 REV1.

[36] JHH Weiler, 'Does Europe Need a Constitution? Demos, Telos and the German Maastricht Decision' (1995) 1(3) *European Law Journal* 219, especially 225ff.

[37] P Craig, 'The Nature of the Community: Integration, Democracy, and Legitimacy' in P Craig and G de Búrca (eds.), *The Evolution of EU Law* (Oxford: Oxford University Press, 1999), 25.

[38] N MacCormick, 'Democracy, Subsidiarity, and Citizenship in the "European Commonwealth"' (1997) 16 *Law and Philosophy* 331–56.

[39] See for example, CR Beitz, *Political Equality: An essay in democratic theory*, chs 2 and 4; RA Dahl, *Democracy and its Critics*, (New Haven: Yale University Press, 1991), 163. See also more specifically, G Majone (ed), *Regulating Europe* (London: Routledge, 1996); FW Scharpf, *Governing in Europe: Effective and Democratic?*, (Oxford: Oxford University Press, 1999), 7ff.

[40] K Featherstone, 'Jean Monnet and the Democratic Deficit in the European Union' (1994) 32(2) *Journal of Common Market Studies* 149, 150.

[41] Featherstone, 155; C Pentland, 'Political Theories of European Integration: Between Science and Ideology', in D Lasok and P Soldatos (eds), *The European Communities in Action* (Brussels: Bruylant, 1981), 545, 550ff; B Rosamond, *Theories of European Integration* (New York: Palgrave Macmillan, 2000), 20ff; D Mitrany,

I do not want to take issue with the implied normativity of this position—a latter day *panem et circenses* approach to democracy—which at some level at least could be considered quite troubling. It is with its empirical reality that I want to take some issue. I do not think that outcome legitimacy explains all or perhaps even most of the mobilizing force of the European construct. Instead, I would argue, that at the conceptual level there is a third type of legitimation which, in my view, played for a long time a much larger role than is currently acknowledged. In fact, in my view, it has been decisive to the legitimacy of Europe and to the positive response of both the political class and citizens at large. I will also argue that it is a key to a crucial element in the Union's political culture. It is a legitimacy rooted in the '*politically messianic*'.

In political 'messianism', the justification for action and its mobilizing force derive not from process, as in classical democracy, or from result and success, but from the ideal pursued, the destiny to be achieved, the 'Promised Land' waiting at the end of the road. Indeed, in messianic visions the end always trumps the means.

Mark Mazower, in his brilliant and original history and historiography of twentieth-century Europe,[42] shows how the Europe of monarchs and emperors which entered the First World War was often rooted in a political messianic narrative in various states (in Germany, and Italy, and Russia, and even Britain and France). It then oscillated after the war towards new democratic orders, that is to process legitimacy, which then oscillated back into new forms of political messianism in fascism and communism. As the tale is usually told, after the Second World War, the Europe of the west was said to oscillate back to democracy and process legitimacy. It is here that I want to point to an interesting quirk, not often noted.

On the one hand, the Western states, which were later to become the Member States of the European Union, became resolutely democratic, their patriotism rooted in their new constitutional values, narratives of glory abandoned and even ridiculed, and messianic notions of the state losing all appeal. Famously, former empires, once defended with repression and blood, were now abandoned with zeal.[43]

And yet, their common venture, European integration, was in my reading a political messianic venture *par excellence*, the messianic becoming a central feature of its original and enduring political culture. The mobilizing force and principle legitimating feature was the vision offered, the dream dreamt, the promise of a better future. It is this feature which explains not only the persistent mobilizing force (especially among elites and youth) but also key structural and institutional choices made. It will also give more depth to explanations of the current circumstance of Europe.

A Working Peace System (Chicago: Quadrangle Books, 1966); EB Haas, *The Uniting of Europe*, (Stanford: Stanford University Press, 1958); EB Haas, 'Turbulent Fields and the Theory of Regional Integration' (Spring 1976) 30 *International Organization* 173; LN Lindberg, *The Political Dynamics of European Economic Integration* (Stanford: Stanford University Press, 1963); LN Lindberg and SA Scheingold (eds), *Regional Integration: Theory and Research* (Cambridge: Cambridge University Press, 1971).

   [42] M Mazower, *Dark Continent –Europe's Twentieth Century* (London: Allen Lane, 1998).
   [43] J Lacroix, 'For a European Constitutional Patriotism' (2002) 50 *Political Studies* 944, at 949ff.

4 The Schuman Declaration as a Manifesto of Political Messianism

The Schuman Declaration is somewhat akin to a European Declaration of Independence in its vision and blueprint. Notably, much of its text found its way into the preamble of the Treaty of Paris, the substance of which was informed by its ideas. It is interesting to re-read the Declaration through the conceptual prism of political messianism. The hallmarks are easily detected as we would expect in its constitutive, magisterial document. It is manifest in what is in the Declaration and, no less importantly, in what is not therein. Please note that European integration is nothing like its European messianic predecessors—that of monarchies and empire and later fascism and communism. It is liberal and noble, but politically messianic it is nonetheless.

The messianic feature is notable in both its rhetoric and substance. Note, first, the language used—ceremonial and sermon-like with plenty of pathos (and bathos).

> *World peace cannot be safeguarded without the making of creative efforts proportionate to the dangers which threaten it . . . .*
>
> *The contribution which an organised and living Europe can bring to civilization is indispensable . . .*
>
> *. . . a first step in the federation of Europe [which] will change the destinies of those regions which have long been devoted to the manufacture of munitions of war . . .*
>
> *[A]ny war between France and Germany becomes not merely unthinkable, but materially impossible.*
>
> *This production will be offered to the world as a whole without distinction or exception . . .*
>
> *[I]t may be the leaven from which may grow a wider and deeper community between countries long opposed to one another by sanguinary divisions.*

It is grand, inspiring, Churchillian, one might even say (with a tad of irony). Some old habits, such as the 'white Man's Burden' and the missionary tradition, die hard:

> *With increased resources Europe will be able to pursue the achievement of one of its essential tasks, namely, the development of the African continent.*

But it is not just the rhetoric. The substance itself is messianic: a compelling vision which has animated generations of European idealists where the 'ever closer union among the peoples of Europe', with peace and prosperity as icing on the cake, constituting the beckoning Promised Land.[44]

It is worth exploring further the mobilizing force of this new plan for Europe. At the level of the surface language, it is its straightforward pragmatic objective of

---

[44] F Piodi, 'From the Schuman Declaration to the Birth of the ECSC: the Role of Jean Monnet', European Parliament, Directorate-General for the Presidency, Archive and Documentation Centre, *CARDOC Journals*, 6: May 2010; T Hoerber, 'The Nature of the Beast: The past and future purpose of European integration' (2006) 1 *L'Europe en formation* 17; JHH Weiler, *The Constitution of Europe 'Do the New Clothes Have an Emperor?' and Other Essays on European Integration*, 'Introduction: We will do, and hearken', 8.

consolidating peace and reconstructing European prosperity. But there is much more within the deep structure of the Schuman Plan.

Peace, at all times an attractive desideratum, would have had its appeal in purely utilitarian terms. But it is readily apparent that in the historical context in which the Schuman Plan was put forward the notion of peace as an ideal probes a far deeper stratum than simple swords into ploughshares, sitting under one's vines and fig trees, lambs and wolves—the classic Biblical metaphors for peace. The dilemma posed was an acute example of the alleged tension between grace and justice which has taxed philosophers and theologians through the ages—from William of Ockham (pre-modern), Friedrich Nietzsche (modernist), and the repugnant but profound Martin Heidegger (postmodern).

These were, after all, the early 1950s with the horrors of war still fresh in the mind and, in particular, the memory of the unspeakable savagery of German occupation. It would take many years for the hatred in countries such as the Netherlands, Denmark, or France to subside fully. The idea in 1950 of a community of equals as providing the structural underpinning for long-term peace among yesterday's enemies, represented more than the wise counsel of experienced statesmen.

It managed to tap into the two pillars of European civilization: the Enlightenment and the heritage of the French Revolution, and the European Christian tradition.[45]

Liberty was already achieved with the defeat of Nazi Germany—and Germans (like their Austrian brethren-in-crime) embraced with zeal the notion that they, too, were liberated from National Socialism. But here was a project, encapsulated in the Schuman Declaration, which added to the transnational level both equality and fraternity. The Versailles version of peace was to take yesterday's enemy, diminish him, and keep his neck firmly under one's heel. Here instead was a vision in which yesterday's enemy was regarded as an equal—Germany was to be treated as a full and equal partner in the venture—and engaged in a fraternal inter-dependent lock that would make the thought of resolving future disputes become unthinkable.[46] This was, in fact, the project of the Enlightenment taken to the international level, as Kant himself had dreamt. To embrace the Schuman Plan was to tap into one of the most powerful idealistic seams in the mines of Europeean civilization.

The Schuman Plan was also a call for forgiveness, a challenge to overcome an understandable hatred. In that particular historical context the Schumanian notion of peace resonated with, was evocative of, the distinct teaching, imagery, and values of the Christian call to forgive one's enemies—values so recently consecrated in their

---

[45] See for example, J Habermas and J Derrida, 'February 15, or, What Binds Europeans Together: Plea for a Common Foreign Policy Beginning in Core Europe', in D Levy *et al.*, *Old Europe, New Europe, Core Europe: Transatlantic Relations after the Iraq War* (London: Verso, 2005), 5, 10–12; A Finkielkraut, *La défaite de la pensée* (Paris: Gallimard, 1987); JHH Weiler, *L'Europe chrétienne: Une excursion* (Paris: Editions du Cerf, 2007); JM Ferry, *La république crépusculaire. Comprendre le projet européen in sensu cosmopolitico* (Paris: Editions du Cerf, 2010); R Schuman, *Pour l'Europe*, 55ff.

[46] A Munoz, 'L'engagement européen de Robert Schuman', in S Schirmann (ed), *Robert Schuman et les pères de l'Europe: cultures politiques et années de formation* (Brussels: Peter Lang, 2008), 39, at 44.

wholesale breach.[47] The Schuman Plan was, in this sense, evocative of both confession and expiation, and redolent with the Christian belief in the power of repentance and renewal and the ultimate goodness of humankind. This evocation is not particularly astonishing given the personal backgrounds of its founding fathers—Adenauer, De Gaspari, Schuman, Monnet himself—all seriously committed Catholics.[48]

The mobilizing force, especially among elites including the political classes who felt more directly responsible for the calamities of which Europe was just exiting, is not surprising given the remarkable subterranean appeal of the two most potent visions of an idyllic kingdom—the humanist and religious combined in one project.[49] This also explains how, for the most part, both right and left, conservative and progressive, could embrace the project.

It is the messianic model which explains (in part) why for so long the Union could operate without a veritable commitment to the principles it demanded of its aspiring members—democracy and human rights. Aspiring states had to become members of the European Convention of Human Rights, but the Union itself did not. They had to prove their democratic credentials, but the Union itself did not—two anomalies which raised hardly an eyebrow.

Note however, that its messianic features are reflected not only in rhetoric. In its original and unedited version, the declaration is also messianic in operational detail,

---

[47] JHH Weiler, *The Constitution of Europe 'Do the New Clothes Have an Emperor?' and Other Essays on European Integration*, 7. Fin-de-siècle Europe: do the new clothes have an emperor?', 241.

[48] A Fimister, 'Integral Humanism and the Re-unification of Europe', in S Schirmann (ed), *Robert Schuman et les pères de l'Europe: cultures politiques et années de formation* (Brussels: Peter Lang, 2008), 25; '*Schuman was an ardent Roman Catholic, and his views about the desirability of political unity in Western Europe owed much to the idea that it was above all the continent's Christian heritage which gave consistence and meaning to the identity of European civilization. And the Europe he knew and loved best was the Carolingian Europe that accorded with his religious faith and his experience of French and German cultures*'; M. Sutton, 'Chapter 1: Before the Schuman Plan', *France and the Construction of Europe, 1944–2007: The Geopolitical Imperative*, (New York and Oxford: Berghan Books, 2007), 34; '*It is with deep faith in our cause that I speak to you, and I am confident that through the will of our free peoples, with your support and with God's help, a new era for Europe will soon begin*'. Extracts from a speech by Alcide De Gasperi at the Constultative Assembly of the Council of Europe in Strasbourd on 16 September 1952—Volume 3, 1952 of the *Official Reports of Debates o the Consultatve Asembly of the Council of Europe*.

[49] One should add that the transnational reach of the Schuman Plan served, as one would expect, a powerful internal interest the discussion of which even today meets with resistance. The challenge of 'fraternity' and the need for forgiveness, love, and grace was even more pressing internally than internationally. Each one of the original Member States was seriously compromised internally. In post-war Germany, to put it bluntly, neither state nor society could function if all those complicit in National Socialism were to be excluded. In the other five, although ostensibly and in a real sense victims of German aggression, important social forces became complicit and were morally compromised. This was obviously true of Fascist Italy and Vichy France. But even Luxembourg contributed one of the most criminally notorious units to the German army and Belgium distinguished itself as the country with the highest number of indigenous volunteers to the occupying German forces. The betrayal of Anne Frank and her family by their Dutch neighbours was not an exception but emblematic of Dutch society and government who tidily handed over their entire Jewish citizenry for deportation and death. All these societies had a serious interest in 'moving on' and putting that compromised past behind them. If one were to forgive and embrace the external enemy, to turn one's back to the past and put one's faith in a better future, how much more so, how much easier, to do the same within one's own nation, society, and even family.

but you will find neither the word 'democracy', nor the term 'human rights'. It is very much a 'let's-just-do-it' programme, animated by great idealism (and a good measure of state interest, as a whole generation of historians such as Alan Milward,[50] Charles Maier,[51] and others have demonstrated). The European double helix has from its inception been Commission and Council: an international (supposedly) a-political transnational administration/executive (the Commission) collaborating not, as we habitually say, with the Member States (Council) but with governments, the executive branch of the Member States, which for years and years had a forum that escaped in day-to-day matters the scrutiny of any parliament, European or national. Democracy is simply not part of the original vision of European integration.[52]

This observation is hardly shocking or even radical. Is it altogether fanciful to tell the narrative of Europe as one in which 'doers and believers' (notably the most original of its institutions, the Commission, coupled with an empowered executive branch of the Member States in the guise of the Council and COREPER), an elitist (and well-paid) vanguard, were the self-appointed leaders from whom grudgingly, over decades, power had to be arrested by the European Parliament? And even the European Parliament has been a strange *vox populi*. For hasn't it been, for most of its life, a champion of European integration, so that to the extent that inevitably, when the thought of Union created fears (only natural in such a radical transformation of European politics), the European Parliament was not the place citizens would go to express those fears and concerns?

5 Law and the Rule of Law

The horrors of the Second World War, but also of the six years leading up to it within Germany, provoked a conceptual reconsideration of the ideal of the rule of law. One may take as an example the degradation and dispossession of the Jews within Germany in the first eight years of the regime prior to their deportation and mass murder. There were of course violent and lawless episodes such as Kristallnacht in 1938 which saw the burning and looting of most synagogues in 1938, and in which the Government was complicit by commission (incitement and encouragement) and omission (failure to prosecute the perpetrators). But what is striking is the exceptional nature of this episode. For the most part, degradation and dispossession were orderly, systematic, following a legal path. The exclusion of Jews from public life was effected by the infamous Nuremberg Law of 1935 which contained elaborate legal definitions and mechanisms. The disposal of Jewish property followed a similar path of legality. Similar legal structures, including courts and judicial procedures, were put in place

---

[50] A Milward, *The European Rescue of the Nation State*, 2nd edn (London and New York: Routledge, 2000).

[51] CS Maier and G Bischof (eds), *The Marshall Plan and Germany: West German Development within the Framework of the European Recovery Program* (Providence: Berg Press, 1991).

[52] K Featherstone, 150; J Delors, *Independent*, 26 July 1993.

to enforce even the most invidious features of the regime. Enemies, real and imagined, were not hunted down by clandestine death squads or simply 'disappeared'. They were arrested, tried, and then, lawfully, executed. The quiet chilling horror of legalized and bureaucratized discrimination, humiliation. and death is captured by a marvellous book, *One Life* by Tom Lampert,[53] which presents some episodes captured through extrapolation from official files and the strength of which is the very absence of blood and gore. In effect, the process was achieved through, and with full respect for, the 'rule of law'.[54]

It is this reality which, already in the context of the Nuremberg Trials, provoked a conceptual reassessment. Since the rule of law was considered as one of the assets of liberal democracies, one could not grace German practice in those years with that appellation. Put differently, one had to move away from a formalist entirely positivist (even Kelsenian) notion of the rule of law and replace it with one which would, for example, incorporate the source and procedure of authority and authorship of the legal rules and procedures, as essential components into an understanding of the rule of law. A legal regime not validated in democratic practices and not respecting human rights would not qualify as a manifestation of the rule of law.[55]

We may return now to the analysis of the Schuman Declaration and the early foundations of European integration. We have already noted the conspicuous lexical and substantive absence of democracy and human rights from the original rhetoric and structures. Equally conspicuous is the heavy reliance on law and legal institutions. The Treaty of Paris—with its explicit reference to supra-nationalism—represents a radical and unprecedented exercise in the legalization of a transnational regime, far exceeding the innovation of the ECHR. It involves institutions of governance, of transnational administration, of adjudication and enforcement. The political project of European integration was to be realized by an economic programme (Coal and Steel Community, European Economic Community) effected through and by the rule of law. Over the years one has celebrated that audacious and fateful choice. Notably, giving such centrality to a judicial organ enabled the European Court of Justice and the law it administered to play in later years, years of political stagnation, the decisive role it played in the construction of European integration.[56]

Electing to place such pronounced reliance on the law and legal institutions for the achievement of their political and economic project was not only an audacious but also a prudentially wise choice. Transnational legality helps prevent 'free riding' and provides stability and continuity to any *acquis* even in periods of political instability

---

[53] T Lampert, *One Life* (Houghton Mifflin Harcourt, 2004).

[54] See also, H Arendt, *Eichmann in Jerusalem: A report on the banality of evil* (New York: Penguin, 1994), 21, 24.

[55] Most famously, J Habermas, 'Paradigms of Law', in M Rosenfeld and A Arato, *Habermas on Law and Democracy: Critical Exchanges* (Berkeley and Los Angeles: University of California Press, 1998), 13; J Habermas, *Between Facts and Norms: Contributions to a discourse theory of law and democracy* (Cambridge: MIT Press, 1998); J Habermas, *Postnational Constellation* (Cambridge: MIT Press, 2001).

[56] See R Lecourt, *L'Europe des juges* (Brussels: Bruylant, 2008).

and wavering commitment. Famously, once the constitutional revolution was effected through the introduction of direct effect, transnational legality harnessed individuals, pursuing their personal interests as a powerful agent of compliance by Member States with their Treaty obligations.[57]

But, inevitably, it also meant an account of the principle of the rule of law which was 'old school': formalist, self-referential, and self-legitimating. Why should I obey? Either—because it is 'The Law' or because it is in the service of the self-legitimating messianic dream. Indeed, I would argue that political messianic projects by their very nature go hand in hand with a formalist, self-referential concept of the rule of law.[58]

It should not need saying that here, too, it is not my intention to argue any substantive similarity with the National Socialist regime. The European integration project is as noble as National Socialism was vile. But I am arguing that the European construct represents an interesting structural and conceptual continuity.

If I am right in this characterization (and I assume it will be contested), interesting implications follow in understanding the relationship between law and politics in the narrative of European integration.[59]

It is quite common when assessing its jurisprudence to cast the European Court, virtuously, in a dialectical relationship with (a typically stalling) political process. The following has been told in many variants over the years:

In the face of political stagnation and stasis in the late 1960s and a lack of 'political will' (a popular if meaningless phrase), the Court steps in and compensates by its remarkable constitutionalizing jurisprudence, virtually salvaging European integration.[60]

In the face of a growing democratic legitimacy crisis, the Court develops its human rights jurisprudence. Community (and Union) norms might suffer from democratic deficiencies, but at least they will be protected against violation of fundamental human rights.[61]

In the face of the failure of the harmonization process in constructing the common market place, the Court steps in with its highly innovative doctrine of functional

---

[57] T Hartley, *The Foundations of European Union Law*, 7th edn (Oxford: Oxford University Press, 2010), '7. Direct effect and national remedies'; A.-M. Burley and W. Mattli, 'Europe Before the Court: A Political Theory of Legal Integration' (1993) 47(1) *International Organization* 41, at 60ff.

[58] JHH Weiler, 'The Transformation of Europe', 2410.

[59] A-M. Burley and W Mattli, 'Europe Before the Court: A Political Theory of Legal Integration' (1993) 47(1) *International Organization* 41, at 60ff; K Alter, *The European Court's Political Power: Selected Essays* (Oxford: Oxford University Press, 2009).

[60] J Bengoetxea, *The Legal Reasoning of the European Court of Justice* (Oxford: Clarendon Press, 1993), 101; JV Louis, 'The Rule of Law', in M Westlake (ed), *The European Union beyond Amsterdam: New concepts of European integration*, 79, at 89ff; J Baquero Cruz, 'Disintegration of the Law of Integration in the External Relations of the European Community' (1997) 3 *Columbia Journal of European Law* 257; JHH Weiler, 'The Transformation of Europe' (June 1991) *Yale Law Journal* 2403, at 2425.

[61] GF Mancini, 'Safeguarding Human Rights: the Role of the European Court of Justice' in GF Mancini, *Democracy and Constitutionalism in the European Union: Collected Essays* (Oxford and Portland: Hart Publihing, 2000), 177, at 185; JHH Weiler, 'Eurocracy and Distrust: Some questions concerning the role of the European Court of Justice in the protection of fundamental human right within the legal order of the European Communities' (1986) 61 *Washington Law Review* 1103.

parallelism (Mutual Recognition) in 'Cassis' providing a jurisprudential breakthrough to move ahead.[62]

There is more than a grain of truth in all the variants, more and less sophisticated, of this narrative. But in all of them, the political problem is extraneous to the Court, which within the limits of its powers, steps in to correct that which politics and politicians are unable to do. According to this view, the Court cannot (and should not) solve all the problems, but it is always cast as part of the solution rather than part of the problem. It is tempting to continue to cast the Court in this role, particularly in the present circumstance of political challenge.

But, in the light of my thesis on rule of law, it becomes possible to see the Court as part of the problem and not only as part of the solution. The argument is obvious enough and follows from the formalist premise of the rule of law. The very same case law, inescapably and inextricably, implicates the Court in the very issues of democratic and social legitimacy which are at least partially at the root of current discontent.[63]

I want to argue further that the Court has responsibilities which do not even fit under the rubric of 'implications'. But before I explain this thesis I want to state clearly what I am not arguing.

My critique is not that the Court has no legitimacy, or that it comprises some kind of *gouvernement des juges*;[64] I do not think Europe has or had a *gouvernement des juges* (whatever that means), nor do I find fundamental fault with the hermeneutics of its essential jurisprudence. On the contrary, in a deep sense I think the Court gave effect, and sought to render effective, the project of the High Contracting Parties encapsulated in their respective Treaties. It is simply that, as I argued, the messianic project was not particularly concerned with democracy (or, at inception, human rights). It sought its legitimacy in the nobility of its cause.[65] Thus, importantly, this critique does not have as its purpose an argument that the constitutional jurisprudence was a normative mistake, a road which should not have been taken. But the road taken had and continues to have consequences inherent in its messianic nature.

My approach rests on two propositions. First, it highlights a certain irony in the constitutional jurisprudence. As noted above it was often perceived (and there are indications in the cases that it was so perceived by the Court itself) as being a response to, and part of, a broader political discourse of integration, often a response to non-functioning dimensions of the political process.[66] But there has been, both by the

---

[62] M Shapiro, 'The European Court of Justice', in P Craig and G de Búrca (eds), *The Evolution of EU Law*, 335; MP Maduro, *We, the Court: The European Court of Justice and the European Economic Constitution; A Critical Reading of Article 30 of the EC Treaty* (Oxford and Portland: Hart Publishing, 1998).

[63] P Allott, 'Preliminary rulings—another infant disease', 538; JHH Weiler, 'The Transformation of Europe' (June 1991) *Yale Law Journal* 2409–10.

[64] For a review of the literature in this regard, see H Rasmussen, *On Law and Policy in the European Court of Justice. A Comparative Study in Judicial Policy-Making* (Dordrecht: Martinus Nijhoff, 1986), 154ff.

[65] P Pescatore, 'The Doctrine of Direct Effects: An Infant Disease of Community Law (1984) 8 *European Law Review* 155, at 157.

[66] GF Mancini, 'The Making of a Constitution for Europe' (1989) 26 *Common Market Law Review* 596; P Pescatore, 'Jusqu'où le juge peut-il aller trop loin?' in K Thorup and J Rosenlov (eds), *Festriskrift til Ole Due*

Court itself and its observers, a myopic view which failed to explore some of the consequences and ramifications of the constitutional jurisprudence.[67] There has been a refusal to see the way in which the essential legal order of constitutional jurisprudence is part and parcel of the political democratic legitimacy crisis. Very often one has the impression that though the political (in the sense of institutions) is well grasped in relation to the case law, the social (in the sense of human dimension and communities) has been far less understood.

How then is the Court implicated in the democratic deficit and legitimacy crisis?

Our starting point can be the fountainhead of this part of the constitutional jurisprudence, *Van Gend en Loos* itself. In arguing for the concept of a new legal order, the Court reasoned in the following two famous passages as follows:

> The conclusion to be drawn from this is that the Community constitutes a new legal order of international law for the benefit of which the states have limited their sovereign rights, albeit within limited fields, and the subjects of which comprise not only Member States but also their nationals. Independently of the legislation of Member States, Community law therefore not only imposes obligations on individuals but is also intended to confer upon them rights which become part of their legal heritage. These rights arise not only where they are expressly granted by the Treaty, but also by reason of obligations which the Treaty imposes in a clearly defined way upon individuals as well as upon the Member States and upon the institutions of the Community.
>
> This view is confirmed by the preamble to the Treaty which refers not only to governments but to peoples. It is also confirmed more specifically by the establishment of institutions endowed with sovereign rights, the exercise of which affects Member States and also their citizens. *Furthermore, it must be noted that the nationals of the states brought together in the Community are called upon to cooperate in the functioning of this Community through the intermediary of the European Parliament and the Economic and Social Committee.* (Emphasis added)

The problem is that this 'cooperation' was extremely weak. This is, in truth, a serious 'dumbing down' of democracy and its meaning by the European Court. At the time, the European Parliament had the right to give its opinion when asked, and it often was not asked. Even in areas where it was meant to be asked, it was well known that Commission and Council would complete their bargaining ahead of such advice which thus became *pro-forma*. But can that level of democratic representation and accountability, *seen through the lenses of normative political theory*, truly justify the immense power of direct governance which the combined doctrines of direct effect and supremacy placed in the hands of the then Community institutions? Surely posing

---

(Copenhagen: GEC Gads Forlag, 1994), 326–7; H Rasmussen, 'Towards a Normative Theory of Interpretation of Community Law' (1992) *The University of Chicago Legal Forum* 135, at 137; CN Kakouris, 'La Cour de Justice des Communautés européennes comme cour constitutionnelle: trois observations' in O Due, M Lutter, and J Schwartze, *Festschrift für Ulrich Everling* (Baden-Baden: Nomos, 1995), 635.

[67] In this regard, see H Rasmussen, *On Law and Policy in the European Court of Justice. A Comparative Study in Judicial Policy-Making.*

the question is to give the answer. In some deep unintended sense, the Court was giving its normative imprimatur to a caricature of democracy, not the thing itself.

The implication of the Court of Justice in the democratic travails of the Union is easily stated even if usually uncomfortably discussed. The late Federico Mancini in his 'Europe: The Case for Statehood', forcefully articulated the democratic malaise of Europe.[68] There were many, myself included, who shied away from Mancini's remedy, a European state, and shied away from his contention that this remedy was the only one which was available. But few quibbled with his trenchant and often caustic denunciation of the democratic deficiencies of European governance.

But could the Court distance itself from this malaise which was so trenchantly and caustically denunciated? It is precisely on these occasions, I argued, that I rejoice most that I am not a judge on the Court. What would I do if I felt, as Mancini did, that the European Community suffered from this deep democratic deficit which he described so unflinchingly and which according to him could only be cured by the creation of a European state? Would I want to give effect to a principle which rendered the Community's undemocratic laws—adopted in his words by 'numberless, faceless and unaccountable committees of senior national experts', and rubber-stamped by the Council—supreme over the very constitutional values of the Member States? If democracy is what one cares about most, could one unambiguously consider much of the Community edifice a major *advance*? Whatever the hermeneutic legitimacy of reaching supremacy and direct effect, the interaction of these principles with the non-democratic decision-making process was and is, highly problematic. Similar dilemmas would of course face national judges.

The paradox is thus that the legitimacy challenge to the Court's constitutional jurisprudence does not rest as often has been assumed in its hermeneutics—a good outcome based on a questionable interpretation—but quite the opposite: an unassail-able interpretation but an outcome which underpins, supports, and legitimates a highly problematic decisional process. Substantively then, the much-vaunted Com-munity rights which serve almost invariably the economic interests of individuals were 'bought' at least in some measure at the expense of democratic legitimation.

Procedurally we find a similar story. The secret of the principle of the rule of law in the legal order of the European Union is that genius process of preliminary references and preliminary rulings. The compliance pull of law in liberal Western democracies does not rest on the gun and coercion. It rests on a political culture which internalizes, especially public authorities, obedience to the law rather than to expediency. Not a perfect, but one good measure of the rule of law is the extent to which public authorities in a country obey the decisions, even uncomfortable ones, of their own courts.

It is by this very measure that international regimes are so often found wanting, and why we cannot quite in the same way speak about the rule of international law. All too

---

[68] GF Mancini, 'Europe: The Case for Statehood' (1998) 4 *European Law Journal* 29. See also JHH Weiler, 'Europe: The Case against the Case for Statehood' (1998) 4 *European Law Journal* 43.

frequently, when a state is faced with an uncomfortable international norm or decision of an international tribunal, it finds ways to evade it.

Statistically, as we know, the preliminary reference procedure is, overwhelmingly, a device for judicial review of Member State compliance with their obligations under the Treaties.[69] It is ingenious for two reasons. First, it deploys individuals, vindicating their own rights as the monitors and enforcers of Community obligations vis-à-vis the Member States.[70] It has been called the private-Attorney-General Model.[71] And second, it deploys national courts.[72] The judgment is spoken through the mouths of Member State courts. The habit of obedience associated with national law is thus attached to European law.[73] The gap between the rule of law and the rule of international law is narrowed, even closed.[74]

However, it is precisely in this context that we can see the problematic nature of the dark side of the moon. The situation implicated in preliminary references always posits an individual vindicating a personal, private interest against the public good. Paradoxically, European rights, in some interesting way, become anti-community rights. If the social reality of the European construct were stronger, this could be seen as mitigating this effect. But the reality of the situation from a social perspective is that—for good legal reason—the principal artefact of the principle of the rule of law in the thin political space constituted by the Union places the individual at odds with his or her thicker national political space. This is how it should be legally. This is what creates the most effective drive for compliance. But this is why it also contributes to the national social and political turn against the Union.[75]

The argument about the rule of law I am trying to make is that formalist and positivist Kelsenian models are no longer accepted as representing a meaningful and normatively acceptable form of the rule of law, if they are not respectful of two conditions: rootedness

---

[69] R Lecourt, 'Quel eut été le droit communautaire sans les arrêts de 1963 et 1964?' in *L'Europe et le droit—Mélanges en hommage à Jean Boulouis* (Paris: Dalloz, 1991), 349; HG Schemers *et al.* (eds), *Art. 177 EEC: Experiences and Problems* (The Hague: Elsevier, 1987); M Broberg and N Fenger, *Preliminary References to the European Court of Justice* (Oxford: Oxford University Press, 2010); T de La Mare, 'Article 177 in Social and Political Context' in P Craig and G De Búrca (eds), *The Evolution of EU Law*, 215.

[70] P Pescatore, 'The Doctrine of Direct Effect: an infant disease of Community law' (June 1983) 8 *European Law Review* 155.

[71] JHH Weiler, 'Cain and Abel—Convergence and Divergence in International Trade Law', in JHH Weiler, *The EU, the WTO, and the NAFTA. Towards a Common Law of International Trade?* (Oxford: Oxford University Press, 2000), 1.

[72] F Grevisse and JC Bonichot, 'Les incidences du droit communautaire sur l'organisation et l'exercice de la fonction juridictionnelle dans les Etats membres' in *L'Europe et le droit—Mélanges en hommage à Jean Boulouis* (Paris: Dalloz, 1991), 297.

[73] See HLA Hart, *The Concept of Law*, especially chapters 3 and 10; Jones, 'The Legal Nature of the European Community: A Jurisprudential Analysis Using H.L.A. Hart's Model of Law and Legal System' (1984) 17(1) *Cornell International Law Journal* 1.

[74] G Bebr, 'Court of Justice: Judicial Protection and the Rule of Law', in D Curtin and T Heukel (eds), *Institutional Dynamics of European Integration. Essays in Honour of H.G. Schemers*, vol II (Dordrecht: Martinus Nijhoff, 1994), 303, at 305; JHH Weiler, 'The Transformation of Europe' (June 1991) *Yale Law Journal* 2403, at 2420ff.

[75] P Allott, 'Preliminary rulings—another infant disease' (2000) 25(2) *European Law Review* 538.

in a democratic process of law making, and respect of fundamental human rights. The European Court of Justice accepted the second of these conditions in an activist jurisprudence beginning in 1969 which proclaimed that European norms not respectful of the common constitutional traditions of the Member States and enshrined in the ECHR would be unacceptable. It understood that even democracies may lead to a tyranny of the majority. Its jurisprudence was bold since there was no hint of that proposition in the Treaties. Indeed, when the Court decided its first cases the terms 'human rights' or 'fundamental rights' were nowhere to be found in the Treaties. There has never been, however, a similar jurisprudence as regards the decision-making processes of the Union. In that respect the Court is complicit in the status quo.

6 Defending Values

The second story, brief and crude, is usually considered a historical curiosity, but it too had a profound effect on the political culture of the Union and European Integration. I refer to the saga of the European Defence Community. A Treaty was actually signed in May 1952 but failed, by a relatively small number of votes, to be ratified in the French Parliament in May 1954 and the project was abandoned.[76]

What is most striking about this historical event is that the governments were actually able to agree among themselves on a treaty concerning this most hallowed of 'sovereign' core. It made huge sense. Quite apart from the fact that, history notwithstanding, a war among the partners of the Union was an unrealistic possibility, this would be a very symbolic and concrete step to make it unthinkable. But even more importantly, in the face of an external threat, and the ambiguity of American patronage, this project at one and the same time brought about considerable savings whilst at the same time enhancing the defence capabilities of European Member States jointly and severally.

My contention is that this 'childhood' trauma, the failure of the European Community, has had profound effects, not just material but principally political and cultural.[77] It became part of European faith that defence, security, and military matters had to be kept separate from the European construct—the argument being that it was neither politically feasible nor politically desirable.[78] It has bred amazing pathologies, not least wasteful replications of the defence efforts of the Member States coupled with a total

---

[76] 'International Organizations: Summary of Activities: III. Political and Regional Organizations—European Defence Community' (1954) 8(4) *International Organizations* 599, at 601.

[77] '*Chosen traumas and chosen glories provide, in other words, the linking objects for later generations to be rediscovered, reinterpreted, and reused*', C Kinval, *Globalization and Religious Nationalism in India: The Search for Ontological Security* (London: Routledge, 2006) 58 cited in I Manners, 'Global Europa: Mythology of the European Union in World Politics', 82.

[78] See for example F Duchêne, 'The European Community and the Uncertainties of Interdependence', in M Kolistamm and W Hager (eds), *Nation Writ Large: Foreign Policy Problems Before the European Communities* (London: Macmillan, 1973), 19ff; JJ Sheehan, *Where Have all the Soldiers Gone?: The transformation of modern Europe*, 222ff; S Rynning, 'Less May Be Better in EU Security and Defence Policy' (2005) 2(1) *Oxford Journal on Global Governance* 45.

reliance on American force. If America has become the 'policeman of the world', it is in part because Europe allowed it to become so, since when in trouble, Europe itself would call not its own police but 911.[79] Paradoxically, the failure to cooperate has also weakened each state individually, since the magnitude of expense simply removed certain projects from national agendas.

Even worse, Europe failed to develop the habits of cooperation and consensus-building in this field which remained outside the European construct. Like its democratization, it had to graft on alien bodies such as European Political Cooperation, Third Pillar, Common Defense and Security, etc.

Worst of all, it developed a whole new rationalization which was grafted on to the original political messianic project—the 'civilian power'[80]—in a questionable attempt to justify the failure of its own early project. Here there has been a veritable spillover also into national politics. Reasonable people can debate the extent of any existential threat to Europe. But there can be no debate that at times, unless one is a pacifist (a comfortable luxury when your friendly neighbour is not), the only way to prevent the worst kind of trampling on the most hallowed values might require decisive use of force. The consequences of this failure are to be found in the graveyards of Bosnia, Darfur, and elsewhere.

7 End Game

The political messianic and its concomitant corollary in a central but formal conception of the rule of law were offered not only for the sake of conceptual clarification but also as an explanation of the formidable success of European integration. It produced a culture of praxis, achievement, ever-expanding agendas. Given the noble dimensions of European integration, one ought to see and acknowledge their virtuous facets.

But that is only part of the story. It also explains some of the story of decline in European legitimacy and mobilizing pull which is so obvious today. Part of the very phenomenology of political messianism is that it always collapses as a mechanism for mobilization and legitimation. It obviously collapses when the messianic project fails, when the revolution does not come. But interestingly, and more germane to the narrative of European integration, even when successful, it sows the seeds of its own collapse. At one level the collapse is inevitable, part of the very phenomenology of a messianic project. Reality is always more complicated, challenging, banal, and ultimately less satisfying than the dream which preceded it. The result is not only absence of mobilization and legitimation, but actual rancour. The original Promised Land,

---

[79] See JJ Sheehan, *Where Have all the Soldiers Gone?: The transformation of modern Europe*, 204ff.

[80] F Duchêne, 'The European Community and the Uncertainties of Interdependence'; A Shonfield, *Europe: Journey to an Unknown Destination* (London: Allen Lane, Penguin Books 1973), 62; H Bull, 'Civilian Power Europe: A Contradiction in Terms?' (1982) 21(2) *Journal of Common Market Studies* 149; K Nicolaïdis and R Howse, '"This is my Eutopia . . .": Narrative as Power' (2002) 40(4) *Journal of Common Market Studies* 767, at 769.

Canaan, was a very different proposition, challenging and hostile, to the dream which preceded it. Independent India, or Kenya, or even the USA were very different to the dreams which preceded them and their ilk. Individually this is the story of many a marriage and love affair. Just as paradise is realized, it is lost. It is part of the ontology of the messianic. The emblematic manifestation of this in the context of European integration is the difference between the 868 inspiring words of the Schuman dream and the 154,183 very real words of the (defunct) European Constitution.

But in the case of Europe, there are additional contingent factors which create the collapse of the messianic narrative as a mobilizing and legitimizing factor. At one level Europe is a victim of its own success. The passage of time coupled with the consolidation of peace, the internalization of the alternative inter-state discourse which Europe presented, has been so successful that to new generations of Europeans, both the pragmatic and idealist appeal of the Schuman vision seem simply incomprehensible. The reality against which their appeal was so powerful—the age-old enmity between France and Germany—is no longer a living memory, and this is a wonderful state of affairs that is in some considerable measure also owed to the European constructs.

At another level, much has changed in societal mores. Europe in large part has become a post-Christian society, and the profound commitment to the individual and his or her rights, relentlessly (and in many respects laudably) placing the individual in the centre of political attention, has contributed to the emergence of the self-centered individuals. Social mobilization in Europe is strongest when the direct interest of the individual is at stake, and at its weakest when it requires tending to the needs of the other, as the recent Euro crisis, immigrant crisis, and other such instances will readily attest. So part of the explanation of the loss of mobilizing force of the Schuman vision is in the fact that what it offers either seems irrelevant or does not appeal to the very different idealistic sensibility of contemporary European society.

The result is that if political messianism is not rapidly anchored in the legitimation that comes from popular ownership, it rapidly becomes alienating and, like the Golem, turns on its creators.

Democracy was not part of the original DNA of European Integration. It still feels like a foreign implant. With the collapse of its original political messianism, the alienation we are now witnessing is only to be expected. And the formal rule of law only serves to augment the alienation. There are no easy fixes to these problems. That is the nature of problems which are not rooted in institutional arrangements but are a reflection of what has become part of a deep-seated political and legal culture.

7

Citizenship and Obligation

Pavlos Eleftheriadis*

Many political philosophers believe that we owe moral obligations to our political communities simply because we are asked. We pay taxes or serve in the army, for example, whenever we are demanded to do so by the competent authorities or agencies. These are obligations of a particular kind because, unlike most other moral obligations, they are not based on the content of the action they require. They are true obligations even when they demand actions that are plainly wrong. Philosophers call this type of obligation 'political obligation' and often connect it to the status of citizenship and to membership in a political community.[1] If political obligation of this kind exists for the citizens of a particular political community, its members are required to adjust their conduct and reasoning accordingly. The obligation exists independently of other moral obligations they owe to each other. Can such moral obligations be created by European Union institutions?

1 European Obligations

The question arises as the European Union is becoming the source of some very important legal duties. I will discuss two examples from the field of asylum and immigration law. Immigration rights concern some of the most important interests human beings have, including their own security and liberty. They presuppose a weak prior connection between the persons burdened by the legal obligation and the institutions making the relevant laws and decisions, that is, normally the host states. If some political obligation can be shown to exist in these examples, it will also exist elsewhere.

* I am grateful to Julie Dickson, Geert De Baere, Fernando Llano, Kalypso Nicolaïdis, and Jeremy Waldron for very helpful comments on an earlier draft. An early version was presented at a workshop at the University of Leuven in May 2011. I am very grateful to Elke Cloots, Triantafyllos Gouvas, George Pavlakos, and H de Schutter for their comments and suggestions.
[1] See for example George Klosko, *Political Obligations* (Oxford: Oxford University Press, 2005) and the works discussed below in Section 2.

A European Union Regulation provides for 'asylum transfers' or, in other words, for criteria and mechanisms for determining the Member State responsible for examining an asylum application lodged in one of the Member States.[2] This regulation, known widely as the 'Dublin II' regulation because it derives from an earlier international convention, provides that asylum seekers that have applied for asylum in one EU Member State, are to be returned to another Member State if the criteria set out in that regulation are met. One such criterion is, for example, that the asylum seeker 'has irregularly crossed the border into a Member State by land, sea, or air having come from a third country'. If this criterion is met, then the Member State thus entered 'shall be responsible for examining the application for asylum'.[3] This entails, however, that the applicant himself or herself is to be forcefully returned to that original state of entry by the relevant authorities.[4] So an asylum seeker, let us call him A, who had travelled to the state where he made his application would be frustrated, since he would be forcefully returned to another Member State. To make the example simple, let us say that A is a genuine refugee, a human rights activist fleeing a well-grounded fear of persecution in the hands of a corrupt and ruthless political regime. Under the regulation, he can be transferred to the first Member State.[5] Having taken the form of a regulation, this set of rules does not depend on any prior implementation by state law.[6]

Does this European Regulation, the set of rules found in its text, create a moral, that is, political obligation, for A to comply? Or are appropriately meritorious applicants, such as A in our example, morally permitted to ignore these rules? Is A morally *permitted* to evade its application by whatever non-violent means, perhaps by absconding? If A has no political obligation to the EU and its laws, he should be able to do so without any moral blame. Of course, the asylum seeker, meritorious or not, may end up arrested by the state exercising its legal powers. A will then face the consequences. But this is not what we are asking. We are asking if he would be morally blameless if he successfully evaded that law. A meritorious applicant would be blameless, if the European Union could not by itself

---

[2] Council Regulation 343/2003 of 18 February 2003, OJ L50/1, 25.2.2003 (known as the Dublin II Regulation). For an interpretation see Ian A Macdonald and Ronal Toal (eds), *Immigration Law and Practice in the United Kingdom*, 8th edn (London: Lexis Nexis, 2010), Vol I, 969–78.

[3] Article 10(1), Regulation 343/2003.

[4] Articles 16 and 20, Regulation 343/2003.

[5] The Regulation provides also that although this decision to send back the asylum seeker may be subject to appeal or review, such an appeal or review 'shall not suspend the implementation of the transfer except when the courts or competent bodies so decide on a case-by-case basis if the national legislation allows for this'; see Article 20(1)(c), Regulation 343/2003. This creates a presumption than any appeal will not prevent the forced return. This is a second way in which EU law has an adverse impact on the applicant, irrespective of what national law says.

[6] For some of the issues raised by this Regulation see the decision of the European Court of Justice in Case C-19/08 *Migrationsverket v Petrosian* [2009] ECR I-495. A more thorough analysis was offered by the House of Lords in *R (Nasseri) v Secretary of State for the Home Department* [2009] UKHL 23; [2010] 1 AC 1 and by the High Court in *The Queen on the application of Saeedi v Secretary of State for the Home Department* [2010] EWHC 705 (Admin) (Cranston J), which is currently on appeal to the Court of Appeal and subject to a preliminary reference to the Court of Justice of the European Union (Case C-411/10 *NS v Secretary of State for the Home Department*).

impose a political obligation to follow its procedures and rules. In the absence of political obligation any EU's legal declarations would have no moral relevance for A as an outsider and non-citizen. The only moral obligations would thus possibly arise out of an argument based on the particular content of what was being asked of him to do. But in our example, A is a meritorious asylum seeker.

The second example is of 'asylum exceptions'. An EU Directive outlines minimum standards for the qualification and status of refugees.[7] This Directive generally recognizes the rights based on the 1951 Geneva Convention and Protocol and also restates their exclusions and obligations. In line with standard refugee law, Article 12 of the Directive provides that a person is excluded from being a refugee where there are serious reasons for considering that '. . . he or she has committed a serious non-political crime outside the country of refuge prior to his or her admission as a refugee . . .'. When the Court of Justice of the European Union was called upon to interpret the relevant provisions it concluded that this exclusion 'is not conditional on the person concerned representing a present danger to the host Member State', and that this exclusion 'is not conditional on an assessment of proportionality in relation to the particular case', and finally, that 'Member States may grant a right of asylum under their national law to a person who is excluded from refugee status pursuant to Article 12(2) of the directive [following more generous provisions of national law] provided that that other kind of protection does not entail a risk of confusion with refugee status within the meaning of the directive'.[8] In all these ways the directive, the Court tells us, has created independent obligations on the third-country nationals seeking refuge. So in this case the European institutions and the Court of Justice create direct obligations on an individual. Let us call this individual B for ease of reference. B cannot get asylum in the Member State, even if the national provisions provide it, unless the EU law conditions outlined by the European Court of Justice are met. But does this judgment create a political obligation on B? If not, he may ignore it without blame.

The two cases give us examples of legal obligations that arise directly from EU laws and institutions. They are legal obligations created by EU institutions that apply directly to persons. I will call both these kinds of legal obligations 'European obligations'. Are they supported by political obligations to EU law and institutions? To answer the question we need to look more closely at the philosophical arguments concerning the idea of political obligation.

2 Political Obligation

Here are some examples of modern political obligation, in ascending order of controversy: an obligation to assist with a police investigation when you are wrongfully

---

[7] Council Directive 2004/83/EC of 29 April 2004 on minimum standards for the qualification and status of third country nationals or stateless persons as refugees or as persons who otherwise need international protection, OJ 2004 L304, 12.

[8] Joined Cases C-57/09 and C-101/09 *Bundesrepublik Deutschland v B and D* (Grand Chamber), 9 November 2010, not yet reported, para 122.

suspected of a crime that you have not committed; an obligation to pursue a claim against another only through the existing system of civil procedure and not through self-help against someone you know is a liar; a requirement to pay a large part of your earnings in income taxation that funds subsidies for well-connected and corrupt businesses; an obligation to apply the law conscientiously whenever you are elected to public office, even when it is a cruel and unjust law; the obligation to serve compulsory military service in an army that you know is often engaged in acts of cruelty to civilians or to your fellow conscripts; the requirement to serve a sentence for a crime you did not commit, if you are convicted by a court of law. All these things entail some injustice, but you have a prima facie reason to do them, at least under the arguments for political obligation.

Arguments that such obligations exist have a very long history. One of the first and best accounts occurs in Aristotle's *Politics*. Having outlined the idea of the rule of law and the separation of powers, Aristotle gives the following advice regarding the preservation of states:

> In all well-attempered governments there is nothing which should be more jealously maintained than the spirit of obedience to law, more especially in small matters; for transgression creeps in unperceived and at last ruins the state, just as the constant recurrence of small expenses in time eats up a fortune.[9]

And, following Plato, he tells us that the laws will always be imperfect, for they tend to miss the details of the particular circumstances.[10] He notes, for example, that: 'the best man, then, must legislate, and laws must be passed, but these laws will have no authority when they miss the mark, though in all other cases retaining their authority'.[11] This does not weaken his commitment to the rule of law, however. This is because in Aristotle's argument the rule of law is not simply rule by a rule-book; rather, it is a constitutional principle about the appropriate function of offices and institutions. The laws become agreeable in all their imperfection, only if they are administered by officers appropriately trained in the law and suitably distant from any dispute. The personal virtues and qualities of these officers are therefore part of the ideal. They are essential, if the law is to be applied without passion or self-interest:

> For magistrates there must be – this is admitted; but then men say that to give authority to any one man when all are equal is unjust. Nay, there may indeed cases which the law seems unable to determine, but in such cases can a man? Nay, it will be replied, the

---

[9] Aristotle, *Politics*, 1307b, trans by B Jowett, in *The Basic Works of Aristotle*, edited by Richard McKeon (New York: The Modern Library, 2001), 1246.

[10] Plato writes, for example, that '. . . law could never accurately embrace what is best and most just for all at the same time, and so prescribe what is best. For the dissimilarities between human beings and their actions, and the fact that practically nothing in human affairs ever remains stable, prevent any sort of expertise whatsoever from making any simple decision in any sphere that covers all cases and will last for all time'; *Statesman*, 294a, in Plato, *The Complete Works*, edited by John M Cooper, trans by CJ Rowe (Indianapolis: Hackett, 1997), 338.

[11] Aristotle, *Politics*, 1286a, 1200.

law trains officers for this express purpose, and appoints them to determine matters which are left undecided by it, to the best of their judgment. Further, it permits them to make any amendment of the existing laws which experience suggests. Therefore he who bids the law rule may be deemed to bid God and Reason alone rule, but he who bids man rule adds an element of the beast; for desire is a wild beast, and passion perverts the minds of rulers, even when they are the best of men. The law is reason unaffected by desire.[12]

Much can be said about this passage. One interpretation is that when Aristotle speaks of law he is not speaking just of the rules but of the institutions, principles, and techniques that are associated with the practice as a whole. This is not just 'ideal' theory. The persons appointed can only work 'to the best of their judgment', implying that their judgment will not always be perfect. The institution is supposed to accommodate our human limitations and indeed derives some of its force from human frailty and weakness of will. It requires us to forgive such failings, under certain conditions. In Aristotle's version, which has been repeated by numerous philosophers through the ages, the rule of law is not just a rule of rules. It is the conscious organization of human life according to basic principles of fairness, justice, or virtue, the only way through which people can have a flourishing life. As a result, political obligation is owed to the institution as a whole, the 'polis', as well as to the individuals administering it on the basis of reciprocity. This has been a standard theme among the classic Greek and Roman philosophers and explains the force and beauty of the examples set in literature by Antigone and in real life by Socrates.

This defence of the rule of law as an ideal for social institutions as a whole is echoed in the modern defence of the 'social contract'. For the very idea of a 'social contract' is itself another metaphor conveying the message of a human union of principles, roles, and procedures with its own moral standing. The social contract marks a union of persons, whose passions and imperfections are always sources of tension and the causes of collapse. At the most abstract end of this tradition Kant echoes the very same ideas when he tells us that 'a *state (civitas)* is a union of a multitude of men under laws of Right'.[13] The multitude is not united by power, but by its laws.

Not everyone agrees with the social contract tradition. Its conclusions are resisted by philosophers, consequentialists, particularists and others, who pursue a different view of political institutions. Political decisions for them may or may not create moral obligations depending on their content or consequences.[14] For such views one may have to cooperate with institutions whose decisions help public coordination or achieve other valuable results, but not otherwise. There is accordingly no general obligation to obey institutions, but only ad hoc requirements to comply with some of their directives. At most, the requirements may cover a whole area of law or indeed,

---

[12] Aristotle, *Politics* 1286b, 1202.

[13] Kant, *Metaphysics of Morals*, in Immanuel Kant, *Practical Philosophy*, translated and edited by Mary J Gregor (Cambridge: Cambridge University Press, 1996), 6: 313, 456.

[14] The doubters include MBE Smith, 'Is there an Obligation to Obey the Law?' (1973) 82 *Yale Law Journal* 950, Leslie Green, *The Authority of the State* (Oxford: Clarendon Press, 1988), 220–47, and Joseph Raz, *The Authority of Law* (Oxford: Clarendon Press, 1979), 233–49.

when certain stringent conditions obtain, a whole jurisdiction. But I will have very little to say about such views. If there is no general political obligation, then the problems I identify here do not arise. Notice, however, that even such theories accept some reasons to comply, although they organize their arguments in a different way. In either case, political obligation need not be conclusive, and here the differences between the theories may seem to be melting away. Like any other moral obligation, political obligation can be overridden by other reasons. So the institutional argument need not differ with the particularist argument on what one has to do in every case.

The theories that affirm the existence of political obligation as a genuine moral obligation are generally divided into 'voluntary' and 'non-voluntary'. The voluntary theories have their origin in Locke's phrase that, '[w]herever, therefore, any number of men so unite into one society as to quit every one his executive power of the law of Nature, and to resign it to the public, there and there only is a political or civil society'.[15] The idea is that the authority of the state is based on the voluntary surrender of the lawless freedom we enjoyed in the state of nature—and this surrender could be taken to be either explicit or implicit. In modern times voluntary theories have found a separate expression in theories of 'fair play', according to which the source of the authority of the state over its citizens is not consent as such, but the active participation in the forms of organization that the state creates, through which we derive tangible benefits. Once we receive the benefits, we are obliged under the principle of fairness, to cooperate with others in the same venture. HLA Hart argued that the mere existence of a cooperative project may create prima facie obligation to those participating in it. He argued that, 'when a number of persons conduct any joint enterprise according to rules and thus restrict their liberty, those who have submitted to these restrictions when required have a right to a similar submission from those who have benefitted by their submission'.[16] This leads to an argument from 'fair play' in political obligation.

By contrast, non-voluntary theories start at the other end. There are principles of justice that oblige us independently of any action we take or promise we give. The clearest argument is offered by John Rawls, who argued for a 'natural duty of justice' to support just institutions:

> From the standpoint of justice as fairness, a fundamental natural duty is the duty of justice. This duty requires us to support and to comply with just institutions that exist and apply to us. It also constrains us to further just arrangements not yet established, at least when this can be done without too much cost to ourselves. Thus if the basic structure of society is just, or as just as it is reasonable to expect in the circumstances, everyone has a natural duty to do his part in the existing scheme. Each is bound to these institutions independent of his voluntary acts, performative or otherwise.[17]

---

[15] John Locke, *Two Treatises of Government*, edited by Peter Laslett (Cambridge: Cambridge University Press, 1988), II, § 89, p 325.

[16] HLA Hart, 'Are there Any Natural Rights?' (1955) 64 *Philosophical Review* 185.

[17] John Rawls, *A Theory of Justice*, revised edition (Oxford: Oxford University Press, 1999), 99 (the text is identical to the 1971 edition at 115). For a discussion of Rawls's arguments see also Jeremy Waldron, 'Special Ties and Natural Duties' (1993) 22 *Philosophy and Public Affairs* 3.

Once the society we find ourselves in can be said to be reasonably just, the duty creates a prima facie moral requirement to obey its institutions. Rawls explains this as the 'duty of civility', namely the duty 'not to invoke the faults of social arrangements as a too ready excuse for not complying with them, nor to exploit inevitable loopholes in the rules to advance our interests'.[18] The main argument behind the duty of civility is that we must accept the 'defects of institutions', at least as we see them from our own point of view, and show a 'certain restraint in taking advantage of them'.[19] There is no other way, Rawls says, for managing a democratic regime. The origin of this idea is with Kant's political philosophy of the social contract, according to which entering a 'civil society' is a 'postulate of public right'.[20] A similarly 'non-voluntary' argument for political obligation is made by Ronald Dworkin, for whom political obligation is an 'associative obligation', namely an obligation that is created as a special responsibility to membership in some social or biological group, when it is organized as a more or less genuine community.[21]

One important difference between voluntary and non-voluntary theories lies in the account they give of the special allegiance we may owe to our own political community. As Jeremy Waldron and A John Simmons have separately argued, consent or fair play explains this special allegiance, because it is this community that we have consented to, or cooperated with. The non-voluntary theories, however, need to explain this special allegiance differently.[22] Assume a state S has just institutions. Do we have a natural duty of justice to serve in its army? Clearly, we do not. Only citizens of S or others suitably connected to S may be conscripted. Political obligation, thus, needs something more than abstract justice. Rawls says that we only have a duty to principles that 'apply to us'. But how do we determine which ones applies to us or, in other words, the scope of political obligation of each state? Legitimacy requires a second type of argument, one that grounds a particular judgment that the political institutions around us are concretely legitimate *for us*, on account of their history and character. To put it in terms of Aristotle's distinction with which we started these thoughts, it is not just the laws that are to be acceptable as abstract precepts, but the particular magistrates appointed to apply these laws must have an appropriate claim on us. So abstract justification and particular legitimacy are different things.[23]

---

[18] Rawls, *A Theory of Justice*, 312.

[19] Rawls explains that 'in adopting some form of majority rule, the parties [to a hypothetical constitutional convention] accept the risks of suffering the defects of one another's knowledge and sense of justice in order to gain the advantages of an effective legislative procedure' (*Theory of Justice*, 312).

[20] Kant, *Metaphysics of Morals*, 6:306, in Kant, *Practical Philosophy*, 450. See Arthur Ripstein, *Force and Freedom: Kant's Legal and Political Philosophy* (Cambridge, Mass.: Harvard University Press, 2009).

[21] Ronald Dworkin, *Law's Empire* (Cambridge, Mass.: Harvard University Press, 1986), 206–15. For a general discussion see also Simmons, 'Associative Political Obligations' in A John Simmons, *Justification and Legitimacy: Essays on Rights and Obligations* (Cambridge: Cambridge University Press, 2001), 65.

[22] See Jeremy Waldron, 'Special Ties and Natural Duties', 3 and John A Simmons, 'Justification and Legitimacy' in his *Justification and Legitimacy*, 122.

[23] A similar point is made by Allen Buchanan, who distinguishes between the 'legitimacy' of institutions and their 'right to rule' over certain people; see Allen Buchanan, 'The Legitimacy of International Law' in

This brings the non-voluntary theories, like Rawls's and Dworkin's, much closer to the voluntary ones. This is because the particular legitimacy of a set of institutions will depend to some extent on the particular facts of one's life. So for example, the laws of state S apply to us only if we live in that state. The explanations offered for legitimacy derive from the justificatory ideal itself, but require this additional step. Waldron explains the point as follows:

> ...the natural duties come into play only where the organization in question passes not only tests of justice and effectiveness, but also a test of legitimacy. What must be established is that there is a good reason to recognize *this* organization, as opposed to any rival organization, as *the one* to do justice in the given territory or with regard to the claims that are at issue. To the extent that such reasons exist, the organization is 'legitimate'. Legitimacy, then, is an exclusive characteristic: only one organization may be legitimate with regard to a given set of claims or with regard to the issues of justice arising in a given territory.[24]

This is a very important point which is often misunderstood. The natural duty of justice relies on the moral distinctiveness of the state as an ideal. A just state is not the result of voluntary agreement. It is meant to be comprehensive or, in more old-fashioned (and somewhat misleading) terminology, a sovereign state.[25] Political philosophers of all persuasions, from Hobbes to Kant, acknowledge that the authority of the just state is not supposed to be challenged by rival authorities. This is what sovereignty is supposed to convey, not as a test for statehood but as an ideal to be achieved. Some modern political philosophers put the problem in terms of coordination and its benefits. The deeper issue, however, is that justice needs institutions and offices that will give practical effect to abstract principles. Justice does not exist otherwise. If the rules of a society are to be public and intelligible and if the rule of law is to be respected, then the institutional machinery in place must be committed to giving effect to a single set of results or conclusions, on the basis of a single set of principles. In that sense, the legitimate set of institutions must enjoy a monopoly of power, not because this achieves coordination, since other divisions of power could also achieve coordination of sorts, but because this is the only way to secure legitimacy.

Different people (or different 'magistrates' in Aristotle's account) will interpret the same principle in different ways. We resolve this ambiguity by selecting one official or one body with the power to make the categorical determination of the rights of parties.

Tasioulas and Besson (eds), *The Philosophy of International Law*, 79, at 80–5. See also Allen Buchanan and RO Keohane, 'The Legitimacy of Global Governance Institutions' (2006) 20 *Ethics and International Affairs* 405. Buchanan's argument is that there is a significant distinction between being 'morally justified in engaging in governance functions' and being 'morally justified in using coercion to secure compliance with the institution's rules'. He uses this distinction to contrast the state (which alone needs the second type of moral relationship) and other political institutions. Buchanan's 'right to rule' captures the requirement for a specific relationship between the ruler and ruled.

[24] Waldron 'Special Ties', 22.

[25] For the ways in which the terminology of 'sovereignty' is misleading see Pavlos Eleftheriadis, 'Law and Sovereignty' (2010) 29 *Law and Philosophy* 535.

We may call this the power of *jurisdiction* (something which is always a feature or ambition of a legal order and never a feature or ambition of a moral order). The monopoly of jurisdiction is required because it protects the justifiability of the relevant legal order. Competing sovereigns would destroy the determinacy of our public rules. Incompatible jurisdictions and diverging rules of conduct would make any rules irrelevant. So the publicity of principles of justice and the availability of a single scheme of institutions and persons that are entrusted with their compulsory application are ideas that are intimately related. Without identifying who is to make our public decisions about these matters and on what basis, there could not have been a public structure of social life. It follows, thus, that the imperfect institutions of the states we observe around us, can be legitimate both because they approximate the ideal and because they are dominant as a single scheme of rules and institutions. Jeremy Waldron brings the two requirements together very effectively when he concludes that: '[t]he sheer existence of an institution as dominant and unchallenged may suffice to establish its salience, whether it is popularly supported or not'.[26]

3 Political Obligation and International Bodies

Can we apply the principles of political obligation to international bodies? Until recently the question might have been just a theoretical problem. There were few direct obligations created by international organizations or laws. Few, if any, such obligations were directed to individuals. The international conventions on refugees, for example, were supposed to be incorporated into domestic law by the signatory states. The same applied to human rights duties or international labour standards. Nevertheless, the law has now changed. There are numerous examples of international treaties or institutions that create direct obligations or other burdens on individuals. The WTO, for example, is a forum where international trade rules affecting millions of lives are debated and decided. The International Criminal Court aims to hold account-able individuals suspected of serious crimes. More distinctly of all, the European Union has created not just rules and legal instruments but also legislative and judicial institutions that aim to apply to persons and states directly, without the intervention of any state. Do such institutions create moral obligations to obey them? If so, how?

The problem is that all examples of international laws and institutions escape the traditional architecture of the state–citizen relationship. The decisions of the WTO or

[26] Waldron, 'Special Ties', 25. Waldron draws the following conclusion from the Rawlsian argument for a natural duty of justice: 'The position we have reached is that an organization that is just, effective, and legitimate (in the sense of being singled out as *the* salient organization for this territory) has *eo ipso* a claim on our allegiance. Though popular consent may be implicated in its justice, its effectiveness, or its legitimacy, the moral requirement that we support and obey such an organization is not itself based on any promise that we have made', 27.

the International Criminal Court take place outside the normal procedures of states. They are not controlled by political mechanisms accountable to the citizens of any single state, but involve state representatives in complex diplomatic conferences and other procedures. And in the case of the European Union, the idea of European citizenship is supplementary to that of the states. So the conventional arguments seem not to apply. This is a problem that has been stressed by a number of political philosophers thinking about recent international law structures. Jeff McMahan, for example, has raised the issue that the international laws of war have a highly question-able justification. He notes that 'it has not been satisfactorily explained how, by establishing political relations among themselves, people could confer on themselves permission to treat others in ways that would be impermissible in the absence of those relations'.[27] He calls this the challenge of 'collectivism' and he deploys it in an argument that seeks to challenge the coherence of a morality and law of the conduct of war, also known as '*ius in bello*'. He notes that killing is wrong even if under the supposed justification of a declaration of war. How can a state declaring war according to the rules of public international law change the wrongness of killing?[28]

Liam Murphy has pursued an analogous argument about the responsibility of individuals for the actions of their own states (the question of 'international responsi-bility'). He argues against the 'political view of the state', namely the view that considers that states have moral standing on the basis of some 'deontological test', according to which 'the state "engages the will" of its subjects when it acts in their name' and therefore creates obligations for them both domestically and internation-ally.[29] Murphy argues that this view in the end 'personifies' the state.[30] It fails to account for the legitimacy of the state system as we have it today, however, because 'deontological accounts...are either implausible on their own terms or if plausible do not in fact show the rule of any states over all their subjects to be legitimate (because few people actually consent, for example)'.[31] For these reasons Murphy suggests an instrumental and therefore contingent and specific justification of the state system. For this view there is no room for a theory of the overall legitimacy of the international system. Each particular measure is to be assessed separately.

The challenge posed by the arguments by Murphy and McMahan are unsettling because they are simple, plausible, and far-reaching. If they are right, then inter-national institutions can create no political obligation. The only political obligations we may have, if at all, derive from internal, state-centred institutions that satisfy

---

[27] Jeff McMahan, 'Laws of War' in Samantha Besson and John Tasioulas (eds), *The Philosophy of International Law* (Oxford: Oxford University Press, 2010), 493, at 503.

[28] Echoing the same idea, A John Simmons observes that: '[s]tates are not entitled to demand from unwilling inhabitants anything that one person may not demand from another independent of states'; Simmons, 'Justification and Legitimacy' in *Justification and Legitimacy*, 122, at 139.

[29] Liam Murphy, 'International Responsibility' in Besson and Tasioulas (eds), *The Philosophy of International Law*, 299, at 308.

[30] Murphy, 'International Responsibility', 313.

[31] Murphy, 'International Responsibility', 308.

stringent conditions of consent, fair play, or due process. Alternatively, political obligation can only arise because of the content of the relevant laws and their likely results. If that is correct, there cannot be any political obligation arising from the actions of institutions of an international body such as the United Nations or a regional body such as the European Union.

4 The Circle of Citizenship

One way of addressing this challenge and understanding European obligations as examples of genuine political obligation would be to reduce them to requirements issued by the Member States. This argument would be based on the idea that political obligation must always be tied to citizenship. Since political obligation is limited to citizenship, then all political obligation must ultimately arise out of one's own citizenship. If we could trace EU laws and requirements to the states themselves, then perhaps the problem would disappear. The legal obligations stemming from the EU would then be seen as political obligations owed to the constituent states by their citizens.

To make this strategy work we must be able to say that any relevant EU regulations and directives would only be taken to be the background to the real sources of obligation, namely the states' laws. So in our examples, A's transfer would be performed just on the authority of the state responsible. Similarly, B's asylum exception would be an obligation created on the asylum giving state by its own laws alone. If all the relevant decisions were reached entirely by the institutions of the states, then the problem would be transformed. The Regulation and the Directive would be the inspiration but not the reason for the relevant obligation. The Court of Justice would be seen either as an advisory body or just another state institution, perhaps simultaneously an institution of the twenty-seven Member States.

This description of the relationship between states and the EU is highly implausible. It contrasts starkly with what all the implicated institutions are actually saying. The States insist that they have no discretion. The EU institutions say that they have competence to make these decisions collectively. Both national courts and the Court of Justice agree that EU law has direct effect and (to some extent, at least) supremacy.[32] This interpretation also clashes with the general institutional structure of the European Union. The EU may not be a fully fledged administrative system, in that it relies on the institutions of the states, but it is an independent bearer of political power. It does not exercise delegated state powers. At the level of high politics, that is, the level of highest

---

[32] See for example Case 106/78 *Amministrazione delle Finanze dello Stato v Simmenthal SpA* [1978] ECR 629; Case C-10–22/97 *Ministero delle Finanze v IN.CO.GE.'90 Srl et al.* [1998] ECR I-6307. See N MacCormick, *Questioning Sovereignty* (Oxford: Oxford University Press, 1999), ch 7, Bruno de Witte, 'Direct Effect, Supremacy and the Nature of the Legal Order', in P Craig and G de Búrca (eds), *The Evolution of EU Law* (Oxford: Oxford University Press, 1999), 177–213.

political decision making, the Union institutions are independent from any govern-ment. The Council and Parliament make regulations and directives that are directly applicable and enjoy supremacy. Decision making in these institutions is mostly majority based, without giving any single state the right of veto. States that have been outvoted routinely insist that they have no option but to comply, even when the issue is one of principle. Moreover, the decisions of the Court of Justice, an institution that is both independent from any state government and outside the civil procedure rules of any Member State, are binding on all states immediately. So for all practical purposes the main EU institutions are entirely independent from any par-ticular set of national institutions. They cannot be seen as the extension of the insti-tutions of any state or of all of them together without serious distortion.

This interpretation of EU decision making would not work, however, even if it was acceptable on the facts. Let us assume that we have reformed the EU institutions and strengthened the role of states to fit this model of state-based decision making. The resulting set of institutions—a new sovereignty-friendly EU, let us say—would still fail to create political obligation in the right way. If the EU was an extension or an arm of all the states, then any resulting political obligation would be wholly *internal* to each Member State and its citizens. Only those who are members of a state, equal stakeholders, or equal co-legislators, would be bound by ties of political obligation in that state. By contrast, the EU is a *universal* project in that its decisions are supposed to apply equally to all the citizens of all Member States at the same time and to any international corporations, to all other states, and all other international bodies. The EU is supposed to have its own international personality and engage in foreign affairs. The circle of citizenship would still not cover this reach of EU law. Non-European Union citizens and corporations would still be outside it, as would all foreign states and international bodies. They could not have any political obligation to comply with the EU's institutions.

The case of such outsiders is particularly telling, because the conclusion conflicts directly with what the law requires and what common sense accepts. Lord Bingham put the case for the authority of the state towards outsiders as a matter of the right of states to regulate the flow of aliens:

> Where removal is proposed in pursuance of a lawful immigration policy, [the] question [whether such interference is necessary in a democratic society in the interests of national security, public safety or the economic well being of the country, the prevention of disorder or crime, for the protection of health or morals or for the protection of the rights and freedoms of others] will almost always fall to be answered affirmatively. This is because the right of sovereign states, subject to treaty obligations, to regulate the entry and expulsion of aliens is recognised in the Strasbourg jurisprudence (see *Ullah* [2004] 3 WLR 23, 29, para 6) and implementation of a firm immigration policy is an important function of government in a modern democratic state. In the absence of bad faith, ulterior motive or deliberate abuse of power it is hard to imagine an adjudicator answering this question other than affirmatively.[33]

---

[33] *Razgar v Secretary of State for the Home Department* [2004] UKHL 27, [2004] 3 WLR 58, para 19. The European Court of Human Rights (Grand Chamber) ruled in *Maaouia v France* ((2001) 33 EHRR 1037, at

This is the legal position. It shows that states have the legal authority to control immigration at their borders.[34] But this is clearly incomplete as a moral account. Where does the 'right' of sovereign states to regulate the entry and expulsion of aliens come from? It cannot simply come from the internal decision of the state to so regulate its borders. If the source is the state itself, then no outsider to the state can be possibly bound. Political obligation, we say, is owed by citizens because of their citizenship. But this means that non-citizens are not so bound. Such outsiders may then not have a moral duty to obey these laws. They would then be morally blameless if they just disregarded them.

The problem is not just a problem for international bodies. It applies equally to all states *vis a vis* non-nationals. If political obligation is tied to citizenship, then it does not extend to aliens even in the case of state laws and directions. So by looking at the activities of the EU we have uncovered a serious gap in the general theory of political obligation. Surprisingly perhaps, this question has not been addressed much by political philosophers. Locke notes that aliens come to be bound by the state where they happen to be simply by 'submitting to the Laws of any Country, living quietly, and enjoying Privileges and Protection under them', and argues that this *'makes not a Man a Member of that Society'*. For this to happen, they need to enter into a 'Commonwealth' by 'positive Engagement, and express Promise and Compact'.[35] But Locke does not explain why aliens who are *not* living quietly and are not yet enjoying any privileges can be bound by the laws of a state. In our examples, the aliens A and B do not have the right to live 'quietly'.

Jeremy Waldron is one of few philosophers to have addressed the problem. He looks again at the arguments for the natural duty to enter the civil condition offered by Rawls and Kant.[36] Waldron builds his analysis on the premise we traced back to Aristotle, namely that any legal principle would need institutions of enforcement and application. Since any principle of conduct will invite disagreements and ambiguities, we therefore need persons with the duty to specify the meaning of principles for particular cases. Waldron uses this argument to draw the conclusion that we owe different duties to the abstract principle and different duties to the particular persons that apply them. To help us draw these distinctions Waldron argues that we ought to draw a distinction between the 'insiders' of a civil condition and its 'outsiders'. The

paragraph 40) that: '...decisions regarding the entry, stay and deportation of aliens do not concern the determination of an applicant's civil rights or obligations or of a criminal charge against him, within the meaning of Article 6(1)'.

[34] Critics of the idea of political obligation could read this problem differently. They may say that the legal authority to control immigration is justified on an ad hoc basis, not on the basis of institutional legitimacy, a notion they reject. But it is very hard to see how, in John Tasioulas' terminology, excluding aliens is justified on the basis of the 'moral interests' of the excluded, who are then bound by the authority of the excluding state. The rule may be reasonable, but it can hardly be said to satisfy their 'interests'.

[35] Locke, Two Treatises, II, §122 349. See Simmons, '"Denisons and "Aliens": Locke's Problem of Political Consent' in *Justification and Legitimacy,* 158. But in what way are aliens bound, if they have not given this consent? Simmons argues that there are degrees and types of consent.

[36] Waldron, 'Special Ties and Natural Duties', 15–19.

insiders may have a natural duty of justice to support the principles and just institutions that apply to them. In this sense they are 'range-limited' principles. Such are the duties of citizenship. Outsiders, by contrast, only have the duty '*not to undermine*' the proper application of the relevant internal principles by the appropriate persons. Waldron argues that only this duty is applicable to everyone, citizens and aliens, alike. Hence, the institutions of New Zealand must not be undermined by the action of French agents, even if the latter have never been to or subjected themselves to the authority of the state of New Zealand (Waldron's own example).

Nevertheless, the cases we are dealing with here go well beyond the negative duty not to undermine the legal order of a state. Those who seek asylum into Europe face European duties that greatly burden their lives and frustrate their plans. These duties go well beyond the duty to respect the decisions of officials as to the relations of persons *within* the jurisdiction. Moreover, such legal obligations are a regular feature of all immigration rules of most, if not all, states. All foreigners have the legal duty to comply with the immigration laws of the chosen host states even where they remain in their own state. They have this obligation, for example, when they go to an embassy or consulate in order to apply to be issued with an entry visa. The laws of the host state seem to apply to them immediately, both legally and morally. The law applies in exactly the same way that it applies to citizens, that is, through similar procedures about rights of appeal, due process or discrimination.

In those cases the outsider, just like Locke's alien who is 'living quietly', may be taken to consent to the process, merely by applying. He is then morally under a political obligation (if we take this consent to be a general consent to all the institutions of the host state). But this leaves open the case of the person not applying at all and choosing to enter *illegally*. This person by definition refuses to consent to any laws and to any institutions. And if we take consent to be the defining criterion of political obligation, then the illegal entrant rules out this ground of obligation by his actions. He seems thus to escape moral obligation. The same must apply to the criterion of 'fair play'. Here is then a paradoxical conclusion of the 'consent' and 'fair play' theories as they apply to aliens. As long as the foreigner refuses to comply with the domestic rules and refuses to derive any 'privileges and protection' or other benefits from the state's law, he avoids being under political obligation. The more of an outlaw he becomes, the less he is bound. Both consent and fair play fail to explain, thus, the ordinary way in which immigration (and other) laws apply extra-territorially in the normal case, even against those who refuse to consent or cooperate.

As it stands, Waldron's argument does not help us explain these non-voluntary obligations. Immigration obligations are not just cases of undermining the institutions of the host state for fun, which is the example used by Waldron, but something far more substantial. We must now return to the idea of special ties. Why does Waldron draw a distinction between duties of citizenship and duties not to undermine a legal order? Waldron's reluctance to recognize any more extensive duties on the part of foreigners is related to the argument he gives for the legitimacy of institutions. Legitimacy responds to a principle of salience. The justice of a set of existing institutions is not enough for the duties it claims on individuals. The legitimacy of a set of institutions needs a particular basis, not merely an abstract justification. On the basis of this point, Waldron argues that for each person there must be *one* salient civil condition that generates the duties of citizenship. There must be only one such civil condition that creates a special tie that triggers the full natural duty of justice, because if there were more than one, then the purpose of the state's institutions in guiding action and achieving coordination would be frustrated. Given the pluralism of views about justice and the partiality we all show to our own causes, we must have in place a single system of institutions attempting to bring about justice. Waldron therefore argues that legitimacy must be exclusive in the following sense:

> What must be established is that there is a good reason to recognize *this* organization, as opposed to any rival organization, as *the one* to do justice in the given territory or with regard to the claims that are at issue. To the extent that such reasons exist, the organization is 'legitimate.' Legitimacy, then, is an exclusive characteristic: only one organization may be legitimate with regard to a given set of claims or with regard to the issues of justice arising in a given territory.[37]

This is an argument for the moral relevance of citizenship. If legitimacy has to be territorial, then there ought to be a distinction between insiders and outsiders. Without it, the idea of a single dominant or exclusive political power over a certain and determinate group of persons cannot work. Hence we assess the salience of institutions over a determinate group over a determinate place. We are thus able to give judgment on its legitimacy for that time and place. If it is legitimate, then the insiders, the citizens, have rights and duties appropriate to their membership.

Nevertheless, Waldron's argument does not even explain why the outsiders have even the minimum duty 'not to undermine' the relations of justice that apply among insiders. To accommodate it, Waldron abandons the general strategy of a natural duty and resorts to a consequentialist argument. He writes: '[this principle], is entirely consequentialist in conception. The claim made in its behalf will be that everyone should recognize that there is value in justice being done, even when they are not those among whom it is being done in this particular instance. For that reason, they should refrain from interfering with it.'[38] But this is surprising. The argument appears to be that the internal procedures of a political community create duties on outsiders even though they do not apply to them (since we have already assumed that they have a 'limited range' which excludes them). Waldron writes: 'When C upsets the distribution between A and B, the *result* is injustice even though C's action is not itself a violation of [a principle of just conduct] in the way that a greedy encroachment by A would be. C's act is wrong because of its consequences.'[39] But if the principles do not apply to them, they have no reason to consider that the internal allocation of benefits and burdens by

---

[37] Waldron, 'Special Ties and Natural Duties', 22.
[38] Waldron, 'Special Ties and Natural Duties', 17.
[39] Walrdon, 'Special Ties'.

the domestic institution according to domestic principles is just. To assume so is to say that the outsider is morally bound by the internal principles of conduct (for no other consequential loss can be established by the violation of the internal rules, other than some kind of moral 'loss').

Moreover, the consequentialist argument does not sit well with Waldron's general account of natural duty as the ground of political obligation. Consequentialist arguments, as we noted at the start, deny the general duty of justice. They accept only ad hoc obligations, depending on circumstances. If consequentialist arguments about the duty of justice apply to foreigners, why not apply to citizens? Moreover, why is it that the consequentialist argument is to consider the welfare of the insiders alone? After all, the insiders will most certainly be outnumbered by the outsiders so that the aggregate interests must tilt the balance the other way. It is very hard to limit the duty in the way Waldron does, on purely consequentialist grounds. It seems, thus, that the real reason is still the natural duty of justice towards the institutions of some states. But how can such a duty apply to outsiders? If the justice of a set of institutions does not create duties to outsiders to subject themselves to it, then it surely cannot create duties 'not to undermine' it. The latter can only follow from the former.

I draw the conclusion that a general argument for political obligation based on the status of citizenship alone fails to give an adequate account of outsiders. And this failure must be a reason to doubt the cogency of the citizenship theory of political obligation as a whole. If political obligation relies on citizenship and exclusivity, as observed by Waldron, then any international obligation seems impossible. For example, in this view the French agents would not owe any moral obligation to the New Zealand authorities. Yet as Waldron notes (and Locke admits) aliens do have moral rights and duties to a state. This commonplace assumption seems inexplicable under the citizenship theory of political obligation.

5 A European Political Order

Could there be a different answer, one concentrating on the ability of the EU to transcend its international origins? The EU has, for example, its own provisions for European Citizenship.[40] Could that change the argument? Could we say that the EU is now an independent political order? This strategy relies on state-based political obligation in a different way. It seeks to show that European Union might itself be the source of the relevant obligation, rather than the States. We are now saying that the states have given way to the new entity, the European Union. Are there any reasons for which the EU succeeds where the separate states fail?

---

[40] See Article 9 TEU and Article 20 TFEU. See also Case C-85/96 *Martinez Sala* [1998] ECR I-2691, Case C-184/99 *Grzelczyk* [2001] ECR I-6193, and Allan Rosas and Lorna Armati, *EU Constitutional Law: An Introduction* (Oxford: Hart, 2010), 128–42.

This strategy may seem hopeless. Political theorists have pointed out that the EU is nowhere near the level of political community required for a democracy or a federal entity.[41] As Professor Anand Menon has summarized, 'Far from being some kind of state in the making, the Union is a tool of existing states'.[42] As we have seen the EU relies on States and not the other way round. Are there not enough examples of unilateral Member State action (in the areas of foreign affairs, security, justice, and economics) that show their continuing political dominance? Not everyone sees it this way. The Court of Justice of the European Union has long spoken of a new legal order and of an autonomous constitutional order. Very recently Advocate General Maduro expressed a similar view in a well-known opinion that the EU Treaties 'have established a "new legal order", beholden to, but distinct from the existing legal order of public international law. In other words, the Treaty has created a municipal legal order of trans-national dimensions, of which it forms the "basic constitutional charter".'[43] But if the Treaty has created a 'municipal' legal order, it has then replaced the municipal legal orders of the Member States.

There are some arguments in support of this strategy. The European Union has its own citizenship. It has its own decision-making mechanisms, which as we noted above, create regulations and directives with direct effect and supremacy. The Commission takes executive decisions, sometimes with huge importance as in competition and state aids. The Court of Justice is an independent court of law. So there are in place at least the building blocks of a federal system that invite the thought that the EU creates political obligation by itself. Such a system remains incomplete, in that the EU relies on the administrative and judicial systems of the Member States for all its functions. Yet, what exists may be sufficient for citizenship.

This argument, however implausible its factual assumptions, appears to solve some of the puzzles of the earlier one, in that it shows how in principle European political obligation could be conceived. But it does not solve all the difficulties. The first problem is that for the argument to work, the EU has to effectively replace all the Member States as the salient political institution. It has to be seen as a successor state and legal order, if its claim to political obligation can be legitimate. This follows from the nature of legitimacy as explained above. Once we draw a distinction between the abstract justification of a set of institutions and its particular legitimacy for a group of people, we must conclude that only one set of political institutions can be legitimate for a given group of people in a given territory at a given time, as Waldron has shown. We are thus left with the impossibility of a dualist answer, namely the position that

---

[41] See Larry Siedentop, *Democracy in Europe* (London: Penguin, 2000), Andrew Moravcsik, 'In Defence of the Democratic Deficit: Reassessing Legitimacy in the European Union' (2002) 40 *Journal of Common Market Studies* 603–24, Alan Milward, *The European Rescue of the Nation State*, 2nd edn (Routledge, 2004), Kalypso Nicolaïdis and Robert Howse (eds), *The Federal Vision: Legitimacy and Levels of Governance in the United States and the European Union* (Oxford: Oxford University Press, 2001).

[42] Anand Menon, *Europe: The State of the Union* (London: Atlantic Books, 2008), 213.

[43] Case C-402/05 P *Yassin Abdullah Kadi v Council of the European Union and Commission of the European Communities* [2008] ECR I-06351.

both the Member States and the EU could be such institutions. If legitimacy is exclusive in this sense, then European Union law and state law cannot be both sources of legitimacy or grounds for political obligation. If they were, they would be rivals and if they were rivals, they would fail to be exclusive. And according to the citizenship theory of political obligation, there cannot be two parallel sources of political obligation for the same place and time.

The argument has further consequences. If only one set of institutions can create political obligation, then no other international set of institutions can create such obligations. So the international courts, for example, or the United Nations Security Council would lack such legitimacy. International institutions cannot create political obligation alongside national institutions. If political obligation is based on the singleness of the political institutions that properly *apply to us*, then any international source of political obligation must be an impossibility. By definition international law assumes that there must be more than one set of sources of legitimate political obligation, namely the states and the existing international institutions. If international political obligation exists, its sources will be the various states of the world and the various international organizations of the world. Exclusivity is not possible.

Mindful of this type of problem, Hans Kelsen argued that the best understanding of law and the legal order is in terms of a 'monist' order, according to which we are to understand the whole of law, domestic and international, as a single entity.[44] Following that kind of argument, we may be drawn to the idea that the only possible avenue for international (and European) obligation is the progressive 'constitutionalization' of international and European law. The closer international law approximates constitutional law, the more legitimate its requirements. This would become both a philosophical position and a policy aim. International law, in order to become more legitimate, ought to be closer to constitutional law. There is a very serious drawback to this position however. There is an inevitable disjunction here. If international law acquires constitutional features and legitimacy, then domestic law will lose these features, and with those, its legitimacy. The issue is one of either/or. The increasing legitimacy of international law will lead to the progressive loss of legitimacy of state law. This argument, in effect, rules out the idea that national and international law can *both* be sources of political obligation. The proponents of this view rarely address these radical and unattractive implications.

An alternative solution, which in a way vindicates monism, is being presented by those defending an instrumentalist view of institutions. For John Tasioulas, no institution creates political obligation independently from the content of its directives.[45] In this sense, Tasioulas dispenses with the idea of political obligation and legitimacy altogether. Instead he proposes that institutions may enjoy 'authority' in the cases where their substantive directives are successful in a certain way. Success is measured

---

[44] Hans Kelsen, *Pure Theory of Law*, Max Knight (trans) (University of California Press, 1967), 328–44.
[45] See John Tasioulas, 'The Legitimacy of International Law' in Besson and Tasioulas (eds), *The Philosophy of International Law*.

by their accuracy in tracking the moral interests that apply to their subjects anyway. In a sense, the legitimate authority is a successful consultancy service. Thus, Tasioulas' account of authority (which is in effect the 'service conception of authority' proposed by Joseph Raz) attributes authority to a person or political body over another person or body, whenever the advisors' directives are more likely to match the correct decisions for the advisee all things considered, than the conclusions the advisee would have reached without deploying any consultancy service at all.[46] The problem with this view is that it makes authority extremely elusive. It allows states to have it. It allows international institutions to have it. But it need not be exclusive. All states or all international entities may enjoy it, at least for a while. Corporations and persons may enjoy it, on the same terms. The argument stops being institutional. In any event, the argument cannot show how any international body can be legitimate or, in Buchanan's phrase, have a 'right to rule'.[47] To have such a right to rule, one needs more than getting the relevant considerations right. Even if it would be good to follow an authority, failing to do so cannot be a duty. Replacing legitimacy with ad hoc authority gives up on the idea of political obligation altogether.

6 The Cosmopolitan Argument

Is there an argument for political obligation that does not proceed from citizenship? We need such an argument in order to make sense of some common-sense beliefs, namely that foreigners are bound by political obligation and that some international entities and EU institutions can be legitimate—or can fail to meet the standards of legitimacy. Citizenship approaches fail to show how those outside the circle of citizenship can be brought under the scope of political obligation or how international institutions can create any true political obligation.

In what follows I wish to defend a different approach. This is the suggestion that political obligation in the cases of international and EU law is not tied to citizenship but is fully *cosmopolitan*. I wish to build on Jeremy Waldron's suggestion that a sufficiently just or simply legitimate state creates moral obligations to everyone. I also wish to rely on the distinction Waldron draws between duties to obey principles of conduct and duties to obey officials administering them. I think that Waldron's argument can be strengthened by a closer look at the overall political arguments made by Rawls and Kant. This new argument shows that political obligation, unlike the obligations of citizenship, is a moral duty that applies universally to all. It can be owed by everyone to any state and to any legitimate international body and institution. The price for this wide scope is paid by the complexity with which, in turn, political

---

[46] See Joseph Raz, *The Authority of Law* (Oxford: Clarendon Press, 1979).

[47] See Buchanan, 'The Legitimacy of International Law' in Besson and Tasioulas (eds). Buchanan's criticism of Tasioulas seems to me entirely parallel to the similar criticism of Raz's view of authority by Stephen Darwall in 'Authority and Reasons: Exclusionary and Second-Personal' (2010) 120 *Ethics* 257–78.

obligation is to be understood. There must be degrees of that obligation and different content to its effects. I wish to distinguish in particular between a natural duty of *jurisdiction* and the natural duty of *civility*. Citizenship should be seen as one central area of political obligation but not its entire domain. Further out from its boundaries, we have duties to comply with some of the requirements emanating from states, but not all. These obligations are to be explained and justified by ordinary moral duties of respect we all owe to each other.

(A) The Duty of Jurisdiction

Waldron writes that 'there is value in justice being done, even when they are not those among whom it is being done in this particular instance'.[48] This seems to me exactly the right way to approach the question. But we must look at the 'justice being done' differently. It need not be justice between two litigants. It may be justice between members of a political community as to the way public force is administered in general. It is justice in the questions of politics, in the way the institutions of the rule of law are being protected and enforced.

Rawls tells us that the natural duty of justice to support legitimate state institutions is separate but on a par with other natural duties, such as the duty of mutual aid, that is, 'the duty of helping another when he is in need or jeopardy, provided that one can do so without excessive risk or loss to oneself', the duty 'not to harm or injure another', and 'the duty not to cause unnecessary suffering'.[49] These are horizontal relations to other persons with whom we come into contact, without having any special relationship with them. These natural duties are moral duties that apply irrespective of one's relationship to a given state. In that sense they are 'natural':

> A further feature of natural duties is that they hold between persons irrespective of their institutional relationships; they obtain between all as equal moral persons. In this sense the natural duties are owed not only to definite individuals, say to those cooperating together in a particular social arrangement, but to persons generally. This feature in particular suggests the propriety of the adjective 'natural'. One aim of the law of nations is to assure the recognition of these duties in the conduct of states.[50]

These duties, Rawls tells us, are owed to every person. But what does this mean in the case of the natural duty of justice to respect the institutions of a foreign state or of international bodies? Rawls does not say much more about it in a *Theory of Justice*.

Kant is clearer. He writes that the civil condition is not simply a union for some common end, but a union which is 'in itself an end' and which is the 'unconditional and first duty in any external relation of people in general, who cannot help mutually affecting one another'.[51] Setting up a commonwealth that complies with the principles

---

[48] Waldron, 'Special Ties', 17.   [49] Rawls, *A Theory of Justice*, 98.   [50] Rawls, *A Theory of Justice*, 99.
[51] Kant, 'On the Common Saying: That May be Correct in Theory, but is of no Use in Practice' in Kant, *Practical Philosophy*, 8: 289 290.

of equal liberty is thus the 'supreme formal condition' (*conditio sine qua non*) of all other external duties, without which no external duty is possible. The principle is necessary and formal because no empirical end can be the focus of a similar agreement: 'for, since people differ in their thinking about happiness and how each would have it constituted, their wills with respect to it cannot be brought under any common principle and so under any external law harmonizing with everyone's freedom'.[52]

The key point of the argument is something emphasized by both Kant and Rawls. Social institutions are entirely human creations. They are not impervious to conscious change. This is why peoples are *responsible* for the basic structure of their own societies and should feel a measure of shame for their failures to make that basic structure at least nearly just. This entails that success in setting up a legitimate basic structure is, conversely, something of value, perhaps something to value more than anything else given how it releases man's creative and moral potential.

A legitimate state is thus an object of moral value because it is created by citizens as co-legislators as a permanent state of affairs. The state is not a set of ephemeral personal encounters, nor is it a contract or a series of contracts. It is meant to be a stable way of living, where we all take our turns as rulers and ruled according to rules of reciprocity. When citizens create a legitimate state in this way they invest it with value, in the same way that an artist creates value in a work of art. Not all such attempts are successful, but they are all valuable. So to say that a civil condition is at least legitimate is to say that it is a partial success in its attempt to set up just institutions. Its value lies not in the goodness of the results it secures, the fact that it perhaps solves our problems or achieves our ends, but in that fact that it is an attempt at securing the rule of law. The value is in what we have been doing, not, strictly speaking. in achieving all our ends. This explains why even imperfect civil conditions have moral value. The value lies in the fact that our collective efforts at legitimacy recognize everyone's equal moral standing. As Rawls and Kant explain, this kind of excellence derives from justice, not goodness, and it is a kind of performance, not a pursuit of any particular end.[53]

Everyone can understand the difficulties and challenges of creating institutions of justice. Because all persons in the world are in the same predicament, burdened by the same passions and weaknesses and aware of the fragility of any political order, all of them understand the difficulties in mustering the self-discipline required for success in setting up a constitution. Aristotle and Plato speak eloquently about the individual virtues required for the excellence of any free state or 'polis', but the modern political philosophers are not unaware of it either. Michael Walzer, for example, has explained that the moral standing of states depends on the political communities that underpin them and on a idea of a 'communal integrity' which 'derives its moral and political force from the rights of contemporary men and women to live as members of a historic

---

[52] Kant, 'On the Common Saying', 8: 290 291.

[53] We could perhaps say that they have 'adverbial' value, as explained by Dworkin in *Justice for Hedgehogs* (Cambridge, Mass.: Harvard University Press, 2011), 88.

community and to express their inherited culture through political forms worked out among themselves'.[54]

This moral standing has been explained by Kant with the metaphor of a tree with its own trunk and roots:

> for a state is not (like the land on which it resides) a belonging (*patrimonium*). It is a society of human beings that no one other than itself can command or dispose of. Like a trunk, it has its own roots; and to annex it to another state as a graft is to do away with its existence as a moral person and to make a moral person into a thing, and so to contradict the idea for the original contract, apart from which no right over a people can be thought.[55]

The metaphor derives its force from Kant's earlier statements that the citizens of a legitimate state have to exhibit the appropriate moral qualities in setting up institutions of the rule of law and due process. If it is legitimate, the state will then apply its public rules through the efforts of those who occupy the offices of government and law.

What does this argument entail for the duties of the alien? When someone who is not a citizen enters a state whose institutions are just or nearly just and which legitimately requires allegiance from its citizens, then he owes them at least minimum recognition of their moral success. He is to address, first of all, the officials of that state, its representatives as it were, with appropriate respect. When these persons address him and ask him to do this or that, they do not speak in their personal capacity. If they are officials, they are speaking in the name of a legitimate state. They are acting not merely on their *personal* reasons but on *public* reasons. Ideally, their decisions and requirements express the 'omnilateral' will of the state they represent. The natural duty of justice entails, conversely, that everyone is to respect these decisions and require-ments as public pronouncements of correctly constituted offices. A duty of justice is thus owed to these individuals, when they so speak. Ignoring the requirements and decisions of such officials would be treating them as if they were not officials at all, but private enforcers. It would imply that the citizens who co-legislated in setting up the offices and appointed the officials achieved nothing. So a refusal to recognize these persons in their public capacity would be tantamount to ignoring the moral value of their collective achievements in having jointly set up a civil condition.

I have outlined a personal duty, a duty of jurisdiction. It is a duty owed primarily to persons who hold office in the name of a community's public law in a legitimate state. The duty of jurisdiction requires us to respect appointed officers in the host state, even though it does not require the full duties of compliance to principles, which applies irrespective of what specific directions the officials address to them, that normally burden the citizens. The duty requires, in effect, to recognize in these officials the moral standing of all the co-legislating citizens and their success in setting up just or

---

[54] Michael Walzer, 'The Moral Standing of States: A Response to Four Critics' (1980) 9 *Philosophy & Public Affairs* (1980) 209–29, at 211.

[55] Kant, Towards Perpetual Peace, 8: 344, in Kant, *Practical Philosophy*, 318.

nearly just institutions. If true, this is a natural duty that binds everyone, irrespective of their actions or the particular way in which they relate to a state. This is why the illegal immigrant cannot avoid moral blame when faced with directions issued by a legitimate state. The duty of jurisdiction exists anyway. It does not depend on him having given his consent or having derived any benefits. We owe such duties of jurisdiction to all states immediately.

The moral basis of jurisdiction, however, has a reciprocal effect. Jurisdiction entails the recognition of reciprocal duties owed by all sates to all persons, citizens, or non-citizens. Kant refers to this as the cosmopolitan right to 'conditions of universal hospitality'. Any foreigner can claim before any state official that they be treated with respect and without violence or mistreatment:

> What he can claim is not the right to be a guest (for this a special beneficent pact would be required, making him a member of the household for a certain time), but the right to visit; this right, to present oneself for society, belongs to all human beings by virtue of the right of possession in common of the earth's surface on which, as a sphere, they cannot disperse infinitely, but must finally put up with being near one another; but originally no one had more right than another to be on a place on the earth.[56]

It is obvious that such a cosmopolitan duty cannot derive from a relation of citizenship. Wherever there is jurisdiction, there ought to be 'hospitality'. The argument is not based on belonging to political community, but on the separate idea of the moral community between all the persons of the world. Our duties are to each other.[57]

(B) A Duty of Civility

Now we need to address the second problem that the citizenship theories were unable to answer. How is it possible that persons or states can owe any political obligation to international entities or international law? The answer must be able to encompass particular decisions of international organizations such as UN Security Council Resolutions, European Union regulations and directives, International Court of Justice judgments, law-making mechanisms such as treaties, customary international law, and even *jus cogens*. We have seen that we cannot transfer the argument about legitimate domestic institution to the international or European domain. The cases are different. So it is obvious that there cannot be a duty of jurisdiction to international entities,

---

[56] Kant, Towards Perpetual Peace, 8: 358, in Kant, PP, 329.

[57] I cannot attempt here to say anything more concrete as to the *content* of these duties and rights, or as to the conditions for the legitimacy of states. Does the duty entail that aliens are to respect everything that the officials require? Obviously not, because there are things that are so extremely wrong, that if the officials of any state required them their whole institutional structure would stop being legitimate. Does the right entail that aliens are to enjoy full equality? The answer seems to me to be no again. Aliens are not to be called to serve in the army, nor are they subject to income tax merely by subjecting themselves to the jurisdiction of a state. They are not citizens. Some equality of treatment is required, but not in everything. But where and how do we draw the line? Here we need further guidance from substantive principles of equality that could possibly determine the relevance of nationality.

since by definition jurisdiction ought to be exclusive. It can only be true for the state where we happen to be. The officials that are to apply the law are state officials according to state public law. And international or European Union law, by recognizing the principle of state sovereignty, does not seek to compete with domestic law. So there cannot be international or European duty of jurisdiction. But this leaves open for a different duty, a duty of civility to the principles and rules of conduct created by international and European Union law.

The key here is again to see this as a problem of the required respect for persons. We saw that a legitimate state has special moral standing because and to the extent to which it sets up institutions guided by just and equal moral concern. But if a state is to recognize the equal moral standing of all persons, it must also at the same time recognize the moral standing of those outside it. They too must at least receive recognition for their efforts to set up legitimate political institutions. This is not an external duty, imposed from outside, after such foreign political entities have been formed, so to speak. It is an internal duty, a duty we owe to other persons. It is a requirement for us and for our state to respect what we owe to each other. To put it another way, our own political institutions cannot be fully just if they are to simply ignore what goes on outside our borders. We have a duty to be prepared to at least recognize and perhaps assist, if we can do with little cost to ourselves other states and their laws in their attempt to satisfy the natural duty of justice. These attempts are objectively valuable, whether they succeed or not. It follows that our state ought to endorse a principle of the mutual recognition of states. Having principles of international law that facilitate this aim is, thus, required by the natural duty of justice. Domestic institutions and rules will always be incomplete without them. So having public international law is a domestic duty of justice, a duty we owe to each other.[58]

How far does this duty go? What does it require? The territorial co-existence of states means both their separateness and mutual dependence. All political communities and all states occupy some territory, effectively a part of the globe. They co-exist with those communities and peoples living beyond their borders to whom they inevitably come into contact. The very nature of borders suggests that no state can ignore these other communities, first, because they pose a potential threat and, second, because they consist of persons with the same moral standing as anyone else. All states are therefore potentially interested in the actions of their neighbours. All states are in this sense mutually dependent and this is why they all arm themselves, organize their defences, and prepare for war. So any state must have a way, a theory, a set of institutions or other public practices, that deal with their borders and their permeability. Every state, if it is to promote institutions of justice, is to be concerned with and

---

[58] A similar argument is made by Leif Wenar who notices that any more directly 'cosmopolitan' argument for the global scope of distributive justice fail to acknowledge the need for principles outlining the rights and duties of states in their mutual relations. In effect, if the scope of justice is the globe, then international law must be replaced by (global) constitutional law—which would rule out treaties, custom, and the other standard sources of international law. See Leif Wenar, 'Why Rawls is not a Cosmopolitan Egalitarian' in Rex Martin and David A Reidy (eds), *Rawls' Law of Peoples: A Realistic Utopia?* (Oxford: Blackwell, 2006), 95–114.

promote peace with its neighbours. Every state must have a foreign policy and send appropriate ambassadors.

A just state must presuppose, at least in principle, the equality of all other states (something captured by the modern idea of state sovereignty in international law). If a state submitted to any international rule which recognized its submissiveness to a stronger neighbour, it would not then enjoy the domestic monopoly of force. Its political institutions would stop being salient for that community. Its own constitution would be undermined as its assurance of enforcement would be conditional on the desires of this powerful neighbour. In that sense, this would not even be a constitution. It follows therefore that international law must in principle be egalitarian in that way, by means of equal and therefore reciprocally limited statehood or 'sovereignty'. This is the only way in which a legitimate state can occupy its place in the world without ignoring the moral standing of all other people and without having its own moral standing being ignored.

This argument shows that the just *domestic* civil condition needs such common or agreed rules that deal with foreign states and foreign nationals with mutual respect, that is, as equals. If states are to be equal, then international law must recognize state consent as one of its organizing principles. But it must also follow that one of the presuppositions of an egalitarian international law is the moral equality of all *persons* and not just states, something which itself can become the subject matter of an international law of human rights. These are very general principles, whose details of course will have to be filled out, just like the details of an egalitarian constitution need to be filled out by constitution-making, legislation, and adjudication.[59] But they show how the justice of the domestic constitution and the framework of international law are elements of the same project of justice. We cannot achieve one without the other.

So the argument entails that every state and every person has reasons to participate in the creation of international law. They must support rules of conduct that cover three dimensions. First they must concern relations between states, that is, public international law. Second, they must regulate relations between states and the citizens of other states, that is, 'cosmopolitan law', including refugee law. Third, they must set up rules about the minimum rules governing relations between states and their own

---

[59] And the most taxing duty of this specification is the determination of relations with states that are not legitimate. How are just states to treat unjust states or even barbaric regimes? This is a highly contested subject of international justice. Public international law has adopted so far a most cautious or conservative stance. It does not use internal political justice as a test for international recognition or legitimacy. If what we have said above is correct, this position is unjustifiable (and to some extent contradicts other parts of international law, such as human rights law or the statute of the international criminal court). See the pertinent comments by Allen Buchanan, *Justice, Legitimacy and Self-Determination: Moral Foundations for International Law* (Oxford: Oxford University Press, 2003). On the other hand, international law is not an independent constitutional order and its tools are limited. States are supposed to be self-governing. Peace and stability is unusually important. As in all public political decisions (where we make decisions that affect the lives of thousands or millions of others) the consequences on others matter much more than the consequences on us. The difficulties are here genuine and deep, because policy and principle are inextricably tied together. This is bound to be an area of great controversy for years to come.

citizens, that is, a law of human rights. These are three different subject matters that are actually currently covered by different areas of international law. Moreover, all three dimensions are covered by European Union law, which includes principles about the relations between the states and the competences of the Union, principles about the rights of citizens vis-à-vis Member States other than their own (for example, free movement rights) and principles about the minimum rules of public law (for example, human rights). So in this account, European Union law is just a special case of international law.

By recognizing the equal statehood of all other states alongside itself, a state recognizes the legitimacy of each one of these states as a subject of international law. It also recognizes the, in principle, symmetrical citizenship rights and duties of all other foreign nationals. In that sense it grants to their statehood and citizenship its own recognition and approval. So the citizenship of any person is, first, a matter of its domestic law, but also the result of the mutual agreement of all other states to respect it. The constitutions of all the states of the world are in a way exclusive, in setting out the criteria for citizenship, but also overlapping and complementary in recognizing the effects of citizenship in their own jurisdiction. Citizenship is therefore by definition a cosmopolitan event, a joint creation of all the constitutions in the world, both of one's own state which grants it but also of all the other states that recognize it. And statehood is equally cosmopolitan. It is created jointly. A state is not fully independent unless it is so recognized by all others and unless it recognizes all others. In this sense, the sovereignty of states or their statehood can only be the joint creation of all civil conditions in the world. Just like property in the domestic case, statehood is a rule of mutual respect. The same must apply to citizenship.

But similarly any treaty in public international law is equally a cosmopolitan event. All citizens of all participating states—and perhaps all citizens of all states, to the extent that the treaty binds them by reason of territory or subject matter—have a moral duty to respect the treaties that have freely and validly been entered into. This begins to explain the moral value of the treaties setting up the European Union. The moral value derives from the moral argument for the legitimacy of international law as an abstract scheme of principles of conduct. We do not need anything stronger than this fundamental premise. If the duty of civility exists for international law, then the EU treaties can be seen to create political obligation simply as treaties of public international law.

This argument is based on the moral force of international law, as one further dimension of human attempt to live side by side with other persons, while complying with the requirements of justice.[60] This is perhaps why Rawls says that the first familiar and traditional principle of justice among free and democratic peoples is that 'peoples are free and independent, and their freedom and independence are to be respected by

---

[60] For an excellent account of the Kantian moral argument for international law, to which my account owes a great debt and to some extent reproduces, see Amanda Perreau-Saussine, 'Immanuel Kant on International Law' in Besson and Tasioulas (eds), *The Philosophy of International Law*, 53.

other peoples'.[61] Kant, like Rawls, concludes that perpetual peace does not need a world state, but the 'federalism of free states' that come together voluntarily in creating a league of nations.[62] Just like the duty of jurisdiction and the right to hospitality, the duty to set up appropriate institutions of international law is a moral requirement. When this duty of setting up international principles of conduct is appropriately exercised, then persons will have a natural duty of civility towards them. The argument proceeds in exactly the same way as in the case for domestic laws.

The moral argument I have outlined creates a justification for some familiar institutions of public international law; for example, the idea of equal sovereign states, the international treaties on human rights and refugee law. It rules out, however, institutions of international law that seek to replace those of the domestic constitution, either through arrangements of dependency or colonization. Such intervention could only be justified in cases where the domestic institutions have failed and the legitimate state has disappeared (perhaps under an authoritarian dictatorship or through civil war). But they would not obtain where the state is legitimate or approximately just. This explains why the arguments for the unconditional supremacy of EU law over national law must be suspect. European Union law, as a creation of international law, finds its inherent limits in the constitutional structures of legitimate or nearly just states. The jurisdiction or powers of EU institutions are in fact delegated powers from states. Their limited scope is outlined in the treaties as supplementary to those of the Member States. EU powers complement and do not antagonize state jurisdiction.[63]

7 What European Political Obligations Do We Have?

Is this argument enough to create political obligation for the current institutions of European Union law? Does it help us answer the question we put at the start regarding the asylum seekers A and B? As we saw above, justification is not enough for legitimacy. We must explain how institutions are justified as abstract objects, but we must also explain how they apply to each person here and now. What kind of special tie can be required for this type of political obligation? The problem is, in my view, exactly the parallel to the domestic case, as identified by Waldron. The abstract justification of international law as an order of principle is not enough by itself to render any treaties legitimate for us. The legitimacy of EU law must depend on a special tie between the institutions that determine its content and the person to whom

---

[61] John Rawls, *The Law of Peoples* (Cambridge, Mass.: Harvard University Press, 1999), 37.

[62] Kant, Towards Perpetual Peace, 8: 354, in Kant, PP, 326.

[63] For a more detailed analysis of this point see Pavlos Eleftheriadis, 'The Structure of European Union Law' (2010) 12 *Cambridge Yearbook of European Legal Studies* 121–50.

they apply. So it may be that EU law of our own day may turn out to be illegitimate, if the conditions we have identified are not met.

We must now take into account the fact that European Union law, just like international law, does not have, strictly speaking, its own jurisdiction. It does not compete with states as orders of public law, that is, schemes of law application, adjudication, and enforcement. And because EU law does not compete with any state legal order, it can co-exist with all of them without contradiction. So the concrete way in which we may or may not be subject to EU law has to be through national officials and institutions. The relevant officials are—in principle—our own state officials. So as long as we are under the jurisdiction of a state that participates in the relevant structures of EU law by being a Member State, we are under the scope of EU law. It does not actually matter which one it is, foreign or domestic, as long as the relevant jurisdiction is properly part of EU law. Both citizens and travellers are equally subject to EU law if they owe a duty of jurisdiction to a Member State of the EU.

It follows that the immigration controls that we started our discussion with will be morally binding on those seeking illegal entry, if those persons are bound by a duty of jurisdiction to a Member State of the EU.[64] What is their special tie? It is the fact that they have left the state of their citizenship and entered the jurisdiction of another state. Once a person leaves the protection of his or her own state, they leave behind some of the duties and privileges of citizenship and submit themselves to a new jurisdiction.[65] The fact of travel (or indeed the intention of travel) is the factual connection, the 'special tie' mentioned by Waldron, with the institutions of the foreign jurisdiction.

This argument from the duty of jurisdiction presents the whole problem in a different light, which avoids the puzzles created by citizenship. It offers the following answer to Jeff McMahan's objection of 'collectivism'. McMahan had complained that the establishment of political relations among one group of people could not create duties on outsiders.[66] But the state is not just a set of agreed relations for those involved in them. The state is a set of impersonal political institutions consisting of both offices of decision making and specific conditions of action. The content of political institutions is never merely domestic. Both constitutional law and international law are essential for satisfying the natural duties of justice.

The same argument provides the answer to Murphy. His objection was that the 'political view of the state' personified the state and gave a false account of

---

[64] For a general discussion of the right to move across borders see Michael Walzer, *Spheres of Justice* (New York: Basic Books, 1983), 31–63, Joseph H Carens, 'Aliens and Citizens: The Case for Open Borders' (1987) 49 *Review of Politics* 251–73, Onora O'Neill, 'Identities, Boundaries and States' in O'Neill, *Bounds of Justice* (Cambridge: Cambridge University Press, 2000), 168–85.

[65] We could even say that by crossing the border, we *consent* to it or indeed take advantage of the openness of borders which is a result of international law. Here both the theory of natural duty and the theory of consent of fair play may be engaged. In some senses, therefore, international obligation has more solid foundations than citizenship.

[66] Jeff McMahan, 'Laws of War' in Samantha Besson and John Tasioulas (eds), *The Philosophy of International Law* (Oxford: Oxford University Press, 2010), 493, at 503.

international responsibility for actions of governments.[67] Yet the cosmopolitan argument offers a different picture. Murphy is right that a despotic government is illegitimate and therefore fails to morally bind its citizens. But this entails the converse result for legitimate government. By electing or otherwise appointing a government, we choose officeholders who will run our political and legal affairs. The role of such offices includes the maintenance of foreign relations and the responsibility for those foreigners that happen to arrive—for whatever reason—at our jurisdiction. Hence, when a government engages in internationally unlawful action it is not merely violating international rules. It is also violating domestic rules, duties that citizenship requires everyone to respect. In a way there is no difference in moral standing or in source between national and international law and in that sense monism is true.

It is thus also true, as Tasioulas insists, that there is nothing special about international duties. International law is part of the duties of citizenship. But monism is false if it insists on the complete analogy between the domestic legal order and the international legal order. There cannot be such an analogy. The domestic legal order is one where public rules and principles are given effect through a complete set of institutions of enforcement and adjudication (or institutions of jurisdiction). International law is not a legal order in that sense. It lacks means and principles of enforcement and adjudication, for which it always relies on state institutions. It therefore makes no assurance of public enforcement of any public rules concerning enforcement and adjudication. Strictly speaking there cannot be an international legal order comparable to the domestic legal order. International law has no parallel process to the domestic setting up of an order of public rules and institutions. It promises no institutional enforcement and provides for no such procedures. International and European institutions complement and do not seek to replace those of the states.

In this sense, the European Union institutions are in a better shape than international institutions as a whole. All Member States of the EU are good constitutional democracies with functioning institutions. They entered into the EU treaties wholly voluntarily. Membership was approved by all other Member States' parliaments. All Member States respect international duties and duties of hospitality. Allowing them some margin for error, we must say that they are all nearly just or legitimate states in the relevant sense. So we may say that if any international laws are legitimate, then the EU treaties must be some of them. It follows, therefore, that in our example the person who faces removal according to the Dublin II regulation, may indeed have a duty of jurisdiction, but not a duty of civility to the host state. His rights are determined by EU laws as well as international laws, since they are part of legitimate international law and institutions that apply to him. In principle, A owes some political obligation to the officials as a matter of the duty of jurisdiction. Of course, the duty is only a prima facie one. The concrete judgment must be made against the background of the other laws that apply to him and the facts of the case. We may say the same thing about B. There

---

[67] Murphy, 'International Responsibility', 313.

is nothing unique in the fact that the relevant decision in this case is reached by the European Court of Justice. That court is a legitimate court under the treaties. Its powers have been delegated by the Member States. Although the Court is not an institution of the host state, it is an institution properly endorsed by that state according to the principles of public international law. Both B's duty of jurisdiction and his duty of civility to international law require him to obey its procedures. Because and to the extent that the relevant cosmopolitan conditions are met, we should conclude that the measures imposed by EU law and enforced by the state officials can be valid sources of political obligation.

Yet we must also be clear about what the argument does not show. The duties of jurisdiction owed by A and B are not owed strictly to the EU institutions themselves. They are owed to the host states, the jurisdictions where A and B happen to be. Since the EU itself relies exclusively on the civil authorities of the Member States, the officials responsible for the application of the relevant laws are those of the host states, as a result of the EU's institutional division of labour. The foreigners that happen to be in the host states that are members of the EU must comply with it because they are within the jurisdiction of those states. It is jurisdiction that takes them into the scope of EU law in the first place. Political obligation, however, is only a moral preliminary. To say that these institutions are in principle legitimate, does not determine fully the justice of the actual decisions they reach. Legitimate institutions may reach unjust results. In fact Aristotle's point starts with precisely this assumption. Legitimacy is not full justice. Justice is satisfied not only when the institutions are appropriately set up but also when they act with appropriate regard to the merits of the case. It is possible, thus, that the decisions of legitimate institutions may end up being unjust for breaching the universal duty of hospitality in the relevant case. Resolving the issue of political obligation clarifies, therefore, the moral responsibilities of the Member States and European institutions, but it is only a preliminary to justice.

8

Constitutionalism in the European Union

Pipe Dream or Possibility?

W.J. Waluchow*

PREAMBLE

The peoples of Europe, in creating an ever closer union among them, are resolved to share a peaceful future based on common values.

Conscious of its spiritual and moral heritage, the Union is founded on the indivisible, universal values of human dignity, freedom, equality and solidarity; it is based on the principles of democracy and the rule of law. It places the individual at the heart of its activities, by establishing the citizenship of the Union and by creating an area of freedom, security and justice.

The Union contributes to the preservation and to the development of these common values while respecting the diversity of the cultures and traditions of the peoples of Europe as well as the national identities of the Member States and the organisation of their public authorities at national, regional and local levels; it seeks to promote balanced and sustainable development and ensures free movement of persons, goods, services and capital, and the freedom of establishment....

1 Introduction

So begins the Charter of Fundamental Rights of the European Union,[1] drafted and officially proclaimed in 2000, and given strengthened legal status by the Treaty of

* McMaster University, Hamilton, Ontario, Canada. I wish to thank Matthew Grellette, Julie Dickson, and Alison Young, for their very helpful comments on earlier drafts of this chapter.
[1] Hereinafter referred to as the Charter.

Lisbon in December 2009.[2] Under the newly adopted Charter, there is now no question but that EU bodies must act and legislate consistently with the Charter's various provisions, and the EU's courts, most notably the European Court of Justice, are explicitly empowered to strike down official EU actions that contravene it.[3] Importantly, the Charter also applies to the official actions of Member States, but only when they are acting within the scope of EU law.[4] In other words, EU courts are not legally empowered to rule on questions concerning the compatibility of EU Charter provisions with the strictly domestic law of a Member State.

Despite these important restrictions on its force and effect, the legal significance of the Charter is not to be underestimated. As judged by its preamble, it seeks to affirm and render more firmly enforceable a joint commitment among EU Member States to a very wide range of common or shared values and principles. These shared norms are said to be founded on 'the universal values of human dignity, freedom, equality and solidarity' and, together with a basic commitment to 'the principles of democracy and the rule of law', serve to establish the EU as a community legally committed to the enforcement of fundamental human rights. The Charter also seeks to affirm a shared commitment that exhibits two further, crucial features: (a) respect for the diversity of the cultures and traditions of the various peoples and nations of Europe, their distinct identities, and 'the organisation of their public authorities at national, regional, and

---

[2] Although the Charter is not, technically, part of the Treaties [The Treaty on European Union (TEU) and the Treaty on the Functioning of the European Union (TFEU)] Article 6 (1) TEU makes it clear that its provisions are to have the same legal effect as articles of the Treaties themselves. '1. The Union recognizes the rights, freedoms and principles set out in the Charter of Fundamental Rights of the European Union of 7 December 2000, as adapted at Strasbourg, on 12 December 2007, which shall have the same legal value as the Treaties'. In Case C-555/07 *Kükükdeveci v Swedex GmbH & Co.* (Grand Chamber judgment, 19 January 2010) the Court of Justice also mentions this point.

[3] In a sense this is nothing new. EU judges have always been empowered to enforce general principles of Union law, and the Charter has for some time been recognized by the Court of Justice as a source of EU law. Furthermore, the Court of Justice judges have also been viewed as empowered to hold Member States and EU institutions to general human rights principles to which Member States committed themselves as signatories of various international human rights treaties. What may have changed is the way in which these commitments are now enforced. As the Charter has the same legal effect as provisions of the TEU and TFEU, contravening a rights provision of the Charter can now be regarded as 'an infringement of the Treaties or of any rule of law relating to their application' (TFEU, Article 263) . It is also important to bear in mind the following. As with many similar instruments, the EU Charter recognizes that the rights and freedoms it affirms are not absolute. On the contrary, a Charter right or freedom may sometimes be overridden or outweighed by competing considerations, including other applicable rights and freedoms affirmed by the Charter and various interests of vital public importance, such as national security or public health. They must also be interpreted and applied with due respect for analogous decisions taken by the various institutions found within the various Member States. More on this later.

[4] In the negotiations leading up to the signing to the Treaty of Lisbon, Poland and the United Kingdom managed to secure a protocol to the treaty concerning the application of the Charter in their respective Member States. 'Protocol: On the Application of the Charter of Fundamental Rights of the European Union to Poland and the United Kingdom' Treaty of Lisbon. Previously, (in October 2009) EU leaders agreed to amend the protocol at the time of the next accession treaty so as to include the Czech Republic as well. It appears as though the aim of these protocols is to grant immunity against claims based on Charter infringement to those Member States to whom it applies. It remains to be seen, of course, how the Court of Justice will interpret this document, and what its precise legal effect will be.

local levels', and (b) respect for the wide range of constitutional traditions and international obligations shared by Member States, the Treaty on European Union (TEU), various other Union Treaties, the European Convention for the Protection of Human Rights and Fundamental Freedoms (ECHR), the Social Charters adopted by the EU and by the Council of Europe, and the case law of both the Court of Justice and the European Court of Human Rights (ECtHR).[5]

These special, somewhat unique features of the Charter and its context, raise a plethora of issues, many having to do with the complex, somewhat bewildering range of different duties and responsibilities now more firmly assigned to the various courts and governments bound by the Charter. For instance, how are decisions of the Court of Justice under the Charter to be reconciled with analogous decisions by the ECtHR under the ECHR and its overlapping (or at the very least similar) provisions? How are governments and courts to deal with a scenario in which a decision by one court requires a course of action that a decision by the other explicitly prohibits? These questions, difficult though they are, are bound to become even more difficult when, as is planned under the Lisbon amendments, the EU itself, *qua* international organization, accedes to the ECHR, thereby becoming the first non-state signatory to it and non-state member of the Council of Europe (COE).[6] Such questions of institutional design, and overlapping and perhaps competing jurisdictions, I will leave to others more qualified than me to address.[7] Instead, I will focus on a number of different, perhaps even more fundamental, questions which emerge quite explicitly with the formal adoption of the Charter but which have been lingering in the background for some time now—since at least 1950 when, in the Preamble to the ECHR, the founding members of the Council of Europe signed on to the following noble, but ambitious moral project:

> *Reaffirming their profound belief in those Fundamental Freedoms which are the foundation of justice and peace in the world and are best maintained on the one hand by an effective political democracy and on the other by a common understanding and observance of the Human Rights upon which they depend;*
>
> *Being resolved, as the Governments of European countries which are like-minded and have a common heritage of political traditions, ideals, freedom and the rule of law to take the first steps for the collective enforcement of certain of the Rights stated in the Universal Declaration.*

---

[5] Charter, preamble. This commitment to respecting diversity within the EU parallels the 'margin of appreciation' doctrine which has figured so prominently in the case law of the ECHR. I will have more to say about this doctrine, and its analogous application within the EU, later, in the final section of this chapter.

[6] TEU, Article 6(2). Arrangements have yet to be made for a non-state body to accede to the Convention.

[7] On the conceptual puzzles that arise from such overlapping, and often competing, jurisdictions, see Julie Dickson's contribution to this volume, as well as the contribution by Culver and Guidice. See also, S Douglas-Scott, 'A Tale of Two Courts: Luxembourg, Strasbourg and the Growing European Human Rights Acquis' [2006] CMLR 43, 629–65, and more generally, M Giudice and K Culver, *Legality's Borders* (Oxford: Oxford University Press, 2010).

Have agreed as follows:
ARTICLE 1
The High Contracting Parties shall secure to everyone within their jurisdiction the rights and freedoms defined in Section I of this Convention . . . .

The rights referred to in Article 1 of the ECHR include, of course, many of those which later were viewed by the Court of Justice as foundational to, and enforceable within, the EU[8] and which have now been explicitly reaffirmed, in canonical form, in its Charter: freedom of religion, expression, association, the right to life and liberty, and so on. This long-standing commitment to the observance of a set of 'common values and principles', the shared 'spiritual and moral heritage' of EU Member States, brings to the forefront a number of related questions that can be summarized as follows:

(i) What precisely is the *nature* or ontological status of these common values and principles to which the European Charter makes reference? What kinds of norms are these?

(ii) What are the basic processes or procedures by which their identity and requirements can be ascertained?[9]

In other words, is it really possible to envisage, let alone put into practice, a set of values that is both shared or common, and yet at the same time rooted in, and sensitive to, the complex, multi-dimensional, and perhaps inconsistent hodge-podge of elements, and variable practices and official decisions, cited in the Charter's preamble—the constitutional traditions and international obligations common to Member States, the EU Treaties in their various manifestations, the plethora of other treaties into which Member States have entered, the ECHR, the case law of both the Court of Justice and the ECtHR, and so on? Is it remotely possible to envisage such a set of 'common values' with any degree of plausibility, especially given the kinds of questions to which the EU Charter, given its very nature as a rights-affirming document, inevitably gives rise— deeply *moral questions* concerning the meaning and import of such things as human dignity, respect for private and family life, freedom of thought, conscience, and religion, freedom of expression and information, the right to life, to integrity of the person, the right not to be subjected to inhuman or degrading treatment or punishment, and the right to property, and to liberty and security? Does its Charter represent little more than a pipe dream, a noble, well-intentioned fantasy that is ultimately destined to failure, cynicism, and possibly the bubbling up of the kinds of 'irreconcilable differences' that, in the marital law of many jurisdictions, often lead to divorce? In short, has the EU bitten off more than it can possibly chew?

---

[8] See eg Case 11/70 *International Handelsgesellschaft mbH v Einfuhr* [1970] ECR 1125, where the Court of Justice asserted that the protection of human rights is an integral element of EU law. In Case 36/75 *Rutilli* [1975] ECR 1219, the Court of Justice further declared that the various rights enshrined in the ECHR are also integral to EU law.

[9] For reasons of verbal economy, and unless the context clearly suggests otherwise, I will henceforth use the phrase 'common values' to refer to the array of values, principles, and basic moral convictions (supposedly) shared among the nations and peoples of the EU and to which reference is made both in the ECHR and the Charter.

My aim in this chapter is to address this troubling family of questions. More specifically, I will attempt to argue for a particular conception or understanding of the moral norms to which a legal instrument like the EU Charter makes reference. I will also attempt to tease out the kinds of considerations upon which we should be focusing if we are to address, in a meaningful way, the question of whether the *Charter* has any chance of meeting the hopes and expectations of its drafters and supporters, to entrench legally a commitment to the rights and freedoms it enumerates. In so doing, I will be drawing on theoretical machinery I have developed elsewhere in response to analogous complaints concerning the feasibility—and moral and political desirability—of *national* charters of rights; eg, the United States Bill of Rights and the Canadian Charter of Rights and Freedoms.[10]

One prominent criticism often made against such national, constitutional instruments is that their advocates invariably ignore, or at the very least seriously underplay, the significance of, what legal philosopher Jeremy Waldron has dubbed 'the circumstances of politics'. These consist in the 'felt need among the members of [pluralistic societies] for a common framework or decision or course of action on some matter, even in the face of disagreement about what that framework, decision or action should be'.[11] Within the context of the constitutional law of a single, pluralistic, national community such as the United States, the United Kingdom (with its Human Rights Act), or Canada, such disagreement is a well-established fact of life; explicit agreement on right answers to the fundamental moral questions posed by a national charter of rights is all but impossible to find in most Western nations. This fact leads some to claim that all talk of a shared commitment to a set of core values and principles, which a nation's constitutional charter of rights can be said to represent, amounts to nothing but the rhetoric of the deluded—or the rhetoric of those willing to betray their democratic heritage and turn important questions of fundamental moral principle over to a group of judicial elites who are, for some unexplained reason, thought better able to discern the moral truth lying behind the fog of uncertainty and rampant disagreement.

If all this is true at the national level, then one might reasonably ask, what hope is there when we turn to the EU where, instead of one national community, we have a collection of no fewer than twenty-seven national communities, each with its own (though no doubt overlapping with the rest) distinct moral, political, and constitutional traditions, and the various institutions to which that community looks for authoritative guidance and legal settlement? I say 'no fewer than twenty-seven' because the number could, in fact, be much higher. For example, even though the United Kingdom constitutes one Member State, it is arguably composed of at least four

---

[10] See eg W Waluchow *A Common Law Theory of Judicial Review: The Living Tree* (Cambridge: Cambridge University Press, 2006); W Waluchow, 'Constitutional Morality and Bills of Rights' in G Huscroft (ed), *Expounding the Constitution* (Cambridge: Cambridge University Press, 2008), 65–92; and W Waluchow, 'The Neutrality of Charter Reasoning' in J Ferrer and JJ Moreso (eds), *Neutrality and Legal Theory* (Madrid: Marcial Pons, forthcoming).

[11] J Waldron, *Law and Disagreement* (Oxford: Oxford University Press), 102.

distinct, and in many ways different, national communities: those of England, Scotland, Wales, and Northern Ireland. *In Re P and others*[12] the House of Lords suggested that Northern Ireland could well have a different human rights culture than England, meaning that what might contravene an ECHR Convention right, as socially and legally understood in England, may not contravene the same Convention right, as it is understood and practised in Northern Ireland. Analogous things might be said with respect to many other Member States, for example, Belgium and Spain (to name but two), and the rights recognized in the EU *Charter*. In this rather complex array of differing contexts and circumstances, there may be even less explicit agreement on the relevant, fundamental questions of political morality than one finds in single nation-states. It might seem nothing short of lunacy, therefore, to propose the possibility that there could be anything approaching the basis for a shared commitment to the particular set of rights, freedoms, and fundamental moral convictions that the EU Charter might meaningfully be said to represent. But courting a charge of lunacy and arguing in favour of such a possibility is exactly what I intend to do. To be clear, my aim is not to support the conclusion that there is less overt disagreement in the EU than meets the eye. My methods are philosophical, not sociological. Rather, I want to say some things about what it might mean to say the following: even if the EU is properly characterized as a community in which deep disagreement on questions of political morality exists, it can nonetheless be true that the EU and its Member States share a set of common values (and concrete moral conclusions drawn from them) to which each has meaningfully committed itself—values to which the EU Charter makes reference and which its authors intended to place front and centre in the minds of those required to exercise public power in accordance with its moral demands.

2 Morality and Charters of Rights[13]

So our primary question is this: to what kind of norms does the EU Charter make reference when it states that 'Everyone has the right to liberty and security of person' (Article 6), or that 'Everyone has the right to freedom of thought, conscience and religion' (Article 10)? Presumably, the norms in question are norms of political morality; more specifically, the morality that concerns the duties and responsibilities that EU governments, agencies, and officials have when acting with the scope of EU law in regard to individuals (and groups of individuals) who reside within the EU.[14] Or putting it the other way, they are norms concerning the correlative rights, liberties, and

---

[12] House of Lords Session, 2007–08 [2008] UKHL 38.

[13] Some of what follows is adapted from my 'Constitutional Morality and Bills of Rights' in G Huscroft, (ed), *Expounding the Constitution: Essays in Constitutional Theory* (Cambridge: Cambridge University Press, 2008), 65–92, and my more recent 'Neutrality and Charter Reasoning' in J Ferrer and JJ Moreso (eds), *Neutrality and Legal Theory* (Madrid: Marcial Pons, forthcoming).

[14] This includes the governments, agencies, and officials of individual Member States, as well as those that pertain to the EU itself, eg, the European Parliament or the European Economic and Social Committee.

privileges of the latter against the former. But what is the ontological status of these norms of political morality? What kind of things are they? Are they the norms moral philosophers often dispute about, that is, ideal moral norms that purport to be universally valid, rationally justified, perhaps even 'objectively true', much as Kant and Plato thought? It is entirely plausible to think that these—I'll call them 'the norms of Platonic morality'—are the intended referent, if only because fundamental rights-affirming instruments are often conceived of in this way and because the Charter's Preamble claims to be recognizing 'indivisible, universal values'.[15] But as we have already seen, the Preamble also claims to be sensitive to the diversity of the cultures and traditions of the peoples of Europe, as well as the national identities of Member States and the organization of their public authorities. In other words, what is being contemplated is a good deal of particularity and, presumably, fully warranted variability or difference. So perhaps what is being recognized are not universal, Platonic moral norms but something more modest; namely, the norms of conventional or positive morality, rooted not in the fabric of the universe and residing quite contentedly in Plato's world of forms unaffected by the messy particularities of real-world law and politics, but in the variable moral beliefs, convictions, practices, and conventions of the EU community and its various constituent Member States. I would like to suggest that it's a little bit of both. What is being recognized—or so I would like to propose and argue—are critically refined, local 'understandings', 'specifications', or 'determinations' of the specific values and principles—the Thomistic 'common notions'—of Platonic morality to which the EU Charter makes reference.[16] This, I shall argue, is not only a plausible way of viewing the Charter and cognate instruments (like the ECHR and the UK's Human Rights Act) it is also one that allows us to deal successfully with a number of persistent worries that often attach to such legal instruments. Let's begin with the worries.

---

[15] A word of caution: in referring to these as norms of Platonic morality, I in no way intend to signal acceptance of Plato's metaphysics, least of all his particular understanding of morality. My intention is simply to take Plato as representing a school of moral philosophy according to which there is a universal, rationally discernible truth of the matter when it comes to questions of moral right and wrong. Anyone who subscribes to this understanding of morality, Kant and Jeremy Bentham included, can be said to subscribe to what I have called 'Platonic morality'.

[16] The same, I would like to suggest, can be said of the norms recognized in the ECHR, although things are quite a bit more complicated given the even wider divergence of understandings of these norms among the various states and sub-communities included within the Council of Europe. Space does not allow me to address this complication fully. Nor will I address any metaphysical questions concerning the identity conditions of communities. I will simply assume that the EU and the Council of Europe represent distinct communities, each of which is composed of, but is not fully reducible to, the various constituent communities which have come together to form these two communities of nations. On Aquinas' theory of 'determination of common notions', see his *Summa Theologica*, I-II, Q 95, AA 1–4. See also, J Finnis, *Natural Law and Natural Rights* (Oxford: Clarendon Press, 1980), 281–90; and W Waluchow, *The Dimensions of Ethics* (Peterborough, Ontario: Broadview Press, 2003), 111–16. The notion of 'determining' or 'specifying' a 'common notion' will be discussed more fully below in Section 7. For now, let me say this. To determine (or specify) a common notion is to choose an understanding of how to comply with a particular value (the common notion) in a scenario whereby a range of acceptable understandings exist, no one of which is uniquely determined by, but each one of which is fully consistent with, the value in question.

Charters of rights are often criticized on the ground that they render the law of a community far too dependent on the subjective moral opinions or predilections of whomever is called on to enforce them. This almost always means judges, most of whom are selected by means other than some form of democratically respectable electoral procedure. Although it is not always so based, this concern is often premised on the implicit assumption that the morality to which charters of rights purport to make reference, and which judges are foolishly expected to discover and apply, is Platonic morality. Since, the critic urges, there is no such morality or we cannot discover and agree on its requirements even if it does exist—witness centuries of dispute about the nature and requirements of morality among moral philosophers, let alone among the wider population—the law ends up depending far too heavily on the subjective, variable, ideologically rooted, moral opinions (and prejudices) of judges. And this cannot possibly be justified, it is claimed, in any society which purports to respect the principles of democracy and the rule of law.

One obvious way round this concern is to suggest that charters of rights need not be taken to refer to Platonic morality, but to the norms of a kind of conventional or positive morality—the morality actually accepted and practised within the relevant population, and whose content a judge can (it might be thought) discover using largely empirical means. The relevant question for a judge, in this alternative, will not be 'What is the ever elusive moral truth on this question?' but rather 'What does my community accept as the moral truth on this ever elusive question?' But this option brings along its own set of difficulties. For instance, discerning the content of positive morality (assuming it exists, about which I'll say something below) is surely not a matter of value-free, empirical discovery. It is risking trouble to suggest that value-free inquiry occurs within the realms of natural science; it is probably sheer foolishness to think that we could have 'pure theory' when the object of discovery is not black holes or the elusive Higgs-boson particle, but the moral views of EU citizens on whether barring a Muslim woman from wearing a face veil when engaged in the practice of teaching primary-school children represents a reasonable limitation on her freedom of religion or expression—a limitation that meets the EU standards of 'proportionality'. If this is true, then 'discovering' the positive morality of the EU community may depend as much on the moral predilections of an interpreter as on any neutral fact of the matter. And if that interpreter ends up being a judge, then we are right back with our concerns about leaving such decisions to the judiciary. Judges end up making the calls on the hard moral questions we and our elected representatives really should be answering instead.

A second equally troublesome difficulty is one already mentioned: the moral disagreement one encounters in pluralistic, multi-cultural communities such as the EU. If moral dissensus is a fact of life in the EU, as it certainly appears to be, then it is far from clear that we could identify a set of norms properly ascribable to the EU community as a whole. If that is so, and if judges in the Court of Justice are being asked to ground their Charter judgments on the norms of positive morality, then presumably they are going to have to pick and choose from among the many options on offer.

If one section of the relevant population thinks one way, say that banning burkas in public space is perfectly acceptable, another strongly disagrees with any such policy, and yet another is wholly indifferent, then the judge is going to have to pick one of the first two perspectives as somehow standing for the community's judgment on the matter.[17] But how could she make such a choice except by relying on her own subjective, moral predilections and preferences as to which view is best? But then we're right back where we started: worried about a legal practice that sees a small group of elite judges deciding the fundamental moral questions that members of a democratic community are supposed to be answering for themselves, in most instances via their elected legislative bodies.

A third possible objection is this. Positive political morality is supposed to be the political morality of 'the community'. But what it really amounts to, practically speaking, is a set of beliefs, norms, and prejudices of the prevailing group(s) within that community, that is, of the *majority*—or perhaps those *minority elites*, eg, the very rich and influential—who happen to enjoy a tight grip on the social and institutional levers of public power. By its very nature, however, a charter of rights is supposed to serve to protect vulnerable minorities and individuals against the errors, prejudices, and excesses of powerful majorities and powerful elites. To view the rights protected by a charter as a function of the moral beliefs of the very majorities and elites against whom protection is thought essential therefore threatens to undermine the very point of having adopted one in the first place.

A fourth, related concern is the degree to which positive moralities are often tinged by, even anchored in, error and misconception. Women have historically been viewed as less 'rational' than men, a conviction shared by philosophical luminaries of no less stature than Aristotle and Kant. People of coloured skin have historically been viewed as less intelligent and mature than whites, as worthy of nothing greater than a state of perpetual servitude. And so on. These moral views, once widely shared among large groups of 'cultured', 'progressive' peoples and societies, and their positive moralities, all rested on patently false factual beliefs. The same is undoubtedly true of other moral views widely currently shared within contemporary societies, although this may, in many instances, become fully apparent only with the benefit of hindsight. In any event, if positive moralities are often based on error and misconception, then one might reasonably ask why judges should look to that source of norms when assessing whether the levers of public power have been exercised in a morally responsible manner? More specifically, what reason could there be to tie their—and our—interpretations of charter rights to such a suspect base? Should we not all be guided by moral truth instead?

So whichever way we turn—Platonic or positive morality—we seem to run into a picture of charters of rights that leads to serious concerns. And, if one's moral and political intuitions suggest that charters of rights can be good things to have, and that

---

[17] On 13 July 2010, France's National Assembly passed a bill banning face-covering veils in all public places. 'French MPs Vote to Ban Islamic Full Veil in Public' <http://www.bbc.co.uk/news/10611398> accessed 1 August 2010, BBC News.

the EU did well in adopting one, then we are going to have to address the serious challenge they pose. That is what I hope to do here. My goal is to sketch a plausible, alternative picture of the morality to which the EU Charter might sensibly be thought to make reference. This morality is not solely the Platonic morality of the philosophers, and though it is in large measure relative to the society(ies) to which it applies and could therefore be viewed as a kind of 'positive morality', it is in no way fully reducible to the moral beliefs and opinions widely shared, at any given point in time, by the majority of people within the EU, or by whatever powerful social and political elites have a firm grip on the levers of public power. Nor is it discoverable using standard methods of social science. Rather, it is a morality which lies somewhere between these two extremes—positive and Platonic morality—combining elements of both. It combines what is normally thought of as positive morality with something along the lines of what HLA Hart termed 'critical morality'. In short, it's positive morality with a critical bite.[18]

3 Two Further Conceptions

So my proposal is that the 'common values' to which the EU Charter makes reference can be viewed as a blend of positive and critical morality that can sensibly be ascribed to the entire EU community. Henceforth I will refer to this morality as the 'EU community's constitutional morality' (EUCCM).[19] Of course, we must not forget that the EU community is made up of a number of smaller units, that is, the various Member States, each with its own possibly distinctive constitutional morality, or moralities.[20] And this will often complicate matters somewhat, especially when, as might have seemed to be the case in *Omega*, the requirements of two moralities diverge.[21] In any event, it is clear that the identity of the relevant community can be a notoriously difficult question—one that can arise in any number of different contexts, not just charters of rights cases. For example, in my country, Canada, Criminal Code provisions are federal in nature. And those governing indecency and obscenity have historically been interpreted in light of what are termed 'community

---

[18] On Hart's distinction between positive and critical morality, see HLA Hart, *Law, Liberty and Morality* (Oxford: Oxford University Press, 1962), 17–24.

[19] The significance of the word 'constitutional' will be explained below.

[20] Whether there is, in a single nation or Member State, something we could meaningfully call that community's constitutional morality is itself open to question. Perhaps, in some Member States, the most we can say that there is a 'community of communities', each with its own distinctive morality, but nothing we could describe as their common, constitutional morality. I will leave this complication aside and assume, for purposes of argument, that each Member State has its own common, constitutional morality understood in a way analogous to the understanding of EU constitutional morality developed herein.

[21] Case C-36/02 *Omega Spielhallen und Automatennaufstellungs GmbH v Oberburger Meisterein der Bundesstadt Bonn* [2004] ECR I-9609. One principal aim of this paper is to explore the sense in which, appearances to the contrary, the decision in *Omega* does not entail that the two moralities in fact diverge from one another. At the very least they did not diverge in a way that threatens the thought that the EU is committed to one and the same set of fundamental Charter rights. More on this, and on the specific facts of *Omega*, later.

standards of tolerance'. But these seem to vary tremendously depending on how one identifies the relevant community.[22] This difficulty is particularly acute within a federal, multicultural, pluralistic society such as Canada. If community standards of tolerance (of obscenity) depend on culture, and the Canadian community includes a plurality of different cultures whose standards lead to significantly different judgments of tolerance, then it may well be a serious mistake to assume that one could somehow discover a single community with a single set of moral norms pertaining to indecency and obscenity which could be said to be recognized or reflected in federal obscenity law. Perhaps, instead, the most that we could find is a collection of different communities, each with its own distinctive culture, and with its own resultant 'community standards of tolerance'. If this is so in a country like Canada, and if positive moralities, like standards of tolerance, are in some way tied to differing cultures, then one might begin seriously to question the possibility that one could somehow discover a common, community morality which we could sensibly attribute to the EU and which could serve as the basis for understanding the EU Charter.

But let's look at all this a bit more carefully. The assumption that there are discoverable norms, properly attributable to a pluralistic, multicultural community like Canada, Spain, the UK, or the EU, may depend on whether or not there is a sufficiently rich overlap in the relevant moral beliefs and norms widely accepted within the various sub-communities in question.[23] It may well be that on at least some of the issues of political morality addressed in the EU Charter there is, in respect of the relevant moralities of the relevant EU countries, something like a Rawlsian 'overlapping consensus'.[24] Rawls explains what he means by this phrase in the following passage:

> There can, in fact, be considerable differences in citizens' conceptions of justice provided that these conceptions lead to similar political judgments. And this is possible, since different premises can yield the same conclusion. In this case there exists what we may refer to as overlapping consensus. Of course, this overlapping need not be perfect; it is enough that a condition of reciprocity is satisfied. Both sides must believe that however much their conceptions of justice differ, their views support the same judgment in the situation at hand, and would do so even should their respective positions be interchanged.[25]

---

[22] eg *R v Butler* [1992] 1 SCR 452; *R v Jacob* [1996] 31 OR (3d) 350; and *Towne Cinema Theatres Ltd v The Queen* [1985] 1 SCR 494.

[23] The same could be said of the situation vis-à-vis each Member State and the various groups or sub-communities within it.

[24] I say 'something like' because Rawls's particular notion has been subject to much discussion and some dispute—and because I do not wish to become embroiled in the intricacies of Rawlsian exegesis.

[25] *A Theory of Justice* (Oxford: Oxford University Press, 1971), 387–8. It is not clear that this is the same notion of overlapping consensus as one finds in Rawls's more recent book *Political Liberalism*, revised edn (New York: Columbia University Press, 1996). There, the object of the overlapping consensus appears to be a political conception of justice upon which all reasonable people, regardless of their acutely differing comprehensive doctrines, can be expected to agree. *Political Liberalism*, 14–15. See, especially, note 17 where Rawls writes: 'The idea of an overlapping consensus, or perhaps better the term, was introduced in *Theory*, 387, as a way to weaken the conditions for the reasonableness of civil disobedience in a nearly just democratic society. Here and later in these lectures I use it in a different sense and in a far wider context.'

Rawls seems to envision a situation where people agree on a range of particular conclusions but disagree about the general premises required to yield them. In this respect, the state of overlapping consensus is like the situation where an appeal court comes to a unanimous decision—for example, the defendant does have the right to wear a burka in public—but the judges disagree on their reasons for judgment, some thinking that a restriction fails the proportionality test in relation to freedom of religion, others believing the relevant norm to be free expression. In other words, the judges agree on a result, but their concurring opinions reveal that they disagree on how that result is to be justified. Whether this is an accurate reading of Rawls need not concern us. The important point to stress at this juncture is that there is no reason to restrict overlapping consensus in the way the passage appears to suggest. The consensus can be on any number of things, including particular concrete judgments about particular cases or types of case, with differing premises yielding shared conclusions. But consensus can also exist with respect to a range of premises of varying degrees of generality, with differences of opinion emerging as to what these shared premises require in the way of particular judgments or rules. We often agree on abstract principles of justice, equality, and the like, but disagree on the implications of these principles—more particular rules, policies, and decisions—for the concrete circumstances of democratic politics. Everyone agrees that we should pursue equality, but there is considerable disagreement about whether, for example, this justifies affirmative action programs, or policies that favour mothers over fathers in custody disputes.

In any event, I hazard to suggest that on at least some of the important questions of political morality that arise in cases under the EU Charter there can be some measure of overlapping consensus within the relevant communities on norms and/or concrete judgments concerning justice, equality, and liberty which would emerge upon careful reflection. Lest I lose the reader instantly, I wish to stress the importance of the phrase 'upon careful reflection' which invokes the critical element mentioned above and about which something further will be said below. There is no doubting the fact that, on many, many issues, people—and peoples—within the EU differ in ways often stressed by critics of charters of rights. But sometimes these disagreements are not as deep as might appear at first blush. Societies which differ in many of their surface moral opinions, are often ones in which there is considerably more basis for informed agreement than initially meets the eye—even if these are agreements which are 'incompletely theorized', and even if they emerge only after an attempt has been made to reconcile conflicting moral views.[26] I also suggest that, on at least some occasions, we can identify the relevant community (or communities) whose moralities enjoy a significant, if imperfect, overlap which can be said to constitute a kind of shared or common morality. When I henceforth speak of a 'community's morality', it is this to which I should be taken to refer.

---

[26] The term 'incompletely theorized agreements' derives from the work of Cass Sunstein in *Legal Reasoning and Political Conflict* (Oxford: Oxford University Press, 1996), ch 2.

4 Elements of a Morality

To this point I have drawn attention to the traditional distinction between positive morality, on the one hand, and critical or Platonic morality, on the other. But what, in more general terms, do we mean by the phrase *a morality*? What do we mean when we say, eg that the morality of the hard-core individualist differs from the morality of a socialist, that the morality of the Catholic Church is different from the morality espoused by Lutherans, or that the morality of Turks is different from the morality of Italians? What sorts of things make up a morality? Let us begin with a number of fairly uncontroversial observations.

(A) Observation 1

Whether we attribute it to a person, a community, a country, or perhaps an institution like an organized religion or sport (eg, golf versus soccer), a morality typically includes a range of different elements. It will usually include (a) a number of very general, basic principles, values, and ideals—or perhaps only one, as in some versions of utilitarianism according to which the principle of utility is the fundamental principle from which all other moral principles are said to follow; (b) more specific rules, principles, and maxims; and (c) opinions and judgments about particular cases and types of cases. It might even include (d) certain meta-ethical rules telling us how we are to go about making our moral decisions. Examples from the first category include Mill's Harm Principle,[27] the value of autonomy, and the ideals of democracy. The second category might include the rule that the consent of a subject is necessary in any scientific study in which that subject's interests are at stake, or the rule that one may keep the truth from one's small children in order to spare them nightmares. The third category might include the belief that same-sex unions are immoral, that gays should not be allowed to adopt, or that overt religious symbols should be barred from public space. As for (d), two prime examples are Kant's categorical imperative and Hare's universal prescriptivism, neither of which tells us directly how to act. Rather, each states a meta-ethical rule we must follow to determine the moral maxims or prescriptions upon which we should act.[28]

---

[27] On many theories of political morality, Mill's Harm Principle functions more or less as a moral axiom. In such cases, the principle clearly belongs in our first category. But it is not so clear that it belongs there if what we have in mind is Mill's own theory. It is tempting, upon reading *On Liberty*, to think that Mill has posited the Harm Principle as a fundamental moral axiom. But Mill is very clear that the Harm Principle is justified by the Principle of Utility: See *On Liberty* (London: Longman, Roberts & Green, 1869), 11, where Mill writes 'It is proper to state that I forego any advantage which could be derived to my argument from the idea of abstract right as a thing independent of utility. I regard utility as the ultimate appeal on all ethical questions; but it must be utility in the largest sense, grounded on the permanent interests of man as a progressive being.' Whether this means that the Harm Principle belongs in category 2, category 1 being reserved for the Principle of Utility alone, is a question which need not concern us, however.

[28] Immanuel Kant, *Groundwork for the Metaphysics of Morals*, Thomas Hill (ed), (Oxford: Oxford University Press, 2003); RM Hare, *Freedom and Reason* (Oxford: Oxford University Press, 1961); and *Moral Thinking: its Levels, Methods, and Point* (Oxford: Oxford University Press, 1981).

(B) Observation 2

It is a commonplace in moral philosophy that an individual's personal morality, understood as including elements of the aforementioned four kinds, can be internally inconsistent, based on false beliefs and prejudices, and otherwise subject to rational critique. None of us gets everything right. It is also a commonplace that it is an individual's moral responsibility to explore and adjust her personal morality so as to avoid as many of the aforementioned deficiencies as possible. This is true whether the agent in question is a utilitarian or a Kantian, a social contract theorist, a feminist, or one who believes that moral judgments express prescriptions capable of being applied universally. It is even true of one who thinks that his moral judgments are in some fundamental way 'subjective' or merely expressive of the speaker's attitudes or emotions. A person who thinks in either of these last two ways will recognize the need to ensure that his subjective moral beliefs or non-cognitive exhortations are based on true non-moral propositions and are relatively consistent with one another.[29] Whatever one's moral stripe, fresh cases, or old cases considered in a new light, lead a responsible moral agent to explore the elements of her morality and to adjust them accordingly. She typically strives, in so doing, to achieve something like a Rawlsian 'reflective equilibrium', where her principles, rules, values, and maxims are internally consistent with one another, based on true beliefs and valid inferences, and in harmony with her 'considered judgments' about particular cases and types of cases.[30] Reflective equilibrium is the state for which a responsible moral agent aims, and moral justification, whatever the nature of morality, partly rests upon how the set of general moral norms to which we subscribe 'fits in with and organizes our considered judgments in reflective equilibrium'.[31] Meeting this condition—which I will henceforth refer to as 'the requirement of reflective equilibrium' or 'RRE'—is a necessary condition of responsible moral decision making and of living a life of moral integrity.[32]

This brief discussion of RRE brings to light a further distinction it would be useful to observe: between mere *moral opinions*, on the one hand, and our *true moral commitments*, on the other. The former phrase will be used to describe moral views, which have not been critically examined (in pursuance of RRE) to some minimally adequate degree and the latter those that have been so examined. In calling the latter 'true' I do not mean to imply that they are all true propositions or beliefs; only that they are ones

---

[29] Various non-cognitivists have developed theories according to which moral utterances, though not truth-bearing, are nonetheless subject to rational governance and critique. A prime example is RM Hare, whose theory of universal prescriptivism includes a logic governing imperative utterances, of which moral utterances are thought to be a species. *Freedom and Reason* (Oxford: Oxford University Press, 1965) and *Moral Thinking: Its Levels, Method, and Point* (Oxford: Oxford University Press, 1981).

[30] Again, I say 'something like' because I do not wish to become embroiled in the intricacies of Rawlsian scholarship.

[31] Rawls, *Theory of Justice* (see n 25) 579.

[32] It is an interesting question, which we will leave unexplored, whether and to what extent RRE is a requirement of all forms of rational decision making, not just decision making of the moral kind. But whatever its extent, I take it to be true that RRE is a requirement of responsible moral decision making.

to which we are, upon due reflection, truly committed. It is the commitments, not the beliefs, which are said to be true—although those who believe that moral sentences express propositions to which truth values can be assigned, will hope that at least most of their beliefs share this further property as well. With this distinction in hand, we are in a position to offer what I hope will be a yet further uncontroversial observation.

(C) Observation 3

Our moral opinions sometimes conflict with our true moral commitments. People's views on some contentious moral issue are sometimes mere opinions so construed; that is, their moral opinions do not reflect their true moral commitments. A person might, for example, believe that it is permissible to ban speech that is deeply offensive to members of a particular religious community only to discover, on sober reflection— that is, on fulfilling RRE—that this particular opinion is deeply inconsistent with general principles and judgments to which she is committed and which she is not prepared to relinquish. Perhaps more importantly for our purposes, people can differ in their moral opinions while sharing the same moral commitments, a source of common ground that often emerges as the product of vigorous, open-ended debate. They discover that they agree on, or are committed to agreeing on, much more than they thought they did. As we shall see shortly, this important observation, when applied at the communal, constitutional level, has crucial implications for our under-standing of charters, and the nature of the morality to which they might sensibly be said to make reference.

5 Charters and Judicial Review

Most of the observations made in the preceding section are relatively straightforward and uncontroversial when applied to personal morality. Of particular interest is Observation 2. Aside from moral nihilists and those who believe that foundational moral principles can be infallibly ascertained through pure reason, moral intuition, or the pronouncements of religious authorities, most individuals approach personal moral questions in the manner described.[33] They work things out as they go along, all the while cognizant of two important facts: (a) that our moral opinions almost never square exactly with our true moral commitments; and (b) that the latter are not always consistent with one another and can sometimes change over time as new facts and circumstances are brought to light. In short, they recognize that, for each of us, meeting the demands of RRE is an *ongoing* requirement of responsible moral decision making.

---

[33] For further discussion of the many ways in which our judgments can be inconsistent with our fundamental beliefs, values, and principles, see W Waluchow, *A Common Law Theory of Judicial Review: The Living Tree*, see n 10, ch 3.

As I said, most of this is uncontroversial when speaking of personal morality. What is surprising, however, is that these commonplace observations are seldom taken to apply when what is at issue is the political morality to which national charters of rights make reference. But there seems no reason that I can think of why this should be so. Communities, no less than individuals and institutions, can be said to make commitments for which they are accountable. They are also as subject to the demands of RRE as any other party, individual or otherwise. RRE applies to any type of moral agent, whether this be a particular person, a country, a community, or an organization such as a church or professional sporting association. Whatever is able to 'act', to exercise agency, and in so doing influence the important interests of other agents, is susceptible to the demands of moral responsibility, including RRE. Among the most prominent ways that a community is able to express its most fundamental true moral commitments is through the adoption and entrenchment of a charter of rights. And among the principal ways of helping to ensure that the community has lived up to those commitments is to have some body of persons overseeing whether those who act on the community's behalf, its governments, officials, and agencies, have acted in ways that do not (unreasonably and/or unjustifiably) infringe those commitments. The most common form of such oversight in the modern world—and in many cases, the best one on offer—is, of course, judicial review of some form or other, an option the EU seems now to have fully embraced with the formal adoption of its Charter.[34]

What I would like to propose, then, is a conception of the EU Charter, and the process of judicial review it contemplates, under which the principal role of EU judges is not to adjudicate on the basis of their own convictions regarding the truths of Platonic political morality, but to hold the EU community to *its* own fundamental commitments on such matters. These commitments are expressed or represented in the EU community's constitutional morality (EUCCM). To be clear, EUCCM is not the personal morality of any particular person or institution, eg the Court of Justice, the Catholic Church, the British Labour Party, or a particular Court of Justice judge who helps decide a case under the Charter. Nor is it the morality decreed by God, inherent in the fabric of the universe, or residing in Plato's world of forms. Rather, it is a kind of community-based, positive morality consisting of the fundamental moral norms and convictions to which the EU community has itself actually committed itself via its Charter and the jurisprudence that has developed, and will continue to develop, as the EU, the Court of Justice, and the various other state actors functioning within the EU come to grips with the concrete implications of those fundamental commitments for everyday life and politics.[35] So construed, EUCCM is

---

[34] For my defence of judicial review in the context of Western domestic legal systems, as well as a discussion of a few of the various forms of judicial review adopted around the world, see WJ Waluchow, *Common Law Theory of Judicial Review: The Living Tree*, see n 10.

[35] Again, many if not all of these commitments were affirmations of commitments made previously in, eg, Court of Justice judgments that invoked the 'common values' for which the EU has been said to stand. But this complication can be safely ignored. Whatever doubt might have existed as to the status of the EU's commitment to the relevant rights and freedoms has now been rendered moot by the Lisbon Treaty.

a subset of the wider set of moral norms and judgments which enjoy some (not insignificant) measure of reflective support within the EU community (or its constituent communities). Some members of this wider set lack any kind of legal recognition whatsoever. Even if there are, within the community morality(ies) of the EU, norms and judgments of positive morality governing non-political matters like friendship, gratitude, and charitable giving, these are not part of the EU's CCM because they lack appropriate constitutional recognition. Constitutional recognition of EUCCM norms includes (though it may not be limited to) enshrinement in the EU Charter and the legislative history and jurisprudence that will continue to flesh out the local, concrete understandings or Thomistic determinations of those principles for that particular community, and for the particular sub-communities which have joined together in forming the EU.

Here are some of the advantages of viewing the EU Charter this way, as expressing EUCCM. Owing to its social origin, EUCCM is a source of moral norms upon which EU judges can draw without seriously compromising democratic legitimacy. Judicial review under the Charter includes, though is by no means limited to, the task of ensuring that the acts of EU and Member-State institutions and officials do not, in ways that could not have been reasonably foreseen by the relevant actors, and which they may have wished to avoid had they had the opportunity to do so, infringe the fundamental moral norms of EUCCM.[36] If this is the role a judge plays in a particular instance of Charter adjudication, then democratic legitimacy is not compromised. The judge is, in effect, helping to implement, and render effective, the democratic will within the EU—helping the relevant community (the EU as a whole, or a Member State with its own distinctive determination of an EUCCM norm) to live up to the moral commitments it made when its officials formally and fully signed up to the Charter upon entering into the Treaty of Lisbon. Furthermore, many other concerns about charters of rights can be successfully parried as well. As we have already seen, one prominent concern is that charter review—the process of judicial review the aim of which is to ensure compliance with the terms of a charter of rights—foolishly asks judges to serve as philosopher kings and queens, asks them to discover Platonic moral truths in respect of matters of justice and equality, and to enforce their understanding or interpretation of those ever-elusive truths against the acts and erroneous interpretations of democratically accountable legislators and officials. Given the deep disagreements on moral matters that seem to prevail in Europe (as elsewhere), together with the fact that judges, no less so than the rest of us, suffer what John Rawls

---

[36] There are at least two importantly different contexts to distinguish here. The first is a context in which the Court of Justice holds an EU body, eg, the EU Parliament, to moral commitments ascribable to the EU as a whole. Then there is a context in which the relevant body is, say, the legislature of a particular Member State whose effort to implement EU law is claimed to violate the Charter. As will be seen below, it seems as though a Member State can quite legitimately have a particular understanding or determination of a Charter provision—and hence of an EUCCM norm—that differs from the understanding or determination of some other Member State, or even of the EU itself. If this is so in a particular case, then the judges of the Court of Justice may be tasked with holding that particular Member State to its own distinctive determination(s) of EUCCM. Whenever I refer to the commitments of EUCCM, and unless the context makes a different meaning evident, I should be understood to be referring to both kinds of context whenever I speak of the commitments of EUCCM.

calls 'the burdens of judgment' in matters moral, having them perform such a task asks them to accomplish the impossible.[37] But if judges, in exercising Charter review, are not seeking—and inevitably failing—to apply Platonic moral truth, but are instead seeking to hold the relevant democratic community to its own constitutionally expressed moral commitments, then the sting of this powerful argument can be largely avoided. Judges are not, on this view, being asked to decide on the basis of *their own* best judgments concerning the demands of Platonic moral truth. Rather they are being asked to decide on the basis of their best judgments as to *the relevant democratic community's* best judgments concerning the demands of moral truth. EU judges can be said, in such circumstances, to be doing nothing more contentious than doing their best to apply, in a fair, impartial manner, standards that originate from an entirely legitimate source; namely, the relevant democratic community's own fundamental moral beliefs and commitments.[38]

6 Further Cause for Concern?

If only matters were this straightforward. But of course they are not. As critics will no doubt be keen to stress, people within the EU seem reasonably to disagree not only about the demands of Platonic moral truth. There is considerable room for disagreement about the demands of an EUCCM as well, especially in the controversial legal cases in which disputes about its concrete requirements come fully to the fore, cases like *Schindler* and *Omega*.[39] The main issue in *Schindler* was whether the UK had the right to restrict, indeed ban, importation of lottery advertisements and tickets for the express purpose of preventing its residents from participating in lotteries operated in other Member States. As the Court of Justice saw it, among the UK's principal grounds were 'public morality considerations' factors which were presumably of little concern in other Member States with their presumably different moral understandings. The

---

[37] The burdens of judgment consist in various limitations on human knowledge, thought, and judgment, as well as the wide diversity of the experiences we bring to bear on moral and political questions. These burdens lead to inevitable disagreements in factual and other judgments among reasonable people, as well as to people having differing life plans, and different religious, philosophical, and moral views. These, Rawls writes, are 'the sources, or causes, of disagreement between reasonable persons...', *Political Liberalism*, see n 25, 55.

[38] That the norms of EUCCM can be largely discovered via a process of reasoning that can plausibly be described as 'impartial' and 'morally neutral' and hence not fully hostage to the personal, moral predilections of EU judges is, itself, a highly contentious claim. It is also one that I cannot explore or defend here. Were I to do so, my argument(s) would be similar to those advanced by Joseph Raz in his discussion of 'detached judgments' and by Julie Dickson in her splendid book *Evaluation and Legal Theory*. (See J Raz, *The Authority of Law* (Oxford: Clarendon Press, 1979), 153–7 and J Dickson, *Evaluation and Legal Theory* (Oxford: Hart Publishing, 2001) but especially her discussion of the agnostic observer of the Roman Catholic mass, 68–9). My own, somewhat under-developed thoughts on the matter are in *Inclusive Legal Positivism* (Oxford: Clarendon Press, 1994), 19–30.

[39] *Omega*, see n 21, Case C-275/92 *Her Majesty's Customs and Excise v Gerhart Schindler and Jörg Schindler* [1994] ECR I-1039.

Court of Justice held that the UK was entitled to have a differential level of protection vis-à-vis restricting lotteries, if this was done in the service of important ends. In other words, banning lottery advertisements and tickets did not breach EU law.[40]

In *Omega* Germany wished to ban one version of a game called 'Laser Quest' which had been developed by a British company (Pulsar Advanced Games Systems Ltd) and which was popular in many Member States. Laser Quest—or, at least, the version of it which Germany wished to ban—is a game in which people 'play at' killing others. At issue was whether such a ban infringed the freedom to provide services established in EU law. In Germany's view, playing at killing others is a practice that seriously violates human dignity, a value of fundamental importance according to German law.[41] Despite other Member States apparently not holding the view that the version of Laser Quest at issue seriously violates human dignity such that it ought to be prohibited, the Court of Justice accepted Germany's claim and ruled the ban to be a justifiable derogation from free movement of services. As in *Omega*, then, what we seem to encounter is a potential clash between differing views concerning the demands of moral values ostensibly shared by EU Member States. Of course, the sheer fact of disagreement in no way implies that there is no fact of the matter in such cases, that EUCCM is therefore incomplete or indeterminate and hence unavailable to ground an EU court's decision. This no more follows than there are no determinate answers available when there is reasonable disagreement about the nature of black holes, or about whether a defendant exercised reasonable care to ensure that his goods arrived safely to market. But there is no getting round the fact that such disagreement threatens to undermine the practical possibility of fair and impartial decision making, and hence democratic legitimacy, of Charter review. How can a decision by the Court of Justice to apply an EUCCM norm in a particular way be properly described as an attempt to implement the common, constitutional morality of the EU if there is so much partisan disagreement within, let alone across, individual Member States, about its proper understanding or interpretation?[42] Will Court of Justice judges not be forced, in the end, to base their choices on their own subjective moral views on the matters in question? What else could they do in such circumstances, short of simply declining to make a decision at all?

I have argued elsewhere, again in relation to national charters, that things are not quite as bleak as might appear at first blush.[43] In national contexts there seems much more basis for agreement and consensus than initially meets the eye. In other words, for reasons such as those sketched above in my discussion of RRE, the limits of

---

[40] It is worth noting that the UK now runs very popular national lotteries, suggesting that whatever 'public morality' concerns there might have been in the UK in 1994 have since dissipated.

[41] According to Article 1(1) of the *Basic Law for the Federal Republic of Germany (Grundgesetz, GC)*: 'Human dignity shall be inviolable. To respect and protect it shall be the duty of all state authority.'

[42] Recall that when I speak of 'the common constitutional morality of the EU' I intend an interpretation of that phrase which is sensitive to the possibility of different, and equally legitimate, Member State determinations of some of the norms of the common morality to which all EU Member States, with the possible exception of the UK and Poland, are committed. This is a possibility I will endeavour to explain and defend below.

[43] Waluchow, see n 10.

justification do not extend only so far as we find explicit agreement. Differing opinions and judgments concerning the commitments of a CCM can often (or, at the very least, can sometimes) be brought into reflective equilibrium with one another. When this happens, members of a community can be led to see that they actually agree, or are *committed to agreeing*, on much more than they think they do. They can, in other words, be led to recognize an implicit basis for explicit agreement on the meaning and implications of the relevant CCM norms, and previous decisions taken under them, when initially this might not have seemed remotely possible. The judge's role in an EU Charter case—enforcing the relevant commitments of EUCCM—may lead her to draw on these bases of agreement and to decide accordingly. When such a basis is found, and a decision is made on its footing, the fact of disagreement may well be replaced by reasonable agreement. We should not reject prematurely the possibility that this might turn out to be true in the EU, even on controversial questions such as those concerning overt religious symbolism, or the suppression of acts of expression that certain religious communities find deeply offensive.

Despite all this, there is no getting round this further potential source of difficulty, one which seems particularly acute within the context of the EU: it is distinctly possible that in some cases arising under a CCM, there is no uniquely correct answer to be found—just answers. What, one might reasonably ask, are Court of Justice judges to do if they encounter a case in which this appears so? Elsewhere I have argued that in national contexts such as one finds in North America, judges should—and in fact often do—engage in a type of moral reasoning traditionally associated with English common law. They should creatively develop or construct the norms of their particular CCM, in an incremental, case-by-case way, in much the same manner as common law judges have historically developed, incrementally, and in a case-by-case manner, the principles of negligence, and the concepts of foreseeability and the reasonable use of force.[44] In so doing, I suggested, they often engage in Thomistic determinations of common notions, deciding among available solutions, none of which is uniquely determined by, but each of which is fully consistent with, the relevant moral notion and with previous efforts by judges and legislators to shape it through the process of determination. Such previous attempts I referred to as 'CCM precedents'. Judges will, in such cases, no doubt be exercising discretion to choose from among non-excluded solutions. But there is, in my view, no better way to proceed in these circumstances. Whether this is always so in the specific context of the EU is an interesting question to which I would now like to turn.

7 The Circumstances of EU Politics

As we saw above, Jeremy Waldron defines the circumstances of politics as combining two key elements: (1) a felt need among the members of a community for 'a common framework or decision or course of action on some matter', and (2) 'disagreement

---

[44] *A Common Law Theory of Judicial Review: The Living Tree*, see n 10, chs 5 and 6.

about what that framework, decision or action should be'.[45] It is in these circumstances, which Waldron takes to be prevalent within Western democracies, that questions concerning the defensibility of judicial review under a charter of rights arise and must be debated. I have already said quite a bit about (2) and how, despite the undeniable existence of extensive disagreement about matters of political morality, it is quite often possible to discover answers which follow from a community's prior commitments—commitments which are, I suggested, to be found in its CCM and the various decisions concerning its demands, including some that have helped shape it via the process of determination. But what about the first element: the need for a common framework, or decision, or course of action on some matter? Within national contexts, it often goes without saying that the need Waldron mentions applies. But one might question whether this is always so in federal nations such as Canada, the United States, or Spain. Must a federal country, if it is to be a nation defined in part by a common set of moral commitments, observe the same concrete ways of implementing these common commitments across all provinces or states? If affirmative action is permitted and practised in Massachusetts, as a way of achieving equality within a community where certain historically disadvantaged groups face barriers to employment to which other groups are not subject, must that practice also be required in Arizona? And if it is not, can the United States be said to be a nation defined in part by its *common* commitment to equality of opportunity? Similar issues arise when we turn to the EU, where analogous questions of uniformity and consistency emerge with respect to the fundamental rights of political morality to which each Member State has fully committed itself.[46] It is far from clear that judges in the EU courts must *always* be concerned to help develop, for all Member States, 'a common framework or decision or course of action' with respect to the various common values constitutionally protected by the Charter. Or so I would now like to argue.

There is a natural tendency to think that commonality of values requires commonality in the way of concrete implementation, in the means by which these values are honoured and applied. When it comes to *fundamental moral matters* of the kind contemplated in the EU Charter, consistent, uniform application of a common frame of action seems, on the face of it, to be an essential requirement. After all, we're talking about matters of fundamental moral right, not matters concerning purely personal or social preferences. When what is at stake is a person's preferred hair colour, or a social preference regarding the appropriate time of day at which to have dinner, variable practices seem perfectly innocent and acceptable. There is, barring unusual circumstances, no need for uniformity. But not so, it might be thought, when questions of fundamental moral rights enter the picture. The thought that what might be right in one community or Member State might not be so in another is a thought which might seem to do violence to the notion of a fundamental moral right—to the very

---

[45] Waldron, see n 11, 102

[46] There are possible exceptions, with regard to Poland and the UK, see n 5.

concept of a universal, human right which all persons, regardless of particular circumstances and preferences, are said to possess in virtue of their shared humanity.

Tempting though this line of thought might be, it is nevertheless mistaken. As I have
alluded to above, and as Aristotle, Aquinas, and Raz have argued, morality does not, as
this picture seems to assume, always provide fully determinate answers to moral questions. In short, many moral norms are, to some extent at least, 'underdetermined'.[47] They
rule out certain options, but leave open ranges of possibility. To be sure, sometimes
morality does provide us with uniquely correct answers: torturing innocent children for
fun is morally wrong, *full stop*, that is, regardless of time, place, and circumstances, and
regardless of personal and social preference or practice. There is no room for Thomistic
determination here. But at other times morality is not quite so definite. Rather, it provides
only 'common notions' on the basis of which determinations or specifications, from
within a range of available options, must be made. In other words, morality sometimes
rules out certain options lying outside the range of the acceptable, but fails to leave us with
one and only one available choice. There may, for example, be no uniquely correct answer
to the question whether freedom of expression is unreasonably infringed by a particular
state's effort to control overt public displays of religious symbols. Even though freedom of
expression unquestionably rules out laws suppressing all forms of political dissent, this
value may well leave open the question whether banning burkas, crucifixes, and ceremonial daggers from classrooms is permissible. It might be open to a society, say France, to
decide to pursue such prohibitions without overstepping the boundaries of the permissible. That option, in other words, might be consistent with freedom of expression. But so
too might a decision by Germany explicitly to permit the display of such symbols. The
relevant value—freedom of expression—might not provide a uniquely correct answer or
solution in respect of this particular set of issues any more than the values of democracy
provide a uniquely correct answer to the question, 'which form of democratic governance
is best?' Is a system incorporating a bicameral legislature better, democratically speaking,
than a unitary system? Is a republican form of government, such as one finds in France
and the United States any more democratic than a constitutional monarchy such as one
finds in the Spain and Canada? Perhaps the most we can say is this: each is permissible
from the perspective of democratic values. That is, neither is ruled out as undemocratic,
as various forms of military dictatorship or oligarchy would be. And this despite the fact
that neither permissible option is, at least from the point of view of democracy, better (or
worse) than the other.[48] In short, the value of democracy *underdetermines* the choice
among the various forms of democratic governance on offer. The United States may be
neither more nor less democratic than the United Kingdom, though each has chosen a

---

[47] For defence of the view that Aristotle accepted the under-determination of value, see TK Seung and
D Bonevac, 'Plural Values and Indeterminate Rankings' 102 *Ethics* (1992), 799–813. For discussion of
Aquinas' view, see works cited n 16 above. Raz's views are presented and defended in *Engaging Reason*
(Oxford: Oxford University Press, 1999), most notably in ch 3, 'Incommensurability and Agency' 46–66.

[48] Even if one option is better, democratically speaking, than the other, it might nevertheless be true that
neither is ruled out as undemocratic, and that a country which, for whatever reason, opted for the lesser option,
could not be charged with having acted undemocratically.

different form of democratic governance than the other. Most importantly for our purposes, there is no reason to complain about a lack of uniformity, the lack of a common framework or course of action across these two undeniably democratic nations.

Now if the above is true when it comes to a common commitment to democratic values, and if, as I've suggested it might, morality underdetermines the issue of controlling overt public displays of religious symbols, then there may be nothing remotely wrong in a state of affairs in which different communities choose different paths on the matters in question, ie, choose different Thomistic determinations. The same might well be true in respect of the question whether prohibiting simulated killing in a laser tag game violates human dignity.[49] Once a particular community's determination is chosen, of course, consistency, fairness, and the demands of moral integrity require that that choice be honoured within that particular community, at least until such time as good reason for a change in policy and practice emerges (if such reason ever does emerge, and of course it might not). The community, in so choosing, has made a further moral commitment. But this kind of consistency is quite different in kind from the one that demands consistency in determinations and resulting practices across the EU and all its Member States in respect of how to implement the scheme of common values members of the EU community share with one another. Why, it might be asked, should we always insist on a consistently applied common framework? Once we recognize there can be more than one legitimate way to recognize and observe a relevant moral value, the possibility emerges that different communities can render different determinations, *and yet be doing so in observance of one and the same, ie, a common, set of values.* So long as all parties are acting within the range of the permissible, as determined by the relevant values, they can all be said to be observing a set of common values on which their shared heritage stands.

So it is far from clear that consistency in determinations and resulting practices is always a requirement of consistent application of a common set of values. I do not mean to deny, I hasten to add, that there might not be in some instances other factors arguing in favour of uniformity and consistency, and that these might tip the balance in favour of common practice. That there are such factors, especially given the EU's founding aim to foster harmonious economic interaction among Member States, seems quite possible. Thus, a case involving a decision of the EU Commission implementing competition law regulations might be one where the need for harmonious economic interaction tips the scales in favour of uniformity across all Member States.[50] Such a need might not be present, at least to a degree sufficient to tip the scales in favour of uniformity, when the action in question is not that of an EU body or official, but of a Member State derogating from EU law, as in *Omega* and *Schmidberger*.[51] To quote from the Court in *Omega*,

---

[49] As in *Omega*, see n 21.

[50] Case 333/85, *Mannesmann-Röhrenwerke and Benteler v Council* [1987] ECR 1381.

[51] *Omega*, see n 21, Case C-112/00 *Schmidberger, Internationale Transporte und Planzüge v Republik Österreich* [2003] ECR I-05659.

37. It is not indispensable in that respect for the restrictive measure issued by the authorities of a Member State to correspond to a conception shared by all Member States as regards the precise way in which the fundamental right or legitimate interest in question is to be protected. Although, in paragraph 60 of *Schindler*, the Court referred to moral, religious or cultural considerations which lead all Member States to make the organisation of lotteries and other games with money subject to restrictions, it was not its intention, by mentioning that common conception, to formulate a general criterion for assessing the proportionality of any national measure which restricts the exercise of an economic activity.

38. On the contrary, as is apparent from well-established case-law subsequent to *Schindler*, the need for, and proportionality of, the provisions adopted are not excluded merely because one Member State has chosen a system of protection different from that adopted by another State (see, to that effect, *Läärä*, paragraph 36; *Zenatti*, paragraph 34; Case C-6/01 *Anomar and Others* [2003] ECR I-0000, para 80).

And then there are the many possible cases where the EU's own determination of a common moral notion—eg, its decision regarding equality of treatment as between married couples and same-sex partners in relation to *EU Staff Regulations*—might differ from analogous determinations within a particular Member State in relation to its own national employment law. In *D and Kingdom of Sweden v Council of the European Union*[52] the Court of Justice adopted its own, distinctive understanding of equality according to which restricting household allowances to EU employed married couples while denying them to members of legally registered (in their own Member State) same-sex partnerships does not unreasonably infringe the norms of equality recognized in what is now Art 157 TEU. This was held to be so despite the acknowledged fact that '[t]he existing situation in the Member States of the Community as regards recognition of partnerships between persons of the same sex or of the opposite sex reflects a great diversity of laws and the absence of any general assimilation of marriage and other forms of statutory union', (para 50)—and the fact that 'Article 1 of Chapter 1 of Lagen (1994:1117) om registrerat partnerskap of 23 June 1994 (the Swedish law on registered partnership) provides that [t]wo persons of the same sex may apply for registration of their partnership . . . and that [a] registered partnership shall have the same legal effects as a marriage . . '. (para 2).[53] So the complex structures and interrelations among the various legislative and administrative bodies operating within the EU make it very difficult, if not impossible, to provide a simple, across-the-board judgment on whether common values require consistent determinations. My aim is only to suggest that there is no distinctly moral reason for uniformity in all cases where the relevant moral norms are under-determined. And if this is so, there is no moral or rational fault in a situation in which varying interpretations of common values are tolerated within a diverse community such as the EU.

---

[52] Joined Cases C-122/99 P and C-125/99 P *Kingdom of Sweden and another v Council of the European Union* [2001] ECR I-04319.

[53] It should be noted that the EU now recognizes same-sex partnerships in a variety of contexts, including its free movement law.

8 The European Convention on Human Rights and the 'Margin of Appreciation'

As a final aside, I would like to draw attention to the ECtHR and the approach it has taken in respect of similar issues of application arising under the ECHR. I have in mind here the 'margin of appreciation' doctrine to which reference was made in, among many other places, *Otto-Preminger Institute v Austria*:[54]

> As in the case of 'morals' it is not possible to discern throughout Europe a uniform conception of the significance of religion in society ... even within a single country such conceptions may vary. For that reason it is not possible to arrive at a comprehensive definition of what constitutes a permissible interference with the exercise of the right to freedom of expression where such expression is directed against the religious feeling of others. A certain margin of appreciation is therefore to be left to the national authorities in assessing the existence and extent of the necessity of such interference.[55]

Attempts to justify the margin of appreciation doctrine often rely on the fact that national courts and legislatures have a better sense of the relevant social, economic, and cultural factors at play within their particular communities. This was described in *Wingrove* as their 'direct and continuous contact with the vital forces of their countries'.[56] It was further claimed that 'State authorities are in principle in a better position than the international judge to give an opinion on the exact content of these requirements with regard to the rights of others as well as on the "necessity" of a "restriction" . . '.[57] Now were it true that moral values were always fully determinate, and in no need of determination or specification, then this epistemic argument would cut little ice, unless radically different sets of non-moral, social circumstances existed among the various Member States, differences which yielded very different moral judgments based on identical principles and values. But this seems unlikely. And so if moral values are always fully determinate, then one might reasonably think that what always matters is the universal, objective, moral truth of the matter, not who has easier access to the 'vital forces' of the relevant community. But if, as I have been suggesting, moral values are often in need of determination, then allowing national authorities to make the appropriate choices for their own communities, choices which might reasonably be based on the vital social, cultural, and perhaps economic forces at play in those different communities, could, in certain cases, be an eminently sensible course of action, one which does not, if my earlier arguments are sound, necessarily threaten the idea that members of the Council of Europe are committed to one and the same common values, the 'common heritage' of Europe.

---

[54] Among the many cases in which the margin of appreciation is invoked to justify allowing variable determinations across EU countries, see *Handyside v UK* (1979–80) 1 EHRR 737; *Wingrove v The United Kingdom* (1997) 24 ECHR 1; *Muller and Others v Switzerland* (1991) 13 EHRR 212.

[55] *Otto-Preminger Institute v Austria* (1995) 19 EHRR 34, para 50.

[56] *Wingrove v The United Kingdom* (1996) 24 EHRR 1.

[57] *Wingrove v The United Kingdom* (1996) 24 EHRR 1, para 58.

None of this means, I hasten to add, that EU courts should pay complete, unquestioning deference to the determinations of Member States—or other EU bodies and officials for that matter. It is important not to forget that although moral values are often *underdetermined*, they are never completely *indeterminate*. That is, although moral values do not always provide uniquely correct answers or solutions, they do rule out some. It is also important not to forget the demands of RRE that apply to all official bodies and officials operating within the EU whenever they act. When an EU court is in a position to make a good faith judgment to the effect that an official act on the part of an EU body or official, or the act of a Member body or official concerned to implement EU law, strays beyond the range of the permissible as defined by its community's prior moral commitments, then that court is under an obligation to intervene, to declare the offending act in breach of the EU Charter. Though choice is sometimes possible, it is always important to remember that some choices are simply not available.

9 Conclusion

In this chapter I have attempted to defend a particular way of conceiving of the Charter of Fundamental Rights of the European Union and the norms of political morality to which that instrument makes reference. I have suggested that the Charter can reasonably be viewed as standing for a set of fundamental moral commitments to which EU Member States have, with the exception of Poland and the United Kingdom, all signed up, though the latter two hold-outs are subject to an equally basic, somewhat analogous set of moral commitments established by the ECHR, subscription to which is a requirement for membership in the Council of Europe.[58] These fundamental Charter commitments are not, I argued, commitments to the norms of a universally valid, Platonic political morality. More accurately, to the extent that they do constitute such a commitment, they do so only in relation to a set of underdetermined norms that require a good deal of shaping through various instances of Thomistic determination. Sometimes, in some contexts, common commitment to a particular value might well demand consistency in or uniformity of determination across the EU. In other contexts, involving, eg actions of a Member State derogating from EU law, something like a 'margin of appreciation' might be perfectly acceptable. Much will depend on the type of action in question, and on the type (EU or Member State) of official, agency, or government body that stands accused of infringing the Charter. But whatever the

---

[58] They are also bound by Court of Justice case law and by the 'general principles' which have for some time now been said by the Court of Justice to lay behind the EU Treaty. As far back as Case 11/70 *International Handelsgesellschaft mbH v Einfuhr etc* [1970] ECR 1125, the Court of Justice declared that it would protect human rights as an integral part of EU law. In Case 4/73 *Nold v Commission* [1974] ECR 491, the Court ruled that international human rights treaties to which Member States were signatories provided further general principles to which Member States and EU institutions were bound.

context, and whatever the demand for consistency might be in that particular situation, the kind of morality to which the Charter makes reference is one that resides somewhere between the universal norms of an unadulterated Platonic morality, and the purely positive morality consisting of the set of whatever moral opinions happen to be prevalent within the relevant community at any given time. It will be, as stated above, a community's positive morality with a critical bite—the bite provided by RRE, the norms of Platonic political morality, and the well-founded, particular determinations of those norms made by the officials and official bodies of that community. Conceiving of the EU Charter in this way allows one not only to circumvent many of the difficulties that have historically plagued national charters of rights. It also provides a promising way forward in dealing with the perplexing set of particular, somewhat unique circumstances in which the EU finds itself—a community of communities, committed to a set of common values, yet sensitive to legitimate differences in local understandings and (official and non-official) practices within the twenty-seven Member States that presently make it up. The morality to which this community has committed itself from the beginning, and which has now been given firm expression by the Treaty of Lisbon and its legally binding commitment to the Charter, is one which might reasonably be described as the EU's shared or common 'spiritual and moral heritage'.

9

The Moral Point of Constitutional Pluralism

Defining the Domain of Legitimate Institutional Civil Disobedience and Conscientious Objection

Mattias Kumm[1]

1 Some Questions about Constitutional Pluralism

Those who embrace constitutional pluralism, notwithstanding important differences between them,[2] take a particular position on how the problem of conflict between different legal orders should be resolved. They emphasize two points.

On the one hand they insist on a *pluralist* account of the world of public law in the following specific sense: they insist that the different legal orders making up the world of public law are not hierarchically integrated. They disagree with the claim put forward by the ECJ in *Costa*, that Member States' courts should always set aside national law, including national constitutional law, when it conflicts with the requirements of EU law as interpreted by the ECJ. And they agree, at least in principle, with most national courts, to the extent they insist that there are red lines, grounded in constitutional commitments, that limit the enforcement of EU decisions domestically.

[1] Inge Rennert Professor of Law, New York University School of Law, Research Professor for 'Rule of Law in the Age of Globalization', WZB, Berlin.

[2] For some basic positions see the debate between Miguel Maduro, Neil Walker, Julio Baquero Cruz, and myself in: M Avbelj, and J Komárek, *Four Visions of Constitutional Pluralism* (2008), EUI Working Paper Law No 2008/21, available at SSRN: <http://ssrn.com/abstract=1334219>. See more generally M Avbelj and J Komarek (eds), *Constitutional Pluralism in the European Union and Beyond* (Oxford: Hart, 2012).

They disagree with the European Court of First Instance in *Kadi* that European Union law should always be set aside when it conflicts with obligations arising under UN Law. And they agree with the ECJ, at least in principle, that EU law may sometimes preclude the enforcement of obligations of UN Law. In other words constitutional pluralists reject the claim that national law is hierarchically integrated into EU law and that EU law is hierarchically integrated into the law of the wider international community.

On the other hand, constitutional pluralists insist that different legal orders don't simply coexist beside one another, as self-enclosed Leibnizian monads with at best contingent relationships between them. Notwithstanding the pluralist nature of legal practice, the relevant actors—and courts in particular—have established mechanisms and designed doctrines that allow for constructive mutual engagement between different legal orders.[3] Legal pluralism in Europe is guided, constrained, and structured in a way that justifies describing that practice in constitutional terms, even in the absence of hierarchical ordering.[4] Constitutional pluralists describe how legal coherence is possible even in the absence of hierarchical integration. The idea of *constitutional pluralism* carves out a third way of conceiving of the legal world between *hierarchical integration* within one legal order on the one hand, and a *radical pluralism* on the other, where actors of each legal order proceed without systemic regard for the coherence of the whole.[5]

It is relatively uncontroversial that the constitutional pluralist account *descriptively* captures two important features of European constitutional practice. What is less clear is its *normative* assessment.[6] How should one make sense of a practice that has this

---

[3] JHH Weiler, 'In Defense of the Status quo: Europe's Constitutional Sonderweg' in JHH Weiler and M Wind (eds), *European Constitutionalism Beyond the State* (2003) 7ff. MP Maduro, 'Contrapunctual Law: Europe's Constitutional Pluralism in Action', in N Walker (ed), *Sovereignty in Transition* (Oxford: Hart, 2006), 501–37; see also M Maduro, 'Europe and the Constitution: What If This Is as Good as It Gets?' in JHH Weiler and M Wind (eds), *European Constitutionalism Beyond the State* (Cambridge: Cambridge University Press, 2003), 74–103. S Besson, 'From European Integration to European Integrity: Should European Law Speak with Just one Voice?' (2004) 10 *European Law Journal* 257–81. M Kumm, 'The Jurisprudence of Constitutional Conflict: Constitutional Supremacy before and after the Constitutional Treaty' (2005) 11(3) *European Law Journal* 262–307. I Pernice, 'After The Lisbon Treaty: Multi-Level Constitutionalism in Action', (2009) 15 *Columbia Journal of European Law* 349–407, A von Bogdandy, 'Overcoming Absolute Primacy: Respect for National Identity under the Lisbon Treaty' (2011) 48 *Common Market Law Review* 1417–53.

[4] See N Walker, 'The Idea of Constitutional Pluralism' (2002) 65 *Modern Law Review* 317–59. For an overview of the state of the debate see also M Avbelj and J Komárek, 'Four Visions of Constitutional Pluralism' (2008) 2(1) *European Journal of Legal Studies* 325–70.

[5] For scepticism regarding a constitutionalist frame for the construction of European Union Law specifically see P Lindseth, *Power and Legitimacy: Reconciling Europe and the Nation State* (Oxford University Press, 2011) and for law beyond the state generally, see N Krisch, *Beyond Constitutionalism* (Oxford University Press, 2010).

[6] What is also less clear is how to make sense of it *jurisprudentially*, see G Letsas in this volume, Chapter 4), as well as P Eleftheriadis, 'Pluralism and Integrity' (2010) 23 *Ratio Juris* 365–89. Both authors are convincing in their argument that constitutional pluralism does not provide a strong argument either way in jurisprudential debates between positivists and interpretivists. But even if constitutional pluralism is not a challenge to any of the more sophisticated positions within classical jurisprudential debates, it poses significant challenges to traditional positions within constitutional theory relating to the grounds of constitutional authority. Those are the focus of this paper.

structure in normative terms? Is it attractive? Are national courts right not to accept the primacy claim of the ECJ about EU law? Is the ECJ right not to accept that UN Law trumps EU law, even when Art. 103 of the UN Charter declares UN law to have primacy over all other Treaty obligations? If so, why? What is it about the ECJ's claim to primacy that is wrong? And what exactly limits and constrains this pluralism to ensure the coherence of legal practice, seen as a whole? What is it about those constraints that justifies calling that legal practice constitutional? In other words, what is the constitutional theory that can provide an account of the normative point, structure, and limits of constitutional pluralism?

There is what some have regarded as a fashionable disposition to embrace legal pluralism[7] without providing an account of the conditions under which it is desirable and the conditions under which it is not. It is not very plausible to believe that legal pluralism is *always* attractive. To illustrate the point, think of the context of a classical federal state and its relationship to its constituent units: if the state Supreme Court of New York were to start questioning the supremacy of US federal law as interpreted by the US Supreme Court on state law grounds, few would conclude that state courts have at last begun to embrace the virtues of legal pluralism. Instead most would insist that something has gone awry. The same is true if Bavaria were to start subjecting the law of the Federal Republic of Germany to state constitutional requirements. What is it about these contexts that justifies the hierarchical integration of state legal orders in the legal order of the larger entity that is different from the EU context? It is not enough to simply presuppose that hierachical integration is appropriate when the more comprehensive legal order is that of a state, whereas pluralism should be embraced when the more comprehensive order is not a state. Even if this were the right answer—and I will argue that it is not—the questions would still remain, which salient features of statehood would justify hierarchical integration that are absent beyond the state, and why pluralism would be a virtue in the relationship between states and non-state legal orders. The general question, then, is the following: under what circumstances is it appropriate to conceive of[8] the relationship between different legal orders in pluralist terms, rather than thinking about them in terms of hierarchical integration? Under what circumstances should, for example, the legal order of the European Union and the legal order of Member States be regarded as a hierarchically integrated whole? Under what circumstances should the European legal order be regarded as an integrative element of an international legal order? What are the conditions under which legal pluralism is a virtue and what are the conditions under which it is a vice? What exactly

---

[7] See JHH Weiler, in JHH Weiler and G de Búrca (eds), *The Worlds of Constitutionalism* (Cambridge: Cambridge University Press, 2011) at 1, calling it 'an academic Pandemic' so dominant that 'Constitutional Pluralism is today the only Party Membership Card which will guarantee a seat at the High Tables of the public law Professoriate'. See also J Baquero Cruz, 'The Legacy of the Maastricht Judgment and the Pluralist Movement (2008) 14 *European Law Journal* 389–422.

[8] This way of talking assumes that law is constructed by lawyers and legal thinkers in the same sense as mathematical models, scientific conjectures or theories are constructed by scientists. Such a position is perfectly compatible with the idea that there are correct and false, plausible and implausible constructions.

is the normative point of pluralism? And what does that imply about the nature of the constraints that ensure the kind of mutual deference and engagement that ensures the coherence of the whole?

From an external point of view—the point of view of a legal sociologist—the answer to the question whether the relationship between legal orders should be conceived in a pluralist or hierarchically way is relatively easy to give. If the highest court of a legal order insists on applying the law of the more encompassing legal order only under conditions defined by its legal order and the decisions of that court are generally taken as authoritative by other officials of that legal order, then the relationship between the legal orders is pluralist *as a matter of fact*. But the perspective to be taken here is not the *external perspective* of the sociologist, but the *internal point of view* taken by *a participant in legal practice*. Here the question changes: under what circumstances *should* a judge on the highest court of a legal order—the ECJ when adjudicating questions involving UN law as in the *Kadi* case, or a national constitutional court adjudicating questions involving EU law—legally recognize or refuse to recognize hierarchical integration in the more encompassing legal order? Or to put it another way: under what circumstances should a court accept the hierarchical integration in the more encompassing[9] legal order? If the ECJ was right to insist on the autonomy of the European legal order in *Kadi*, what would need to happen for the ECJ to accept that primacy of UN law as indicated by Article 103? If Member States courts are right not to accept the ECJ's claim that EU law has primacy over national law at the current state of integration, what would need to happen for that to change? What is the right conceptual framework for thinking about these issues? *What kind of constitutional theory provides the most plausible account of these issues?*

In order to develop the broad contours of a constitutional theory that makes normative sense of constitutional pluralism, I will first discuss the structure, implications, and shortcomings of two widely endorsed theoretical frameworks used by different courts at different times that I claim are incompatible with constitutional pluralism properly so-called. I will refer to them as Democratic Statism and Legal Monism respectively.[10] Democratic Statism insists on a pluralist construction of the legal world, but insists that constitutionalism properly so-called is tied to a genuine political community establishing a supreme legal authority within the framework of a sovereign state. There can be no constitutionalism properly so-called beyond the state, even though states might sometimes have good reasons to open up their respective legal orders to the law beyond the state and that law can be institutionally complex. Legal Monism, on the other hand, is sceptical about any kind of legal pluralism and can analyse it only it as a case of law in crisis. If either of these positions is right, there

---

[9] 'More encompassing' merely refers to the fact that the international legal order is a legal order of all states, the EU legal order is a legal order of some states, and a domestic legal order is the legal order of only one state (itself perhaps made up of a number of constituent states).

[10] The description and analysis of the competing frameworks draws heavily on M Kumm, 'How does EU Law Fit into the World of Public Law?', in J Neyer and A Wiener (eds), *Political Theory of the European Union* (Oxford University Press, 2011), 111–38.

can be no constitutional pluralism in any meaningful sense. These positions are incompatible with constitutional pluralism properly so called. Conversely constitutional pluralists implicitly claim that Democratic Statism and Legalist Monism provide misguided interpretations of the world of law, and are ultimately based on untenable accounts of the grounds of constitutional authority.

After analysing the structure of these positions and their implications for conflict between legal orders, I will briefly describe the contours of what I have called Constitutionalism.[11] Constitutionalism is the name of a conceptual framework that can help make sense of the idea of constitutional pluralism both analytically and normatively, while also being able to generate an account of the conditions under which hierarchical integration is preferable to pluralism. *The refusal of a legal order to recognize itself as hierarchically integrated into a more comprehensive legal order is justified, if the more comprehensive legal order suffers from a structural legitimacy deficit that the less comprehensive legal order does not suffer from. The concrete doctrines governing the management of the interface between legal orders are justified, if they are designed to ensure that the legitimacy conditions for liberal democratic governance are secured. In practice that means that there are a variety reasons that support a presumption in favour of applying the law of the more comprehensive order over the law of the more parochial one, unless there are countervailing concerns of sufficient weight. The point of constitutional pluralism, I will argue, is to create a normative space both for justified institutionalized civil disobedience and justified institutionalized collective conscientious objection.*

2 The Old World of Public Law: Democratic Statism and the Deep Divide

(A) Statism in Three Historical Versions: Conceptual, Realist, and Democratic

The core feature of statist accounts of the world of law is a deep divide: there is national or state law on the one hand and there is international or interstate law on the other. State law is the paradigmatic case of law. International law is the impoverished stepchild of state law. The former is in some sense derived from the latter and yet it seems lacking in some basic way. Historically three different accounts of that divide were offered, each distinguishable by their account of what exactly international law lacked.

During much of the nineteenth century, legal theorists spent a great deal of time grappling with the *conceptual question* whether international law properly so called

---

[11] I have on other occasions also referred to the theory as 'Cosmopolitan Constitutionalism', see M Kumm, 'The Cosmopolitan Turn in Constitutionalism: On the Relationship between Constitutionalism in and beyond the state', in JL Dunoff and J Trachtman (eds), *Ruling the World: Constitutionalism, International Law, Global Governance* (Cambridge: Cambridge University Press, 2009) or 'Constitutionalism beyond the State', see M Kumm, n 3.

could exist, or whether it was really just a kind of positive morality, given the absence of an international sovereign. If law was the command of a sovereign,[12] or sovereignty was a predicate that precluded being subject to legal obligations,[13] how could international law exist as law?

Even though conceptual arguments lost their sway in the twentieth century, after the Second World War so-called 'realism'[14] provided what was believed to be an *empirically grounded* account of why the structure of the international system made the establishment of the rule of law beyond the state a utopian exercise. In an international system where states simply followed their national interests, international law could not function as an independent guide or constraint for state action.

But by the end of the Cold War, with the spread of failed states on the one hand and the rise of relatively effective Treaty regimes and practices of global governance on the other, that argument too, fell out of favour. The terms of the debate shifted again. General scepticism was in retreat as a rich literature burgeoned that tried to explain the widespread phenomenon of compliance with international law.[15] As liberal constitutional democracies were increasingly constrained perhaps not by a Weberian iron cage but at least a strong web of transnational legal norms, *statism took a democratic turn*: now the deep divide between national law and international law was justified with reference to democratic constitutional theory. State law ultimately derives its authority from, 'We the People' imagined as having acted as a *pouvoir constituant* to establish a national constitution as a supreme legal framework for democratic self-government.[16] International law, on the other hand, derives its authority from the consent of states. Of course, states may decide to establish all kinds of international institutions to address specific issues. They can also establish courts and tribunals and even establish treaties that create rights and obligations for individuals. But no matter how important these treaties might be to address basic collective action or coordination problems, no matter the internal complexity of the institutions they set up, none of this takes away from the fact that these international institutions are ultimately based on treaties requiring the ratification by states following national constitutional requirements. Member States remain the masters of international treaties, for as long as they are not replaced by genuine constitutions attributable to a constitutive act of 'We the People'.

There are two important consequences connected to a construction of the legal world informed by democratic statism. First, democratic statism insists that national constitutional law, as the supreme law of the land, determines if and under what conditions international law is to be enforced domestically. The authority of

---

[12] J Austin, *The Province of Jurisprudence Determined* (London: John Murray, 1832).

[13] See for example A Lasson, *Prinzip und Zukunft des Völkerrechts* (Berlin: Hertz, 1871). The argument was actually pleaded and dismissed by the Permanent Court of Justice, the predecessor of the ICJ, see the S.S. Wimbledon Case, *U.K. v Japan*, 1923 PCIJ (series A) No 1, at 25.

[14] For a classical statement see HJ Morgenthau, *Politics Among Nations: The Struggle for Power and Peace*, 5th edn, revised, (New York: Alfred A. Knopf, 1978), 4–15.

[15] An overview of the debate as it stood in the nineties and further references can be found in H Koh, 'Why Do Nations Obey International Law?' (1997) 106 *Yale Law Journal* 2634.

[16] See E-J Sieyes, 'Qu'est-ce que le tiers etat' (1985), in *Ecrits Politiques* 115, 160.

international law, from the perspective of national law, remains a matter to be determined by national constitutional law. Of course a violation of international law may trigger the responsibility of the violating state on the international level, but as a matter of domestic law such a consequence might well be legally irrelevant. The legal world thus has a dualist structure. Second, given that state law is connected to the idea of the citizenry governing themselves democratically, and the institutional and social infrastructure for collective self-government is absent beyond the state, international law is inherently infected by a democratic deficit. That deficit is less when there is a close and concrete link between a specific international legal obligation and state consent. But even then there is a residual problem, because many international obligations can't be unilaterally revoked by the state as a matter of international law, even when the majority of citizens using democratic procedures wants to do so. Problems of democratic legitimacy become even more serious, when treaties authorize international institutions to make important social and political choices. Even if ultimately problem-solving or cooperation-enhancing benefits associated with international law may legitimate international law, there remains an aura of a legitimacy deficit that hangs over international law.

(B) Democratic Statism and the ECJ's Claim to Primacy over Domestic Constitutional Law

When the ECJ made the claim in *Costa v ENEL* that EU law has primacy over national law, even national constitutional law, the Court implicitly rejected Democratic Statism and embraced an alternative account of public law. That will be described below. Here the focus is on how to make sense of such a claim from the point of view of Democratic Statism, a framework adopted by some Member States' highest courts, perhaps most prominently the German Federal Constitutional Court in its *Maastricht*[17] and *Lisbon*[18] decisions. Within the framework of Democratic Statism a claim to primacy is plausible only if the European Union has in fact become a federal state with a constitution properly so called. The central question becomes: is the EU an international organization, ultimately based on Treaties deriving their authority from the ratification of Member States according to their national constitutional requirements? Or has the EU become a federal state, based on an act by the citizenry acting as a *pouvoir constituant*? If it is the former EU law cannot, at least as a matter of domestic law, claim primacy over national constitutional law. If it is the latter, Member States have lost their ultimate authority as their national constitutional order has been hierarchically integrated into the legal order of the new federal superstate.

Note that within the democratic statist model there is no third alternative. The EU qualifies either as a state or as an international institution. Calling the EU an institution *sui generis*, as has become customary in EU legal circles to avoid asking that

---

[17] BVerfGE 89, 155—*Maastricht* (12.10.1993), file number 2 BvR 2134, 2159/92.
[18] BVerfG 2 BvE 2/08, Judgment of 30 June 2009.

question, just clouds the issue. The EU may be *sui generis* in all kinds of ways, but it will be either a *sui generis* state or a *sui generis* international institution, *tertium non datur*. The question is whether it is one or the other.

i The Test for Establishing Statehood: Why the EU is no State

So how would one go about establishing whether it is one or the other? Courts and scholars using a Democratic Statist framework generally focus on a combination of three factors.[19] The first is *institutional* and focuses on the structure of the EU Treaties. Here the general focus tends to be whether Member States can still plausibly be described as the 'Masters of the Treaty' or whether EU institutions have emancipated themselves from the control of Member States to a sufficient degree. The focus is on a variety of factors that include but are not limited to the amendment procedure (is the unanimity required to amend the Treaties or is a qualified majority enough?), the ordinary legislative procedure (is the Council in charge or does Parliament dominate the legislative process and even if it does, is it constituted in a way that reflects the idea of equality of citizens), competencies (how far does EU law authorize legislation in core traditional areas of sovereignty, such as taxes, defence, social security, and criminal law?). The second factor is *procedural*. Were the Treaties the result of an ordinary treaty ratification procedure or was there a constitutional convention or some other mechanism which allowed for the kind of high-level participation and deliberation associated with actions appropriately attributable to 'We the People'? Third, there are *sociological* factors: do EU citizens have the kind of cohesion, do they share the kind of bond characteristic of 'the people'? Do they have what it takes to be a '*demos*'? To determine whether that is the case some authors focus on shared history, culture, religion, language etc. Others focus on the structure of the public sphere and the institutions of civil society relating to media, political parties, interest groups, etc. These differences cannot be addressed here and it must suffice to point to the basic structure of the argument.

Even though applying these factors to the EU might plausibly give rise to debate as to whether or not the EU qualifies as a state, there is not a single court or author I am aware of that has embraced the democratic statist framework and then concluded that, on applying some set of criteria along these lines, the EU qualifies as a state. Among democratic statists there seems to be a consensus that the EU is based on treaties, not a constitution properly so called, and that it qualifies not as a state but as an international institution. Democratic Statists thus conclude that the primacy claim made by the ECJ is mistaken, at least if it is understood as a claim that national courts should apply EU law even in the face of opposing national constitutional norms. Since there is no European Constitution plausibly grounded in an act of a European '*pouvoir constituant*' and ensuring the democratic self-government of a 'European People',

---

[19]   See M Kumm, 'The Jurisprudence of Constitutional Conflict: Constitutional Supremacy in Europe before and after the Constitutional Treaty' (2005) 11(3) *European Law Journal* 262 and 275–8. For an account of a similarly structured discussion in the US pre-Civil War context see D Golove, 'New Confederalism: Treaty Delegations, Executive and Judicial Authority' (2003) 55 *Stanford Law Review* 1697.

European law cannot plausibly be conceived as the supreme law of the land in the European Union. Recognizing the position of the ECJ would undermine commitments to democratic self-government central to Democratic Statism. Instead EU law, on this view, ultimately derives its authority from Member States who have ratified the treaties according to their national constitutional requirements. The status of EU law as a matter of domestic law depends ultimately on what the national constitution determines. EU law trumps national law only to the extent prescribed by the national constitution. National constitutional law remains the supreme law of the land.

ii Consequences for the Domestic Application of EU Law

Where does that leave the application of EU law by national courts? Those who adopt a Democratic Statist framework insist that such a commitment is distinct from national constitutional parochialism. It does not necessarily entail a commitment to national constitutional doctrines that are inimical to the application of EU law and the functional imperatives of European integration. States might well adopt an 'open constitution', allowing for far-reaching openness to and engagement with the international legal order. Fears invoked by those advocating European law's primacy in the name of ensuring the effective and uniform enforcement are overblown. It is a mistake to believe that only the recognition that EU law is the supreme law of the land ensures the effective and uniform functioning of EU law. National constitutions may well contain norms that specifically authorize the enforcement of EU law in most cases. There is no problem inherent to the idea of constitutional self-government as it is conceived by democratic statists. The real question is merely *how to conceive of the self that governs itself constitutionally,*[20] and how that identity translates into national constitutional conflict norms. The core point is this: following the disasters of the First and Second World Wars, the national selves that govern themselves constitutionally within the framework of the state have committed themselves to constitutionally tolerate European laws enacted collectively by Member States and their peoples. On this, authors ranging from conservatives such as Paul Kirchhof,[21] Judge Rapporteur of the Maastricht judgment,[22] to liberal constitutionalists, such as Dieter Grimm[23] or Joseph Weiler,[24] notwithstanding important differences among them, would agree. The idea of constitutional tolerance lies at the heart of what makes European integration possible and describes its normative core.[25] Most national constitutions have been

---

[20] The idea and its deeper normative significance is developed in JHH Weiler, 'To Be a European Citizen: Eros and Civilization' in JHH Weiler, *The Constitution of Europe* 324. Practical doctrinal implications for thinking about constitutional conflict within this paradigm are developed in M Kumm, 'Who Is the Final Arbiter of Constitutionality in Europe?' (1999) 36 *Common Market Law Review* 356.

[21] P Kirchhof, 'The Balance of Powers Between National and European Institutions' (1999) 5 *European Law Journal* 225–42.

[22] See BVErfGE 89, 189 (1993).

[23] D Grimm, 'Does Europe Need a Constitution?' (1995) 1 *European Law Journal* 282.

[24] JHH Weiler, *Constitutionalism Beyond the State*, (Cambridge: Cambridge University Press, 2003), 7.

[25] JHH Weiler, see n 24.

amended in the process of European integration. All of them are interpreted by national courts to require the enforcement of EU law, even when it conflicts with national statutory law. Constitutional tolerance of EU law—the openness of national legal orders to EU law—is hardwired into national constitutional law as it is interpreted by Member States' highest courts. But tolerance remains very much a feature of the *national* constitution and those who interpret it. Tolerance is, from the perspective of those who decide upon the contours of the constitutional framework within which they govern themselves, *voluntary*.[26] Conceptually, Democratic Statism and its connection between the supremacy of the constitution and the idea of constitutional self-government remain untouched. Focusing on the Schmittian question—who has the final say?—misses the point. It obscures the remarkable fact that in Europe, the everyday enforcement of European law is guaranteed by national constitutional provisions and their interpretation by national courts. The true innovation in European integration is not the establishment of a new ultimate constitutional authority on the European level. And it is not the abdication of national constitutional authority. Europe's genius and the key to understanding its *sui generis* character lies in the reinterpretation of national constitutional traditions to reflect a commitment to constitutional tolerance. National constitutional authority, structured and exercised to reflect a commitment to constitutional tolerance, lies at the heart of the European integration process. The challenge is to amend and interpret national constitutions in such a way that it reflects appropriate respect for national democratic commitments, while enabling appropriate engagement with European law. European integration is inherently beset by a tension between genuine democratic self-government that takes place on the national level, and functional considerations that justify some delegation of powers to the European Union and some degree of opening up of the national legal orders to EU law. That tension has to be carefully calibrated and reflected in the constitutional doctrines that national courts as ultimate guardians of constitutional legality enforce. EU law, no doubt in many ways *sui generis*, ultimately remains treaty-based international law and not constitutional law properly so called.

(C) Democratic Statism and the Relationship between UN Law and European Law

Democratic Statists would have an easy time addressing the central issue in *Kadi*:[27] whether the ECJ had the authority to effectively review a UN Security Council Resolution on the grounds that it violated European fundamental rights. The EU is, like the UN, a treaty-based organization. It came about by states negotiating, signing, and ratifying a treaty according to their national constitutional requirements. Given that both treaties derive their authority from the same source and are both equally

---

[26] JHH Weiler and 'Global and Pluralist Constitutionalism – some doubts', in JHH Weiler G de Búrca *Worlds of Constitutionalism* (Cambridge University Press, forthcoming 2011).

[27] C-402/05 P *Yassin Abdullah Kadi v Council of the EU and Commission of the EC* [2008] ECR I-6351.

international law, the relationship between the two cannot be resolved with reference to source-based conflict rules. Instead the issue is one of conflicting treaty provisions. Conflicts between treaties are resolved first of all with reference to stipulations made by the treaties themselves about their status in case of conflict.[28] Luckily both treaties contain concurring propositions that indicate what should be done in case of conflict. Both the UN Treaties and the EU Treaties require or permit that EU primary law is not applied to prevent the effective implementation to UN law. On the one hand Article 103 UN Charter in conjunction with Article 25 UN Charter clearly stipulates that in case of a conflict between the obligations of the members of the United Nations under the Charter and their obligations under any other international agreement the Charter shall prevail. On the EU side, Article 351 of the Treaty on the Functioning of European Union (hereinafter: TFEU) specifically provides that nothing in the Treaty is to be considered as incompatible with previously assumed international obligations by Member States.[29] Since UN obligations were assumed before Member States joined the EU, the EU Treaties should not preclude the application of UN law. Nothing suggests that the Treaties should have primacy over the UN. Clearly, therefore, the ultimate conclusion reached by the ECFI that UN law is not to be effectively subjected to EU law fundamental rights review is correct and the position of the ECJ is wrong.

The position of the ECJ in *Kadi* does become more plausible, however, if one starts off with the assumption *that the EU is a state* and that EU primary law is like the constitution of a state the supreme law in the European Union. Is that how the ECJ justifies its claim that it can effectively subject UN law to EU fundamental rights review? At the crucial juncture of the decision the Court is remarkably obscure in its reasoning and apodictic in its formulation: the EU is committed to the rule of law and cannot avoid reviewing acts it undertakes on the basis of its own constitutional charter, that establishes an autonomous legal order.[30] Obligations imposed by international agreements cannot change the allocation of powers under that constitutional charter and cannot have the effect of prejudicing constitutional principles that form part of the foundations of the Community.[31] Ultimately the ECJ is only pronouncing on an EU measure, not a UN measure, and it is doing so applying EU fundamental principles.

One obvious criticism of this type of rhetoric is that it is statist in the worst sense: it is not even Democratic Statist. It may sound like some of the more recalcitrant Member States' courts asserting the supremacy of their national constitutions, when confronted with the ECJ's claim that EU law takes primacy over national law, including national constitutional law. The only difference is that the rhetoric of 'the EU as an

---

[28] For the interpretation of Treaties see Vienna Convention on the Law of Treaties (VCLT), done at Vienna on 23 May 1969. Entered into force on 27 January 1980, Arts 31–33. Note that Art 30 VCLT contains a specific set of conflict rules governing Treaties relating to the same subject matter.

[29] According to Art 30(2) VCLT, when a Treaty specifies that it is not to be incompatible with an earlier Treaty, the provision of the earlier Treaty shall prevail.

[30] *Kadi*, see n 27, paras 281 and 282.

[31] *Kadi*, paras 282 and 285.

autonomous legal order' substitutes for the invocation of state sovereignty. But notice how this kind of argument resembles a pre-democratic conceptual statism: a conceptual claim—this time not 'statehood' or sovereignty', but the idea of an 'autonomous legal order'—substitutes for an argument relating to 'We the People' and democracy. The idea of an autonomous legal order is not enriched by arguments about what it is about an order that has certain features that justifies according primacy to it. Read in this way, the ECJ's *Kadi* decision is even worse than national constitutional decisions that make claim to supreme authority. If you take the more articulate cases of national recalcitrance, perhaps best exemplified by the German Constitutional Court in its *Maastricht*[32] and more recent *Lisbon* decision,[33] these decisions at least provide a theoretical basis for their recalcitrant approach: they provide for a democratic statist constitutional theory. Democratic Statism may be ultimately unconvincing, but it is made explicit and allows for serious engagement and criticism.[34]

Of course it is not surprising that the ECJ does not draw on Democratic Statism to justify the EU's primacy over UN law. Arguments about democracy and the role of a *pouvoir constituant* would not resonate when applied to the EU. As discussed above, the perceived absence of a *demos* and the perception that the EU is based on Treaties rather than an act of a European *pouvoir constituant* has made it plausible for many national courts to insist on limiting the extent to which the primacy claim of the ECJ is enforced over specific national constitutional commitments. Not surprisingly the ECJ in *Costa* did not rely on democracy-based arguments to justify the primacy of EU law over Member States' law either. So if the ECJ did not embrace Democratic Statism to justify its claim to primacy in *Costa v ENEL*, what did it rely on? And how might that justification fit with the Court's position with regard to UN law in *Kadi*?

3 The Modernist Challenge: Legalist Monism

Democratic Statism has, over time, been challenged by another model of the world of public law: Legalist Monism.[35] Legalist Monism is the position that underlies the ECJ's jurisprudence in *Costa v ENEL*, justifying the primacy of EU law over all national law, including national constitutional law. The ECJ justified the primacy of EU law not by coming up with a competing interpretation of the criteria established by Democratic Statism as they concern the EU. Instead, the ECJ insisted on using a very different conceptual framework to justify that EU law trumps national law. The following will briefly analyse the justification of that position in *Costa v ENEL* and then assess what

---

[32] BVerfG 89, 155 (1993).

[33] BVerfG, 2 BvE 2/08, Judgment of 30 June 2009.

[34] eg M Kumm, 'The Jurisprudence of Constitutional Conflict: Supremacy before and after the Constitutional Treaty' (2005) 11(3) *European Law Journal* 262–307.

[35] The classic literature on Monism includes H Kelsen, *General Theory of Law and State* (1945), 363–80; A Verdross, *Die Einheit des rechtlichen Weltbildes auf Grundlage der Völkerrechtsverfassung* (1923); H Lauterpacht, *International Law and Human Rights* (1950).

the implication of such an account of the world of public law would be for assessing the relationship between EU and UN law. As will become apparent, there is a tension between *Costa* and *Kadi*. The Legal Monist position in *Costa* should have led the ECJ to confirm the ECFI's decision that it should not review acts implementing UN Law on European fundamental rights grounds.

(B) The Primacy of EU Law

As every student of EU law knows, since the 1960s the ECJ has consistently held that in case of a conflict between European and national law Member States courts are under an obligation to set aside all national law, even national constitutional law.[36] For all practical purposes, European law as interpreted by the ECJ is claimed to be the supreme law of the land in the European Union. The ECJ has supported that claim with the proposition that the EC Treaties established a new legal order and later referred to the Treaties as Europe's 'constitutional charter'.[37] To substantiate this claim the ECJ employed three arguments.

First, the Court makes a conceptual argument. If the Treaty is to establish legal obligation properly so-called, it cannot be permissible for a Member State to unilaterally set it aside unless authorized to do so by EU law. Such unilateral unauthorized action would undermine the status of EU law as law binding on all Member States. This argument is of Kelsenian heritage. According to Kelsen, the world of law has to be conceived in monist terms. Taking a legal point of view is incompatible with the claim that from the point of view of one legal order (say, the European legal order), X is the case, but from the point of view of another legal order (the legal order of Member States), Y is the case. There can be no coexistence of different legal systems constituted by different ultimate legal rules. The world of law is unified not as an empirically contingent matter, but as a conceptual matter.[38]

This is not the place to provide a comprehensive discussion and critique of the argument. Here it must suffice to point out that the argument is not at all obvious. It is

---

[36] Case 6/44 *Costa v ENEL* [1964] ECR 585; Case 43/76, *Comet BV v Produktschap voor Siergewassen* [1976] ECR 2043; Case 106/77 *Amministrazione delle Finanze dello Stato v Simmenthal* [1978] ECR 629.

[37] Case 294/83 *Parti Ecologiste 'Les Verts' v European Parliament* [1986] ECR 1339.

[38] According to Kelsen, the demand that the world of law be monist does not require a *Grundnorm* according to which transnational law trumps national law. It is also possible to posit a *Grundnorm* according to which there is no law except as established by national law. But the choice of the latter *Grundnorm* would imply a kind of national solipsism, comparable to a Cartesian subject that denies the existence of other such subjects and claims that all other persons are nothing but emanations of his consciousness. Adopting such a position is logically possible. Notwithstanding significant efforts by generations of philosophers, solipsism is a position remarkably difficult to refute conclusively. On the other hand there are just no plausible arguments in its favour, so only the most anxious foundationalists have been troubled by the problem. Others have been happy to assume the reality of other subjects as the more plausible starting point. Similarly lawyers, it might be implied from Kelsen, would do well to posit that there is a European legal order and that the legal orders of Member States are equally subject to it. But of course the whole argument depends on the non-obvious claim that there can only be one legal order and that the idea of legal pluralism is untenable for conceptual reasons. That is an issue not to be discussed further here.

not clear why it would undermine the status of EU law as law that there is another legal system that incorporates EU law on its own terms. It is unclear why it should be *conceptually impossible*, as opposed to say, undesirable on pragmatic grounds, to imagine the legal world in pluralist terms. What is *conceptually* wrong with acknowledging the possibility of the existence of different legal orders, each of which recognize the authority of the law of the other on its own terms? There does not *have to be* only one legal point of view, even though it *might* be desirable that there be only one on other normative grounds. Member States may or may not be doing the right thing if they insist on determining the status of EU law in light of their own national constitutional requirements. But they are not thereby undermining the status of EU law as law properly so-called.

The second argument put forward by the ECJ is, at first sight, no less mysterious. The Court lists a number of features of the Treaties that distinguish it from ordinary Treaties of international law: within the considerable competencies defined in the Treaty, EC institutions can enact legislation directly binding citizens in Member States. Furthermore since the enactment of the Single European Act, most decisions concerning the Common Market and, increasingly in other domains as well, are made following a procedure that allows valid legislation to be passed by qualified majority vote and the participation of a European Parliament, even in the face of resistance of some Member States. European law, then, has emancipated itself in its day-to-day workings from its international law foundations and the idea of state consent. It has established its own autonomous legal order.

It is not easy to make sense of this argument. It might be understood in one of two ways. First, it could be understood as a weak claim that the EU is sufficiently different from ordinary treaties that it should not be assessed within the conventional statist paradigm, which constructs international law in contractualist terms based on state consent. But for that argument to be persuasive it would have been necessary to point out how exactly the highlighted features and the relative autonomy of EU law are relevant to the claim of primacy. The Treaties of Rome might be different from most run-of-the-mill treaties, but they are still Treaties and not a genuine constitution of a new state. At least that would be the claim made by a Democratic Statist. What exactly is wrong with that claim? The ECJ does not say.

But the listing of ways in which the EU is different from other Treaties might just have the function of opening the door to the third argument that lies at the heart of the case for primacy. It turns out that the particular features of the EU and the autonomy of the legal order matter for *functional* reasons. A treaty regime that has these features and has been designed to fulfil ambitious purposes—including the establishment of a common market—can only function in a coherent way if the laws it establishes have primacy over national law. Without primacy, the effective and uniform enforcement of Europe's laws would be endangered. The purpose of the European Union to fulfil its various objectives, including the establishment of a common market, could not be achieved if Member States did not accept the primacy of EU law. An aggressively purposive interpretation of the Treaties leads the ECJ to conclude that for all practical purposes, EU law has to be accepted as the supreme law of the land in order to fulfil its purpose. This is a contestable empirical claim about the consequences of not accepting the unconditional primacy of EU law connected to a normatively contestable functional account of the basis of public authority.

The claim to primacy is further strengthened by two further arguments, not explicitly made in *Costa*, but standard fare in the literature supporting that decision. The first concerns democratic empowerment and has been made most forcefully by Christian Jörges and Miguel Maduro. It is not only the case that EU institutions can solve coordination and cooperation problems, thereby providing a functional justification for their legitimacy. They also make available procedures that empower those who are affected by the policies to participate in the process, even if participation is generally more mediated than in the national process. The point is that national processes by themselves are lacking in a central range of cases: they lack the capacity to address certain classes of problems that require coordination and cooperation between states (think of a national fisheries policy trying to establish standards for sustainable use in the North Sea). Self-government exclusively on the level of the state leaves out too much that is of importance for anyone seeking effective self-government. Beyond the national level the idea of self-government requires the availability of jurisgenerative processes—open to participation even if in a more mediated form than electoral democracy—beyond the state level. Furthermore without a transnational check, states are left to decide on policies that have significant externalities, without those who are affected having a say (think of the monetary policy of the Bundesbank before Monetary Union, which effectively set monetary policies for much of Europe). The second argument is historically informed: legally constraining the relationship between Member States is an effective remedy against the great evils that have haunted the continent throughout much of the nineteenth and first half of the twentieth century: clashes of interest between nation-states have a dangerous propensity to degenerate into bloody wars. Within the framework of a coherent legal order the definition, articulation, and negotiation of national interests occurs in such a manner as to make such a development highly unlikely. Legal integration can be seen as a mechanism which tends to immunize nationally organized peoples from the kind of passionate political eruptions that have led to totalitarian or authoritarian governments and/or discrimination of minorities that have characterized European history in the nineteenth and twentieth centuries. This could not be achieved to the same degree, so the argument goes, if the final decision concerning what is to be applied as law in a Member State rests on a decision ultimately made by Member States themselves.

Clearly these arguments have to be read as a critique of Democratic Statism and they embrace a different account of the grounds of public law. Those who claim that the Treaties as the constitution of the European Union are the supreme law of the land in Europe in fact claim that Democratic Statism, which connects the idea of an ultimate legal authority with a strong conception of democratic self-government, is mistaken and needs to be modified. Democratic Statism is unable to incorporate into its account of supremacy the importance of expanding the idea of effective legal authority beyond the boundaries of the nation-state. There may not be a European people and a European democracy in a meaningful sense, but the value of national constitutional self-government is not absolute. The idea of Europe as a legal community—a Rechtsgemeinschaft[39]—integrated by European institutions and European law in the service of prosperity and peace trumps the limitations this imposes on constitutional self-government.

(B) EU Law and International Law: *Kadi*

What are the implications of such a position for deciding whether the ECJ should subject an EU Regulation implementing a UN Security Council obligation to EU fundamental rights law? It turns out that the arguments for the primacy of EU law in *Costa* should also push the ECJ towards recognizing the primacy of UN law over EU law. First, if the conceptual argument is plausible in the context of the relationship between EU law and the law of Member States, there is no reason why it should not also be determinative in the relation between UN law and EU law. If the fact that Member States subject EU law to national constitutional standards subverts the very idea that EU law is law properly so called, does not the fact that the ECJ effectively subjects UN Resolutions to review based on EU standards undermine the very idea that UN law is law properly so called? Second, there are many features of the UN that distinguish it from an ordinary treaty. The UN Charter establishes complex institutions with their own competencies. It allows the UN Security Council to create new legal obligations following a qualified majority procedure among the fifteen states represented on the UN Security Council that generate binding obligations for all Member States (affirmative votes of nine states can therefore bind 193 states). And is the UN Charter not also a constitutional charter of an autonomous legal order? Of course there are differences between the UN and the EU: the ECJ has compulsory jurisdiction over issues of EU law, for example, whereas the ICJ does not have compulsory jurisdiction over issues arising under the UN Charter. There is no comparable doctrine of direct effect with regard to UN law. But not all differences suggest that the EU is more of an 'autonomous legal order' than the UN. Some differences point in the opposite direction. Take the name: the UN is called a charter, not a treaty. Think of the explicit claim to primacy in Article 103 UN Charter, a claim still not explicitly made by the EU Treaties even after the latest rounds of reform.[40] At any rate, whatever differences may exist between the UN and the EU, it remains unclear why these differences should be decisive for the purpose of establishing that the EU is an autonomous legal order that makes a claim to primacy, whereas the UN is

---

[39] See W Hallstein, *Der unvollendete Bundesstaat: Europäische Erfahrungen und Erkenntnisse* (Düsseldorf–Wien: Econ Verlag, 1969).

[40] Of course the failed 'Treaty establishing a Constitution for Europe' (TCE, 2004) had a qualified supremacy clause. The Treaty of Lisbon ('Treaty of Lisbon amending the Treaty on European Union and the Treaty establishing the European Community, signed at Lisbon, 13 December 2007', 2007/C306/01) on the other hand, merely confirms the ECJ's jurisprudence in the 'Declarations annexed to the final act of the intergovernmental conference which adopted the *Treaty of Lisbon*' (signed on 13 December 2007, C115/335) attached to the Treaty.

not. Third, the functional reasons supporting primacy of EU law over Member States law also support the claim to primacy of UN law of EU law. If the UN is to effectively succeed in 'maintaining peace and security', and if the UN Security Council is to effectively take up its 'primary responsibility for the maintenance of international peace and security', does that not require that other actors accept the primacy of UN Security Council Resolutions? Would anything else not undermine the effective and uniform enforcement of UN law? The judgment of the ECFI, with its emphasis on functional arguments, to a large extent reflects the Legal Monist positions embraced by the ECJ in *Costa*. But the position of the ECJ does not. Is the only way to make sense of the ECJ's *Kadi* decision to understand it as the ECJ having taken a statist turn, albeit a statist turn without the resources of democratic constitutional theory to back it up?

4 Second Modernity: Cosmopolitan Constitutionalism in a Pluralist Key

There seems to be an irresolvable tension between *Kadi* and *Costa*, just as there seems to be an irresolvable tension between *Costa* and most of the decisions of national constitutional courts, that insist on drawing constitutional red lines in the sand. But there is a way to reread *Kadi*, *Costa,* and national constitutional court decisions that suggests all three in fact embrace a very similar conception of public law. But that conception is neither Democratic Statist, nor is it Legal Monist. Instead it is what I call Cosmopolitan Constitutionalist.[41] Constitutionalism refers to a position according to which a set of universal principles central to liberal democratic constitutionalism undergird the authority of public law. Constitutionalist principles constitute the law and guide its interpretation and progressive development. They also determine which norms take precedence over others in particular circumstances. Contrary to Democratic Statism, it is not the case that the idea of 'democracy' and 'national self-government' connected to statehood and sovereignty provide the decisive principles to determine where ultimate authority lies. But nor is it the case that the idea of legality and the functional reasons in support of it are sufficient to justify a hierarchically structured, source-based monist account of the legal world. Both of these competing conceptions address relevant moral concerns, but neither one is persuasive because both are one-sided. Instead constitutionalism provides an integrative framework that guides the resolution of constitutional conflicts.

First, Legalist Monism is right that the idea of legality—respect for the rule of law—and the functional and procedural considerations that support extending it to the level beyond the state plausibly provide for a presumption of some weight: that the law of the more expansive community should be respected by public authorities, regional or

---

[41] M Kumm, 'The Cosmopolitan Turn in Constitutionalism: On the Relationship between Constitutionalism in and beyond the State', in JL Dunoff and JP Trachtman (eds), *Ruling the World? Constitutionalism, International Law and Global Governance* (Cambridge: Cambridge University Press, 2009).

national law to the contrary notwithstanding. *There is a presumption that UN law trumps EU law and that EU law trumps Member States' law ultimately grounded in functional and participatory considerations. Given the collective action and coordination problems that these regimes are trying to solve that States individually are unable to address effectively, the resolution provided for by the more expansive regimes ought to carry with them a presumption of authoritativeness.* But in liberal democracies, legitimate authority is not tied to formal and functional considerations alone. It is also tied to procedural and substantive requirements that are reflected in constitutional commitments to democracy and the protection of rights. And it takes seriously the idea of self-government of a national community. That does not mean that the authority of UN law, from the perspective of EU law, should be determined exclusively by EU primary law or that the authority of EU law should be determined exclusively by Member States' constitutions. Both Legalist Monism and the Democratic Statist conception of the legal world provided by the statist version of national constitutionalism ultimately provide one-sided and thus unpersuasive accounts of the principle of legality. What it suggests instead is that the presumption in favour of applying the law of the more expansive community can be rebutted if, in a specific context, the law of the more expansive community violates countervailing principles in a sufficiently serious way.

What then are those countervailing principles and what is the implication of them being violated? Here it must suffice to name them and then briefly illustrate how they operate: besides the principle of legality, which establishes a presumptive duty to enforce international law, the normatively complementary but potentially countervailing principles are the jurisdictional principle of subsidiarity, the procedural principle of due process, and the substantive principle of respect for human rights and reasonableness.[42]

The basic building blocks of a conception of legality that is tied to a framework of constitutionalism are now in place: the law of the more expansive community should presumptively be applied even against conflicting national law, unless there is a sufficiently serious violation of countervailing constitutional principles relating to jurisdiction, procedure, or substance.

To illustrate the idea of Constitutionalism as a distinct model of the world of public law I will first provide an alternative account of the approach taken by some Member States' courts in their engagement with the ECJ's primacy claim (A), then revisit *Costa* (B), and finally provide another reading of *Kadi* (C). The point is to illustrate how central elements of these decisions can be understood as reflecting a commitment to Constitutionalism, rather than Statism, or Legalist Monism. It will also become clear that the kind of resistance by courts to the claims to authority by the more comprehensive legal orders is best understood as a form of either institutionalized civil disobedience[43] or identity-based conscientious objection demanding asymmetric accommodation.

---

[42] For a fuller account, see M Kumm, 'The Jurisprudence of Constitutional Conflict: Constitutional Supremacy before and after the Constitutional Treaty' (2005) 11(3) *European Law Journal* 262–307.

[43] For the idea of linking the pluralism debate to institutional disobedience, see J Baquero Cruz, 'Legal Pluralism and Institutional Disobedience in the European Union' in J Komarek and M Avbelj (eds), *Constitutional Pluralism in the European Union and Beyond* (Oxford: Hart, 2011).

(A) Constitutionalism and the German Constitutional Court's Response to *Costa*

One important consequence of conceiving of legal authority as a function of the realization of a set of principles is that whether or not EU law should be recognized as having primacy over national constitutional law is a question that allows for qualified answers. It admits to more nuanced answers than just yes or no. Even if the European Union law does not, without some qualification, establish the supreme law of the land, it could still effectively reconstitute legal and political authority in Europe. The authority of EU law is possibly a question of degree. It may depend on the degree to which constitutional principles are realized by EU institutions. It admits of the possibility that neither EU law nor national constitutional law effectively establishes the supreme law of the land. In this way, constitutionalism can help shed light on a fascinating aspect of national courts reception of EU law. For the most part national courts have not accepted that EU law is the supreme law of the land. But nor have they simply assumed that national constitutional law is the supreme law of the land and that EU law is applied only to the extent authorized by the national constitution. There is something deeply misleading in claiming that, to the extent that national courts have not accepted EU law as the supreme law of the land, they are merely interpreting their national constitutions to establish what the status of EU law should be as a matter of domestic law. National courts have generally adopted an intermediate position. They generally accept neither EU law nor the national constitution as the supreme law of the land. Instead they look to both EU law and the national constitution and try to make sense of what the best understanding of the competing principles in play requires them to do.[44] Theirs is a constitutionalist conception of public law. To flesh out what this means practically and provide an example, a brief and somewhat schematic analysis of the German Federal Constitutional Court's approach to the authority of EU law will follow. The jurisprudence of the Court may be widely known by European Union lawyers, but its reconstruction in terms of a commitment to constitutionalism may prove illuminating, even if it can only be brief and schematic.

The German Constitution, until the early 1990s,[45] contained no specific provisions addressing European integration, though the Preamble mentions Germany's commitment to strive for peace in a united Europe. The Constitution did authorize Germany to enter into treaties establishing international institutions,[46] and it contained general provisions giving international treaties the same status as domestic statutes.[47] Yet the

---

[44] For a fully developed argument to this effect see M Kumm, 'The Jurisprudence of Constitutional Conflict: Constitutional Supremacy before and after the Constitutional Treaty' (2005) 11(3) *European Law Journal* 262–307.

[45] In the context of the ratification of the Maastricht Treaty Art 23, the Basic Law was amended to address questions of European integration.

[46] See Art 24 Basic Law.

[47] This is the dominant interpretation of Art 59 II Basic Law.

ECJ had claimed that EU law was to be regarded as the supreme law of the land in the European Union requiring Member States' courts to set aside any national law, even national constitutional law, if it was in conflict. How were national courts to respond? Was the ECJ's claim really plausible that Member States had established a new supreme law of the land by signing and ratifying a set of treaties the core objective of which was to establish a common market? On the other hand, was it plausible to claim that the EU Treaties, which established institutions that had been endowed with significant legislative authority, and played a significant role to secure peace and prosperity in war-ravaged Europe, should be treated like any other treaty? Was it really adequate to apply the general rule applicable to treaties according to which an ordinary statute enacted after the treaty was ratified would trump it? If the national courts simply accepted the basic ideas underlying Democratic Statism and its idea of constitutional self-government, this is probably the conclusion the court would have reached. If, on the other hand, the court accepted EU law as legitimate constitutional authority on legalist grounds, it would follow the ECJ. But the court chose neither of these options. It embraced an intermediate solution. That intermediate solution illustrates the connection between a constitutionalism and the complex set of doctrines that national courts have in fact developed for assessing the ECJ's claims concerning the supremacy of EU law.

First the German Federal Constitutional Court (hereinafter: FCC) accepted without much ado that EU law trumps ordinary statutes, even statutes enacted later in time, because of the importance of securing an effective and uniformly enforced European legal order.[48] The principle of ensuring the effective and uniform enforcement of EU law—expanding the rule of law beyond the nation-state—was a central reason for the court to recognize the authority of EU law over national statutes. This meant that in Germany, EU Treaties were effectively granted a more elevated status than ordinary treaties, to which a 'last-in-time' conflict rule generally applies.

Yet, contrary to the position of the ECJ, the court recognized that that principle was insufficient to justify the supremacy of EU law over all national law. The principle of legality matters, but it is not all that matters. The *second* issue before the court was whether it should subject EU law to national constitutional rights scrutiny. Could a resident in Germany rely on German constitutional rights against EU law? Could the protection of national residents against rights violations guaranteed in the national constitution be sacrificed on the altar of European integration? Like other questions concerning the relationship between EU law and national law, the German Constitution provided no specific guidance on that question. In *Solange I*[49] the FCC balanced the need to secure the fundamental rights of residents against the needs of effective and uniform enforcement of EU law and established a flexible approach: for as long as the EU did not provide for a protection of fundamental rights that is the equivalent to the protection provided on the national level, the court would subject EU law to national constitutional scrutiny. At a later point in *Solange II*[50] the court determined that the

---

[48] BVerfGE 22, 293 (1967) and BVerfGE 31, 145 (1971).
[49] BVerfGE 37, 271 (1974).   [50] BVErfGE 73, 339 (1986).

ECJ had significantly developed its review of EU legislation and held that the standard applied by the ECJ was essentially equivalent to the protection provided by the FCC's interpretation of the German Constitution. For so long as that remained the case, the FCC would not exercise its jurisdiction to review EU law on national constitutional grounds. Because the ECJ through its own jurisprudence provided the structural guarantees that fundamental rights violations by EU institutions would generally be prevented, it conditionally accepted the authority of EU law. To put it another way, structural deficits in the protection of fundamental rights on the European level were the reason for the FCC to originally insist that it should not accept the authority of EU law, insofar as constitutional rights claims were in play. When those specific concerns were effectively addressed by the ECJ, the authority of EU law extended also over national constitutional rights guarantees and the FCC as their interpreter. The authority of EU law, then, was in part a function of the substantive and procedural fundamental rights protections available to citizens as a matter of EU law against acts of the European Union. If within such a framework the court was to refuse to enforce EU law, it would amount to a form of civil disobedience: a public act refusing compliance, based on principles that are imagined to be shared by both EU and national law, also taken with a view to change European law. The whole threat of exercising jurisdiction with regard to fundamental rights at all is tied to existence of a structural deficit on the European level. Only because there are structural concerns relating to fundamental rights protection does the German court assert jurisdiction. Once the structural concern is addressed at the EU level, concerns relating to uniform and effective enforcement of EU law trump any possibility that, in a given case, the FCC might to a better job at identifying the disputed proper scope and limits of a right.

But there is a third issue. In its Maastricht decision,[51] and later in its Lisbon decision,[52] the FCC determined that it had jurisdiction to review whether or not legislative acts by the European Union were enacted *ultra vires* or not. If such legislation were enacted *ultra vires*, it would not be applicable in Germany. As a matter of EU law it is up to the ECJ, of course, to determine as the ultimate arbiter of EU law whether or not acts of the European Union are within the competencies established by the Treaties.[53] But the ECJ had adopted an extremely expansive approach to the interpretation of the EU's competencies, raising the charge that it allowed for Treaty amendments under the auspices of Treaty interpretation. Under these circumstances the FCC believed it appropriate for it to play a subsidiary role as the enforcer of limitations on EU competencies of last resort. Both in the Maastricht and Lisbon decisions, arguments from democracy played a central role. Democracy in Europe remains underdeveloped, with electoral politics playing a marginal role. The national domain remains the primary locus of democratic politics. Under those circumstances, ensuring that EU institutions would remain within the competencies established in the Treaties is of paramount importance. Yet even while insisting that it

---

[51] BVerfGE 89, 155 (1993).   [52] BVerfG, 2 BvE 2/08, Judgment of 30 June 2009.
[53] See Art 230 ECT.

had the competency to review EU law on jurisdictional grounds, the FCC made it clear that that review would be highly deferential:[54] only if the transgression of the EU competencies is *sufficiently serious* and the act in question leads to a *structurally significant* shift in the allocation of competencies, would the acts be deemed *ultra vires* and inapplicable in Germany.[55] This deferential standard reflects concerns for the rule of law and effective functioning of a transnationally integrated community, where reasonable interpretative disagreement about the jurisdictional limits of the EU is possible, in particular given open-ended jurisdictional norms such as subsidiarity and proportionality. These doctrinal tests can thus be understood to determine the conditions under which claims to justified institutional disobedience in the name of the protection of democracy and subsidiarity can be made.

This points to a final line of national resistance. When a national constitution contains a specific rule containing a concrete national commitment—say a commitment to free secondary education,[56] or a restriction to national citizens of the right to vote in municipal elections,[57] or a categorical prohibition of extradition of citizens to another country[58]—these commitments will not generally be set aside by national courts. Instead, national courts will insist that the constitution is politically amended to ensure compliance with EU law. This line of cases reflects an understanding that the realm of the national remains the primary locus of democratic politics and primary focal point for the identification of citizens. For as long as that remains the case, a commitment to democracy is interpreted by some Member States' courts as precluding setting aside specific national constitutional commitments, to the extent they are embodied in concrete and specific rules. It is then up to the constitutional legislature to initiate the necessary constitutional amendments.

To the extent that such commitments are understood as part of a national constitutional identity, the claim made by a court in the name of constitutional identity is structurally equivalent to a person demanding to be exempt from a generally applicable rule as a conscientious objector: it is a demand to accommodate a specific addressee of a legal obligation because of deeply held commitments that it would, on balance, be unreasonable for the legal order to require the addressee to give up. Unlike civil disobedience, conscientious objection is not directed towards legal reform. The claim is merely to be left alone with regard to an obligation whose appropriateness for others is not put into question. When a national court invokes the constitutional identity of the national community as an argument not to comply with a legal

---

[54] Decision of 6 July 2010, 2 BvR 2661/06—*Honeywell*. See also Judgment of 7 September 2011, 2 BvR 987/10, 2 BvR 1485/10, 2 BvR 1099/10 (Greece aid and Euro rescue package).

[55] See M Payandeh, 'Constitutional Review of EU Law after *Honeywell*: Contextualizing the Relationship between the German Constitutional Court and the EU Court of Justice' (2011) 48 *Common Market Law Review* 9–38.

[56] Belgian Constitutional Court, European Schools, Arbitragehof, Arrest no. 12/94, B.S. 1994, 6137–46.

[57] Spanish Constitutional Court, Municipal Electoral Rights, 3 Common Law Reports 101 (1994).

[58] Polish Constitutional Court, Judgment of 27th April 2005, P 1/05.

obligation, it is thus not implausible to understand this claim as the democratically 'constitutionalized' version of what on an individual basis would be recognized as conscientious objection.[59]

This highly stylized and schematic account illustrates the operation of a conception of legitimate constitutional authority that puts the principles of constitutionalism front and centre.[60] The principle of legality and its extension beyond the nation-state has an important role to play to support the authority of EU law, but concerns relating to subsidiarity, democracy, and human rights may provide countervailing reasons for limiting the authority of EU law in certain circumstances. Furthermore, the principles that govern the relationship between national and EU law do not themselves derive their authority from either the national constitution or EU law. The relative authority of EU and national constitutions is a question to be determined by striking the appropriate balance between competing principles of constitutionalism in a concrete context. The result of such an exercise is a doctrinal framework that defines the conditions under which either institutionalized civil disobedience or constitution-based conscientious objection are justified.

(B) Constitutionalist Elements in *Costa* and Beyond

As was argued above, *Costa v ENEL* more than any other decision reflects a commitment to Legal Monism, not Constitutionalism. But in the following I will demonstrate that there are elements in *Costa* that make better sense when interpreted in a Constitutionalist, rather than Legal Monist prism (i). Furthermore I will argue that EU law has evolved in a way that suggests that the courts' continued insistence on primacy may not only be justifiable in Constitutionalist terms, but also be generally compatible with the positions actually taken by Member States' courts (ii).

i *Costa* and Constitutionalism: Making Sense of the Idea of an Autonomous Legal Order

So how does Constitutionalism make sense of the claim that the authority of EU law is not simply derived from the fact that Member States have signed and ratified the founding EU following their respective constitutional requirements? What, if anything, justifies the claim that EU law establishes an autonomous legal order and what follows from it?

Whether a treaty qualifies as a constitution of an autonomous legal order or merely as an ordinary treaty under international law depends on how its claim to legal authority is best understood. If its claim to legal authority is best understood to rest exclusively on the fact that Member States have signed and ratified it, then it is an

---

[59] I thank Victor Ferreres Comella for bringing this analogy to my attention. For a general discussion on civil disobedience and conscientious objection and their different justification see J Raz, *The Authority of Law* (Oxford: Oxford University Press, 1979), 263–89.

[60] For a more fully developed account see M Kumm, 'The Jurisprudence of Constitutional Conflict: Constitutional Supremacy before and after the Constitutional Treaty' (2005) 11(3) *European Law Journal* 262–307.

ordinary treaty of international law. The decisive feature of constitutional treaties establishing an autonomous legal order in some sense is that its claim to authority is in part directly grounded in constitutional principles.[61] Its claim to authority is not grounded exclusively in the fact that Member States have signed and ratified it, even if it would not have come into existence had Member States not signed and ratified it. The idea of a constitutional treaty, then, is contrary to claims by Democratic Statists, not a contradiction in terms. Nor does it matter that the Treaties of the European Union have gradually evolved in a piecemeal fashion, rather than having being created in a legal revolutionary moment, a kind of constitutional 'big bang' or a 'creatio ex nihilo'. Whether or not something that takes the form of a treaty is in fact merely a treaty of international law or a form of transnational constitutional law that has greater authority is a question of interpretation.

The European Union explicitly claims to be founded on constitutional principles. Article 6 of the Treaty on European Union[62] states that the 'Union is founded on the principles of liberty, democracy, respect for human rights and fundamental freedoms and the rule of law, principles which are common to the Member States'. The EU, in its self-presentation, is neither founded on the will of a European 'We the People', nor is it founded on the 'will of Member States'. It is founded on the constitutional principles that are a common heritage of the European constitutional tradition as it has emerged in the second half of the twentieth century. And, as the ECJ found more than forty years ago and as is now recognized in Declaration 17 of Appended to the EUT,[63] EU law makes a claim to primacy. Whether and to what extent that claim to authority deserves to be recognized by Member States' courts is not an easy question and it gives rise the kind of concerns that were described above. But an answer to that question will not make use of unhelpful dichotomies between treaties and constitutions or the 'will of Member States' or 'We the People'.

ii *Costa* Today

When the ECJ made the claim that EU law has primacy over all national law, including national constitutional law, it was making a claim that national courts were right not to

---

[61] Compare also A von Bogdandy, 'The Prospect of a European Republic: What European Citizens are Voting on' (2005) 42 *Common Market Law Review* 913–41.

[62] *Treaty of Lisbon* ('Treaty of Lisbon amending the Treaty on European Union and the Treaty establishing the European Community, signed at Lisbon, 13 December 2007', 2007/C 306/01).

[63] Declaration 17 states: 'The Conference recalls that, in accordance with well settled case law of the Court of Justice of the European Union, the Treaties and the law adopted by the Union on the basis of the Treaties have primacy over the law of Member States, under the conditions laid down by the said case law. The Conference has also decided to attach as an Annex to this Final Act the Opinion of the Council Legal Service on the primacy of EC law as set out in 11197/07 (JUR 260): '*Opinion of the Council Legal Service of 22 June 2007: It results from the case-law of the Court of Justice that primacy of EC law is a cornerstone principle of Community law. According to the Court, this principle is inherent to the specific nature of the European Community. At the time of the first judgment of this established case law (Costa/ENEL,15 July 1964, Case 6/641 (1) there was no mention of primacy in the treaty. It is still the case today. The fact that the principle of primacy will not be included in the future treaty shall not in any way change the existence of the principle and the existing case-law of the Court of Justice.'*

accept it in an unqualified way. At the time EU law did not provide for adequate constitutional rights protection, it did not provide for an adequate democratic legislative procedure, and there was no indication that the Court took seriously the limits of competencies in the Treaty. These concerns became more serious as the decision making moved from unanimity to qualified majority voting in more and more areas since the mid-1980s. To a significant extent, the response of Member States' courts can be understood as a general acceptance of the ECJ's claim to primacy, but with the proviso that EU law does not violate fundamental rights, remains within its competencies, and does not encroach on fundamental constitutional commitments that defined the democratic identity of the Member State. To the extent that Member States' responses fit this description, they generally comply with constitutionalist requirements. What is remarkable, however, is that all of these concerns are now addressed to a large extent, even if not always effectively, by EU law itself. The story about the evolution of the EU's fundamental rights guarantees is well known and has finally led to the entry into force of the European Charter of Fundamental Rights in December 2009. The concerns relating to competencies have arguably led the ECJ to pay greater attention to delimitation of competencies, even though here there are still good grounds for scepticism.[64] Furthermore, the Treaty of Lisbon contains interesting procedural innovations involving national parliaments that might make some contribution to help establish a culture of subsidiarity in Europe. Finally the structural problems relating to democracy have not really been addressed so far by EU actors even though the legal framework established by the Treaty of Lisbon might allow for the evolution of greater electoral accountability of the Commission in the future, thereby making the elections of the European Parliament more meaningful.[65] But more importantly, EU law now specifically requires that Member States' constitutional identity be respected.[66] A plausible interpretation of that provision suggests that it might not violate EU law if a Member State refused to apply EU law in a situation where a fundamental national constitutional commitment is in play.[67] If that is correct, it is not implausible that a claim to primacy made by EU law that shares these features may no longer be implausible from a constitutionalist point of view. The justification for the primacy of EU law at the time *Costa* was decided might not have been plausible. And the limited acceptance by Member States might in most instances have been justified. But to a significant extent EU law has absorbed the concerns that fostered legitimate resistance by Member States, just as Member States have, over time, opened up their legal orders to accept the application of EU over national law in most instances. Shared constitutional principles seem to have provided the focal point of

---

[64] See M Kumm, 'Constitutionalizing Subsidiarity in Integrated Markets' (2006) 12 *European Law Journal* 503.

[65] See M Kumm, 'Why Europeans Are Not Constitutional Patriots' (2008) 6 ICON 117.

[66] See Art 4, Sect 2 EUT: 'The Union shall respect the equality of Member States before the Treaties as well as their national identities, inherent in their fundamental structures, political and constitutional (. . .)'.

[67] See M Kumm and V Ferreres Comella, 'The Primacy Clause of the Constitutional Treaty and the Future of Constitutional Conflict in the European Union' (2005) 3 ICON 473, 491, and 492.

complementary evolutions of both EU law and national constitutional law. The tensions created by a conflict between Legalist Monism and Democratic Statism have to a large extent been replaced by a common commitment to Constitutionalism. That still leaves open the possibility of conflict on application, but it ensures a common framework within which concrete disagreements are addressed.

(C) A Constitutionalist Reading of *Kadi*

But is *Kadi* compatible with an account that emphasizes the spread of constitutionalism? On the surface the ECJ may seem to have adopted a relatively conventional dualist, statist approach. It insisted on the primacy of EU constitutional principles and explicitly rejected applying these principles deferentially, even though the EU Regulation implemented a UN Security Council Resolution. But on close examination it becomes apparent that important elements of that decision reflect constitutionalist analysis. First, the court specifically acknowledges the function of the UN Security Council as the body with primary responsibility to make determinations regarding the maintenance of international peace and security.[68] Second, the Court examines the argument whether it should grant deference to the UN decisions and rejects such an approach only because at the time the complaint was filed, there were no meaningful review procedures at the UN level, and even those that had been established since then[69] still provide no judicial protection.[70] Only after an assessment of the UN review procedures does the Court conclude that full review is the appropriate standard. This suggests that, echoing the ECHR's approach in *Bosphorus*,[71] more adequate procedures on the UN level might have justified more deferential review. This is further supported by the ECJ's conclusion that under the circumstances the plaintiff's right to be heard and the right to effective judicial review were *patently* not respected. This language suggests that even under a more deferential form of judicial review, the Court would have had to come to the same conclusion. It also suggests that the Court was fully attuned to Constitutionalist sensibilities. It just turns out that the procedures used by the UN Sanctions Committee established by the UN Security Council Resolution were so manifestly inappropriate given what was at stake for the black-listed individuals, that any jurisdictional considerations in favour of deference were trumped by these procedural deficiencies, thus undermining the case not just for abstaining from judicial review altogether, but also for engaging in a more deferential form of review. Third, the Court shows itself attuned to the functional division of labour between the UN Security Council and itself when discussing judicial remedies: the Court does not

---

[68] *Kadi*, Recital 297.

[69] See Security Council Resolution SC Res 1730, UN Doc. S/Res/1730 (19 December 2006); SC 1735, UN Doc. S/Res/1735 (22 December 2006); SC Res 1822, UN Doc. S/Res/1822 (30 June 2008).

[70] *Kadi*, Recital 321, 322. See most recently SC Res 1904 (17 December 2009) that provides at least certain minimal guarantees.

[71] *Bosphorus Hava Yollari Turizm v Ireland* [2005] ECHR.

determine that the sanctions must be lifted immediately, but instead permits them to be maintained for three months, allowing the Council to find a way to bring about a review procedure that meets fundamental rights requirements. Finally, during all of this the Court is careful to emphasize that nothing it does violates the UN resolution, given that international law leaves it to states to determine by which procedures obligations are enforced. Notwithstanding serious problems that remain, it seems that forceful judicial intervention has had a salutary effect, with serious reform proposals discussed and in part enacted at the UN level.[72] An ECJ committed to Constitutionalism takes international law seriously. But taking international law seriously does not require unqualified deference to a seriously flawed global security regime. On the contrary, the threat of subjecting these decisions to meaningful review might help bring about reforms on the UN level. Only once these efforts bear more significant fruit will the ECJ have reasons not to insist on meaningful independent review of individual cases in the future.

Even if the above suggests that it is a mistake to read *Kadi* merely as a case of entrepreneurial but jurisprudentially dubious state-building by the ECJ,[73] there are still plausible grounds to criticize *Kadi* on constitutionalist grounds: why did the Court not emphasize the universal nature of the human rights it was applying? Why did the Court not follow the Advocate General's lead and be more explicit about the conditional nature of its lack of deference? And was it justifiable for the Court to preclude Member States from finding their own ways to address the tensions between compliance with UN sanctions and the relevant human rights concerns? But notwithstanding scope for legitimate criticism, Constitutionalist sensibilities were not lacking in *Kadi*.

5 Challenges and a Response to Critics

Constitutionalism establishes a framework of principles that provide the grounds and limits of legal authority of any legal order within the liberal democratic tradition. These principles guide the inquiry into whether the result of certain jurisgenerative procedures on the level of the more comprehensive legal order effectively establish legal obligations or whether, in a particular context, non-compliance on the level of the more parochial legal order is justified. The principle of establishing the rule of law beyond the state and the functional and procedural concerns that support it, provide a presumption that the outcomes of law generating procedures on the level of the more comprehensive legal order should be respected by its addressees. That presumption can be rebutted if and to the extent that non-compliance is necessary to further countervailing principles relating to jurisdiction, procedure, or substance that in the

---

[72] See most recently Security Council Resolution 1904 (17 December 2009) that finally provides at least minimal, even if still inadequate, procedural guarantees.

[73] See J Goldsmith and E Posner, 'Does Europe Believe in International Law?' (25 November 2008), *Wall Street Journal*.

relevant context, have greater weight. The doctrines used by courts to structure the relationship between different legal orders establish the jurisdictional, procedural, and substantive conditions under which courts claim to be justified to practice institution-alized civil disobedience or protect the constitutional identity—the institutionalized collective equivalent of individual conscience—of the more parochial legal order. Those doctrines are justified, if, all things considered they can be reconstructed as the result of balancing the relevant competing normative concerns.

This account of constitutional pluralism can help clarify what is right and what is wrong about a number of criticisms to which constitutional pluralist accounts have recently been subjected. According to one view Constitutional Pluralists with their happy-go-lucky embrace of 'discourse among courts' and 'heterarchy rather than hierarchy' or 'contrapuntal harmonics' are insufficiently attuned to the functional prerogatives of European integration[74] or virtues of obedience.[75] There is something to that claim. On the one hand, talking about the structure of pluralism in terms of a discourse among courts or contrapuntal harmonics does capture the reasoned and dynamic form that engagement with the more comprehensive legal order frequently takes. But it falls short conceptually. This way of talking is not sufficiently sensitive to the graduated claims of authority that various doctrinal frameworks have built into them. The really interesting questions concern the structures of graduated authority built into doctrinal frameworks: who needs to look at what and give what kind of consideration to what is being said and done. This is still the world of law. It takes the form of constitutional principles generating doctrinal structures, not a Habermasian world of 'herrschaftsfreier Diskurs', or a world of contrapuntally structured discre-tional improvization or diplomatic negotiation based on 'comity' between well-mannered gentleman judges. In the relationship between different legal orders, plur-alism takes the form of a limited but legally structured space constrained by a presumption of authority in favour of the more comprehensive legal order.

But is the account perhaps still too permissive? In a brilliant article, Julio Baquero Cruz has recently argued that the talk of pluralism is exaggerated and misguided, and that instead of constitutional pluralism, the best way to make sense of constitutional conflict in the European Union is to see it as a form of institutional disobedience.[76] As I have argued above, there are good grounds to believe that much of what national courts do can best be understood along those lines. But there are two points of disagreement worth

---

[74] See eg J Baquero Cruz, 'The Legacy of the *Maastricht*-Urteil and the Pluralist Movement' (2008) 14 *European Law Journal* 398.

[75] JHH Weiler, 'Prologue: Global and Pluralist Constitutionalism—Some Doubts', in JHH Weiler and G de Búrca (eds), *The Worlds of European Constitutionalism* (Cambridge: Cambridge University Press, 2011).

[76] See J Baquero Cruz, 'Legal Pluralism and Institutional Disobedience in the European Union', in J Komarek and M Avbelj (eds), *Constitutional Pluralism in the European Union and Beyond* (Hart, forthcom-ing 2012). The issue was first broached in an exchange between Cruz and myself also involving M Maduro and N Walker documented in M Avbelj and J Komarek, 'Four Visions of Constitutional Pluralism' (2008) 2(1) *European Journal of Legal Studies* 325–70. Furthermore an illuminating article by NT Isiksel has recently linked the jurisprudence of the ECJ in the *Kadi* case to the ideal of institutional civil disobedience, see 'Fundamental Rights in the EU after Kadi and Al-Barakaat' (2010) 15(5) *European Law Journal* 551–77.

noting. First, the moral point of pluralism is not just to define the space of legitimate space for institutional disobedience but also institutional conscientious objection. And second and more importantly such a claim does not stand in opposition to the idea of constitutional pluralism as it is defended here. On the contrary, a constitutional theory of constitutional pluralism provides an account of the conditions under which such practices of resistance are justified. Without an account of the moral stakes, that only some version of constitutional theory (even if it is only the bare-bone structure of an account as provided here) can provide, no account of the legitimate grounds of institutionalized civil disobedience or conscientious objection or the nature of the trade-offs necessary can be offered. However the argument Cruz provides has persuaded me that along with the idea of 'identity based' constitutional conscientious objection, the idea of official disobedience captures well the moral point of the kind of pluralism that is justified by the Constitutionalist account.[77] When courts develop doctrines managing the interface between different legal orders, derived from the correct interpretation of principles of Constitutionalism as they apply them to the relevant context, we might say that they are seeking to lay down the jurisdictional, procedural, and substantive conditions for the exercise of institutionalized civil disobedience or conscientious objection. The idea of institutionalized conscientious objection and civil disobedience, then, provides a good way of capturing the moral point of constitutional pluralism.

Finally there are those who insist that the kind of account of constitutional pluralism provided here is not really pluralist, but effectively monist.[78] Ultimately Constitutionalism as it is described here is based on a framework of principles that defines the grounds of law both on the state level and beyond. This is not pluralism, so the claim goes, but monism. I think that claim is correct on one level, even though it is misleading on another. It is correct on the level of jurisprudential reconstruction. Jurisprudentially speaking, the account provided here is monist in the following sense: The moral principles that ground law—that is the principles that determine which social facts are relevant and how exactly they are relevant in establishing something as a correct legal proposition—hang together and form a coherent whole, whether they concern national, European, or UN law. It is difficult to make sense of the idea of a deep discontinuity on the level of principles that ground the practice of law.[79] But even if Constitutional Pluralism is accounted for within unified framework of principles—a monist jurisprudential account—the idea of legal pluralism describes something morally important and jurisprudentially interesting.[80] The type of account provided here insists that whether a

---

[77] The contours of that account were first presented in M Kumm, 'Who is the Final Arbiter of Constitutionality in Europe? Three conceptions of the Relationship between the Federal Constitutional Court and the European Court of Justice' (1999) 36 *Common Market Law Review* 351–86 and more fully developed in M Kumm, 'The Jurisprudence of Constitutional Conflict: Constitutional Supremacy before and after the Constitutional Treaty' (2005) 11(3) *European Law Journal* 262–307. It is only here that I connect this account with the idea of institutional disobedience and conscientious objection as the moral point of constitutional pluralism.

[78] See P Eleftheriadis, 'Pluralism and Integrity' (2010) *Ratio Juris* 365–89 (387) and G Letsas, 'Harmonic Law: The Case against Pluralism' (in this volume).

[79] For an exploration of these themes, see R Dworkin, *Justice for Hedgehogs* (Harvard, 2011).

[80] See G Letsas, see n 78, at 34, claiming that within an 'interpretivist' account the problem of constitutional conflict is not a genuine problem, and can be debunked as a pseudo-problem.

lower legal order should be conceived as being hierarchically integrated within a larger legal order depends on contingent features of the structure of the legal world. The states that are part of the German Federation are right to interpret state law as being hierarchically integrated and inferior to the law of the more comprehensive legal order. There are ultimately Constitutionalist grounds—that is, grounds of moral principle—that justify the recognition of such a hierarchy in some contexts, just as there are Constitutionalist grounds for not recognizing such a hierarchy in other contexts. That is neither a trivial nor uncontested proposition. As I hope to have shown above, it is not possible to make sense of constitutional pluralism within either a Democratic Statist or Monist Legalist framework. If the correct theory of European public law has a Democratic Statist or Legalist Monist structure, there is no place for a meaningful idea of constitutional pluralism. But if the correct theory of European public law has a Constitutionalist structure, then there is an important space for constitutional pluralism.

So what are the core characteristics of a world of public law described in constitutionalist terms? First, unlike the world imagined within the framework of Democratic Statism, the world of public law is imagined as constituted and held together by a shared commitment to constitutional principles. There is no fundamental distinction between state law and law beyond the state. State law and law beyond the state have more in common than statists suggest. Constitutional authority and constitutional principles are constitutive not only of national law and politics, but of law and politics *tout court*. In that sense Constitutionalism is reconceived in a *cosmopolitan* and not statist framework. Second, nor is the legal world of imagined as a monist whole, if what is meant by that is a hierarchically unified structure of norms, in which all conflicts can be resolved by reference to source-based conflict rules. Instead Constitutionalism helps give an account of the principled, but deeply pluralist and fragmentized nature of the world of public law.

There are two ways in which Constitutionalism and pluralism are connected. First, Constitutionalism explains how there can be a plurality of legal regimes that make claims to authority which go beyond their origin in the consent of states. These regimes may be based on a treaty, but these treaties are, just like domestic constitutions in traditional constitutional theory, genuinely constitutive: with them, a new legal authority comes into being. Instead of deriving their authority from the legal acts that made them possible, their claims to authority derive at least in part directly from the constitutional principles they embody and help realize. Second, constitutional principles provide the mediating principles for a deeply pluralist structure of public law. In practice, regime pluralism sometimes leads to the enactment of rules that conflict with one another. When they do, there is no guarantee that conflicts between them will be resolved in the same way by each regime. So there is a distinct possibility of contradictory claims that are part of the legal world without law having the resources to resolve them conclusively. But notwithstanding the possibility of irresolvable legal conflict, *this kind of pluralism* is not deep and hard, but shallow and soft. It is shallow and not deep because Constitutionalist principles are the shared *grounds* of public law practices. And it is not hard but soft, because Constitutionalist principles serve as a *common framework* to mediate potential disputes and give rise to principled practices of engagement and deference that reduce the occasions and limit the stakes of conflict. The moral point of pluralism in such a world is to create a space for justified institutionalized disobedience and constitutional identity based conscientious objection without inappropriately undermining the integrity of the whole.

10

The Idea of European Demoicracy

Kalypso Nicolaïdis[*]

Introduction

How can an 'ever-closer union' between distinct democratic peoples be democratically legitimate? The idea of European 'demoicracy' provides a deceptively simple answer: one is not to cross the Rubicon which separates a European Union ruled by and for multiple *demoi* from a Europe ruled by and for one single *demos*.[1] By crossing the Rubicon in 49 BC, a shallow and red river in northern Italy, Caesar violated the old constitutional rules concerning his own 'imperium' and dramatically changed Rome and his own place within it. There has been a strong temptation for Europe to cross its own Rubicon, the point of no return on the road to integration, in search of its own glorious destiny. But this temptation should be resisted.

To be sure, the idea of a notional barrier between a Europe of demoi and that grounded on the assumption of a single European demos should not be seen as the familiar story about sovereignty and its denial. Instead, there is enough space to enter

* For comments on a previous version of this paper I would like to thank Francis Cheneval, Pavlos Eleftheriadis, Frank Schimmelfennig, Tristan Storme, and Rebecca Welge. I would also like to thank participants in the workshop on 'Demoicracy: Government of the Peoples', 22–23 March 2012, University of Zurich.

[1] The term 'demoicracy' is derived from demoi (δῆμοι in ancient Greek is the plural form of δῆμος), meaning peoples, and kratos (κράτος), meaning power—or to govern oneself with strength. Peoples here are understood both individually, as citizens who happen to be born or reside in the territory of the Union, and collectively as states, that is the separate political units under popular sovereignty which constitute the Union. For previous discussions of the term see K Nicolaïdis, 'We The Peoples of Europe' (2004) 83 *Foreign Affairs* 97; S Besson 'Deliberative Demoi-cracy in the EU: Towards the Deterritorialisation of Democracy' in S Besson and JL Marti (eds), *Deliberative Democracy and its Discontents* (Farnham: Ashgate, 2006); K Nicolaïdis and J Pelabay, 'One Union, One Story? In Praise of Europe's Narrative Diversity' in A Warleigh-Lack (ed) *Reflections on European Integration* (London/New York: Palgrave, 2008); F Cheneval, *The Government of the Peoples: On the idea and Principles of Multilateral Democracy* (New York: Palgrave MacMillan, 2011); J-W Mueller, 'The Promise of Demoi-cracy: Diversity and Domination in the European Public Order' in J Neyer and A Wiener, *The Political Theory of the European Union* (Oxford: Oxford University Press, 2010), 187–205.

and navigate this Rubicon, away from the safe shores of classic nation-statehood or public international law on one side and federal statehood on the other.[2] As a 'demoicracy', the European Union requires its many peoples not only to open up to one another but to recognize mutually their respective polities and all that constitutes them: their respective pasts, their social pacts, their political systems, their cultural traditions, their democratic practices. Such mutual recognition is highly demanding. Today's EU is both a demoicracy-in-the-making and is prey to many age-old anti-democratic demons standing in the way.

If this Rubicon of ours is a narrow and turbulent third way between the two familiar alternatives, the challenge is to resist landing on these two state-centric shores. That we need to deploy new understandings of European constitutionalism, cosmopolitanism, or federalism short of their 'statist' connotation as 'state-writ-large' is not an in itself original position. So for instance, Neil McCormick's advocacy in favour of a pluralist philosophy which sought to resolve or at least address the tensions of a multiplicity of competing legal orders with overlapping supremacy claims has inspired a growing corpus of thought on constitutional pluralism.[3] Others, starting with Pavlos Eleftheriadis in Chapter 7 in this volume, seek to demonstrate that the EU has not lost its 'international' law pedigree even while at the same time pushing the frontier of what is meant by 'obligation' in this inter-state realm.[4] And others have built on the insight that the EU can be understood as a federal union, not a federal state.[5] Perhaps the most wide-ranging and consistent inspiration for such a third way can be found in the writings of Joseph Weiler and his long-standing vision of the EU at its best as aspiring to community rather than unity, a community of others committed to a philosophy of constitutional tolerance.[6]

All these approaches share a concern with preserving the boundary between a non-statist and a statist reading of the EU's legal order: not crossing the Rubicon. The idea of demoicracy builds on these insights to better connect the sophisticated world of legal philosophy and its controversies with the simpler world of politics, that is the political imagination, discourses, and practices which make up the EU polity.

---

[2] On the ubiquity of the image of the EU as a ship of states, see the wonderfully illustrated paper by S Leibfried, S Gaines, and L Frisina (eds), *Through the Funhouse Looking Glass: Europe's Ship of States,* (TransState Working Papers 90, Bremen, 2009). For a playful and insightful use of the ship metaphor for political theory purposes see also 'Introduction' and 'Conclusion' in J Neyer and A Wiener (eds), *Political Theory of the European Union* (Oxford: Oxford University Press, 2010).

[3] See Kumm 'The Idea of Constitutional Pluralism' (2002) 65 *Modern Law Review* 317–59; M Maduro, 'Contrapunctual Law: Europe's Constitutional Pluralism in Action', in Neil Walker (ed), *Sovereignty in Transition: Essays in European Law* (Oxford: Hart Publishing, 2003), 3–32; N Krisch, *Beyond Constitutionalism: The Pluralist Structure of Postnational Law* (Oxford: Oxford University Press, 2010).

[4] Chapter 7 in this volume.

[5] R Howse and K Nicolaïdis (eds), *The Federal Vision: Legitimacy and Levels of Governance in the US and the EU,* (Oxford: Oxford University Press, 2001). See also O Beaud, *Fédéralisme et fédération en France: histoire d'un concept impossible?* (Strasbourg: Presses universitaires de Strasbourg, 1999).

[6] See J Weiler, 'The Transformation of Europe' (1991) 100 *Yale Law Journal* 2403–83. See also J Weiler, *The Constitution of Europe: 'Do the New Clothes Have an Emperor?' and Other Essays on European Integration.* (Cambridge: Cambridge University Press, 1998).

In this chapter, I stop short from offering a 'demoicratic theory' for Europe. Indeed, the general concept of demoicracy can accommodate many contending conceptions on how it can be achieved and it would be presumptuous at this stage to offer more than the broad parameters for discussion. Such a conversation can bring into relief the meeting points, lines of convergence, and perhaps more crucially, misunderstandings between the many traditions and fields which are relevant to the endeavour, from legal theory to philosophy, sociology, and normative theories of international relations. Among contentious points, I would suggest the following.

First, when are neologisms justified? Indeed, demoicracy could be but another word for what others have explored as multilateral democracy,[7] transnational democracy,[8] compound democracy,[9] directly deliberative polyarchy,[10] agonistic democracy,[11] or for that matter the numerous variants on federal democracy.[12] I hope to make the case, however, that words matter and that the idea of a 'European demoicracy' has the potential to ground normative claims about the EU which encapsulate intuitions that analysts and protagonists actually share.

There are, secondly, methodological questions. We may disagree on the relationship between making the case for describing or understanding the EU as a demoicracy-in-the-making in a positive sense, and deploying the concept of demoicracy as a normative benchmark by which to assess developments of the EU's legal, political, and economic order. We may also disagree on what kind of practices fall short of the normative benchmark in question. And we may disagree on how such a descriptive-cum-normative concept may also render unable to *explain* the evolution of the enterprise. In short, what should be the relationship between the 'ought', the 'what', and the 'why' of European demoicracy?

A third issue is the vexed question of the *sui generis* nature of the Union. It has become something of a commonplace to discuss the EU—understood as some version of the international, cosmopolitan, constitutional, Kantian, or otherwise federal—as an instantiation of more general theories of democracy beyond the state, of global law or global governance. And so with European demoicracy. For my part, I have long argued against constitutionalism as an appropriate analytical or prescriptive take on global governance.[13] One need not deny that there may be realms where the 'international'

---

[7] F Cheneval, see n 1.

[8] J Bohman, *Democracy Across Borders: From Demos to Demoi* (Cambridge: MIT Press, 2007).

[9] S Fabbrini, *Compound Democracy* (Oxford: Oxford University Press, 2010).

[10] C Sabel and J Zeitlin (eds), *Experimentalist Governance in the European Union: Towards a New Architecture* (Oxford: Oxford University Press, 2010).

[11] C Mouffe, *The Democracy Paradox* (London: Verso, 2000).

[12] Conversely, and somewhat confusedly for our purposes the philosopher Philippe van Parijs used the compound term *demoi*-cracy to refer precisely to what we do not mean by demoicracy, eg *merely* a nation-state-centric view of indirect democracy in the EU which he thought ought to be transcended by European demos-cracy. See P van Parijs, 'Should the European Union become More Democratic?' in A Follesdal and P Koslowski (eds), *Democracy and the European Union* (Berlin: Springer-Verlag, 1998), 32.

[13] Nicolaïdis, 'Legitimacy through "Higher Law?" Why Constitutionalizing the WTO is a Step Too Far,' in T Cottier, P Mavroidis, and P Blatter (eds), *The Role of the Judge: Lessons for the WTO* (Bern: The World Trade Forum, 2002).

meets bits of the 'constitutional'. This does not make the constitutionalization of global institutions a plausible or desirable prospect.

Last but not least, we may disagree on what our theories on the nature of the EU have to say about the likely aftershocks of its greatest crisis yet. If the EU is a demoicracy-in-the-making, which stage are we at, and how fragile and incipient is it still? Here, those who are seduced by the idea of demoicracy itself may disagree with the more speculative part of my argument. That is that because Europeans have generally failed to see their political construct as a demoicracy they have allowed their political space to be monopolized by two antagonists integrationist and anti-integrationist camps. This in turn has made the European demoicratic construct vulnerable to functionally driven calls for fusion and the unavoidable backlash into fission. So the same third-way character which makes it attractive also makes highly demanding. As a tragic political animal, our demoicracy may very well be an unstable and temporary equilibrium.

1 Ontology: On the Possibility of Demoicracy as a Third Way

The diagnosis of the EU's democratic deficit usually revolves around questions of representation and accountability. Who is to be accountable to whom? If the focus is on parliamentarianism, what parliaments should there be, and by what kind of representation should they come about? Whose interests ought to be aggregated and at which level of government? But all these questions, which belong to the *story of governance*, cannot be addressed appropriately without *a story of the polity*. What does it mean for citizens to 'belong to the Union,' as individuals, as groups of individuals, or as constituted states? The force of the German Constitutional Court in its famous 1993 Maastricht judgment, was to connect these two questions of belonging: how the Union may come to belong to its citizens will depend on how citizens feel they belong to this Union.[14] The 'no-demos' thesis was an empirical statement meant to justify caution about unchecked integration *for the time being*. Paradoxically, since ultimately the Court looked forward to the eventual emergence of a 'European demos', the no-demos thesis has come to be restated as the empirical grounds for sovereignist arguments ever since.

The idea of demoicracy was put forth as a way to appropriate and subvert the no-demos thesis, as a response to proposals for creating the missing 'demos'.[15] These proposals were uttered by a majority of those attending the initial convention to establish the EU, and said to motivate their quest for a Europe Constitution. Jurgen Habermas and the former German foreign minister Joschka Fischer sought to weigh in

[14] *Brunner*, 89 BVerfGE 155, [1994] 1 CMLR 57.
[15] Nicolaidis, (2004), see n 1; K Nicolaidis, 'Our European Demoicracy: Is this Constitution a Third Way for Europe?' (2003) in Nicolaidis and Weatherill (eds), *Whose Europe? National Models and the Constitution of the European Union*, European Studies at Oxford Series, Oxford University Press.

the Constitutional debates by arguing that a European demos could and should be 'forged' as the foundation for formal constitutionalization of European integration: there may be no European demos quite yet, but there is a European demos in the making.[16]

The demoicratic response to both sides was this: the Court was right in its *no-demos* diagnosis, but so what? This does not mean that the EU cannot be democratically legitimated by a plural *pouvoir constituant*. A Constitutional moment need not wait for Frenchmen (and Dutch and Portuguese) to be turned into 'Euromen', as peasants were turned into Frenchmen two hundred years ago. Instead we have actually been inventing a different kind of democracy at the European level which does not need to reinvent the state-centric model.

(A) A Philosophical Triangle

The EU as a political entity failed to capture the imagination of philosophers and other intellectuals during its first three decades.[17] But they were, finally, awakened by the turbulent events surrounding the end of the Cold War, German reunification, and the debates about the Maastricht Treaty. And while national debates were mostly conducted in intellectual silos, a similar pattern, a kind of 'EU philosophical triangle' can be found across countries.[18]

At one end we find what we may call theories of national sovereignty, or 'national-civic' approaches which essentially criticize the idea of democracy at the European level in the name of the primacy of the nation-state.[19] At its most general, this school of thought is based on the idea that the cradle of both modern democracy and the welfare state is the nation-state, which cannot be reproduced at the European level. As democracy presupposes a polity with a common language and common representations, which originates in a shared history and exists thanks to its very differences from other communities, and as Europe cannot meet such prerequisites, the idea of a European democracy is at best an illusion.[20]

---

[16] Indeed for Habermas and Derrida, such European demos was thankfully born on 21 February 2003 with the pan-European demonstrations against the Iraq war. J Habermas and J Derrida, *Le Monde*, February 2003.

[17] For possible explanations, see 'Introduction' in J Lacroix and K Nicolaïdis, *European Stories: Intellectual Debates on Europe in National Contexts* (Oxford: Oxford University Press, 2010).

[18] For a discussion see Lacroix and Nicolaidis, see n 17.

[19] Proponents are myriad, including, David Miller in the UK or Pierre Manent in France. See David Miller, *On Nationality* (Oxford University Press, 1995); Justine Lacroix, *La pensée française à l'épreuve de l'Europe* (Cerf, 2009). In Central Europe, we find the many who reject what they see as a 'moral hazard', a one size-fits-all EU-led hegemonic interpretation of European modernity (such as Roman Dmowski in Poland or the followers of Nocia's calling for the revival of metaphysics in Romania). In Southern Europe, we find all the variants of what Nikiforos Diamandouros has termed 'the culture of the underdog'. For a discussion across twelve member states, see *European Stories*, see n 17.

[20] This school of thought could itself be divided into two strands—a conservative strand which sees Europe as a threat to national identity and cultural values, and a progressive strand which sees it as a threat to self-government and social justice. For both, the mutual sacrifices required by fiscal solidarity as we are discussing today in the EU suppose the kind of mutual trust and identification found within bound political communities.

In contrast and at the other end of the spectrum are all those who equate more (supra-national) Europe with the promise of economic, social, moral, and eventually political progress. This side often calls for variants of a 'Federal Europe' which would also be the only way to 'rescue' the achievements of the national welfare state—achievements that are threatened by the pace of globalization. If a common language and shared values are necessary to consolidate a democratic political community, these have been the result of a long historical process at the nation-state level: a similar process should and could take place at the European level.[21] Jürgen Habermas has come to embrace this belief in both the desirability and possibility of a European federal state.[22]

The third philosophical family—to which the idea of demoicracy belongs—can be referred to as 'transnational' for its stress on the horizontal and mutual opening between peoples in a shared polity.[23] It assumes that Europe is not constituted by separate demoi nor demoi-made-into-one but by distinct political demoi progressively opening to each other and to each other's democratic systems. This openness can be seen as, in a way, asymptotic: it is sharing, pooling, enmeshing, but not unifying. Thus, the third way approach sees as its brief to analyse the uneasy coexistence between peoples, both peoples-as-states and peoples-as-citizens. It is translating in democratic language what legal theorists see as the duality of Member States and Community legitimacy.[24] This third school includes many thinkers in the 'post-national' constellation[25] as well as those

---

[21] Clearly there are many disagreements within this school itself, including on the necessary conditions for the emergence of a true continental democracy (whatever this may mean), or the development of a European public space underpinning and ultimately embodying European political identity. But all seem to agree that these developments are desirable to the furthering of the European cause. Conceived as a supranational project, the ideal-type Europe of this school of thought would potentially be a multinational federal state or a consociational polity.

[22] J Habermas, 'Why Europe Needs a Constitution' (2001) New Left Review 11. For a critical discussion see J Lacroix, 'Does Europe Need Common Values: Habermas against Habermas' (2009) 8 European Journal of Political Theory 141–56.

[23] See inter alia, J Weiler, 'The Transformation of Europe' (1991) 100, 8 Yale Law Journal 2403 83 and The Constitution of Europe, above; See also R Bellamy and D Castiglione, 'Between Cosmopolis and Community: Three Models of Rights and Democracy within the European Union' in D Archibugi, D Held, and M Koehler, (eds), Re-Imagining Political Community (Cambridge: Polity, 1998); D Castiglione, R Bellamy, and J Shaw, Making European Citizens: Civic Inclusion in a Transnational Context (London: Palgrave-MacMillan, 2006); M Maduro, 'Contrapunctual Law: Europe's Constitutional Pluralism in Action' in Neil Walker (ed), Sovereignty in Transition, (Oxford: Hart Publishing, 2003), 502–37; Joerges (2011) Unity in Diversity as Europe's Vocation and Conflicts Law as Europe's Constitutional Form in Joerges (ed), After Globalisation, RECON Report No 15, Oslo, August 2011; P Eleftheriadis, 'The Moral Distinctiveness of the European Union' (2011) International Journal of Constitutional Law 43; Nicholas Aroney, 'Federal Constitutionalism/European Constitutionalism in Comparative Perspective,' The Federal Trust, March 2009; A Menon, The State of the Union (Atlantic, 2008); See also the three democratic orders discussed in E Eriksen and J Fossum (eds), Rethinking Democracy and the European Union (New York: Routledge, 2012); S Fabbrini, see n 9; C Mouffe, see n 11; Nicolaïdis and Pelabay, see n 1.

[24] And therefore to transform reigning legal paradigms, as the constellation of constitutional pluralist would argue and as opposed to those who believe that we can infer from either domestic or from municipal law the broad features of European law.

[25] See inter alia, Habermas, The Post-National Constellation (1998); and discussion in J-W Müller, Constitutional Patriotism (Princeton: Princeton University Press, 2007).

who chose to describe the EU through the lens of 'empire'[26]—although in my view these labels are ultimately misleading both descriptively or normatively.[27] I prefer the evocative label of 'borderland' suggested by the philosopher Etienne Balibar.[28] Yet those who could be identified with this school of thought do not always recognize its character as a *third way* because they are focused on steering away from one or the other side of the Rubicon.

This is an amorphous constellation regrouping those who oppose *both* other camps which, while seeming to stand at the two ends of the normative spectrum, equally maintain that democratic ideals and practices require equating the boundary of the democratic polity with that of *a* single demos (whether national or European). It seems symptomatic of the pervasiveness of such an equation which demoicracy seeks to escape that some thinkers may ultimately support both camps, such as the German jurist Carl Schmitt, usually associated with the most radical version of our first school of thought.[29] Similarly, Lacroix shows how French national-republican thinking, while criticizing communitarianism at home, tends to promote a similar 'closed' vision of the European polity.[30]

While the strength of a demoicratic third way rests on the plausibility of lumping together its two opponents as part of the same cognitive straightjacket, it does share traits with both sides. It shares with the champions of the 'national-civic' credo the idea that representative democracy within the Member States, and therefore indirect accountability, ought to remain at the very centre of the EU construct. In contrast, however, it considers that the European 'constraint' as a body of laws destined to 'tame' the national (or empower constituencies within it) including through the

[26] U Beck and E Grande, *Cosmopolitan Europe*, (London: Polity Press, 2007) and U Beck and E Grand, 'Empire Europe' in J Neyer and A Wiener (eds) above; J Zielonka, *Europe as Empire: The Nature of the Enlarged European Union.* (Oxford: Oxford University Press, 2006). See also Gary Marks, 'Europe and its Empires' (January 2012) *Journal of Common Market Studies*.

[27] While I find fundamental affinities between Europe-as-demoicracy and as-Empire, including on the issue of enlargement, the 'Empire' lens lacks a normative benchmark against which to pit the realities of domination, subjugation, and Eurocentricism which Empire connotes. As for the 'post-national' label it is unfortunate in suggesting the obsolescence of the 'national', even if in theory the 'post' only applies beyond the state. This flirtation with the second, supra-national school of thought is reinforced by the attempts to export the concept of 'constitutional patriotism,' from the German to the European level. See Nicolaidis, 'Notre Demoï-cratie européenne: La Constellation post-nationale à l'horizon Patriotisme Constitutionnel' (Spring 2006) in *Politique européenne*, No 19.

[28] See E Balibar, *Europe Constitution Frontieres* (Paris: Editions du Passant, 2005).

[29] For Schmitt, sovereignty was always associated with the unshakable conceptual triad of 'demos-state-constitution' which justified his call for states to remain unitary and sovereign within the European space. But he also came to accept the alternative of a continental State, with his 'theory of the federation (*Bund*)' which would be based on a 'pact' and would unite many peoples, with the political conservation of all members of the federation as a 'common goal'. Crucially, Schmitt believed that such a federation would not be here to stay as such but would lead to a unitary state and a single people. Note that Schmitt's position had a significant posterity, including authors such as Ernst-Wolfgang Böckenförde. For a discussion see Tristan Storme, *Carl Schmitt, Europe and Universal Democracy. The question of Schmitt's Europe and its impact on the current French debate about the European construction* (PhD thesis, Université libre de Bruxelles, Brussels, May 2011). See also *inter alia*, J-W Müller, 'Carl Schmitt and the Constitution of Europe' (2000) 21(6) *Cardozo Law Review* 1780.

[30] J Lacroix, *Communautarisme versus libéralisme. Quel modèle d'intégration politique ?* (Bruxelles, Editions de l'Université libre de Bruxelles, collection Philosophie et société, 2003).

promotion of human rights, is not the source of dissolution of national democracies, but rather a potential means of perfecting them. Such constitutional discipline which rests on degrees of supra-nationality—and the partial cessions of sovereignty which ensue—can be seen as a commitment shared with traditional federalists, but with one crucial caveats: supra-nationality (eg non-veto and delegation) follows an instrumental logic not an ontological one, and it can be (at least theoretically) withdrawn.[31] In this spirit, proponents of a demoicratic approach welcome the right to exit and its actual possibility which 'federalists' decry.

Crucially, such a third way may look like the traditional 'in-between' (international organization v federal state) and empirically borrows from both sides, but contrary to a *via media,* it is also normatively opposed to both. As with every third way, the idea of demoicracy holds the promise of escape from an entrapping dialectic—the tyranny of dichotomies which dominates EU debates, from champions of the European Council v European Parliament, all the way down the path of ascription in the war between 'nationalists' and 'federalists'. It is its own thing, as it were.

In summary, European demoicracy can be defined as follows:

> European demoicracy is a Union of peoples, understood both as states and as citizens, who govern together but not as one. It represents a third way against two alternatives which both equate democracy with a single demos: as a demoicracy-in-the-making, the EU is neither a Union of democratic states as 'sovereigntists' would have it, nor a Union-as-a-democratic state *to be* as 'federalists' would have it. A Union-as-demoicracy should remain an open-ended process of transformation which seeks to accommodate the tensions inherent in the pursuit of radical mutual opening between separate peoples.[32]

(B) Debating European Demoicracy

If we analyse European demoicracy through the lens of democratic theory, we may see it as having acquired a truly 'transformative' character in the sense of Robert Dahl's 'transformation of democracy'—as opposed to a 'mimetic' logic leading to a continental state.[33] In this intellectual tradition, we need to stretch the background theories of domestic democracy (eg liberal, republican) to accommodate the kind of mutual opening involved and analyse the radical nature of demoicracy.

---

[31] A logic Joseph Weiler described as 'Constitutional tolerance'. J Weiler, 'Federalism and Constitutionalism: Europe's Sonderweg', in K Nicolaïdis and R Howse (eds), *The Federal Vision* (Oxford: Oxford University Press, 2001).

[32] I would like to thank participants in the Zurich workshop on demoicracy for their feedback on this definition. See acknowledgements, above.

[33] Dahl's 'transformations of democracy' (initially from direct to representative democracy) in R Dahl, (1989) *Democracy and its Critics* (New Haven: Yale University Press); R Dahl, *A Preface to Democratic Theory* (Chicago: University of Chicago Press, 2006). See also Cheneval, see n 1. Bohman (see n 8) speaks of a gradualist logic, but the term is misleading to describe the obsolescence of the national/state level of jurisdiction. On the mimetic logic in EU national discourse, see also Nicolaidis and Weatherill, see n 15.

More generally, the broad idea of demoicracy as a radically transformative process raises a number of questions to which I now turn.

Why should we narrow our geographical scope to 'European' demoicracy? Are we in fact discussing demoicracy *tout court?* In probing the philosophical foundations of EU law, we are inevitably confronted with the tendency among scholars to apprehend the EU as a particular instantiation of a broader universal form of integration between states short of statism writ-large.[34] If we follow Rawls's constructivist method, for instance, where this universal vision itself can be deduced from first principles, European demoicracy could be fruitfully 'deduced' from more abstract characterizations of justice or democracy beyond the state as potentially universally valid, at least among liberal democracies.[35] But while universalizing and deductive viewpoints are often illuminating—in my view Rawls understood 'European peoples' better than many Europeans—should our normative beliefs about the EU be held hostage to our normative beliefs regarding the potential or desirable evolution of the international system?

There might have been historically, and there might yet be, other demoicracies in the making. But the EU appears to have been the product of a unique historical context. Nowhere else and at no other time have such deeply entrenched albeit relatively recent constructs as 'nation-states' been so collectively bent on taming their own nationalism, and shielded in doing so by a hegemon's security umbrella. As a result, even while it may be possible to argue that other regions around the world as well as the global governance system may borrow from bits of EU governance, using it as an experimental tool box, this does not mean that the deeper part of its structure, the kind of democratic bond we are concerned with here, ought to be 'reproduced' beyond Europe too.[36] A global ethics within a pluralist international system may provide more realistic prospects for global peace.[37] To put it crudely, if it is desirable to embrace a transformative logic when thinking about Europe, why fall prey to mimetism or gradualism, this time from the European to the global level?

If we should remain agnostic about the validity of 'demoicracy' beyond the confines of the EU, this is I believe also in light of the implicit or explicit eurocentrism pervading much of the scholarship on global governance and the constitutional

[34] These are more often framed through the question of global justice rather than democracy per se, whether in political theory, legal theory or international relations- from Linklater's cosmopolitanism, to Wendt's constructivism, Bohman's transnational democracy, or Krisch's constitutional pluralism to state but a few.

[35] J Rawls, *The Idea of Public Reason Revisited* (Cambridge, Mass.: Harvard University Press, 2002); In this tradition, see Cheneval, n 1 on the generation of the basic structure of multilateral democracy.

[36] See Howse and Nicolaïdis, see n 13; K Nicolaïdis and R Howse, 'This is my EUtopia... Narrative as Power', (2002) 40(4), JCMS. In a similar vein see also D Cass, *The Constitutionalization of the World Trade Organization: Legitimacy, Democracy, and Community in the International Trading System* (Oxford: Oxford University Press, 2005).

[37] R Howse and K Nicolaïdis, 'Towards a Global Trade Ethics' in Eagleton-Pierce, Jones, and Nicolaïdis (eds), *Building Blocks Towards a Global Trade Ethics* (Oxford GTE Programme, WP Series, July 2009).

evolution of the international legal system. Presenting the EU as a (demoicratic) pluralist, cosmopolitan, *avant-garde* heralding a possible future world order recalls the 'standards of civilization' that pervaded Europe's imperial era. As if the contemporary echoes of colonialism could be wished away if only we could 'get it right' this time around.[38] Even if we restrict our claims to relations between states which are themselves democratic, modernity obviously comes in many shapes and accents. And others may be more interested in our debates about demoicracy and its trials and errors than in its substantive features.[39]

Crucially, the idea of demoicracy resists recourse to a notion of 'European identity' as underpinning the EU polity, as many, if not all, federalists would have it. The EU is a community of others, as Weiler famously put it, not brothers.[40] That only a small minority of rooted cosmopolitans would describe the EU (and even 'Europe') as a chosen identity is a sociological fact.[41] But the argument against 'identity' is above all grounded and normatively in the imperative to reject the European demon of 'othering' non-Europeans (as any identity discourse ultimately requires). Nevertheless, is it not possible to imagine more positive variants? Is there a way to speak of 'European values' not as identity markers ('our' values, 'invented here') but as principles for action? When we explore the many debates about the EU around Europe, what we do find is a bewildering array of criss-crossing stories, or 'a kind of European ambivalence refracted through multiple identities informed by many cleavages between winners and losers, optimists and pessimists, movers and stayers in the EU'.[42] Indeed, the idea of demoicracy allows for many stories about what 'it is' as long as we can discuss the grounds for our 'reasonable disagreements'.[43] Translated in democratic theory, this means that the loss of democracy inherent in the process of integration cannot be recouped directly through a change of democratic identity scale: there is no EU-wide polity in which most citizens would be willing to accept to be subjected to the rule of a pan-European majority.

---

[38] See R Rao, *Third World Protest: Between Home and the World* (Oxford: Oxford University Press, 2010); N Fisher Onar and K Nicolaidis 'The Decentering Agenda: Rethinking Europe in a Non-European World,' *Cooperation and Conflict*, 2013; T Lenz. PhD Thesis, Oxford University, Spring 2012.

[39] More generally, perhaps we can both emphasize European uniqueness and recognize a universal pattern at a higher level of abstraction—eg the search for the elusive equilibrium between the one and the many whereby neither does the one dominate over the many, nor do the many dominate the one. It may simply be that what is of universal relevance is not the specific form of demoicracy that the EU has stumbled upon but this quest for balance through experimentation.

[40] In this sense, van Parijs is wrong to assimilate Weiler and Habermas, as both representatives of those who believe in the 'family variant' rather than in the '(isolated) peoples' variant of the EU. See Philippe van Parijs and John Rawls, 'Three Letters on the Law of Peoples and the European Union,' (2003) *Revue de philosophie économique*.

[41] In 2010, the proportion of Europeans who define themselves as 'Europeans' and 'national' was less than a third while two-thirds defined themselves as 'national' only. See S Duchesnes, *L'identité européenne, entre science politique et science fiction* (Paris: L'Harmattan, 2010).

[42] 'Introduction' in J Checkel and P Katzenstein (eds) *European Identity* (Cambridge: Cambridge University Press, 2009). See also, J Lacroix and K Nicolaïdis (2010), see n 17.

[43] K Nicolaïdis and J Pelabay, see n 1.

What then is the glue that holds Europeans together in a demoicracy? If it is not a community of identity, what kind of community is it? A community of purpose, of destiny, of project? A collective of peoples pooling risk in an era of global existential threats? If citizens tend to complain about the obligations stemming from the EU in the same way as they might about their own government—not questioning the underlying existence of their country—is this where the real legitimacy of Europe lies: a disenchanted acceptance, a pragmatic consequentialist attitude? But does euro-indifference (or resignation) continue to trump Euro-scepticism among European electorates even at times of crisis? Can the idea of European citizenship constitute 'the glue', short of European identity *per se*? In a demoicratic framework, we need to consider the various ways in which EU citizenship expands the rights and opportunities of citizens without superimposing a new 'citizenship granting and monitoring' authority over them. And EU citizenship needs to be meaningful both for nomads and settlers in Europe. It may for instance empower non-movers over and above their domestic political circumstances as with the recent ECJ's move to grounding rights beyond free movement.[44] Can we interpret this move as reflecting a certain idea of integrity of the separate demoi under a shared set of standards? But does such an evolution require the actual autonomy of the idea and status of European citizenship? Can it not rather be framed as a change in the substance of national citizenship to reflect the openness of 'europeanized' citizenship?

And how do we know one of these constitutive demoi when we see one?[45] Perhaps it is enough that citizens conceive of their core democratic involvement as centered around their respective consolidated (and highly imperfect) liberal institutions. But even as we retain the primacy of the nation-state as the core unit of the Union, should we reify national demoi as the only legitimate unit of interest aggregation?[46] It may be that the idea of demoicracy is an invitation to live with the under-defined or at least to move away from essentialist debates about what might constitute a 'people' and to question the separation between 'peoples' and 'persons' that provides the moral foundation for international law.[47] In doing so, we may be able to accommodate understandings of such 'peoples' both as collective entities which in the modern era has usually meant 'states' or 'nations', and as networks of persons endowed with individual rights and participatory claims. To complicate matters, states may acknowledge several peoples in their midst, and some of these demoi might not be defined in national terms at all. Does it matter to the plural conception if the constituent demoi are delineated through linguistic, cultural, religious homogeneity, or some vaguer

---

[44] See for example Case C-34/09 *Ruiz Zambrano*, 8 March 2011, nyr.

[45] For a recent review of the literature through a demoicratic lens see Antoinette Scherz 'What Is the Demos and Who Should Be Included? Membership Principles and Democratic Performance', *Living Reviews in Democracy* (forthcoming)

[46] For a discussion see M Maduro, 'Europe and the Constitution: What If This Is As Good As It Gets?' in Marlene Wind and Joseph Weiler (eds), *Constitutionalism Beyond the State* (Cambridge: Cambridge University Press, 2003), 74–102.

[47] See F Cheneval 2011, see n 1.

measure of community, shared trust, and the like? Should the idea not also accommodate individuals who do not identify with a single 'people' but either none or several?

Is demoicracy then simply an EU version of liberal pluralism? Not if we consider that pluralism is what states make of it. Indeed, one can argue that its two alternatives are also compatible with different forms of pluralism or toleration, but that neither has embarked consistently on the project of reconciling the plurality of states and the pluralism of individuals within states. Moreover, to say that the EU remains and should remain not-a-state while progressively adopting a constitutional 'operating system'—as Weiler would say—is a two-way statement: however much shared *kratos*, we still have demoi; but also crucially, however many demoi, we need a common *kratos*. In this sense demoicracy displays a compound character—a polity of polities, a *community* of communities, an overlapping consensus of overlapping consensus which must amalgamate pre-existing political and social bargains while respecting the say of the peoples-as-states (whereby interests have already been aggregated) *and* peoples-as-citizens (whereby disperse individual interests may or may not recognize themselves in pre-existing national bargains). This is a tall order as these peoples may have organized their national democracies around widely different models of capitalism and state–society relationships. Yet there is no necessary tension between the preservation of pluralism and a common purpose expressed through common projects (be it a single market or a single currency): the question is *how* such project are implemented to respect the plurality of peoples.[48]

Is demoicracy a defence of the status quo, of the EU-as-is? Or could it provide arguments for change in the EU legal or constitutional order? To be sure, the idea of demoicracy was initially meant optimistically as a pointer to the EU's many *existing* demoicratic attributes, partially echoing Moravcsik's denial of a serious 'democratic deficit', or Weiler's advice, 'if it ain't broke don't fix it'.[49] The Treaty of Rome, both in its institutional set up and the 'community method' can be seen as almost quintessentially demoicratic—even if large Member States have regularly been prone to question some of its tenets.[50] Thus a demoicratic lens makes the need for remedies to the so-called democratic deficit both less and more daunting. Less, to the extent that it gives

---

[48] In this sense, Rawls overstates the threat stemming from common projects against van Parijs's 'federalist' creed when he asks in their exchange of letters on the EU: 'Isn't there a conflict between a large free and open market comprising all of Europe and the individual nation-states, each with its separate political and social institutions, historical memories, and forms and traditions of social policy. Surely these are great value to the citizens of these countries and give meaning to their life.' (See van Parijs and Rawls, n 40). If a single market is obtained through 'managed mutual recognition' rather than harmonization, it need not threaten national diversity of policies and regulations. See *inter alia*, K Nicolaïdis, 'Mutual Recognition of Regulatory Regimes: Some Lessons and Prospects,' *Jean Monnet Paper Series* (Cambridge, MA: Harvard Law School, 1997); K Nicolaïdis, 'Kir Forever? The Journey of a Political Scientist in the landscape of recognition', in Maduro, (ed), *The Past and Future of EU Law; The Classics of EU Law Revisited on the 50th Anniversary of the Rome Treaty* (Oxford: Hart Publishing, 2010).

[49] Moravcsik, 'The European Constitutional Compromise and the Neofunctionalist Legacy' (2005) 12(2) *Journal of European Public Policy*.

[50] See Paul Magnette and K Nicolaïdis, *Big vs Small States in the EU* (Paris: Notre Europe, 2003).

more weight to existing indirect accountability and checks and balance factors; more, as the horizontal openings demanded of a demoicracy (such as cooperation between national parliaments) can be more difficult than traditional vertical remedies (such as giving more power to the European Parliament). In short, the current demoicratic practices of the Union are both more democratically valuable than federalists recognize, and more perfectible than sovereigntists can live with.

But the idea of demoicracy was also meant to change the term of the debate and free up political energies from teleological tropes bent on describing the EU as a political form or endgame rather than a process of ongoing transformation. The ongoing debates over constitutionalism and the EU provide a particularly apt foil in this regard.[51] Under one reading, the Constitutional Treaty could have been the EU's 'coming out' as demoicracy in the making, as the substance of the text, including its provisions on democracy and its exit clause (more than the process), fared pretty well against the demoicracy benchmark.[52] On the other hand, it could be argued that the very adoption of a 'Constitution' itself would have changed the character of the EU, that it was bound to do what Constitutions do: proclaim the creation of a political community where the One (henceforth 'constituted') overrides the Many, where the direct relationship established between citizens and the highest level of governance not only takes on a life of its own but supersedes national state–society relationships. Perhaps constitutionalism simply consists in 'putting into form' as well as 'proclaiming' a given political endeavour; but can citizens apprehend the direct link created by a Constitution as something else than that with a *bona fide* 'state'? Yes, if we adopt non-statist understandings of European constitutional pluralism. No, if we believe Habermas when he declared at the time of the Convention, 'I support the idea of a European Constitution, and consequently of the adoption by Europe of a new principle of legitimacy and of Europe acquiring the status of a State'.[53]

Enshrined or not in a Constitution, theorists have asked whether European demoicracy might be just another way of speaking of 'federal democracy' without the name.[54] It could indeed be argued that the 'real' federal vision (as opposed to the above 'federalist' school) predates its capture by the state during the nineteenth century. Or that 'federalism' only refers to a process in the centralization of powers,

---

[51] See for instance J Weiler and M Wind, see n 46. JE Fossum and A J Menedez speak of the 'constitutional synthesis' in *The Constitution's Gift: A Constitutional theory for Democratic European Union* (Plymouth: Rowan, 2011); T Borzel and T Risse. 'Who Is Afraid of a European Federation? How to Constitutionalize a Multi-Level Governance System?' in C Joerges, Y Meny, and JHH Weiler (eds), *What Kind of Constitution for What Kind of Polity?* (Florence: European University Institute, 2000). See also P Eleftheriadis, K Nicolaïdis, and J Weiler (eds), 'Symposium on European Constitutionalism' (2011) *International Journal of Constitutional Law* 43.

[52] K Nicolaïdis (2004) n 1.

[53] J Habermas, 2001, see n 22.

[54] See Mueller, n 1. On this question see Nicolaïdis and Howse, 2001 above; A Menon and M Schain (eds), *Comparative Federalism* (Oxford: Oxford University Press, 2006); Kelemen and K Nicolaïdis, 'Bringing Federalism Back In', KE Jorgensen *et al.* (eds), *Handbook of European Union Politics* (Thousand Oaks: Sage Publishing, 2007).

consistent with the continued position of the state as the dominant organizing unit in the system, as opposed to 'federation' as the end-point of that process.[55] Or one can attempt to rescue federalism from its statist incarnation by presenting EU demoicracy as a federal union not a federal state.[56] But we can also view the concept as too tainted by the particular conception of a 'federal state' to serve as background theory for the idea of demoicracy—as is certainly the case for the use of the term 'federal' in the public sphere, not only in the UK.[57]

Debates over the interpretation of Kant's cosmopolitan federal union may provide the most fruitful ground for a demoicratic reading of federalism.[58] For one, given Kant's emphasis on *jus cosmopolitius*, eg the (transnational) rights of individuals outside their own states which constitute in turn the core engine for the 'opening up' of democracies we are discussing here. Precisely because he stressed the necessary mediation of the state in a possible federal union, a demoicratic reading of Kant from a twenty-first-century perspective may well give more flesh to the bare bones of cosmopolitan law conceived originally as minimal rights of residence and duties of hospitality. In short, effective cosmopolitan law must rely on the institutions of the host state.[59]

In summary, we may ask what is lost and what is gained by the conceptual innovation of 'demoicracy'. Much of the inspiration for the idea comes from intellectual traditions (federalism, cosmopolitanism, constitutionalism), which themselves accommodate conflicting views over the desirability of statism on a wider scale. The beauty of these traditions is that they come with baggage, concepts, insights, controversies, and exegesis; in short, intellectual gravitas. But with such baggage, we are also burdened with semantic connotations, obfuscations, and interpretative turf battles. A scholarly debate aimed at refining a new concept such as demoicracy enables us to

---

[55]   Michael Burgess (2000), 28; P King, *Federalism & Federation*. Baltimore, MD: Johns Hopkins University Press, 1982.

[56]   See Nicolaïdis, 'We, the Peoples...' (see n 1). For a critical viewpoint see P Eleftheriadis, 'Federalism and Jurisdiction' in Geert De Baere and Elke Cloots (eds), *Federalism and EU Law* (Oxford: Hart Publishing, 2012).

[57]   For an account of the battle-lines drawn at and around the European convention over federalism and its many composites, including Delors' call for a federation of nation-states see K Nicolaïdis, 'What is in a Name: Europe's Federal Future and the Convention on the Future of Europe' (2004) *The Journal of European Law*.

[58]   For interpretations of cosmopolitanism as a non-statist political vision applied to Europe, see J-M Ferry, *La Republique crepusculaire: comprendre le projet européen in sensu cosmopolitico* (Paris: Cerf, 2010); J-M Ferry, *Europe, la voie kantienne: essai sur l'identité postnationale* (Paris: Cerf, 2005); Beck and Grande 2007, see n 26, and F Cheneval, *La Cité des peuples: Mémoires de cosmopolitismes* (Paris: Cerf, 2005) see also D Archibugi (ed), *Debating Cosmopolitics* (London: Verso, 2003).

[59]   In this spirit, Ferry lambasted Habermas for his reading of Kant's 'permanent alliance between peoples' in *Perpetual Peace* as incompatible with Kant's own presuppositions in *The Metaphysics of Morals*, which had grounded the general principles of law on human rights. In Habermas' view Kant erred in considering that individual liberty depended on state sovereignty. For his critics, Habermas failed to see that the permanence of states was essential in the making of a cosmopolitan entity 'which cannot simply be buttressed on the universal constitutionalization of fundamental rights, but should stem from the constitutional recognition of the fundamental rights of the peoples' J-M Ferry, *La Question de l'Etat européen* (Paris: Gallimard, 2000); see also S Glendinning, 'Europe, for Example,' *LSE Europe in Question*' Discussion Paper Series, March 2011; A Hurrell. 'Kant and the Kantian Paradigm in International Relations' (1990) 16 *Review of International Studies* 183–205.

use these alternative frames as background theories, while allowing us to start the conversation afresh without the baggage of extant theory and authority.

In this spirit, defenders of demoicracy may appeal to affinities with the very 'essence' of these traditions, an essence anterior to or distinct from the particular variant of the 'state writ large' which might have tainted each of them in the public and scholarly imagination. To make up for the latter, they may also side with composite notions such as constitutional *pluralism*, federal *union*, or *moral* cosmopolitanism. Moreover, in the spirit of Beck's cosmopolitan realism, demoicracy can also help reconcile philosophical debate and normative arguments with the positive methods which prevail in the social sciences of the EU, starting with the extremely fruitful concept of multilevel governance to describe the EU's journey on the Rubicon.[60]

2 Ethos: European Demoicracy's Normative Core

How then are we to derive the normative core of the EU as demoicracy that may underpin our assessment of legal and political developments therein? Political philosophers like to debate the relative merits of non-ideal versus ideal theory as put forth by Rawls, or whether one should start with the imperfect but perfectible world as is, or from 'first principles', derived from an hypothetic original position which allows to balance fairly all possible conflicting views. I argue here for a normative inductive methodology which can draw on both sides. On one hand, historical contextualization does not mean that we have to accept what Waltz called the inductivist illusion and simply infer the normative core of European demoicracy from empirical observation.[61] We do need a normative benchmark, an analytically autonomous standpoint from which to assess the demoicratic quality of the European project today.[62] But is there not a risk that conclusions may already be contained, even if implicitly, in the premises of theories of demoicracy 'inspired' mostly by one case, and applied or tested on that same case?

In this spirit, I would argue that the normative core of European demoicracy can be found as immanent in the reality that one observes in the European Union as it is today thus allowing for real life approximation of Rawls's 'original position' but only under certain conditions: that one selects underlying norms *to the extent* that they are consistent with the idea of European demoicracy as a third way, and that the EU-as-is is pregnant with other normative possibilities as well as numerous pathologies; that it is itself the product of negotiations about norms where

---

[60] Beck and Grande, see n 26. An analytical framework with strong affinities to the *descriptive* understanding of European demoicracy. L Hooghe and G Marks, *Multi-level Governance and European Integration*, (Lanham: Rowman and LittleField Publishers, 2001). See also M Jachtenfuchs and B Kohler-Koch, *Governance and Institutional Development*; Simona Piattoni, *The Theory of Multi-Level Governance Conceptual, Empirical, and Normative Challenges* (Oxford: Oxford University Press, 2010).

[61] K Waltz, *Theory of International Politics* (Boston: Addson-Wesley, 1979).

[62] As cogently argued in F Cheneval and F Schimmelfenning 'The Case for Demoicracy in the EU' (*EUSA Conference*, 2011). See also Cheneval, n 1.

various actors and cleavages are represented; but that in turn, the outcomes of these actors' interactions and negotiations can be granted normative status only to the extent that underlying power asymmetries have been sufficiently mitigated by procedural constraint towards compromise-and-consensus.[63] In contrast to Rawlsian constructivism, this kind of 'inductive normativism' learns from the bargaining, deliberation, and contestation which we find in EU practice. This observation can give us some confidence that a balance has been reached in the evolving EU order between opposing camps of sovereigntists and supra-nationalists; of big and small states; of Left and Right; of republican and liberal states, and last but not least, of nomads and settlers in the EU. We learn in ways, not only more subtle (that would be a drawback from a philosopher's view point), but perhaps more innovative than any scholar can conjure up deductively.

Accordingly, a normative inductive argument may be inspired by historically contextual and empirically informed normative reasoning in ways we observe in much political theory today. While we do not need to go back to Hegel or Marx to look for an ideal in the real itself, immanent principles have been necessary weapons in the struggle for progressive social change because they provide a basis for critique within historical reality and for emancipation from it.[64] We are reminded of Arendt's commitment to political action as a worldly activity and her call for singling out judgment as a distinct capacity of our minds.[65] So in the case of the EU, the transformative potential lies not in pursuing an ideal to its extreme but in pursuing such balancing, through a kind of fanatical moderation, in which the EU political actors unrelentingly pursue compromise under the shadow of consensus, and the Court pursues balance under the shadow of politics.[66] Combined with ways of making 'agreements to disagree' sustainable, this is not just a process-constraint but compromise and balance elevated to a normative good.

First things first. The EU was born from the ashes of a less than ideal world. The EU's normative core starts from what Europeans wanted to escape. But the point can be made more generally. As Michael Waltzer writes in *On Toleration*: 'the things we admire in a particular historical arrangement are functionally related to the things we fear or dislike'.[67] This method appeals to our intuition: the importance of something

---

[63] If we take account of Rawls's process of reflective equilibrium (between the principles he generates and their real world application) normative inductivism is all the more compatible with to a proceduralist Rawlsian approach to demoicracy, the greater the weight granted to such reflectivity.

[64] This was the intention of those like Adorno and his *immanent critique* who by locating contradictions within the world observed, sought to contextualize not only the object of investigation, but also its ideological basis. For a discussion in a similar vein as normative inductivism see A Azmanova, *The Scandal of Reason: A Critical Theory of Political Judgment*, (New York: Columbia University Press, 2012).

[65] Hanna Arendt. *Responsibility and Judgment* (New York: Schocken, 2003).

[66] W Mattli and A-M Slaughter. 'Law and Politics in the European Union: A Reply to Garrett' (1995) 49 *International Organization* 183–90. See also P Magnette and K Nicolaidis, 'The European Convention: Bargaining in the Shadow of Rhetoric' (April 2004)*West European Politics*.

[67] M Walzer, *On Toleration* (New Haven: Yale University Press, 1997), 5.

we might value is often best understood when it is denied to us—in other words, we tend to recognize specific norms like 'the rule of law' in the breach.[68] Or, as Hobbes powerfully demonstrated, one way to capture an ideal is not to capture how it is for it to be fully instantiated, but what happens without it. Many political theorists have followed suit to this day.[69] As Avishai Margalit puts it most starkly, 'it is much more urgent to remove painful evils than to create enjoyable benefits'—asymmetries of urgency concentrate the mind.[70] What greater evil could concentrate European minds then European wars? Not only did the initial foundations of European demoi-cracy initially result from what Europeans wanted to escape, but such a 'drive to escape' is still with us today. For, I would argue, behind 'war' we had two underlying anti-values: the will to subordinate and the denial of recognition.

But at the very same time, our normative core can be and has been stated positively as an ideal which we are striving to approximate. For behind 'peace' (hopefully perpetual), we have two ideal values which mirror the anti-values behind 'war': transnational non-domination (or non-subordination), and transnational mutual recognition. In this and at least for our purposes ideal and non-ideal theory bring us to the same place.

Following political theorists like Bohman and Cheneval, in elucidating these anti-values/values we can make great use of background theories, including domestic and international political theory.[71] But they can only take us part of the way, especially as the norms in question are likely to be transformed in the process of European integration, including from the major key of war and peace to the minor key of political and bureaucratic games or what Kojeve saw as the end of history.[72] I do not believe that we necessarily need to privilege one background democratic theory over another, or that these two sets of anti-values/values are incompatible normative grounds for demoicracy.[73] I prefer to argue that a demoicratic theory should combine background theories of democracy—eg republicanism and liberalism— and should not be reduced to one or the other.[74] In this spirit, we can bring together related norms with clear elective affinities into 'normative clusters', organizing the

---

[68] See M Krygier's insightful 'Four Puzzles about the Rule of Law': Why, What, Where and Who Cares?' in J Fleming (ed) *Getting to the Rule of Law* (London and New York: New York University Press, 2011).

[69] Philip Selznik urges us to start with the conditions of existence themselves if we are to create a 'moral commonwealth'. See *The Moral Commonwealth: Social Theory and the Promise of Community* (Berkeley: University of California Press, 1994). Judith Shklar with her freedom from fear asks of a norm not where it may deliver us *to* but what it may deliver us *from*; Amartya Sen invites us to focus on eliminating injustice and Avishai Margalit on eliminating humiliation if we seek to live in decent societies; Thomas Pogge shows how far we can go by embracing a no harm principle on a global scale; and Nancy Fraser and Charles Taylor's enquiries start with social denials of recognition.

[70] A Margalit, *The Decent Society* (Cambridge: Havard, 1996), 4.

[71] Bohman, see n 8; Cheneval, see n 1.

[72] F Fukuyama, 'The End of History?' *The National Interest* (1989).

[73] *Contra* JW Mueller, 'The Promise . . .', see n 1.

[74] F Cheneval (2011), see n 1.

meaning of demoicracy around the three core norms of 'non-domination', 'mutual recognition', and 'internal/external consistency'.

(A) Transnational Non-domination

The EU was born as an anti-hegemonic project when it left the shore of an anarchical system based on great power politics and wars. Peace would require not only the taming of nationalism in general but a more concrete set of mechanisms to contain the historical appetite for power of continental big states. The people of France or Germany *qua states* will never again be allowed to subjugate others or the continent, but will respect instead their mutual autonomy as separate demoi.

The threat of war may have receded but the norm of non-domination *among peoples* remains. While originally this meant an 'institutionalized balance of power between states', we have come to understand it as the requirement for checks and balance within an institutional framework. As the stakes change from survival to autonomy of demoi, we shift from the major key of international relations theory to the minor key of democratic theory, which in its republican guise casts the goal of non-domination as one by which 'the condition of liberty is explicated as the status of someone, who, unlike the slave, is not subject to the arbitrary power of another: that is someone who is not dominated by someone else'.[75] And indeed freedom as non-domination in a transnational context calls for practices in the EU which are far from embedded in the political culture of some of the larger Member States, often subject to a pervasive Gulliver syndrome. Instead, we are witness to the fact that the EU can easily become prey to new patterns of what we could call soft domination.

As the Union strengthens and the self-government of the Member States gives way to shared self-government, the risk of domination, albeit soft domination, reasserts itself in another guise, this time as vertical domination. As pre-Civil War US federalists so passionately reminded their contemporaries, when power is transferred from the units to a new centre, however 'decentralized', this centre is always prone to capture by permanent majorities or otherwise tyrannical agents. One needs to escape empires, be they that of Charlemagne or of Angela Merkel. One also needs to escape federal states, be they a United States of Europe or an EU-as-Germany. That is because neither empires nor federal states have addressed the fear of domination in a satisfactory way.[76] Napoleons and Bismarks would not do in the halls of Brussels, nor should Brussels supersede London, Madrid, Prague, or indeed, Athens.

So when it comes to vertical subordination, we need to enrich our normative vocabulary. This can be done, I believe, by returning to Joseph Weiler's principle of constitutional

---

[75] Philip Pettit, *Republicanism: A Theory of Freedom and Government* (Oxford University Press, 1997); J Bohman, 'Transnational Democracy and Nondomination' in C Laborde and J Maynor (eds), *Republicanism and Political Theory* (London: Blackwell, 2008), 190–216.

[76] We may of course ask ourselves if these two Scylla and Charybdis are necessarily part of the mainland or if they cannot be imagined as part of the ride, still on the Rubicon, be it in the benign medieval version of empire or the benign commonwealth version of federation.

tolerance—for its appeal to the ideal of non-coercion, choice, or free association, the idea that peoples in a demoicracy merge their national democratic orders by choice, a choice that needs to be seen as ultimately reversible and where consent cannot be assumed as given once and for all.[77] What is more, such an idea of non-presumed consent calls for tempering with legal hierarchy. Constitutional pluralists like Maduro and Kumm push this idea further and start from the empirical observation that the question of final constitutional authority in the EU remains open in law, in order, ultimately to ground their normative claim that the question of final authority (between European and national courts) ought to be left open.[78] For this view, 'heterarchy'—defined as the 'networks of elements in which each element shares the same horizontal position of power and authority'—is seen as superior to hierarchy as a normative ideal in circumstances of competing constitutional claims. It suggests that neither the EU nor the Member States ought to prevail in their constitutional claims.[79] But the key in this context is to develop the capacity for each 'demos' to defend itself against domination through various representative, deliberative, and participatory channels.

There are clearly tensions in this narrative once we envisage it operationally. A demoicracy faces a precarious balance between the pathologies associated with international anarchy and hierarchy. If the normative ideal is to overcome these pathologies, then it should recognize its continuous vulnerability to both. Demoicracy is an exercise in power mitigation not denial. As theorists of the English school like Bull and Wright would have it, international order and peace demand that we put power to work, that collective expectations be built and institutionalized to entrench great power responsibly.[80] In an order characterized by the rule of law, be it domestic or international, it is the arbitrary use of power that needs to be curbed and not power per se.[81] This is true all the more in a demoicratic context embracing polities of great wealth and demographic asymmetries.

In sum, the first core normative cluster comes with tensions and questions of its own. Under the imperative of non-domination, transfers of power and competences to the centre are preferred to the extent that they are used to empower local actors, such as minorities. This is true in general for the democratic value added of international institutions.[82] But the so called 'constitutionalization' of the EU amplifies both the potential for such empowerment and the potential for ignoring it. We need to ask how the EU's political and legal order has affected the fabric of domestic and local

---

[77] J Weiler, see n 23.

[78] Kumm (2002) and Maduro (2003), see n 3.

[79] D Halberstam 'Constitutional Heterarchy: The Centrality of Conflict in the European Union and the United States', in J Dunoff and J Trachtman (eds), *Ruling the World? Constitutionalism, International Law and Global Governance* (Cambridge: Cambridge University Press, 2009), 326–55.

[80] H Bull, *The Anarchical Society* (New York: Columbia University Press, 1977).

[81] See Walker and Palombella (eds), *Relocating the Rule of Law* (Oxford: Hart, 2008). For a discussion of the difficulties in applying this ethos in the context of EU enlargement see *inter alia*, K Nicolaïdis and R Kleinfeld, *Rethinking Europe's Rule of Law and Enlargement Agenda: The Fundamental Dilemma*' OECD-SIGMA Strategy Papers Series, March 2012.

[82] See R Keohane, S Macedo, and A Moravcsik, 'Democracy-Enhancing Multilateralism' (2009) 63 *International Organization* 1–31.

democracy and how the EU's centralizing functional logic can be checked against a localist preference.[83] How should a demoicracy adjudicate between risks of domination between people as states and between the individuals that compose it? How should non-hierarchy between peoples translate in shades of political hierarchy? When does the institutionalized balance between equality and non-equality principles become *de facto* domination? To what extent does the responsibility that comes with power mitigate the primary object of this preoccupation from domination? And while a demoicratic norm of non-subordination ought to serve as a constant warning against both the Union as a cover for horizontal domination and the Union as an instrument of domination itself, what if some of one is necessary to curb the other?

Hence, for instance, Pavlos Eleftheriadis argues in this volume that we should understand the EU as a community of 'obligation', but he does not tell us how and to what extent this may come into conflict with the republican primary concern with 'non-domination' adapted to a transnational context or the idea that social obligations of solidarity should not be imposed but chosen in a demoicracy.[84]

(B) Transnational Mutual Recognition

If the basic constraint of non-domination is meant to keep the European ship away from the two state-centric mainlands prone to the travails of domination, would we rest content with it staying put and vulnerable in the middle of the river? Political projects need to catch winds in their sails, some kind of animating force. Hence this second normative cluster, which in my view ultimately forms the essence of demoicracy, revolves around transnational mutual recognition and its variants.

There is a complex connection between denial of recognition within sovereign boundaries and the need for recognition between states.[85] Like non-domination, the normative cluster around mutual recognition is rooted in anti-values, what a demoicracy seeks to avoid, including variants of the denial of recognition through assimilation.[86] Lest the will

---

[83] On granting autonomy to lower level actors to experiment with solutions of their own devising in exchange for their support of the centre, see Gráinne de Búrca and Joanne Scott (eds), *Law and New Governance in the EU and the US* (Oxford: Hart Publishing, 2006). See also Sabel and Zeitlin, see n 10.

[84] On non-domination, see Pettit, above. For a discussion of the kind of solidarity called for in the EU context as a subtle balance between political obligation versus altruism on one hand and self-regarding interest versus other-regarding community on the other see Nicolaïdis and Viehoff, 'The Choice for Sustainable Solidarity in the EU' in *Solidarity for Sale? The Social Dimension of the New European Economic Governance* (Bertelsmann Stiftung Foundation, January 2012).

[85] See N Fraser, 'From Redistribution to Recognition? Dilemmas of justice in a "postsocialist" age' (1995) I (212) *New Left Review* 68–93. See also, C Taylor 'The politics of recognition', in A Gutman (ed), *Multiculturalism: Examining the Politics of Recognition* (Princeton: Princeton University Press, 1994), 25–73; see also K Nicolaïdis, 'Trusting the Poles? Constructing Europe through mutual recognition' (2007) 14 *Journal of European Public Policy* 682–98.

[86] Mutual recognition is clearly related to non-subordination but in complex ways: to the extent that non-subordination is a prerequisite for genuine *mutual* recognition, mutual recognition subsumes it. Conversely, mutual recognition can be a prerequisite to subjugation—states need to recognize each other as enemies to be able to raise armies.

to subordinate by one great European power be singled out, we need only recall the pervasive absolute denials of recognition of close others, neighbours as intimate enemies, which led to the appalling crimes committed in the myriads of local battles for supremacy throughout Europe after the Second World War.[87]

So demoicracy arises with the need to both supplement and mitigate the diplomatic norm of mutual recognition with a social norm of transnational mutual recognition. At the same time, it avoids reaching the other shore where the degree of institutionalized convergence, harmonization, and assimilation renders such recognition mute. In federal states, mutual recognition becomes subsumed under the requisite of unity.

In short, if the EU is to be more than an alliance of states while remaining a community of others, it is because its peoples are increasingly connected through multifaceted and deep forms of political and historical mutual recognition.[88] As I wrote previously:

> To really celebrate the EU as a *demoicracy* consists in recognizing that Europeans are part of 'a community of others', who are somewhat at home anywhere in Europe. European demoicracy is predicated on the mutual recognition of the many European identities—not on their merger. Not only does it promote respect for their differences, in a classic communitarian sense, it also urges engaging with each other and sharing these identities. In an apt metaphor, existing European treaties allow nationals of EU member states to use each other's consular services outside of the union: A Spaniard's belonging to the EU allows her to be a bit Italian or a bit British when traveling outside the union. In the same spirit, today's constitution [2003] does not call for a homogeneous community or for laws grounded on the will of a single European *demos*. Rather, it makes mutual respect for national identities and institutions one of its foremost principles... Why spin the rainbow white?[89]

Mutual recognition across borders is a holistic ideal referring to the entire realm of social interactions: identities and cultures, political traditions, social contracts, historical grievances and memories. It is on this basis that European peoples may accept, or better wish, to mutually open their democracies to the peoples of other member states. At the outset, this does not require a singularly European public space but asks only that citizens have 'an informed curiosity about the opinions and political lives of their neighbors'.[90] In time, multinational politics and perhaps even a new citizenship will emerge from the confrontation, accommodation, and inclusiveness of Europe's varied political cultures. And from this in turn, an enlarged mentality may even emerge, as Kant would have it, of thinking and judging from the point of view of everyone else.[91] If Europe is a community of others then we need to learn to justify our political

---

[87] See *inter alia* K Lowe, *Savage Continent: Europe in the Aftermath of World War II* (Viking, 2012).

[88] On philosophical roots see A Honneth, *The Struggle for Recognition: The Moral Grammar of Social Conflicts* (Cambridge: Polity Press, 1996).

[89] In Nicolaïdis, 'We the Peoples...', 102. See n 1.

[90] M Maduro, 'So close and yet so far: the paradoxes of mutual recognition' (2007) 14(5) *Journal of European Public Policy* 814–25.

[91] Kant, *Critique of Judgment*, section 40. Quoted in Bohman (2007), see n 8.

judgments not from a perspective we argue should be 'ours', *this* people, but from what we believe may be theirs, *that* people, and find ways to creatively confront and pool different perspectives without pretending that they can be merged.[92]

More generally, denial of recognition is present as an obsession with 'oneness' which prevails in many European quarters. But mutual recognition also reaffirms resistance to isolation through a kind of openness which leads to changing one's own nature. Under genuine mutual recognition, it is not quite the same any more to be French or Greek or British—a theme to be revisited in the context of crisis.[93]

In this sense, mutual recognition presupposes toleration but does not finish there. The European dream is that enemies can become neighbours and neighbours can become friends. Recognition forces us to assess circumstances where mutual tolerance is not enough, eg the peaceful coexistence of groups of people with different histories, cultures, and identities, which is what toleration makes possible.[94] It may indeed guard against 'oppressive tolerance' or point to when the act of tolerance itself must either be supported by 'more' or risks degenerating into conflict if it is based on ignorance.

Where Walzer only needs an aspiration to peaceful coexistence for his normative core (and can therefore encompass under his umbrella associations ranging from empires to nation-states), a demoicracy is preoccupied with a much more demanding engagement of the demoi in such a process. Some would say that this is the true meaning of 'reconciliations' at the heart of European project (and not only between France and Germany). And, as reconciliation is translated into functional cooperation, the level of interdependence and common projects engineered by their governments and managed by their respective states is such that it requires peoples to care *both* about what their governments do together and about the inter-societal interactions which underpin this action.

So demoicracy cannot be reduced to the continued existence and desirability of diversity in an interdependent world threatened by powerful homogenizing forces. There may be enduring demoi but the challenge of demoicracy is for them to engage enough with each other in order to deliver *kratos* as part of the equation. This is why this second cluster includes a host of variants which can be adapted to a demoicratic lens, from binding trust to ideals of community, friendship, mutuality, inclusiveness, solidarity, loyalty, or fidelity, each of which deserves a longer discussion. Moreover, it is our modern understanding that the ideal of openness discussed here commands deliberation. But if we consider the normative core of demoicracy without adjective, then transnational deliberation is not necessarily part of its core essence; there are many ways in which democratic polities can interrelate including social bargaining, contestation, and mobilization. When Samantha Besson writes about deliberative democracy she does so precisely by arguing that, in her view, demoicracy as an ideal is not sufficient in and of itself to fulfil transnational liberal demoicratic aspirations.[95]

---

[92] Bohman (2007), see n 1.   [93] J Weiler, 'To be a European: Eros and Civilization' (1999).
[94] M Walzer, see n 67.   [95] S Besson (2006), see n 1.

Finally, mutual recognition is tested as a normative core through the ways in which the peoples in a demoicracy relate to the mosaic of stories which they respectively hold about the Union as a whole. Embracing the narrative diversity about the EU which prevails both within and across European countries is a tall order. Yet if the EU is to be described as an overlapping consensus of overlapping consensus, then traditional EU integrationists will exclude dissenting voices at their peril. The EU rests on practices of interpretation and negotiation reflecting strong—yet reasonable—disagreements between its many component parts on the norms and goals that underpin the process of integration.[96] Taken together, all these stories are part of a logic of reflexive appropriation, decentring, and mutual learning which together provide the narrative backdrop for mutual recognition.

A demoicratic ethos of transnational engagement and mutual recognition focuses more than its alternatives on how the Union constrains and binds the ways in which a country treats other Union nationals beyond some shared customary norm of 'hospitality', as with Kant's cosmopolitan law. It focuses in particular on whether the rules of free movement/non discrimination are genuinely applied. It is open to the idea that people who move across borders bring with them the laws and social contracts of their home country, but asks how laws written solely in one country affect citizens of another (directly or through their effects on domestic welfare states), and how this in turn affects the quality of democracies. And it suggests that citizens should have a say in the rules that might affect them as consumers, clients, or school parents, but are emanating from other countries.

Here again, many question arise from the narrative core. How is the emancipatory potential of mutual recognition actualized? Can we sustain mutuality under profound inequality? Under what conditions can mutual recognition suffice in providing the 'ties that bind'? To what extent is the demand for recognition between peoples only a function of recognition between states' laws and regulations? And how can recognition be non-discriminatory when it is in part conditional on the features of the other side? If countering the tendency to deny recognition (through discrimination) is at the core of the (liberal) EU single market project, what of denials to recognition in the social realm, from gay marriage to refugee status, or the tendency to use mutual recognition in illiberal ways to bolster the exercise of state coercive powers against individuals?[97]

(C) Internal/External Consistency

EU officials, academics, and commentators have been struggling with a third normative cluster: the application of internal principles to external relations. This has meant, on the one hand, heralding the need for consistency between the internal and the

---

[96] K Nicolaïdis, 'Germany as Europe: How the Constitutional Court unwittingly embraced EU demoi-cracy' (2011) 9 *International Journal on Constitutional Law* 786–92. Nicolaïdis and Pelabay, see n 1; Lacroix and Nicolaïdis, see n 17.

[97] For a discussion see S Lavenex 'Mutual Recognition and the Monopoly of Force: Limits of the single market analogy' (2007) 14(5) *Journal of European Public Policy* 762–79. See also Fichen and Massimo, Criminal Law Beyond the States: The European Model (19 April 2011), Helsinki Legal Studies Research Paper no 4.

external; but on the other hand, living in a world often 'inconsistent' with the EU's normative core. So we need to translate transnational non-domination and transnational mutual recognition from the internal to the external under such constraints.

Most simply, the kind of essentialism connected with the ideal of a European demos (defining ourselves through who we are) is bound to have something to do with 'othering', eg defining ourselves against some other, which in turn is the root of nationalism, this time Euro-nationalism. Is it desirable to see Europe built against an 'other'—be it Islam, the United States, China, or simply the non-European world— especially when such 'other' is so present within (Muslim communities in Europe)? Would Euro-patriotism be true to the EU's normative foundation?

It may be that the idea of demoicracy is grounded—and for some of us perhaps primarily motivated—by a commitment to 'no othering' both internally and externally, in spite of the reigning denial of Europe's colonial past. It is for this reason that when he chose to uphold the ideal of a European Union defined *against* that of the United States, it is fair to say that Habermas stepped outside the demoicratic ethos.[98]

(D) Synthesis? Horizontality and Transnationalism

Should we try to set forth a singly overarching norm that can define the project of European demoicracy? Some might simply refer to transnationalism as such a norm, a broader overarching norm in international relation, and a norm which connects to deeper roots in transnational histories.[99] In a minor key, I would be inclined to elevate the ideal of horizontality from a positive concept (describing the nature of international or European cooperation without government) to normative status to the extent that it can convey both the ideal of non-domination and that of mutual engagement and recognition. The 'mutual opening up of democracies' which is the signature of a demoicracy is not the pre-condition but the result of a political-legal order centred around horizontal transfers of sovereignty between demoi and their representative institutions.[100] If in a demoicratic polity like the EU, such horizontal transfers tend to be preferred to vertical transfers of sovereignty, this is no less demanding a process as we now explore.

3 Genealogy: Resilience and Pathologies

There are at least two options if we want to ask how these general norms are to be operationalized. We can propose to deduce practical implications directly from the

---

[98] J Lacroix (2009), see n 19.

[99] For an early discussion see T Kappen (ed), *Bringing Transnational Relations Back in* (Cambridge: Cambridge University Press, 1995).

[100] See K Nicolaïdis and G Shaffer, 'Transnational Mutual Recognition Regimes: Governance without Global Government' (2005) 68 *Michigan Review of International Law* 267–322.

norms themselves. Or we can pursue a normative-inductive approach and avail our-selves of the rich historical material provided by decades of trial and error in European legal and political development.[101] In other words, we can use the EU's historical experience to refine the guiding principles that may sustain demoicracy over time.

So, how does a demoicratic system come about and develop? Can we have demoi-cracy without demoicrats? Can it be the case that we do not find a demoicratic grand design in the EU but what Hallstein labelled 'creative opportunism', namely a balance that no-one intended to begin with? Or on the contrary, could demoicracy be the result not only of 'rhetoric entrapment' but also 'normative entrapment'? Is the ethos of demoicracy pervasive enough in the EU that a critical mass of actors 'do it' without labelling it, as Mr Jourdain spoken prose?

In these last pages I can only sketch elements of a response regarding the root cause of demoicratic resilience and the pathologies that may threaten it as is apparent in the current crisis.

(A) Resilience through Transformation

If we were to write a story of resilience of demoicracy in Europe, we would need to distinguish between two periods. First, during the foundational period, the basic structure of a demoicratic polity of peoples-as-states was put in place as 'the commu-nity method'. During this time, the organizing principles were not tested against the mettle of peoples-as-citizens and indirect political accountability seemed to suffice as a proxy for 'democracy in Europe'. During the second, current, period, which started with the end of the Cold War, the peoples-as-citizens entered the scene along with a more public and explicit engagement with the democratic question. Resilience would have to do in part with the ways in which these two logics work together.

Joseph Weiler's analysis in 'The Transformation of Europe' did much to convince us that we cannot and should not try to encapsulate the EU under a static political form.[102] From its inception, the EU has been in a process of adaptive transformation. The fundamental pattern of European politics can be seen as a dance between law and power, judges and politicians, respectively and reflexively engaged in trading off a gradual foreclosing of exit (hardening EU law through the chemistry of combining supremacy and direct effect) with the retaining of Member States' voice through their insistence on unanimous consent ('hard law making' in Weiler's terminology). This was a deal struck less by design than by necessity. In this way and through the first three decades, a constitutionalized arrangement between states emerged with increas-ing legal bite but a bite of their own design. Letting go and asserting control as the *yin*

---

[101] For a synthetic overview see E Bomberg and J Peterson, *Decision-Making in the European Union* (London: Palgrave MacMillan, 1999).

[102] J Weiler, 'The Transformation of Europe' see n 6. And A Hirschman, *Exit, Voice and Loyalty—Responses to Decline in Firms, Organizations and States* (Cambridge: Harvard University Press, 1970).

and *yang* of European politics can serve the first analytic building bloc of this demoicratic story. And this tension explained the paradox that integration had been seen to increase (by lawyers) and stagnate (by political scientists) at one and the same time. In this way, a common purpose could be pursued—the single market—through the management of managed mutual recognition among states while guarding against supra-national subordination, or total harmonization of standards. As the principle of indirect democracy (peoples-as-states) reigned supreme, citizens were not asked to own the process but its results.[103]

But what would happen next? At the time, Weiler expressed his judgment that such foundational equilibrium was precious and that we should worry about dismantling that which 'helps explain the uniqueness and stability of the Community for much of its life'.[104] Formally, we may consider that the demoicratic bargain was unhinged at Maastricht and the years that followed. The perceived combination of creeping EU competence with shrinking indirect accountability was not matched by an appropriate renewal of democratic stories and practices. The peoples-as-citizens were knocking at the door and the seeds of a 'demoicratic deficit' were planted in spite, or rather because of, a quasi-exclusionary focus on the European parliament as the political answer.

Nevertheless, I would argue that EU politics have continued to deliver the basic ingredients of a demoicratic polity. It has done so through rebalancing, taking small steps to reinvent the foundational equilibrium in other guise, at least when considering peoples-as-states: the generalization of opt-outs as well as most recently the highly symbolic 'exit clause' introduced the Lisbon Treaty (even while one might question its *de facto* feasibility); the retaining of elements of formal state equality through the continued (now headless) rotation for the Councils of Ministers; the collective reasser-tion of voice on the part of Member States in the face of growing EU (including Commission) competence in the financial area; and, in spite of the pressures of scale, enlargement has not meant an abandonment of the consensus-and-compromise method of decision making.[105]

The EU has radically transformed itself since 1958, as the functionalist currents have constantly been steered by demoicratic preferences.[106] But these developments, important as they are from an institutional perspective, have left the matter of popular democratic legitimacy unresolved. What of Hirschman's third part of the triptych, the

---

[103] The work of Friz Scharf and Giandomenico Majone both cogently analyse this logic. Majone, *Regulating Europe* (Routledge, September 1996); *Dilemmas of European Integration* (Oxford University Press, 2005); *Governing in Europe. Effective and Democratic?* (Oxford/New York: Oxford University Press).

[104] Weiler, see n 46.

[105] Renaud Dehousse, Florence Deloche-Gaudez, and Olivier Duhamel, *Elargissement—Comment l'Europe s'adapte* (Paris, Presses de Sciences Po, 2006).

[106] This story of demoicratic transformation can be read in various ways. Andrew Moravcsik's master narrative emphasizes choices but overlooks the normative core; others the reverse. See A Moravcsik, *The Choice for Europe: Social Purpose and State Power from Messina to Maastricht* (New York: Routledge, 1998). See also S Benhabid, 'Transformations of Citizenship: The Case of Contemporary Europe' (2002) 37(4) *Government and Opposition* 439–65.

kind of loyalty to an institution which activates the commitment to voice in the first place rather then its alternative of exit?[107]

(B) From Pathologies to Crisis

European democracy ultimately depends on the health of national democracies. This is both an asset and a problem for demoicracy, so we need to ask what happens to national pathologies once democracies open up to each other. Does the EU level magnify such pathologies or does it help reduce them? It may be that the EU often helps entrench domestic democratic flaws, starting with the weakening of the rule of law by the use of managerial channels of power and executive decision making. At the same time, in Weiler's formulation, the DNA of EU politics since its inception has been the pursuit of a political messianic venture where legitimacy is to be derived from the destiny pursued rather than the peoples.[108] And messianism as a force of fusion amplifies political dynamic of disintegration and anti-EU populism, which then justifies its own rhetoric: further integration to counter the Eurosceptic bogeyman— which leads us back to the quality of national democracies.

It is of course in times of crisis that such pathologies can come to seriously threaten the EU's demoicratic ethos: can the demoicratic logic still accommodate more centralization of functions, loss of voice, and foreclosure of exit at one and the same time? At which point will we have crossed the Rubicon whereby the EU's legal order has taken on undeniable statist characteristics? What are the demoicratic safeguards against the alliance between the logic of messianism and the determinism of 'market pressure'? And what is the line between the legitimate exercise of disproportionate 'responsible' power in the pursuit of common purposes and illegitimate albeit 'soft' domination by a member state and its people?

Spelling out concrete and generalizeable principles to address these questions is perhaps the most pressing research agenda attached to the idea of demoicracy at a time of crisis in the EU, and one which is also suggested by several contributions to this volume.[109] Indeed, guiding principles for legal and policy praxis have been honed through the history of the EU which need to be protected and perfected. Among such principles I would include the autonomy of peoples, safeguards at the centre against power imbalances, preference for pluralities over majorities, transnational rights, legal recognition of equivalence, domestic mediation of supranational disciplines, empowerment of lower levels of governance and individuals, complementarity

---

[107] Hirschman, see n 102.

[108] Chapter 6. Such a belief in the rightfulness of deeper integration for its own sake backed up by elite networks of cooperation impervious to the demands of the 'peoples' is in sharp contrast with the pattern of 'cycles of federalism' which we can observe in more mature federation. *Federal Vision*, see n 31. See also K Nicolaïdis 'Our Democratic Atonement: Why we Need an Agora Europe' in *The People's Project? New European Treaty and the Prospects for Future Negotiations* (Brussels: European Policy Centre, December 2007).

[109] K Nicolaïdis, "European Democracy and its Crisis" (2012), *Journal of Common Market Studies*.

between direct and indirect accountability, co-citizenship among peoples, and commitment to political diversity.

4 Conclusion

In the last two decades, philosophers have been discovering the EU and its new brand of democracy across states and hailed its radical transformative logic. But if we move our focus from the transformation of the state as our unit of analysis to the transformation of the European system of states as a whole, the European Union can be understood as an original choice to incrementally transform the latter rather than to transcend it altogether. We are not creating a united Europe. We are changing the way in which its various states can remain separate while at the same time opening up their institutions and democratic politics to each other. Paradoxically, the transformative logic of European demoicracy therefore owes its radical nature to the conservative refusal to do away with the core tenet of nation-state-based democracy.

In this chapter, I have sought to make the case for demoicracy as a philosophical idea that illuminates extant EU law. I have argued that the radical mutual opening of national democracies that a genuine demoicracy would involve ought to serve as a beacon for the EU's further development. Scholars and actors alike must resist the pull of 'oneness'—be it one people, one state, one voice on the world stage, or indeed one story—to concentrate instead on drawing strength from the accommodation of differences. A 'demoicratic' ethics for Europe can sometimes be reflected in law, but not always. In the end, it is borne in our collective imagination.

11

Statecraft and the Foundations of European Union Law

Ari Afilalo[1] and Dennis Patterson[2]

1 Introduction

In this chapter, we use the lens of Statecraft to analyse the philosophical foundations of the European integration enterprise. We advance a theory of Statecraft that posits that the state evolves through successive eras that are characterized by distinctive hallmarks. The 'state-nation' of the Industrial Revolution drew on the resources of its subjects and garnered for itself as much international resources as possible to strengthen and solidify the economic base of the polity. More laissez-faire policies internally, mercantilism and gunboat diplomacy on the trade front, as well as competition for colonial resources, accorded with the ethos of the state-nation. In time, the state-nation evolved into a 'nation-state' dedicated internally to providing 'welfare' (which we define to encompass both entitlements and welfare-enhancing regulation) to its nation. Collaboration with other states in an international trade framework dedicated to liberalizing trade while theoretically allowing each participant to set its chosen welfare level accorded with this model. Decolonization of nations artificially established by the colonial powers, the establishment of a United Nations based on territorial integrity and sovereign equals, and a general system of international law

[1] Professor of Law, Rutgers University School of Law (Camden). This chapter was written while the author was an Emile Noel Fellow at New York University's Jean Monnet Center for International and Regional Economic Law and Justice.

[2] Professor of Law and Chair in Legal Philosophy and Legal Theory, European University Institute, Florence; Board of Governors Professor of Law and Philosophy, Rutgers University, New Jersey, USA; Professor of Law and Chair in International Trade and Legal Philosophy, Swansea University, Wales, UK. The author gratefully acknowledges comments received at a discussion of this chapter at a meeting of the EUI Legal Philosophy and Legal Theory Working Group. Special thanks to Professor Sven Steimo for helpful remarks and suggestions.

providing few encroachments on national sovereignty were twentieth-century phenomena consistent with the age of the nation-state.

The evolutionary nature of Statecraft is grounded in the constant interaction
between the 'inner' and 'outer' faces of the State, and the constitutional and structural
changes it generates. For example, the nation-state of the twentieth century evolved in
time into the nascent 'market-state' of the twenty-first. The shift was structurally
ingrained into the very constitution of the nation-state. Its legitimacy depended on
the supply of welfare to the nation, an eminently sovereign function of the State. To
maximize global resources and avoid the trade wars of the 1930s, the nation-states
entered into an international legal order liberalizing the free movement of goods and
services, consistent initially (in theory at least) with the exercise of sovereignty. But with
globalized trade, the participating states could no longer remain independent and
sovereign 'black boxes'. As a natural corollary, ownership of assets became internation-
alized, money became a commodity, regulation travelled with goods, production
became outsourced. Together with unprecedented progress in information technology
as a means of linking a trading world, these factors all added up to what has loosely been
described as 'globalization'. As we will explain, one of the hallmarks of the market-state
age is the inability of any one state to shelter itself from crises in others, a loss of control
over the ability to deliver welfare, and a shift from welfare delivery to the enablement of
global economic opportunity as the legitimating basis for the State.

In this chapter, our focus is on exposing and explaining how these fundamental
political ideas have affected the development of the law and institutions of the
European Communities and their successor Union. We apply our theory of Statecraft
to explain and contextualize essential constitutional provisions and historical milestones of Europe. Why does unification of control over budgetary and fiscal policies,
(or a Euro bond) become a possibility today, while in the mid-1960s the Community
almost broke up over the question whether to transition to some form of majority
voting on matters much less threatening to national sovereignty? How did the nature
of the State after the Second World War make it desirable to establish a deeply
integrated territory? Why did the integration of Europe accelerate in the latter part
of the twentieth century, which witnessed the introduction of a common currency,
common citizenship, increased integration of legal norms, and free movement of all
persons within the Schengen zone? We posit that these events are neither accidents of
history nor phenomena born of the increased habit of cohabitation of the European
nations under one tent, nor of their struggling with the challenges *du jour*. Rather, the
hallmarks of the State in each particular era explain those developments. The Luxembourg crisis reflects the nation-state's adherence to its regulatory welfare-legitimating
ethos. The accelerated integration of Europe reflects its transition into the era of the
market-state. Its financial crises and Europe's need to unite politically to manage them
reflect the demands of market-state policies and the need to make sure that all parts of
the integrated area adhere to them.

The 'leaps and bounds' of European evolution that Schuman spoke of are informed
by the then-current Statecraft constitution. To be sure, Europe's unique history has a

profound influence on its integration enterprise. We believe, for example, that Europe lunged forward into the market-state age faster than most because the Second World War and its attendant tragedies instilled a sense of urgency into the enterprise. We also obviously acknowledge the complexity and breadth of the historical, economic, political, cultural, and other influences on the European enterprise. However, a full understanding of the essential drives that pushed European integration forward necessitates an analysis of its history using the tools of Statecraft theory.

Our thesis is that the State[3] goes through successive iterations that are properly described as 'constitutional orders'. Each constitutional order is characterized by certain foundational hallmarks. These are fundamental constitutional principles that define how states behave, both internally and externally, vis-à-vis other states. With each successive passage into a new constitutional order, states must adjust their internal foundational law and external strategic and commercial behavior to accord with the epochal hallmarks of Statecraft. The failure to do so leads to deep structural crises, such as the trade wars of the 1930s, and the financial crises of 2008 and 2010.

The European enterprise, its milestones, its crises, its limitations, and its accomplishments, can be perspicuously rendered with this theory of Statecraft. European integration surely could have occurred earlier than it did: after the First World War and the Treaty of Versailles, Europe comprised nation-states that readily could have begun the integration process into a single market area with common institutions.[4] After the Second World War, early European treaties reflect a constitutional design characteristic of the nation-state that could have been launched when the nation-state epoch was ushered in after the First World War. The first European crises and challenges, including the Luxembourg crisis, the so-called 'democracy deficit', and the political resistance to the European Court's integration jurisprudence and its aggressive interpretation and application of the European economic constitution, reflect a tension between integration and the protection of sovereignty that are typical of the nation-state era. The acceleration of the integration of Europe, in particular in the latter part of the twentieth century, including increased harmonization, the Single European Act, the Maastricht Treaty, European citizenship, and the Schengen arrangements, the single currency, and other significant developments, is consistent with the transition from a nation-state to a 'market-state'[5] constitutional order.

Most recently, the Lisbon Treaty gives concrete legal and political form to European experimentation with institutions that respond, in large part, to market-state

---

[3] We use the word 'state' in two different senses. When we write 'State', we are referring to the conceptual political entity that has evolved in the Western world over roughly the last five hundred years. See JS McClelland, *A History of Western Political Thought* (Routledge: London, 1996), 280 (dating the birth of the modern state at 1500). The State is manifested in many territorially and politically distinct 'states' such as Italy or the Republic of Latvia. When we refer to these individual states, we refer to them as a 'state'.

[4] Disparities in economic power between the nation-states of Europe as well as animosity engendered by the Treaty of Versailles are possible explanations for the delay in integration.

[5] As we detail later, the legitimacy of the market-state is grounded in its ability to provide economic opportunity for the citizenry. This is its purpose and its ethos.

challenges.[6] The debt crisis and other recent challenges to Europe also reflect tensions that are characteristic of a market-state age where states are interdependent and where financial and other crises reverberate throughout an enlarged, deeply integrated market. Much as the nation-states of the twentieth century failed for three decades to recognize that they should develop their welfare national systems whilst integrating their commercial relationships with other nation-states, the emerging market-states of the twenty-first century have thus far failed to recognize that the market-state age demands that welfare programs from the nation-state era be substantially curtailed. The State's legitimacy will depend on its ability to stabilize and shore up markets. Even this mandate is inconsistent with budgetary and monetary policies that once lay at the foundation of the nation-state's legislative programme, failure to adhere to the market-state ethos will not only lead to the demise of the culprit state but reverberate throughout the collectivity. Similarities to the twentieth-century trade wars also extend to the strategic realm. The modern liberal democratic nation-states had to struggle against fascism and communism at the same time as their economic architecture faltered as a result of the failure to change policy. Postmodern liberal democratic market-states are devoting an inordinate amount of resources to the existential financial crises arising out of their most recent policy failures, at the time when they have to struggle with global networked terrorism, the commodification of weapons of mass destruction, and Islamic extremism.

We begin our chapter with a brief overview of Statecraft and our understanding of the State. We then proceed to weave a narrative of the European integration project that is infused with our Statecraft analysis. Our contention is that the philosophical foundations of a united Europe cannot be properly understood without examining them in light of the philosophy of the State. We do not purport to present an all-encompassing theory explaining why and how Europe has evolved. It is obvious that a single theoretical tool cannot explain such a vast and complex enterprise. Rather, we posit that Statecraft theory is a lucid tool in explaining how the edifice of Europe has been constructed, how it addressed its existential crises, and the challenges and difficulties that it may encounter in the future.

We contend that Europe is a unique phenomenon. It is a theatre where *sui generis* historical *rebondissements* have mixed with Statecraft evolution[7] to engender a 'new legal order' that reflects the hallmarks of the Statecraft of its age but also goes beyond it. We believe that, by and large, history can be explained through ideas and

---

[6] Some see the 'end' of the State marked by a transition to other, more complicated organizing forms. *See* Martin Van Creveld, *The Rise and Decline of the State* (Cambridge University Press, 1999, vii) ('Globally speaking, the international system is moving away from an assembly of distinct, territorial, sovereign, legally equal states toward different, more hierarchical, and in many ways more complicated structures'.). See also Anne-Marie Slaughter, *A New World Order* (Princeton University Press, 2004), 32 ('The conception of the unitary state is a fiction'.)

[7] We use the word 'evolution' throughout this article to describe the development of the State. The key concept in our evolutionary narrative is 'legitimacy'. How the State legitimates itself and how it responds to crises of legitimacy are the fundamental features of our evolutionary narrative.

intellectual history rather than the random intersection of material events. Throughout this essay, we articulate and describe how European historical particularism is consistent, and has coalesced, with the evolution of Statecraft to produce the European integration area.

2 The State: An Overview

We start with a brief overview of the evolution of the State through its various epochal iterations and introduce concepts that are relevant for the balance of our exposition. The 'State' is not a static entity. The State has evolved through distinct constitutional orders. As the State evolves, the grounds of its legitimacy vis-à-vis its subjects change. States establish legal systems consistent with the demands of legitimacy, which feature discrete hallmarks. For example, as we argue below, the European 'state-nations' of the seventeenth and eighteenth centuries sought to solidify the metropolis, drew on their subjects and on external resources to foster the consolidation enterprise, and minimized collaboration with other states. The 'nation-states', which succeeded the state-nations in the twentieth century, marshalled their resources to ensure the welfare of the nation, and were better suited to collaborate in a free trade and integration enterprise with other states. Market-states face a diffuse, interdependent, and intertwined market that cuts across boundaries and, while formally sovereign to establish their welfare systems, those states are in practice required to coordinate entitlements and regulation with other market-states because a structural crisis in one state (such as the Greek debt crisis) will reverberate and endanger the other states in much the same manner as protectionist policies shook the international commercial system in the nation-state eras. The legitimacy of market-states will depend on their ability to protect the foundational stability of the globalized markets that have grown out of the nation-state era thereby enabling and fostering economic opportunity. This will require them to adopt legislation that shifts away from the top-down welfare regulatory entitlements structures of the twentieth century, converge towards fiscal and monetary policies that are consistent with sound budget management, and generally attempt to solidify and stimulate market activities. The transition from a welfare state to an era of economic opportunity raises resistance and opposition from the beneficiaries of welfare policies, much like the industrial beneficiaries of protectionism opposed liberalized trade. However, governments that fail to ensure market stability will not meet the legitimacy test in this age of Statecraft; they will inevitably fail. This constitutional architecture would, as we explain below, change fundamentally in the nation-state era that followed the epochal iteration of the state-nation.

Over the course of the last five hundred years, the State has evolved through a series of configurations. Its last three iterations are relevant to our narrative: the 'state-nation' (French Revolution to the First World War); the 'nation-state' (1917 up until 1990); and the 'market-state' (since 1990). We shall discuss each iteration in greater detail as we review Europe's passage through the relevant epoch. As the State evolves over time, its constitutive features change both in themselves and in relation to one another. At all times, the most important aspect of the evolution of the State is the degree to which it responds to the demands of its citizens in the course of legitimizing itself. With respect to each era, the ethos of the State is a function of the legitimacy demands of its citizenry. In turn, different constitutional architectures result in different internal legal systems and a different mode of relating to other states in the collective system. In this essay, we will summarize the essential aspects of each epochal iteration of Statecraft and describe how they affected Europe.

The State has two faces, an inner and an outer one. The outer face of the State has two dimensions: strategy and trade. At all times, states have a strategic relationship to other states, the most basic of which are peace and war. Trade is the second dimension of the outer face of the State. Trade ideology (for example, mercantilism or comparative advantage) follows the constitutional order of the society of states in that each form of the State is complemented by a particular trade regime. For instance, mercantilism may be understood as complementary to the state-nation form of the State. In an age where Statecraft was focused on the solidification of a central State,[8] and the resources of its subjects marshalled to achieve that goal, an international policy focused on mercantilist drives, 'gunboat' diplomacy, and a set of commercial relations driven more by power struggles than the rule of international law, was more consistent with domestic Statecraft than twentieth-century comparative advantage.[9] Strategy follows the same patterns. The colonization enterprise aimed, in substantial part, to amass resources for the metropolis. It carved out foreign territories based on the result of struggles and compromises among European powers bent on strengthening their home-state-nation bases. States went to war to appropriate disputed border territories. No League of Nations, United Nations, or other formal institutions based on balance of powers, sovereignty, and collaboration among states resting on fully formed nations existed. No general agreement on comparative advantage-based trade was entered into by commercial states. Instead of the plethora of treaties that characterized the second half of the twentieth century, states entered into a relatively small number of agreements that, by and large, would be acceptable only if they furthered the solidification enterprise of the state-nation. This international landscape, too, was entirely consistent with the ethos of the state-nation.

The inner face of the State is law and 'welfare'. We understand welfare capaciously as both subventions by the State as well as the production of legal regimes designed to improve the lives of citizens. The latter is what we term 'regulatory welfare'. Regulatory welfare refers to the regulation of the economic and social aspects of the State. Health, labour, environmental regulations, resource conservation, worker safety, competition laws, consumer and investor protection, are examples of regulatory welfare. We call

---

[8] *See* Phyllis Deane, *The Evolution of Economic Ideas* (Cambridge University Press, 1978), 2.

[9] Mercantilism has classically been understood as a set of economic policies seeking to encourage exports and restrain imports with a view to enriching the exporting state to the greatest extent possible. Such policies are often described as 'beggar-thy-neighbour'. They were prevalent in the nineteenth century and the era of the State that we describe as 'state-nation'. See Lars Magnusson, *Mercantilism: The Shaping of an Economic Language* (Routledge, 1994).

the subvention part of welfare 'entitlements welfare'. It encompasses the various regimes adopted by European states to ensure minimum standards of living for their subjects. These include unemployment benefits, retirement, health insurance, minimum income guarantees, housing aid, aid to families with children, education, and other welfare tools adopted by European states to ensure that their nation will not fall below a minimal safety-net level.

'Statecraft' embodies the outer and the inner faces of the State. Our argument is that these two dimensions of Statecraft interact with one another over time, and that the trade and strategic outer faces of the State must be structured so as to accord with the inner dimensions of Statecraft, as well as with each other. Thus, when we say that the trade order 'follows' the constitutional order of states, we mean that each constitutional order of the State (that is, each epochal iteration of the State) embraces a complementary trade ideology.

Our theory posits that the inner constitutional dimension of the State, the law, is directly linked to the outer face of the State; that the inner constitution of the State varies from one epochal manifestation to the next; and that the interaction between the inner and outer faces of the State ultimately brings about transformative patterns that, over time, usher in the next era of Statecraft.[10] Thus, the state-nation's solidification enterprise, drawing on its subjects to consolidate the metropolis, wound up establishing a distinct 'nation' that became associated with the state and its boundaries. This nation would become the foundational interlocutor of the nation-state, and the legitimating enterprise of the State would be to provide for its welfare. We are sceptical of sweeping pronouncements to the effect that an optimal form of government, or a timeless trade order, have been found. For example, we believe Francis Fukuyama was mistaken when he declared that modern liberal democratic Statecraft portended the 'end of history'.[11] Rather, we believe Fukuyama only glimpsed the modern nation-state at its apex.[12]

---

[10] Cooper writes: 'The kind of world we have depends on the kind of states that compose it: for the pre-modern world, success is empire and failure is chaos. For the modern, success entails managing the balance of power and failure means falling back into war or empire. For the postmodern state, success means openness and transnational cooperation.' Robert Cooper, *The Breaking of Nations* (Atlantic Books, 2003), 76.

[11] Fukuyama has continued to massage his initial claim. Recently he had this to say:

The End of History was never linked to a specifically American model of social or political organization. Following Alexandre Kojeve, the Russian-French philosopher who inspired my original argument, I believe that the European Union more accurately reflects what the world will look like at the end of history than the contemporary United States. The EU's attempt to transcend sovereignty and traditional power politics by establishing a transnational rule of law is much more in line with a 'post-historical' world than the Americans' continuing belief in God, national sovereignty, and their military. Francis Fukuyama, *The History at the End of History*. Available at: <http://www.project-syndicate.org/commentary/fukuyama3/English>.

[12] According to Fukuyama, the liberal democratic model soundly beat fascism and communism because, simply put, it was a better idea. The liberal democratic model had no problem besting the fascist ideology of expansionism and racial superiority. In time, it defeated the Marxist ideology—in part because the growth of a strong and expansive middle class, resulting from (among other factors) the welfare policies of the nation-state—as it had radically changed the social reality in which Marx wrote. In the end, Fukuyama argued, all good government would be organized along the lines of the liberal democratic model, which would be applied to

Likewise, we argue that a united Europe is not a timeless concept. The European enterprise could not have been launched until after the First World War, when the European state-nations graduated to their nation-state form. Schuman, in his famed Declaration, understood the historical context for his 'United States of Europe' vision. He properly understood that his enterprise could not have been launched before the transformation of the State into its nation-state evolution, and the failure to integrate that he identified was that which occurred *entre deux guerres*, not earlier.

In this chapter, we seek to understand the European enterprise in light of a theory of Statecraft that views the State as undergoing successive epochal transformations. This theory holds that, in each era, a prevailing form of the State operates characterized by foundational features that define the nature of its internal law and its relations with other states. We review the historical and legal background of the European collectivity in light of our Statecraft theory, and explain how Statecraft sheds light and insight into the political, legal, and institutional evolution of Europe and its crises, both past and present.

3 Pre-Modern Era: No Possible Europe

We posit that the pre-modern era started with the French Revolution, spanned the Industrial Revolution, and ended with the First World War. In this age of Statecraft, the State focused on its own consolidation. Internally, the pre-modern era involved a foundational laissez-faire policy coupled with the growth of a legal system designed to protect private property and contract rights. Externally, the State adhered principally to a zero-sum game intended to amass wealth. Taken together, these policies had the design and purpose of strengthening the industrial base of the developing states.

The state-nation legitimated itself by bringing unity out of diversity. It arose from the unification into one entity of largely unrelated territories, such as dukedoms, feudal territories, and princely states. The state-nation founded a single entity within discrete boundaries. Economically, it saw the rise of capital investment in the industrial base. Its ethos was to increase the power of the emerging sovereign. The internal legal system of the state-nation enabled its essential purpose. The state-nation adopted an economic legal structure designed to protect contractual and private property, rather than to extend entitlements to its subjects. Legal codes such as the Napoleonic Code were drafted.[13] They protected the expectations of capital holders, and they did so by ensuring that in the common cycles of 'boom-and-bust' policies that later in history came to be known as 'Keynesian' did not interfere with the free evolution of the market.

---

govern an ethnic or otherwise discrete nation and would protect the rights of minorities. See Francis Fukuyama, *The End of History?* (Summer, 1989) The National Interest.

[13] Al Grab, *Napoleon and the Transformation of Europe* (Palgrave Macmillan, 2003), 50–1. PAJ van den Berg, *The Politics of European codification: A history of the unification of law in France, Prussia, the Austrian Monarchy and the Netherlands*, 4–5 (Europa Law Pub. 2007), 206.

Another way to conceptualize this era of Statecraft is to think of it as a 'minimal welfare' constitutional era. A regime of entitlements welfare was inconsistent with the protection of capital. Industrialization and the concentration of capital required a freer market than a sophisticated system of welfare entitlements would permit. The same result obtained for regulatory welfare. Here, as well, the state-nation did not legitimize itself by providing protection for its nation. It had not even yet generated the concept of a nation. Instead, it drew on its subjects to amass resources and strengthen itself and, in the process, created the unified State resting on the nation that characterized the twentieth century. In that context, regulatory systems like labour or consumer protection, environmental, or resource conservation (generally, any of the twentieth-century administrative laws that we are familiar with) were not part of the internal legal fabric of the states. They would have burdened and hampered the solidification of the emerging industrial concerns at a time when the State derived its legitimacy from the protection of this very process.

Externally, the state-nation followed trade and strategic foundational policies that furthered a similar purpose: the consolidation of the state-nation. The state-nations of Europe colonized foreign territories and drew upon their resources to bolster their own commercial and industrial base.[14] These foreign territories were viewed as resources with respect to which they were in competition with their neighbours. The colonial map of Africa bears witness to these struggles. It comprised states that carved through traditional tribal boundary lines, lumping together ethnic groups that historically had never been part of the same polity, reflecting territorial struggles and compromises among England, France, Belgium, Germany, Italy, and other European colonial powers.[15] The European state-nations also followed a predominantly mercantilist policy, seeking to sell as much as possible and buy as little as possible from their trading interlocutors.[16]

In this environment, there was no foundation for a European Union. Each entity comprising the whole dedicated itself to consolidating its own base. The very ethos of the state-nation was antithetical to unity. States could not engage in an economic and strategic zero-sum game to strengthening themselves while at the same time seeking collaboration. Whether in the colonial battle field or in the realm of economic competition, the nature of Statecraft called for mustering the available resources to build a unified state.

The state-nation needed to build its industrial and commercial base. The state-nation process achieved that goal and, in the course of its enterprise, also created a

---

[14] Francois Crouzet, *A History of European Economy, 1000–2000*, (The University Press of Virginia, 2001), 50–4, 165.

[15] Thomas Pakenham, *The Scramble for Africa*, (New York: Avon Books, 1991), 21. HL Wesseling, *Imperialism and Colonialism, Essays on the History of European Expansion* (Greenwood Press, 1997), 12–20. On colonization of Africa see also Vincent B Khapoya, *The African Experience: An Introduction* (Prentice Hall, 2009).

[16] Peter Mathias and Sidney Polland, *The Cambridge Economic History of Europe*, Vol VIII, (Cambridge: Cambridge University Press, 1989), 103.

nation associated with its physical boundaries. The Schuman Declaration may be read to understand that the European enterprise was not a matter of destiny. It described the failures of the nations of Europe, after the First World War, to begin creating a unified whole. It did not argue, as Fukuyama or Ricardo did, that history had ended because we had reached a timeless and ultimate state of democratic rule or of economic organization. Instead, it acknowledged that the tragedy of Europe lay in its failure to recognize that, after the First World War, a 'united Europe was not created and we had war'.[17] It recognized that in the post-World War I era, Europeans adopted a Treaty which reflected the state-nation era values of competition, zero-sum game, lack of cooperation, and domination. The result was a foundational rupture between the architecture of a basic treaty defining the relations among European states and the Statecraft of the age.

Of course no-one could have accurately predicted whether the Second World War, and the rise of fascism and Nazism, could have been avoided had the Weimar Republic been brought into the fold of a collaborative Europe including France, Italy, and possibly Great Britain. However, much as the global trade wars of the *entre-guerre* that came at a time when modern liberal democracies needed to structure their commerce based on comparative advantage to solidify their economic base, the fracture of Europe certainly created fertile ground for the rise of totalitarian forces opposed to modern liberal democracies.

Scholars such as Philip Bobbitt view the 'modern', twentieth-century period as a 'Long War', one that featured a struggle among three competing ideologies for domination of the nation-state: democracy, fascism, and communism.[18] Their common denominator was adherence to a theory of Statecraft that gathered the power of the State to serve the nation. Communism did so by theoretically granting all subjects a joint and undivided interest in the whole. 'From each according to his abilities, to each according to his needs',[19] would ensure that each member of society would, in theory, enjoy a minimum level of entitlements. Fascism provided a corporatist organization to those who, racially, managed to become part of the nation. It gave its subjects an expansionist and dominating ideology whereby they would rule over inferior nations.[20] Modern liberal democracies followed suit with the welfare, administrative state that gave its subjects regulatory and entitlements welfare.

As we describe below in the next section of this chapter, the modern liberal democratic nation-states were uniquely suited for a collaborative architecture that would solidify their commercial base. Strategically, bringing Germany and Italy

---

[17] The Schuman Declaration was delivered by Robert Schuman, then French Foreign Minister, on 9 May 1950, announcing the creation of the European Coal and Steel Community (ECSC). For the full text of the declaration, visit <http://www.robert-schuman.eu/declaration_9mai.php>.

[18] Philip Bobbitt, *The Shield of Achilles: War, Peace and the Course of History* (Knopf, 2002), 24–33.

[19] Phrase first elucidated in Karl Marx's 'Critique of the Gotha Program'. The article was first published in the journal *Die Neue Zeit* (Bd. 1, No. 18, 1890–91).

[20] See Benito Mussolini, *Fascism Doctrine and Institutions* (Rome: Ardita Publishers, 1935), 7–42.

into the fold of a unified Europe, instead of addressing the 'German problem'[21] with a state-nation, zero-sum game approach, might have given the modern liberal democratic world a better chance of eliminating (or at least weakening at the outset) fascism as a candidate for delivering welfare in the Statecraft modern age. If that had happened, then the balance of powers in the twentieth century (starting with the 1920s) would have been devoted to a struggle between democracy and communism for the soul of the nation-state and, perhaps, it would have led to an earlier victory of the modern liberal democratic ideal.

Europe was the prime battleground for the Long War's ideological competition: its failure to recognize early enough that Statecraft had graduated to a new age hampered the Continent's liberal democratic movements in their struggle against totalitarianism. The unique European historical background sharpened the conflict and amplified the consequences of the failure to read Statecraft evolution correctly. To be sure, the global trade wars that resulted from the failure to move the trading system to one grounded on comparative advantage also damaged the United States' and other economies' ability to emerge faster from the Great Depression. Only in Europe, however, did the failure to tame totalitarianism result in an 'unthinkable' war the likes of which had never been seen on the Continent.

The Second World War was a catalyst for the adoption of the treaties and programmes that shaped the world in the second half of the twentieth century. Those treaties, as we explain below, are consistent with a nation-state, modern age of Statecraft. The GATT was signed at Bretton Woods and ushered in the trade liberalization enterprise, rejecting mercantilism and protectionism.[22] It 'embedded liberalism' in that each state participant enjoys, at least in theory, the sovereign right to establish and operate a welfare system of its choice, and at the same time removed barriers to trade and create a more efficient trading system. France could stay France and maintain programmes ranging from universal education to the supply of subsidized *metro* tickets to large families, all the while participating in a liberalized system of trade that generated more global resources to share. The Marshall Plan ensured that the European trading partners had sufficient economic strength to be meaningful commercial interlocutors for the United States. The new modern order relied on balance of powers, alongside liberalized trade and integration among sovereign equals, and the Marshall Plan fostered European powers so as to bring about greater balance.

Europe, because of its unique suffering during the Second World War, engaged in a deeply integrationist enterprise that went well beyond what any other free trade area would aspire to accomplish. Nevertheless, its roots can be traced to a modern enterprise, albeit amplified by historical circumstances.

---

[21] On 'the German Problem' see Roger H Wells, 'The German Problem in 1948' (June 1949) 2(2) *Political Research Quarterly* 208–16.

[22] After the initiation of Bretton Woods, international trade proliferated sixfold from 1948–1973. See <http://econ2.econ.iastate.edu/classes/econ355/choi/bre.htm>.

4 Europe: The Early Years

In the course of the state-nation building process, a nation associated with the boundaries of the state was formed. The state-nation had drawn on its subjects and created institutional systems to administer its building effort. Statecraft evolves from one era to the next, because the inner and external systems adopted in any age will transform the economic and social conditions of the participating states. As we will observe later, for example, the nation-states' liberalized trading system brought about a globalized economy that slowly eroded the association between the nation and its state's boundaries, the ability of states to provide for regulatory and entitlements welfare, and transformed the legitimating ethos of the State from providing welfare to enabling economic opportunity in a market-state. In the state-nation era, the consolidation of the State contributed to the creation of a nation. Among other things, conscription became the norm. Administrative control mechanisms were put in place. Power became centralized in a bureaucracy. The laissez-faire policies of the state-nations, coupled with industrialization and urbanization, left substantial segments of the citizenry in precarious economic and social conditions. A nation with an identity associated with the boundaries of the states looked to political institutions to address their welfare needs.

By the end of the First World War, after the adoption of the Treaty of Versailles, the European states had graduated to the early stages of the nation-state era. During that era, the State would marshall its power to provide for the welfare of its nation. At that time, the seeds that had been sown for the establishment of a European collectivity based on free trade, and common political institutions had yielded a collectivity of states ready to engage in the European endeavour.[23] The European Union was ready to proceed as a project of integration of discrete nations into a whole that would be inextricably bound but would at the same time respect national sovereignty.[24]

The historical basis of Europe is succinctly expressed in the Schuman Declaration: 'A united Europe was not achieved, and we had war.' By binding France and Germany to a union and partnership for coal and steel, the resources of war, the community of Europe would make war not only 'unthinkable but materially impossible'. Europe would not be achieved overnight. It would focus on concrete achievements and, in leaps and bounds, become a polity that could in time fairly be labelled as the 'United States of Europe'. In the meantime, foundational treaties were designed to shelter the sovereign right of the Member State to engage in regulatory and entitlements welfare.

European exceptionalism joined Statecraft to create a highly integrated Europe. The European Treaties went well beyond the free trade treaties (for example, the GATT)

---

[23] Anthony Sutcliffe, *An Economic and Social History of Western Europe Since 1945* (New York: Longman, 1996) 106.

[24] Damian Chalmers, Gareth Davies, and Giorgio Monti, *European Union Law. Cases and materials*, (Cambridge University Press, 2010), 7–9; Neill Nugent, *The Government and Politics of the European Union*, 5th edn (Duke University Press, 2003), 9–16.

that were adopted after the Second World War. They included a commitment to a single, tariff-free market and the removal of non-tariff barriers to trade. The GATT, on the other hand, contemplated a gradual reduction of the applicable tariffs through a 'binding system' that capped the tariff each state could apply in any product category, and a most-favoured-nation system that (save for regional commitments) required that the lowest tariff extended by the GATT members to any trading partner be extended to all. The European Economic Community, as successor to the European Coal and Steel Community, also established common institutions mirroring those of the ECSC that the GATT and other integration systems did not come close to achieving. As explained in greater depth below, Europe attempted to replicate the institutional structure of modern liberal democracies by instituting legislative bodies, an executive-like agency, and a constitutional court. The Treaties also gave individuals a right of access to national courts to enforce rights granted under European law.[25]

At the same time, the European Treaties followed the same sovereignty-protecting strictures as were found in the GATT. They banned discriminatory taxation, but they did not mandate tax policy on the part of the Member States. They banned quantitative restrictions and measures having an equivalent effect, but they did not mandate harmonization of regulatory levels among the Member States. Moreover, although the Treaties referenced qualified majority voting, the institutional voting rules as a general rule provided that, initially, unanimity would be required before any measure was adopted. The Treaties did not specifically state that European law would have direct effect, and they did not include any supremacy clause. While the European Treaties were bolder and more ambitious than any international treaty in force at the time, this overall design still provided a substantial level of protection of the Member States' ability to legislate both regulatory and entitlements welfare. Each Member State could, to a certain extent, remain free to determine how best to support the welfare of its nations, free from interference by European law, which we refer to as a 'black box' model.[26]

The initial challenges of Europe involved the familiar questions attendant to the integration of discrete nation-states into a single market. The early crises of Europe reflected the classical tension between preservation of sovereignty and opening borders to trade. States operating under a black box model have, by definition, disparate levels of regulation. France may choose a higher pesticide or worker protection level than the Netherlands. Italy may choose to permit the market of a certain type of wheat only under the 'pasta' label. Germany may have alcohol content laws that ban the marketing of light liquors. In all instances, the disparate regulations have the effect of hindering trade among Member States. When borders are open to trade, although

---

[25] See Case 14/83 *Sabine von Colson and Elisabeth Kamann v Land Nordrhein-Westfalen* [1984] ECR 1891.

[26] For quite some time the constitutional courts of the Member States contested the European Court of Justice's position on fundamental rights issues. Thus, in 1970 the German and Italian Constitutional Courts stated they would not apply provisions of EU law that failed to respect the fundamental rights and values set out in their national constitutions. See in this respect *Internationale Handelsgesellschaft* [1974] 2 CMLR 540 and *Frontini v Ministero delle Finanze* [1974] CMLR 386.

formally regulatory welfare remains unaffected, the disparate regulatory levels travel along with the goods.

European judicial and political institutions reacted to this challenge of integration with a significantly greater pro-trade approach than other integration projects that did not feature the European commitment to creation of a new legal order.[27] Here again, European exceptionalism thrust Europe into an exacerbated tension characteristic of the Statecraft era of the day. Europe experienced a sharp conflict between sovereignty and integrationist pressures well before other trade areas experienced it, and to a much greater extent. In its early decisions, the European Court of Justice made certain that any measure that actually or potentially, directly or indirectly, hindered trade, would be subject to its judicial scrutiny.[28] This brought before the Court a wide array of domestic laws, ranging from health measures to pornography or store closing laws, and including worker safety, consumer protection, product safety, and virtually every regulation of the marketplace with the potential to slow trade down. If France did not permit the marketing of apples exceeding its allowed pesticide level, any apple coming from a European state adhering to a more lax regulatory standard would be excluded from the French market. If Britain followed stringent obscenity rules, materials produced under more permissive Danish standards would not be allowed access to the British market. If Germany relied on worker training to ensure operator safety with respect to particular machinery, and France chose an automation philosophy, then German machines would not satisfy standards necessary to be operated in France.

In all cases, barriers to trade arose out of the disparity among national regulations. The nation-state's welfare ethos directly conflicted with the European drive to integration. The European Court scrutinized a wide array of national measures and in all instances (until it retreated in 1990 from its initial, aggressively pro-integration stance), the Court found that the measure at issue was a non-tariff barrier requiring review to evaluate whether the State's purpose at issue justified the burden on trade. In so doing, the European Court adopted a 'presumption of mutual reciprocity', holding that a measure that satisfied the laws of the exporting Member State should be presumed to be satisfactory to the importing State.[29] The European Court found many national measures to be in violation of European law, and even when it upheld a national measure it required the defending State to justify it and overcome the presumption of mutual reciprocity.[30]

The unbridled integrationist purpose of the European Court of Justice thrust it in the midst of a European review of national measures. At the same time, the Court found that European law would have direct effect as long as it was clear and

---

[27] See MP Egan, *Constructing a European Market* (Oxford: Oxford University Press, 2001), ch 4.

[28] See Case 41/74 *Van Duyn v Home Office* [1974] ECR 1337.

[29] This presumption is also known as the principle of equivalence or mutual recognition. For its application see, for instance, Case 272/80 *Frans-Nederlandse Maatschappij voor Biologische Producten* [1981] ECR 3277; Case 120/78 *Rewe-Zentral AG v Bundesmonopolverwaltung fur Branntwein* [1979] ECR 649.

[30] Sacha Prechal, 'Free Movement and Procedural Requirements: Proportionality Reconsidered' (2008) 35(3) *Legal Issues of Economic Integration* 201–16.

unconditional.[31] It implied a supremacy clause in the Treaties.[32] It also found an implicit 'Bill of Rights' in the common traditions of the Member States, thereby assuaging the national judicial fears that an all-powerful European law would trump national constitutional human rights provisions. Altogether, in its early work, the Court went a long way in finding in the Treaties a mandate for a new constitutional order.

As Professor Weiler observed in his seminal article 'The Transformation of Europe',[33] the political institutions of the Member States (in particular, France) did not expect that the Treaties would be interpreted in such an aggressive integrationist manner. As construed by the Court, European law went a long way toward infringing upon the sovereign regulatory welfare rights of the Member States. This is precisely why France threatened to withdraw from the integration enterprise and precipitated the so-called 'empty chair crisis' or 'Luxembourg crisis', and the subsequent Luxembourg accords or Luxembourg compromise.[34]

As we explain below, every modern trade-liberalizing system ultimately erodes sovereignty and sows the seeds of its own demise. Modern Statecraft is based on sovereignty and the notion that liberalizing trade can be done without infringing sovereignty. While each trade system will, by definition, seek to balance these conflicting values (often choosing sovereignty-protection), over time, the diffuseness and interloped nature of liberalized integrated markets erodes the black box nature of the participating states. This destroys the conditions that made modern trade interaction desirable, and necessitates a new system.

Owing to its unique history, Europe witnessed this phenomenon very early (at the height of the modern era), hence the significance and political sensitivity of the Luxembourg crisis. The Member States rejected the combination of aggressive economic constitutional jurisprudence, passage to less-than-unanimity voting, and closure of selective exit through hardening of law because they could not fathom a situation where other States would outvote them and dictate welfare policy. The sensitivity to welfare and sovereignty, however, was no accident: it was a unique product of the modern age. As we explain later, the Member States had no issue abandoning the Luxembourg compromise whereby each State could veto European legislation that it disliked later in the twentieth century, because by then they had graduated to a postmodern market-state age. The protective reflex that led to the Luxembourg accords, thereby saving the European enterprise, stemmed from

---

[31] See Case 26/62 *NV Algemene Transport- en Expeditie Onderneming van Gend & Loos v Netherlands Inland Revenue Administration* [1963] ECR 1.

[32] See Case 6/64 *Flaminio Costa v ENEL* [1964] ECR 585; C-106/77 *Simmenthal II* [1978] ECR 629; C-106/89 *Marleasing* [1991] ECR I-7321.

[33] JHH Weiler 'The Transformation of Europe' (June 1991) 100(8) *The Yale Law Journal*, Symposium: International Law.

[34] N Piers Ludlow, 'De-commissioning the Empty Chair Crisis: The community institutions and the crisis of 1965-6', in *Visions, Votes and Vetoes: The empty chair crisis and the Luxembourg compromise forty years on* (Peter Lang: Brussels, 2006), 79–96.

fundamental nation-state constitutional principles: preservation of regulatory welfare, sovereign right to legislate in that area free of international and supra-national interference, and sovereign limitation on the import of foreign standards into the domestic market.

As Professor Weiler pointed out, the aggressive jurisprudence of the European Court of Justice would likely not have triggered the Luxembourg constitutional crisis, if it had not been joined with the planned transition away from unanimity voting and the possibility of a group of nations imposing binding law on others. The European Court dealt with issues that came to be characteristic of trade, centring on the extent to which a state should be required to accept goods that meet the regulatory standards of the country of export but not of the import jurisdiction. While the European Court took a much more aggressive stance than, say, the GATT panels, it still operated under a constitutional system that recognized sovereign regulation to implement welfare. Europe did not unify fiscal or budgetary policy, and allowed each Member State to adopt its own welfare system on any issue not harmonized or preempted by European law. The European Court formally recognized the right of the Member States to adopt laws furthering any of the specified exceptions to the free movement of goods, and other 'mandatory requirements' recognized by the Court. Protests may have been launched against what some criticized as European judicial activism but sovereignty would not have been threatened on an existential level had the Member States retained their ability to, in Weiler's words, 'selectively exit' the system.[35]

The closure of selective exit was unpalatable because it would have established a foundational system more characteristic of the market-state, where sovereignty is subordinate to international measures to solidify and protect markets. The European plan to install such a system was scheduled to take effect in the thick of the modern nation-state era. This was inconsistent with the legitimacy demands on the State, and with its need to provide welfare unimpeded by international regulatory schemes. This explains why France among other Member States viewed the combination of low Exit and low Voice as an existential crisis.

5 Democracy Deficit

Statecraft also explains the institutional challenges that arose in the formative years of Europe, and how those challenges were met. In the modern nation-state age, the global collectivity of states agreed to open up borders to trade, all the while preserving in theory each individual state's ability to establish the welfare system of its choice.[36] France could remain France and extend half-price metro tickets to families with many

---

[35] *See* Weiler, *The Transformation of Europe*, 2457.

[36] See John Gerard Ruggie, 'International Regimes, Transactions, and Change: Embedded liberalism in the postwar economic order', (Spring 1982) 36(2) *International Organization*, International Regimes 385–8.

children, Great Britain could continue to adhere to cradle-to-grave programmes, Japan could engage in indicative planning, and the United States could tax and spend.

The GATT was established along these lines.[37] Of course, the import of products from one state to another raised the quintessential modern age question whether a regime of regulatory comparative advantage should give way to domestic regulation or whether goods should be allowed to move freely. The GATT, however, dealt with these questions infrequently because of the state-to-state nature of its dispute resolution systems and the inherent deterrents to challenges it carried. Until 1994, the GATT also would only impose a judgment against a Contracting (state) Party if all Contracting Parties, including the losing state, agreed.[38]

Additionally, the jurisprudence of the GATT did not take as aggressive a stance as Europe's. The definition of what constituted a measure 'having an effect equivalent to a quantitative restriction' adopted by Europe was much broader than the GATT's approach to what constitutes a quota. It would have been unthinkable for the GATT, or for that matter any integrated area other than Europe, to engage in a review of measures such as Sunday trading rules, worker safety, or consumer protection, as the European Court did.[39]

In addition, the GATT's political institutions focused initially only on the gradual reduction of tariffs. Although the members of the 'Green Room' can be said to have led the way for states sharing their ideological orientation, no Contracting Party could formally be required to agree to reduce its tariffs.[40] The rounds of tariff-reduction that the GATT Contracting Parties engaged in would result in packages that reduced tariffs, and that left it to the GATT dispute resolution panels to balance sovereign protection of domestic regulation against free movement of goods.

Europe, on the other hand, had to adopt a political decision-making structure for crafting laws that would harmonize the single market and that, in light of the decisions of the European Court on constitutional issues, would be binding throughout the Member States. This was another manifestation of European exceptionalism. Even though the Luxembourg accords shielded the Member States from too rapid a move towards a majority or qualified majority voting principle, Europe still had significant institutional machinery intended to produce supra-national laws. These laws would cover a wide array of subject matter areas, including harmonization of regulatory welfare rules. Therefore, the debate over the political decision-making institutions and how they should operate had a profound impact on the welfare systems of the Member States. Unanimity ensured that European regulation would not spread as quickly as

---

[37] Information on the GATT, its background, legal framework, etc, is available at: <http://www.gatt.org/>.

[38] Information on the GATT dispute settlement procedure, legal framework, figures, and case law is available at: <http://www.worldtradelaw.net/history/urdsu/w4.pdf>.

[39] The European Court's case law on issues such as taxation, free movement of goods, social policy, freedom to provide services, etc is available at: <http://curia.europa.eu/jurisp/cgi-bin/form.pl?lang=en>.

[40] 'The "Green Room" is a phrase taken from the informal name of the director-general's conference room. It is used to refer to meetings of 20–40 delegations, usually at the level of heads of delegations'. <http://www.wto.org/english/thewto_e/whatis_e/tif_e/org1_e.htm>.

the Treaties, as written and as strengthened by the European Court, could have. However, Europe still produced from the outset a bureaucracy and legislation-producing institutions dedicated to making and implementing Europe-wide laws. One of its initial foundational challenges, then, was how to design those institutions.

Europe quickly fell into the trap of trying to resolve this issue by replicating the political institutions of the nation-state, attempting, in effect, to create a European 'super-nation-state', one that would protect the welfare of the European collectivity. Europe adapted the institutions with which the Member States were familiar. A Council was created to legislate. A Commission would include the administrative bureaucracy necessary to craft and enforce laws. A Court would review their legality. A Parliament, initially endowed with only minimal powers, would consult and legislate along with the Council. Europe, in effect, adopted its Court's presumption of mutual reciprocity and attempted to create an enlarged collectivity that would approximate or harmonize welfare, thereby accomplishing integration without relinquishing the welfare goal in selected areas. Europe would leave to its Member States a substantial area of competence. Where it acted for the whole, Europe would replicate the European modern liberal democratic state.

This is what led to what came to be known as the 'European democracy deficit'. The democracy deficit debate often took the form of a critique of Europe's failure to adopt institutions that better replicated those of modern liberal democracies.[41] In particular, European institutions were blamed for the lack of accessibility to the ordinary citizens, lack of accountability of its institutions, inadequate checks and balances, and general excess of executive powers. For example, an oft-heard complaint related to the relative lack of powers granted to the European Parliament, especially in the early days of Europe. The Parliament slowly and gradually moved from a principally consulting role to that of a decision-maker with powers parallel to those of the Council in certain subject matter areas. Some observers critiqued this institutional arrangement on the grounds that the only institution directly elected by the European people lacked basic legislative powers. Indeed, legislative powers of the European Parliament are weaker than those of national parliaments.[42] As a result, the European Parliament had no exclusive jurisdiction over any legislative proposal or power of initiative in any significant area of policy-making.[43] The Council, on the other hand, which comprised members of the executive branch of each government, was perceived during the formative years of Europe as the main legislative institution.[44]

---

[41] For extended argumentation on democracy deficit in EU see: Andreas Follesdal and Simon Hix, *Why there is a Democratic Deficit in the EU: A response to Majone and Moravcsik*, European Governance Papers, N C-05-02, *Journal of Common Market Studies* (2006) 44(3) 533–62, and Andrew Moravcsik, 'In Defense of the Democratic Deficit: Reassessing Legitimacy in the European Union' (40)4 *Journal of Common Market Studies* 603–524, available at: <http://www.princeton.edu/~amoravcs/library/deficit.pdf>.

[42] Paul Craig and Gráinne de Búrca (eds), *The Evolution of the EU Law* (Oxford: Oxford University Press, 2010), 30.

[43] Chalmers, Davies, and Monti, see n 24, at 86.

[44] Alina Kaczorowska, *European Union Law* (New York: Routledge-Cavendish, 2009).

Europe also sought to replicate the modern constitutional protections of minority rights. After it announced its supremacy jurisprudence, the European Court of Justice assuaged the fears of national judiciaries and other interlocutors by implying a Bill of Rights in the European Treaties, which included none.[45] The fundamental rights guaranteed by this jurisprudence would be inspired by the common values of the Member States. They would ensure that European law, although supreme, would not conflict with basic rights recognized by the Member States.[46]

However, as more insightful observers commented, this nation-state reflex to determine welfare by majority or other democratically endorsed voting quorum missed the core question of integration in the modern nation-state era: how to craft rules for the whole all the while respecting national sovereignty. Whether an alliance of national members of Parliament voted down another set of Member State representatives directly elected by the people, or whether this happened through a vote of the executives delegated to the Council, the integrated area would overrule national choices that were the essence of Statecraft in action in the modern age. No matter how much representative democracy was infused in the system, the malaise caused by the democracy deficit would not dissipate.[47]

This malaise was typical of the era of the nation-state. The State's ethos was to deliver welfare to the nation. Integration, principally in the realm of regulatory welfare, threatened to limit the State's accomplishment of this essential purpose. The GATT responded by limiting the interference of international law in domestic systems. Europe first responded by demanding unanimous decision making, and then sought to adjust its institutions to create a super-nation-state.

The first response saved Europe. The second created the illusion of protecting sovereignty but, in point of fact, it perpetuated the malaise of the democracy deficit throughout the first thirty years of European integration. Some limited measures may be taken, such as increasing transparency and access to information in the European bureaucracy. By and large, however, until the waning days of the nation-state era, there was no institutional or political way to resolve the democracy deficit. The European judiciary, true to the historical foundations of Europe and anxious to integrate, accelerated the integration enterprise. The Luxembourg political accords saved Europe from self-implosion caused by an overly rapid move to integration.[48] As explained below, until the market-state epochal transformation began, Europe was bound, as it

---

[45] JHH Weiler, 'Eurocracy and Distrust: Some Questions Concerning the Role of the European Court of Justice in the Protection of Fundamental Human Rights within the Legal Order of the European Communities', (July 1986) 61(3) *Washington Law Review* 1105.

[46] On the Doctrine of Supremacy, see Weiler, *The Transformation of Europe*, at 2414.

[47] Weiler, see n 33, 2466–74.

[48] The Luxembourg Compromise, signed on 30 January 1966, provides that '[w]here, in the case of decisions which may be taken by majority vote on a proposal of the Commission, very important interests of one or more partners are at stake, the Members of the Council will endeavour, within a reasonable time, to reach solutions which can be adopted by all the Members of the Council while respecting their mutual interests and those of the Community'. More at: <http://europa.eu/legislation_summaries/glossary/luxembourg_compromise_en.htm>.

did, to slowly evolve away from a polity where nation-states, although forced to obey their courts, would not relinquish their voice over legislation.

Professor Weiler was right that the slowing down of European law-making saved Europe and made aggressive judicial integration palatable. To put the matter differently, while the European Court took a resolutely market-state approach ahead of its time, the political institutions of Europe made sure that a clash of ideologies that was not possible in the nation-state age would not destroy Europe. This allowed Europe to proceed, in the latter part of the twentieth and early twenty-first century, to deepen the integration enterprise at a time when market-state Statecraft permitted integrative legislation to be adopted that would never have passed the legitimacy test in the heart of the nation-state era.

6 From Luxembourg to Maastricht: Accession to the Age of the Market-State

The Luxembourg crisis both saved and tempered the integration enterprise of Europe. Bargaining 'in the shadow of the veto'[49] sheltered sovereignty but slowed the adoption of European integration measures. By the 1980s and 1990s, however, Europe picked up speed and moved rapidly ahead with the harmonization or approximation of its laws on a larger scale. Complementing the more perfect unification of its single market, Europe then proceeded to adopt a single currency, European citizenship, an agreement for the removal of border controls among Member States belonging to the Schengen zone, and other institutional and political breakthroughs that pushed Europe significantly along the integration road.

We posit that while other factors surely contributed to it, the acceleration of the integration of Europe was made possible by the accession to the age of the market-state. Nation-states are bound to evolve into market-states over time. Their inner ethos, welfare for the nation, corresponds to their outer face: integration through trade while preserving sovereignty. Trade in goods and services inevitably leads to capital flows and interloping ownership of global assets. This is true especially in an integrated area like Europe, where the movement of capital and people is ensured and encouraged to a much greater extent than in other trade regulatory schemes. The integrated area will then tend to become more diffuse and use its 'black box aggregation character'. Industries and other commercial sectors will tend to be dissociated from the nation. Regulatory welfare will be disrupted by the growing import of goods manufactured under other regulatory conditions. In time, jobs and production will be increasingly outsourced.

In this environment, the State loses control over regulatory and entitlements welfare. Traditional tools such as exchange rates become regulated by the market to

---

[49] Weiler, see n 33, 2450.

a much greater extent than by the State. States gradually lose their ability to incur national debt because foreign debt holders gradually displace nationals. The free flow of goods carries with it disparate regulation. With the ageing of a population that boomed after the Second World War with renewed birth rates and immigration, budgets for entitlements welfare come under excessive strain. In turn, the nature of sovereignty changes as the ethos of the State shifts away from providing top-down regulatory and entitlements welfare, to fostering and preserving market conditions where economic opportunity can be maximized.

This is the legitimating ethos of the market-state. Instead of providing top-down welfare, the postmodern market-state unleashes its power to ground the market and maximize the enablement of economic opportunity for its citizens. This may translate into legislation that is similar to that which obtained in the nation-state. Securities disclosure or bank capitalization laws, for example, protect consumer welfare while fostering market stability. Even entitlements such as aid to education may belong to both ages, although vouchers and other market-based solutions may be more appropriate to the market-state era. In the changed postmodern globalized terrain, market failures in one segment of the market can travel rapidly to threaten and infect other segments across borders. The collectivity of states must dedicate itself to create conditions that stabilize and solidify the enlarged market. The process is not unlike that of the state-nation; even if it infringes on what would have been viewed as unassailable welfare sovereign rights in the middle of the twentieth century, it is necessary to maintain the architecture of the twenty-first. This is the pattern that Europe followed.

We place the emergence of the market-state toward the end of the twentieth century, when global economies started to integrate to such an extent that black box Statecraft eroded enough to give way to a more diffuse, interconnected set of market-states whose ethos focused on the preservation of the market and the maximization of opportunity, rather than top-down welfare entitlements. Europe's expansion into market-state regulatory territory coincided with this timetable. In effect, '[i]n the late 1980s the Single European Act was passed to facilitate the creation of a single market by streamlining the method by which harmonization laws were made. These laws were designed to complete the single market by the end of 1992.[50] Prior to 1993, over 300 measures were passed into law.'[51] Thereafter, hundreds more measures were adopted, thereby bringing the regulatory welfare landscape of Europe into substantial conformity.

---

[50] Article 13 of the Single European Act ('SEA'), which entered into force in 1987 amended, *inter alia*, Article 8a of the Treaty Establishing the European Economic Community ('EEC Treaty') so that it read: 'The Community shall adopt measures with the aim of progressively establishing the internal market over a period expiring on 31 December 1992 . . . The internal market shall comprise an area without internal frontiers in which the free movement of goods, persons, services and capital is ensured in accordance with the provisions of this Treaty.' The SEA is available at: <http://ec.europa.eu/economy_finance/emu_history/documents/treaties/singleuropeanact.pdf>.

[51] More at: <http://www.lavellecoleman.ie/cuuploads/editor/file/England%20and%20Wales%20pdfs/Using-EuropeanLaw2/5_%20Harmonistions%20of%20Laws.pdf>.

The Single European Act's main contribution was the establishment of the Single Market as a progressive goal to be reached by 31 December 1992. To that end, it provided for an 'increasing number of cases in which the Council can take decisions by qualified majority voting instead of unanimity. This facilitated decision making and avoided the frequent delays inherent to the search for a unanimous agreement among the twelve Member States. Unanimity was no longer required for measures designed to establish the Single Market, with the exception of measures concerning taxation, the free movement of persons, and the rights and interests of employed persons.'[52] The Treaty of Maastricht built upon the SEA by completing the Single Market and establishing the European Monetary Union. The Treaty requires the Member States to 'ensure coordination of their economic policies' (a significant move to which we will come back later in this chapter), and to 'provide for multilateral surveillance of this coordination'. In addition, the States 'are subject to financial and budgetary discipline'. Monetary unification was an extremely significant step in the evolution of Europe, which was also consistent with accession to the market-state. The objective of monetary policy is to create a single currency and to ensure this currency's stability by maintaining price stability, economic policy coordination, and respect for the market economy.[53]

The Economic and Monetary Union (EMU), which 'is the process of harmonizing the economic and monetary policies of the Member States of the Union with a view to the introduction of a single currency, the euro',[54] was implemented in three successive stages:

- The first stage, from 1 July 1990 to 31 December 1993, liberalized the movement of capital, and called for closer coordination between the central banks and closer coordination of economic policies;

- The second stage, from 1 January 1994 to 31 December 1998, provided for the convergence of the Member States' economic policies and the establishment of the European Monetary Institute (EMI) and, in 1998, of the European Central Bank (ECB);[55]

- The third stage began on 1 January 1999 and involved the fixing of the exchange rates and the introduction of the single currency on the foreign-exchange markets and for electronic payments.

---

[52] <http://europa.eu/legislation_summaries/institutional_affairs/treaties/treaties_singleact_en.htm>.   See Articles 6, 14, 16, 18, and 25 of the SEA concerning qualified majority and Articles 17 and 18 concerning unanimity.

[53] See   <http://europa.eu/legislation_summaries/economic_and_monetary_affairs/institutional_and_economic_ framework/treaties_maastricht_en.htm>. See also article 105 of the Treaty on European Union (TEU) added by the Maastricht Treaty. The consolidated version of the TEU is available at: <http://eur-lex.europa.eu/LexUriServ/LexUr-iServ.do?uri=OJ:C:2006:321E:0001:0331:EN:PDF>.

[54] See <http://europa.eu/legislation_summaries/glossary/economic_monetary_union_en.htm>.

[55] See Articles 4a and 109f of the TEU, as well as the Protocol on the Statute of the European Monetary Institute, and Protocol on the Statute of the European System of Central Banks and of the European Central Bank, added by the Maastricht Treaty.

When the third stage of the EMU was launched, eleven Member States adopted the euro as the single currency.

The convergence of economic policy that came with monetary unification goes to the heart of welfare entitlements. Although Europe did not adopt a common fiscal policy, it did not infringe on the welfare system of Member States in that it left them free to craft social security and health, education, pensions, and other mainstays of welfare as they saw fit. But entry to the Eurozone demanded that participating Member States adhere to specified macroeconomic goals.[56] These European requirements made sense in a market-state age where protecting market opportunity becomes the ethos of the State and an animating principle of the relationship among states. The limitations that it places on welfare Statecraft would in all likelihood not have been palatable in the age of the nation-state. Macroeconomic policy has an obvious impact on the ability of any individual state to establish its welfare policies. In the emerging age of the market-state, however, the legitimacy of the State depends on its ability to maximize opportunity and preserve the market, and these measures became consistent with the State's ethos and its marching orders of the day.

7 European Citizenship

The European citizenship arm of Maastricht also accorded with the market-state's ethos and was made possible by Statecraft's accession to its new market-state iteration. In the age of the nation-state, despite Europe's attempt to integrate into a single market, the nationality of the European countries remained the stronghold of the State's identity. While it was true that Europe attempted to create a super-nation-state, and that a pan-European citizenship would accord with that goal, the enterprise was initially viewed by many scholars as a 'flag which fails to cover its cargo'.[57] Citizenship could be construed as an attempt to replicate the hallmarks of a modern liberal democratic nation-state on a European level. However, until the nature of sovereignty began to erode in the age of the market-state, individual nation-state

---

[56] These criteria, established by the Maastricht Treaty and referred to as the 'Maastricht Criteria', were enshrined in Articles 104 and 121(1) of the TEU, as well as in Protocol (No 20) on the Excessive Deficit Procedure, and Protocol (No 21) on the Convergence Criteria referred to in Article 121 of the Treaty on European Union. Such criteria may be summarized as follows: '1) inflation of no more than 1.5 percentage points above the average rate of the three EU member states with the lowest inflation over the previous year. 2) A national budget deficit at or below 3 per cent of gross domestic product (GDP). 3) National public debt not exceeding 60 per cent of gross domestic product. A country with a higher level of debt can still adopt the euro provided its debt level is falling steadily. 4) Long-term interest rates should be no more than two percentage points above the rate in the three EU countries with the lowest inflation over the previous year. 5) The national currency is required to enter the ERM 2 exchange rate mechanism two years prior to entry [to the Eurozone]', <http://glossary.reuters.com/index.php/Maastricht_Criteria>.

[57] See Norbert Reich, *Union Citizenship—yesterday, today and tomorrow!*, RGSL Working Papers No 3 (RGSL, 2001), 5.

citizenship as an identifier of the nation-state could not be superseded by a vague supra-national identity.[58]

There also was much debate over the idea of a widely shared set of social values among European Union citizens. Many observers argue that a demos would never develop in the EU, while others claimed that Europe possessed enough shared values to create a 'European people'. A third group argued that the EU does not need a traditional demos in order to support a democratic system.[59] The market-state cut through this debate by precluding the need for a common demos to create European citizenship. A pan-European *espace*, akin to Schengen, conformed with the shoring up of a wider and intertwined market where economic interests become dissociated from the nation. It supplemented the integration of Europe into a single market with a single currency.

The same evolutionary patterns explain major aspects of the Treaty of Lisbon.[60] Lisbon amended Maastricht and the Treaty of Rome without replacing them.[61] It introduced a number of important innovations in the structure of the European Union. Lisbon abolished the three-pillar system initiated by Maastricht.[62] The three-pillar system included the European Community, Common Foreign and Security Policy, and Justice and Home Affairs. With the adoption of the Lisbon Treaty the first pillar, the EC pillar, was replaced by the EU, and was brought with the other two pillars into the same framework. Justice and home affairs policy moves into the generally applicable mechanisms of the Union (based on those of the old, first pillar, Community). The Common Foreign and Security Policy remains subject to specific procedures.

The EU also obtained a consolidated legal personality. Before Lisbon only the European Community and the Euratom had express legal personalities. Conferring legal personality expressly on the EU meant that, among other things, it would have the ability to join international organizations or to take, or be subject to, proceedings in international tribunals, and enter into agreements with other parties.[63]

The Lisbon Treaty introduced several institutional innovations. It established the positions of a full-time President of the European Council to lead its work, and of a High Representative to preside over the Foreign Affairs Council and conduct the Union's common foreign and security policy. The Lisbon Treaty fortified the role

---

[58] Dimitry Kochenov, 'Ius Tractum of Many Faces: European Citizenship and the Difficult Relationship Between Status and Rights' (2009) 15(2) *Columbia Journal of European Law* 171–2.

[59] Stephen C Sieberson, 'The Proposed European Union Constitution—Will it Eliminate the EU's Democratic Deficit?' (2004) 10(1) *Columbia Journal of European Law* 200.

[60] The full text of the Lisbon Treaty is available at: <.http://eurlex.europa.eu/JOHtml.do?uri=OJ:C:2007:306: SOM:EN:HTML>.

[61] Rome was renamed as the Treaty on the Functioning of the European Community.

[62] See<http://europa.eu/legislation_summaries/institutional_affairs/treaties/lisbon_treaty/ai0020_en.htm>.

[63] For more on the legal personality of the European Union, see Philippe de Schoutheete and Sami Andoura, *The Legal Personality of the European Union*. Studia Diplomatica Vol. LX: 2007, No 1.

of the European Parliament (EP) by extending the application of co-decision procedures where the Parliament is on an equal footing with the Council. The EP was given an enhanced role in deliberations on any future revisions of the Treaties, the EP's powers regarding the appointment of the Commission were strengthened and its budgetary powers extended. The Lisbon Treaty also significantly expanded the role of the European Court. It gained jurisdiction over the Justice and Home Affairs area. For the first time, Member States may be taken to the Court for failure to implement EU legislation in the area of criminal law and policing properly. Moreover, the role of national parliaments was enhanced. They were given additional time to review proposals and increased powers to call for a proposal to be reviewed. The Lisbon Treaty also facilitated cooperation between national parliaments and the EP.

The Lisbon Treaty also brought changes to the decision-making process. Qualified majority voting (QMV) became the default voting method in the Council. The previous default voting method was simple majority. Sensitive areas like tax and social security remain decided by unanimity, but significantly, a number of areas moved from decision in the Council by unanimity to decision by QMV. These include policy areas such as Justice and Home Affairs, a number of matters relating to foreign and defence policy, plus certain internal matters. Finally, the Lisbon Treaty changed the status of the Charter of Fundamental Rights, making it by virtue of Article 6 of TEU a legally binding document, rather than only declaratory as previously.

Lisbon is an eminently early market-state-era treaty. While it continues the European tendency to replicate the structure of the nation-state at the integrated area level, it does not hesitate to give the European polity powers that nation-state Statecraft could never have tolerated be transferred from the nation. Lisbon gives Europe an important foreign policy unified voice. It consolidates it into a legal personality that will make it easier to accede to agreements and international institutions. It gives more power to the European Parliament while making qualified majority at the Council level the default. It transfers to the European Court jurisdiction over areas that are traditionally associated with the nation-state's competence in the previous Statecraft age. It further Europeanizes human rights by strengthening the legal status of the Charter of Fundamental Rights. It increases the coordination between national and European institutions, strengthens the concept of subsidiarity, and moves Europe theoretically further down the role of a quasi-federal entity.

Altogether, these developments are consistent with the diffusion of an integrated area that arose out of its nation-state iteration, in the early age of the market-state evolution. They reflect attempts to shore up the collective whole by strengthening the power of its institutions and loosening the decision-making capacities, all the while addressing some of the remnants of the nation-state age issues, such as the democracy deficit.

In this respect, Lisbon is most conspicuous for what it does not include: a coordination of budget and tax policies in the integrated single market for goods, services, capital, and persons. These aspects of integration are some of the last frontiers of the dismantlement of nation-state welfare. Welfare entitlements depend on the budget and tax choices made by the nation-state. While the Eurozone nation-states of Europe committed to a certain degree of convergence, Europe fell short of unifying or harmonizing budget and tax choices. The nation-state's reflex, whether it is expressed in French strikes to protest the proposed raising of the retirement age or Greek debt issuance, evidently does not allow Europe to strip its members of welfare entitlements sovereignty at this early market-state age.

The situation just described is akin to the state-nation reflex of the post-First World War era that prevented the emerging nation-states from trading among themselves based on comparative advantage and the preservation of sovereignty. Architecturally, Europe had to shed its mercantilist skin in exchange for an economically collaborative one. Today, Europe must begin to shed its national welfare entitlements skin and trade it in for a market-state budget and tax policy that will inevitably cut deep into the welfare entitlements programmes of the twentieth century. Failure to do so will lead to existential crises akin to the trade wars of the 1920s and 1930s. The reason is this: in a diffuse and intertwined market, the welfare entitlements choices made by one national component reverberate and threaten those made by others. The Greek and Irish debt crises illustrate this claim.

After Greece adopted the euro in 2001, the country borrowed and spent heavily. Due to years of unrestrained spending, cheap lending, and failure to implement financial reforms, Greece was vulnerable when the global economic downturn occurred. When the global financial crisis broke, Greece's national debt rose to €262bn from €168bn in 2004. In 2009 Greece's credit rating was downgraded to the lowest in the Eurozone. This caused the cost of borrowing to be so high that the country's overdraft facility was cancelled overnight. The credit-rating downgrade also left the country struggling to pay its bills as interest rates on existing debts rose. All this reflected badly on the Euro and had the potential to infect other members of the single currency. The poor ratings officially gave Greece the lowest sovereign debt rating in the world. In May 2010, the IMF and EU agreed to a €110bn rescue package over three years. The agreement was followed by a forty-eight-hour strike in Greece, with three people killed after a bank was set on fire in Athens. In July 2011, the European Union approved another round of bailouts for the Greek government. It allowed Greece to default on part of its debt and included 109 billion euros in new aid from the EU, ECB, and IMF, with a 3.5 per cent interest rate, a ten-year repayment grace period, and a thirty-year maturity.

Ireland's sovereign debt crisis was mainly caused by its blanket guarantee of the banking sector. Prior to the financial crisis, the banking sector was over-leveraged, over-sized, and fuelled the country's economic and real estate bubble. After the collapse of the economy and housing market, Irish banks were left with major losses. Ireland then bailed out its banks and guaranteed all of their unsecured senior debt. Ireland's economy suffered because of a collapse in housing prices, unemployment, and a financial sector meltdown. Salaries were lowered, and pensions and health benefits were reduced. The crisis also led to a reduction of Ireland's debt rating and increased borrowing costs for the government. In November 2010 Ireland agreed to an 85-billion-euro (113 billion US dollars) bailout loan from the EU and the IMF at an average interest rate of 5.8 per cent.

In both instances, the rest of Europe was left with two stark choices: to alter its own budgetary choices to a significant extent in order to save the defaulting country from its own choice, thereby preserving the Eurozone intact; or to allow (or even push) those countries to cut themselves off from the Eurozone. Such is the nature of a market-state integrated area. Welfare entitlements cannot operate on a nation-state model without creating pockets of imbalance that threaten the whole. The market-state's ethos, to maximize the creation of economic opportunity within a system that fosters market-state stability, must become the animating principle. States that do not move towards establishing those foundational Statecraft hallmarks as the basis for their inner law and external relations will become burdens that, ultimately, will either drag down the collectivity or will be evicted from it.

8 Conclusion: A Three-Speed Europe?

Much has been said about the possibility of a two-speed Europe. With the recent crises of Greece and Ireland, Germany and France have agreed to propose alternatives for backing up those countries within the Eurozone system. Those measures call for closer and more integrated ties within the Eurozone.[64] For its part, Britain, which has historically opposed the two-speed Europe (because it fears it might marginalize it), has recently supported it. The reason is that Britain will not agree to join the Eurozone, especially with the current crisis, and yet it is imperative that the Eurozone be rescued (mainly because of Britain's trading interests with the Eurozone).[65]

The Eurozone is not the only area where multi-speed integration is present. The Schengen zone is another example, as are certain guidelines concerning political issues, such as asylum policy.[66]

An outstanding issue is how this differentiated integration will take place. The main question is whether this will happen within the EU or outside of it. But there are other, more subtle and critical issues, such as the legal and institutional consequences of different guidelines for integration.[67]

---

[64] Philip Stephens, *All aboard for a new two-speed Europe*, Financial Times, 10 February 2011. Available at <http://www.ft.com/intl/cms/s/0/95357aa6-3548-11e0-aa6c-00144feabdc0.html#axzz1VKZRLGq4>.

[65] Bagehot, 'Britain changes its mind about a two-speed Europe', *The Economist*, 21 July 2011. Available at: <http://www.economist.com/node/21524364>. See also James Chapman, *Leave them to it: Osborne backs 'two-speed Europe' with Britain taking a back seat*, MailOnline, 22 July 2011. Available at: <http://www.dailymail.co.uk/news/article-2017488/Eurozone-crisis-George-Osborne-backs-speed-Europe.html>.

[66] Werner Weidenfeld, *Making the Case for a Multi-Speed Europe*, Centrum für angewandte Politikforschung and der LMU München, 30 July 2008. Available at: <http://www.cap-lmu.de/aktuell/pressespiegel/2008/multi-speed-integration.php>.

[67] See David Král, *Multi-speed Europe and the Lisbon Treaty—threat or opportunity?*, at 3. EUROPEUM Institute for European Policy (November 2008). Available at: <http://www.europeum.org/doc/pdf/895.pdf>.

Differentiated integration is both a political and practical issue. There is an argument that a more integrated Europe will grow at a slower pace than a less integrated one, because it requires subventions from richer countries to poorer ones, and because it establishes more restrictions.[68]

There is a practical issue as well: the newer European members are not able to join integration at the speed of the other, older members. In June 2001, Jean-Noel Jeanneney, Pascal Lamy, Henri Nallet, and Dominique Strauss-Kahn wrote an article in *Le Monde* called '*Europe: Pour aller plus loin*', in which they proposed the idea of a 'two-speed Europe'; the authors argued that if the EU lets in large numbers of Central and East European countries, it will no longer be capable of developing the political will or the mechanisms that stronger social, industrial and foreign policies will require. So they revived the idea put forward in 2000 by Joschka Fischer (in his Humboldt University speech) and by Jacques Delors (in CER Bulletin No 14): a core group of countries, committed to 'an ambitious idea of Europe . . . which would show the way and the direction we prefer'.[69]

There is no agreement as to whether a two-speed Europe is a good or bad idea. Some argue that those countries willing and able to integrate further should be able to do it.[70] Some argue that a two-speed Europe is inevitable and also desirable.[71] Some others think it is unworkable because of the legal and institutional issues it raises.[72]

The advent of the age of the market-state age may bring the debate beyond considering a two-speed Europe to whether a three-speed Europe will become necessary. Within the European family, two speeds may make sense in certain subject matter areas. Great Britain can safely stay out of the Schengen *espace* without threatening the European enterprise. Its adherence to a separate currency can also be accommodated with a single market. Ireland can be bailed out because of its relatively small size without threatening the Eurozone. However, on a fundamental Statecraft level, Member States cannot afford to perpetuate a principally nation-state approach to Statecraft without endangering the rest of the system. Continued adherence to a welfare nation-state overall programme and agenda is bound to create more financial crises that will reverberate throughout Europe. Much as mercantilism fractured democracies' trade in goods, and should have been cast away in the modern era, adherence to welfare nation-state policies is bound to fracture the integrated financial and other postmodern markets.

The collectivity of postmodern states is bound to converge towards market-state policies to create an architecture that accords with the Statecraft of the day in order to

---

[68] Hamish McRae, 'A multi-speed Europe is inevitable—and right', *The Independent*, 17 September 2003. Available at: <http://www.independent.co.uk/opinion/commentators/hamish-mcrae/a-multispeed-europe-is-inevitable—and-right-580164.html>.

[69] Charles Grant, *France, Germany and a 'Hard-Core' Europe*, CER Bulletin, Issue 19 (August/September, 2001). Available at: <http://www.cer.org.uk/articles/n_19_grant.html>.

[70] Král, see n 67.

[71] McRae, see n 68.

[72] Grant, see n 69.

foster and preserve markets that are essential to the good functioning of the system. This does not apply only to Europe. China, for example, has traversed in the last two to three decades a state-nation-like consolidation, a selective opening of its boundaries to modern trade, and is now inextricably intertwined in the globalized postmodern market. A failure of its banks on account of a real estate bubble that is not properly managed would send shock waves around the world. A retreat from the Chinese commitment to purchase US and European debt to fund deficits would significantly damage the Western economies, and in turn harm the Chinese export-based manu-facturing capacity. Conversely, the failure of the United States and Europe to rein in borrowing will result in downgrading of the quality of their debts, and in Chinese reluctance to continue to finance it.

European exceptionalism again brings the Continent to the forefront of the State-craft issues of the day. The Greek and Irish bailouts, and the Italian and French fears, are threatening to fracture the Continent. In order to preserve its one- or two-speed core, Europe may have to adopt a third gear to leave behind, temporarily or perman-ently, Member States that fail to adopt postmodern policies of the type necessary to preserve the Eurozone and the integrated markets of Europe. In the postmodern age, a Member State will not be able to remain in a market-state area without converging towards market stabilization and solidification policies intended to enable and maxi-mize economic opportunity. However unthinkable it might seem to the European institution-building mind, the *acquis européen* may need to be revisited in order to save Europe.

We believe that the philosophical foundations of Europe include a fair amount of Statecraft cement. We have attempted in this chapter to show how its integrative and disintegrative impulses can be better understood through our Statecraft lens. European exceptionalism will, we predict, continue to show the evolving postmodern world the cutting-edge issues of this new epochal iteration. Europe is most likely to be, yet again, an experimental incubator. In order to draw lessons from its troubled past, the Continent must craft its constitutional architecture and resulting policies to conform to the State-craft foundational principles of the day, no matter what the costs of doing so.

PART III
CONSTITUTIONAL VIRTUES

12

Precedent and the Court of Justice

A Jurisprudence of Doubt?

Takis Tridimas

Bred in a civil law tradition, the European Court of Justice (ECJ) does not adhere to the doctrine of binding precedent.[1] But what is the real value of precedent in its case law? Where does it stand in the formal hierarchy of sources of law? How often does the Court depart from its previous rulings and what does that tell us about the role of judges in the EU[2] legal order? The influence of the ECJ in the shaping of the EU polity has been unprecedented yet its attitude to precedent has remained something of a puzzle.[3] One may identify three constituencies. The precedential value attributed by the Court itself to its rulings, their binding effect on the General Court of the EU, and their binding effect on national courts. This chapter examines the doctrine of *stare decisis* in relation to the first and the third constituency.[4] It looks at the Court's methodology in distinguishing precedent, express and implicit overruling, and the

---

[1] The expression 'jurisprudence of doubt' used in the title is a quote from the Supreme Court of the United States in *Planned Parenthood of Southeastern Pennsylvania v Casey* 505 US 833, at 844 (1992).

[2] The term 'European Union' or 'EU' will be used throughout this chapter to refer both to the EU and its predecessors, namely the European Community and the European Economic Community.

[3] For bibliography, see J Komarek, 'Judicial Lawmaking and Precedent in Supreme Courts: The European Court of Justice Compared to the US Supreme Court and the French Cour de Cassation' (2008–2009) 11 CYELS 399; A Arnull, *The European Union and its Court of Justice* 2nd edn (Oxford: Oxford University Press, 2006); M de SOL'E Lasser, *Judicial Deliberations: A Comparative Analysis of Judicial Transparency and Legitimacy* (Oxford: Oxford University Press, 2004); J Barceló, 'Precedent in European Community Law', in DN MacCormick, RS Summers, and A Goodhart, *Interpreting Precedents* (Ashgate: Dartmouth, 1997), 407–36; A Arnull, 'Owing Up to Fallability: Precedent and the Court of Justice' (1993) 30 CMLR 247; AG Toth, 'The authority of judgments of the European Court of Justice: Binding force and legal effects' (1984) 4 YEL 1; T Koopmans, *Stare decisis* in European Law', in D O'Keeffe and HG Schermers, *Essays in European Law and Integration* (Deventer: Kluwer, 1982), 11–27.

[4] As far as the General Court (GC) is concerned, suffice it to say that, according to the Statute of the ECJ, it is formally bound by ECJ precedent only in two cases: where the ECJ decides a point of law on appeal and remits the case to the GC for a decision (Article 61) and where the ECJ decides that a case falls within the jurisdiction of the GC and remands the case to it (Article 54). In all other cases, the GC is not bound formally but failure to follow the interpretation of law provided by the ECJ may lead to a successful appeal.

quasi-normative effect of precedent. The picture that emerges is that of a judicial behaviour which is close in result, albeit not in methodology, to that of Ango-Saxon supreme courts which adhere to the doctrine of *stare decisis*.

1 The Value of Precedent in EU Law: A Transformation in the Making

The ECJ was modelled on the French *Conseil d'Etat* and traditionally precedent played little role in its case law. There are good historical, legal, and political reasons which explain its limited value. The Court's civil law ancestry has had a defining influence. Binding precedent has no place in a tradition where, at least in formal terms, courts are perceived to be *la bouche de la loi*.[5] This, in turn, influenced the Court's methodology. Nurtured in a French legal tradition, the style of its judgment and its reasoning were highly formal. Collective judgment and terse reasoning are not fertile grounds for *stare decisis*. The Court did not view reference to precedent as being part of its reasoning, in contrast to Advocates General[6] who, from an early stage, saw analysis of previous case law as a core part of their function.[7] This bifurcation under which the development of the law rests in the interplay between the 'magisterial' tone of the judgment and the expansive reasoning of the Advocate General is a distinct feature of the EU judicial process.[8] The Court was comfortable with formality: the terse, *ex cathedra* style of the judgment radiated 'imperial confidence'[9] and enhanced judicial authority.

The Court also had little incentive to rely on national law precedents. To the extent that it perceived the European Union not only as an economic organization but as a political experiment, adherence to legal tradition was to be avoided rather than to be encouraged. The journey towards European integration required the dismantling of traditional perceptions about law, constitutional authority, and sovereignty. A new

---

[5] The expression comes from Montesquieu's seminal work *De L'esprit des lois* (1748) who stated that judges should be 'the mouth that pronounces the words of the law, inanimate beings who can moderate neither its force nor its rigor' (see Montesquieu, *The Spirit of the Laws* Cambridge: Cambridge University Press, 1989, bk II, Ch 6, 156). In the French legal tradition, the quote is intended to signify the allegiance of the judges to the legislature's monopoly of legislative power and exemplifies the doctrine of the separation of powers. The conception of judges as servants of the law came as a reaction to the excessive power enjoyed by the French judiciary under the pre-revolutionary regime. For the background to this in comparative perspective, see, among others, JWF Allison, *A Continental Distinction in the Common Law* (Oxford: Oxford University Press, 1996) and Lasser, see n 3, ch 27.

[6] Advocates General are full members of the Court. Under Article 252 TFEU, their function is to deliver an impartial opinion on how the case in issue should be resolved. The opinion is not binding on the Court although it is followed in the overwhelming majority of cases.

[7] See eg Joined Cases 19/60, 21/60, 2/61, and 3/61 *Fives Lille Cail v High Authority* [1961] ECR 281 at 308 per Roemer AG.

[8] For a detailed analysis, see Lasser, see n 3, ch 4, esp. 107.

[9] Lasser, see n 3, 107.

legal order could not be built on strict adherence to precedent. The Court sought the emancipation of the EU from the legal systems of its constituent states and, as *Internationale Handelsgesellschaft*[10] testifies, it viewed the national constitutional traditions as a launching pad rather than as a constraining force. Seen in that context, any reliance on national law precedents would negate the distinctiveness and autonomy of the integration rationale.

In any event, as far as the Court's own rulings were concerned, at least in the early years of the Union's development there was not much precedent to rely upon. As the Union legal order started to evolve and the case law acquired more importance, the ECJ began to develop its own precedent-based methodology. The Court's change of attitude coincides with the development of the *acquis communautaire*. Once a sufficiently articulate and distinct corpus of case law began to morph in key areas, solutions to pending disputes could be justified by reference to earlier judgments thus granting them precedential value. Reliance on precedent fulfilled in effect a dual role. It enhanced judicial legitimacy whilst, at the same time, preserving the Court's own legacy. It was, in effect, a kind of self-legitimation. References by the ECJ to earlier judgments were sporadic in the 1970s,[11] became much more prevalent in the 1980s,[12] and standard practice in the 1990s. Precedent became both enabling in that it allowed the ECJ to develop the law and self-empowering in that it committed its development along established pathways laid down by the ECJ itself. In effect, the importance of previous rulings as a source of authority can be traced back to the seminal rulings of *Van Gend en Loos* and *Costa v ENEL*.[13] These judgments laid down the principles of direct effect and primacy and set in motion a process towards the constitutionalization of the Treaties. How could the ECJ not attribute authority to its own rulings which, in the Court's own words, are the fundamental attributes of EU law? The result of the Court's activist case law was to abolish the nation-state's monopoly to grant individual rights, which hitherto had remained unchallenged. By doing so, it encouraged the formation of a direct bond between citizens and the EU and dispersed political authority. Through increasing reliance on precedent, the immediacy of EU law and its authority to grant rights became self-preserving. Seen from this perspective, the establishment of rights and respect for precedent developed hand in hand.

In formal terms, reliance on precedent by the ECJ did not entail the usurpation of law-making authority. Its previous rulings possess a declaratory character. A distinction has validly been drawn between precedent of solution and precedent of interpretation.[14] In the former, a judicial decision provides a binding rule which has normative

---

[10] Case 11/70 *Internationale Handelsgesellschaft* [1970] ECR 1125.

[11] See eg Case 13/76 *Donà v Matero* [1976] ECR 1333; Case 47/76 *De Norre v Brouwerij Concordia* [1977] ECR 65.

[12] See eg Case 187/80 *Merck v Stephar and Exler* [1981] ECR 2063, para 12 (free movement of goods); Case 107/82 *AEG v Commission* [1983] ECR 3151, para 35 (competition law); Case 264/82 *Timex v Council and Commission* [1985] ECR 849, para 15 (standing of individuals in actions for judicial review).

[13] Case 26/62 *Van Gend en Loos* [1963] ECR 1; Case 6/64 *Costa v ENEL* [1964] ECR 585.

[14] Z Bankowski, D Neil MacCormick, 1 Morawski, and A Ruiz Miguel, 'Rationales for Precedent in MacCormick *et al.*', n 3 above, 484.

value per se and determines the outcome in subsequent cases, hence the need to extrapolate the *ratio decidendi*. In the latter case, a judgment is seen as determining the correct, or at least a reasonable, interpretation of a pre-existing rule or principle. It does not bear any regulatory value in itself but expresses the best interpretation of the law. ECJ judgments provide precedents of interpretation. They are not sources of law in the way understood by Cross and Harris, that is, as premises from which norms derive their validity as rules of law.[15] They are interpretative rather than normative in nature, the formal sources of law being the Treaties, international agreements, and legislation. This statement however must be read subject to three *caveats* which make ECJ rulings distinct. First, the general and nebulous terms of the EU Treaties grant the rulings of the Court a heightened value of interpretation since the Treaties predetermine less than statutes what the correct interpretation of the law might be. Secondly, the ECJ recognizes unwritten general principles of law, such as the principle of non-discrimination, as sources of EU law. These appear to exist independently or above written provisions. To the extent that it is impossible to establish whether they exist and what is their minimum content prior to their judicial recognition, it may be said that judgments of the Court cease to have a declaratory character and acquire a constitutive force. Judgments serve not simply as their recognition but as their embodiment. Thirdly, the principle of primacy and the obligation of national laws to provide effective remedies for the protection of EU rights commit the national courts to follow the rulings of the ECJ. The interpretation of EU law is accepted by the national courts not because it emerges effortlessly from the ultimate principles of the Treaties and written EU law but because it is derived from them by the ECJ. We will return to this below.

2 Respect and Reversal: Drawing the Balance

Before looking in more detail at the way the ECJ handles its earlier rulings, it is salutary to look at the wider picture. Precedent should not be viewed from the perspective of binding–non-binding dichotomy but rather as a continuum.[16] It is beyond doubt that it plays a role also in legal systems which do not follow the doctrine of *stare decisis*. There are many good reasons why courts should decide new cases according to their previous judgments. Fairness and justice require that the factual situations which are materially the same must be decided in the same way. Precedent is a fundamental attribute of the principle of equality. It honours citizens' expectations and faith in equality before the law.[17] It is, at the very least, 'the moral presence of our past'.[18]

---

[15] R Cross and JW Harris, *Precedent in English Law*, 4th edn (Oxford: Clarendon Press, 1991), 167.

[16] Bankowski *et al.*, see n 14, 497.

[17] See Benjamin N Cardozo, *The Nature of the Judicial Process* (New Haven: Yale University Press, 1921), 33–4.

[18] See GJ Postema, 'On the Moral Presence of Our Past' (1991) 36 *McGill Law Journal* 1153.

Reasons of efficiency also dictate respect for precedent, especially by a court of last instance. A fundamental function of any developed dispute resolution mechanism is not only to solve a dispute but also signal to prospective parties how the decision-maker approaches the law so that they can assess their chances of success before engaging in future litigation. In short, a court that fails to honour its previous judgments will soon find that its legitimacy suffers and its authority is eroded. As a result, Continental supreme courts tend to develop and respect *jurisprudence constante* in key areas of law and lower courts can only ignore it at the cost of a successful appeal. The civil and the common law systems appear closer than they used to be although this is not to hide important differences among specific legal systems.[19] Also, constitutional courts in Continental Europe appear to depart from the traditional civil law model in that they tend to follow more discursive reasoning and are more willing to refer to their own earlier rulings. The ECJ's approach to precedent can be seen as an extension of the judicial engagement with precedent prevalent in the constitutional traditions of the Member States. Furthermore, it should be borne in mind that even in English law, which recognizes precedent as a stronger restraining force than it is recognized in US law, the binding effect of earlier judgments is best viewed as an exercise in judicial self-limitation. It is not an innate feature of the legal system but a self-imposed discipline for managing uncertainty.[20]

There appears to be a broad consensus across legal systems that a balance must be struck. Too much adherence to precedent and there is a risk of injustice and stagnation.[21] Too little observance of it, and certainty, predictability, and fairness will suffer. Supreme courts should therefore enjoy some flexibility in departing from their own precedent. As the US Supreme Court has declared *stare decisis* 'is not an inexorable command'.[22] It 'is a principle of policy and not a mechanical formula of adherence to the latest decision',[23] which reflects a judgment that 'in most matters it is more important that the applicable rule of law be settled than that it be settled right'.[24] The value of flexibility has also been recognized by the House of Lords which in 1966 declared that it did not feel bound to follow its previous decisions in all cases.[25] Where courts draw the balance and what they consider to be good reason for departing from precedent differs from country to country. English courts for example are perceived to

---

[19] See E Hondius, Precedent and the Law, in K Boele-Woelki and S van Erp (eds), *General Reports of the XVIIth Congress of the International Academy of Comparative Law* (The Hague: Eleven International Publishing, 2007), 31–50.

[20] See Cross and Harris, see n 15, 165ff.

[21] See, for a forceful expression of this point, Lord Denning, *The Discipline of the Law* (London: Butterworths, 1979) at 292.

[22] See eg *Lawrence v Texas* 539 US 558 at 577; (2003); *Casey*, see n 1, 854.

[23] *Helvering v Hallock*, 309 US 106, 119 (1940).

[24] *Burnet v Coronado Oil & Gas Co.*, 285 US 393, 406 (1932).

[25] *Practice Statement (Judicial Precedent)* [1966] 1 WLR 1234 (HL). The House of Lords announced that, in contrast to its previous position, it would consider departing from its own precedent on the ground that 'too rigid adherence to precedent may lead to injustice in a particular case and also unduly restrict the proper development of the law'.

be more conservative than US courts, and attribute more importance to self-restraint.[26] It is generally and rightly acknowledged, however, that the mere fact that a court disagrees with one of its earlier rulings is not in itself sufficient to justify overruling.[27] Overruling demands 'special justification'.[28] There must be a 'cogent reason'[29] or it must 'appear right to do so'.[30] Sticking to precedent is a value in itself and there must be an interest outweighing that value to persuade the court to overrule.

Borrowing from the approach of the United States Supreme Court, which is more open in acknowledging pragmatism and viewing the decision whether to overrule as a cost-effectiveness exercise,[31] one may outline the following factors that may be taken into account in deciding whether to overrule. A court will be more deferential to *stare decisis* where property rights, contractual relations, or commercial transactions are at issue[32] or where the issues involved are politically sensitive and give rise to partisan controversy.[33] By contrast, a court will be more willing to overrule where procedural issues or constitutional issues are involved.[34] The US Supreme Court also accepts that the doctrine of binding precedent is at its weakest in the interpretation of the Constitution because such interpretation can be altered only by constitutional amendment or by overruling.[35] By contrast, *stare decisis* carries more weight on issues of statutory interpretation since legislative changes should be left to Congress.[36]

Notably, the House of Lords has placed emphasis on different areas. When in its 1966 Practice Direction announced that it would consider departing from its precedents in appropriate cases, it outlined special concerns which imposed limits on overruling. It was however preoccupied with private and criminal law interests rather than constitutional ones.[37] This in turn illustrates the understated role that the highest

---

[26] Note however that there have been overrulings by the House of Lords even in areas, such as criminal law, where the House has declared that particular importance should be attached to precedent. See *R v Shivpuri* [1987] AC 1 and n 38.

[27] See eg for the House of Lords *Fitzleet Estates Ltd v Cherry (Inspector of Taxes)* [1977] 3 All ER 996 and for the Canadian Supreme Court, McRuer CJHC in *R v Nor Elec Co* [1955] OR 431.

[28] *Patterson v McLean Credit Union* 491 US 164, 172 (1989).

[29] See *Scoppola v Italy (No 2)*, ECtHR, Judgment of 17 September 2009 (Appl No 10249/03), para 104.

[30] House of Lords Practice Statement, see n 25.

[31] See eg *Casey*, see n 1, 854–5.

[32] For a useful restatement, including a brief history of the development of *stare decisis* in Anglo-American law, see *In re Livingston* 379 BR 711 (2007, United States Bankruptcy Court, WD Michigan) and also *Casey*, op. cit.

[33] *Bush v Vera* 517 US 952 (1996), at 985.

[34] See *In re Livingston*, see n 32 and *Hohn v US*, 524 US 236, 251–2, (1998) (involving issues of criminal procedure), *Agostini v Felton*, 521 US 203, 235, 117 S Ct 1997, 138 L.Ed.2d 391 (1997) (constitutional issues).

[35] See eg *Agostini v Felton* 521 US 203 (1997), at 235; *Seminole Tribe of Fla v Florida*, 517 US 44, 63.

[36] *Leegin Creative Leather Products, Inc. v PSKS, Inc.*, 127 S Ct 2705 (2007). Still, US courts accept that that rule should not be applied mechanically to prohibit in all cases overruling of earlier decisions on statutory interpretation (see eg *Shi Liang Lin v U.S. Dept. of Justice*, 494 F.3d 296 (2007)) and that it has less force in relation to statutes which are treated as 'common law' statutes (*Leegin Creative Leather Products*, see n 36).

[37] See 1966 Practice Direction, n 25. The House of Lords stated that, in deciding whether to depart from a previous decision, it 'will bear in mind the danger of disturbing retroactively the basis on which contracts, settlements of property and fiscal arrangements have been entered into and also the especial need for certainty as to the criminal law'.

court in the land played at that time in public law. Still, any judicial effort to lay down general guidelines is of relative value and should be treated with caution. It is true that there have been few cases where the House of Lords has departed from its precedent since 1966, but these have included criminal law, one of the areas where certainty was identified as being of particular importance.[38]

A further factor appears to be whether the ruling is in the sphere of private or public law. Although this is not articulated expressly in judicial dicta, overruling may be easier to justify in the field of public law for the following reasons. Private law transactions have to do with contracts and/or the allocation of property rights, areas in which both the US Supreme Court and the House of Lords have identified the need for certainty as being paramount. Also, private law relations are regulated mostly by statutes. To the extent that overruling is more easily justified in the interpretation of constitutional texts rather than statutory law, a good reason for overruling is less likely to exist in relation to private law. Finally, to the extent that overruling requires the existence of public policy reasons such a reason might be easier to establish in relations between the individual and the state rather than relations between individuals.

It will be noted that, since in EU law there is no formal doctrine of *stare decisis,* the distinction between *ratio decidendi* and *obiter dictum* does not exist.[39] A prime example is provided by the judgment in *Marshall I*[40] where the ECJ held that directives do not have horizontal effect. The statement was treated as establishing authority but was strictly speaking *obiter* since the applicant in the main proceedings was working for a public authority and it was therefore not necessary for the ECJ to pronounce on the possible effect of directives on private relations.[41] Given the lack of formal doctrine of precedent, Arnull argues that all dicta in a court's judgment are capable of carrying the same force.[42]

3 Distinguishing Precedent

The ECJ regularly refers to its 'settled' case law.[43] Although its methodology is not as developed as that of common law courts, given the rich jurisprudence that has evolved on the interpretation of the Treaties and EU legislation, much judicial work involves

---

[38] See *R v Shivpuri* [1987] AC 1 overruling *Anderton v Ryan* [1985] AC 560.

[39] Occasionally references to *ratio decidendi* are made by Advocates General. See eg Case 112/76 *Manzoni v FNORM* [1977] ECR 1647 at 1662, per Warner AG and also the Opinion of Maduro AG in Case C-127/08 *Metock and others v Minister for Justice, Equality and Law Reform* [2008] ECR I-6241 at paras 11ff of the Opinion. See also the comments of Maduro AG in Joined Cases C-99/04 and C-202/94 *Cipolla and Others* [2006] ECR I-11421, at para 28 of the Opinion.

[40] Case 152/84 *Marshall v Southampton and South-West Hampshire Area Health Authority* [1986] ECR 723.

[41] The lack of horizontal effect of directives was confirmed in Case C-91/92 *Faccini Dori v Recreb* [1994] ECR I-3325.

[42] See Arnull, *The European Union and its Court of Justice* (n 3 above), 631.

[43] See eg Case C-188/92 *TWD Textilwerke Deggendorf* [1994] ECR I-833, para 13; Case C-255/02 *Halifax v Commissioners of Customs and Excise* [2006] ECR I-1609, para 68.

application or distinguishing of precedent. An interesting example is provided by the leading judgment in *TWD*.[44] There it was held that, where an undertaking clearly has standing to challenge an EU measure directly before the EU courts and fails to do so within the requisite time limit, it cannot subsequently seek to challenge that measure indirectly before a national court. In its earlier judgment in *Rau*[45] the Court had held that the possibility of bringing a direct action for judicial review of a Commission decision before the ECJ did not preclude the possibility of challenging that decision indirectly via a national court. On its face, *TWD* ran counter to *Rau* but it was in fact a case of successful distinguishing. In *TWD* the Court pointed out that in *Rau* the applicants had sought to challenge the contested decision directly before the ECJ and, therefore, had not been inactive prior to the expiry of the time limit. The two cases were therefore factually distinguishable. Nevertheless, a subsequent development in this area shows a less skilful handling of precedent. In *Casa di Risparmio* the ECJ appeared to narrow considerably the scope of *TWD* by stating that it does not apply where the national court questions the validity of an EU measure on its own motion.[46] The introduction of such a broad exception to an important principle occurred without any explanation, almost casually, showing in effect an unwillingness to engage with precedent.

Instances of detailed and skilful engagement with precedent are provided by a series of cases on corporate mobility[47] or the post-*Mangold* case law.[48] Although in many cases, reference to previous rulings appears selective and superficial, the process of adjudication inevitably draws the ECJ to engaging with its own precedent as litigants rely on earlier rulings. Distinguishing precedent involves identifying factual differences between cases such that they make the *ratio* of the earlier judgment inapplicable to the new case. Distinguishing is not an easy task. For one thing, it may not be easy to establish the *ratio* of a case or its precise limits. For another, what matters is not establishing a distinction but a material one. The limits between distinguishing and overruling are relative. Where rulings are broadly formulated, distinguishing becomes more challenging. Where distinguishing occurs all too often, precedent is disturbed even in the absence of explicit overruling. One may identify different kinds of distinguishing. In its simplest form it takes place where a court accepts the *ratio decidendi* of an earlier judgment and finds that the new case does not fall within it because of a material difference of fact. But a more nuanced and more restrictive form of

---

[44] *TWD*, n 43.

[45] Joined Cases 133 to 136/85 *Rau v ALM* [1987] ECR 2289.

[46] Case C-222/04 *Ministero dell'Economia e delle Finanze v Cassa di Risparmio di Firenze SpA* [2006] ECR I-289, para 74.

[47] See Case 81/87 *R v HM Treasury and IRC, ex parte Daily Mail and General Trust* [1988] ECR 5483; Case C-208/00 *Überseering BV v Nordic Construction Company* [2002] ECR I-9919; Case C-210/06 *Cartesio Oktató és Szolgáltató bt* [2008] ECR I- 9641.

[48] See Case C-144/04 *Werner Mangold v Rüdiger Helm* [2005] ECR I-9981 and its progeny which includes, *inter alia*, Case C-212/04 *Adeneler v ELOG* [2006] ECR I-6057; Case C-427/06 *Bartsch v BSH* [2008] ECR I-7245; Case C-411/05 *Palacios de la Villa* [2007] ECR I-8531; Case C-555/07 *Kükükdeveci v Swedex GmbH* [2010] ECR I-365.

distinguishing exists where the court makes an earlier ruling conditional on the presence of additional facts which were treated as immaterial in the earlier judgment.[49] This, in effect, restricts the ratio of the earlier judgment and contributes to the incremental development of the law. Although, given the lack of a clear differentiation between *ratio decidendi* and *obiter*, such forms of distinguishing cannot be applied directly to the ECJ, analogies could be drawn. Under that categorization, *TWD* would be a non-restrictive distinction of precedent whilst, for example, the case of *Sapod Audic* where the Court tempered its previous ruling in *Unilever* may be seen as a case of restrictive distinguishing.[50]

In some cases, the ECJ refers to a previous judgment as authority for a proposition which, however, does not flow from it. Such liberal methodology obscures the nuanced development of the law and confuses the legal community. A prime example is provided by the *First Tobacco Advertising Directive* case.[51] The ECJ stated that, in examining the lawfulness of a directive adopted on the basis of Article 100a EC (now Article 114 TFEU), the Court must verify whether the distortion of competition which the measure purports to eliminate is appreciable.[52] It referred as authority for this proposition to paragraph 23 of its judgment in *Titanium Dioxide*.[53] The point made in that paragraph, however, was different. The issue in *Titanium Dioxide* was whether a directive seeking the elimination of industrial pollution should be adopted on the basis of Article 100a as a measure affecting the internal market or under the legal basis of environmental protection. It does not follow from that judgment that only appreciable distortions of competition may trigger the harmonization powers of the Union under internal market competence. Indeed, the emphasis in *Titanium Dioxide* was on the existence of distortions of competition rather than in verifying that they are appreciable ones, and no *de minimis* requirement appears to emerge from that case.

Engagement with precedent is not aided by the collective character of the judgments of the ECJ. The lack of discursive reasoning, which is typically present in individual judgments of Anglo-Saxon courts,[54] makes it more difficult for the Court to engage in detailed discussion of its previous judgments. However, collective judgment need not

---

[49] See N Duxbury, *The Nature and Authority of Precedent* (Cambridge: Cambridge University Press, 2008), 115.

[50] In Case C-443/98 *Unilever Italia SpA v Central Food SpA* [2000] ECR I-7535, the Court held that an individual may rely on Directive 83/189 to set aside national technical standards which had not been approved by the Commission and thus force its contractual counterparty to accept delivery of goods which did not comply with those standards. Subsequently, in Case C-159/00 *Sapod Audic v Eco-Emballages SA* [2002] ECR I-5031 the Court confirmed that technical standards that have not been notified to the Commission are not enforceable but held that it was for the national court to decide what the consequences of unenforceability would be for the contract in question.

[51] Case C-376/98 *Germany v Parliament and Council* [2000] ECR I-8419.

[52] See n 51, at para 106.

[53] Case C-300/89 *Commission v Council* [1991] ECR I-2867.

[54] Even where one of the members of the US Supreme Court delivers the majority or the only opinion of the court, the judgment is more expansive and individual in style than the collective judgment of the ECJ. The same applies to majority opinions delivered by the UK Supreme Court, a practice which the Supreme Court appears to encourage.

amount to lack of expansive reasoning. The Court does engage in some cases in detailed examination of earlier judgments and this makes for a more transparent and persuasive judicial law making.[55]

An important judgment is often followed by a series of new cases where the Court is asked to determine the scope and the ramifications of its ruling. The ensuing litigation inevitably requires revisiting the initial judgment, assessing its implications, refining its reasoning and articulating adaptations or exceptions to suit factual variations. This often leads to corrective readjustments of the original principle. Such corrective readjustments may occur, in particular, where there is departure from precedent,[56] where the court introduces a new principle or makes a quantum leap,[57] where it extends an existing principle to a new area of law,[58] or where a national measure, which is representative of a trend in many Member States, comes to be questioned.[59]

4 Express Overruling

Whilst distinguishing may be seen as an integral part of the ordinary exercise of judicial function, overruling makes a break with the past: to be legitimate, it requires special justification. The ECJ has in fact expressly overruled precedent only in very few cases. It is not accidental that the first wave of reversals came in the 1990s, that is, after the internal market era where EU law entered a stage of post-adolescent maturity. The first case of express overruling was *HAG II*.[60] In *HAG I*,[61] the Court had given preference to free trade over the protection of trademarks by adopting the doctrine of common origin. It held that the proprietor of a trademark could not prohibit the marketing in its own Member State of goods lawfully produced by the proprietor of an identical trademark in another Member State if the two trademarks had a common origin. Such readiness to sacrifice proprietary rights in favour of free movement was perceived as erroneous by Jacobs AG in *HAG II*. He invited the Court to overrule its precedent and to make it clear that it was doing so.[62] The Court followed and made the

---

[55] See eg Joined Cases C-444/09 and C-456/09 *Gavieiro v Consellería de Educación e Ordenación*, judgment of 22 December 2010, paras 91ff.

[56] See eg Joined Cases C-267 and C-268/91 *Keck* [1993] ECR I-6097.

[57] See eg *Mangold*, see n 48, and the post-*Francovich* case law, especially, Joined Cases C-178, 179, 188–190/94 *Dillenkofer and others v Germany* [1996] ECR I-4845, where the ECJ revisited and interpreted its judgment in Joined Cases C-6 and C-9/90 *Francovich* [1991] ECR I-5357.

[58] See eg the successive generations of cases which followed the ruling Case C-279/93 *Schumacker* [1995] ECR I-225 applying the free movement provisions of the Treaty on direct taxation. See eg Case C-446/03 *Marks & Spencer v David Halsey (Her Majesty's Inspector of Taxes)* [2005] ECR I-10837; Case C-446/04 *Test Claimants in the FII Group Litigation v Commissioner of Inland Revenue* [2006] ECR-11753.

[59] See eg the 'golden shares' cases which include Case C-282 & 283/04 *Commission v Netherlands* [2006] ECR I-9141; Case C-112/05 *Commission v Germany* [2007] ECR I-8895.

[60] Case C-10/89 *CNL-Sucal v HAG GF (HAG II)* [1990] ECR I-3711.

[61] Case 192/73 *Van Zuylen v HAG (HAG I)* [1974] ECR 731.

[62] *HAG II*, see n 60, 3749–50.

determinant factor for reliance on a trademark the criterion of consent rather than the criterion of common origin. The reason for reversal in *HAG II* was that the ruling in *HAG I*, which had been delivered sixteen years earlier, was out of step with subsequent developments in the case law on intellectual property rights and out of step with the evolving perception of the internal market.

In contrast to *HAG II*, where the Court reversed precedent at the instigation of the Advocate General, in *Keck*[63] it did so on its own initiative. *Keck* introduced a new approach to the interpretation of Article 30 (now Article 34 TFEU) drawing a distinction between rules concerning the physical characteristics of goods and rules concerning selling arrangements. *Keck* represents the most spectacular departure from precedent in the Court's history. To justify it, the Court used cost considerations and a consequential and pragmatic reasoning. It referred to 'the increasing tendency of traders to invoke Article 30 of the Treaty as a means of challenging any rule whose effect is to limit their commercial freedom even where such rules are not aimed at products from other Member States'.[64] *Keck* can only be understood in historical perspective. In *Dassonville*[65] and *Cassis de Dijon*[66] the Court had interpreted the notion of restrictions on free movement of goods very broadly. The emphasis shifted from the criterion of equal treatment between national and imported products to the criterion of justification on grounds of mandatory requirements. That brought within the ambit of Article 34 a host of national market-regulation measures many of which were by no means designed to affect imports, were dictated by non-economic considerations, and had evolved over the ages, crystallizing local preferences.[67] Such measures were suddenly put under scrutiny in the light of a new pan-European economic constitutional order. As the case law moved away from the notion of discrimination, the Court had no option but to rely on the principle of proportionality in order to draw the demarcation line between lawful and unlawful impediments to trade. That, as one of the judges extra-judicially acknowledged,[68] led the Court to make choices of a broadly political nature which many of its members thought exceeded the judicial province.

There is a second reason which led the Court to revise the interpretation of Article 34. The previous case law was not devoid of inconsistencies. The uncertain state of the law encouraged unmeritorious claims and led to an increase in litigation. In short, following *Dassonville* and *Cassis de Dijon*, the scope of Article 34 seemed to have become over-ambitious: questionable in conceptual terms and counterproductive in its practical application. In the light of those problems, *Keck* sought to increase legal certainty by offering a more predictable filtering mechanism.

---

[63] Joined Cases C-267 and C-268/91 [1993] ECR I-6097.

[64] See n 63, at para 15.

[65] Case 8/74 *Procureur du Roi v Dassonville* [1974] ECR 837, para 5.

[66] Case 120/78 *Rewe v Bundesmonopolverwaltung für Branntwein* [1979] ECR 649.

[67] See S Weatherill, *Law and Integration in the European Union* (Oxford: Oxford University Press, 1995), ch 7.

[68] R Joliet, 'La Libre Circulation des Merchandises: L'arrêt *Keck et Mithouard* et les nouvelles orientations de la jurisprudence' (1994) Journal des tribunaux, Droit Européen, 145 at 149.

Whilst *HAG II* and *Keck* were instances of overruling on the interpretation of the Treaty, *Cabanis Issarte*[69] represents a departure from precedent on statutory interpretation. The Court expanded Regulation No 1408/71 on social security[70] to encompass not only derived rights, namely rights derived by members of the family of a migrant worker from their status as family members, but also personal rights. *Cabanis Issarte* is by no means the only example of overruling in the field of statutory interpretation. *Brown v Rentokil Ltd,*[71] overruling *Larsson,*[72] provided a more favourable interpretation of the Sex Equality Directive for pregnant employees. *Brown* is interesting because it came only some thirteen months after *Larsson* and four of the five judges who decided *Larsson* also took part in *Brown.*[73] Colomer AG, who agreed with the Court, attributed reversal to the fact that *Larsson* was out of line with consistent case law and, effectively, decided *per incuriam.*[74] Still, Brown appears somewhat tactless. No compelling reason was invoked and it appears that the Court simply changed its mind.

In *Bidar,*[75] overruling *Lair* and *Brown,*[76] the ECJ reconsidered its earlier view that maintenance grants for attendance of university studies fell outside the scope of EU law. The Court identified two developments since the judgments in *Lair* and *Brown*: the establishment of Union citizenship and the addition to the EC Treaty by the TEU of the Chapter on education and vocational training. In view of those developments, it held that the situation of a Union citizen who is lawfully resident in another Member State falls within the scope of Article 12 EC (now 18 TFEU) for the purposes of obtaining a student maintenance grant or a subsidized loan.[77] The ECJ reversed precedent on the basis of an evolutionary interpretation of EU law recapturing the spirit of *les Verts*[78] and *Chernobyl,*[79] only this time in the social field. *Collins*[80] signalled a similar departure. In earlier rulings[81] the ECJ had held that the right to equal treatment with regard to social and tax advantages could be claimed only by migrant workers and did not extend to those moving borders in search of employment. In

---

[69] Case C-308/93 *Bestuur van de Sociale Verzekeringsbank v Cabanis-Issarte* [1996] ECR I-2097.

[70] Council Regulation (EEC) No 1408/71 of 14 June 1971 on the application of social security schemes to employed persons, to self-employed persons and to members of their families moving within the Community, as amended and updated by Council Regulation (EEC) No 2001/83, OJ 1983 L230/6.

[71] Case C-394/96 *Brown v Rentokil Ltd* [1998] ECR I-4185.

[72] Case C- 400/95 *Larsson v Føtex Supermarked* [1997] ECR I-2757, para 23.

[73] *Larsson* was a delivered by a five member chamber whilst *Brown* was a petit plenum judgment; The only judge who took part in the first but not the second was Judge Hirsch. The *juge rapporteur* was the same (Kapteyn).

[74] Note that Colomer AG was also the Advocate General in *Larsson* where he had not been followed by the Court.

[75] Case C-209/03 *The Queen on the application of Dany Bidar v London Borough of Ealing and Secretary of State for Education and Skills* [2005] ECR I-2119. See also now Case C-158/07 *Förster* [2008] ECR I-8507.

[76] Case 39/86 *Lair* [1988] ECR 3161 and Case 197/86 *Brown* [1988] ECR 3205.

[77] *Bidar,* see n 75, para 42.

[78] Case 294/83 *Partie Ecologiste 'Les Verts' v European Parliament* [1986] ECR 1339.

[79] Case C-70/88 *Parliament v Council (Chernobyl case)* [1990] ECR I-2041.

[80] Case C-138/02 *Collins v Secretary of State for Work and Pensions* [2004] ECR I-2703.

[81] Case 316/85 *Lebon* [1987] ECR 2811 and Case C-278/94 *Commission v Belgium* [1996] ECR I-4307.

Collins it held that, in view of the establishment of EU citizenship, which 'is destined to be the fundamental status of nationals of the Member States',[82] it was no longer possible to exclude from the scope of free movement financial benefits intended to facilitate access to the labour market.[83]

Metock,[84] like *Brown*, involved reversal of precedent on the interpretation of EU legislation. The case concerned the right of residence of third-country nationals who are family members of a Union citizen and raised some politically sensitive issues as it related to the power of Member States to conduct immigration policy.

Article 10 of Regulation No 1612/68 granted to third-country nationals who were family members of an EU migrant worker, the right to accompany the EU worker in the state where he was employed. In *Akrich*,[85] the Court held that, to benefit from the rights of Article 10, the spouse of an EU worker must already be lawfully resident in a Member State when he moves to another Member State to accompany the EU worker. In *Metock*, the ECJ did away with the requirement of prior lawful residence. It held that Directive 2004/38,[86] which replaced Regulation No 1612/68, confers on family members rights of entry and residence in the host Member State, without requiring that they must have already resided lawfully in another Member State.[87] The Court did not make any effort to distinguish the cases on the facts. It relied instead on two supervening judgments[88] neither of which, however, suggested that *Akrich* was bad law. In *Metock* the ECJ relied on a textual interpretation of Directive 2004/38 and employed a results-driven reasoning: the refusal of the host Member State to grant rights of entry and residence to her family members would discourage an EU citizen from inter-state movement.

Metock is surprising. It came only five years after *Akrich* and the ECJ reversed its previous case law in the face of fierce opposition. Ten governments presented observations whilst only one government had presented observations in *Akrich*. Both judgments were decided by the plenum but by a different formation: only two judges sat in both cases.[89] Critics of judicial activism would also argue that there was nothing in the history of Directive 2004/38 to suggest that it intended to change the judgment in *Akrich* but this argument may be reversed: there was nothing to suggest that the drafters intended to follow *Akrich* or indeed that they had considered its possible impact on such a factual situation. The truth is that the text of the directive is much less conclusive than the judgment appeared to suggest. It thus seems that in *Metock* reversal of precedent was the

---

[82] *Collins*, see n 80, para 61.

[83] *Collins*, see n 80, para 64.

[84] Case C-127/08 *Metock and others v Minister for Justice, Equality and Law Reform* [2008] ECR I-6241.

[85] Case C-109/01 *Akrich* [2003] ECR I-9607.

[86] Directive 2004/38/EC on the right of citizens of the Union and their family members to move and reside freely within the territory of the Member States OJ 2004 L158/77.

[87] *Metock*, see n 84, para 58.

[88] Case C-459/99 *MRAX* [2002] ECR I-6591; Case C-157/03 *Commission v Spain*, judgment of 14 April 2005.

[89] These were Judge Timmermans and Judge Jann. There were eleven judges in *Akrich* and thirteen judges in *Metock*.

result of the combination of factors. The change in the Court's composition, the development of a favourable, albeit inconclusive, trend in the case law, the adoption of a new directive and, perhaps, the fact that in *Akrich* the Court overshot: the generality of the ruling appeared to go beyond what was necessary on the facts.

5 Implicit Overruling

Implicit or covert overruling occurs where the Court reverses an earlier principle without acknowledging it expressly. The problem with covert overruling is that it is not easy to establish whether overruling has taken place and, if so, exactly what has been overruled.[90] A prime example of implicit overruling is provided by *Bergaderm*.[91] In standard case law developed from the 1970s the ECJ had laid down the conditions under which the EU institutions would incur liability for breach of EU law.[92] The case law attributed importance to whether the breach was the result of administrative or legislative action and varied the conditions of liability accordingly. In *Bergaderm,* the Court held that the determining criterion is no longer the administrative or legislative character of the measure but the degree of discretion available to the institution in question.

Bergaderm was a welcome development. It did away with artificial distinctions made in earlier cases and recognized that the EU administration may enjoy ample discretion and be called upon to make choices which are equally difficult, complex, and sensitive as those of the legislature. In that respect, *Bergaderm* is a recognition of the growth of the EU administrative state. The trouble is that the ECJ did not expressly state that it had abandoned its well-established case law nor did it give any indication as to the extent of change that it envisaged. The judgment does not score high on clarity and it is indicative that it took time for the Court of First Instance to follow the new approach. In a number of cases decided after *Bergaderm* that court continued to attribute importance to the legislative or administrative character of the measure.[93]

The difference between overruling and distinguishing precedent may be very difficult to draw. A possible test to employ is to ask the following question: is it possible to envisage any factual situations to which the earlier judgment still applies? If so, the earlier judgment still has some life left in it and cannot be said to have been overruled. If this test were to be applied, it is clear that *Bergaderm* is a case of implicit overruling. *Francovich*[94] itself can be seen as an overruling of *Russo v AIMA*.[95] There, the Court

---

[90] The same problem, however, may arise where a court expressly states that it overrules previous case law but does not explain which cases it overrules: see *Keck*, n 63, para 16.

[91] Case C-352/98 P *Laboratoires Pharmaceutiques Bergaderm and Goupil v Commission* [2000] ECR I-5291.

[92] See eg Case 5/71 *Aktien-Zuckerfabrik Schöppenstedt v Council* [1971] ECR 975.

[93] See eg Case T-178/98 *Fresh Marine Company AS v Commission* [2000] ECR II-3331; on appeal C-472/00 P judgment of 10 July 2003. Joined Cases T-198/95, T-171/96, T-230/97, T-174/98 and T-225/99 *Comafrica and Dole Fresh Fruit Europe v Commission* [2001] ECR II-1975.

[94] See n 57.

[95] Case 60/75 [1976] ECR 45.

held that, if a national authority has caused damage to an undertaking as a result of breaching EU law, it is for the domestic legal system to determine the possible liability of the authority. The finding of the Court in *Russo* could not even be classified as *obiter*, assuming that the distinction between *ratio* and *obiter* could be transposed to EU law, as it was the reply to a specific question asked by the national court.

The test suggested above, however, is not without problems. First, in many cases, it will not be clear whether the earlier judgment still applies until the court has had the opportunity to consider many factual variances and determine the scope of application of its new ruling. The truth is that when courts make general pronouncements of principle, they do so with specific facts in mind and do not necessarily take a view as to whether, and if so under what modifications, that principle might be applied in different factual situations. It may in fact not be possible to determine the true scope of change until several cases have been decided and a trend begins to develop.[96] Law is about incrementalism. Focusing too much on overruling is liable to convey a static conception of the law and does not give the true measure of changes in judicial law.

Secondly, it is important to define the above test carefully. The correct criterion to determine whether overruling has taken place is not whether certain facts that were considered in an earlier judgment would have been decided in the same way notwithstanding the new ruling, but whether the legal principle articulated in the earlier case law still holds valid. The point can be illustrated by the volte-face relating to the standing of the European Parliament. In the *Comitology* case,[97] the Parliament sought to challenge the validity of a Council decision which laid down procedures governing the way the Commission could exercise implementing powers. At that time, Article 173 EEC, the predecessor to Article 263 TFEU, did not mention the Parliament as a potential plaintiff, and the Court rejected the Parliament's action as inadmissible. Less than two years later, however, in *Chernobyl*[98] the ECJ entertained an application brought by the Parliament against the Council on the ground that it intended to safeguard its prerogatives.[99] The Court's reasoning stood on two pillars: respect for institutional balance and the need to ensure that the Parliament's prerogatives, like those of the other institutions, cannot be breached without it having available a legal remedy.[100]

Chernobyl is a bold and iconoclastic judgment. In terms of reasoning, it signalled that unwritten general principles of law, such as the right to judicial protection, are on a par with the founding treaties as sources of law. In policy terms, it opened the way for Parliament to use the judicial process for overtly political purposes. Strictly speaking, *Chernobyl* is not a reversal of *Comitology*. Whereas in *Comitology* the emphasis was on the Parliament's role as a general defender of EU law in circumstances where its own powers were not at stake, in *Chernobyl* the emphasis was entirely on the Parliament's

---

[96] See Lord Simon in *FA and AB Ltd v Lupton* [1972] AC 634 at 658.

[97] Case 302/87 *Parliament v Council* [1988] ECR 5615.

[98] Case C-70/88 *Parliament v Council* [1990] ECR I-2041.

[99] This judicial development was subsequently inserted in Article 173(3) of the EC Treaty by the Treaty on the European Union. The Parliament now enjoys unlimited standing: see Article 263(2) TFEU.

[100] *Chernobyl case*, see n 98, para 25.

defence of its own prerogatives. If a factual situation similar to *Comitology* arose after *Chernobyl* it would not have been decided differently. Nevertheless, it is best to view *Chernobyl* as a reversal of authority. The ECJ articulated a different test for determining the *locus standi* of Parliament and signalled a resounding overruling of principle.

There is no escape from the fact that, in some cases, drawing bright lines between overruling and distinguishing precedent is virtually impossible. In the case of the US Supreme Court, dissenting judgments often bring to the surface underlying tensions and show that the difference is artificial or may be impossible to draw.[101] Part of the reason for this is that, when judges revisit an earlier ruling, they have to interpret it, but that is not a neutral exercise. The interpretation of precedent will depend on the interpreter's own perception of the objectives of the court which delivered the previous ruling, his or her own preferences as to the outcome of the new case facing the court, and the inferences that he or she would be prepared to draw from the previous ruling. Courts like continuity and, where possible, prefer to rule on the basis of distinction rather than proclaim reversal. However, too much eagerness to distinguish might reveal a 'faux judicial restraint' that leads to 'judicial obfuscation'.[102] In the context of the ECJ, the danger arises not so much from seeking to make fine esoteric distinctions but rather from not making clear the way its judgments interrelate with, and might affect, earlier rulings.

In *Extramet*[103] and *Codorniu*[104] the Court expanded, albeit in a limited way, the *locus standi* of individuals to bring actions for annulment of EU measures not addressed to them. Both cases represent a controlled expansion of the *Plaumann* test[105] rather than reversal as there was no antithesis with any specific earlier ruling. The *Emmott* line of case law is more difficult to classify. It is best viewed as representing a gradual restriction of an earlier judicial principle to the point of asphyxiation but not overruling since the possibility exists that *Emmott* may still find application on certain facts and the legal principle established therein still remains valid.[106] *Familiarpress*,[107] on the other hand, represents a tacit departure from *Cinéthèque*.[108] In that

---

[101] Note, for example, that Justice Scalia prefers overruling and has been critical of Chief Justice Roberts's and Justice Alito's preference to distinguish previous cases rather than overrule: see S Low Bloch, CC Jackson and TG Krattenmaker, *Inside the Supreme Court: The Institution and its Procedures*, 2nd edn (St Paul, Minnesota: Thompson West 2008), 650 where further bibliography is provided.

[102] See *FEC v Wisconsin Right to Life*, 127 S.Ct.2652 (2007) at 2683, n 7 Justice Scalia.

[103] Case C-358/89 *Extramet Industrie v Council* [1991] ECR I-2501.

[104] Case C-309/89 *Codorniu SA v Council* [1994] ECR I-1853.

[105] Case 25/62 *Plaumann* [1963] ECR 95.

[106] In Case C-208/90 *Emmott* [1991] ECR 4269, it was held that that, so long as a directive has not properly been transposed into national law, individuals are unable to ascertain the full extent of their rights. Consequently, a limitation period laid down by national law within which proceedings to protect rights conferred by the directive must be initiated cannot begin to run before proper implementation has occurred. Subsequently, in a number of cases the Court narrowed down the scope of that ruling and, eventually, in Case C-188/95 *Fantask A/S and Others v Industriministeriet (Erhvervsministeriet)* [1997] ECR I-6783 it declared it applicable only on its facts.

[107] C-368/95 *Vereinigte Familiapress Zeitungsverlags- und Vertriebs GmbH v Bauer Verlag* [1997] ECR I-3689.

[108] Joined Cases 60 and 61/84 *Cinéthèque v Fédération Nationale des Cinémas Français* [1985] ECR 2605.

case, having found that a French law on videos which restricted the free movement of goods was compatible with Article 30 EC [Article 34 TFEU], the Court declined to test its compatibility with the freedom of expression on the ground that the French legislation in issue fell within the powers of the national legislator. Subsequently, in *Familiarpress*, the Court held that any national measure which poses a restriction on free movement of goods must comply with fundamental rights, including freedom of expression, in order to take advantage of a derogation. *Familiapress* is a case of implicit overruling, the critical reason being that in the meantime the case law on fundamental rights had expanded.

6 Does the ECJ Treat Precedent with Respect?

It becomes evident from the above analysis that the ECJ has overruled precedent only on few occasions. The main reason for overruling has been the shifting constitutional landscape. The unacknowledged judicial assumption appears to be that, if the underlying rules of the game change, the Court is entitled to review its internalized notion of justice. Under this model, uncertainty in EU law is not the result of a judiciary prone to prevarication but the constant movement of the constitutional tectonic plates. This narrative gains support from the provisionary caveat that the ECJ sometimes inserts in its judgments explaining its rulings taking account of the 'present state' of EU law.[109]

It may be said that overruling falls into the following categories. Cases where it is necessitated by the evolution of EU integration (*Chernobyl, Francovich, Bergaderm, Bidar, Collins*); cases where it has been predicated on the lack of workability of the earlier ruling (*Keck*), and cases where it has been justified on the ground that the earlier interpretation has been erroneous (*HAG II, Cabanis Issarte, Brown*). This classification is no doubt relative. In some of the above cases departure from an earlier ruling could be attributed to a political realignment within the Court (*Metock, Brown*) or to a quest for greater legitimacy (*Keck*). Courts at the apex of a jurisdiction are, to a good extent, masters of their own destiny. Two things, however, are clear: in none of the cases where departure from precedent may be attributed to the evolution of EU law can it be said that overruling was inevitable or flowed effortlessly from the applicable provisions. The overruling was itself an integral part of, or even anticipated, change. Secondly, the Court has not shied away from overruling in areas which are highly politically sensitive such as social rights (*Bidar, Collins*) or immigration policies (*Metock*). Although pragmatic in its approach to precedent, the ECJ remains principled in its pursuit of pro-integration policies.

Cross and Harris suggest, among others, the following reasons which justify North American courts being more lax in their adherence to precedent than English courts.[110] The existence of a formal constitution makes that document the central

---

[109] See eg Case 81/87 *The Queen v H. M. Treasury and Commissioners of Inland Revenue, ex parte Daily Mail and General Trust* [1988] ECR 5483, para 19.

[110] See R Cross and JW Harris, *Precedent in English Law*, 4th edn (Oxford: Clarendon Press, 1991), 19–20.

point of reference and the case law a correspondingly secondary consideration. Also, North American courts, especially the US Supreme Court, often have to deal with momentous political and social issues. Strict adherence to precedent would be less appropriate in that it might commit the Supreme Court to a static construction of constitutional texts which would be incompatible with political, social, and economic developments. These considerations apply with equal force to the ECJ. Add to those the constant movement of the EU constitutional arrangements and it becomes clear that pious respect for precedent would be inappropriate.

It is interesting to consider at this juncture the criteria used by the US Supreme Court in deciding overruling and see how the ECJ would fare in relation to them. A number of reasons justify looking at the US Supreme Court as a measure of comparison. It is more open than English or other European courts in discussing reasons for overruling and thus providing a framework for determining the justification of overruling. It also exercises constitutional jurisdiction in a pluralist judicial system applying an abstract founding law. Whilst the differences with the ECJ are readily obvious so are the similarities. In *Casey*[111] the Supreme Court held that, when it examines a prior ruling, its judgment is 'informed by a series of prudential and pragmatic considerations designed to test the consistency of overruling a prior decision with the ideal of the rule of law'. This cost-effectiveness exercise includes the following considerations: (a) whether the rule 'has proven to be intolerable simply in defying practical workability', (b) whether it 'is subject to a kind of reliance that would lend a special hardship to the consequences of overruling and add inequity to the cost of repudiation', (c) whether related principles of law have developed as to make the old rule 'a remnant of abandoned doctrine', or (d) whether 'facts have so changed, or come to be seen so differently, as to have robbed the old rule of significant application or justification'.[112] Whether the above conditions are fulfilled is, of course, a matter of judgment. Thus, in a notable example of overruling, in *Lawrence v Texas*[113] the Supreme Court held that a Texas law which criminalized sexual intercourse between two persons of the same sex was unconstitutional because it violated the liberty and privacy of the individual. To be sure, the Supreme Court's reversal was subjected to much criticism. *Lawrence* suggests that there must be a combination of both subjective and objective reasons for departing from precedent. The judges must subjectively be of the view that the previous case was incorrectly decided and also objectively the ruling must have been eroded by readily ascertainable subsequent legal and societal developments.

One could justify the cases where the ECJ has overruled precedent on the basis of the above criteria. Thus, to mention but a few, *Keck* would belong to the first category (practical workability), whilst *Bidar*, *Collins*, *Metock*, and *Familiapress* to the third (supervening changes in the law). If there is one consideration which the ECJ appears to pay less attention to it is the second, that is, legal certainty. Whilst in some cases the

---

[111] *Casey*, see n 1, 854–5.   [112] *Casey*, see n 1, 854–5.
[113] *Lawrence v Texas* 539 US 558 (2003) overruling *Bowers v Hardwick* 478 US 186 (1986).

ECJ would limit the retroactive effect of its ruling in order not to disturb existing legal relations, the exercise of this discretion does not appear to be linked directly to departure from precedent.

Although the ECJ remains measured in its readiness to overrule, this must be seen in the following context. First, the ECJ's adherence to precedent should not hide that the development of the case law is less predictable than in the context of a national legal system. The teleological and evolutionary interpretation of the Treaties has been a defining attribute of the case law. Secondly, the case remains that departure from precedent by the ECJ appears to occur ad hoc and not within any explicitly recognized conceptual framework. The approach of the ECJ is less structured and less transparent not only than that of the US Supreme Court but also than the approach of the European Court of Human Rights. Although it is not formally bound by *stare decisis*, the Strasbourg court accepts that, in the interests of legal certainty, foreseeability, and equality before the law, it should not depart from its precedents without cogent reason.[114] The extent to which the ECtHR is willing to review its own precedent is determined by the need to maintain a dynamic and evolutionary approach to the interpretation of the Convention so as to ensure that it provides human rights protection which is practical and effective rather than theoretical and illusory.[115]

On the basis of its judgment in *Scoppola v Italy (No 2)*[116] it appears that, for the ECtHR to overrule an earlier ruling, in principle, the following conditions should be satisfied: there must be a sufficiently ascertainable emerging consensus as to a new standard of protection of fundamental rights; such standard must have demonstrably crystallized in at least some of the following: national or pan-European measures, international treaties, the national constitutional traditions, and case law; a considerable time must have elapsed since the ruling which is being overturned; the new interpretation of the Convention must be necessary to ensure effective protection of human rights and promote the objectives of the Convention. These conditions are to be used as guidance and not as imposing inflexible requirements. Still, the Strasbourg court appears readier to confront and systematize overruling. Its approach may be illustrative of a more general difference in the interpretative outlook of the two courts. Whilst both courts engage in the extrapolation of general principles of law, the reasoning of the ECtHR tends to be more detailed and transparent than that of the ECJ whose laconic pronouncements are characterized by conceptual density rather than expansive justification.[117]

---

[114] *Scoppola*, see n 29, para 104. See for similar dicta *Cossey v the United Kingdom, 27 September 1990*, § 35, Series A no 184; 1990) 13 EHRR 622, [1990] ECHR 10843/84; *Chapman v the United Kingdom* [GC], no 27238/95, § 70, ECHR 2001-I); *Coster v United Kingdom* [2001] ECHR 24876/94, (2001) Times, 30 January.

[115] *Scoppola*, see n 29, para 104.

[116] *Scoppola*, see n 29.

[117] Compare the establishment of the general principle of prohibition of discrimination on grounds of age in *Mangold* by the ECJ (see n 48) with the establishment of the right to retroactive application of the more favourable criminal law in *Scoppola*, see n 29.

7 Binding Effect on National Courts

Rulings delivered by the Court in preliminary reference proceedings bind not only the court that made the reference but also have a wider precedential value which, in certain cases, reaches a quasi-normative effect. Thus, when it comes to the effect of ECJ precedents on national courts, the distinction between precedent of interpretation and precedent of outcome becomes even more difficult to draw.

Already at an early stage, *Da Costa*[118] held that a national court of last instance is not under an obligation to make a preliminary reference if the ECJ had already pronounced on the point of interpretation in issue. In *CILFIT*[119] the precedential value of case law was reiterated and extended. *CILFIT* marked an important stage in the development of EU law precisely because it recognized the precedential value of ECJ rulings turning the preliminary reference procedure from a dialogue between the ECJ and the referring court to a wider conversation involving all national courts.[120] It may be said that in *Da Costa* and in *CILFIT* the precedential force of earlier judgments is negative rather than positive: the existence of a ruling does not require the national court to follow it but removes its obligation to make a reference. In both cases however an earlier judgment is treated as binding in that it forecloses the option of a national court not following the legal principle established by it.

A ruling declaring an EU act invalid has general application. It applies *erga omnes* and binds all courts and authorities in the EU.[121] A ruling on interpretation also produces wider effects. It defines the meaning of the EU norm in issue as it ought to have been understood and applied from the time of its coming into force unless the Court itself restricts the retroactive effect of its ruling.[122] Thus the national administrative authorities must apply the interpretation provided by the ECJ even to legal relationships which arose before its judgment. Whilst that duty is subject to limits imposed by the principle of legal certainty, it is far reaching. In *Kühne & Heitz*,[123] the Court held that, under certain conditions, the national authorities must review a final administrative decision in order to take into account the interpretation of EU law provided by a subsequent ruling of the ECJ. Whilst this case relates to the binding effect of judgments vis-à-vis the executive and not the judiciary, it illustrates the far reaching binding effect that even a single judgment of the ECJ can produce.[124]

---

[118] Joined Cases 28–30/62 *Da Costa v Nederlandse Belasting-administratie* [1963] ECR 31, para 13.

[119] 283/81 *CILFIT v Ministry of Health* [1982] ECR 3415, para 14.

[120] See P Craig and G De Búrca, *EU Law*, 4th edn (Oxford: Oxford University Press, 2008), 478.

[121] See Case 66/80 *International Chemical Corporation v Amministrazione Finanze* [1981] ECR. In Case 314/85 *Foto-Frost v Hauptzollamt Lübeck-Ost* [1987] ECR 4199, the ECJ held that it has exclusive jurisdiction to declare EU acts invalid. For an early acknowledgment of the binding effect of ECJ rulings, see Case 112/76 *Manzoni v FNORM* [1977] ECR 1647 at 1662, per Warner AG.

[122] See eg Case 61/79 *Denkavit Italiana* [1980] ECR 1205, para 16.

[123] C-453/00 *Kühne & Heitz NV v Productschap voor Pluimvee en Eieren* [2004] ECR I-837.

[124] Note that there is no general obligation to reopen national judgments on the ground that they conflict with subsequent case law of the ECJ: Case C-234/04 *Kapferer v Schlank & Schlink* [2006] ECR I-2585.

The binding force of precedent has further been recognized in the context of state liability for breach of EU law. In *Factortame* the Court held that a factor of particular, indeed absolute, importance to be taken into account in determining whether a breach of EU law is serious is the existence of precedent. A breach will be serious, and may therefore give rise to a right to reparation, if it has persisted despite existing case law that establishes the breach in question.[125] Previous rulings here appear to have a strong foreclosure effect and come perilously close to being elevated to formal sources of law. The possibility of state liability for breach of EU law by the national judiciary may in fact go as far as to undermine in practice the finality of judicial rulings delivered at the national level.[126]

One may identify, more broadly, instances where ECJ judgments acquire heightened precedential value. Where the Court breaks new ground, reverses precedent, or rules on an important provision which is general in scope, its guidelines acquire almost a quasi-legislative character. This was the case, for example, in *Rewe* and *Comet*,[127] where the ECJ articulated the principles of equivalence and effectiveness for the protection of EU rights in national courts and in *Altmark*,[128] where it provided guidelines in relation to the application of competition law to undertakings offering services of general economic interest. In such cases, the quasi-binding effect of the ruling is intensified and much of the subsequent case law turns on applying and refining the judicial guidelines in a process no different from the building of the common law by Anglo-Saxon courts. The precedential value of the ruling also depends on its generality. In answering preliminary references, the ECJ may be very specific, providing the referring court with an outcome to the dispute or more general providing guidelines or even deferring to the national court. The guidance approach lends itself to the establishment of precedent since the Court's guidelines must be followed by all national courts.[129]

It may be argued that the Court's expansive understanding of the legal force of its own precedents lacks constitutional authority. A reply to this argument may be found in Hart's *The Concept of Law*. Whatever one might think of the correctness or otherwise of the Court's activism, the truth is that it has not been seriously challenged in its foundations. Whilst national courts may question specific rulings or jurisprudential trends and politicians may sometimes reject forcefully what they perceive as the ECJ's unwarranted law making, the bottom line is that, essentially, they have been willing to cooperate. National courts, the EU political institutions, and national governments have, as a whole, played by the rules thus bestowing legitimacy and

---

[125] Joined Cases C-46 and 48/93 *Brasserie du Pêcheur v Germany and the Queen v SS for Transport, ex parte Factortame* [1996] ECR I-1029, para 57. For a recent confirmation, see Case C-429/09 *Günter Fuß v Stadt Halle,* judgment of 25 November 2010, paras 52 and 57.

[126] See Case C-224/01 *Köbler v Austria* [2003] I-10239, para 125.

[127] Case 33/76 *Rewe v Landwirtschaftskammer für das Saarland* [1976] ECR 1989; Case 45/76 *Comet v Productschap voor Siergewassen* [1976] ECR 2043.

[128] Case C-280/00 *Altmark Trans GmbH v Nahverkehrsgesellschaft Altmark GmbH* [2003] ECR I-7747.

[129] See T Tridimas, 'Constitutional Review of Member State Action: The virtues and vices of an incomplete jurisdiction' *International Journal of Constitutional Law* 737.

authority to the ECJ's perception of justice. Authority and legitimacy can here be derived *ex posto facto* by the conduct of those subject to the Court's rulings. As Duxbury puts it, 'the proof of constitutionality is in the pudding'.[130] It is important to highlight here the role of the ECJ's most crucial constituency: the national courts. The process towards the constitutionalization of the EU Treaties could not have advanced without the cooperation of the national courts. Such cooperation has taken a variety of forms ranging from encouragement to acquiescence or even sceptical and conditional tolerance. It would be incorrect to conceive of national courts as passive receivers of judicial wisdom from above. They influence the ECJ and the development of EU law. They may criticize previous rulings, invite the Court to reconsider, or lay red lights in their own case law thus engaging in a process of protest through cooperation. Essentially, however, national courts have been willing to play a constructive role in building the EU edifice.[131]

Finally, it is to be noted that the force of precedent has received recognition by the ECJ's Rules of Procedure. Article 104(3), as amended in 2000,[132] introduces a summary procedure under which the Court may dispose of a reference by order, *inter alia*, where the question referred is identical to a question on which the Court has already ruled or where the answer may be clearly deduced from existing case law. In such instances, the case need not proceed to judgment. The Court may reply by way of an order without the parties presenting oral argument and without the Advocate General delivering an opinion. The ECJ, in other words, may refuse to engage in a dialogue because precedent exists and the matter can be considered as closed. Although on the face of it, Article 104(3) appears to be an uncontroversial housekeeping measure, it could conceivably have considerable potential to operate as a quasi-filtering mechanism since it enables the Court to decide which precedents to revisit. In fact, the ECJ has made only measured use of this procedure. The number of such orders has been small and, in disposing of cases by order, it has not engaged in creative application of precedent but remained squarely within the confines of its previous rulings.[133]

8 Conclusion

Although precedent falls short of being a formal source of EU law, it has progressively acquired prime place in the 'juristic consciousness'[134] of EU lawyers. This has been the

---

[130] *Mangold*, see n 48, 136.

[131] Notably, a study found that ECJ rulings are implemented in 96.3 per cent of the cases studied: S Nyikos, 'The Preliminary Reference Process, National Implementation, Changing Opportunity Structures and Litigant Desistment' (2003) 3 EUP 397.

[132] See consolidated version of the Rules of Procedure, OJ 2010, C171/1.

[133] See eg Case C-307/99 *OGT Fruchthandelsgesellschaft* [2001] ECR I-3159; Case C-288/10 *Wamo BVBA v JBC NV, Modemakers Fashion NV*, Order 30 June 2011.

[134] U Bindreiter, *Why Grundnorm?: A treatise on the implications of Kelsen's doctrine* (The Hague: Kluwer, 2002), 73.

result of a multitude of factors. The Court itself has seen greater reliance on precedent as a form of self-legitimation and as preserving and reinforcing the legal value and the distinctiveness of EU law. Calls for transparency in judicial reasoning and the need to rationalize the growing political authority of the EU have led the Court to adopt a more discursive approach in its reasoning. The substantial presence and influence of the Anglo-Saxon Bar has put further pressure on the ECJ to engage with its earlier rulings. But more than anything, the principles of primacy and effectiveness, themselves generated by the judiciary, have granted a quasi-normative effect to the rulings of the ECJ vis-à-vis national courts. Although it remains interpretative in character, ECJ precedents have come to provide the embodiment of true interpretation, the key to coherence and legal argumentation. Despite its self-referential origins, the value of precedent has been accepted by the political constituencies to such an extent that it can now be said to have a quasi-normative character. This in turn requires the ECJ to be more careful in its use.

A leading treatise identifies three models of reasoning from precedent.[135] The model of analogy under which a ruling is treated as an example of a correct decision and thus a guide to resolving future similar cases; the rule-stating model which treats a judicial decision as laying down a rule which binds courts in the future unless they can distinguish or overrule it; and the principle-exemplifying model where a ruling can be understood as exhibiting a legal principle which may be relevant in deciding future cases. Whilst this distinction is not free from difficulties, it is correct to observe that in systems which do not recognize precedent as a formal source of law, the function of earlier judicial rulings can be better explained by the first and the third model.[136] In the context of the ECJ, an interesting bifurcation emerges. Whilst the third model comes closer to explaining the effect of ECJ's precedents on its own subsequent judgments, the rigidity of primacy, and the possibility of state liability where a national court departs from the ECJ's interpretative choices, might tempt one to conclude that the second model provides a plausible narrative. From the point of view of a national court, justification for its ruling may be found in the very pronouncement of the ECJ rather that the principle that it embodies. This is exemplified by the inherent bias of Treaty-based norms in favour of abstract principles rather than concrete rules: the greater the generality and abstraction of the text of the law, the higher the normative function of interpretative precedents.

It may be said that in the EU legal order precedent fulfils the following functions. It promotes the goal of uniform interpretation and application of EU law; it advances the establishment of a strong central political authority which is the perceived intention of the authors of the Treaties; and enables the establishment of legal principles from general and vague Treaty provisions.

---

[135] Z Bankowski, D Neil MacCormick, l Morawski, and A Ruiz Miguel, 'Rationales for Precedent' in D Neil MacCormick, RS Summers, and A Goodhart, *Interpreting Precedents* (Ashgate, Dartmouth, 1997), 481, 497.

[136] Bankowski *et al.*, see n 135, 498.

The ECJ has in fact overruled precedent only in very few cases. The justification in most of those cases appears to be the ever-changing constitutional landscape of the EU. Still, this is not to hide the fact that the development of the case law is less incremental than in more 'mature' legal systems. There is no doubt that the evolutionary interpretation of the Treaties has been a defining attribute of the case law and that judicial quantum leaps have anticipated and even, on occasion, hijacked the political agenda. The ECJ's approach to overruling precedent appears more ad hoc and less structured than that of the European Court of Human Rights or the US Supreme Court. It has not sought to provide any theoretical framework or general guidelines as to when overruling might be justified. Still, the difference should not be exaggerated. Even where courts attempt to draw bright lines, it is not easy to tell whether they have crossed them.

13

Monism and Fundamental Rights

Lorenzo Zucca[*]

Europe boasts the most developed transnational system of protection of fundamental rights. Individuals whose rights have been violated can have satisfaction at the national level through domestic constitutional courts, at the EU level through the Court of Justice, and at the level of the Council of Europe through the ECtHR. Each court has its own domain, but the possibility of overlap is not excluded since fundamental rights have a very expansive reach. While the existence of various layers of protection of fundamental rights could be celebrated, the possibility of diverging views between courts on the same cases poses a real challenge: who is the ultimate authority on matters of interpretation of fundamental rights? This question is far from purely theoretical since individual litigants need clear and predictable guidance as to what they are entitled to in terms of European fundamental rights. Irish women, for example, need to know whether, and under which conditions, they can travel abroad in order to undergo abortion and without being singled out negatively at home where abortion is constitutionally prohibited.[1]

The challenge is often described as a matter of conflicts of rights.[2] It is however imprecise to describe it in this way. Conflicts between rights take place between two norms or principles that require from individuals' incompatible behaviours.[3] These

[*] Reader in Jurisprudence, King's College London. This chapter has benefited from comments by Matej Avbelj, Marco Dani, Pavlos Elefteriadis, Peter Eeckhout, Francis Jacobs, Giuseppe Martinico, George Letsas, Federico Ortino, Andrea Sangiovanni, and the participants to a seminar organized at the EUI, Florence, the participants of a workshop organized in Cracow, the participants of a seminar organized in Dundee, and the participants of the STALS workshop at Sant'Anna School of Advanced Studies, University of Pisa.

[1] The Irish abortion saga contains several chapters over the last twenty-five years or so and saw litigation at every European level; European courts held divergent views without entering into an open confrontation. This did not, however, contribute to the overall clarity of the guidance provided to women in need of information. The last case in time is an example of confusion and lack of appropriate legislation: *A, B and C v Ireland* [2010] ECHR 2032.

[2] Aida Torres Perez, for example, conflates the notion of conflicts of rights with that of conflicts between courts in her book, *Conflicts of Rights in Europe* (Oxford: Oxford University Press, 2009).

[3] For a fuller discussion, see my *Constitutional Dilemmas—Conflicts of Fundamental Legal Rights in Europe and the USA* (Oxford: Oxford University Press, 2007).

conflicts are a normal occurrence in every domestic constitutional system: free speech conflicts with privacy and courts attempt to strike a balance between the two. The European scenario, however, poses a different problem: who deals with conflicts between jurisdictions? In this case the issue is not about finding the best compromise between two rights, but it is about which system of rights takes priority. Naturally, since fundamental rights go to the very root of any legal system, each court is very protective of its own terrain of authority.

In this chapter, I argue that there are two opposite ways of conceiving the relationship between law and fundamental rights in a way that makes jurisdictional conflicts manageable. Both ways are monistic, although in a completely different way: one posits the superiority of fundamental rights as moral principles over the law (what I crudely call *Moralism*). The other claims that fundamental rights should be treated as any other rule, only encapsulating very important interests by way of stipulation (what I crudely call *Positivism*). *Moralism*, as I understand it here, relies on value monism, which maintains that any system of values—including fundamental rights—can be presented as a reduction to the one overarching value that makes the whole morally coherent. *Positivism*, as I understand it here, relies instead on a formal understanding of law as a system of rules which are produced, applied, and interpreted according to one single master rule which give unity to the overall framework—what we could call legal monism. Under both these monist views, jurisdictional conflicts are merely apparent: value monism suggests that institutions ought to interpret rights in a coherent and harmonious way, which would prevent the possibility of discrepancies. To this extent, value monism subordinates the resolution of jurisdictional conflicts to the debunking of conflicts between rights.[4] Legal monism, on the other hand, suggests that an appropriate legal world view posits the unity of plural legal systems, unity without which we could hardly make sense of the juridical phenomenon in a comprehensive way. Given that unity of perspective, it would then be possible to observe that different legal sub-systems organize themselves in a more or less centralized way that aims at the resolution of jurisdictional conflicts amongst other things.

Both monist views put forward here are at odds with mainstream legal pluralism. Legal pluralists resist legal monism in particular, while they are unclear as to value monism. Some pluralists, for example, claim that jurisdictional conflicts can be solved by appeal to an overarching ethos, which makes their views very close to value monism.[5] Others claim that jurisdictional conflicts are dealt with by engaging in judicial politics; that is, strictly speaking, in a non-legal way.[6] Most legal pluralists insist that while in theory conflicts are everywhere, in practice they are extremely

---

[4] See George Letsas (Chapter 4 in this book) for this endeavour.

[5] Kumm is a good example as he embraces Dworkin's value monist position. See M Kumm, 'The Jurisprudence of Constitutional Conflicts: Constitutional Supremacy in Europe before and after the Constitutional Treaty' (2005) 11 *European Law Journal* 262.

[6] N Krisch, *Beyond Constitutionalism—The Pluralist Structure of Post-National Law* (Oxford: Oxford University Press, 2010). See also N Krisch, 'The Open Architecture of European Human Rights Law' (2008) 71(2) MLR 183–216, reproduced in the book.

limited and explain this by the idea of cooperation between judicial institutions. However, cooperation cannot happen without a shared understanding of the relationship between law and fundamental rights. Sometimes courts avoid jurisdictional conflicts by suggesting that their protection of fundamental rights is equivalent.[7] In order to establish this, they must have at least a shared understanding of what fundamental rights require. This does not mean that there cannot be divergence as to the interpretation of rights; it simply means that in order for reasonable divergence to take place there needs to be a common monistic understanding of what fundamental rights require.

In recent years, however, that minimum common understanding has been questioned, so much so that the EU had to come up with a Charter of Fundamental Rights to reassert its fundamental rights commitment, while a project of accession of the EU to the ECHR is being implemented. This legalistic turn on fundamental rights highlights the fact that in practice institutions are acutely aware of the possibility of jurisdictional conflicts and they seem intent on building a closer, more unified, legal framework of fundamental rights within which conflicts will be managed. It therefore seems that a legal monistic understanding of the law as regulating fundamental rights is emerging and imposing itself from the practice of the institutions themselves.[8]

This chapter aims to offer a theoretical reconstruction of the practice of fundamental rights in Europe. Firstly, it engages in a genealogy of fundamental rights in the EU and shows that their foundation is rooted in a string of pronouncements of the Court of Justice which can be described as having one single moral foundation. Secondly, it argues that hitherto the European architecture of fundamental rights adjudication was based on a value monistic understanding of fundamental rights. Thirdly, it suggests that the value monistic understanding of fundamental rights is less appealing than a legal monistic foundation, which is more transparent, more predictable, and finally mirrors better the recent reforms concerning the relationship between the EU and the Council of Europe.

1 Genealogy: Is there a Foundation to the Order of Fundamental Rights?

(A) Preliminaries

The genealogy of fundamental rights in Europe can be traced back to the aftermath of the Second World War. Between 1947 and 1949 Germany and Italy adopted their constitutions which both contained a list of constitutional rights and a strong mechanism of implementation crowned by their constitutional courts. The entrenchment of

---

[7] *Bosphorus Hava Yollari Turizm v Ireland* (2006) 42 EHRR 1.

[8] For an interesting practice-based theory of human rights, see Charles Beitz, *The Idea of Human Rights* (Oxford: Oxford University Press, 2009).

constitutional rights meant for them a very robust and symbolic role in the new constitutional democracies. It also meant a shift of power toward higher judicial institutions. In
parallel with European constitutions came the Universal Declaration of Human Rights
(UDHR) in 1948 which set out a list of international human rights as leading guidelines for
the conduct of international relations. These rights, however, did not come with a
mechanism of protection akin to domestic constitution. International human rights as
recognized by the UDHR and other international treaties exercise moral, symbolical,
pressure on the sovereign states without empowering individuals or groups against them.[9]

On 4 November 1950, the ECHR was signed in Rome. The ECHR is an international
treaty that singles out a list of rights largely inspired by the UDHR. The Treaty,
however, has a revolutionary innovation: individuals and groups can bring an action
against states to a supra-national court created by the Treaty. This mechanism of
individual petition transforms international human rights, whose strength is largely
symbolic, into enforceable legal rights. Fundamental rights protected by the ECHR
form the bulk of what the Court came to recognize as the European public order.[10] To
this extent, they claim to give a common (minimum) core of rights protected by an
institution endowed with important powers.

(B) Fundamental Rights without Foundations

Fundamental rights in the European Union have no original legal (textual) foundation.
Most EU lawyers candidly acknowledge that fundamental rights were the product of a
judicial construction by the Court of Justice.[11] The EU project was born as a trade
agreement and largely remains centred on that project as the kernel of a broader
political outlook.[12] Fundamental rights were an afterthought formalized by the Court
of Justice when it realized that the legitimacy of the economic construction also
depended on the respect of some fundamental rights enshrined in domestic constitutions and in the European Convention of Human Rights.[13]

While rights at the domestic and ECHR level have a textual foundation that
ascertain an agreement in principle over some basic rights of the individual, at the
EU level there used to be no such support.[14] Thus, the status of EU fundamental rights
as legal norms is problematic. In most domestic constitutions, the primacy of rights is

---

[9] Some, limited, empowerment today (eg Optional Protocol complaints mechanism).

[10] *Loizidou v* Turkey, 310 ECtHR (series A) 23 March 1995.

[11] See for instance S Douglas Scott, *Constitutional Law of the European Union* (London: Longmans, 2009).

[12] Of course, there are growing areas of EU law where human rights become important either through
political or judicial fiat, albeit in a very limited way.

[13] Some believe that according to the ordo-liberal type of market integration, the European economic
project disempowers the state and furthers individual autonomy as part of a broader post-totalitarian political
project: MP Maduro, *We The Court: The European Court of Justice and the European Economic Constitution.
A Critical Reading of Article 30 of the EC Treaty* (Oxford: Hart Publishing, 1998), 126–9.

[14] The Charter of Fundamental Rights was only given binding legal effect on December 2009, ten years after
the first meeting of the Convention that drafted the text.

clearly formalized in a bill of rights and is manifested in the possibility for national supreme courts to strike down legislation inconsistent with some of those rights. In the EU, because of the lack of a clear formalization, the list and content of fundamental rights is formulated by the Court of Justice. It includes, for example, economic freedoms that need to be balanced against social rights (*Viking, Laval*).[15] Among other problems, the lack of a clear formal status for fundamental rights' norms undermines their ability to withstand the challenge posed by other norms that are in breach of fundamental rights. Where norms are formally ranked, the hierarchy provides a tool for the resolution of conflicts between inconsistent norms. For example, a state legislation that breaches US constitutional principles will be struck down on the basis that it does not respect a superior norm. But this is not the case any more if many items qualify as belonging to the same category of general principles. The more capacious the category, the greater the likelihood of conflicts between the norms that qualify as members of that group. The greater the number of conflicts read in by the court, the greater its power to rank interests as it thinks best.

Their scope is unclear and hard to define as well. Since there is no clear foundation, nor any other constitutional way of establishing a list of rights, the scope of rights in the EU is determined by successive interpretations of the judicial institution that has a very thin basis to work on. Moreover, any extension of the scope of a right increases the possibility of conflict with other rights. A classical example of this situation is the conflict between free speech and privacy. Both rights in the abstract have far-reaching scope that needs to be narrowed down by a competent interpreter. Instead, their scope has been greatly expanded in the last fifty years or so with the result that their conflict is more than likely in various situations. The extension of the scope of a right also implies the dilution of its strength. For example, if free speech extends from political contexts to commercial ones, its strength will be lower in latter cases.

Finally, because the judicial construction of the EU fundamental rights does not proceed on the basis of a clear textual foundation, most of the decisions tend to start with the paramount concern of efficiency in market transactions. Supra-national courts do not always articulate the reasons for protecting fundamental rights and the importance of doing so. As a consequence, the stringency that accompanies the application of a right is always open to a very difficult balancing exercise between market and other interests. Because of all these reasons EU fundamental rights rest on very thin ice. Against this background it is not surprising that several treaties and charters have been subsequently enacted in order to provide the practice of rights with a textual basis.

The EU Charter of Fundamental Rights is a good example of an *ex post facto* textual foundation.[16] The document covers all previous rights recognized by the Court of Justice and goes far beyond that, listing many other rights but without giving any

---

[15] Case C-438/05 *International Transport Workers' Federation and Finnish Seamen's Union v Viking Line* (Judgment 11 December 2007) and Case C-341/05 *Laval v Svenska Byggnadsarbetareförbundet* (Judgment 18 December 2007).

[16] Will Waluchow (Chapter 8 in this book) attempts to show that the EU Charter is the building block of European constitutionalism. I find the Charter a belated attempt to give a legal basis to the practice of fundamental rights as developed by the EU Court of Justice.

guidance on what would happen in case of a clash between competing interests. It is also a poorly concocted list of rights as former AG Francis Jacobs points out in his 2006 Hamlyn Lectures 2006.[17] Some of the rights coincide with those of the ECHR, but are phrased differently. Some are justiciable, while others are not. Their scope is limited by explanatory notes that are not included in the main text. They only limit the action of the EU and Member States when applying EU law. These limitations can be a source of great confusion and of very difficult implementation.

Moreover, those who claim that it is the job of courts to balance competing rights underestimate the range of interests encapsulated in the EU Charter of Fundamental Rights. The Charter contains a great number of rights ranging from economic freedoms, to liberty rights, and to social rights thereby opening the door for intractable clashes. Thus, the Charter of Fundamental Rights broadens and deepens the possibility of conflicts between various interests; it would also enormously increase the transfer of power to the Court of Justice. It broadens the likelihood of conflict by the simple fact that if there are more interests protected by legal rights, the statistical probability of a clash is higher. It also deepens the conflict insofar as the Charter does not give guidance as to how to decide clashes of interest. It is essentially up to the Court of Justice to decide the appropriate tools and the hierarchy of values applicable.

(C) Foundational Fiction

Fundamental legal rights in the EU are the result of a foundational fiction. A fiction is a statement that claims to be true, it can be empirically tested, and is false. In common law, for example, a legal fiction is a fact or statement invented by the courts in order to extend the application of a legal rule. The Court of Justice posited a foundational commitment to fundamental rights in *Stauder* (1969) and reiterated it several times. It is with *Internationale Handelsgesellschaft* that the fictional foundation is best articulated: 'respect for fundamental rights forms an integral part of the general principles of Community law protected by the Court of Justice'.[18] This was stated notwithstanding the fact that the founding treaties were totally silent with respect to fundamental rights provisions. So if one applies the definition of fiction given above: (1) the statement of principle made by the Court of Justice in *Internationale Handelsgesellschaft* claims to be true; (2) it is empirically testable since it can be tested against the foundational commitments stated in the Treaty of Rome; (3) it is false since there is no mention of fundamental rights in the original Treaty. Yet it forms the basis for the EU protection of fundamental rights.

The foundational fiction can be encapsulated in a very simple and general moral principle: '*fundamental rights must be respected*'. There is no contestation about this statement of principle of the Court of Justice. On the contrary, the most important actors and commentators celebrate this foundational moment as a great achievement

---

[17] See Francis Jacobs, *The Sovereignty of Law—The European Way* (Cambridge: Cambridge University Press, 2007), 150–1.
[18] *Internationale Handelsgesellschaft*, 11/70 [1970] ECR 1125.

on the part of the Court of Justice. From this point on, every act of the EU is potentially reviewable on the basis of its compatibility with fundamental rights. As with any fiction, however, the problem arises with its actualization. It took many years for the court to articulate its understanding of fundamental rights flowing from the foundational fiction. Needless to say, it encountered a major problem in relation to the place of fundamental rights in its overall project. The EU's self-avowed aim was to create a well-functioning common market. Economic integration drove the evolution of the institution, while political integration came as an additional aim, which was then presented as increasingly important.[19] But because the relation between economic and political integration has never been spelled out clearly, the Court of Justice was left with a much more difficult job than the ECHR. The Court of Justice is in the business of dealing with issues of social economic and political governance. This has a major consequence in terms of fundamental rights: the Court of Justice has to constantly struggle to find the best balance between the preservation of economic freedoms and the protection of other values. Cases like *Schmidberger* and *Omega* point to the tentative way in which the Court of Justice strikes that balance.[20]

The problem with such an approach is that it is open to criticism from both market enthusiasts and rights advocates, leaving the door open to issues of uncertainty as to the appropriate ranking of interests. The Court of Justice has to single out each time which interests are at stake and how to balance them. This used to be the job of domestic legislatures, but the EU increasingly encroached upon that state prerogative. This means that the Court of Justice had to engage in a complex area of overlapping political and economic interests. In particular, the Court of Justice had to decide cases that raise crucial problems such as the best balance between economic efficiency and welfare models that may raise issues of social dumping (*Viking & Laval*).[21] At the supra-national level, it is much more difficult to reach agreement on what may be a good compromise in this area rather than a good compromise on how to limit free expression.[22] The majority of Europeans agrees on the importance of free expression and disagrees on how to best protect it. But European states vary considerably, and harshly disagree on the very principle of social welfare. So, disagreement is likely to be much more extreme on issues of social rights rather than on issues of civil and political rights.[23]

Given this background, it would be surprising if the Court of Justice was not challenged by domestic courts as well as by the ECtHR on its interpretation of

[19] Subsequent treaties have insisted on the need for an ever closer union, etc.

[20] Case C-112/00 *Schmidberger v Austria* (12 June 2003) and Case C-36/02 *Omega* (2004).

[21] Case C-438/05 *International Transport Workers' Federation and Finnish Seamen's Union v Viking Line* (Judgment 11 December 2007) and Case C-341/05 *Laval v Svenska Byggnadsarbetareförbundet* (Judgment 18 December 2007).

[22] See for instance the US Congress today: it is much more likely to divide on an issue of social security than on a bill on freedom of expression. The agreement in principle on the latter is such that nobody would challenge the role of free speech in the US.

[23] For this reason, some states (including the UK, Poland, and Czech Republic) negotiated opt-out clause from the Charter of Fundamental Rights. See Council of the European Union (1 December 2009), *Brussels European Council 29/30 October 2009: Presidency Conclusions*, 15265/1/09 REV 1, accessed 23 January 2010.

fundamental rights. Yet things are very different in practice: conflicts are seldom acknowledged by competing jurisdictions. They are an exception to the rule, where the rule is collaboration between jurisdictions. But institutions cannot cooperate for the sake of cooperation. They have to do so in a way that pursues a common goal, or a project. When it comes to fundamental rights, the implicit common project is the harmonious and homogeneous protection of rights.[24] In other words, judicial institutions seem to converge because they share the belief in one common foundational fiction: *fundamental rights must be respected.*

2 Order and Conflicts

In this section, I sketch the contours of the Moralist understanding of European fundamental rights as based on the fictional principle, *fundamental rights must be respected.*[25] I believe that this implicit assumption best explains the fact that conflicts between legal orders should be everywhere, but in practice they are very seldom acknowledged by institutions. Others believe that conflicts are not pervasive because inter-institutional interactions are characterized by mutual reference between courts[26] or judicial dialogue. Yet to engage in a meaningful dialogue one has to agree on the basic object of discussion, before one can disagree about it, which brings us back to the implicit assumptions of Moralism.[27]

(A) Moralism: A Value Monistic order

As we saw above, the practice of fundamental rights in the EU can be explained by reference to a foundational fiction which I have called *fundamental rights must be respected* and which was established by the Court of Justice in search of a basis for its judicial review and under the pressure of National Courts, in particular the German and the Italian Constitutional Courts. The German Court promoted and then accepted the establishment of such a foundational fiction. It is therefore possible to speak of an order between the two levels on the basis of a shared understanding of the fictional foundation. Later on, the ECHR came to recognize that very principle when faced with the examination of the system of protection of fundamental rights at the EU level in the *Bosphorus* case.[28] The ECtHR accepted the fact that the EU protects fundamental rights, and that it does so in a way that is equivalent to its own.

---

[24] See the Draft Agreement on the Accession of the European Union to the convention for the Protection of Human rights and Fundamental Freedoms, <http://www.statewatch.org/news/2011/jul/eu-coe-echr-final.pdf>. See also the Joint Communication from Presidents Costa and Skouris, available at: <http://www.echr.coe.int/NR/rdonlyres/02164A4C-0B63-44C3-80C7-FC594EE16297/0/2011Communication_CEDHCJUE_EN.pdf>.

[25] For a defence of a Moralist Approach, see George Letsas (Chapter 4 in this book).

[26] For this terminology, See Culver and Giudice (Chapter 3 in this book).

[27] For this position, see Culver and Giudice (Chapter 3 in this book).

[28] *Bosphorus Hava Yollari Turizm v Ireland* (2006) 42 EHRR 1.

It could be suggested that the maxim *fundamental rights must be respected* was implicitly posited as the common and ultimate value on the basis of which national, supra-national, and international courts organize the protection of fundamental rights. The value monist moralist position is that disagreement is possible and encouraged to the extent that it does not erode the fundamental commitment to the protection of fundamental rights. In other words, it is possible to suggest that the maxim *fundamental rights must be respected* promotes the belief in the unity of value of all the norms in the European constitutional environment.[29] Beyond the pluralism of those different systems, the unity of value would point to the fact that the order of fundamental rights in Europe is monist as it is based on a single overarching commitment of principle that is implicitly or explicitly shared by all the judicial actors. This consequence can of course be tempered in the sense that each legal system claims autonomy as to the adjudication of fundamental rights claims. But this autonomy is validated by the acceptance of the common principle *fundamental rights must be respected*, which precedes the declaration of autonomy of each legal system within the European legal space.

In theory those legal systems would have to conflict one another if they were truly plurals. In practice they seldom conflict, and if they do, then there is a regulative principle that solves the conflicts by creating a mechanism of mutual deference (*Solange*), which is itself dependent upon the foundational principle *fundamental rights must be respected*. Institutions agree on the foundational principle, only to disagree on what it requires in practice. *Solange* from this viewpoint can be interpreted as the twin requirement of value monism: it stands for a form of deference according to which each institution is prepared to bow one to another as long as they share the basic understanding that fundamental rights should be protected appropriately.

Unity of value and deference stand together for the affirmation of Moralism.[30] Within this value monistic order of fundamental rights, all rules and principles must be traced back to the ultimate foundation *fundamental rights must be respected*. Moreover, if there is a conflict between rules this will be solved by reference to the regulative norm *Solange*. In the following section we will explore a little further how *Solange* works in situations of conflict. But let me add here that the order of fundamental rights which we just presented is monistic insofar that it is based on a fictional principle that has no textual basis, but which was implicitly accepted and explicitly articulated by all the jurisdictions in Europe. The value monistic order explains the practice at least as far as it tells us what justifies the thinking of the actors engaged in the adjudication of fundamental rights' claims. It shows that behind any talk of pluralism lies a monist fictional foundation, without which institutions would be hard pressed to defer to one another. Deference in matters of fundamental rights is only possible if there is a belief that the other institution protects rights as well as

---

[29] Dworkin defends the thesis of the unity of value in his latest book, *Justice for Hedgehogs* (Cambridge, Mass: Harvard University Press, 2010).

[30] A Somek, 'Monism: A Tale of the Undead', in M Avbelj and J Komárek (eds), *Constitutional Pluralism in Europe and Beyond* (Oxford: Hart, 2011).

everyone else (this is the gist of *Bosphorus*). The existence of a fictional foundation also explains why the practice displays such a limited amount of conflicts.

(B) Conflicts

Conflicts between jurisdictions should be the norm; instead they are the exception. Courts play down confrontations as they have nothing to gain from them. They engage in a game that we can deem 'the politics of deference', where courts agree to a mutual pact of non-aggression. This situation is presented as desirable by radical pluralists who welcome the resolution of jurisdictional conflicts on the basis of politics rather than law. The problem here is that this kind of judicial politics is primarily geared to the preservation of relative power of the courts rather than to the upholding of fundamental rights: if a decision is believed to be mandated by fundamental rights, but happens to be very hard to accept, then any court will think twice before taking it. In this way, any decision of principle is watered down by institutional strategic thinking; the Irish abortion saga is a good illustration of this.

More importantly from a general viewpoint, it would be impossible to settle on a pact of non-aggression if there was no minimal agreement as to the rationale for this pact. As shown above, in practice, that minimal agreement is encapsulated in the idea *fundamental rights must be respected*, which keeps all the actors happy about their mission whilst free to disagree as to what that foundational norm really entails. From a constitutional pluralist viewpoint, the suggestion is that there is an emerging constitutional order within which competing authorities find a way to settle disagreement, while preserving autonomy. The problem with this position is that settling disagreement on such fundamental issues requires once again an agreement in principle on a basic norm, which brings us back to the same idea. Officials are not so keen on recognizing conflicts, especially at the supra-national level. Conflicts are generally raised by national courts to resist the imposition of an interpretation of their most fundamental commitments. The original resistance, as the story goes, came from the BVG which was not prepared to recognize the authority of the Court of Justice unless it displayed an equivalent protection of fundamental rights as to its own case law.

The first *Solange* case expressed the resistance, while the second *Solange* case eventually expressed acceptance of the EU level of protection of fundamental rights. It can be added to that that *Solange I* was about efficient protection: the Court of Justice had to demonstrate that it had a mechanism of judicial review of fundamental rights. *Solange II* was instead about equivalent protection: once the system was in place, the question was whether it afforded enough protection to the individuals. The *Solange* regulative principle was also applied by the ECtHR vis-à-vis the Court of Justice in the well-rehearsed *Bosphorus* case.[31] In this case, the ECtHR had to *de facto* review the Court of Justice decision to uphold an EU regulation implementing a UN sanction

---

[31] *Bosphorus Hava Yollari Turizm v Ireland* (2006) 42 EHRR 1.

regime against Yugoslavia, which had as a consequence the impounding of an aircraft leased to the Bosphorus company. In this context, Strasbourg developed its doctrine of equivalent protection which is visibly derived from the previous *Solange* jurisprudence of the BVG. It is not easy to establish exactly what equivalent protection may mean here. It is clear that it does not mean identical protection, so it has to be somehow short of it. As a matter of fact, the Strasbourg court limits itself to a cursory review of the fundamental rights mechanism as established and articulated by the Court of Justice since its original introduction. It is interesting to note here that respect for fundamental rights becomes a purely formal, institutional issue. It seems sufficient for each court to ascertain the existence of a mechanism of judicial review to establish a presumption of compatibility between the systems. Of course, the possibility of intervention remains, but we have no clue as to what kind of case would trigger a rebuttal of the presumption of compatibility.

Commentators have criticized the decision on the basis that it is a compromise that waters down further the protection of fundamental rights. The President of the ECtHR Jean Paul Costa has defended the decision arguing that '[the decision] can be seen as an important expression of our Court's plea for harmonious co-existence of both legal orders'.[32] The question, however, is the following: at what price should the myth of harmonious coexistence be entertained? It seems that the interest behind this harmonious coexistence is preservation of relative power rather than protection of fundamental rights: both courts would accept a less than satisfactory protection of fundamental rights for the sake of maintaining good institutional relationships. Coexistence in this context may mean two different things. Either it means that there is mutual indifference between the two orders and this entails peaceable, albeit largely formal relationships. Or it means that at bottom, courts are more interested in keeping a good institutional façade rather than protecting fundamental rights at the appropriate level, as is the case in a growing number of cases; for example, the Irish abortion saga.[33]

President Costa's plea propounds the myth of harmony at the level of basic values as well as between jurisdictions; this is a confirmation of the implicit belief in the legal fiction *fundamental rights must be respected*—which guarantees a minimal overarching agreement without committing institutions to any given positions as to the articulation of fundamental rights. In addition to that, President Costa suggests that rather than conflicts, we should speak of cooperation, and here he echoes Judge Garlicki who insists that: '[c]ooperation between Courts may only exist if there is, on both sides, a mutual respect and a common will to act together. The judges are, in principle, reasonable creatures and the very nature of their training should encourage them to avoid unnecessary confrontations.'[34] It is hard to make sense of this

---

[32] JP Costa, 'The Relationship between the European Convention on Human Rights and European Union Law—A Jurisprudential Dialogue between the European Court of Human Rights and the European Court of Justice,' unpublished Lecture at King's College London, 7 October 2008.

[33] *A, B and C v Ireland* [2010] ECHR 2032.

[34] Lech Garlicki, 'Cooperation of Courts: The role of supranational jurisdictions in Europe' (2008) 6(3–4) *Int J Constitutional Law* 509–30.

suggestion without postulating a common foundational commitment which guides the behaviour of judges, for cooperation can only happen on the basis of a common project or at least a common goal. Anything short of that would only amount to judicial diplomacy that has little to do with effective protection of fundamental rights: sometimes to protect rights, it is necessary to take strong, unpalatable stances vis-à-vis other institutional actors. I argued until now that in the mind of judges, that common goal can be expressed with a formal commitment to the respect of fundamental rights in Europe. It is unclear, however, to what extent that belief guarantees the effective protection of fundamental rights. Moreover, it is also unclear whether the European order of fundamental right as judicially constructed hitherto has any purchase beyond Europe.

3 The Ultimate Conflict

The value monistic understanding of fundamental rights conveys the belief that all European legal orders must respect a common set of fundamental rights. These fundamental rights are at the foundation of each legal order; by and large the foundation, and more importantly the protection of fundamental rights attached to it, is equivalent as acknowledged by all the major European courts. It nonetheless remains the case that when the UNSC issued the infamous resolutions freezing the assets of a number of individuals, the response of European Courts was very mixed and cautious on the very issue of fundamental rights protection. The relationship between the International legal order and European fundamental rights provides the scenario for testing some assumptions that are built into competing theories.

I want to suggest that these cases represent the ultimate clash between two completely different understandings of law and fundamental rights. One view, Moralism, believes that any legal order is based on a substantive foundation of fundamental principles amongst which fundamental rights are the most important. The other view, Positivism, believes that the only possible foundation of legal orders is formal and corresponds to what positivists regard as a *Grundnorm* or rule of recognition. As a consequence fundamental rights only exist insofar as they have been recognized by a valid legal act. Needless to say, the value monistic understanding of fundamental rights belongs to the first understanding, while the idea that international law is based on legal monism, however imperfect, belongs to the second.

(A) Moralism versus Positivism

One way of examining the ultimate clash between international law and European fundamental rights is by opposing *Moralism* to *Positivism*. I will delve a little more into this distinction since I believe that it can help dispel the great confusion which is presently surrounding the recent developments and debates following from it. The first important point to bear in mind is that both Moralism and Positivism are theories of norms. The difference lies in the fact that Moralism believes in the distinction in kind between rules and principles and goes on to suggest that principles are at the foundation of any other rule. Positivism suggests instead that all legal norms are rules that can be ascertained by reference to one formal fundamental norm. Interestingly, Neil MacCormick, who first used the notion of pluralism in the context of European law, distinguishes between two forms of pluralism and then opts for one which is in fact legal monism based on *Pacta Sunt Servanda* by MacCormick's own admission: 'Since this position involves pluralistic relationships between the law of the Community and the Member States [...], *albeit within a 'monistic' framework of international law*, I shall in subsequent discussion refer to this position as that of 'pluralism under international law.'[35] I have no quarrel with this general stance. Any plurality of objects within a monistic framework is at bottom a monism, which is the position that I defend from the positivistic viewpoint of law understood as a system of norms.

Most of the confusion about pluralism comes from another aspect of MacCormick's legal philosophy, which he deems 'Institutional Theory of Law' and which defines law as an institutional normative order.[36] There is no room here to evaluate his theoretical effort.[37] Here, it is important to stress that this theory introduces a tension between the understanding of law as a system of norms and the understanding of law as a web of institutional practices. The difference with more established philosophical theories of law is its focus on institutions which is very interesting but also potentially misleading. In order to dispel that tension we can look at the practice of law as characterized by plural institutions *within a monistic framework of law,* paraphrasing only slightly MacCormick's very insight on the relationship between European and International law.

It is important to stress all this because many pluralists defend a somewhat simplified institutional understanding of law, which regards law as an institutional matter casting shadows over the most fundamental understanding of law as a system of norms.[38] Thus EU lawyers often speak of pluralism with reference to the fact that there are many judicial institutions (that is, a plurality of courts) in Europe. It should be stressed at the outset that even this perspective has built into it a strong monistic component insofar that it requires the identification of a common juridical space in Europe. But what I really want to stress here is the fact that institutional pluralism is subordinated to the existence of law as a set of organized norms which establish and regulate legal institutions; that is, courts.

---

[35] Neil MacCormick, 'Risking Constitutional Collision in Europe?' (1998) 18(3) *Oxford J Legal Studies* 517–32.

[36] See N MacCormick, *Institutions of Law* (Oxford: Oxford University Press, 2007).

[37] Culver and Giudice engage in this endeavour by developing a theory of legal order based on the idea that law is a complex pattern of institutions of law.

[38] The efforts of Culver and Giudice in this book (Chapter 3) are to be welcomed here. They rightly insist on distinguishing legal institutions from institutions of law. It would be a mistake to base legal pluralism only on the competition between legal institutions, ie courts. Yet many legal pluralists seem to fall in this trap when they devote excessive time to the discussion of dialogue between courts. See Anthony Arnull's chapter in this book (Chapter 5).

There is a second complication that has to do with the understanding of fundamental rights as either moral principles or legal rules. When fundamental rights are described as moral principles, the purpose of this manoeuvre is to show that there is no sharp distinction between law as rules, and morality as principles encapsulating fundamental values. Those who hold this position are inclined to argue that there is a fusion between law and morality at the level of fundamental rights. Law and morality are one, but there is more. According to Dworkin, for example, morality as best understood speaks with one voice: this means two separate things. Firstly, there is a harmonious set of moral values that under-girds any legal system. This means that there is no real conflict between these values at the deeper level since (secondly) morality can be described as a coherent practice organized according to one paramount value.[39] On the other hand, to understand fundamental rights as legal rules means two things: firstly, fundamental rights are entrenched in bills of rights. Secondly, their implementation and interpretation depends on rules laid down by a prior legal instrument. In this understanding, legal systems do not open themselves up to morality but only mediate their relationship on the very terms stated by law. Thus the realm of values is kept separate from the realm of law.

The latter view is represented by Positivism, while the former can be expressed through Moralism. If this is correct, then there is an immediate striking conclusion that flows from it. From the viewpoint of values, Moralism has to commit to a demanding form of value monism, while Positivism is indifferent to this and is compatible with both value monism and value pluralism. To this extent, at least, Positivism is more receptive to value pluralism than Moralism would be. This is easy to understand if one thinks of conflicts between two values; for example, free speech and privacy. Those committed to fundamental rights as moral principles have to claim that it is always possible for the judge to solve those conflicts on the basis of the reasoning of moral principles alone. If genuine conflicts between rights existed, then the project of value monism would be doomed to fail.[40] Thus in every given case, the judge should be able to say that free speech is more important than privacy or vice versa. This judgment of importance, which is encapsulated in the so-called balancing exercise necessarily involve a judgment of value that needs to be stable over time, otherwise the process would be arbitrary. In order to be stable, it has to be based on a coherent moral theory which is capable of ranking the importance of each principle.[41]

Positivism does not have to open the Pandora's Box of values underpinning fundamental rights. It is largely indifferent to that and focuses on the way fundamental rights as legal rules can be implemented and interpreted so as to avoid conflicts at the practical level. But it is compatible with the fact that conflicts of values are very possible at the abstract moral level, which in turn may present in very occasional

---

[39] These two theses are defended in the most recent work of R Dworkin, *Justice for Hedgehogs* (Cambridge, Mass.: Harvard University Press, 2011).

[40] See L Zucca, *Constitutional Dilemmas- Conflicts of Fundamental Legal Rights in Europe and the USA,* (Oxford: Oxford University Press, 2007).

[41] See George Letsas's criticism of pluralism from that viewpoint, Chapter 4 in this book.

cases dilemmas for the judge.[42] In any case, Positivism gives a much clearer picture of law as it focuses exclusively on law as a theory of norms. Moralism on the other hand has to present law as a theory of norms, institutions, and values which ultimately makes the picture very confused and disorderly and opens the gate to a number of constitutional theories that attempts to extol the virtues of pluralism as window-dressing for lack of order or sheer disorder.[43]

This table summarizes the possible variables described above:

	Moralism	Positivism
Norms	Fundamental rights as moral principles	Fundamental rights as legal rules
Institutions	Disagreement between: -Pluralism of Institutions -Coherent Institutional Framework	INDIFFERENT (but perfectly compatible with institutional pluralism)
Values	Disagreement between: -value pluralism -value monism	INDIFFERENT (but perfectly compatible with value pluralism)

(B) The Ultimate Test

The value monistic order of fundamental rights was recently put to test in a number of cases where the United Nations Security Council (UNSC) norms infringed fundamental rights as protected in Europe. These cases included the now famous assets freezing saga. In this context, the value monistic order collided with the legal order of international law. The facts of the saga are very well known. The Security Council set up a list of potential terrorists in the aftermath of 9/11. Being on that list entails having one's assets frozen for an indeterminate time. There is no mechanism for reviewing that decision, so target individuals have a major curtailment of their rights.

The central issue is the relationship between the international legal order and the European legal orders, and the point of intersection is the respect of fundamental rights. Should European (domestic?) fundamental rights prevail over international law or vice versa? Pluralist legal theories would allow for the potential override of international law since according to them there are no more hierarchies. But European Courts responded in various different ways that are not all pluralist.

---

[42] See L Zucca, *Constitutional Dilemmas*, op. cit.

[43] Neil Walker, 'Beyond Boundary Disputes and Basic Grids: Mapping the global disorder of normative orders' (2008) 6(3–4), *Int J Constitutional Law* 373–96.

In its *Berhami* case, the ECtHR took a legal monistic position vis-à-vis international law.[44] The scene was set out for an open conflict: the UN Security Council authorized some coercive measures which resulted in a series of accidents with the civilians in Kosovo. The civilians blamed the UN Security Council for that and asked for the recognition of its responsibility in the violation of fundamental rights including the right to life. The ECHR had to decide whether to subject the acts of the Security Council to judicial review or to defer to the authority of the international organization deriving from public international law. These were the words used by the ECtHR: 'While it is equally clear that ensuring *respect for human rights* represents an important contribution to achieving international peace ... the fact remains that the UNSC has primary responsibility, as well as extensive means under Chapter VII, to fulfil this objective, notably through the use of coercive measures.'[45] Contrary to many expectations, the ECtHR decided to defer and therefore to exempt those international legal acts from fundamental rights review. In other words, the ECtHR upheld a classical understanding of international law based on *Pacta Sunt Servanda*, that is a legal monist viewpoint.

In its *Kadi I* case, the General Court did not take a fundamentally different view.[46] The Security Council resolutions were imposing a draconian regime of assets freezing incompatible with fundamental rights as protected by the Court of Justice. However, the General Court reasoned that international law could not be reviewed on the basis of European fundamental rights, but only in extreme cases of violation of *jus cogens*. Here the Latin formula betrays a certain hesitation. On the one hand, *jus cogens* goes in the direction of a minimal moral content which should never be trumped. However, the legal contours of *jus cogens* are so hazy and empty, that the practical conclusion of the General Court goes toward the respect of international law even if it is clear by now that those measures seriously breached recognized rights. At this point, AG Maduro enters the scene, in theory a prominent defender of legal pluralism. The AG's opinion, however, bears all the features of Moralism coupled with a *Solange* approach: in his opinion, fundamental rights lies at the foundation of the municipal constitutional order of the EU which is itself based on the original foundational fiction explored in Section 2; it follows that the Court of Justice cannot give way to obligations of international law 'so as to silence the general principles of Community law and deprive individuals of their fundamental rights'.[47] Rather than a legal pluralist position, this amounts to a version of Moralism whereby municipal constitutional law takes precedence over International law on the basis of the *fundamental rights must be respected* foundational fiction.

The second stage of the opinion applies a *Solange I*-type of solicitation, which requires that effective protection of fundamental rights through a judicial mechanism as a precondition for collaboration and mutual deference with international institutions:

---

[44] ECtHR Grand Chamber, *Berhami and Saramati*, Appl No 71412/01, 2 May 2007.

[45] *Berhami and Saramati* (note 45), para 148.

[46] For an interesting discussion of Kadi see Geert De Baere in this book (Chapter 14), who takes a moralist perspective that regards fundamental rights as mandated by the respect of the rule of law.

[47] *Kadi*, Opinion of Advocate General Maduro, Case C-402/05 *Kadi v Council*, para. 34.

Had there been a genuine and effective mechanism of judicial control by an independent tribunal at the level of the United Nations, then this might have released the Community from the obligation to provide for judicial control of implementing measures that apply within the Community legal order. However, no such mechanism currently exists. As the Commission and the Council themselves have stressed in their pleadings, the decision whether or not to remove a person from the United Nations sanctions list remains within the full discretion of the Sanctions Committee – a diplomatic organ. In those circumstances, it must be held that the right to judicial review by an independent tribunal has not been secured at the level of the United Nations. As a consequence, the Community institutions cannot dispense with proper judicial review proceedings when implementing the Security Council resolutions in question within the Community legal order.[48]

Let me reiterate here the idea that a *Solange* approach works if courts are agreed at least in principle on the respect of fundamental rights. Now, there is no international mechanism to protect fundamental rights, so some steps are required for the international legal system to put in place a form of review. The way to answer to that is either by having an international court declare itself competent to review the resolutions on the basis of fundamental rights or alternatively to set up through political agreement a mechanism that allows for the review of those resolutions. The latter option is more difficult but it makes sure that every international actor is on board, while the former solution only triggers a number of extra legal problems which cannot be solved by a court alone. In this game, the loser is the individual petitioner and the lame winner is institutional respectability. After the whole saga of *Kadi I*, the petitioner was still left unsatisfied to the extent that he had to bring a second complaint ending with *Kadi II*.

Eventually, the Court of Justice took its own moralist approach with priority of its domestic constitutional law based on the foundational fiction *fundamental rights must be respected*. First it states as clearly as possible the principle: 'It is also clear from the case-law that respect for human rights is a condition of the lawfulness of Community Acts (Opinion 2/94, paragraph 34) and that measures incompatible with respect for human rights are not acceptable in the Community (*Schmidberger*)'.[49] The Court of Justice then reaches the inevitable conclusion that: '[i]t follows . . . that the Community judicature must, in accordance with the powers conferred on it by the EC Treaty, ensure the review, in principle the full review, of the lawfulness of all Community acts in the light of the fundamental rights forming an integral part of the general principles of Community law . . .'.[50]

The ultimate conflict staged in the 'freezing of assets sagas' is that between two monistic conceptions of the relationship between fundamental rights and law. One is

---

[48] *Kadi*, Opinion of Advocate General Maduro, Case C-402/05 *Kadi v Council*, para 54.

[49] Joined Cases C-402/05 P and C-415/05 P, *Kadi*, para 284.

[50] Joined Cases C-402/05 P and C-415/05 P, *Kadi*, para 326. This saga is not at the end, since new cases have emerged since then. The Swiss Constitutional Tribunal followed the General Court in its *Nada* case, which asserts the immunity of UNSC regulations provided that they are compatible with *jus cogens*. The case has now been fast-forwarded to the Grand Chamber of the ECHR who will write a new chapter of the saga.

the classical positivist conception reaffirmed in the cases of the ECtHR and some national constitutional courts. The other is the moralist conception put forward in two versions by the Court of Justice and the Advocate General. Doubts have been voiced about the compatibility of the Court of Justice's positions and the EU obligations under international law, in particular with regard to the maintenance of international peace and security. Those doubts were recorded and partly vetted by an astounding passage of the General Court itself when it decided *Kadi II*, the remake of the same film with the EU as the main culprit: 'The General Court acknowledges that those criticisms are not entirely without foundation .... However, it is for the Court of Justice itself to provide an answer in the context of future cases before it.'[51] Those doubts capture the fundamental tension between Moralism and Positivism. But Moralism has even greater problems to face. The Court of Justice's affirmation of respect of fundamental rights met many times before with great criticism.

(C) The Limits of Moralism and the Necessity of Institutional Reforms

Fundamental rights in the EU were not an immediate success. As many have pointed out, it took a long time for the fundamental rights language to become salient within the EU.[52] It is only recently that cases like *Schmidberger* and *Omega* asserted the importance of fundamental rights vis-à-vis even interests embedded in the common market. And it is not a long time ago either that the ECtHR recognized that the protection of rights afforded by the EU is equivalent to its own.[53] Even so, in the eyes of some commentators, the EU only adhered to a commitment on paper. It lacked more substantive engagement with fundamental rights.[54] The judicial pronouncement of respect for fundamental rights did not entail a full-blown policy for the implementation of rights. In Europe, more generally, both the Strasbourg and the Luxembourg regimes of fundamental rights are of a limited type. They only protect individuals from the interference of the state in some of their core interests. But they do not necessarily allow for the promotion of policies that strengthen fundamental rights.

Those kinds of criticisms are welcome and important. They are only possible if we are able to distinguish between the role of politics and that of the law. Judicial actors can stretch the respect of fundamental rights only to a point, but they cannot design whole policies for the promotion of fundamental rights.[55] It is the responsibility of

---

[51] Case T-85/09 *Kadi II*, para 121.

[52] See for instance, Alston and Weiler, 'An "Ever Closer Union" in Need of a Human Rights Policy: The European Union and Human Rights', available at: <http://centers.law.nyu.edu/jeanmonnet/chapters/99/990101.html>.

[53] *Bosphorus Hava Yollari Turizm v Ireland* (2006) 42 EHRR 1.

[54] *Bosphorus* (see n 53).

[55] A Williams, 'Promoting Justice after Lisbon: Groundwork for a New Philosophy of EU Law' (2010) 30(4) *Oxford J Legal Studies* 663–93.

political institutions to do so, and from a fundamental rights perspective they are responsible if they do not act in this direction.

The Council of Europe is conscious that its system of protection is plagued by the case load; the ECtHR should be given greater powers of case selection, or it risks collapse. More importantly, its relationship with the Luxembourg regime is both strained and unclear. The moment has come to clarify that relationship on the basis of a legal agreement. The same feeling is shared at the level of the EU, which is willing to build a more transparent order of fundamental rights by entrenching a Charter of Rights and by accessing the Strasbourg system. These developments should come as a lesson to those who believe that courts are perfectly happy to manage all the conflicts and tensions arising between legal orders, including those concerning fundamental rights. Moreover, these legal arrangements make it clear that informal cooperation is insufficient and that a proper system of fundamental rights can only be achieved by establishing an official legal link between those legal orders.

The Lisbon Treaty opens the door for the EU to sign up to Strasbourg as a whole. This will not be an easy process, but it may start a process of consolidation of the relationships between existing institutions. Indeed, Article 6.2 of the Lisbon Treaty states in very clear terms that 'the Union shall accede to the ECHR'. That is to say, the Lisbon Treaty creates an obligation for the EU to become a member of the ECHR. I read this disposition to require as a necessity the simplification and formalization of the relationships between judicial institutions on matters of right.

The accession of the EU to the ECHR is made possible by Protocol 14 to the ECHR. Protocol 14, besides making the EU accession possible, also allows the ECHR to pick and choose its own cases (see the idea of pilot cases). In more emphatic terms, Protocol 14 leads the ECHR towards a more explicit role as a constitutional court of Europe broadly understood. This development is not only made possible by the Protocol, but it is actively advocated for by the Court's president himself who had opportunities to voice that preference in judicial and extrajudicial opinions. In *Vo v France*, for example, President Costa argued in a separate opinion: 'is there any reason why the Court, which aspires to the role of a constitutional court within the European human rights order should be less bold?'[56]

If one reads all these developments together, the overwhelming impression is that judicial and political actors are willing to establish more explicit links between European institutions rather than maintain an informal coordination organized by the principles that are at the core of so-called legal or constitutional pluralism. Institutions themselves understand that it is more desirable to gesture towards an explicitly coherent fundamental rights order rather than have multiple conflicting orders. On this point, the Draft legal instrument on the accession of the EU to the ECHR is clear in its Preamble: 'Considering that the accession of the EU to the Convention will enhance coherence in human rights protection'. Let us make no mistake on this point:

---

[56] *Vo v France*, Appl No 53924/00, EurCtHR, 8 July 2004, para 12.

on matters of fundamental rights, the accession of the EU to the ECHR aims at creating a hierarchical relationship between the Courts. Here are the words of the registrar of the ECHR which are worth reporting:

> Imagine you have a company and you have been fined by the European Commission for breach of EU competition law. You can appeal to the General Court (formerly the Court of First Instance) and then to the Court of Justice which will give judgement on the merits. That is currently the end of the story, for there is *currently no appeal* to the Strasbourg Court against an act or a judgement by the Court of Justice. *Accession would fill that gap.*[57]

The accession process is now advancing and is expected to happen fairly soon. The objectives of the process are clear to everyone:

> As a result of acceding to the ECHR the Union will be integrated into its fundamental rights protection system. In addition to the internal protection of these rights by the internal law of the Union and the Court of Justice, which is strengthened by the incorporation of the Charter of Fundamental Rights into its primary law, the Union will be bound to respect the ECHR and placed under the external control of the European Court of Human Rights. This will close a gap in human rights protection and enhance consistency between the Strasbourg and the Luxembourg human rights systems. Accession to the ECHR will afford citizens protection against the action of the Union similar to that which they already enjoy against action by all the Member States, thereby improving judicial protection of fundamental rights in Europe for the individuals.[58]

The Draft Agreement on the Accession of the European Union to the Convention for the Protection of Human Rights and Fundamental Freedoms[59] gives us more insights into this process and brings me to my conclusion: legal monism is the appropriate way of describing the way in which European fundamental rights are gradually being organized. I will illustrate this by reference to the Preamble of the Draft Accession which lists the following general principles:

1. Considering that the European Union is founded on the respect for human rights and fundamental freedoms;

2. Considering that the accession of the European Union to the Convention will enhance coherence in human rights protection in Europe;

---

[57] Interview given on 5 July 2010 by Johan Callewaert, Deputy Grand Chamber Registrar, European Court of Human Rights, to a delegation of ELSA International on the accession of the EU to the European Convention on Human Rights (my italics). Available at: <http://www.coe.int/t/dc/files/themes/eu_and_coe/interview_callewaert_en.asp>.

[58] Official page of the Council of Europe monitoring the accession process, available at: <http://www.coe.int/t/dghl/standardsetting/hrpolicy/cddh-ue/>.

[59] See the Draft Agreement on the Accession of the European Union to the convention for the Protection of Human Rights and Fundamental Freedoms, <http://www.statewatch.org/news/2011/jul/eu-coe-echr-final.pdf>.

3. Considering, in particular, that the individual should have the right to submit the acts, measures or omissions of the European Union to the external control of the European Court of Human Rights (hereinafter referred to as 'the Court');

4. Considering that, having regard to the specific legal order of the European Union, its accession requires certain adjustments to the Convention system to be made by common agreement,

The first principle reasserts in a legal document the basic foundational fiction; the more it is repeated, the more one thinks that it was not self-evident from the beginning. In any case, the fact of restating it in a legal document gives to it the necessary legal basis which was not there from the beginning. The second 'considering' states that the coherence of human rights protection will be enhanced. This means that as things stand the protection is not sufficiently coherent and that something is needed to make it more coherent! So what is it that will bring more coherence? The answer is in the third 'considering'. Individuals will have the right to submit the acts of the EU to the external control of the ECHR! This is a formidable statement: when accession takes place, individuals will have a further layer of judicial review on the basis of fundamental rights. This is closely comparable to the rights of plaintiffs to have their case heard by an appellate court in domestic cases. It means concretely that the ECtHR will sit at the top of the judicial hierarchy and *this* is what brings more coherence to fundamental rights protection: legal monism will enhance the coherence of fundamental rights protection! The fourth 'considering' introduces a final important idea: the Convention system will have to be modified in order to take into account the special nature of the EU legal order. The biggest modification to the Convention system concerns the so-called co-respondent mechanism (Article 3 Draft Agreement). This mechanism allows the EU and EU Member States to intervene in cases where an obligation arising from the respect of fundamental rights is in conflict with an obligation arising from EU law. When the EU is co-respondent, the Court of Justice of the EU will have a chance to pronounce itself before the ECtHR in case it has not yet pronounced itself on the compatibility between EU law and Convention Rights (Article 3.6). This mechanism recognizes a great degree of autonomy to the EU legal order. It nevertheless remains the case that the ECtHR will keep the last word as a matter of principle and ultimate authority. In practice, it is likely that the ECtHR will leave to the EU a great margin of appreciation, but in theory it will always be possible to step in to rectify a situation of less-than-satisfactory protection of fundamental rights. More importantly, the protection of fundamental rights is organized along a legal monistic way, while preserving the necessary autonomy to all legal orders.

I have to add a note of caution. I am not saying that these institutional reforms would definitely improve the protection of fundamental rights. When the EU accedes to the ECHR, it will greatly formalize the relations between the two supra-national institutions. What I am saying here is that both legal and constitutional pluralism are based on the false assumption that institutional pluralism is an accurate way of describing the practice of fundamental rights in Europe. That assumption is clearly wiped away by the most important institutional reforms in Strasbourg and Luxembourg. It should be replaced by the idea of legal monism.

4 Conclusion

The practice of fundamental rights in Europe, while very rich and sophisticated in comparison with any other international organization, has not yet reached its full development and the necessary degree of organization. European courts have played an important role in pushing for the recognition, at least in principle, of concerns expressed in the language of fundamental rights. The Court of Justice single-handedly introduced the idea of respect of fundamental rights back in the 1970s. It subsequently built upon that fictional foundation a growing body of cases taking fundamental rights into account, and this was done in collaboration with national courts and the ECtHR. But after over forty years that fictional order of fundamental rights still falls short of a fully developed and working system of protection of fundamental rights.

It is high time today to reassess that value monistic understanding of fundamental rights and examine the possibility of moving towards a working and integrated legal system which includes strong protection of fundamental rights in Europe and beyond. The route to follow has been timidly paved by recent institutional reforms which expressed the political will to establish a common legal framework for the protection of fundamental rights in Europe. Protocol 14 of the ECHR and the Lisbon Treaty are a first step, although certainly not the last, toward the creation of a common legal framework for the protection of fundamental rights. More is needed both at the European and international level in order to promote institutions that really respect the rule of law through fundamental rights.[60]

What is important to stress at this point is that a more just European and international legal order can only be effectively promoted if there is the required political will expressed in clear and binding legal terms. Fundamental rights policies can only be brought forward by political institutions willing to commit time and money to the pursuit of a more just supra-national and international order. Crucially, it has to be noted, it is not the task of courts to promote those policies, but the task of political actors at every level. The most efficient promotion will be carried out if there is explicit, formalized, cooperation between those political institutions under a legal monistic framework, as the negotiations between the Council of Europe and the EU are increasingly showing.[61]

Last, but not least, it must be stressed that the role of a philosophy of European law is to help to understand what exists and whether it makes sense. It can play an important role, for example, in demystifying some of the implications of fundamental

---

[60] This is not to say that the Rule of Law is founded on Fundamental Rights as De Baere suggests in his paper. It is perfectly possible to say that the Rule of Law helps to shape the fundamental values to which any given community aspires. Those fundamental rights are not there to be unveiled, but are defined by agreement of the various parties.

[61] See the Draft Agreement on the Accession of the European Union to the convention for the Protection of Human Rights and Fundamental Freedoms, <http://www.statewatch.org/news/2011/jul/eu-coe-echr-final.pdf>.

rights at the international and European level. The language and practice of fundamental rights is filled with rhetorical claims and great expectations that often boil
down to limited commitments in practice. This can be explained when the value
monistic understanding of fundamental rights faces the reality of competing interests
at different levels, municipal, supra-national, and international. It is in these situations
that we understand very clearly that fundamental rights are far from being the only
currency at the level of European and international politics. I tried to argue that their
effective promotion could only happen if political actors agreed first that the new
world order should be organized in the respect of international law.[62] Only if that was
established, would it then be possible to raise some claims of a more just legal order.[63]
At a slightly smaller scale—the European scale—it is only when there is a coherent set
of institutions formally organized according to hierarchical principles and clear rules
that we can improve on the protection of fundamental rights.

---

[62] The killing of Osama Bin Laden raised few international legal eyebrows. Antonio Cassese, for example,
criticizes the primacy of realpolitik over the respect of international law, see his brief op-ed on the 'three
American violations' available at: <http://temi.repubblica.it/micromega-online/osama-le-tre-violazioni-amer-
icane/>.

[63] *Contra* A Williams, *The Ethos of Europe—Values, Law and Justice in the EU* (Cambridge: Cambridge
University Press, 2010).

14

European Integration and the Rule of Law in Foreign Policy

*Geert De Baere**

1 Introduction

This chapter puts forward a simple argument; namely, that the core aspect of the rule of law as applied to foreign policy forms the cornerstone of European integration. That core aspect is expressed cogently and concisely in Thomas Fuller's phrase 'Be you never so high, the Law is above you'.[1] That phrase reflects a principle that all individuals and entities, including states and international organizations,[2] are to be

* Assistant Professor of International Law and EU Law at the Faculty of Law and senior member at the Leuven Centre for Global Governance Studies, University of Leuven. Special thanks are due to Advocate General Eleanor Sharpston, who was originally invited to write the present chapter and who provided crucial inspiration at the initial conceptual stage. Earlier versions of the present chapter were presented as an inaugural lecture at the Faculty of Law of the University of Leuven on 11 January 2011 and as a Durham European Law Institute seminar on 3 March 2011. Many thanks to both institutions for allowing some of the ideas to be presented and tested and to those present for inspirational discussions. Many thanks also to Professor Helder De Schutter, Dr Pavlos Eleftheriadis, Professor Kathleen Gutman, Mr Nicolas Hachez, Mr Henry Mares, Dr Alex Mills, Dr Nikolas Stürchler, and Dr Isabelle Van Damme for their comments and suggestions either on earlier drafts or on some of the questions raised. The usual disclaimer applies.

[1] T Fuller, *Gnomologia: Adagies and Proverbs; Wise Sentences and Witty Sayings, Ancient and Modern, Foreign and British* (London: Barker and Bettesworth and Hitch, 1732), sentence no 943, quoted by Lord Denning MR in *Gouriet v Union of Post Office Workers* [1977] QB 729, 762, and by T Bingham, *The Rule of Law* (London: Allen Lane, 2010), 4.

[2] This chapter leaves to one side the fact that the rule of law (or its equivalents in other languages) was originally developed to be applied to states, as a glance at the names of the equivalent (though not entirely identical) concepts in the four other (apart from English) 'pivotal' languages of the Court of Justice of the EU ('the Court of Justice' or 'the Court') makes clear: *Rechtsstaat, Etat de droit, Stato di diritto, Estado de derecho*. This does not seem to stand in the way of the application of the rule of law, in its core meaning, to other entities such as the EU. Cf TRS Allan, *Constitutional Justice: a Liberal Theory of the Rule of Law* (Oxford: Oxford University Press, 2001), 11, arguing that from the appropriate moral perspective, concerned with the elimination of arbitrary power, there can be no clear-cut distinction between the state and other 'quasi-public' bodies (including private associations). See N Walker, 'The Rule of Law and the EU: Necessity's Mixed Virtue' in G Palombella and N Walker (eds), *Relocating the Rule of Law* (Oxford and Portland, OR: Hart Publishing, 2009), 136, for some doubting reflections. This chapter acknowledges the divergent meanings given to the

subject to and accountable to the law. This chapter suggests that that principle as applied to public authorities, particularly those involved in foreign policy, is the cornerstone of European integration.

A distinction could be drawn between an external and an internal aspect of the rule of law depending on the sources of rule of law constraints and the public authorities to which they apply. The sources of external rule of law constraints are legal orders which include but are broader in scope than the legal order whose public authorities they are meant to constrain; for example, constraints on states imposed by an international organization of which they are a member, but equally constraints on international organizations imposed by general international law. The sources of internal rule of law constraints are the legal orders themselves whose public authorities are to be constrained; for example, constraints imposed by the internal law of those states or international organizations. In both cases, those constraints can pertain to public authority action within the legal order; that is, domestic policy, and public authority action outside the legal order; that is, foreign policy. An example of an external rule of law constraint on foreign policy is the prohibition on the threat or use of force in international relations contained in Article 2(4) of the UN Charter. An example of an external rule of law constraint on domestic policy is the right not to be subjected to torture as guaranteed by Article 3 of the European Convention on Human Rights (ECHR). An example of an internal rule of law constraint to foreign policy would be the possibility for courts to review government action in the sphere of foreign policy. An example of an internal rule of law constraint to domestic policy would be that same possibility as regards internal police action by the state.

This chapter examines how the EU has imposed external rule of law constraints on the Member States both as regards their domestic and foreign policies, and how both EU law itself internally, and international law externally, have imposed rule of law constraints on the EU. The argument will proceed as follows. This chapter first sets out what it regards as the core of the rule of law. It then explains how European integration has used a particular method; that is, the 'Community method' or what could now be called the 'ordinary Union method',[3] to enhance the observance of the rule of law among the nations of Europe. It then explores how that method explains both the undeniable success and some of the failures of the EU project. In particular, it is argued that that particular choice of method for European integration has led to a failure of the imposition of rule of law constraints on the area of 'high politics' foreign policy.

---

equivalent concepts in the various European traditions. However, they broadly appear to agree that the concept implies the subjection of public power to legal constraints with a view to guaranteeing the protection of the individual against its arbitrary or unlawful use: see L Pech, 'The Rule of Law as a Constitutional Principle of the European Union' (Jean Monnet Working Paper 04/09, NYU School of Law, 2009), 70, and 22–47.

[3] G De Baere, 'The Basics of EU External Relations Law: An Overview of the Post-Lisbon Constitutional Framework for Developing the External Dimensions of EU Asylum and Migration Policy' in M Maes, M-C Foblets, and Ph De Bruycker (eds), *External Dimensions of EU Migration and Asylum Law and Policy*, (Brussels: Bruylant, 2011), 122. See Section 3.

The lack of jurisdiction of the Court of Justice within the common foreign and security policy (CFSP) is used as an illustration of that shortcoming, which consists in considering the ordinary Union method as the only option for subjecting Member States' behaviour to the rule of law, leaving other alternatives unconsidered. At the same time, the possibility of extending the Court's jurisdiction to the CFSP is used as an illustration of how the rule of law can be advanced outside the original Community paradigm. It is then argued that such advancement is only possible if the Union simultaneously strives for a reinforcement of the rule of law at the international level. This chapter concludes that the cornerstone of European integration is not the ordinary Union method as the particular method chosen to subject Member States' behaviour to the rule of law, but the rule of law itself.

The external relations of the EU *sensu lato*[4] feature prominently in the present chapter, both because that area provides the paradigmatic example for the argument put forward here, and because the development of the EU can be seen as an extraordinary attempt to bring foreign policy further within the realm of law and thereby to constrain its possible destructive force. Having 'domesticated'[5] the Member States' foreign policies with regard to each other, the EU is gradually bringing their foreign policies with regard to third countries within the constraining and enabling framework of EU law and hence under the rule of law at the EU level.[6]

2 The Core of the Rule of Law

This chapter regards as the core aspect of the rule of law what could be described as 'rule by law',[7] which has been depicted as either too obvious to deserve any attention,

---

[4] Ie the relations of the EU with all that is external to it including, for example, the United Nations and external human rights standards.

[5] Cf F Duchêne, 'The European Community and the Uncertainties of Interdependence' in M Kohnstamm and W Hager (eds), *A Nation Writ Large? Foreign-Policy Problems before the European Community* (London and Basingstoke: Macmillan, 1973), 19–20: 'This means trying to bring to international problems the sense of common responsibility and structures of contractual politics which have in the past been associated almost exclusively with "home" and not foreign, that is *alien*, affairs'.

[6] Cf G De Baere, *Constitutional Principles of EU External Relations* (Oxford: Oxford University Press, 2008), 315.

[7] See similarly on the international rule of law: W Bishop, 'The International Rule of Law' (1961) 59 *Michigan L Rev* 553; M Kumm, 'International Law in National Courts: The International Rule of Law and the Limits of the Internationalist Model' (2003–2004) 44 *Virginia J of Intl L* 22; and S Beaulac, 'The Rule of Law in International Law Today' in G Palombella and N Walker (eds), *Relocating the Rule of Law* (Oxford and Portland, OR: Hart Publishing, 2009), 205. Specifically on the rule of law in the EU: FG Jacobs, *The Sovereignty of Law: the European Way* (Cambridge: Cambridge University Press, 2007), who argues *inter alia* that the traditional concept of sovereignty is incompatible with the rule of law (Jacobs, 5). Cf J Rawls, *Lectures in the History of Political Philosophy* (S Freeman (ed), (Cambridge, MA: Belknap Press, 2007), 86; and P Eleftheriadis, 'Law and Sovereignty' (2010) 29 *L and Philosophy* 535–69. Further: N MacCormick, *Questioning Sovereignty: Law, State, and Practical Reason* (Oxford: Oxford University Press, 1999); K Flikschuh, 'Kant's Sovereignty Dilemma: A Contemporary Analysis' (2010) 18 *The J of Political Philosophy* 469–93. This chapter therefore understands 'rule by law' in a different way from the description in M Krygier, 'Rule of Law' in M Rosenfeld and A Sajó (eds), *The Oxford Handbook of Comparative Constitutional Law* (Oxford: Oxford University Press,

uninteresting, or not even part of the rule of law, but rather of what law is or of 'the concept of law'.[8] This chapter adopts a conception[9] of the rule of law that cannot be divorced from the concept of law itself.[10] The rule of law aims to correct abuses of power that arise when political power is exercised by insisting on a particular mode of exercise of that power; that is, governance through law.[11] This chapter is not intended as a further examination of that conception. It merely sets out what is arguably the function of the rule of law in European integration,[12] and builds on the more fundamental work on such a conception of the rule of law by other authors.[13] It

2012), 234, where it is understood as a situation in which 'political power is exercised by legal means but key elements of the rule of law are lacking'.

[8] Pech, see n 2, 25–6.

[9] The distinction between 'concept' and 'conception' used here is taken from HLA Hart, *The Concept of Law*, 2nd edn (Oxford: Oxford University Press, 1994), 155–9.

[10] See NE Simmonds, *Law as a Moral Idea* (Oxford: Oxford University Press, 2007), 46: '[M]ight we not reasonably assume that 'the rule of law' refers to a state of affairs where law rules?', also noting that perhaps 'social practices count as instances of law only when they partially embody an idea that they can never fully realize' (Simmonds, 5); cf J Finnis, *Natural Law and Natural Rights*, 2nd edn (Oxford: Oxford University Press, 2011), 270, defining the rule of law as the 'name commonly given to the state of affairs in which a legal system is legally in good shape'; Allan, see n 2, 1–2; J Waldron, 'The Concept and the Rule of Law' (2008) 43 *Georgia L Rev* 59; J Oberdiek and D Patterson, 'Moral Evaluation and Conceptual Analysis in Jurisprudential Methodology' in M Freeman and R Harrison (eds), *Law and Philosophy* (Oxford: Oxford University Press, 2007), 66–71. The phrase 'rule of law' itself originates from AV Dicey, *Introduction to the Study of the Law of the Constitution*, 6th edn (London: Macmillan, 1902). The present chapter uses the phrase similarly to the first meaning ascribed to it by Dicey, namely 'the absolute supremacy or predominance of regular law as opposed to the influence of arbitrary power' (Dicey, 198).

[11] Waldron, see n 10, 11. That also entails a number of minimal characteristics, such as that law must be prospective, public, general, clear, stable, certain, and applied to everyone equally according to its terms: BZ Tamanaha, 'A Concise Guide to the Rule of Law' in G Palombella and N Walker (eds), *Relocating the Rule of Law*, (Oxford and Portland, OR: Hart Publishing, 2009), 3. Cf the eight desiderata in L Fuller, *The Morality of Law* (Revised edn, New Haven and London: Yale University Press, 1969), 38–9; the eight desiderata in Finnis, see n 10, 270–1; and the eight principles in J Raz, *The Authority of Law*, 2nd edn (Oxford: Oxford University Press, 2009), 214–19; and compare the definition of the rule of law in F Hayek, *The Road to Serfdom* (Abingdon: Routledge, 1944), 54.

[12] One is perhaps reminded of Wittgenstein's point about the meaning of a concept being its use: 'For a *large* class of cases of the employment of the word "meaning"—though not for *all*—this word can be explained in this way: the meaning of a word is its use in the language': L Wittgenstein, *Philosophical Investigations* (1953), GEM Anscombe, PMS Hacker, and J Schulte (eds), 4th edn, (Chichester: Wiley-Blackwell, 2009), 25, para 43, though of course the implications of Wittgenstein's argument must not be oversimplified and are beyond the scope of the present chapter. Cf Beaulac, see n 7, 222–3, who argues that 'the rule of law' is a formulation of 'Hurrah!' words, ie words that provoke a positive emotion (as used by CK Ogden and IA Richards, *The Meaning of Meaning: A Study of the Influence of Language upon Thought and of the Science of Symbolism* (1923, San Diego, CA, New York, NY, London: Harcourt Brace Jovanovich, 1989); and, famously but less charitably, JN Shklar, 'Political Theory and the Rule of Law' in A Hutchinson and P Monahan (eds), *The Rule of Law: Ideal or Ideology* (Toronto, Calgary, Vancouver: Carswell, 1987) 1: 'It would not be very difficult to show that the phrase "the Rule of Law" has become meaningless thanks to ideological abuse and general over-use. [...] No intellectual effort need therefore be wasted on this bit of ruling-class chatter'.) Further: J Waldron, 'Is the Rule of Law an Essentially Contested Concept (In Florida)?' (2002) 21 *L and Philosophy* 137–64, referring to R Fallon, '"The Rule of Law" as a concept in Constitutional Discourse' (1997) 97 *Columbia L Rev* 6, citing WB Gallie, 'Essentially Contested Concepts' (1955–1956) 56 *Proceedings of the Aristotelian Society* 167.

[13] See eg Allan, see n 2; Simmonds, see n 10; and Waldron, see n 10.

rests on the belief that, simply put, the fact of moving a state of affairs from being governed by power to one governed by law is the most foundational aspect both of the rule of law, whether at national or international level, and of the project of European integration. The state of affairs specifically addressed by the project of European integration that started with the European Coal and Steel Community is the until not very long ago conflict-prone relationship between the states of Europe. Why would infusing law into that relationship be a good idea?

Rule of law requirements apply to states for the sake of individuals. The purpose of law is not primarily the efficient attainment of governmental objectives, but the provision of a stable constitutional framework for interaction between citizens and between citizens and the state.[14] Kant considered 'right' to be 'the sum of the conditions under which the choice of one can be united with the choice of another in accordance with a universal law of freedom'.[15] International law attempts to constrain the unlimited exercise of power by states through subjecting their behaviour to a set of rules. That not only makes their behaviour compatible with similar behaviour of other states and actors in international law, but also makes it more predictable and hence creates opportunities for individuals to act freely and autonomously.[16] If we define a legal system, with Rawls, as 'a coercive order of public rules addressed to rational persons for the purpose of regulating their conduct and providing the framework for social cooperation', we can see that these rules establish expectations for individuals. If the bases of these rules and claims are unsure, 'so are the boundaries of men's liberties'.[17] Crucially, men's liberties are as much at stake when the state acts externally as when it acts internally. Indeed, many more individuals may be affected by the state's

---

[14] Allan, see n 2, 58.

[15] I Kant, *Metaphysics of Morals* (1797, M Gregor (ed), Cambridge: Cambridge University Press, 1996), 24, para 6:230.

[16] This is the '*raison d'être* of the rule of law': J Waldron, 'The Rule of International Law' (2008) 30 *Harvard J of L & Public Policy* 17. Cf A Perreau-Saussine, 'Immanual Kant on International Law' in S Besson and J Tasioulas (eds), *The Philosophy of International Law* (Oxford: Oxford University Press, 2010), 55, noting that for Kant, 'the closer a state approaches perpetual peace with its potential enemies, the more secure citizens' juridical freedom will be'. Cf G Dworkin, *The Theory and Practice of Autonomy* (Cambridge: Cambridge University Press, 1988), 12, connecting the central idea underlying the concept of autonomy to its etymology: αυτος [autos] (self) and νομος [nomos] (rule or law). As argued by JW Devine, 'Privacy and Hypocrisy' (2011) 3 *J of Media L* 173, an important dimension of self-rule is 'the capacity to make decisions without being subject to coercion or influences that may prevent those decisions from being products of one's own judgement'.

[17] J Rawls, *A Theory of Justice* (Revised edn, Cambridge, MA: Belknap, 1999), 207, noting that 'the rule of law is obviously closely related to liberty'. In that sense, might too extensive a conferral of discretion upon public officials not invite the judgement that the regime in question is but a marginal instance of a legal ordering? If discretion is too broadly conferred, individuals will have to guide their conduct by prediction of official behaviour, rather than by legal rules: Simmonds, see n 10, 46. This also implies that 'the virtue of the rule of law consists in its embodiment of our independence of the power of others, not in its realization of mere predictability in governmental action: even when we are fully under the power of the unconstrained will of our governors, the exercise of that power may be highly predictable' (Simmonds, 90, also 98). Cf Allan, see n 2, 174, arguing that 'the notion of a purely administrative or discretionary act that determines a citizen's fate, without recourse to legal safeguards, is a flagrant contradiction of the rule of law'.

external action than by its internal action. Moreover, lawless state action in the international realm may entail lawless state action at home.[18]

Waldron has observed that 'although from the citizens' perspective "the more law the better" is definitely not true, something like that is true for the government'.[19] That would seem to be the core conundrum of the international rule of law. Indeed, though the absence of regulation presents an opportunity for individual freedom, for the state it means that official discretion is unregulated and that power exists without a process to channel and discipline its exercise. Such absence of regulation is not an opportunity for freedom, but rather a defect and a matter of regret for the rule of law.[20] Governments should therefore proceed on the basis that they are to act in accordance with law in all of their operations, and thus subject themselves to constraint by law so that citizens can enjoy freedom under law.[21]

For states, external rule of law constraints are often seen as a nuisance and a hindrance to their freedom of action. Could it not be said that states' antecedent expectations are entitled to the same rule of law respect as individuals' legitimate expectations? Waldron argues that they are not, noting that on a rule of law account, the value of the government's freedom of action has no value or negative value if it is not in accordance with law. Bringing it under law when it was previously thought to be lawless must therefore count as a positive thing.[22]

That assessment appears correct, but one must not overlook the fact that the antecedent expectations of states may have a direct impact on the rule of law for individuals, which is especially clear in the area of foreign policy. Arguably one of the main reasons why states prefer not to be constrained by too much law in their external action is that they perceive the environment in which they are acting to be mostly power- and not law-governed. The less the international environment in which states operate is governed by law, the less willing states will be to have their own behaviour internally or externally constrained by law. To put it differently, in an unpredictable world, states must not be constrained by rules that prevent them from acting quickly and decisively. States can only allow themselves to be so constrained if the behaviour of other international actors can be predicted because it is governed by rules. That is why

---

[18] J Waldron, 'Are Sovereigns Entitled to the Benefit of the International Rule of Law?' (2011) 22 *Eur J Intl L* 341–2, noting that abuses in the government's treatment of others abroad can creep back in and insinuate themselves into domestic state practice, infecting and contaminating the culture of legality at home, and that the 'governmental character of the nation-state does not evaporate when we move up a level to the international realm'. Cf MR Reiff, 'The Attack on Liberalism' in M Freeman and R Harrison (eds), *Law and Philosophy* (Oxford: Oxford University Press, 2007), 181–3. Cf regarding the EU: Walker, see n 2, 131, noting that the external rule of law profile of the EU has provided an ideological resource for people wishing either to reinforce or to question the EU's internal commitment to making the 'law rule'.

[19] Waldron, see n 16, 18.

[20] Even if other ideals that apply to the government need to be brought into the equation: Waldron, see n 18, 339.

[21] Waldron, see n 18, 340, arguing also that the government's own freedom of action is not an intrinsic value as it is for individual citizens.

[22] Waldron, see n 18, 340.

foreign policy has frequently been claimed to escape any grasp of law.[23] On the internal level, it is widely held that the penetration of law into foreign policy should be kept to a minimum: the executive must have its hands free to react to international developments quickly and effectively, without interference from the legislature or the judiciary.[24] Lon Fuller referred in that regard to a scale, starting at the bottom with the duties most obviously necessary to social existence, and ending at the top with the highest and most difficult achievements of which human beings are capable. At the bottom of that scale are the rules of duty set by the government to control human conduct. The example Fuller chooses for the other end of the scale is telling: 'the President conducting . . . our relations with foreign countries, relations that *obviously* cannot be set by fixed rules of duty, if for no other reason, because they involve decisions by powers beyond the reach of our law'.[25] Whence the 'obviousness' of the absence of rules of duty in the conduct of foreign relations? On the international level, a similar attitude has sometimes led to the rejection of the legal character of inter-national law,[26] or the downplaying of its significance.[27]

The argument in this chapter is not meant to deny that international law can often also be actively used by states to achieve particular objectives that they find difficult to achieve using purely internal means. It can, for example, be used to entrench rules that are not easily subject to entrenchment by ordinary statute.[28] Moreover, states often do regard themselves bound by certain constraints regardless of whether other international actors

---

[23] Cf the US Fifth Circuit Court of Appeals in *Occidental of Umm al Qaywayn, Inc. v A Certain Cargo of Petroleum*, 577 F.2d 1196 (5th Cir. 1978), *cert. denied sub nom. Occidental of Umm Qaywayn, Inc. v Cities Serv. Oil Co.*, 442 US (1979), 1204–5, holding that in 'their external relations, sovereigns are bound by no law; they are like our ancestors before the recognition or imposition of the social contract': see TM Franck, *Political Questions/Judicial Answers: Does the Rule of Law Apply to Foreign Affairs?* (Princeton: Princeton University Press, 1992), 49, reviewed in A-M Slaughter, 'Are Foreign Affairs Different?' (1993) *Harvard L Rev* 1980–2008.

[24] Cf Franck see n 23, 3–4, who refers to 'a constitutional theory, still asserted by many lawyers and judges, that foreign affairs are *different* from all other matters of state in some crucial fashion . . . Carried to its logical extreme, this doctrine holds that the political authorities are suit-proof as long as they purport to act in pursuance of their "foreign-affairs" power.'

[25] Fuller, see n 11, 170 (emphasis added).

[26] Famously J Austin, *The Province of Jurisprudence Determined* (1832, WE Rumble (ed) Cambridge: Cambridge University Press, 1995), 20 *et passim*, also classifying constitutional law as 'positive morality merely': Austin, 216 *et passim*. But see T Franck, *Fairness in International Law and Institutions* (Oxford: Clarendon Press, 1995), 6, arguing that international law has entered a 'post-ontological era', enabling international lawyers to 'undertake critical assessment' of their subject, instead of continuously having to defend its existence. See also Finnis, see n 10, 277–8, who points out that too often one particular characteristic of 'the central case of law' is emphasized, and any system not displaying that characteristic (eg a system without easily enforceable sanctions) is then brand-marked as not really being law, thus banishing it to another discipline; and cf JL Brierly, *The Law of Nations: An Introduction to the International Law of Peace*, 4th edn (Oxford: Clarendon Press, 1949), 73.

[27] eg Hart, see n 9, 198, remarking that law in the international system has been confined to matters that do not 'affect "vital" issues'.

[28] For example, bilateral investment treaties (BITs) can resolve the problem that a state cannot make a commitment to an investor under national law, because it may be unable securely to bind itself domestically: A Mills, 'The Public-Private Dualities of International Investment Law and Arbitration' in C Brown and K Miles (eds), *Evolution in Investment Treaty Law and Arbitration* (Cambridge: Cambridge University Press, 2011), 97.

are so constrained. For example, many states would hold themselves bound by an obligation not to torture prisoners, regardless of whether other states or international actors are under the same obligation.[29] This chapter submits that states or other international actors may wish to limit the rule of law constraints that they are subject to in their foreign policies to the extent that they perceive the international environment in which they are acting to lack such rule of law constraints. It does not deny that other considerations may sometimes override that concern and motivate states voluntarily to submit to external rule of law constraints or to impose internal rule of law constraints.

European integration was designed to address the conundrum of the international rule of law in a specific region. It did so by means of a specific method: the 'ordinary Union method'. That term denotes the traditional form of integration within the Community or the first pillar of the Union, based on market integration.[30] As a method of institutional decision making, it is characterized by (i) the central role of the Commission in formulating proposals; (ii) qualified majority voting (QMV) in the Council; (iii) involvement of the European Parliament with varying intensity depending on the decision making procedure; and (iv) the role of the Court of Justice in ensuring judicial accountability.[31] As a corollary thereof, the first pillar or Community legal order has been characterized by the Court as a 'new legal order', which implies the application of certain fundamental principles, such as primacy and the potential for direct effect,[32] or the potential for shared competences to become exclusive through exercise.[33] The ordinary Union method and the areas of policy in which it applies are often seen as the cornerstone of European integration.[34] However, this chapter argues that while it has proven to be a very successful method, it is still

---

[29] A liberal state may, for example, take the view that resorting to torture would undermine the basis of the proper constitutional relationship between state and citizen: see Allan, see n 2, 83–4. Further: J Waldron, *Torture, Terror, and Trade-Offs: Philosophy for the White House* (Oxford: Oxford University Press, 2010).

[30] See the next section.

[31] De Baere, see n 6, 73.

[32] See Opinion 1/91 *Draft agreement between the Community, on the one hand, and the countries of the European Free Trade Association, on the other, relating to the creation of the European Economic Area* [1991] ECR I-6079, para 21. Note that the Court has now characterized the entire Union as a 'new legal order': Opinion 1/09 *European and Community Patents Court* [2011] ECR I-0000, para 65: 'It is apparent from the Court's settled case-law that the founding treaties of the European Union, unlike ordinary international treaties, established a new legal order, possessing its own institutions, for the benefit of which the states have limited their sovereign rights, in ever wider fields, and the subjects of which comprise not only Member States but also their nationals.... The essential characteristics of the European Union legal order thus constituted are in particular its primacy over the laws of the Member States and the direct effect of a whole series of provisions which are applicable to their nationals and to the Member States themselves [...].' It is unclear what this implies for primacy and direct effect in areas outside the former first pillar. For some thoughts on the applicability of these principles to the CFSP: De Baere, see n 6, 201–13.

[33] Art 2(2) TFEU.

[34] See eg the Opinion of Mazák AG in Case C-440/05 *Commission v Council* [2007] ECR I-9097, point 46, who refers to the distinction between the former first (Community) and second (CFSP) pillars as 'the line between what is essentially the Community method, characterising the "hard core" of European integration under the European Communities, and the more "intergovernmental" policies and forms of cooperation established by the EU Treaty'.

precisely that: a method. The essence and object of European integration is subjecting
Member State action to the rule of law, which in itself is also a means to an ultimate end,
namely the liberty of individual human beings.[35] The equation of progress in rule of law
constraints on the Union and the Member States with the ordinary Union method has
prevented the rule of law from becoming effective in areas of policy that do not fit
within the ordinary Union method, notably the common foreign and security policy
(CFSP). This chapter argues that one of the principal reasons why the CFSP does not fit
within the ordinary Union method, is the—perceived or actual—lack of rule-governed
behaviour of other international actors, which arguably induces Member States to
accept as few as possible internal or external rule of law constraints on their international actions.[36] There is therefore an intimate connection between the international
rule of law and the rule of law at the level of the EU and of the Member States.

Finally, the conception of the rule of law espoused by the present chapter is not one
of simply 'rule by a rule-book', but fundamentally of a constitutional principle
regarding the appropriate functions of institutions.[37] As noted by Waldron, principles
(such as the rule of law) 'cannot conduct distributions by themselves: they must be
administered by working institutions', and 'to the extent that the avoidance of injustice
is a moral imperative, the establishment of coordinating institutions is a moral
imperative'.[38] The establishment of the Union and its institutions and the rule of
law as the cornerstone of that project of European integration are to be understood
against that background.

3 Integration Through Law: The Ordinary Union Method

Article 2 EU in its post-Lisbon version states that the Union is founded on, *inter alia*,
the rule of law. Furthermore, Article 21(1) EU provides for the Union's action on the
international scene to be guided by the principles which have inspired its own creation,
development, and enlargement and which it seeks to advance in the wider world,
among which figures the rule of law. In other words, the EU Treaty makes two
assertions: on the one hand, that the EU is founded on the rule of law, and on the
other hand that that foundational value guides the international action of the Union.

---

[35] Cf Allan, see n 2, 2.

[36] This chapter does not deny that foreign policy is in many states subject to internal and/or external rule of
law constraints. The argument is merely that the perceived or actual lack of rule of law constraints at the
international level arguably provides a reason for states to minimize the rule of law constraints on their own
international acts.

[37] See P Eleftheriadis, Chapter 7 in the present volume.

[38] J Waldron, 'Special Ties and Natural Duties' (1993) 22 *Philosophy & Public Affairs* 15 and 28. Cf
P Eleftheriadis, *Legal Rights* (Oxford: Oxford University Press, 2008), 56, arguing that the creation of legal
institutions is a matter of a special moral duty and that the successful function of law is therefore a distinct
moral requirement.

This chapter examines both of these assertions and argues that there is an intimate link between them.

As a preliminary remark, it should be noted that the rule of law did not appear in the original Treaties. The concept was only introduced by the Treaty of Maastricht, first in what was then Article J.1(2) EU (on the CFSP) and in Article 130u(2) EC (on development cooperation).[39] In other words, the rule of law as a concept was first introduced explicitly in the Treaties as regards external relations. After the Lisbon Treaty, the rule of law can now be found in the EU Treaty, but not in the Treaty on the Functioning of the EU (FEU Treaty or TFEU). That would seem to follow the logic of the EU Treaty as the basic treaty setting out the constitutional principles of the EU, with the FEU Treaty setting out the more substantive policies.[40] The rule of law is now mentioned in the second and fourth recitals in the preamble to the EU Treaty, as well as in Articles 2, which lists the rule of law among the values on which the Union is founded, 21(1), which lists the principles by which the Union's action on the international scene is to be guided, and 21(2), which lists the objectives for the pursuit of which the Union is to define and pursue common policies and actions, and to work for a high degree of cooperation in all fields of international relations. Nonetheless, the concept has always been implicit in the EU legal order.[41]

The project of European integration is essentially one of legalization.[42] European integration is an attempt to infuse often destructive political processes with law in order to prevent war[43] and to infuse international relations with predictability—not for the sake of the states taking part in those inter-state relations, but for the sake of the individuals who make up the states and for the sake of whom states ultimately exist. Making international relations more predictable allows individuals the freedom to live the lives of their choice and make plans without having to worry about war or any form of discretionary and illegitimate use of governmental power impinging on those plans.[44] That important link between constraint on governmental powers and the

---

[39] After the Amsterdam Treaty, these became ex Art 11(1) EU and ex Art 177(2) EC, respectively. Both articles were amended by the Lisbon Treaty (becoming Arts 24 EU and 208 TFEU, respectively) the effect of which was to remove the explicit referral to the rule of law, which is subsumed under the general objectives of the Union's external action in Art 21 EU.

[40] That distinction only goes so far, as the FEU Treaty sets out the categories of competences (Arts 2–6 TFEU), which are clearly of general constitutional significance for the entire Union.

[41] A Arnull, 'The Rule of Law in the European Union' in AM Arnull and D Wincott (eds), *Accountability and Legitimacy in the European Union* (Oxford: Oxford University Press, 2002), 239–41.

[42] Cf eg M Cappelletti, M Seccombe, and JHH Weiler (eds), *Integration Through Law. Europe and the American Federal Experience* (Berlin: Walter de Gruyter, 1986).

[43] See Art 3(1) EU: 'The Union's aim is to promote peace, its values and the well-being of its peoples.' Cf Shklar, see n 12, 5: 'The ultimate spiritual and political struggle is always between war and law', viewing this as integral to Montesquieu's conception of the rule of law; and S Pinker, *The Better Angels of Our Nature: The Decline of Violence in History and Its Causes* (London: Allen Lane, 2011), arguing that the 'international entity with the best track record for implementing world peace is probably not the United Nations, but the European Coal and Steel Community...'.

[44] Cf Waldron, see n 18, 338.

rights of individuals was expressed by the Court of Justice in its seminal *Van Gend & Loos* judgment:[45]

> ... [T]he Community constitutes a new legal order of international law for the benefit of which the states have limited their sovereign rights, albeit within limited fields, and the subjects of which comprise not only Member States but also their nationals. Independently of the legislation of Member States, Community law therefore not only imposes obligations on individuals but is also intended to confer upon them rights which become part of their legal heritage.

The EU is therefore essentially a society in which law has been the main building material. It is a system constructed on the basis of law, which has created its own distinctive legal system, and which is dominated by law in its everyday functioning.[46] The approach chosen for that project of legalization was both classic and novel.

The approach was classic in that, especially after the failure of the European Defence Community (EDC),[47] the method chosen was that of market integration and free trade.[48] The idea of achieving peace through trade liberalization is not novel. Kant argued that peace among nations could be achieved by relying on their 'mutual self-interest'. Allowing free trade among nations and creating commercial links between citizens of different nations will promote peace, 'for the spirit of commerce sooner or later takes hold of every people, and it cannot exist side by side with war. ... Thus states find themselves compelled to promote the noble cause of peace, though not exactly from motives of morality'.[49] The rule of law in turn enhances certainty, predictability,

---

[45] Case 26/62 *Van Gend en Loos v Administratie der Belastingen ('Van Gend en Loos')* [1963] ECR 1.

[46] P Allott, 'The Concept of European Union' in A Dashwood and A Ward (eds) (Oxford and Portland, OR: Hart Publishing, 2000) 2 *The Cambridge Ybk of Eur Legal Studies* 1999 37 and 46.

[47] On which M Trybus, 'The Vision of the European Defence Community and a Common Defence for the European Union' in M Trybus and N White (eds), *European Security Law* (Oxford: Oxford University Press, 2007), 13–42; and D Scannell, 'Third Time Lucky: The Pre-history of the Common Security and Defence Policy' in A Arnull, C Barnard, M Dougan, and E Spaventa (eds), *A Constitutional Order of States? Essays in EU Law in Honour of Alan Dashwood* (Oxford and Portland, OR: Hart Publishing, 2011), 565–88.

[48] De Baere, see n 6, 220–1. Cf A Williams, *The Ethos of Europe: Values, Law and Justice in the EU* (Cambridge: Cambridge University Press, 2010), 64, calling this 'a brilliant if not original response to the age old rivalries of European history'.

[49] I Kant, *Perpetual Peace: A Philosophical Sketch* (1795, HS Reiss (ed), Cambridge: Cambridge University Press, 2003), 114, adding that '[i]n this way, nature guarantees perpetual peace by the actual mechanism of human inclinations'. Perreau-Saussine, see n 16, 54, notes that Kant's essay, structured 'as if itself a peace treaty aims to show how writing books really *could* challenge a prince's confidence in his own wisdom, and as such help to transform a perpetual state of war into one of perpetual peace'. See also CL de Secondat, Baron de La Brède et de Montesquieu, *The Spirit of the Laws* (1748, AM Cohler, BC Miller, and HS Stone (eds), Cambridge: Cambridge University Press, 1989), Book 20, ch 2: 'The natural effect of commerce is to lead to peace.' See also Pinker, see n 43, 284–94 on whether the post-SecondWorld War 'Long Peace' is liberal and Kantian. The idea of 'peace through trade' can be found in much of modern international law and institutions not in the least in the GATT/WTO and the EU: S Marks, *The Riddle of All Constitutions: International Law, Democracy and the Critique of Ideology* (Oxford: Oxford University Press, 2000), 35; and G De Baere and I Van Damme, 'Co-adaptation in the International Legal Order: The EU And The WTO' in J Crawford and S Nouwen (eds), *Select Proceedings of the European Society of International Law, Volume 3, 2010* (Oxford and Portland, OR: Hart Publishing, 2011), 311–25.

and security and thereby benefits market economies, *inter alia* by protecting contracts and property.[50]

The approach was, however, also novel in that European integration substituted the strategy of dealing with a political problem (the prevention of war in Europe) through economic means for that of dealing with economics through politics.[51] European integration became a functional enterprise,[52] or it was, at least from an internal perspective, perceived as such. That strategy could be described as a successful example of politics by dissociation: political problems are solved not directly by confronting them as such, but indirectly, by dealing with them as economic and hence technical ones.[53]

This approach carries within it the seeds both of its undeniable success in doing exactly what it said on the tin, that is, bringing peace in Europe, and of some of the problematic aspects of European integration. Indeed, the Community quickly found out that political problems could not be made to go away by not confronting them directly. The political character of the Community's policies, in particular its external aspects, moved the Member States to attach political forums to its technical core, first through the European Political Cooperation (EPC),[54] and after Maastricht through the CFSP. The Community's success, however, was based on its technicality, and the political aspects of foreign policy were not integrated in the paradigmatic Community. This forced the Community to re-invent itself as a divided subject: the Union. By its very nature, the Community was thus not well equipped to confront political problems directly. The 'technocratic' approach that seems to work so well in the 'technical' core business does not work nearly as well outside that core. It also prompts questions with regard to transparency and democratic accountability. Deficiencies in that regard may impact upon the stability of the rule of law in the EU,[55] as both democratic government and the rule of law may be traced back to an ideal of equal liberty and dignity of citizens. Legal systems that fail to elicit the consent of their subjects must therefore be

---

[50] Tamanaha, see n 11 9; Walker, see n 2, 123. The link between the rule of law and the free market was already present in A Smith, *An Inquiry into the Nature and Causes of the Wealth of Nations* (London: Strahan and Cadell, 1776).

[51] As notably proposed by Aristide Briand in 1929: M Koskenniemi, *The Gentle Civilizer of Nations: The Rise and Fall of International Law 1870–1960* (Cambridge: Cambridge University Press, 2002), 342.

[52] Koskenniemi, see n 51, 347, adding that in so doing, European integration 'effectively set aside federalist views that were based on political or moral axioms, generalizations about human nature or the good society'. A Verhoeven, *The European Union in Search of a Democratic and Constitutional Theory* (The Hague, London, and New York: Kluwer Law International, 2002), 111, questions the assumption that an important part of positive integration such as the completion of the common market can be achieved in a non-political way, by following a logic of rationality and efficiency alone.

[53] De Baere, see n 6, 221. Mannheim would possibly have pointed out that this is part of what bureaucracy does: 'The fundamental tendency of all bureaucratic thought is to turn all problems of politics into problems of administration': K Mannheim, *Ideology and Utopia. An Introduction to the Sociology of Knowledge* (London: Routledge & Kegan Paul, 1936), 105.

[54] On which: M Smith, *Europe's Foreign and Security Policy: The Institutionalization of Cooperation* (Cambridge: Cambridge University Press, 2004), 63–175.

[55] Walker, see n 2, 134–5.

regarded as substandard instances of the ideal to which they aspire.[56] However, without denying their eminent importance, this chapter does not examine in detail the problematic aspects of the democratic accountability of the Union. Instead it focuses on the consequences that the integration method chosen had on the legalization of the policy most resistant to rule of law constraints: the CFSP. Specifically, the role of the Court of Justice within the CFSP will be examined as an example of how the confusion between the ordinary Union method and its *ratio*, that is, establishing the rule of law in Europe, has led to the failure of the imposition of rule of law constraints on the Member States' foreign policies, and a failure of the operation of the rule of law within the CFSP. Conversely, imagining a broader role of the Court of Justice without expanding the ordinary Union method in its entirety will be explained as an example of how the rule of law as the cornerstone of European integration can be advanced without necessarily using the ordinary Union method with all its trappings.

4 *Extra Communitatem nulla salus*: the particularity of the CFSP

(A) The nature of the CFSP

Considered too political for the Community, the CFSP was created by the Maastricht Treaty in a separate second pillar. This entails a number of striking particularities. First, the way in which competences are attributed within the CFSP is very different from how they are attributed in ordinary Union policies: the technique of detailed and specific attribution of competences typical of the Community and now of policies in the FEU Treaty, is absent in the CFSP. Second, CFSP legal instruments are essentially used for making executive decisions legally binding, which explains the absence of any legislative character in most (though not all) of them. Third, the particularity of CFSP decision making lies in the predominance of the institutions in which the Member States are directly represented: the European Council and the Council. Moreover, the Court of Justice lacks jurisdiction within the CFSP.[57] Finally, neither the Commission nor the Parliament have any real supervisory powers over the Council or the Member States as regards CFSP action. This makes the EU operate much more like an 'ordinary' international organization in the CFSP than under the other Union policies.[58]

The dearth of normative constraints such as detailed and specific attribution and legislation and the absence of judicial review appear particularly relevant from a rule of law perspective. The CFSP seems to have scarce characteristics of positive general norms that govern the actions of the Member States and of the Union.[59]

---

[56] Allan, see n 2, 29 and 65.   [57] With two exceptions: see below.   [58] See De Baere, see n 6, 101–58.
[59] Waldron, see n 10, 28, argues that this requirement of 'positivity' is one of the main characteristics of a legal system.

CFSP legal instruments as a rule do not envisage legislative action in a direct way like regulations, or in an indirect way, by aiming to harmonize Member State legislation, in the manner of directives. Indeed, the second subparagraph of Article 24(1) EU explicitly provides that the adoption of legislative acts[60] within the CFSP is to be excluded. This touches upon one of the central elements of the nature of foreign policy. The CFSP operates with a *modus operandi* rather different from the norm-creating and norm-applying pursuant to the ordinary Union method. The Union is not unique as regards this specificity of foreign policy-making, which seems to be largely conducted through executive measures, rather than through legislation.[61] That is so because foreign policy is not as easily susceptible to legislative instruments setting out norms for international behaviour, given the difficulty in gathering information about external affairs and the need to preserve flexibility in the face of changing circumstances. As argued, part of those unpredictably changing circumstances consists of the dearth of rule-governed behaviour by actors on the international level.

However, some CFSP legal instruments do contain obligations for the Member States to take legislative action or to harmonize their legislation, and therefore bear a distinct resemblance to such legislative instruments as a directive, and a growing number of CFSP legal instruments have substantial consequences not only for the Union and the Member States, but also for individuals.[62] Despite that, the fact that the CFSP was kept out of the Community also meant that it was kept outside the jurisdiction of the Court of Justice.

(B) The Shifting Sands of the Law: The Rule of Law and the Role of the Court in the CFSP

The possibility of access to an independent judiciary and of judicial review is an essential aspect in most understandings of the rule of law.[63] The Union's professed

---

[60] Art 289(3) TFEU provides that legal acts adopted by legislative procedure (ie the ordinary legislative procedure (Arts 289(1) and 294 TFEU) or a special legislative procedure (Art 289(2) TFEU)) are to constitute legislative acts.

[61] For a diagnosis of the reasons for this dominance of the executive in foreign relations: P Allott, *Eunomia: New Order For a New World* (Oxford: Oxford University Press, 2001), 279, paras 15.45ff, especially paras 15.47–15.48.

[62] eg Council Decision 2012/285/CFSP of 31 May 2012 concerning restrictive measures directed against certain persons, entities and bodies threatening the peace, security or stability of the Republic of Guinea-Bissau and repealing Decision 2012/237/CFSP [2012] OJ L142/36.

[63] On the merits and demerits of judicial review: J Waldron, 'The Core of the Case against Judicial Review' (2006) *Yale LJ* 1346–406; R Fallon, 'The Core of an Uneasy Case For Judicial Review' (2008) *Harvard L Rev* 1693–763; M Tushnet, 'How Different are Waldron's and Fallon's Core Cases For and Against Judicial Review?' (2010) 30 OJLS 49–70; CF Zurn, *Deliberative Democracy and the Institutions of Judicial Review* (Cambridge: Cambridge University Press, 2007); WJ Waluchow, *A Common Law Theory of Judicial Review: The Living Tree* (Cambridge: Cambridge University Press, 2009). Cf J Rawls, *Political Liberalism*, Expanded edn (New York, NY: Columbia University Press, 2005), 339, arguing that a constitution specifying a just political procedure and incorporating restrictions which protect the basic liberties and secure their priority, while the rest is left to the legislator, conforms to the traditional idea of democratic government, while allowing a place for the institution of judicial review.

attachment to the rule of law in both its internal and its external policies thus prompts the question to what extent judicial review plays a role in the Union's foreign policy.[64] The judiciary's crucial role in a democratic system of preventing discrepancy between the law as declared and as administered[65] makes the courts an obvious focal point for a discussion of the rule of law in the EU.

The core meaning of the rule of law, that is, that no authority should remain unchecked by law, applies as much to the Union as it does to the Member States. The Community was, and the Union is, 'based on the rule of law, inasmuch as neither its Member States nor its institutions can avoid a review of the question whether the measures adopted by them are in conformity with the basic constitutional charter, the Treaty'.[66] An important aspect thereof is that the Union is an organization based on conferred competences,[67] that is, the Union and its institutions can only act when allowed to do so by the Treaties and hence by a framework of law. It would have been inconsonant with the legal traditions of the Member States for institutions enjoying such far-reaching competences to have escaped judicial control.[68] The Court of Justice has therefore from the start provided judicial protection in case of a violation of EU law. Its task is to ensure that in the interpretation and application of the Treaties the law is observed.[69] However, the Maastricht Treaty excluded the jurisdiction of the Court from the CFSP, except for its jurisdiction under ex Article 47 EU of ensuring that CFSP acts capable of having legal effects did not encroach upon the powers conferred on the Community.[70] The possibility also existed of subjecting CFSP measures to an indirect judicial review in cases where CFSP acts were implemented by Community acts.[71] A specific problem arose where persons or entities were originally listed in a UN Security Council resolution and the EU was merely implementing such a UN listing. That issue will be addressed in the next section.

---

[64] Cf the Opinion of Mengozzi AG in Case C-354/04 P *Gestoras Pro Amnistía and Others v Council* ('*Gestoras*') [2007] ECR I-1579 and Case C-355/04 *SEGI and Others v Council* ('*SEGI*') [2007] ECR I-1657, point 77.

[65] Fuller, see n 11, 81; cf Waldron, see n 10, 20, arguing that absent the existence and operation of the sort of institutions we call courts, something should not be regarded as a legal system. See also Allan, n 2, 43; and Jacobs, n 7, 35.

[66] Case 294/83 *Parti écologiste 'Les Verts' v European Parliament* [1986] ECR 1339, para 23. See also Joined Cases C-402/05 P and C-415/05 P *Kadi and Al Barakaat International Foundation v Council and Commission* ('*ECJ Kadi I*') [2008] ECR I-6351, para 81; and, most recently, Case C-533/10 *Compagnie internationale pour la vente à distance (CIVAD) SA v Receveur des douanes de Roubaix and Others* ('*CIVAD*') [2012] ECR I-0000, para 30.

[67] Arts 5(2) EU and 13(2) EU. These two articles could be said to reflect the idea of a *Rechtsstaat*. The latter is generally held to contain both the separation of powers and the principle of legality. Cf Allan, see n 2, 2–3, 56. See already Montesquieu, n 49, Book 6, ch 6.

[68] Lord Mackenzie Stuart, *The European Communities and the Rule of Law* (London: Stevens, 1977), 6–14.

[69] Art 19(1) EU.

[70] See eg Case C-91/05 *Commission v Council* [2008] ECR I-3651.

[71] See eg Case C-550/09 *E and F* [2010] ECR I-6213. For further potential avenues for judicial review, see A Hinarejos, *Judicial Control in the European Union: Reforming Jurisdiction in the Intergovernmental Pillars* (Oxford: Oxford University Press, 2009), 128–49; and De Baere, see n 6, 177–88.

The Court's role in the CFSP has not fundamentally changed after the Treaty of Lisbon. Articles 24(1) EU and 275 TFEU exclude the Court's jurisdiction in the CFSP, except 'to rule on proceedings, brought in accordance with the conditions laid down in the fourth paragraph of Article 263 [TFEU], reviewing the legality of decisions providing for restrictive measures against natural or legal persons adopted by the Council [within the CFSP]', and policing the borderline between CFSP and other Union policies pursuant to Article 40 EU,[72] the successor to ex Article 47 EU.[73]

It is to be welcomed that Article 275 TFEU gives the Court jurisdiction to review the legality of CFSP decisions providing for restrictive measures against natural or legal persons. Such an extension of jurisdiction had become necessary from the point of view of fundamental rights[74] and the rule of law. However, there are no other avenues for the Court to provide judicial protection within the CFSP, for example through references for a preliminary ruling,[75] actions for damages,[76] or infringement proceedings.[77] Moreover, any direct action brought by an individual[78] will be subject to the *locus standi* requirements of Article 263(4) TFEU: a challenge is only possible with respect to an act addressed to that person or that is of direct and individual concern to him or her, and against a regulatory act that is of direct concern to him or her and does not entail implementing measures. When a measure explicitly lists a person as the target of restrictive measures, that threshold to *locus standi* should normally not be a problem.[79] However, individuals affected by restrictive measures while not listed *nominatim* will face the usual uphill struggle. Moreover, in case of an CFSP measure affecting individuals and needing implementation by Member States, the individual would be left to rely on the competent national courts, on the assumption that they would not be barred from assuming jurisdiction under national law.[80] If the national court does assume jurisdiction, it cannot ask the Court of Justice for help in interpreting the CFSP measure at issue, which would be likely to affect the internal coherence of the EU legal order.[81]

---

[72] Arts 24(1) EU and 275 TFEU.

[73] Art 40 EU now prohibits any mutual invasion of territory between the 'Union competences referred to in Articles 3 to 6 of the Treaty on the Functioning of the European Union' (*viz* the former first pillar competences) and the CFSP.

[74] Especially the right to an effective remedy as guaranteed by Art 6 ECHR and Art 47 of the Charter of Fundamental Rights of the EU.

[75] Art 267 TFEU.

[76] Arts 268 and 340 TFEU; cf K Gutman, 'The Evolution of the Action for Damages Against the European Union and Its Place in the System of Judicial Protection' (2011) 48 CML Rev 700–1.

[77] Arts 258–260 TFEU.

[78] Note that Article 275 TFEU refers to 'proceedings, brought in accordance with the conditions laid down in the fourth paragraph of Article 263 [TFEU]', ie proceedings brought by individuals. That appears, rather anomalously, to exclude privileged applicants (Member States, the European Parliament, the Council, and the Commission) from bringing such an action: Hinarejos, see n 71, 158–9.

[79] eg T-253/04 *Kongra-Gel and Others v Council* [2008] ECR II-46, paras 77–78.

[80] Though see the second subparagraph of Art 19(1) EU, which obliges Member States to 'provide remedies sufficient to ensure effective legal protection in the fields covered by Union law'.

[81] Hinarejos, see n 71, 166.

The Court itself has acknowledged that, while its jurisdiction in the former third pillar was less extensive than under the first pillar,[82] '[i]t is even less extensive under [the CFSP]', adding that '[w]hile a system of legal remedies, in particular a body of rules governing non-contractual liability, other than that established by the treaties can indeed be envisaged, it is for the Member States, should the case arise, to reform the system currently in force in accordance with Article 48 EU'.[83]

However, even where the absence of judicial review in the CFSP is identified as a fundamental problem for the rule of law in the Union, it is often considered not to be a decisive argument in itself, given the similar position of foreign policy matters within the constitutional systems of many states. Foreign policy questions are considered non-justiciable in many jurisdictions, given the complexity and the sensitivity of the issues at hand.[84] While substantive judicial review in foreign policy matters within any constitutional system is very uncommon indeed,[85] this should not distract from fundamental questions about the implications of this constitutional position of foreign policy for *any* entity—state, international organization, or otherwise—that presents itself as subject to the rule of law. The EU probably does not differ much from other constitutional systems with regard to the absence of substantive judicial review of foreign policy decisions, but this does not answer the question of the implications of this absence for the characterization of the EU as based on the rule of law, in the same way that it does not make this question disappear with regard to any other constitutional system.[86]

The absence of judicial review also poses a potential problem for the Union's compliance with the international rule of law. In combination with the fact that there is little or no possibility for the Union in general, and the Commission in particular, to ensure compliance of the Member States with CFSP acts, the absence of judicial review might lead third countries to doubt whether the Member States can be made to comply at all. In other words, doubts may be cast on the predictability of the international behaviour of the Union, which may in turn have an impact on the international action of the third countries and international organizations dealing with the Union. This could damage the credibility of the Union as a reliable partner, as well as create problems with regard to the international responsibility of the Union and the Member States. There would therefore be scope for an enforcement jurisdiction of the Court of Justice, akin to the one existing for the ordinary Union policies pursuant to Articles 258 to 260 TFEU. The lack of such a procedure under the current constitutional system is liable to damage the abilities of the Union as an international actor.[87]

---

[82] And still is during a transitional period, pursuant to Art 10 of Protocol No 36, annexed to the TEU, TFEU and EAEC Treaty, on Transitional Provisions [2010] OJ C83/322.

[83] See *Gestoras,* see n 64, para 50 and *SEGI* see n 64, para 50.

[84] W van Gerven, *The European Union: A Polity of States and Peoples* (Oxford and Portland, OR: Hart Publishing, 2005), 120.

[85] Cf T Koopmans, *Courts and Political Institutions: A Comparative View* (Cambridge: Cambridge University Press, 2003), 98–104. In general: Franck, see n 23.

[86] De Baere, see n 6, 200.   [87] De Baere, see n 6, 200.

The argument for limiting the role of the judiciary in foreign policy is partly the same as for limiting the role of parliament: the need to be able to react quickly and efficiently to international developments.[88] That justification assumes that there is a scarce amount of law on the international scene to provide the desired predictability. This does not, however, prevent the courts in many of the world's democratic systems from playing a role in external relations, even though the extent of this role differs. Constitutional systems that do allow the judiciary to get involved often limit its functions to arbitrating competence quarrels between different levels of government, and scrutinizing international agreements on their compliance with the constitution.[89]

Noteworthy in that regard is Advocate General Jacobs' response to the Commission's argument that the embargo established by Greece against the Former Yugoslav Republic of Macedonia (FYROM) would increase rather than decrease tension between the two countries and would thus have detrimental consequences for the internal and external security of Greece: such a line of argument was based on a political appreciation of an eminently political subject. It was simply not possible to apply any legal standards to determine what the wisest course of action for Greece under the circumstances would be.[90] The Advocate General here identified a clear example of a situation on which courts are probably not properly equipped to pass judgment.[91] Indeed, it is probably fair to say that no institution is completely equipped to judge what the repercussions of such actions as taken by Greece would be on the international scene.

Has Advocate General Jacobs hereby introduced a 'political question doctrine' into the EU legal order?[92] Perhaps so, but only a political question doctrine 'lite'.[93] Indeed, while the Advocate General emphasized that there are no legal standards to review the

---

[88] For a rebuttal of many of the 'prudential' arguments ('courts are ill-equipped to deal with foreign policy') against a role for the judiciary in foreign policy: Franck, see n 23, 45–60. But see the dissenting opinion of Breyer J in *Zivotofsky v Clinton*, 566 U.S. _(2012): 'Decision making in this area typically is highly political. It is "delicate" and "complex." *Chicago & Southern Air Lines*, 333 U. S., at 111. It often rests upon information readily available to the Executive Branch and to the intelligence committees of Congress, but not readily available to the courts. Ibid. It frequently is highly dependent upon what Justice Jackson called "prophecy." Ibid. And the creation of wise foreign policy typically lies well beyond the experience or professional capacity of a judge. Ibid. At the same time, where foreign affairs is at issue, the practical need for the United States to speak "with one voice and ac[t] as one," is particularly important.'

[89] eg, the United States Supreme Court and the German *Bundesverfasssungsgericht* refuse to abdicate automatically their role as constitutional arbiters as soon as any question of foreign policy arises, albeit that their approach is rather different: see Franck, n 23; specifically on Germany: and 107–25, noting for example that for the German courts, the issue is not '*whether* but *how* judges should decide'. See also Hinarejos, n 71, 169–71, on Germany and France.

[90] Opinion in Case C-120/94 *Commission v Greece*, removed from the register [1996] ECR I-1513, points 59 and 65.

[91] See, for a similar argument, the Opinion of Kokott AG in Case C-420/07 *Apostolides* [2009] ECR I-3571, points 43–48, and G De Baere, 'Case C-420/07, Meletis Apostolides v. David Charles Orams, Linda Elizabeth Orams, Judgment of the Grand Chamber of 28 April 2009, [2009] ECR I-3571' (2010) 47 CML Rev 1135–6.

[92] Further on political questions in EU law eg K Lenaerts, *Le juge et la constitution aux États-Unis d'Amérique et dans l'ordre juridique européen* (Brussels: Bruylant, 1988), 440–58.

[93] De Baere, see n 6, 195–6.

substance of Greece's action to avoid the threat of war, he seemed equally adamant that such legal standards did exist with regard to the possibility of internal disturbances and accordingly brushed aside Greece's claims. The same should be true for independent measures that a Member State may be called upon to take in order to carry out obligations it has accepted for the purpose of maintaining peace and international security.[94] Legal analysis is clearly required in determining Member States' obligations under international law, and there would seem to be no reason why a court could not exercise judicial review in these circumstances, even if it would only be a marginal review.[95] Nonetheless, the Commission referred to the political question doctrine in the proceedings before the Court of Justice in *Kadi I*, which will be analysed in the next section.

A survey of the world's constitutional traditions suggests that courts tend not to get involved in substantive foreign policy decisions and leave the political institutions (normally the executive) a considerable margin of discretion, although the desirability and extent of this margin is open to discussion.[96] While a comprehensive substantive review of CFSP measures would be problematic, it is difficult to maintain that a procedural review, of which examples in other areas of EU law exist,[97] would be equally unimaginable.

Fear of granting the Court a role in the CFSP is often based on a conception of the Court as activist and integrationist, and a concern that it might extend this approach to sensitive areas of foreign policy. However, 'activism' must not be confused with constitutional adjudication,[98] which arguably requires a Court equally to take into account the principles on which the legal order in question is founded. More in general, adjudication may appear to be only partly a matter of the application of law when in penumbral cases reference is made to principles rather than clearly identifiable rules. However, if we think of law and of the rule of law as an ideal imperfectly

---

[94] Art 347 TFEU (ex Art 297 EC).

[95] P Eeckhout, *EU External Relations Law*, 2nd edn (Oxford: Oxford University Press, 2011), 545.

[96] eg, as regards the US, *Zivotofsky v Clinton*, 566 US (2012): 'We have explained that a controversy "involves a political question...where there is 'a textually demonstrable constitutional commitment of the issue to a coordinate political department; or a lack of judicially discoverable and manageable standards for resolving it.'" *Nixon v United States*, 506 U.S. 224, 228 (1993) (quoting *Baker v Carr*, 369 U. S. 186, 217 (1962))' (Roberts CJ delivering the opinion of the Court). Further: L Henkin, 'Is There a Political Question Doctrine?' (1976) 85 *Yale LJ* 597–625; Franck, see n 23; J Nzelibe, 'The Uniqueness of Foreign Affairs' (2004) 89 *Iowa L Rev* 941–1009; R Fallon, 'Judicially Manageable Standards and Constitutional Meaning' (2006) 119 *Harvard L Rev* 1274–332. In general: Allan, see n 2, 161–99; and TRS Allan, 'Judicial Deference and Judicial Review: Legal doctrine and legal theory' (2011) 127 LQR 96–117.

[97] eg Case 191/82 *Fediol v Commission* [1983] ECR 2913, para 30; Case 187/85 *Fediol v Commission* [1988] ECR 4155, para 6; Case C-121/86 *Anonymos Etaireia Epichirisseon Metalleftikon Viomichanikon kai Naftiliakon AE and Others v Council* [1989] ECR 3919, para 8. Cf the Opinion of Jacobs AG in Case C-70/94 *Werner v Germany* [1995] ECR I-3189, point 45, arguing that judicial review as regards an assessment of whether the export of certain dual-use goods could raise security concerns 'is confined to ensuring that manifest errors of appraisal have not occurred and that national authorities have not abused the powers conferred [...]'.

[98] FG Jacobs, 'Is the Court of Justice of the European Communities a Constitutional Court?' in DM Curtin and D O'Keeffe (eds), *Constitutional Adjudication in European Community and National Law: Essays for the Hon. Mr. Justice O'Higgins* (Dublin: Butterworth, 1992), 32.

incarnated by existing legal systems, legal reasoning can be considered as guided by fidelity to that idea of law. The guiding idea will then be capable of exerting its influence 'beyond the "core of settled meaning" of the rules'.[99] By and large, the Court of Justice's case law can be explained in that light.[100]

The equation of integration with the ordinary Union method—a result of the original Community's place as the paradigmatic core of the Union—appears to be an example of a false dichotomy, whereby alternatives are presented in terms of stark oppositions, in which one alternative and its polar opposite appear as the only options (the ordinary Union method is the only way to make progress in European integration, so either we apply the ordinary Union method to the CFSP or no progress can be made). It rules out moderate intermediate possibilities and makes change seem unfeasible, leading to a confirmation of the existing situation.[101] The apparent impossibility of fundamentally reconsidering the Court of Justice's role in the CFSP can be regarded as partly a result of this approach. The debate on the Court's jurisdiction is often seen by the Member States as so inherently linked to the debate on the extension of the ordinary Union method to the CFSP, that the former can hardly be imagined without the latter. More moderate possibilities, of for example a limited or procedural judicial review, are left unconsidered. While it is true that they are more present in the first than in the second pillar, it does not follow that the only way to attain more accountability and more compliance with the rule of law over the whole field of foreign policy is to apply the ordinary Union method in its entirety to the CFSP.[102]

As argued, an important reason for the lack of normative standards and of judicial review, and hence the reason why the Member States regarded the CFSP as 'too political' to be integrated within the Community, is the perceived or actual dearth of satisfactory rule of law standards at the international level, and hence the lack of predictability on the international plane. The Union and the Member States therefore wish to be constrained as little as possible when they are acting in international fora. Nevertheless, the common commercial policy (Arts 206–207 TFEU) essentially applies the idea of free trade for peace to trade with third states and therefore falls within the original Community paradigm. That is arguably precisely because international trade is subject to a more rigorous application of the international rule of law, especially through the WTO. However, even in international trade the willingness of the Union and its Member States to subject themselves to external rule of law constraints reaches

---

[99] Simmonds, see n 10, 189. Compare as regards 'constitutional cases' R Dworkin, *Taking Rights Seriously* (London: Duckworth, 1977), 131–49 and in general R Dworkin, *Law's Empire* (Oxford and Portland, OR: Hart Publishing, 1986).

[100] Cf J Bengoetxea, N MacCormick, and L Moral Soriano, 'Integration and Integrity in the Legal Reasoning of the European Court of Justice' in G de Búrca and JHH Weiler (eds), *The European Court of Justice* (Oxford: Oxford University Press, 2001), 43–85. Further: E Sharpston and G De Baere, 'The Court of Justice as a Constitutional Adjudicator' in A Arnull, C Barnard, M Dougan, and E Spaventa (eds), *A Constitutional Order of States? Essays in EU Law in Honour of Alan Dashwood* (Oxford and Portland, OR: Hart Publishing, 2011), 123–50.

[101] Cf Marks, n 49, 22.   [102] De Baere, n 6, 226–7.

its limits when these standards are considered insufficiently rigorous, which in turn leads to defects in internal Union rule of law standards.[103]

The perceived or actual dearth of satisfactory rule of law standards at the international level has also had an impact on the compliance of the Union with the international legal standards in place, in that the EU has challenged the external rule of law standards on the international plane on the basis of its internal rule of law. That issue will now be examined within the context of the possibility for the Court of subjecting CFSP measures to an indirect judicial review in cases where CFSP acts were implemented by Community acts while the CFSP measure in question was in turn merely implementing a UN Security Council resolution. While the next section therefore concerns the review of 'first pillar measures', their judicial review by the Court implies a measure of control over the way in which CFSP competences are generally exercised and amounts to judicial protection within the realm of the CFSP *sensu lato*.[104]

5 The Mutual Impact of the International Rule of Law and the Rule of Law within the Union: the *Kadi* Saga

Pursuant to Article 3(5) EU, the Union is to contribute to 'the strict observance and the development of international law, including respect for the principles of the United Nations Charter'. The Court of Justice has interpreted that provision as obliging the Union 'to observe international law in its entirety, including customary international law, which is binding upon the institutions of the European Union'.[105] The Court has

---

[103] An (in)famous example is the lack of direct effect of WTO law in EU law. See eg Case C-149/96 *Portugal v Council* [1999] ECR I-8395, para 46: 'To accept that the role of ensuring that Community law complies with [WTO] rules devolves directly on the Community judicature would deprive the legislative or executive organs of the Community of the scope for manoeuvre enjoyed by their counterparts in the Community's trading partners.' For the latest episode in that saga: Joined Cases C-120/06 P and C-121/06 P *FIAMM and FIAMM Technologies and Fedon & Figli and Fedon America v Council and Commission* [2008] ECR I-6513, in which the Court *inter alia* held that notwithstanding the expiry of the period of time allowed for implementing a decision of the WTO Dispute Settlement Body (DSB), the EU courts could not review the legality of the conduct of the EU institutions in the light of WTO rules (para 133); see M Dani, 'Remedying European Legal Pluralism: The *FIAMM* and *Fedon* Litigation and the Judicial Protection of International Trade Bystanders' (2010) 21 *Eur J Intl L* 303–40. See also, more recently, *CIVAD*, see n 66, paras 36–44, in which the Court held that since it alone has jurisdiction to declare an act of the EU invalid and the purpose of that jurisdiction is to ensure legal certainty through the uniform application of EU law, the fact that the DSB has found that an anti-dumping regulation is not in accordance with the Agreement on Implementation of Article VI of the General Agreement on Tariffs and Trade 1994 [1994] OJ L336/103, does not affect the presumption that such a regulation is lawful.

[104] Hinarejos, see n 71, 133–4.

[105] Case C-366/10 *Air Transport Association of America and Others* [2012] OJ C49/7, para 101. See further G De Baere and C Ryngaert, '*Air Transport Association of America* and the EU's Contribution to the "Strict Observance And Development of International Law" ', in preparation for the *ICLQ*.

also held a number of times that the Union must respect international law in the exercise of its powers,[106] and that a measure adopted by virtue of those powers must be interpreted, and its scope limited, in the light of the relevant rules of international law.[107] Furthermore, the first paragraph of Article 21(1) EU provides for the Union's action on the international scene to be guided by the principles which have inspired its own creation, which include 'respect for the principles of the United Nations Charter and international law'. In other words, respect for the international rule of law is written into the basic constitutional charter of the Union.

However, what does it actually mean for the Union to respect the principles of the United Nations ('UN') Charter? The Union Courts were faced with that issue in the *Kadi* cases, in which an individual challenged the lawfulness, in the light of fundamental rights, of EU regulations ordering the freezing of his funds so as to give effect to a resolution adopted by the UN Security Council under Chapter VII of the UN Charter. In *Kadi I*, the General Court held that both international law and Union law required the Union institutions to implement the Security Council resolution, without there being any possibility of judicial review of the lawfulness of such implementing measure in the light of fundamental rights.[108] However, the Court of Justice set aside the judgment of the General Court, holding that the Union judicature must 'ensure the review, in principle the full review, of the lawfulness of all Community acts in the light of the fundamental rights forming an integral part of the general principles of Community law, including review of Community measures which, like the contested regulation, are designed to give effect to the resolutions adopted by the Security Council under Chapter VII of the Charter of the United Nations'.[109] The Court concluded that it was not a consequence of the principles governing the international legal order under the UN that any judicial review of the internal lawfulness of the contested regulation in the light of fundamental freedoms is excluded by virtue of the fact that that measure is intended to give effect to a resolution of the Security Council adopted under Chapter VII of the UN Charter.[110]

The Commission, the Council, and the United Kingdom had contended that the specific subject matter at issue in *Kadi I* did not lend itself to judicial review, claiming that the European Court of Human Rights (ECtHR) takes a similar position. The

---

[106] Case C-286/90 *Poulsen and Diva Navigation ('Poulsen')* [1992] ECR I-6019, para 9; Case C-162/96 *Racke* [1998] ECR I-3655, para 45; *ECJ Kadi I*, see n 66, para 291.

[107] *Poulsen*, see n 106, para 9; and *ECJ Kadi I*, see n 66, para 291.

[108] Case T-315/01 *Kadi v Council and Commission ('GC Kadi I')* [2005] ECR II-33649, paras 181–225; and Case T-301/01 *Yusuf and Al Barakaat International Foundation v Council and Commission* [2005] ECR II-3533. The General Court held that it could only indirectly check the lawfulness of the Security Council resolutions with regard to *ius cogens*, but found no breach (*GC Kadi I*, paras 226–291).

[109] *ECJ Kadi I* (n 66 above) para 326. See for a discussion, eg D Halberstam and E Stein, 'The United Nations, the European Union, and the King of Sweden: Economic Sanctions and Individual Rights in a Plural World Order' (2009) 46 CML Rev 13–72; T Tridimas and J Gutiérrez-Fons, 'EU Law, International Law and Economic Sanctions against Terrorism: The Judiciary in Distress?' (2009) *Fordham Intl LJ* 660–730; G de Búrca, 'The EU, the European Court of Justice and the International Legal Order after Kadi' (2009) *Harvard Intl LJ* 1–49.

[110] *ECJ Kadi I*, see n 66, paras 292–299.

Commission specifically referred to the concept of 'political questions'. Advocate General Poiares Maduro forcefully dismissed that claim:[111]

> The claim that a measure is necessary for the maintenance of international peace and security cannot operate so as to silence the general principles of Community law and deprive individuals of their fundamental rights. This does not detract from the importance of the interest in maintaining international peace and security; it simply means that it remains the duty of the courts to assess the lawfulness of measures that may conflict with other interests that are equally of great importance and with the protection of which the courts are entrusted.

The Advocate General acknowledged that extraordinary circumstances may justify restrictions on individual freedom that would be unacceptable under normal conditions, but added that such 'should not induce us to say that "there are cases in which a veil should be drawn for a while over liberty, as it was customary to cover the statues of the gods"'.[112]

The judgment of the Court of Justice in *Kadi I* has been one of the most commented on in the history of the Court, generating a veritable '*petite industrie*' of literature and dividing international and EU lawyers into camps of supporters and detractors cutting across both disciplines. Most notably, the Court has been obliquely but unmistakably criticized in the judgment of the General Court in *Kadi II*, brought by Mr Kadi essentially because the Council, in taking renewed restrictive measures against him, had not complied to a sufficient extent with the standard set out by the Court of Justice in *Kadi I*. After recalling that in the context of these new proceedings, it was not bound by the points of law decided by the Court of Justice in *Kadi I*, the General Court noted that 'certain doubts may have been voiced in legal circles as to whether the judgment of the Court of Justice in *Kadi* is wholly consistent with … international law … and … the EC and EU Treaties . . '.[113] In a rather remarkable couple of paragraphs, the General Court then went on to outline some of those doubts, and concluded that, while it acknowledged 'that those criticisms are not entirely without foundation, … in circumstances such as those of the present case … the appellate principle itself and the hierarchical judicial structure which is its corollary generally advise against the General Court revisiting points of law which have been decided by the Court of Justice. That is a fortiori the case when, as here, the Court of Justice was sitting in Grand Chamber formation and clearly intended to deliver a judgment establishing certain principles. Accordingly, if an answer is to be given to the questions raised by the institutions, Member States and interested legal quarters following the judgment of

---

[111] Opinion in *ECJ Kadi I*, see n 66, point 34, also referring to the dissenting opinion of Justice Murphy in US Supreme Court, *Korematsu v United States*, 323 US 214, 233–4 (1944). See also the Opinion of Sharpston AG in Case C-27/09 P *France v People's Mojahedin Organization of Iran* [2012] OJ C49/2, points 253–255.

[112] Opinion in *ECJ Kadi I*, see n 66, point 35, referring to Montesquieu, see n 49, Book 12, ch 19. The AG also (rightly) expressed serious doubt as to whether the claim on the limitation of the ECtHR's jurisdiction was correct (*ECJ Kadi I*, point 36).

[113] T-85/09 *Kadi v Commission* ('*GC Kadi II*') [2010] ECR II-5177, paras 112–115.

the Court of Justice in *Kadi*, it is for the Court of Justice itself to provide that answer in the context of future cases before it.'[114]

The General Court therefore considered that its task was to ensure 'in principle the full review' of the lawfulness of the contested regulation in the light of fundamental rights, without affording the regulation any immunity from jurisdiction on the ground that it gives effect to resolutions adopted by the Security Council under Chapter VII of the UN Charter. The General Court pointed out that that had to remain the case, at the very least, so long as the re-examination procedure operated by the Security Council's Sanctions Committee clearly fails to offer guarantees of effective judicial protection.[115] It then went on to clarify why it felt that that was the case. The General Court explained that what the Court of Justice had considered in *Kadi I* remained fundamentally valid today, even if account is taken of the 'Office of the Ombudsperson', the creation of which was decided in 2009.[116] The General Court held that, in essence, the Security Council had still not deemed it appropriate to establish an independent and impartial body responsible for hearing and determining, as regards matters of law and fact, actions against individual decisions taken by the Sanctions Committee. Furthermore, removal of a person from the Sanctions Committee's list still requires consensus within the Committee. Moreover, the evidence which may be disclosed to the person concerned continues to be a matter entirely at the discretion of the state which proposed that he be included on the Sanctions Committee's list and there is no mechanism to ensure that sufficient information be made available to the person concerned in order to allow him to defend himself effectively (he need not even be informed of the identity of the state which has requested his inclusion on the Sanctions Committee's list). The General Court concluded that, for those reasons at least, the creation of a 'focal point' and the Office of the Ombudsperson could not be equated with the provision of an effective judicial procedure for review of decisions of the Sanctions Committee.[117]

The scope of the present chapter is too limited to provide a full assessment of the remarkable judgment of the General Court. It suffices for the purposes of the argument here that the General Court followed the lead of the Court of Justice in providing a full judicial review of the Union decision in question despite the fact that it implemented a Security Council resolution taken under Chapter VII of the UN Charter, essentially because the General Court considered the review mechanisms at the level of the UN not to live up to internal EU rule of law standards.

---

[114] *GC Kadi II*, see n 113, paras 116–121. The Court of Justice will have a chance to do precisely that or, of course, to confirm what it said in *Kadi I*, as the appeals to *Kadi II* are pending before it: Case C-584/10 P *Commission v Kadi* [2011] OJ C72/9; Case C-593/10 P *Council v Kadi* [2011] OJ C72/9; and Case C-595/10 P *United Kingdom v Kadi* [2011] OJ C72/10. The cases were joined by order of the President of the Court of 9 February 2011.

[115] *GC Kadi II*, see n 113, paras 126–127, referring to *ECJ Kadi I*, see n 66, para 322 and the Opinion of Poiares Maduro AG, point 54.

[116] UN Doc. S/RES/1904 (2009).

[117] *GC Kadi II*, see n 113, para 128 and the national case law referred to there.

This provides a clear illustration of the connection between the rule of law at the international and EU levels. The defects in how the rule of law operates at the international level bring the Union to a partial rejection of the existing international rules to the extent that they do not comply with internal rule of law standards. The *Kadi I* and *II* judgments expose a system failure in the relationship between EU law and international law in general and between EU law and UN law in particular. A definitive solution does not appear to be immediately forthcoming,[118] particularly not if requiring amendment of the UN Charter.[119]

On balance, however, these judgments are to be supported from the perspective of furtherance of the rule of law, just as the *Bundesverfassungsgericht* was arguably to be commended for helping to convince the Court of Justice to take fundamental rights seriously. As is well known, after the Court of Justice's judgment in *Internationale Handelsgesellschaft*,[120] the *Bundesverfassungsgericht* in *Solange I*[121] considered that it was necessary to conduct a second review of Community legislation in the light of the fundamental rights guaranteed by the Basic Law *so long as* the Community legal order lacked a democratically elected parliament with legislative powers and powers of scrutiny and a codified catalogue of fundamental rights. The Court of Justice then confirmed 'that fundamental rights form an integral part of the general principles of the law, the observance of which it ensures',[122] after which the *Bundesverfassungsgericht* declared that an additional review of Community legislation in the light of the fundamental rights guaranteed by the Basic Law was no longer necessary *so long as* the case law of the Court of Justice continued to afford the level of protection found.[123] It could be argued that part of the reason the Court of Justice in *Kadi I* came out so strongly in favour of fundamental rights was that it was well aware that national

---

[118] See eg the dissenting opinion of President Schwebel in *Questions of Interpretation and Application of the 1971 Montreal Convention arising from the Aerial Incident at Lockerbie (Libyan Arab Jamahiriya v United States of America), Preliminary Objections, Judgment, ICJ Reports 1998*, p 115, concluding from the *travaux préparatoires* (especially the episode of the failed Belgian proposal to introduce a limited possibility of review by the International Court of Justice (ICJ)) that the ICJ was not and was not meant to be invested with a power of judicial review of decisions of the Security Council (dissenting opinion of President Schwebel, 171). See, however, UN Security Council, *Tenth report of the Analytical Support and Sanctions Implementation Monitoring Team submitted pursuant to resolution 1822 (2008) concerning Al-Qaida and the Taliban and associated individuals and entities* (UN Doc. S/2009/502), 5: 'Although there is no obvious or immediate solution to the problem faced by several Member States, particularly in the European Union ..., in its report the Monitoring Team argues that the Council and the Committee would be ill-advised to do nothing. The Council and the Committee should exercise their authority in this matter rather than cede it to others'. See further *Prosecutor v Tadic*, Case No IT-94-1, International Criminal Tribunal for Yugoslavia Appeals Chamber Decision on the Defence Motion for Interlocutory Appeal on Jurisdiction, (2 October 1995), para 28: 'neither the text nor the spirit of the Charter conceives of the Security Council as *legibus solutus* (unbound by law)'. The latter is a reference to Ulpian's dictum '*Princeps legibus solutus est*': *Digesta*, 1.3.31.

[119] Cf JM Farrall, *United Nations Sanctions and the Rule of Law* (Cambridge: Cambridge University Press, 2007), 38–9, and 230–40 (for some pragmatic suggestions).

[120] Case 11/70 *Internationale Handelsgesellschaft* [1970] ECR 1125, paras 3–20.

[121] Judgment of 29 May 1974, BVerfGE 37, at 271, [1974] 2 CMLR 540.

[122] Case 44/79 *Hauer* [1979] ECR 3727, para 15.

[123] Judgment of 22 October 1986, BVerfGE 73 at 339; [1987] 3 CMLR 225.

constitutional courts might be tempted to review EU measures considered unreviewable by the Court of Justice.[124] The General Court appears to have hinted at the parallel with the *Solange* cases in its judgment, by noting that it was its task to ensure the full review of the lawfulness of the contested regulation in the light of fundamental rights '*so long as* the re-examination procedure operated by the Sanctions Committee clearly fails to offer guarantees of effective judicial protection'.[125]

It is regrettable that the Court of Justice supported its argument in favour of protection of fundamental rights and judicial review on the internal EU rule of law standards without referring to the reformative potential of the international rule of law.[126] It is of course true that the Court could not be seen directly to be reviewing Security Council resolutions, and referring to UN standards might have given that impression. Nonetheless, it must surely be possible for the Union courts to make it clear that they are *only* reviewing EU law measures, but doing so on the basis of internal *and* external rule of law constraints. The Court could possibly add a phrase indicating that its thoughts might perhaps be of use to the UN, while making it clear that it does not pass judgment directly on it, by analogy to the phrase it sometimes adds after ruling that a situation is purely internal to a Member States and therefore falls outside the scope of EU law.[127]

The EU can only make progress in internal rule of law standards and in the normative character of its foreign policy if it strives for a more rigorous application of the rule of law at the international level, and the judgments of the Court of Justice and the General Court in *Kadi* can be understood in that light. However, it must be emphasized that the Member States too can only maintain and reinforce their internal rule of law standards if they strive for a more rigorous application of the rule of law at the level of the EU. In doing so, the Member States may in turn often find support in the international rule of law. That is strikingly illustrated by the judgment of the ECtHR in *M.S.S. v Belgium and Greece*, which relies heavily on reports of the Office of

---

[124] Which they may still be tempted to do as regards the CFSP measures that have remained unreviewable after Lisbon: Hinarejos, see n 71, 177.

[125] *GC Kadi II,* (see n 115), paras 126–127 (emphasis added), referring to *ECJ Kadi I,* see n 66, para 322 and the Opinion of Poiares Maduro AG, point 54.

[126] See also Halberstam and Stein, see n 109, 72. The rule of law is of course equally at the heart of the mission of the United Nations: *The rule of law and transitional justice in conflict and post-conflict societies.* Report of the Secretary-General (UN Doc. S/2004/616), para 6; and *Strengthening and coordinating United Nations rule of law activities.* Report of the Secretary-General (UN Doc. A/66/133), para 6: 'Rule of law at the international level is the very foundation of the Charter of the United Nations'. See further <http://www.un.org/en/ruleoflaw/and http://www.unrol.org/>. See, however, S Chesterman, 'An International Rule of Law?' (2008) 56 AJCL 354, who questions whether the UN may properly be said to embody the rule of law in a meaningful way, in large part due to the peace and security powers given to or asserted by its Security Council and the unusual relationship to other legal regimes due to Art 103 of the UN Charter.

[127] See, for example, Case C-84/11 *Susisalo and Others* [2012] ECR I-0000, para 20 (reference for a preliminary ruling from the Korkein hallinto-oikeus, Finland): 'However, even in a purely internal situation such as those at issue in the main proceedings, the Court's answer may nevertheless be useful to the referring court, in particular if its national law required it to grant the same rights to a Finnish national as those which a national of another Member State in the same situation would derive from European Union law.'

the UN High Commissioner for Refugees (UNHCR) in holding Belgium responsible for transferring asylum seekers to Greece pursuant to the Dublin II Regulation[128] where they may be mistreated or risk of being sent back to war zones in breach of the principle of *non-refoulement*.[129] The ECtHR also recalled its *Bosphorus* judgment, in which it held that the protection of fundamental rights afforded by Community law was equivalent to that provided by the Convention system.[130] However, it added that, in reaching that conclusion, it attached great importance to the role and powers of the Court of Justice of the EU in the matter, considering in practice that the effectiveness of the substantive guarantees of fundamental rights depended on the mechanisms of control set in place to ensure their observance. Significantly, the ECtHR observed that it 'also took care to limit the scope of the *Bosphorus* judgment to Community law in the strict sense—at the time the "first pillar" of European Union law'.[131] Though not an unequivocally clear statement, it would not seem too far-fetched to suggest that this implies that the ECtHR would not feel inhibited in exercising (one is perhaps tempted to say) 'in principle the full review'[132] of Union measures taken under CFSP competences. As and when the Union accedes to the ECHR,[133] the exclusion of the jurisdiction of the Court of Justice from CFSP competences appears difficult to sustain.[134] In its judgment in *N.S. v Secretary of State* and *M.E. v Refugee Applications Commissioner*, the Court of Justice adopted the ECtHR's analysis in *M.S.S. v Belgium and Greece* and held that Member States of the EU, including their national courts, may not transfer an asylum seeker back to the Member State where he or she first entered the Union when there are substantial grounds for believing that individual would face a real risk of being subjected to inhuman or degrading treatment contrary to Article 4 of the Charter of Fundamental Rights of the EU.[135] As the EU may encourage the reinforcement of external rule of law constraints (for example, at the level of the UN) by contesting the current standards as inadequate, the EU in turn may be caused to reinforce its internal rule of law by more rigorous existing external rule of law standards (for example, at the level of the ECHR). Indeed, in the words of Advocate General Poiares Maduro, the EU's municipal legal order and the international legal order do not 'pass by each other like ships in the night'.[136]

---

[128] Council Regulation (EC) No 343/2003 of 18 February 2003 establishing the criteria and mechanisms for determining the Member State responsible for examining an asylum application lodged in one of the Member States by a third-country national [2003] OJ L50/1.

[129] *M.S.S. v. Belgium and Greece ('M.S.S'.)* [GC], no 30696/09, 21 January 2011.

[130] *Bosphorus Hava Yolları Turizm ve Ticaret Anonim Şirketi v Ireland* [GC], no 45036/98, § 165, ECHR 2005-VI.

[131] *M.S.S.*, para 338.

[132] In the words of *GC Kadi II*, see n 113, para 126, referring to *ECJ Kadi I*, see n 66, paras 326–327.

[133] As it must pursuant to Art 6(2) EU.

[134] De Baere, see n 6, 196–7.

[135] Joined Cases C-411/10 and C-493/10 *N.S. and M.E. and Others* [2012] OJ C49/8, paras 106 and 113. See G De Baere, 'N.S. v. Secretary of State for the Home Department. Joined Cases C-411/10 & C-493/10', forthcoming in (2012) 106 AJIL.

[136] Opinion of Poiares Maduro in *ECJ Kadi I*, see n 66, point 22.

6 Conclusion

This chapter has argued that the rule of law is the cornerstone of European integration. It has also suggested that the equation of European integration and the ordinary Union method has prevented the rule of law from becoming operational effectively in areas of policy that do not fit within that original paradigm, notably the CFSP. It was argued that one of the principal reasons why the CFSP does not fit within the ordinary Union method, is the—perceived or actual—lack of rule-governed behaviour of other international actors, which induces Member States to accept as few as possible internal or external rule of law constraints on their international actions. There is therefore an intimate connection between the international rule of law and the rule of law at the level of the EU. In order to strengthen the rule of law internally, the EU must search for new and creative ways of bringing more law into the CFSP without necessarily importing the ordinary Union method. This chapter argued that this must go hand in hand with striving for a reinforcement of the rule of law at the international level.

The role of law should of course not be overestimated. As Lon Fuller reminded us: 'the most we can expect of constitutions and courts is that they save us from the abyss; they cannot be expected to lay out very many compulsory steps toward truly significant accomplishment'.[137] Law, in the form of Treaty amendments or otherwise, cannot be the solution to all the Union's quandaries. An important reason why neither the Union nor the Member States wish to be subjected to too many external rule of law constraints in their foreign policy is arguably the perceived or actual lack of international rule of law standards. However, a further crucial reason why the Member States are resistant against rule of law constraints imposed by the Union on their foreign policies would seem to be their lack of political will and their different visions on matters of foreign policy.[138] The Member States' foreign policies are inherently part of their identities, and creating a more common foreign policy for the Union would arguably require a more common EU identity composed of principles and values made concrete in aims.[139] As a 'defining virtue' of the Union, the rule of law could contribute to the formation of such a common identity.[140]

This does not, however, mean that the Union should portray itself as the world centre of political virtue, which is the impression the judgments in the *Kadi* cases tend to give. The EU should not give the impression of basing its identity on the negation of the 'non-European otherness'[141] of the wider world, as it did during its colonial past.[142] Instead of

---

[137] Fuller, see n 11, 44.

[138] See De Baere, see n 6, 312–13.

[139] This may be as true for the EU as for any collectivity. cf Rawls (n 17 above), 456–64; Finnis, see n 10 above, 152: '...sharing of aim, rather than multiplicity of interaction is constitutive of human groups, communities, societies'. Recall that the Treaty of Lisbon has provided a set of values that are to govern all EU action, as well as a single set of objectives for the entire field of EU foreign policy: see Arts 2, 3(5), and 21 EU.

[140] Walker, see n 2, 124.

[141] Koskenniemi, see n 51, 112.

[142] Cf R Kleinfeld and K Nicolaïdis, 'Can a Post-colonial Power Export the Rule of Law?' in G Palombella and N Walker (eds), *Relocating the Rule of Law* (Oxford and Portland, OR: Hart Publishing, 2009), 139–69, arguing that, 'at a minimum, the EU must be self-aware of its post-colonial legacy in choosing both the objects

taking the moral high ground, Europe could show that it has learned from its terrible mistakes in the past. It could do worse than letting its foreign policy be guided, as Article 21(1) EU requires, by the principles that have inspired its own creation, development, and enlargement: 'democracy, the rule of law, the universality and indivisibility of human rights and fundamental freedoms, respect for human dignity, the principles of equality and solidarity, and respect for the principles of the United Nations Charter and international law'.[143] Significantly, that would seem to call for a rejection of the traditional conception of foreign policy as purely the pursuit of national—or Union—interests.[144] The duty to recognize the equal moral standing of all persons, whether inside or outside the Union, is therefore an internal duty fundamentally linked to the rule of law, and the Union cannot be fully just without observing it.[145]

The role of law in EU integration should equally not be downplayed. As argued, European integration is an attempt to infuse often destructive political processes with law in order to prevent war and to infuse international relations with predictability—not for the sake of the states taking part in those inter-state relations, but for the sake of the individuals who make up the states and for the sake of whom states ultimately exist.

The core of the Union is therefore not the ordinary Union method, which is a means—albeit a very successful one in large areas—but checking foreign policy's possible destructive force by subjecting it to rule of law constraints. Having brought the Member States' foreign policies with regard to each other under the rule of law, the EU is gradually bringing the Member States' foreign policies with regard to third countries within the constraining and enabling framework of EU law.

However, the Union will never succeed in that endeavour if it does not at the same time strive towards a more rigorous application of the rule of law at the international level.[146] This chapter argued that the judgments in *Kadi I* and *Kadi II* should be seen in

---

of reform and the strategies it uses to pursue such reform' (at 142). See on the alleged uniqueness of Western values: AK Sen, *Identity and Violence: The Illusion of Destiny* (London: Allen Lane, 2006), 49–58.

[143] See also Arts 2 and 3(5) EU.

[144] De Baere, see n 6, 314. Though see of course Art 3(5) EU, which provides for the Union to 'uphold and promote its values and interests and contribute to the protection of its citizens' in its relations with the wider world, and Art 21(2)(a) EU, which lists as one of the objectives of EU external action the safeguarding of 'its values, fundamental interests, security, independence and integrity'. For an argument against traditional foreign policy: T Nagel, *Equality and Partiality* (New York and Oxford: Oxford University Press, 1991), 179: 'The collective pursuit of prosperity and justice for themselves by the citizens of a nation remains under a shadow while it goes on in a world like ours, where a minority of nations are islands of relative decency in a sea of tyranny and crushing poverty, and the preservation of a high standard of life depends absolutely on strict controls on immigration'. Cf AK Sen, *The Idea of Justice* (London: Allen Lane, 2010), 128–30, concluding that 'assessment of justice demands engagement with "the eyes of mankind"', referring to A Smith, *The Theory of Moral Sentiments* (London: Cadell, 1790), III, i, 2.

[145] Cf Eleftheriadis, see n 37.

[146] And hence, towards making international law 'a better example of a legal system': Waldron, see n 10, 46–7. Cf Simmonds, see n 10, 99, proposing an archetypal concept of law: to count as 'law', a regime or system must approximate to the archetype to some degree. That archetype can be reached to varying degrees, which implies that it also serves as a guiding ideal 'to which legal systems ought to strive to conform more closely'; cf Rawls, see n 17, 207, arguing that the precepts of justice associated with the rule of law 'are those that would be followed by any system of rules which perfectly embodied the idea of a legal system'; and cf H Kelsen, *Peace*

that light. While the Union courts ought to have relied both on the reformative potential of internal and external rule of law standards, these judgments should be seen as positive attempts to convince other actors in international law of a more rigorous application of the rule of law and thereby to conform more with the real purpose of international law and of the rule of law in the international realm: not the protection of sovereign states, but the protection of the populations committed to their charge. States are indeed not ends in themselves, but instruments for the well-being of human individuals, who are ends in themselves.[147] The Member States have limited their sovereign rights, so that rights are conferred upon individuals which become 'part of their legal heritage' independently of the power of the individual Member States.[148] Such liberty as independence from the power of others, including public authorities, can only be realized by that form of moral association we call 'the rule of law'.[149] That idea is the cornerstone of European integration.

Through Law (Chapel Hill: The University of North Carolina Press, 1944), ix, describing the approach to the aim of world peace as 'one of slow and steady perfection of the international legal order'.

[147] Cf Waldron, see n 16, 24 and I Kant, *Groundwork of the Metaphysics of Morals* (1785, M Gregor (ed), Cambridge: Cambridge University Press, 1999), 78–9: 'Now I say that the human being and in general every rational being *exists* as an end in itself, *not merely as a means* to be used by this or that will at its discretion; instead he must in all his actions, whether directed to himself or also to other rational beings, always be regarded *at the same time as an end.*'

[148] *Van Gend en Loos*, see n 45.

[149] Simmonds, see n 10, 152, describing it as 'a common good that is intrinsic to law's nature'.

15

Solidarity in the European Union

Problems and Prospects

*Andrea Sangiovanni**

Solidarity has long been a fundamental value underpinning the project of European integration. In the ECSC Treaty of 1951, the Preamble recognized that 'Europe can be built only through real practical achievements which will first of all create real solidarity, and through the establishment of common bases for economic development'. In both the Single European Act (1986) and the Maastricht Treaty (1992), 'solidarity' appeared alongside 'cohesion' as one of the central objectives of the EC/EU. The Treaty of Lisbon not only continues this commitment but also expands it, mentioning it both as a value binding together Member States and as a value binding together the citizens of each and every Member State.[1] The text of these articles recognizes that each Member State is defined and distinguished by its commitment to social justice, and it is one of the fundamental aims of the Union to preserve such commitments 'while', as the Preamble to the Charter of Fundamental Rights puts it, 'respecting the diversity of the cultures and traditions of the peoples of Europe as well as the national identities of the Member States and the organization of their public authorities at national, regional and local levels'.

The double commitment to preserving the national solidarity at the basis of the 'European Social Model' as well as deepening and strengthening solidarity across Member States has developed in reaction to widespread uneasiness with regard to the liberalizing effects of European integration—effects which are seen to reinforce rather than allay the impact of globalization and demographic change on the viability of the welfare state. This was evident already in the late 1990s with the coming of the Lisbon European Council, which sought to rebalance the internal market agenda with an

---

* Department of Philosophy, King's College London.

[1] The Preamble to the Lisbon TEU commits its signatories 'to deepen the solidarity between their peoples while respecting their history, their culture and their traditions'. Cf Arts 2, 3, 21 TEU; Arts 67, 80, 122, 194 TFEU and again in various protocols. See also the Preamble to the Charter of Fundamental Rights.

ambitious project to modernize the European Social Model. But the Treaties and European Councils were not the only sites for renewed emphasis on 'social protection' and 'solidarity'. The ambit of both values, and the public disquiet that has accompanied them, has recently been growing. To see this, one need look no further than the anxiety at the heart of the Dutch and French rejections of the Constitutional Treaty, fraught debates over the drafting (and redrafting) of the Services Directive, more general discussion about 'social services of general interest', 'social dumping' (for example, *Viking, Laval, Rüffert*), 'benefit tourism', and the prospect (and now reality) of eastward enlargement.[2] Sensing danger in the growing malaise, the Commission has been quick to respond with a steady stream of new communications peppered with references to 'solidarity', the launching of a new 'Social Agenda', a draft for future development in this area ('Europe 2020'), and myriad consultations with social partners. This is not mere rhetoric. The ECJ has now developed a line of jurisprudence (in the area of competition and freedom of movement law) in which it routinely refers to 'principles of solidarity' to determine the proper balance between market principles and social protection objectives in EU law.[3] And, to name but one further example, the Community legislator is steadily at work on a new framework for health services in which the balance between market access and principles of solidarity is centre stage.

Yet, despite such prolific use of 'solidarity', there is very little analysis of what the nature of solidarity in fact *is*, or why we should feel particularly moved by it.[4] Referring to the convention on the ill-fated Constitution, then-Advocate General Miguel Poiares Maduro bemoans this fact and calls for deeper reflection on the 'criterion of distributive justice' that should guide European reform. 'Without such a debate,' he writes, 'there can be no true social contract capable of legitimizing the emerging European polity and the consequences would be either a return to a less advanced form of integration . . . or, if the current model continues to be stretched, a crisis of social legitimacy which may manifest itself in increased national challenges to European policies (whose redistributive effects are not understood and accepted)'.[5] But what

---

[2] See eg Gráinne De Búrca, 'Reflections on the Path from the Constitutional Treaty to the Lisbon Treaty', *Jean Monnet Working Paper No 3/2008*); Paul Craig, 'Competence and Member State Autonomy: Causality, Consequence and Legitimacy', in *The European Court of Justice and the Autonomy of the Member States* (eds) HW Micklitz and B de Witte, forthcoming.

[3] See eg Jo Shaw (ed), *Social Law and Policy in an Evolving EU* (Oxford: Hart, 2000); G De Búrca (ed) *EU Law and the Welfare State: In Search of Solidarity* (Oxford: Oxford University Press, 2005); Eleanor Spaventa and Michael Dougan (eds), *Social Welfare and EU Law* (Oxford: Hart, 2005).

[4] For the Court's own approach, see eg Joined Cases C-159/91 and C-160/91 *Poucet and Pistre v AGF and Cancava* [1993] ECR I-637 paras 15 and 18; but cf FFSA (Case C-244/94 *Fédération Française des Sociétés d'Assurances* [1995] ECR I-4013) and discussion in Siofra O'Leary, 'Solidarity and Citizenship Rights in the Charter of Fundamental Rights of the European Union' in *EU Law and the Welfare State: In Search of Solidarity*, G De Búrca (ed) (Oxford: Oxford University Press, 2005).

[5] Miguel Poiares Maduro, 'Europe's Social Self: 'The Sickness Unto Death'', in *Social Law and Policy in an Evolving European Union*, J Shaw (ed) (Oxford: Hart, 2000), 325–49, at 347. Cf Delors: '[a]ny attempt to give new depth to the Common Market which neglected this social dimension would be doomed to failure' (Delors, 1985: xviii, Delors, J (1985) 'Preface', in J Vandamme (ed), *New Dimensions in European Social Policy*, ix–xx. London: Croom Helm).

kinds of principles, policies, and ideals should an affirmation of solidarity commit us to?

This is not simply an empirical or legal question. We are not trying to gauge the current degree of attachment to the EU or the depth of European fellow-feeling by, for example, citing the latest poll. We are also not attempting to state the implicit rationale followed by the ECJ in its recent 'solidarity' jurisprudence or trying to fix what the Commission might mean by it. Rather, we want to know the answer to the more fundamental question underlying both the legal and the empirical questions: can a more demanding criterion of solidarity—beyond, say, a humanitarian minimum—conceivably apply between states and citizens of the emerging European polity? And, if so, how demanding is it? Should we, for example, aim for a truly European solidarity, in which we judge the EU according to the standards of social justice and protection traditionally thought to apply to states? If not, how do we conceive of the 'middle ground' occupied by the EU (between states and the international order)? Or is talk of 'social justice' and solidarity inappropriate at the EU level? These are, it should be clear, manifestly philosophical questions: while the answers depend on getting the law and facts right, merely legal or empirical reflection cannot provide them. But they are not *only* philosophical questions: the way in which we conceive of the future of the European project—including the balance between 'market access' and 'solidarity' in EU law, the shape and character of future reform in healthcare, pensions, public services, the boundaries of enlargement and our responsibilities to new members, and the precise balance between monetary stability and fiscal autonomy in EMU—depends on our answers to them.

One might, as a result, expect the current literature on the 'political theory of the EU'—by which I mean the literature that aims at a normative analysis of the process, policies, laws, effects, and institutions of European integration—to address these questions. Yet, despite the rich potential of the EU as a basis for deeper reflection upon the nature of distributive justice 'beyond the state', this literature is strikingly narrow. Two questions dominate. The first is whether there is or is not a 'democratic deficit'; the second whether there is or is not a 'European identity'.[6] These two, closely related, questions have received abundant scholarly attention in recent years. Much less attention, however, has been paid to the question of what a fully-fledged European democracy and identity should be used, ultimately, *for*.[7] To be sure, the 'identity' literature makes much of the commitments of Europeans to social protection and social justice, but it is never in the context of the substantive question—are there any obligations of distributive justice among Europeans? If so, what are their grounds? Rather, these concerns are considered merely instrumental in enlisting general support either for deepening and widening the project of European integration or for

---

[6] The literature is extensive, but three recent surveys of the normative debates are indicative, namely H Friese and P Wagner, 'Survey Article: The Nascent Political Philosophy of the European Polity', *Journal of Political Philosophy* (2002) 10, 342–64; JP Olsen, 'Unity, Diversity and Democratic Institutions: Lessons from the European Union' (2004) 12 *Journal of Political Philosophy* 461–95.

[7] For this point, I am indebted to Glyn Morgan, *The Idea of a European Superstate: Public Justification and European Integration* (Princeton, NJ: Princeton University Press, 2004).

underwriting the democratization of the EU. This is also true of some of the most sophisticated and nuanced accounts of the EU's impact on social solidarity both within and across borders, such as Fritz Scharpf's *Governing in Europe*, where policy recommendations aimed at preserving the 'European Social Model' are cast within the framework of increasing the EU's 'output legitimacy'.[8] The judgment and demand is echoed in a recent article by Andrew T Williams, who complains that 'the existing philosophy of EU law rests upon a *theory of interpretation* at the expense of a *theory of justice*', concluding that 'a satisfactory theory of justice needs to be constructed and adopted constitutionally if EU law is to be presented as the guardian of an "ideal constitution" which possesses a coherent ethical vision for the EU'.[9]

I have raised a question about cross-national justice, so one might think that the political theory literature on international *cum* global justice would have something to say. But, focused almost exclusively on the problem of global poverty and the global institutional order (as represented, for example, in the WTO, UN, IMF, and so on), it too offers few tools for answering our set of substantive questions regarding *regional* but still *international* social and political inequalities—inequalities which, moreover, do not in most cases involve the severe absolute deprivation present in the developing world.[10] To my knowledge, no-one contributing to the international *cum* global justice literature has tried to outline what kinds of principles of social justice, if any, apply to the EU. So we are entering largely uncharted territory here.[11]

It is instructive at this point to consider a private exchange between John Rawls and Philippe van Parijs (now public) on whether principles of distributive justice apply to the EU.[12] In that exchange, van Parijs puts a challenge to Rawls's *Law of Peoples*. Probing Rawls's conception of a people, van Parijs asks what factual criteria Rawls believes bound concern for distributive justice. He worries that Rawls's argument provides grist for nationalist mills (as in the Belgian [Walloon-Flemish] case), supporting those who would argue that, between cultural nations, only duties of assistance rather than more demanding duties of distributive justice should apply. He goes on to suggest that, at best, it is the bounds of *social cooperation* rather than *national identity* that are more appropriate for bounding egalitarian concern within a Rawlsian framework.[13] It is at this point that he asks 'whether the emerging political entity [that is, the

---

[8] Fritz W Scharpf, *Governing in Europe: Effective and Democratic?* (Oxford: Oxford University Press, 1999).

[9] AT Williams, 'Taking Values Seriously: Towards a Philosophy of EU Law' (2009) 29 *Oxford Journal of Legal Studies* 549–77, at 552.

[10] Cf Rawls's brief remarks on 'cooperative [international] organizations' in John Rawls, *The Law of Peoples* (Cambridge: Harvard University Press, 1999), 42–3.

[11] On Habermas, see below.

[12] Philippe van Parijs and John Rawls, 'Three Letters on the *Law of Peoples* and the European Union', (2003) 8 *Revue de philosophie économique* 7–20, available at: <http://www.etes.ucl.ac.be/Activites/semdoc/RawlsVanParijs1.R.Phil.Econ.pdf>.

[13] Van Parijs writes: 'the relevant factual question is then not whether there is one or more ethnoi involved (a matter of cultural distance), nor whether there currently happens to be a common demos (a matter of political institutions and of sufficiently common public space), but whether the circumstances (mobility, contact, interdependencies, etc.) are such that there *should* be a common demos—if only to enforce the

EU] will never be more than a conglomerate of ethnoi-demoi, between which only assistance is required on grounds of justice, or whether it can constitute a poly-ethnic demos to which a more demanding conception of distributive justice can conceivably apply'.[14] This is a revealing case for Rawls: forcing Rawls to confront the EU would force him to confront not only whether social cooperation takes precedence over national identity but also *what kind* of social cooperation.

Rawls's response is, to my mind, evasive. He does not deny that the nation-state is the relevant unit of distributive concern. But nor does he explicitly affirm it. Instead, he writes as if the emphasis on the nation-state were only a matter of methodological priority, and further qualifications can be introduced for more complicated cases (that is, for multi-nation states, which Rawls believes can still count as peoples, and hence can be units within which distributive concerns matter). This is obscure: part of van Parijs's charge is surely to demand a justification for beginning with the nation-state at all. Why not begin, once again, with facts relating to social cooperation and leave the existence of nations to the side when discussing distributive justice? Rawls's response is just as evasive with regards to the EU. Rawls does not confront the EU as it is. Instead, he asks what we should think if 'Belgium and the Netherlands, or the two together with France and Germany, decide they want to join and form a single society, or a single federal union'. It is of course true that, *if* these countries explicitly agreed to join and form 'a single society, or a single federal union', principles of liberal justice would now apply to their union (just as in the case of multi-nation peoples). But even if we knew what Rawls meant by a 'single society, or single federal union' (a state?), no Member State in the actually existing EU has explicitly agreed to join such a single society. So the question remains: do principles more demanding than assistance but less demanding than the full extent of liberal justice apply to the EU, or not? If so, what are they, and how would we go about constructing them?[15]

The aim of this chapter is to clear the ground for an answer to van Parijs and Maduro's challenge. More specifically, I shall reconstruct and criticize three different arguments regarding how and whether solidarity, as a value, applies to the EU, and what implications each one has for our understanding of distributive justice beyond the state. The three arguments, in brief, are that (1) because the EU is a voluntary association, Member States should be held liable for the consequences of joining, and

---

requirements of justice'. I take it that this is not a statement of van Parijs's own position on these matters. Rather, it is his attempt to work from within Rawlsian premises to what seems like a position more consonant with Rawls's views in both *Political Liberalism* and *A Theory of Justice*.

[14] First Letter, van Parijs and Rawls, 'Three Letters on the *Law of Peoples* and the European Union'.

[15] Cf the *Law of Peoples*, in the section on 'cooperative organizations' (40–3): 'Should cooperative organizations [such as the EU] have unjustified distributive effects between peoples, these would have to be corrected, and taken into account by the duty of assistance.' Does Rawls here mean that distributive effects between peoples are unjustified if they fail to satisfy the duty of assistance, or does he mean that the there are further principles of distributive justice beyond the duty of assistance (and principles of fair trade) that apply in such cases?

hence distributive justice concerns are irrelevant to its evaluation; (2) the EU should be transformed into a federal welfare state in order to discharge obligations of 'post-national' solidarity to the worst off individuals in the EU; (3) there are no obligations of solidarity across EU borders because the EU lacks an encompassing societal culture necessary for such obligations to apply. I discuss these three because they strike me as the most promising arguments currently available for thinking about solidarity at the EU level, yet I believe they all fail. While I will not outline a fully fledged alternative criterion of trans-, inter-, and intra-national solidarity here (a task I undertake else-where),[16] I hope that the more modest aim I have set will serve to demonstrate the need for more careful, philosophical reflection on one the most important of the fundamental values animating the European project.

1 Statist Solidarity

The first model of solidarity I will discuss accepts that we have obligations of social justice at the domestic level, but denies that we have any obligations of solidarity or justice beyond the nation-state. I shall refer to it, for reasons that will become evident in a moment, as *statist solidarity*.

The argument in favor of *statist solidarity* is best outlined by a transposition to the EU level of an argument made by Thomas Nagel in a seminal article entitled 'The Problem of Global Justice'. The argument picks up, explains, and then generalizes an intuition that many have about obligations of social justice, namely that they only apply to organizations—such as the state—whose membership is *nonvoluntary*. The importance of such a conclusion to the EU, if warranted, should be clear (although Nagel does not himself draw this connection): If Nagel is right, and if the EU legal order is the product of *voluntary* intergovernmental bargaining, then Member States or their citizens cannot reasonably have a complaint in justice about the results. There are, on this view, no obligations of distributive justice or solidarity which traverse Member State boundaries other than the ones expressly agreed to by Member States. Is the argument a good one?

Nagel's argument sets out two conditions that he claims are necessary and jointly sufficient for obligations of social—and in Nagel's case, egalitarian—justice to hold among members of an norm-governed association: (1) The association in question must 'claim to speak in our name' insofar as we can rightly considered to be, in some relevant sense, the *authors* of the norms governing the association; (2) we must be forced to comply with the norms in question; we must have, that is, no reasonable option but to comply. If one or both of these conditions fail to hold of a given association, then obligations of socio-economic justice more demanding than humani-tarianism fail to hold. The two conditions, Nagel believes, also express the moral distinctiveness of the state, and serve to explain why norms of social justice do not

---

[16] Andrea Sangiovanni, *Domains of Justice* (Harvard University Press, forthcoming).

apply at the international level. Nagel's argument is complex, so it is worth quoting him at length:

> Equality as a demand of justice comes from a special involvement of agency or the will that is inseparable from membership in a political society. Not the will to become or remain a member, for most people have no choice in that regard, but the engagement of the will…in the dual role each member plays both as one of the society's subjects and as one of those in whose name its authority is exercised. One might even say that we are all participants in the general will.
>
> A sovereign state is not just a cooperative enterprise for mutual advantage. The societal rules determining its basic structure are coercively imposed: it is not a voluntary association. I submit that it is this complex fact—that we are both putative joint authors of the coercively imposed system, and subject to its norms, i.e., expected to accept their authority even when the collective decision diverges from our personal preferences—that creates the special presumption against arbitrary inequalities in our treatment by the system.
> without being given a choice, we are assigned a role in the collective life of a particular society. The society makes us responsible for its acts, which are taken in our name and on which, in a democracy, we may even have some influence; and it holds us responsible for obeying its laws and conforming to its norms, thereby supporting the institutions through which advantages and disadvantages are created and distributed. Insofar as those institutions admit arbitrary inequalities, we are, even though the responsibility has been simply handed to us, responsible for them, and we therefore have standing to ask why we should accept them.[17]

Let us assume that the first condition (which I will refer to as the 'authorship' condition) is satisfied in the case of the EU: we are rightly considered to be the authors of the norms governing the EU, which in turn claims to 'speak in our name' and on our behalf. An important clarification: the authorship condition is very weak. It does not apply only to legitimate democracies. Of a colonial power 'imposed from outside', Nagel writes, 'it purports not to rule by force alone. It is providing and enforcing a system of law that those subject to it are expected to uphold as participants, and which is intended to serve their interests even if they are not its legislators. Since their normative engagement is required, there is a sense in which it is being imposed in their name.'[18] The crucial feature of 'authorship', for Nagel, is that the order of rules claim to be in the interest of those who are expected to uphold it. The claim in turn triggers a demand for special justification: 'Does the order *really* serve the interests of those it claims to represent?' And it is this demand for a special justification, Nagel claims, that requires a special, egalitarian concern for how well each subject is doing when compared with all the rest. For our purposes, this means that the authorship condition would be satisfied even if one considered the EU to be a highly undemocratic regime. It is uncontroversial that the EU purports not to rule by force alone; it claims to serve the interests of the citizens and states who are expected to uphold its norms.

---

[17] Thomas Nagel, 'The Problem of Global Justice' (2005) 33 *Philosophy & Public Affairs* 113–47 at 128–9.
[18] Nagel, 'Global Justice' at 129n.

The premise I will focus on in this article is the second one: associations whose membership is voluntary and whose rules are not directly enforced are not properly subject to norms of social justice.[19] If this premise is correct, then talk of social justice at the EU level seems, as we said before, misplaced: it seems uncontroversial that no Member State is literally forced either to be a member of the EU or to comply with its norms. Unlike its Member States, the EU lacks an autonomous coercive apparatus with a monopoly over the legitimate uses of coercion within its borders, ultimately relying on Member States to enforce its norms. Furthermore, exit from the EU is no more difficult than exit from any international organization: although a non-negotiated withdrawal would be illegal from the point of view of international (and now EU) law,[20] there is little that any Member State or the EU could do in the event. Should, for example, the British Parliament repeal the 1972 European Communities Act while failing to successfully negotiate withdrawal (for example, by not getting the required qualified majority under the Lisbon Treaty), EU law would no longer be enforced in the UK. Other Member States would rightly claim a breach of treaty obligations, but short of (illegal) military intervention or other (illegal) retaliatory economic and political sanctions (for example, trade embargoes—which, assuming Britain had not also violated legal obligations under the GATT/WTO Treaties, would be declared illegal by the WTO's dispute resolution panel—diplomatic restrictions, etc), Britain would have, in practice, freed itself of its European obligations.[21]

Summarizing, we can state the argument in schematic form:

(1) Social justice norms more demanding than humanitarianism apply to the rules and regulations of an association if and only if (a) the association claims to speak in the name of its members and to rule in their interests; and (b) membership in the association is non-voluntary and compliance with its norms directly enforced.

---

[19] Nagel writes: 'Justice applies, in other words, only to a form of organization that claims political legitimacy and the right to impose decisions by force, and not to a voluntary association or contract among independent parties concerned to advance their common interests' (Nagel, 'Global Justice', 140).

[20] The Lisbon Treaty stipulates a procedure for negotiated withdrawal requiring *inter alia* a qualified majority of other Member States. See Art 50, TEU. But even before the Lisbon Treaty, it was generally recognized (at least among international and EU lawyers) that there was no unilateral right to withdraw. See, for example, J Herbst, 'Observations on the Right to Withdraw from the European Union: Who are the "Masters of the Treaties"?' (2005) 6 *German Law Journal* 1755: 'there can be no serious doubt that, currently, there exists no unlimited right of an EU Member State to withdraw from the Union, ie without any further prerequisites and simply at the free discretion of the respective Member State, within the confines of its internal (constitutional) law provisions'. This is contested by national courts; see eg the German Maastricht and Lisbon decisions. Similarly, under international law, there is no unilateral right of withdrawal unless circumstances have significantly, unequivocally, and unforeseeably changed or unless a joint decision to implicitly grant a right to unilateral withdrawal can be inferred (*rebus sic stantibus* under customary law; see also Arts 61 and 62 of the 'Vienna Convention').

[21] Cf J Hill: '[A]s a practical matter if a Member State were determined to withdraw, the EEC has no sanctions that can be applied to compel lawful compliance with the Treaty. Thus, from this point of view, it really is of no consequence whether a legal right of withdrawal exists', 'The European Economic Community: The Right of Member State Withdrawal' (1982) 12 *Georgia Journal of International and Comparative Law* 335.

(2) The EU claims to speak in the name of both its Member States and its citizens and purports to rule in their interests.

(3) BUT: membership in the EU is voluntary and its rules and regulations are not directly enforced (the EU depends on Member States to enforce its rules and regulations).

(4) Therefore, social justice norms more demanding than humanitarianism do not apply at the EU level.

The argument fails for two reasons. First, in the sense relevant to Nagel's argument, I will argue that the EU is not in fact a voluntary organization (Premise 3 is false). But, second, I will contend that the non-voluntariness condition is anyway implausible: social justice norms can also apply to (some) *voluntary* organizations (Premise 1b is false). If Premise 1b is false, then we might ask: could the authorship condition alone be both necessary and sufficient for triggering the full panoply of social justice norms (which would mean that the full panoply of social justice norms would apply at the EU level)? I will argue that the answer is no (Premise 1a without 1b is implausible). This means that we would do better to look elsewhere for a plausible model of solidarity in the EU.

(A) Is the EU a Voluntary Association, in the Relevant Sense? (Premise 3 is False)

To see why the membership in the EU and the EU legal order are in fact *non-voluntary* in the relevant sense required for *statist solidarity* to go through, we first need to understand the rationale for the premise. The rationale for Premise 1b turns on the thought that different standards apply to voluntary as opposed to non-voluntary schemes. To illustrate: suppose there is a large and important social networking site, called 'Phasebook I', which provides a tool for people to maintain contacts and exchange information over the internet. Phasebook I, however, does not allow its users to protect privacy settings, so whatever information is placed on your Phasebook profile becomes fully public. Many feel that users should be allowed to control the level of information revealed. Indeed, they feel that Phasebook's use of information is *unjust*, and believe it would therefore be justifiable to force Phasebook I to comply through sanctions. Here it seems reasonable to say, in response, 'if you don't like the way Phasebook runs things, then don't join! No-one is forcing you to join and thereby forcing you to reveal your information to the whole world.' (If you're not convinced that this response *is* reasonable, imagine there was another social networking site, MySpays, exactly the same as Phasebook I, except that it allows users to control access to profile information.) But now consider Phasebook II (thirty years on). Phasebook II works exactly in the same way as Phasebook I except that now membership in Phasebook II is either required in order to have access to the job market (MySpays died out long ago) or enforced through fines and in some cases imprisonment. In this case, it *does* seem reasonable to protest the injustice of making people's private information public. Phasebook II forces people to reveal their private information to the rest of the world. Because Phasebook II bends our will into joining, because we are left with no reasonable option but to join, we have a special demand for justification that we lacked for Phasebook I—a demand that can be met only if Phasebook II meets much more stringent criteria. And, according to Nagel, in the case of associations that claim to speak in our name and serve our interests over central areas of our life and liberty, the more stringent criteria will include ones that require egalitarian concern for each person's prospects within the association.

Notice that, in this example and others like it, the 'voluntariness' of an arrangement weakens the stringency of the justice norms which apply to it only if the arrangement is one of several reasonably eligible alternatives. It is only in those cases that it is reasonable to say, 'love it or leave it!' If the alternatives are excessively and unreasonably burdensome for the agent in question, then the arrangement is not voluntary in the relevant sense (that is, not sufficiently voluntary to significantly weaken the stringency of the demands we can reasonably make of it). But if this is the case, then it seems clear that the EU is *not* voluntary in the relevant sense required for less demanding norms to apply: withdrawing carries large and significant costs for all of its members (for example, in market access); and the longer the membership the worse the costs (for example, given adaptation in the presence of legitimate expectations regarding market access). While it might be argued that the decision to join the EU for either the founding or acceding generation was voluntary in the relevant sense, this is certainly not the case for succeeding generations. Given that all members will eventually be members for longer than a generation, the argument would have an exceedingly narrow scope.

(B) The Non-Voluntariness Condition is Implausible (Premise 1b is False)

If I am right and if we accept the Nagelian argument, then it looks like we should be led to the *opposite* conclusion, namely that the EU—at least with respect to those Member States that have been part of the EU for at least a generation—should be subject to the same principles of social justice as have traditionally been thought to apply to states. I now want to argue that we should resist this further conclusion because the non-voluntariness condition is itself implausible.[22] Without it, Nagel's argument—and therefore its implications for the EU—collapses. Recall Phasebook I and II. In those cases, it seemed plausible to argue that what didn't seem like an injustice in Phasebook I (where membership was voluntary) did seem like an injustice in Phasebook II (where membership was non-voluntary). It seemed plausible, that is, to argue that there exist obligations of justice in the second, non-voluntary case that do not exist in the first. But this appearance is illusory. Contrary to the Nagelian thesis, the justice-based

---

[22] I elaborate and extend the argument presented in the text in 'The Irrelevance of Coercion, Imposition, and Framing to Distributive Justice' *Philosophy & Public Affairs* (Winter 2012, forthcoming).

entitlements in the two cases remain constant, namely the justice-based entitlement *not to have one's private information made public.* So what explains our different reactions to the two cases? The difference between Phasebook I and II is that in Phasebook I we can plausibly be understood to have either tacitly or expressly *consented* to release our information by joining. (We can imagine here signing a list of 'terms and conditions' upon joining.) Phasebook's I justice-based obligation not to release our information, we say, is waived when we so consent; *volenti non fit injuria.* But it would be a mistake to claim that the obligation not to release our private information is only *triggered* when membership in Phasebook was non-voluntary. That seems to get things exactly backwards. The case is analogous to someone's waiving, say, their right to receive a state-based pension: it gets things backwards to argue that we *acquire* the right to receive a state-based pension only by virtue of the fact that we have not consented to waive it. Our not having consented to waive it satisfies a necessary condition for us to claim the pension, but it doesn't in any sense ground or otherwise qualify the content and scope of the obligation. In cases like this (and unlike promises or contracts), consent only plays a role *after* the obligations have already been defined.

To see the importance of this point, we need to consider if there are cases in which strong egalitarian obligations obtain in a non-voluntary scheme that would still obtain even if membership in that scheme were voluntary, and where there is no question of consent (either because the right in question is inalienable, or because the relevant conditions for consent do not obtain). This would show that *statist solidarity* fails, and would serve to bring our discussion to a close. Such an example is ready to hand. Suppose that you are a well-to-do French immigrant living and working in the US. Imagine your move was fully voluntary: there is no plausible sense in which you could claim you were *forced* to relocate because of economic, social, or political conditions (although by moving to the US you live a much better life than you would have had you remained in France). But now suppose you were to suffer discrimination on the job: you are not paid equal pay for equal work. You protest the injustice. Would the US government or your employer be justified in saying: 'look, you might be right in saying that a citizen of this country who has, in the relevant sense, no choice but to remain in this country would have a claim in justice against our policy. But you are free to return to your country; since your residence in the US is fully voluntary, you have no complaint in justice against our treatment of you'? This strikes me as straightforwardly implausible. There is no relevant sense in which you have (knowingly and willingly) consented to unequal treatment (that was not part of your work contract and the policy was enacted only after you had already arrived). Non-voluntarist views at most establish that *some* obligations can be waived by consent (but who would object to that?), *not* that obligations of strong social justice arise only among individuals whose interaction is forced.

It might be retorted that, as long as she remains in the US, she *is* being coerced. If she were to break the law, she would, after all, be sent to jail. To see why this is an irrelevant sense of coercion in this context, let's further distil the example: imagine that, if she were to break any US law she would be able, with absolute certainty, to escape back to France without suffering punishment,[23] and let us further suppose that she knows this, but she does not want or intend to break any laws. I submit that this makes no difference to our evaluation of the injustice of this case.

We can reinforce the argument by considering another case. Suppose that Barbara gets in to a number of universities. She decides to go to what is far and away the best one, University X (the others are fully adequate but not as good). Imagine further that it turns out that University X (but not other universities) only supports scholarships for students from wealthy backgrounds, and no such scholarships for poor and middle class students (the university claims that this is necessary to support a ruling elite). Suppose that, once there, Barbara protests the policy's injustice. Would it be plausible for the university to respond, 'your attendance at this university is entirely voluntary; if you don't like its policies, you are free to switch and attend one of the others. While you may be right in saying that the policy would be unjust if everyone were coerced or otherwise forced to attend *this* university, this is not the case, so stronger norms of social justice do not apply to it'? This strikes me as implausible: is the fact that her attendance to University X was voluntary in the relevant sense mean that she cannot appropriately make justice-based assessments of the university's policies as they develop over time? (Notice once again that though voluntary, she has not in any way *consented* to being unfairly treated, and, even if she had so consented, she would have been *waiving* rights that she had rather than failing to acquire them in the first place.)[24]

The consequences for our analysis of solidarity in the EU should be clear. Even if we assume that Member States voluntarily join the EU (and voluntarily remain in afterwards), there are no grounds for denying the appropriateness of justice-based objections to the EU's policies, laws, and effects. To be sure, I have not yet made an argument for what the content of such standards might be or what types of relations might trigger them, but I hope to have cleared away an important argument for the conclusion that there can be *no* such standards.

One might object that the case with accession to the EU is quite different from the Barbara example (or the immigrant one). *Unlike* Barbara and the immigrant, acceding states have not only voluntarily joined the EU but also *consented* to its laws, policies, and effects, and it is for this reason that justice-based criticism is inappropriate. But when put it in this way, the objection says something that is clearly false. Acceding

---

[23] This would be analogous to a classic highway gunman case in which we know with absolute certainty that the gun the highwayman carries isn't loaded, and he is too weak to threaten you in any other way. When you walk away, or willingly give him your wallet nonetheless, you have not been coerced.

[24] Of course, at the limit, namely where there are an infinite number of choices, including one in which she is given everything that she could morally expect, and the transaction costs of choosing one over the other are negligible, the choice of one over another can be considered a case of tacit consent. But all I need for the example to go through is a sufficiently wide range of choices such that she is not forced to choose any one, but none of which offers an optimal solution. On the stringency of tacit consent, and why less than optimal circumstances work to make the imputation of tacit consent implausible, see A John Simmons, *Moral Principles and Political Obligations* (Princeton, NJ: Princeton University Press, 1979).

Member States consent to be governed by the framework of treaties constituting and regulating the EU, but they do not consent to waive any justice-based entitlements that they may have upon entering. The situation is the same with Barbara and the immigrant, who both agree to be bound by the terms of their contract and admission, but not to lay down any justice-based entitlements that they may have once they begin work. Once we more clearly distinguish voluntary membership and compliance from consent, Premise 1b collapses.

(C) Authorship Alone? (Premise 1a is Implausible)

At this point in the discussion, it may seem that we can safely push *statist solidarity* to the side. But there is one last move that a Nagelian might make to sustain the force of the argument, although in a *federalist* rather than *statist* direction. One might hold that the authorship condition is both necessary *and* sufficient for strong social justice norms to apply. This would imply, of course, that the same norms of social justice as have traditionally been applied to the state would apply to the EU, since the EU, as we have seen, clearly satisfies the authorship condition. The problem with this argument is that it is very implausible, and it is no coincidence that Nagel (and others) have emphasized the non-voluntariness condition.[25] If the authorship condition alone were necessary and sufficient, then it would imply that the members of *any* organization that claims to be representative of its members would incur obligations to share responsibility for others members' educational, health, employment, pension, etc, prospects over an entire life. This would be true, that is, even of local chess and tennis clubs. Why would sharing in 'authorship' of such organizations alone create such a strong demand?[26]

2 Postnational Solidarity

Jürgen Habermas is one of the most prominent political philosophers to write about the EU. In this section, I want to reconstruct Habermas's arguments for what I will call *postnational solidarity*. According to *postnational solidarity*, the EU should be reorganized as a pan-European welfare state whose central purpose is to take us beyond the classical nation-state and the nationalism associated with it. I shall claim that the arguments for *postnational solidarity* all fail.

---

[25] See eg Michael Blake, 'Distributive Justice, State Coercion, and Autonomy', (2001) 30 *Philosophy & Public Affairs* 257–96; Mathias Risse, 'What to Say About the State' (2006) 32 *Social Theory and Practice* 671–98.

[26] Views like Nagel's also suffer from several other flaws, the most important of which is that they cannot explain how some morally relevant features of will-bending fix the content and scope of distributive obligations. I discuss these problems in more detail in 'The Irrelevance of Coercion, Imposition, and Framing to Distributive Justice', *Philosophy & Public Affairs* (forthcoming) and 'International Justice and the Morality of Coercion, Imposition, and Framing' in Andrea Sangiovanni, 'Justice and the Priority of Politics to Morality' (2008) 16 *Journal of Political Philosophy* 137–64.

Habermas does not believe that obligations of distributive justice apply to us independently of the social and political relations in which we stand. He is not, that is, a thoroughgoing cosmopolitan: he rejects the idea that we owe distributive obligations to persons *as such*. But which social and political relations trigger the concern for social justice? For Habermas, what matters are our relations as consociates in a determinate legal association. To see why, we need to turn to Habermas's 'discourse-theoretic' understanding of basic rights.

Habermas understands distributive justice in terms of a substantive conception of *social rights*. The justification of social rights (to a decent standard of living, adequate housing, etc) is understood as part of a more general justification of a 'system of rights', which includes the classical liberal-democratic list of civil and political rights. The argument, in brief, is this. According to Habermas, individuals who want to regulate their common life via a legitimate legal order must respect what he calls the 'democratic principle'; namely, the idea that 'only those statutes may claim legitimacy that can meet with the assent of all citizens in a discursive process of legislation that in turn has been legally constituted'.[27] And, in turn, the only way to institutionalize a democratic legal order is to enact social rights along with civil and political rights. This is because social rights are necessary to give *fair value* to our civil and political liberties, which in turn are necessary to enable and constitute our private and public autonomy as citizens.

In view of our discussion here, the key point is that the group of civil, political, and social rights are not binding as *external* constraints on a democratic sovereign. To understand this point, consider Habermas's ambition in Chapter 3 of *Between Facts and Norms*, namely to demonstrate how civil, political, and social rights are *constitutive* of democratic self-legislation. 'The idea of self-legislation by citizens . . . requires that those subject to law as its addressees can at the same time understand themselves as authors of the law.' But, he continues, '[w]e cannot meet this requirement simply by conceiving the right to equal liberties as a morally grounded right that the political legislator merely has to enact'. To do so would be to subordinate law to morality, a 'move incompatible with the idea of an autonomy realized in the medium of law itself'.[28] To construe: the concept of law (viz, any legal system, even the most unjust) presupposes (a) that liberty is defined as the silence of the law, and (b) that laws must be made and enacted by a legislator. The concept of law presupposes, that is, both a space in which we are free to do as we like and a mode of public law-making. To be legitimate, the law must, in turn, respect the democratic principle, and hence guarantee our freedom as both authors and addressees. To meet this requirement, we must be guaranteed the capabilities required to be both 'publicly autonomous' *qua* co-legislators (authors) and 'privately autonomous' *qua* subjects (addressees). It is these capabilities (required for the realization of our legally mediated private and public autonomy) which the 'system of rights' guarantees. Civil, political, and social rights are therefore not moral rights which exist independently of law. They constrain us if

---

[27] Jürgen Habermas, *Between Facts and Norms*, trans W Rehg (Cambridge, MA: MIT Press, 1996a), 110.
[28] Habermas, *Between Facts and Norms*, 120.

and only if we share a legal order; indeed, they can only be understood *in terms of* a legal order of which we are co-authors and addressees. This is why Habermas calls them 'juridical *by their very nature*'.[29] In summary: no law without democracy; no democracy without rights; and no rights without law.

It is useful to compare Habermas's account of social rights to Nagel's argument for why equality is a demand of justice only among subjects of a sovereign. Habermas and Nagel both agree that civil, political, and social rights—the equivalent of Nagel's 'equal concern, equal opportunity, and equal respect'—only apply to citizens who share subjection to a (coercive) body of law. They also agree that it our relationship as both authors and addressees of the law that explains why principles of distributive justice apply only among members of that legal order.[30] Given the structural similarity between Nagel and Habermas, one would think that Habermas would also endorse Nagel's statist conclusions. Yet, quite on the contrary, Habermas has consistently endorsed a much more thorough-going cosmopolitan position on issues of global justice.

This is most evident with regard to Habermas's advocacy of a European federalism securely anchored in a pan-European constitution, which Habermas sees as the first step on the way to realizing 'an obligatory cosmopolitan solidarity'. Habermas writes: the 'form of civil solidarity that has been limited to the nation-state until now has to expand to include all citizens of the union, so that, for example, Swedes and Portuguese are willing to take responsibility for one another'.[31] Given the structure of Habermas's justification of the 'system of rights', how does he arrive at this conclusion?

There are four arguments Habermas gives for extending the bounds of egalitarian justice beyond the state, all of which follow from his advocacy of EU federalism. I will now argue that none of these is successful.

(A) 'Politics Must Catch Up with Markets'

The first argument follows directly from Habermas's empirical assessment of the negative impact of globalization and European integration on what he calls the *Sozialstaat*, or the redistributive-egalitarian welfare state. Habermas cites a number of familiar explanations for why globalization and integration limit the capacity of states to adjust and, most importantly, to maintain domestic commitments to egalitarian redistribution. These include: regulatory competition among states in an open economy, which causes a 'race to the bottom' in many areas of social policy; limitations on the capacity of states to intervene in the economy due to delegation of monetary policy to the European

---

[29] Jürgen Habermas, 'Kant's Idea of Perpetual Peace: At Two Hundred Years' Historical Remove', in *The Inclusion of the Other* (Cambridge: MIT Press, 1998b), 190, emphasis in original.

[30] Of course, they diverge on the explanation of *how* our relations as authors and addressees generates a demand for equality. For Habermas, as we have seen, the 'system of rights' is an institutional precondition for the successful institutionalization of the 'democratic principle' (itself generated by the 'interpenetration' of the legal form with his discourse principle (D)). For Nagel, the pressure for equality is generated via the fact that state law demands our compliance, on pain of sanctions, while at the same time claiming to speak in our name.

[31] Jürgen Habermas, 'The Postnational Constellation and the Future of Democracy', in *The Postnational Constellation: Political Essays* (Oxford: Polity Press, 2001a), 99.

Central Bank (ECB), and exacerbated by the Growth and Stability Pact; limitations on state capacities to tax mobile forms of capital with predictable constraints on the generation of revenue; and so on. Gone are the days in which 'deployment of neo-corporative negotiating systems and regulated industrial relations, mass political parties with social-structural anchoring, reliably functioning social security systems, nuclear families with inherited sexual division of labor, normalized labor relations with stand-ardized career paths' formed 'the background for a more or less stable society based on mass production and mass consumption'.[32] Habermas's diagnosis is that either Europe must federate to maintain its commitments to social protection, or it must 'eliminate the pressure of these problems by consigning them to the market', which means, in effect, to give in to a 'neo-liberal' Europe prone to 'de-differentiation, alienation, and anomie'.[33]

Throughout his writings on Europe, this is the argument to which Habermas refers most often, although it is one of his weakest. Even if we grant that globalization and European integration have had a negative impact on the sustainability of *current* welfare states, it does not follow that the only solution available is a continental *Sozialstaatsverbund*. In particular, Habermas provides no evidence suggesting that well-designed domestic reform of the welfare state, coupled with EU reform well short of 'full harmonization of social policy',[34] would be unsuccessful in harnessing the benefits of integration and globalization, while maintaining a commitment to fully fledged egalitarian redistribution. We could grant that a federation on an EU scale would be a *sufficient* condition for maintaining the European social model (itself highly questionable, given the diversity in welfare regimes across Europe).[35] Taken on its own, however, Habermas's empirical argument fails to show that a federal EU is *necessary* for maintaining commitments to social solidarity.

Ample evidence for the argument that a federal EU is not in fact a necessary condition for maintaining (and even increasing) levels of social protection and spend-ing can be garnered from recent studies of the impact of globalization on the welfare state. There is by now a quite extensive literature that demonstrates that the impact of globalization on the nation-state (increased openness to trade and investment, in part the result of the loss of capital controls, floating exchange rates, etc) varies tremen-dously by regime type.[36] Indeed, some of the most open economies—for example, small states such as Denmark—have not only done quite well in terms of productivity growth, but have also been able to retain high levels of social spending and social protection.[37] Others, on the other hand, have fared much more poorly (for example,

---

[32] Habermas, 'Postnational Constellation', 87.   [33] Habermas, 'Postnational Constellation', 97, 83.

[34] Habermas, 'Postnational Constellation', 97.   [35] Scharpf, *Governing in Europe*.

[36] Geoffrey Garrett, *Partisan Politics in the Global Economy* (Cambridge, UK: Cambridge University Press, 1998); Peter A Hall and David W Soskice (eds), *Varieties of Capitalism: the Institutional Foundations of Comparative Advantage* (Oxford: Oxford University Press, 2001); Dani Rodrik, *Has Globalization Gone Too Far?* (Washington, DC: Institute for International Economics, 1997); Linda Weiss, *The Myth of the Powerless State* (Ithaca, NY: Cornell University Press, 1998); Scharpf, *Governing in Europe*; Peter J Katzenstein, *Small States in World Markets: Industrial Policy in Europe* (Ithaca, NY: Cornell University Press, 1985).

[37] See eg Garrett, *Partisan Politics in the Global Economy*; Katzenstein, *Small States in World Markets: Industrial Policy in Europe*.

France and Italy).[38] What the literature suggests is that there is much that can be done at the domestic level to adapt to changing conditions. Furthermore, it is relevant that there is a strong correlation, even in an era of globalization, between the level of development and degree of social spending: less-developed states which have achieved higher than average growth rates recently have also increased their social spending in conjunction with this growth, just as more developed countries did previously.[39] By treating globalization and integration as having a uniformly and universally negative effect, Habermas makes the conclusion he endorses seem functionally inescapable, when it is nothing of the sort. Habermas's urgent call for a new welfare Europe therefore rings false.

(B) Constitutional Patriotism and Postnational Solidarity

Habermas's second argument draws on the idea of 'constitutional patriotism'. Constitutional patriotism aims to provide a basis of political unity strong enough to bind together modern societies in conditions of ethnic, religious, and value pluralism. This unity is forged out of universalist commitments to principles of justice and democracy embodied in liberal constitutions, rather than particularist attachments to shared cultures, ethnicities, languages, religions, or even territories.

Constitutional patriotism represents an alternative to nationalism that is intended to serve the same sociological functions but in a very different way. Late-eighteenth and nineteenth-century nationalism—by which Habermas means the political ideology which claims rights of self-governance for groups bound by ethnic and cultural ties, shared characteristics, a sense of belonging together, and common myths of origin—historically served an important sociological function. Disseminated through new forms of mass communication and the 'educated bourgeois public', nationalism provided a motivational spur intended to foster people's identification with the state. Nationalism's ideal of the citizen was based on sacrifice and loyalty: to die for one's country and one's people was not only an honour but also an obligation one owed to the nation personified as an objective 'spirit'.[40] Nationalism thus became the 'vehicle for the emergence of' the republicanism of the so-called 'democratic revolutions' of the late eighteenth century.[41] But Habermas is clear that there is no *conceptual* relation between nationalism and republicanism. Once nationalism has served its purpose of breaking apart the corporative ties of early modern society, and then uniting disparate groups of people under a single flag and a single 'fate', its connection with republicanism can and indeed should be severed. According to Habermas, 'the modern understanding of this republican freedom can, at a later point, cut its umbilical cord to the

---

[38] See eg Scharpf, *Governing in Europe*.
[39] See eg European Values in the Globalised World, COM(2005).
[40] See his lecture on German historiography, entitled 'What is a People? The Frankfurt "Germanists' Assembly" of 1846 and the Self-Understanding of the Humanities in the *Vormärz*' in Jürgen Habermas, *The Postnational Constellation: Political Essays*, trans M Pensky (Cambridge: MIT Press, 2001c).
[41] Habermas, *Between Facts and Norms*, 495.

womb of the national consciousness of freedom that originally gave it birth'.[42] Nationalism can now be replaced, Habermas tells us, by a 'legally mediated social integration' established via the democratic process itself. Citizens reorient their attachments from the nation personified as an organic spirit to procedures that secure the possibility of a democratically structured 'opinion- and will-formation'. The basis of this new attachment is the justice of the procedures, which reflect citizens' desire to 'regulate their living together according to principles that are in the equal interest of each and thus can meet with the justified assent of all'.[43]

This new basis of civic solidarity centred on a constitution, which is only now beginning to take shape (very imperfectly) across Europe, is also under threat from globalization. Habermas writes, as 'nation-states increasingly lose both their capacities for action and the stability of their collective identities, they will find it more and more difficult to meet the need for self-legitimation'.[44] The limits on the scope of state action imposed by cultural, economic, and social globalization (exacerbated by the EU) strain the basis of civic solidarity in each Member State. As older forms of national 'homogeneity' weaken (for example, with increasing immigration), cultural communication across borders increases, social inequalities grow, and post-war commitments between capital and labour fray, the resources available for a 'social integration based on mutual understanding, intersubjectively shared norms, and collective values' dwindle, and along with it a commitment to joint redistribution.[45] Whereas in the first argument, globalization worked to undermine the welfare state at an institutional level, according to this argument, it works to undermine it at a *sociological* level.

Habermas recommends a revived constitutional patriotism at a *European* level to overcome the solidarity deficit at the domestic level.[46] He argues that the EU provides an opportunity to revive 'an interest in and a particular affective attachment to a particular ethos: in other words, an attraction to a particular way of life' necessary to replenish the reserves of social solidarity sapped at the national level.[47] Against those who claim that a *demos* is impossible at an EU level, Habermas counters that such an affective attachment can be centred on a European Constitution, itself rooted in common European experiences of conflict and cooperation, which 'have acted as a spur toward the decentering of perspectives; as an impulse toward critical reflection on, and distancing from, prejudices and biases; as a motive for the overcoming of particularisms, toward tolerance and the institutionalization of disputes'. This political culture will represent a common 'egalitarian universalism', which 'can ease the

---

[42] Jürgen Habermas, 'Citizenship and National Identity', in *Between Facts and Norms* (Cambridge: MIT Press, 1996b), 295. See also Habermas, 'Nation, the Rule of Law, and Democracy', 131–3.

[43] Habermas, 'Citizenship', 496.

[44] Habermas, 'Postnational Constellation', 80.

[45] Habermas, 'Postnational Constellation', 83.

[46] See also Justine Lacroix, 'For a European Constitutional Patriotism' (2002) 50 *Political Studies* 944–58 and Richard Bellamy and Dario Castiglione, 'Lacroix's European Constitutional Patriotism: A Response' (2004) 52 *Political Studies* 187–93.

[47] Jürgen Habermas, 'Why Europe Needs a Constitution' (2001b) 11 *New Left Review* 5–26, at 8.

transition to postnational democracy's demanding contexts of mutual recognition for all of us'. He continues; 'we, the sons, daughters, and grandchildren of a barbaric nationalism'.[48] If national and democratic forms of collective identity emerged (in the eighteenth and nineteenth centuries) from local and dynastic identities through 'a painful process of abstraction', why, Habermas asks, should this process be 'doomed to come to a final halt just at the borders of our classical nation-states?'[49]

I have two simple counter-arguments to this line of reasoning. First, either (a) the argument depends on the empirical premise that Member States are no longer able, institutionally, to sustain commitments to social protection domestically or (b) it can stand independently. If (a), then the argument from constitutional patriotism is redundant or, if not redundant, then it collapses into a form of the first argument already discussed. If (b), Habermas gives us no reason to believe that a *European* constitutional patriotism will be, as a sociological matter, any more successful than a *domestic* constitutional patriotism in motivating people to sustain egalitarian forms of redistribution. Habermas's point here seems to be that the ghosts of nationalism past can best be exorcised at the supra-national level, since the possibility of a reversion to ethnocentric nationalism is less likely at that level. But, if this is the idea, then a European constitutional patriotism would either come too early or too late. If it is true that ethnic nationalism is still lurking, then a European constitutional patriotism will come too early, since nationalist feeling will preclude a move to a European federation. And if it is not true that resurgent ethnic nationalisms would preclude the emergence of a European federation, then the call for a European constitutional patriotism comes too late, when the nationalist ghosts are fading anyway.

This leads me to my second point. It seems that general support for constitutional patriotism should, if anything, lead one more naturally to support *euroscepticism* rather than federalism. Consider, for example, Michael Howard, ex Leader of the Conservative Party in Britain. In a 2004 speech in Berlin, he tried to rein in the aspirations of European federalists like Habermas and Joschka Fischer: 'We in Britain came through the war with our national institutions strong. When we seek to preserve those institutions, we are defending a constitutional settlement that has survived great stresses and strains and which continues to work well and be understood by people in Britain. To undermine these institutions and ways of life, whether they have developed uninterrupted over hundreds of years or only recently re-emerged, and which are seen as legitimate by their people, would be an act of folly.' Howard is concerned that further integration would unjustifiably corrupt British constitutional practices; he is not worried that 'Europe' will destroy the legacy of Shakespeare and Shaftesbury, dismember the Anglican Church, or make French the national language. What worries him is that the EU will undermine the principles, practices, and ideals implicit in

---

[48] Habermas, 'Postnational Constellation', 103. For similar passages, see also Habermas, 'Nation, the Rule of Law, and Democracy', 152; Habermas, 'Does Europe Need a Constitution? Response to Dieter Grimm', 161; Habermas, 'What Is a People?' 18–19.

[49] Habermas, 'Why Europe Needs a Constitution', 16.

Britain's unwritten constitution. In an allusion to the particularly *constitutional* upheavals of 1641, 1649, 1653, 1660, and 1689, Howard avers: 'What is proposed is perhaps the biggest change in Britain's constitutional arrangements since the seventeenth century'.[50] It would be misleading to claim that Howard is an ethnic or even ethnocultural nationalist. In these passages, he is the very image of a constitutional patriot. So the puzzle remains: why does Habermas believe that a defence of constitutional patriotism commits us to further European integration?

(C) Cosmopolitanism, Human Rights, and Constitutional Patriotism

Perhaps the answer to this question can be found by turning to the *object* of patriotic attachment. If the object of the patriot's allegiance are values, including human rights, whose 'mode of validity . . . points beyond the legal orders of nation-states', then it might be argued that, in affirming one's own constitutional order, one implicitly also affirms (albeit only potentially) a cosmopolitan order.[51] And if this is true, then it might also be true that we have an obligation to integrate with other states *on the way* to such a truly cosmopolitan order, where we can feasibly do so without dissolving our commitments to joint redistribution. The EU, in this argument, would form precisely such a Kantian focal point. Transforming the EU into a federation would become a demand of 'cosmopolitan solidarity'. This third argument for expanding the bounds of egalitarian justice beyond the state is much more explicitly normative and abstract than the first two we have considered, and returns us to Habermas's derivation of the 'system of rights' from the 'interpenetration' of law with the discourse principle. Recall that we wondered how Habermas's insistence that the 'system of rights' was 'juridical *by its very nature*'—which included his rejection of a moralized conception of human rights *external* to a constitutional-legal order—could lead him anywhere but to a statist conclusion similar to Nagel's. Here we have the beginning of an answer.

As we have seen, the structure and content of human rights cannot be understood apart from their being embedded in legal systems of adjudication and protection. This is not simply a conceptual point. To treat human rights as if they existed prior to legal orders, and positive legal norms as if they were simply dressed up moral norms invites, Habermas argues, a dangerous moralization of international relations.[52] Habermas therefore accepts the 'kernel of truth' of the argument made famous by Carl Schmitt, namely that 'an *unmediated* moralization of law and politics does in fact break through

---

[50] All passages from Michael Howard's speech, entitled 'A New Deal for Europe', delivered to the Konrad Adenauer Stiftung in Berlin, Thursday, 12 February 2004.

[51] Robert Fine and Will Smith, 'Jürgen Habermas's Theory of Cosmopolitanism' (2003) 10 *Constellations* 469–87, 190.

[52] Carl Schmitt of course famously inveighed against liberalism for presuming to speak in the name of all of humanity, and in the process trying to deny the political distinction between friend and enemy. In so doing, liberalism invites the most inhuman of all wars. In wars which are fought on behalf of humanity, the enemy is denied his dignity *qua* opponent. If he rejects the norms and standards of all of humanity, then he must be *necessarily* inhuman, no better than an animal. He deserves no recognition or standing, only a 'total annihilation'. See Carl Schmitt, *The Concept of the Political*, G Schwab (ed) (Chicago: University of Chicago Press, 1996).

those protective zones that we want to have secured for legal persons for good, indeed moral, reasons'.[53]

But he resists the conclusion Schmitt draws: 'It is a mistake to assume that this moralization can only be prevented by keeping international politics free from law and the law free from or purged of morality.'[54] Rather, the opposite is true. By submitting the international order to the rule of law, we ensure that all 'unmediated' moral claims are filtered through legal procedures designed to protect the accused and to submit claims to public, indeed multilateral, evaluation. As in the domestic case, such 'filtering' gives decision outcomes a rebuttable presumption of rational acceptability, and hence legitimacy. This 'cosmopolitan transformation of law' follows from the fact that human rights, while juridical in structure and content, have a universal justification, a 'validity claim', that transcends all borders and boundaries: 'Human rights fundamentalism is avoided not by renouncing the politics of human rights, but only through a cosmopolitan transformation of the state of nature among states into a legal order.'[55]

If Habermas grants Schmitt the idea that human rights should not be conceived as *moral* rights—if we accept, with Habermas, that human rights are 'juridical by their very nature'—then I do not see the force of his claim that we have an obligation to embed the enforcement of human rights in a system of cosmopolitan law. To whom do we owe this obligation? If the answer is that we owe this obligation to those (either actually or potentially) subject to human rights violations, then they clearly have a moral claim and right to have the international legal order extended to them. And if they do have such a moral right, then we might reasonably wonder what the basis of this right is. I see no other answer to this question, within a Habermasian framework, than the one he is trying to resist; namely, that those at risk are entitled to have their human rights protected *even if they do not yet form the basis of a legal order*. In responding to Schmitt, Habermas is therefore caught on the horns of a dilemma. He can either accept that we have an obligation to extend a cosmopolitan order to all human beings. But human rights, on this view, would be *external* to any system of law, and hence his conception of the 'internal relation' between rights, law, and democracy would fail. Or, on the other hand, he could accept that basic rights only hold within the bounds of legal orders, in which case there would be no obligation to extend the bounds of solidarity beyond the nation-state.

(D) The Democratic Deficit

Habermas's fourth argument for a European federation is the most straightforward. Beginning from the premise that the EU is a legal order, and that legitimate law requires democracy, one could argue that the EU must be democratized. Once democratized, social rights would need to be extended equally to all European citizens to ensure the fair value of civil and political liberties. Habermas writes:

---

[53] Habermas, 'Kant's Perpetual Peace', 199.
[54] Habermas, 'Kant's Perpetual Peace', 199.
[55] Habermas, 'Kant's Perpetual Peace', 201.

At present, legitimacy flows more or less through the channels of democratic institutions and procedures within each nation-state. This level of legitimation is appropriate for inter-governmental negotiations and treaties. But it falls short of what is needed for the kind of supranational and transnational decision-making that has long since developed within the institutional framework of the Union and its huge network of committees. It is estimated that European directives already affect up to 70 per cent of the regulations of national agencies. But they lack any serious exposure to a timely and careful public opinion or will-formation in those national arenas that are today alone accessible to holders of a European passport.[56]

We need not doubt that the EU could benefit (in legitimacy terms) by more open and transparent procedures (for example, Council meetings) as well as a more active (and truly European) 'public sphere'. But why must *any* legal order—regardless of its particular character, scope, functions, etc—trigger the full panoply of rights, controls, and institutions typical of a constitutional state? While we can (for the sake of argument) concede Habermas's claim that a *comprehensive* legal system typical of a modern state requires the legitimacy conditions he outlines, it is not clear why less comprehensive legal systems, including the EU (but also international law more generally), should meet the same demanding standards. This is all the more true if we take into account the fact that European institutions specialize in areas—anti-trust prosecution, central banking, various forms of social regulation—which are already delegated to non-majority institutions domestically. Seen from this point of view, it is not at all clear that domestic non-majoritarian institutions are any more constrained by public 'opinion- and will-formation' than European institutions. Indeed, in many cases, especially given the wide range of 'veto points' and checks and balances at the European level, the opposite often seems to be the case.[57]

The point stands even if we concede that more needs to be done to make the EU responsive and accountable to European publics (not to mention domestic non-majoritian institutions).[58] Even if we make this concession, the move from 'law' to 'democracy' to 'social rights' is still too quick. If Habermas's central argument for an egalitarian distribution is an instrumental one—strong social rights are required to sustain the fair value of civil and political liberties—then, in the view of the limited capacity of European institutions, it seems far-fetched to argue that until pan-European egalitarian justice is secured, civil and political liberties will remain insecure. While the argument has force at a domestic level, where there is a legal order securing the full range of collective goods and services, criminal law, torts, etc, it has

---

[56] Habermas, 'Why Europe Needs a Constitution', 14.

[57] See A Moravcsik, 'In Defence of the 'Democratic Deficit': Reassessing Legitimacy in the European Union', *Journal of Common Market Studies* (2002) 40: 603–24; Giandomenico Majone, *Dilemmas of European Integration: the Ambiguities and Pitfalls of Integration by Stealth* (Oxford: Oxford University Press, 2005); Giandomenico Majone, 'The Common Sense of European Integration' (2006) 13 *Journal of European Public Policy* 607–26, at 618ff.

[58] See eg Andreas Føllesdal and S Hix, 'Why There Is a Democratic Deficit in the EU: A Response to Majone and Moravcsik' (2006) 44 *Journal of Common Market Studies* 533–62, and Richard Bellamy, 'Still in Deficit: Rights, Regulation, and Democracy in the EU' (2006) 12 *European Law Journal* 725–42.

less force at an EU level. Because of the different range of authority exercised by EU vis-à-vis national institutions, EU citizens are, to put it starkly, much more vulnerable to domination as a result of *intra*-Member State inequalities than *inter*-Member State ones. Of course, if Habermas could show that democratizing the EU *required* expanding its range of competences, including its budget, then he could argue that pan-European egalitarianism would have to follow. But increasing the accountability and responsiveness of EU institutions does not require increasing its range of competences or expanding its budget. Habermas's argument that the 'form of civil solidarity that has been limited to the nation-state until now has to expand to include all citizens of the union, so that, for example, Swedes and Portuguese are willing to take responsibility for one another', once again, fails.[59] There is no argument available along Habermasian lines that demonstrates that the EU must be transformed into a federal *Sozialstaatsverbund*, or that distributive justice extends beyond the borders of the nation-state.

3 Solidarity as Fraternity

The third model of solidarity, like the statist one, also challenges the idea that obligations of distributive justice and solidarity can extend beyond the nation-state, but in a very different way. The most plausible versions of the argument for *solidarity as fraternity* take one of two forms, both of which are variants of liberal nationalism. The first and most common version emphasizes the link between trust and nationality; the second, more nuanced version emphasizes the link between collective agency and nationality.

According to the first form of the argument, distributive justice cannot be realized with a motivational basis in a sense of fellow-feeling. David Miller, for example, asks: 'What can motivate people to make the sacrifices that distributive justice requires, whether this takes the form of supporting parties that promise redistribution, or simply behaving in a fair way in their everyday lives?' Miller continues, there 'is a wealth of evidence that shows that people are more willing to make such sacrifices the more closely they feel themselves tied to the likely beneficiaries of their actions'. Joint redistribution requires, that is, a 'common identity or common values'.[60] The reason people are more willing to make sacrifices to others with whom they share an identity is that 'ties of community are an important source of . . . trust between individuals who do not know one another'.[61] Without such mutual trust, we cannot be sure that others will be prepared to return the benefits which we provide through our sacrifices, should we come to need them. Miller's most striking and well-known claim is that the *only* viable source for such a common identity in modern societies is shared *nationality*:

---

[59] Habermas, 'Postnational Constellation', 99.
[60] David Miller, 'The Left, the Nation-State, and European Citizenship' (1998) 45 *Dissent* 48.
[61] David Miller, *On Nationality* (Oxford: Oxford University Press, 1995), 92.

In states lacking a common national identity . . . politics at best takes the form of group bargaining and compromise and at worst degenerates into a struggle for domination. Trust may exist within the groups, but not across them.[62]

In summary, distributive justice requires solidarity, solidarity requires mutual trust, and mutual trust requires a common identity grounded in a shared nationality.[63] The extension of the argument to the EU, given these premises, is straightforward: because the EU lacks a common national identity, distributive justice cannot apply at that level. The argument has many adherents, including Streeck, Scharpf, Offe, and Grimm.[64]

It is, however, implausible as it stands. First, *solidarity as fraternity* is a purely instrumental justification of liberal nationalism. It does not say that citizens have good reason to restrict the scope of egalitarian concern to those with whom they share a national identity. Rather, it simply asserts that, as a matter of *fact*, the bounds of egalitarian concern only extend thus far and no further. But if we accept that feelings of national fellow-feeling and solidarity are not simply urges, like nausea and hunger, but judgment-sensitive attitudes, then they must also be responsive to reasons. From a first-person perspective, we can always ask: while it may be true that my fellow compatriots feel no inclination to trust non-nationals, and that they therefore do not support extending the bounds of egalitarian concern to them, why should *I* believe that relations of shared nationality constitute *good grounds* for restricting the scope of distributive justice in this way? The argument just canvassed squarely begs this question, which is the question we are ultimately interested in.[65]

The first form of *solidarity as fraternity* has a further and deeper weakness. The empirical premise on which the argument relies is false: it is not true that shared culture or nationality or even common identity is necessary for the existence of mutual trust. While it is true that a common identity (though not necessarily a national one) increases the chances of successful cooperation, there are many other circumstances which favour the formation of mutual trust in the absence of such a common identity. For example, a wide range of studies demonstrates that relationships of sustained reciprocity (whether specific or diffuse) can generate and reproduce relations of trust.[66] This is unsurprising: continued and positive interaction under a generally

---

[62] Miller, *On Nationality*, 92.

[63] Notice that, according to this argument, shared nationality is a necessary condition of solidarity but not a sufficient one (eg the US). The explanation is obvious: the disposition to aid the worst off requires a sense of justice which is independent of merely sharing a common identity or nationality. While there are national identities which define themselves in terms of their commitment to solidarity, solidarity is not a constitutive feature of national identity as such.

[64] Claus Offe, 'The Democratic Welfare State in an Integrating Europe', in *Democracy Beyond the State? The European Dilemma and the Emerging Global Order* MT Greven and LW Pauly (eds) (Lanham, MD: Rowman & Littlefield, 2000); Scharpf, *Governing in Europe*; W Streeck, 'Neo-Voluntarism: A New European Social Policy Regime?' (1995) 1 *European Law Journal* 31–59; D Grimm, 'Does Europe Need a Constitution?' (1995) 1 *European Law Journal* 282–302.

[65] For more on this argument, see Sangiovanni, *Domains of Justice*, chapter 3.

[66] See eg K Binmore, 'Reciprocity and the Social Contract' (2004) 3 *Politics, Philosophy & Economics* 5–35 and the useful survey in E Fehr and U Fischbacher, 'The Nature of Human Altruism' (2003) 425 *Nature* 785–91.

recognized system of norms promotes trust that people will continue to comply in the future. This effect is enhanced, in turn, when it is possible to build reputations—when knowledge of people's past willingness to contribute is widely available. In such cases, reputation functions as a signal of trustworthiness. In none of these cases is a common identity a necessary condition for the existence of the mutual trust required for stable patterns of generalized reciprocity.

But even if we concede that the thorough-going relations of solidarity typical of egalitarian welfare states cannot be sustained at the European level for the reasons given by *solidarity as fraternity*, there is no reason given why weaker relations of solidarity that are more demanding than humanitarianism but less demanding than full equality cannot develop at the European level. Indeed, if it is true that sustained relations of generalized reciprocity can generate mutual trust independently of common identity, and if it is true that such mutual trust is required for solidarity, then there seems to be at least a prima facie case why such weaker relations of solidarity could in fact develop, given the right conditions. The argument that norms of distributive justice and solidarity cannot apply at the European level because there is no sense of shared identity grounded in a common nationality therefore fails.

The second, more nuanced argument for *solidarity as fraternity* focuses on the link between nationality and collective agency. The argument turns on the idea that principles of distributive justice can only apply to persons who together constitute a viable collective political agent. According to this second version of the argument, there are a number of conditions which a 'people' organized for collective political agency must meet before principles of distributive justice can apply to it. I will use Pettit's recent interpretation of Rawls's argument in the *Law of Peoples* to make the point. Pettit writes:

> [A] people will be organized for agency... in a manner that goes precisely with its having a well-ordered structure. This involves continuous interaction between a[]...representative government and a[]...responsive citizenry. The members of any well-ordered people will be party to certain shared ideas that are capable of being articulated into a theory of justice. And they will control the government that represents them, they will constitute it as their representative to the extent that the government is ordered or regulated by those common reasons, and by the corresponding conception of justice.[67]

When a 'people' meets these conditions, it can be considered a collective agent proper. This is because, in these circumstances, a 'people' (1) has shared goals that the group pursues, and has procedures (not necessarily formal) for their selection, revision, and promotion; (2) it will act 'under the guidance of a body of judgments that members authorize as common property'; and (3) it displays 'a modicum of rationality' (to avoid, for example, familiar inconsistencies given by the nature of collective decision making).[68]

---

[67] Philip Pettit, 'Rawls's Peoples', in *Rawls's Law of Peoples: A Realistic Utopia?* R Martin and DA Reidy (eds) (Oxford: Blackwell, 2006), 48.

[68] Pettit, 'Rawls's Peoples', 46, 8. On Pettit's conception of collective agency, see Philip Pettit, *The Common Mind* (Oxford: Oxford University Press, 1993); cf Christopher Kutz, *Complicity: Ethics and Law for a Collective Age* (Cambridge: Cambridge University Press, 2000); Michael Bratman, 'I Intend That We J', in *Faces of*

The key condition for the liberal nationalist is (2). The liberal nationalist makes the further claim that persons which are a 'party to shared ideas [and common reasons] that are capable of being articulated into a theory of justice' must share what Miller calls 'a public culture'—a shared fund of beliefs, values, attitudes, and ritual observances which together are constitutive of nationality.[69] Once again, no shared nationality, no distributive justice; no pan-European national identity, no pan-European distributive justice.

There are at least two reasons why collective agency of this sort is necessary and sufficient for principles of distributive justice to apply. First, for the exercise of political authority in the name of distributive justice to be legitimate, directives must be capable of acceptance by those subject to them. The directives must, that is, not only track *common* interests but also *shared* goals and reasons. (Two people going on vacation to Greece *together* have a *shared* aim; two strangers on the same boat who happen both to be going to Greece on vacation merely have an aim *in common*.) The argument under consideration says that this justification can be successful only if it can be cast in terms of reasons widely available in the public political culture, including the political texts and traditions central to it. If there is no fund of shared reasons available or if the regime is not accountable to them, then the regime (even if it acts, say, to maximize the prospects of the worst off) can only be legitimate if all parties unanimously agree on the outcome.

Second, publicity—the idea that justice must not only be done but must also be seen to be done—is also a fundamental requirement of legitimate authority. The shared reasons there are must not only motivate policy but must also be known to motivate policy. But publicity, the argument goes, cannot be realized in the absence of a shared institutional system of rules and procedures ensuring both a 'modicum of rationality' and responsiveness to shared reasons. Coordinated and accountable political institutions create circumstances in which governing regimes can be relied on to act on shared reasons rather than on reasons serving merely special or private interests (for example, those of a ruling class). In the absence of a responsive institutional structure for making decisions, and given normal time constraints as well as the complexity of government policies for any citizen, directives cannot be known to reliably track shared reasons, and so cannot act either legitimately or *a fortiori* justly.

Both of these rationales for making this kind of collective political agency a condition for the application of principles of distributive justice more demanding than humanitarianism seem to me correct.[70] The mistake in the argument lies in the further, specifically liberal nationalist, premise which states that *only* nations, and therefore *not* the EU, are capable of the collective agency required for distributive

---

Intention, M Bratman (ed) (Cambridge: Cambridge University Press, 1999); J David Velleman, 'How to Share an Intention' (1997) 57 *Philosophy and Phenomenological Research* 28–49.

[69] Rawls can be interpreted as making a similar claim. See Rawls, *The Law of Peoples*; van Parijs and Rawls, 'Three Letters on the *Law of Peoples* and the European Union'.

[70] Indeed, although I cannot show this here, I believe they can be marshalled in support of the practice-dependence thesis.

justice to apply. After all, the EU—and, I would add, other international institutions such as the WTO, UN, and so on—do have a unified system of institutions which ensures both a 'modicum of rationality' and the selection and pursuit of shared goals; furthermore, the operation of each one, over time, has produced a fund of shared reasons (rooted in texts, traditions of argument, and so on) which can serve as a basis of both support and criticism. In the EU case, the fund is surely much thinner than at the domestic level, but there is enough there from which to construct a conception of solidarity adequate to the type of social cooperation made possible by the EU (recall the texts and debates with which we began this paper). It is important to emphasize, moreover, that this shared fund need not represent any consensus on values or beliefs. The shared fund of reasons could be constituted, for example, by a typical, recurring, and characteristic set of *disagreements* (just as it can at the domestic level). So, while the argument could be used to show that principles of distributive justice more demanding than humanitarianism cannot apply to 'the global institutional order' writ large (which is not organized as a collective agent of the relevant type), it cannot be used to establish the conclusion intended, namely that principles of distributive justice cannot apply to the EU.

4 Conclusion

In this chapter, I have reconstructed and rejected three strategies for answering our initial question regarding the nature of solidarity at the EU level. The aim, as I said in the introduction, was to demonstrate the need for more careful philosophical reflection on one of the fundamental values underpinning the EU, and to clear the ground of some of the most promising views currently available. One might naturally wonder at this point what a plausible alternative might look like. We can, I believe, draw several conclusions from our discussion. A plausible account of European solidarity should not begin with the EU's capacity (or incapacity) to coerce its members and citizens, with the depth and richness of European identity or fellow-feeling, or with the democratic quality of European institutions. Rather, the most plausible view will begin with the special character and nature of European social, political, legal, and economic *cooperation*, or, to put it another way, with the special character and nature of the *public goods* generated by participation in European institutions. On this view, it is our relation as participants in the maintenance and reproduction of such public goods (rather than our relations as subjects of coercion, bearers of an identity, or democratic citizens) that trigger stronger social justice norms, which are in turn interpreted as demands of *reciprocity*. To make this plausible, much more would need to be said regarding what this reciprocity involves and among whom it applies. We would also need to provide a precise characterization of the public goods generated by European cooperation, and, more generally, an account of the point and purpose of the EU against which we can make sense of the idea of a fair return.

If, for example, we conceive of the EU as a way for Member States to enhance their domestic problem-solving capacities in an era of globalization, while indemnifying each other against the risks and losses associated with pooled decision-making authority, then what would count as a fair allocation of those risks? To what extent should Member States and their citizens share in the economic and social fate of their fellow members and citizens? I cannot hope to provide a satisfactory answer to these questions here.[71] But I do hope to have at least made the questions raised, and the lines of inquiry traced, interesting ones.

---

[71] I answer this question in 'Solidarity in the European Union', *Oxford Journal of Legal Studies* (forthcoming); see also Sangiovanni, *Domains of Justice,* Part III.

16

The Problem of Justice in the European Union

Values, Pluralism, and Critical Legal Justice

Sionaidh Douglas-Scott*

Achieving justice in the EU is problematic. The many differences between Member State legal systems, and their varied attitudes towards, for example, redistribution of wealth, render an overarching concept of justice for the EU seemingly unattainable. Indeed, the complex, pluralist landscape of EU law and governance, with its fragmented lines of authority and near invisible accountabilities, seems to render injustice all the more likely. Further, it might seem that the concept of justice itself is pluralist, capable of many understandings and interpretations. How is justice achievable, given this complexity? Yet EU law must seek to promote justice—what would we say of a legal system that did not seek to do so? In this chapter, I argue for justice as a value to be promoted by the EU. In order to aid its realization, I argue for the recasting and re-imagining of the rule of law as *Critical Legal Justice*—a vibrant concept of justice able to span the Byzantine complexities of the EU.

1 Values

Values have somehow found their way into key EU texts in the early years of the twenty-first century. For example, the Treaty of Lisbon introduces the following values (in wording identical to that of the defunct Constitutional Treaty) into Article 2 TEU:

Article 2
    The Union is founded on the values of respect for human dignity, freedom, democracy, equality, the rule of law and respect for human rights, including the rights of persons belonging to minorities. These values are common to the Member States in a society in

* Professor of European and Human Rights Law, University of Oxford.

which pluralism, non-discrimination, tolerance, justice, solidarity and equality between women and men prevail.

On the other hand, other elements, not described as 'values', are clearly also apparently presented as important, and follow on in Article 3, in imperative form. For example, the EU 'shall offer its citizens an area of freedom, security and justice', 'shall work for . . . a highly competitive social market economy', 'shall promote social justice', and 'shall contribute to peace, security, the sustainable development of the Earth, solidarity and mutual respect among peoples, free and fair trade, eradication of poverty and the protection of human rights'.

There are many observations that one could make about this twenty-first-century insertion of values into EU Treaty texts. One is that, after the failed Constitutional Treaty, and a lukewarm (or even negative, in the case of the Irish referendum) response to the Lisbon Treaty, it is not the best of times to be introducing 'values' into a project in which the public obviously has so little interest, other than as a perceived means to prosperity. Yet the retention of 'values' from the failed Constitutional Treaty suggests a continuing optimism as to the capacity of the EU to function as something beyond that of a Common Market, or an economic entity. Is such optimism misplaced? The crisis of the Eurozone from 2010, and the austerity conditions imposed on some of its members, might seem to undermine any EU claims to democracy or social justice at the very least.

An immediate problem lies in the incoherence of presentation of all of these values and objectives in the Treaties. This does not bode well for their fulfilment. Why are some ambitions described as aims or objectives rather than values? Surely this lessens their importance, renders them less compelling? Why should peace, or social justice, be classified as aims rather than values? And what to make of the fact that so many different values and aims, and principles, of a different ideological bent appear grouped together? Is it really possible for the EU to fulfil its aim of being 'a highly competitive social market economy, aiming at full employment and social progress',[1] and to promote 'social justice', especially in these days of world recession, and crisis of the Eurozone, when at its very centre for over fifty years has been free trade and competition? Can the EU really contribute to 'peace, security and sustainable development of the Earth'? Or are these just nice-sounding words? Such an extraordinarily (over) ambitious set of values and goals for the EU tends to suggest either an immodest belief in the EU's capabilities or a rather cavalier inclusion of all 'good things', in order to make the first part of the EU treaties acceptable and alluring to all. We might note that the Preamble to the TEU states that these 'universal values' have developed from 'the cultural, religious and humanist inheritance of Europe'. Are they universal, and if so, can they truly have developed from the singular, particular European inheritance? And do all the peoples of the EU share a religious and humanist heritage in any case? Overall, the early Treaty provisions present themselves as a rather incoherent jumble.

---

[1] The terminology used in Art 3 TEU.

My central observation however, and the concern of this chapter, turns on what seems to me to be a significant omission. Justice is notably not presented as one of the EU's founding values in Article 2 TEU. We are told that justice 'should prevail' in this society but not that justice is one of its values. Why not? Surely, in the many years in which the EU has interrogated itself, its identity and its ambitions, it must acknowledge the crucial importance of justice. If it does not set justice as a fundamental value then what is its worth? What might we say of any society or legal entity that would not embrace justice as a founding value, especially one such as the EU which has, from its earliest days, set a premium on 'integration through law'[2] (law and justice of course being intimately related)? One might believe it possible to infer justice as a value for the EU from the sum total of all the other values, aims, objectives, and principles that it embraces. Yet this seems unsatisfactory—one should not have to extract or distil justice as a value from a range of clauses and provisions—its salience surely renders its importance freestanding. For after all, as John Rawls stipulated, 'Justice is the first virtue of social institutions'[3]—a suggestion to be taken very seriously, even if one does not concur with Rawls's actual proposed substantive theory of justice. Note that at this stage, I am not suggesting that we should understand justice in any particular sense, thick or thin;[4] rather, that it is a value whose importance is immediately recognizable in some sort of Dworkinian 'pre-interpretive' sense,[5] and should surely be acknowledged by an EU which wishes to proclaim its values.

A recent study, *The Ethos of Europe: Values, Law and Justice in the EU*, by Andrew Williams,[6] castigates the EU for lacking any coherence in its values or ethos, and for an absence of a clear moral purpose. Everyone might agree that peace and prosperity are desirable, but beyond this, the EU presents an 'unresolved political problem'.[7] It has not found its 'soul'[8] (Jacques Delors' aspiration for the EU). The values identified by the Lisbon Treaty amendments may present, as Tridimas[9] has suggested, a 'moral identity' for the EU, but if so, accompanied by an overabundance of other objectives, principles, and policy statements, their expression in the Lisbon Treaty provides a confusing and particularly inept way to construct a meaningful moral identity or philosophical framework for the EU. I agree with Williams. The omission of justice as an explicit value, even if it might eventually be found to be lurking around or hiding behind or deducible from other provisions, suggests a lack of clear vision, coherence, and insight at the very centre of the EU.

---

[2] See eg M Cappelletti, M Seccombe, and J Weiler (eds), *Integration Through Law* (Berlin and New York: Walter de Gruyter, 1986).

[3] J Rawls, *A Theory of Justice* (Cambridge, MA: Harvard University Press, 1971), 3.

[4] 'Thick' and 'thin' senses of justice are discussed below.

[5] See R Dworkin *Law's Empire* (Cambridge, MA: Harvard University Press, 1986).

[6] A Williams, *The Ethos of Europe* (Cambridge, UK: Cambridge University Press, 2010).

[7] Étienne Balibar, *We, the People of Europe? Reflections on Transnational Citizenship* (Princeton NJ: Princeton University Press, 2003).

[8] President Delors, Speech to the churches. Brussels, 4 February 1992.

[9] See T Tridimas, *The General Principles of EU Law*, 2nd edn (Oxford: Oxford University Press, 2006), 16.

Williams' conclusion is that the EU has adopted a largely pragmatic concentration on principles rather than on defining or realizing values. Its ethos has been technical rather than ethical, with the requirements of the market providing a 'value surrogacy'. It has not taken justice seriously. This seems to me very plausible. This is a highly critical state of affairs and a brief reflection on three areas of EU activity—its self-presentation as 'an area of freedom, security and justice' (especially its action in the field of criminal law), and on what might loosely be described as matters affecting the field of social policy and social justice, as well as its actions in the field of economic and monetary union and attempted resolutions of the Eurozone debt and financial crisis, serve to illustrate this.

2 Injustice in the EU

In 1997, in the context of the Treaty of Amsterdam, the EU created an 'Area of Freedom, Security and Justice' (AFSJ)—an area which has constitutional status in EU law due to its inclusion in Article 3 TEU, although EU law nowhere provides a definition of the concepts of 'freedom', security', or 'justice'. However, as a concept including the term 'justice', the AFSJ seems at least a good place to start in an examination of whether and how EU law delivers justice. The concept of an AFSJ was supposed to make the EU citizen feel closer to the EU and more included by it. But what is most notable is that within the scope of the AFSJ, the EU is able to adopt all sorts of measures which have not traditionally been associated with EU action, including measures on terrorism, migration management, visa policies, asylum, privacy and security, the fight against organized crime, and criminal justice.

Unfortunately, it has become almost a commonplace to state that, in the context of the EU's AFSJ, freedom and justice are being sacrificed to the needs of security. The 'justice' of the AFSJ seems to have been understood by the EU as merely the technical administration of justice. Although the AFSJ is intended to be an 'an area of rights' according to the European Commission,[10] and, since the Lisbon Treaty came into force on 1 December 2009, the EU's Charter of Fundamental Rights at last has binding force, the EU has generally been slow to adopt measures on rights,[11] and too quick to adopt more coercive and potentially rights-violating measures such as the European Arrest Warrant, or the extremely broad EU definition of terrorism. Furthermore, at least until the Lisbon Treaty amendments, access to justice, in terms of court review of AFSJ measures, has been severely lacking. There has been an overall deficit of justice.

---

[10] See Commission, 'Report on the practical operation of the methodology for a systematic and rigorous monitoring of compliance with the Charter of Fundamental Rights', COM(2009) 205 final.

[11] A draft Procedural Rights framework decision under discussion for some years had not been adopted at time of writing. See however, Directive 2010/64/(EU) of the European Parliament and of the Council L280/1 on the right to interpretation and translation in criminal proceedings. Also, an EU Framework decision on data protection was adopted in 2009 after years of discussion, as well as the EU's Framework decision on combating certain forms and expressions of racism and xenophobia.

The nature of all of this activity undermines the claim made by some theorists that the legitimacy, or morality, of EU action should not be of primary concern because the EU lacks all of the competences of a traditional state and its powers are mainly economic. Such an approach focuses on so-called 'output legitimacy'—namely, the EU's activities are seen as legitimized in terms of effective and efficient output.[12] Yet within the scope of the AFSJ are matters that are crucial, for example, the relation between the individual and public authorities. It is therefore crucial that the AFSJ be developed in the spirit of a 'constitutional moment', as a space of hope, rather than what Pocock has called a 'Machiavellian moment'[13] (that is, an attempt to remain stable by any means in the face of a stream of irrational events). To this end, justice and human rights should play a crucial role.

In the domain of social justice, the problem is even more critical. As long ago as 1975, AG Trabucchi famously stated: 'If we want Community law to be more than a mere mechanical system of economics and to constitute instead a system commensurate with the society which it has to govern, if we wish it to be a legal system corresponding to the concept of social justice and European integration, not only of the economy but of the people, we cannot fail to live up to what is expected of us.'[14] Less was expected in 1975 than now, given the more restricted competences and membership of the EEC in those days. Yet even applying a lower expectation of justice, it cannot be said that the EEC and then EU, has lived up to expectations.

Yet what possible meaning can be given to 'social justice' as an aspiration in Article 3 TEU, for an EU which has for so long focused on a market-driven ideology? The problem of course is a complex one. One cannot deny the benefits of EU law and Court of Justice case law, for example, in the field of the equal treatment of men and women. However, even these benefits have been market-driven, by the need to secure a level playing field in an area of free movement, rather than by a freestanding concern for equality. For so many years of the EU's existence, equal treatment law failed to extend beyond the field of employment and beyond the equal treatment of men and women to discrimination of other sorts; for example, of sexual orientation, or race. It is not necessarily that the EU has turned its back on redistribution of wealth, nor on social justice, rather that such a policy remains well-nigh impossible as a harmonized common policy for the EU when its Member States differ and are so divided as to whether social welfare should be market-driven or redistributionist and 'welfarist'. Unlike in the context of the fight against terrorism and organized crime within the AFSJ, where there appears to be a consensus[15] among both the European publics and

---

[12] See F Scharpf, *Governing in Europe: Effective and Democratic?* (Oxford: Oxford University Press, 1999); A Moravscik, 'In defence of democratic deficit: reassessing legitimacy in the EU' (2002) 40 *Journal of Common Market Studies* 4.

[13] J Pocock, *The Machiavellian Moment: Florentine Political Thought and the Atlantic Republican Tradition* Revised edn (Princeton, NJ: Princeton University Press, 2003).

[14] Opinion of Advocate General Trabucchi in Case 7/75 *Mr. and Mrs. F v Belgium* [1975] 6 ECR 679.

[15] eg Eurobaromoter, *Opinions on organised, cross-border crime and corruption,* European Commission March 2006.

governments in favour of active EU policies, there is no consensus as to the desirability of a redistributive EU social policy. Indeed, if anything, there exists a mutual mistrust, as illustrated by polarized reactions to the Lisbon Treaty, with some states seeing earlier drafts as too free-market and Anglo-Saxon in approach. In such an environment, EU joint action is restricted to low minimum standards acceptable to all states, or the very limited redistributive functions in the fields of regional development policy and the varying budgetary contributions of its Member States.

Given these circumstances, as Fritz Scharpf has asserted,

> European integration has created a constitutional asymmetry between policies promoting market efficiencies and policies promoting social protection and equality. National welfare states are legally and economically constrained by European rules of economic integration, liberalization, and competition law, whereas efforts to adopt European social policies are politically impeded by the diversity of national welfare states, differing not only in levels of economic development and hence in their ability to pay for social transfers and services but, even more significantly, in their normative aspirations and institutional structures.[16]

Perhaps most critical is that the Court of Justice has been willing to assert the equivalence of fundamental market freedoms and fundamental rights, with no positive outcome for fundamental rights. In both *Viking Line* and *Laval*[17] it was claimed that the applicant undertakings' market freedoms had been restricted by trade union collective action. Although the right to take such action was at least acknowledged by the Court as a 'fundamental right', in both cases it was interpreted as a 'restriction' on a fundamental market freedom. The Court took a broad approach to the application of EU law, holding that collective action could restrict market access. It then went on to weigh the freedom to provide services against this fundamental right to strike, in effect interpreting the right to strike as a *restriction* on the market freedom. The Court found that the right to strike must be exercised proportionately. Such reasoning is antipathetic to fundamental rights and has been strongly criticized. As has so often been the case in the EU, the Internal Market lies at the centre of things, and proportionality's essential function is to ensure that market integration is not too greatly compromised. In such a mindset,[18] social justice will always be compromised. And yet, 'social justice' here carries further complexities, capable of morphing into a means of protecting labour privileges of the more prosperous EU states at the expense of newer EU states keen to gain access to new labour markets. In this highly complex minefield, whither social justice for the EU?

In any case, it is difficult to see how the EU can promote itself as the sort of social market community urged by Habermas,[19] when so many of its members would veto

---

[16] F Scharpf, 'The European Social Model: Coping with the Challenges of Diversity', MPIfG Working Paper 02/8.

[17] Case C-438/05 *Viking Line* [2007] ECR I-10779; Case C-341/05 *Laval* [2007] ECR-I 11767.

[18] Also, see eg F Scharpf, 'The double asymmetry of European integration—or why the EU cannot be a social market economy' MPIfG Paper 09/12; C Joerges 'Rechtstaat and Social Europe' (2010) *Journal of Comparative Sociology* 65–85.

[19] See eg J Habermas, 'Why Europe Needs a Constitution' (2001) *New Left Review* 11. Habermas' theory is discussed further below.

such a role for it. In the absence of such a common policy, developments in the social law field have been incremental, ad hoc, tangential to free movement concerns, rather than comprehensive in nature, and inevitably also derived from litigation before the Court of Justice, which has had other motivations (usually enjoyment of free movement, such as in *Viking Line* and *Laval*) as its immediate inspiration.

The handling of the recent financial crisis, within the Eurozone states in particular, perhaps provides the most critical example of injustice. The original legal arrangements for Economic and Monetary Union (EMU) did not provide explicit mechanisms to deal with a debt crisis, probably because the original premise for EMU was that there should be no debt and no deficit within states and hence no need for bailouts. Notably, Article 122 TFEU, the provision which was partly used as a basis to deal with the Greek bailout, refers to 'severe difficulties caused by natural disasters or exceptional occurrences' beyond a Member State's control, rather than financial or economic crisis. The EU has had to remedy this situation by further action since 2010.

Since the onset of the crisis, EU Member States and institutions have limped from summit to summit, instigating a seemingly incessant series of measures in an ad hoc and reactive way. New measures on economic governance have been adopted, and austerity measures have been institutionalized through mandatory limits on public spending and adjustment of labour market policies in favour of more flexibility and lower wages. These dramatic changes have been advanced speedily and without great transparency, under the pretext of restoring stability in the Eurozone. Such measures have not always taken the form of traditional EU legal instruments but have also consisted of international agreements between the Member States.[20]

The scope and impact of these measures has often been breathtaking, as for example, those imposed by the 'conditionality' clauses in bailout agreements. The conditions imposed by the Greek bailout in 2010 provide a good example. These required Greece to end its deficit situation by adopting measures (described by one author as 'the most drastic intervention in a member State's economic and social policy ever decided by the EU')[21] including, for example, to reduce pensions, the reduction of public investment, and a reform of wage legislation in the public sector.[22] Forty-five measures in all were required and Greece was given until December 2011 for implementation.[23]

---

[20] As in the case of the European Stability Mechanism (ESM)—see xxx.

[21] R Bieber, 'Observer, Policeman Pilot: On lacunae of legitimacy and the contradictions of financial crisis management in the EU' EUI Law Working Paper 2011/16.

[22] Council Decision 2010/320, [2010] OJ L145/6 (as amended by Council Decision 2010/486 [2010] OJ L241/12) respectively Articles 2(1)(e), 2(1)(n), 2(2)(d).

[23] Further measures in Council Decision 2010/320 also included: a law to reform the wage bargaining system in the private sector, which should provide for a reduction in pay rates for overtime work, enhanced flexibility in the management of working time and allow local territorial pacts to set wage growth below sectoral agreements (Art 2(3)(d)); and a reform of employment protection legislation to extend the probationary period for new jobs to one year, reduce the overall level of severance payments and ensure that the same severance payment conditions apply to blue- and white-collar workers, raise the minimum threshold for the rules on collective dismissals to apply, especially for larger companies, and facilitate a greater use of temporary contracts (Art 2(3)(e)).

In May 2010, the EU Commission made further proposals to aid financial stability in the EU—specifically a European Financial Stabilization Mechanism (EFSM)[24] established by Council regulation and European Financial Stability Facility (EFSF)[25] taking the form of an intergovernmental agreement. Further bailouts were made of Ireland and Portugal under these measures, along with IMF contributions, which imposed conditions similar to those under the Greek bailout. Yet more measures followed, namely a permanent European Stability Mechanism (ESM),[26] established by treaty between Eurozone Member States, which is to replace the EFSF and EFSM. The ESM is to provide financial assistance on the basis of strict conditionality, following a macro-economic adjustment programme and robust analysis of public debt sustainability conducted by the Commission along with the IMF and ECB. At the same time the ESM was negotiated, a 'Euro pact' was concluded in March 2011,[27] requiring Member States to monitor labour law and wages to ensure competitiveness, and stipulating that regard to 'sustainability of pensions, health care and social benefits' should be the primary means of ensuring 'sound public finances'. However, as the Euro pact does not include strong enforcement measures, even more action was needed, and a range of binding provisions in a package of six legislative measures on economic governance (sometimes referred to colloquially as the 'six pack') was adopted later in 2011.[28] This 'six pack', consisting of five regulations and one directive, was approved by all twenty-seven Member States and the European Parliament and represents the most comprehensive reinforcement of economic governance in the EU and the Eurozone since the launch of EMU. From 2012, the European Parliament and Commission will have the power to scrutinize national budgets before even national parliaments have the chance to do so. If Member States fail to reduce their debts or refuse budgetary suggestions from Brussels, they can be subject to enforcement measures, which can lead to fines of up to 0.05 per cent of GDP. The most serious breaches are those of the reinforced Stability Pact's[29] two requirements (to keep deficits below 3 per cent of GDP and debt below 60 per cent). Further, Member States will only be able to avoid fines or other sanctions if a qualified majority in the Council

---

[24] Council Regulation 407/2010 establishing a European financial stabilization mechanism [2010] OJ L118/1.

[25] Terms of reference of the Eurogroup, European Financial Stability Facility, Luxembourg, 7 June 2010. EFSF Framework Agreement, Execution Version, 7 June 2010.

[26] Treaty Establishing the European Stability Mechanism, 11 July 2011.

[27] 'The Euro Plus Pact: Stronger Economic Policy Coordination For Competitiveness And Convergence', annexed to European Council Conclusions, Brussels, 20 April 2011, EUCO 10/1/11, REV 1.

[28] For details see Council briefing of 8 November 2011, accessible at: <http://www.consilium.europa.eu/uedocs/cms_data/docs/pressdata/en/ecofin/125952.pdf>.

[29] The Stability and Growth Pact was concluded by the European Council in December 1996. It lays out the rules for the budgetary discipline of the Euro member states and binds all parties to engage in the prompt implementation of the 'Excessive deficit procedure', should any of them fail to meet the agreements of the pact. The procedure is enforced when a member state runs a public deficit of over 3 per cent of its GDP in any year, and, additionally, governments may not allow total government debt to exceed 60 per cent of GDP. The 'six pack' measures reinforce its provisions.

vote against them, a procedure which might be seen as amounting to 'semi-automatic' sanctions.

As if this were not enough, in 2012 the Eurozone adopted yet another crisis measure, this time taking the form of an international agreement[30] on a 'reinforced economic union' (Treaty on stability, coordination and governance in the economic and monetary union, often referred to as the 'Fiscal Compact Treaty' 2012) which raises further serious issues of democratic accountability, not to mention this projected treaty's relationship with, and compatibility with, EU law.

All of these measures were adopted with little debate and a minimum of public awareness. Most Europeans have little idea that such changes, involving such inroads into their governments' economic sovereignty, have taken place.

In the light of these measures, the warnings of those such as Alex Callinicos, who counselled against the original adoption of the single currency ('the introduction of this currency, the euro, in present circumstances is likely to have a devastating effect on the jobs, wages, and collective consumption of the European working class')[31] seem prescient. The EU and its Member States' response to the crisis of its currency has been characterized by a continuous flurry of non-transparent and undemocratic measures, distancing economic governance from the control of elected governments and national parliaments, in an extremely complex and confusing melée of arrangements of EU law and international agreements between the states.

Further, it would seem that many of these measures have brought the EU into conflict with both human rights and its own Treaties and proclaimed values. For example, the Lisbon Treaty's objective of 'a highly competitive social market economy' (Article 3(3)) has already been noted. It would be hard to argue that the measures and reforms detailed above are compatible with a social market economy, nor with the provisions of Article 9 TFEU which states that '[i]n defining and implementing its policies and activities, the Union shall take into account requirements linked to the promotion of a high level of employment, the guarantee of adequate social protection, the fight against social exclusion, and a high level of education, training and protection of human health'. Further, the conditionality clauses in the bailout agreements, imposing restrictions on the availability of collective bargaining, show little concern for the special status of the social partners recognized by Article 152 TFEU: 'The Union recognises and promotes the role of the social partners at its level, taking into account the diversity of national systems. It shall facilitate dialogue between the social

---

[30] An intergovernmental treaty, signed by all members of the EU, except the Czech Republic and the UK, on 2 March 2012. In a referendum held on 31 May 2012, the Irish voted in favour of the Fiscal Compact treaty. The treaty will come into effect on 1 January 2013, if by then twelve or more of its signatories who are members of the euro area have ratified it.

[31] See A Callinicos, 'Europe: The Mounting Crisis' (1997) 75 *International Socialism* 23 at 41. A critique of the euro and the EU's handling of the euro crisis goes well beyond those commenting from a socialist perspective. For a recent critique of the imposition of austerity through untransparent Eurozone measures see eg F Scharpf, 'Monetary Union, Fiscal Crisis and the Preemption of Democracy' MPIfG Discussion Paper 11/11.

partners, respecting their autonomy', or with the freedom of association recognized in both the ECHR and EU Charter of Fundamental Rights.[32]

The handling of the Eurozone crisis also reveals a very serious deficit of democracy in the EU. Elected politicians (prime ministers, in the case of Greece and Italy) have been forced out of office, to be replaced by unelected bureaucrats, or 'economic experts', without any electoral mandate. National budgets will become the property of EU institutions as much as of national governments and parliaments. This is hugely troubling, but the challenges of democracy for the EU are beyond the scope of this chapter. Although some theorists have challenged any essential difference between democracy and justice,[33] or propose substituting discourse on the democratic deficit with that of transnational justice,[34] this approach will not be taken here, and the discussion of this chapter is confined to justice, while acknowledging that justice and democracy can be related, and that many of the Eurozone crisis measures might be regarded as a travesty of democracy.

This short reflection on three areas of EU law might suggest that it is the lack of justice, or the presence of injustice, which is more to be observed than justice within the EU. What is to be done? Andrew Williams' suggested solution to the EU's failure to take justice seriously is to propose a human rights centred concept of justice—one which understands human rights primarily as a response to suffering. I agree with much of what Williams suggests. Human rights are of course crucial and should play a vital role in European integration. In particular, collective rights, which have a presence (albeit a rather slim one)[35] in the Charter of Fundamental Rights, can enable justice to be done. But as in the case of democracy, I would suggest that human rights are not the same thing as justice, or at least, they may only be part of an understanding of justice. Not every situation of injustice can be framed in terms of human rights.[36] This is not to belittle the role of human rights in any way—indeed, I have written elsewhere, urging the importance of their full recognition in the EU and in the wider European context.[37] However in this chapter, rather than eliding justice with human rights, I seek to focus more directly on the concept of justice itself, to give it its own

---

[32] Further, all twenty-seven EU member States have ratified the International Labour Organization (ILO) Convention no 154 on promotion of collective bargaining and ILO Convention no 87 on freedom of association. Greek Trade Unions complained to the ILO regarding the imposition of bailout conditions, and in particular restrictions on collective bargaining. In this context, the CEACR (2011 Report of the Committee of Experts on the Application of Conventions and Recommendations) of the ILO held that 'restrictions on collective bargaining should only be imposed as exceptional measures and only to the extent necessary, without exceeding a reasonable period' (Report, 83).

[33] eg R Forst, 'Transnational Justice and democracy' RECON Working Paper 2011/12 Oslo 2011.

[34] J Neyer, 'Justice, not Democracy: Legitimacy in the EU' (2010) 48 *Journal of Common Market Studies* 903.

[35] See eg the somewhat qualified provisions on 'Solidarity' in Title IV of the Charter of Fundamental Rights of the European Union.

[36] For example, Rawls's Difference Principle, which permits redistribution of wealth, in order to benefit the least well off in society is not based on human rights principles.

[37] eg S Douglas-Scott, 'Europe's Constitutional Mosaic: Human rights in the European legal space—utopia, dystopia, monotopia or polytopia?' in N Walker, J Shaw and S Tierney (eds), *Europe's Constitutional Mosaic*, (Oxford: Hart Publishing, 2011).

meaning, as a freestanding concept, to engage more deeply with what particular form it should take in the EU, given the peculiarities and singularities of the EU legal order. In order to do this, one must first engage with the pluralism of the EU itself, which has made some authors question the possibility of a workable, overarching concept of justice. Pluralism, soft law, governance, and networks—all recognizable aspects of the EU legal space—create particular problems for the provision of justice. This does not end the complexity of the investigation, however, for it will also be necessary to consider the possible pluralism of the concept of justice itself.

3 Pluralism in the EU

European law reveals many complex, interesting interactions and relationships between pluralities of laws and legal systems; indeed, it is probably one of the best contemporary examples of legal pluralism. On the one hand, EU law is a distinct legal order—it has acquired what MacCormick described as 'self-referentiality'.[38] Yet EU law also interlocks and interacts with municipal laws in a post-sovereign Europe, where there are no longer any absolutely sovereign states. EU law illustrates that legal systems are not, or at least no longer are, solid and palpable entities.[39]

European law is a sphere of overlapping jurisdictions, segmented authority, and multiple loyalties, carrying with it the risk of constitutional crisis and of officials being compelled to choose between their loyalties to different public institutions. In such circumstances, it is perhaps no wonder that the EU Treaties present an incoherent jumble of values and aims. Mireille Delmas-Marty, writing about European law generally, has described it as a zone in which, 'incomplete pyramids surrounded by strange loops are mocking the old hierarchies'.[40] The plurality of European human rights jurisdictions—national, EU, and ECHR—is a good example of these phenomena,[41] as illustrated by the well-known *Bosphorus* case, in which a Turkish airline, whose aircraft (leased from a Yugoslav company) had been seized under sanctions against former Yugoslavia, sued in all three of these jurisdictions over a total of

---

[38] N MacCormick, *Questioning Sovereignty* (Oxford: Oxford University Press, 1999).

[39] For theories which challenge, or aim to advance on, the understanding of law in terms of solid, palpable systems, see Chapter 2, J Dickson (arguing that while the concept of a legal system, and of distinct legal systems, remains of explanatory importance for the contemporary EU, the nature of the EU raises particular problems for that concept that need to be addressed); also the contribution of K Culver and M Giudice in Chapter 3 (arguing that the concept of a legal system is inadequate to explain the dynamic and other special features of the contemporary EU and that an alternative 'inter-institutional account' is necessary).

[40] M Delmas-Marty, *Pour un droit commun* (Paris: Seuil, 1994).

[41] But so is the Eurozone, with its melée of different legal arrangements, and different participants in different agreements, making it a paradigm example of legal pluralism and multi-level governance—see eg F Snyder, 'EMU—Integration and Differentiation: Metaphor for European Union', in P Craig and G de Búrca, *The Evolution of EU Law* (Oxford: Oxford University Press, 2011).

thirteen years—and lost in all three, illustrating that more choice does not always necessarily equate with success for litigants.[42]

The fluidity, crossovers, and spatial morphologies of the European legal world recall innovations of recent science—of chaos theory, twister space, Borromean knots, Moebius bands, and 'rubber maths', whereby figures are pulled and twisted and reshaped in different ways. Zygmunt Bauman has characterized this situation as a 'liquid modernity', recalling the Communist Manifesto's evocation of 'all that is solid melts into air'.[43] Others might prefer to characterize this legal space as 'postmodern'.[44] In any case, it presents a sharp contrast to an earlier modernist paradigm that tends towards a more mechanical order—with a precise, clockwork-like nature.[45]

It is impossible to categorize such complex legal landscapes by referring to a neat, self-contained conception of law, such as those associated with various theories of twentieth-century legal positivism—for example, the orderly Kelsonian pyramid, or Hart's systematic concept of law as the union of primary and secondary rules.[46] Instead, legal pluralism has become a popular paradigm,[47] and it is not a paradigm that I wish to challenge, or at least not if pluralism is taken as a statement of fact or description of the contemporary legal landscape.[48] Legal pluralism describes a state of affairs in which two or more legal orders occupy the same legal area, sometimes peacefully coexisting but sometimes in direct competition with each other. Pluralism is extolled by its adherents as a model that more genuinely captures the legal world than monism or legal positivism, and pluralism is often promoted with a breathless enthusiasm.[49] The assumption is also that it is less oppressive than earlier unifying modernist paradigms, less silencing of voices and other ways of doing things. Yet legal pluralism brings its own worries, which are all too often ignored, or downplayed, in the urge for flexible, diverse regulation.

For example, the complex legal pluralism of the EU carries increased risks of a lack of accountability, of self-regulating institutions or localized laws being captured by

---

[42] For a comment on *Bosphorus*, see S Douglas-Scott (2006) 43 CML Rev 83, also S Douglas-Scott, 'A Tale of Two Courts' (2006) 43 CML Rev 629.

[43] Z Bauman, *Liquid Modernity* (Cambridge: Polity Press, 2000).

[44] See eg B Sousa Santos, *Toward a New Common Sense: Law, Science and Politics in the Paradigmatic Transition* (London: Routledge, 1995); I Ward, 'Identity and Difference: The European Union and Postmodernism', in J Shaw and G More (eds), *New Legal Dynamics Of European Union* (Oxford: Oxford University Press, 1995), 15, 21–6.

[45] See eg R Dawkins, *The Blind Watchmaker* (London: Penguin, 1988).

[46] H Kelsen, *The Pure Theory of Law* (Berkeley and Los Angeles: University of California Press, 1967); HLA Hart, *The Concept of Law* (Oxford: The Clarendon Press, 1961); see also Chapters 2 and 3 in this volume for a different view.

[47] For more general theories of pluralism see eg S Falk Moore, 'Law and Social Change: The semi autonomous social field as an appropriate object of study' (1973) 7 *Law & Society Review* 719; S Engle Merry, 'Legal Pluralism' (1988) 22 *Law & Society Review* 869; J Griffiths, 'What is Legal Pluralism?' (1986) 24 *Journal of Legal Pluralism* 2–55; for the particular relevance of legal pluralism in the EU and in international law, see also MacCormick (see n 38); N Krisch, *Beyond Constitutionalism: The pluralist structure of postnational law*) (Oxford: Oxford University Press, 2010).

[48] As will become apparent, I am concerned with, and critical of, legal pluralism when it is presented as a normative model, ie not only as a description of legal affairs but also as a desirable model for them.

[49] eg AM Slaughter, *A New World Order* (Princeton NJ: Princeton University Press, 2005).

special interests, and of 'a fragmented and impotent polity in which the public interest is emptied of meaning'.[50] Accountability can be very weak in this pluralistic landscape, and institutional design and effective tutelage become ever more important. An example of this is provided by the transfer of criminal law competences from Member State to EU level, resulting in (at least pre-Lisbon) a change from national parliamentary control to a situation of intergovernmental legislation by the Council of Ministers, with very little, if any, parliamentary control. Furthermore, relationships of authority can be difficult to trace because what might appear to be strictly hierarchical relationships in fact involve mutual incorporation or mutual influence. How to attribute motive or agency where injustice is fragmented, systemic, and impersonal? How are conflicts to be settled, and by which standards? How will we identify those 'like' cases that are to be treated alike? How will we treat persons with equal concern and respect if there is no uniform system? How may law be legitimate? Does the overwhelming complexity of the legal world diminish the prospects for justice?

Indeed, to conclude this section, I would suggest that justice is *the key* issue for law in the era of legal pluralism. Rather than, or at least in addition to, questions of ordering[51] or interpreting pluralism, we should ask how is justice achievable, given this complexity? Ultimately, therefore, how is justice possible?

4 Justice

The concept of justice is thus doubly crucial for the EU. First, because the EU has failed to deliver justice in high-profile areas such as the AFSJ, social policy or EMU, and has failed explicitly to embrace justice as a value. But secondly, given the EU's complicated brand of legal pluralism (that is, situations of great complexity, in which traditional mechanisms of democracy and accountability may no longer apply) the question of how to achieve justice becomes highly salient.

How to interrogate the concept of justice for the EU? The obvious concern is that achieving justice in a supra-national community, and in the context of pluralism, raises particularly complicated issues. Furthermore, confronting the nature of justice for the EU raises justice in all of its manifold forms—substantive and procedural, distributive and corrective. It is not only one type, or aspect, of justice that is at issue. For example, the question of securing social justice in the EU raises very thorny issues of distributive justice, whereas the problems of the AFSJ will often turn on issues of corrective justice, which raise different concerns, but may be equally problematic for a

---

[50] P Nonet and P Selznick, *Law in Society: Toward Responsive Law* (New York: Harper Colophon, 1979), 103; T Lowi, *The End of Liberalism* (New York: Norton, 1989); also C Scott 'Analysing Regulatory Space: Fragmented Resources and Institutional Design' (2001) PL 329, for the view that institutional design is increasingly important.

[51] See eg M Delmas Marty, *Ordering Pluralism* (Oxford: Hart Publishing, 2009).

transnational community. The parties involved are also multiple—EU [i]nstitutions, Member States and even individuals, may all owe duties of justice.

Yet complex though these issues are, it is notable that general scholarship on justice contains a wealth of resources that may be applied in the EU context. These resources span the immense scope of justice, and its requirement as a moral imperative in so many varied circumstances. Justice has a pervasive aspect—it is hard to imagine that any community, however large, might escape its remit. It is a necessary part of our moral landscape.[52] According to Walzer, nothing can be omitted, 'no feature of our common life can escape its scrutiny'.[53]

(A) The Search for an Overarching, Transnational Justice

Yet there remain theorists who believe that justice is only capable of having a local form or expression, and can only function within the nation-state or smaller community, and not across boundaries. If this were so, a theory of justice for the EU, overall, as a polity, would be an elusive or impossible quest. John Rawls, in his late career work, *The Law of Peoples*,[54] denied the applicability of the twofold principles of justice articulated in his earlier *Theory of Justice* (namely, first that of equal access to basic liberties, and second, the 'Difference Principle', which ensures that unequal social distributions are only permissible if they benefit the worst off in society) in a global context, preferring instead something akin to the principles of existing international law. Rawls believed his theory of justice to be inapplicable to the international arena, considering that, due to a lack of any 'international society', justice could only be *interstatal* and not trans- or supra-national. Other philosophers, such as Nagel, have shared this view, although Nagel's view derives from the argument that justice depends on the coordinated conduct of large numbers of people that must be backed up by a centralized monopoly of force.[55]

Even if one disagrees with Rawls or Nagel as to the possibility of application of justice on a global or regional level,[56] it is admittedly hard to conceive of the operation of a redistributive policy, such as Rawls' Difference Principle, at EU level. Theories such as those of Rawls, or Nagel, applied to the EU context, suggest that the lack of a

---

[52] W Sadurski, 'Social Justice and Legal Justice' (1984) *Law and Philosophy* 329.

[53] M Walzer, *Spheres of Justice* (New York: Basic Books, 1984).

[54] J Rawls, *The Law of Peoples* (Cambridge MA: Harvard University Press 2001).

[55] See T Nagel, 'The Problem of Global Justice' (2005) 33 *Philosophy and `Public Affairs* 115, in which Nagel prefers to look to other standards such as 'minimal humanitarian morality'.

[56] And many do disagree—eg for theories of justice applied to international level, see T Pogge (ed), *Global Justice* (Oxford: Blackwell, 2001); D Held, *Democracy and the Global Order: From the Modern State to Cosmopolitan Governance* (Stanford: Stanford University Press, 1996); C Beitz, *Political Theory and International Relations* (Princeton: Princeton University Press, 1979) (looking to a Kantian justification of international justice principles); B Barry, *Theories of Justice* (London: Harvester Wheatsheaf, 1989); M Nussbaum, 'Patriotism and Cosmopolitanism' in J Cohen (ed) *For Love of Country, debating the limits of patriotism* (Boston: Beacon Press, 1996).

European identity, or a European people, with true cross-national bonds of solidarity[57] and meaningful ties,[58] raises real problems, particularly with regard to the level of mutual cooperation and engagement with others thought necessary for social justice of the redistributive sort. There currently exists at EU level no deeply rooted supra-national community based on a substantive value consensus—even Habermas con-cedes that at present the EU lacks a sense of mutual political belonging (although he asserts the possibility of a future stronger EU identity grounded on a community of civic values rather than ethnic ties).[59]

Rawls's theory raises problems of distributive justice in the EU context, but prob-lems of corrective justice in the context of the AFSJ are equally salient. Although the phenomena of global terrorism, or organized crime, have been recognized to require regional or international approaches, criminal justice is often perceived as a matter that identifies the state. Criminal laws and procedures, it is argued, are cultural artefacts that reflect a wide, deep embedded background, and are problematic to transpose to a transnational context. This view is expressed in the work of jurists such as Pierre Legrand, Carol Harlow, and also sometimes that of Gunther Teubner.[60] Such theories raise arguments of a cultural nature against the possibility of a trans-national, EU corrective justice.

(B) The Pluralism of Justice

Therefore, one need not be a North American liberal philosopher to doubt the possibility of an overarching concept of justice for the EU. Further arguments, deriving from postmodern philosophy, relate theories of justice not to state sovereignty, but to pluralism and difference. For if EU law is pluralist, in the sense of encompassing many different and sometimes competing conceptions of law, then so also may be justice, with no single, unifying concept of it possible. Justice may need to be contemplated in three, or even manifold dimensions.[61] On this account, a unitary concept of justice,

---

[57] It is suggested that the Eurozone bailouts do not provide an example of interstate solidarity, as will be discussed below.

[58] See eg R Bellamy, 'The liberty of the postmoderns? Market and civic freedom within the EU?' LSE Working Paper, 2009.

[59] J Habermas, *The Divided West* (Cambridge: Polity Press, 2006).

[60] eg G Teubner, 'Legal Irritants: Good Faith in British law, or How Unifying Law Ends Up in New Differences' in F Snyder (ed) *The Europeanization of Law: The Legal Effects of European Integration* (Oxford: Hart Publishing, 2000); C Harlow, 'Voices of Difference in a Plural Community', in P Beaumont, C Lyons, and N Walker (eds), *Convergence and Divergence in European Public Law* (Oxford: Hart Publishing, 2002) 199–204; P Legrand, 'Against a European Civil Code', (1997) 60 MLR 44. On the other hand, some jurists point to a developing or even already existing 'harmonious convergence' in this area, as evidenced by measures such as the European definition of terrorism. eg Delmas-Marty, one of the expert proponents of the *Corpus Juris* project, asserts such a convergence, deeming it 'a new design of the legal landscape', M Delmas-Marty, *Towards a Truly Common Law: Europe as a laboratory for legal pluralism* (New York: Cambridge University Press, 2002), 13.

[61] eg N Fraser, *Scales of Justice: Reimagining political space in a globalizing world* (New York: Columbia University Press, 2009), 16, who writes of a 'three dimensional theory of justice'.

even if theoretically or practically possible, is inadequate, as a unitary concept denies to justice a multiplicity of perspectives, localities, and frames.

Postmodern accounts of justice, such as those Derrida or of Lyotard, which relate it strictly to context, to different 'language games', seem well suited to a multiplicity of laws. Contemporary theorists have cited 'otherness' as the basis of a postmodern justice[62] and impose a mandate on law to recognize the 'demand of the suffering other' as 'the non-essential essence, which the legal system needs in order to merit its necessary but currently absent claim to do justice'.[63] Such a demand requires us to recognize a plurality of different justices. Derrida's injunction is to embrace an ethics of responsibility, imposing the requirement of abandoning the abstract reason,[64] and to open scholarship to other disciplines, to pluralism, and to difference. As Peter Goodrich writes,

> (Derrida's) acknowledgement of the heteronomy of disciplines and knowledge fits well with the chaos of surfaces, of rhetorical fronts, of facades that Venturi and others had invoked in architecture and that Lyotard had already formulated neatly in stating that 'any attempt to state the law, for example, to place oneself in the position of enunciator of the universal prescription is obviously infatuation itself and absolute injustice.' Derrida's warning is that to impose a universal principle of justice is to ensure injustice to some. Justice, and in this the postmodern accounts concur, is plurality.[65]

Yet such a conclusion is not necessarily a morally attractive one. Just as legal pluralism has its downsides, so too does a pluralism of justice. A plurality of justices would not be only those of the suffering Other. Much contemporary law is privately created, and so may it be the case with justice. For example, much EU law occurs at a sub-state and operational level, agreed by groups of experts and professionals—almost acts of private law-creating with little state input (certainly very little from any parliament). Within the EU, good illustrations of this point may be found in the work of technical standardization (and also, indeed, in the many measures produced by committees in the Comitology process). In these fields, privately produced rules have played an important part in furthering EU integration—such as those of the technical experts who make up the European Committee for Standardization (CEN) who draw up harmonized technical standards for products throughout the EU. Nor can these just be dismissed as committees of technocrats—the issues that they deal with can prove surprisingly controversial—such as the BSE crisis, which converted animal feed into a political issue, and conveyed much publicity to the veterinary standards committee.

---

[62] Eg C Douzinas and R Warrington, *Justice Miscarried: Ethics and Aesthetics in Law* (New York/London: Harvester Wheatsheaf, 1994), 17.

[63] Douzinas and Warrington, 19.

[64] J Derrida, 'Force of Law' in D Cornell, M Rosenfeld, and D Carlson (eds), *Deconstruction and the Possibility of Justice* (New York: Routledge, 1992), 9.

[65] P Goodrich, 'Postmodern Justice' in A Sarat *et al.* (eds) *Law and the Humanities* (Cambridge: Cambridge University Press, 2010), 204, citing J Lyotard and J Thébaud, *Just Gaming* (Manchester: Manchester University Press, 1985), 99.

In the context of international commercial law, Günther Teubner highlighted a similar development of a new private, global 'lex mercatoria' as a 'Global Bukowina'.[66] Teubner took the term 'Global Bukowina' from the work of Eugen Ehrlich, a jurist working at the dawn of the twentieth century in Bukowina, a town then situated on the fringes of the Austro-Hungarian Empire, and now in Romania. Ehrlich's important observation was that what he called 'living law'—namely the measures and rules which local people actually worked with and observed, proved more important than official law created many hundreds of miles away in Imperial Vienna. Teubner finds similar moves afoot in contemporary global legal practice, in which global law firms and other corporate entities create their own brand of 'living law'—namely, rules best suited for themselves and their clients, often choosing to ignore any apparently relevant state law. For Teubner, this latter-day Global Bukowina reveals not only a fragmentation of and proliferation of laws, but also a burgeoning role for private law-making.[67]

Within EU criminal law and justice, there is the particular concern that such a phenomenon not only suffers problems of accountability, but also human rights and justice concerns where coercive law is enforced in private. For example, although systems such as the Schengen Information System[68] (which is an EU-wide system for the collection and exchange of information relating to immigration, policing and criminal law, for the purposes of law enforcement and immigration control) and Eurodac[69] (which is the European fingerprint database for identifying asylum seekers and irregular border-crossers) were set up with the involvement of EU Member States, and are associated or contained within EU institutions, 'once the various systems are up and going, they interlock through informal agreements and arrangements, rapidly expanding their practices—a kind of customary law, again in the diffuse zone around valid formal law. In other words, the systems are increasingly integrated "horizontally".'[70] Such a development has been described as a 'lex vigilatoria',[71] paralleling Teubner's 'lex merca-toria' in the public law field. It is just this sort of arrangement that is liable to fall under the radar of traditional constitutional law (or national criminal law).

Beyond such examples, there exists a danger of private, tailor-made interpretations of 'justice' substituting for publicly held and shared conceptions of justice. For example, the danger of custom-made justice of large multinationals, or private security firms in, for example, Iraq or Afghanistan, being asserted as equally valid as the justice of law courts and official law. If justice is acknowledged as a concept with a plurality of

---

[66] See G Teubner, '"Global Bukowina": Legal Pluralism in the World Society', in G Teubner (ed), *Global Law without a State* (Dartmouth: Aldershot, 1997).

[67] Some of the Eurozone crisis measures, detailed above, exemplify aspects of this, being rules crafted largely by and for technocrats and economists, extremely non-transparent to the European citizen.

[68] Council and Parliament Regulation (EC) 1987/2006 on the setting up of SIS II [2006] OJ L381/4.

[69] Council Regulation 2725/2000 concerning the establishment of 'Eurodac' for the comparison of finger-prints for the effective application of the Dublin Convention [2000] OJ L316/1.

[70] T Mathiesen, 'Lex Vigilatoria—Towards a control system without a state?' European Civil Liberties network, *Essays for Civil Liberties and Democracy in Europe,* available at: <http://www.ecln.org/essays/essay-7.pdf>

[71] Mathiesen, 3.

dimensions, contextualized in the form of 'language games', would it still be possible for it to retain any public, shared dimension? Even if we exclude 'private' justice, the issue of how to assess the justice of pluralistic law is an essential theme. How can we be sure which 'scale' of justice—local, national, regional, transnational, or even a combination (as in the interplay of various human rights mechanisms in Europe illustrated by the *Bosphorus* case) actually delivers justice? An embrace of pluralism does not necessarily solve the problem of justice in the EU.

A most anti-universalist, postmodern account, such as Lyotard's, asserts the pluralism of distinct and incompatible language games. Different concepts of justice are perceived as incommensurable, rather like a host of computer programs that will not speak to each other. Lyotard's account rejects both the possibility and desirability of a global concept of justice. To attempt legal convergence may result in what Teubner terms legal transplants as 'irritants'[72]—or an interference like that on the TV screen when the picture is blocked. The experience of implementing the European Arrest Warrant in EU states, which resulted in several constitutional courts finding its implementing provisions unconstitutional due to incompatibility with, for example, national prohibitions on the extradition of nationals,[73] has illustrated the problems and disruptions of introducing an EU criminal justice regime. Nancy Fraser has characterized the situation of incommensurability of different visions of justice as one of 'abnormal justice'—citing the furore over the Danish Mohammed cartoons as an example—in which theories of justice lack shared understandings and assumptions regarding the scope, agents, subjects, and spaces of justice, and thus debates about justice have, as she puts it, a 'freewheeling character'.[74]

At this point, justice may seem so elusive as to be a utopian ideal. Indeed, Derrida interprets justice as a complex of aporia—demanding immediate action, yet infinite time, knowledge, and wisdom in order to do 'justice'. According to Derrida,[75] justice is unquantifiable, it is 'deconstruction' but not, unlike law, deconstructible. Justice may also operate as a surrogate for value in a modern 'valueless' world, holding out the promise or hope of what is right, but always to come—never to be achieved in the here and now—a utopian ideal. Deleuze and Guattari, in their writings about Kafka, present a similar interpretation. For them, justice represents the desire for what is lacking in our life, what we yearn for in an empty, valueless world, for them, 'Justice is desire and not law'.[76] In this way justice is rendered far more ephemeral, extremely subjective, a subject of our fantasies.

---

[72] G Teubner, 'Legal Irritants: Good Faith in British Law' 61 MLR, 11.

[73] eg Polish Constitutional Court, *Re Enforcement of a European Arrest Warrant*, [2006] 1 CMLR 36; *Judgment of the German Constitutional Court of 18 July 2005*, 2 BvR 2236/04.

[74] Fraser (see n 61), 49. For accounts of 'abnormal' discourse see eg J Lyotard, *The Differend: Phrases in dispute* (Minneapolis: Minnesota University Press, 1988). See also Rorty, who distinguishes 'normal' discourse as conducted 'within an agreed-open set of conventions about what counts as relevant contribution' and 'abnormal' which sets them aside or ignores them: R Rorty, *Philosophy and the Mirror of Nature* (Princeton: Princeton University Press, 1979), 320.

[75] Derrida, (see n 62).

[76] G Deleuze and F Guattari, *Kafka: Toward A Minor Literature* (D Polan trans, Minneapolis: University of Minnesota Press, 1986), 43.

This might be one conclusion—justice as desire, as what is lacking, what will always be lacking, in the EU, in the world at large. But should we conclude here?

For perhaps we should be aware of the irony of Pascal's comment: 'A funny justice that ends at a river. Truth this side of the Pyrenees. Error on that.'[77] The post-war growth of international law, and of human rights treaties, undermines state-bounded claims for the realm of justice. Pressing problems which cut across boundaries—such as environment, global poverty, and terrorism—raise issues of justice which demand global or regional solutions. The denial of the possibility of international justice seems neither realistic nor normatively desirable. Kant might have feared the concept of a world-governing Leviathan, but he wrote in *On Perpetual Peace* that 'a violation of rights in one part of the world is felt everywhere',[78] a statement echoed by Martin Luther King, who wrote in 1963 in his *Letter from Birmingham City Jail*, 'Injustice anywhere is a threat to justice anywhere'.[79] Both statements reflect the interdependence of human life, outside of bounded communities, and, therefore, we cannot ignore the global or supranational dimensions of justice.

Pace Rawls or Lyotard, there exists no overwhelming scepticism as to the possibility of a concept of justice going beyond the state. For example, Williams interprets the EU as a cooperative enterprise, rather than one of mere coordination, asserting that cooperation implies development of an international community, or even society, which accepts a sense of solidarity and engagement with ethical commitments transcending borders.[80] However, I believe Williams to be overly optimistic as to the current state of solidarity and cooperation within the EU, especially given the pressures of recent enlargements, and the challenges of the financial crisis. *Contra* Williams, I do not believe that there currently exists sufficient solidarity and social community within the EU to support the substantive, social theory of justice which he proposes. It is the case that the Greek bailout, for example, was partly implemented under Article 122(1) TFEU, which states '...the Council, on a proposal from the Commission, may decide, in a spirit of solidarity between Member States, upon the measures appropriate to the economic situation ...'. However, aside from the fact that Article 122 was intended to apply in the case of natural disasters and energy catastrophes, and bailouts were specifically not intended under the mechanisms of EMU, these bailouts hardly provide examples of solidarity between Member States.[81] Who

---

[77] B Pascal, *Pensees* (AJ Krailsheimer trans, London: Penguin Books, 1966), 294.

[78] I Kant, 'Perpetual Peace: A Philosophical Sketch' in HS Reiss (ed), *Kant: Political Writings* (Cambridge: Cambridge University Press, 1991), 108.

[79] Martin Luther King, 'Letter from Birmingham city Jail' in H Bedau (ed), *Civil Disobedience in Focus* (London: Routledge 1991), 69.

[80] A Williams, 'Promoting Justice after Lisbon; groundwork for a new philosophy of EU law' (2010) OJLS 1.

[81] Notably, Art 125(1) TFEU, which could be seen as a 'no solidarity clause', provides: 'The Union shall not be liable for or assume the commitments of central governments, regional, local or other public authorities, other bodies governed by public law, or public undertakings of any Member State, without prejudice to mutual financial guarantees for the joint execution of a specific project. A Member State shall not be liable for or assume the commitments of central governments, regional, local or other public authorities, other bodies governed by public law, or public undertakings of another Member State, without prejudice to mutual financial

benefits from these 'solidarity' measures, undertaken with reluctance by states, and only under conditions of extreme austerity? It would seem to be indebted banks, or creditors, in other Member States, rather than the citizens of the states in difficulty who must face years of shrinking wages, unemployment, and shrivelling of public services and welfare.

This may not, however, mean that such solidarity is incapable of existing in the future. Perhaps the most well-known contemporary theory of post-national justice and solidarity is that of Jürgen Habermas.[82] Although Habermas acknowledges that no overarching EU political identity currently exists, he asserts that civic solidarity across borders is possible if certain conditions are fulfilled. For Habermas, the key question is not whether an EU identity exists, but whether processes of shared political opinion and will formation can develop through public discourse, in the way that national identities were constructed in the nineteenth century, and so produce the type of popular support formerly attracted by the state.[83] Although it may be very hard, given the lack of consensus as to social policy in the EU, to develop sufficient mutual solidarity necessary for redistributive principles of justice, requiring large transfers of wealth and heavier taxation, this does not rule out transnational justice of a less financially demanding kind in the EU based on the type of civil values vaunted by Habermas.

I believe views such as those of Derrida or Lyotard to be extreme, dictating a radical pluralism and isolationism of an almost hermetically sealed nature, which militate against shared and overarching notions of law and justice, and do not sit squarely with the history of EU integration. They also ignore a pluralism of a more accommodating kind. They miss, for example, a genuine desire and striving for convergence in much of EU law, as well as a willingness to work by way of *mutual recognition* in many areas rather than by harmonization. They ignore the existence of pan-European standards such as those of the ECHR, which work in tandem with a contrapunctual[84] margin of appreciation. They further ignore a crucial imperative of actually *doing justice*, which cannot be ignored just because legal systems are thought to be incompatible and justice immeasurably complex. We cannot end our quest for transnational justice with a counsel of despair or a yearning for unrealizable utopia.

5 Addressing the Confusion of Justice

One might ask, perhaps with a postmodern twist, how may we do justice to justice? The many conflicting and complex accounts of justice examined above are not

---

guarantees for the joint execution of a specific project.' It was necessary to introduce new measures, notably the ESM, in order to make provision for future loans to troubled Member States.

[82] Habermas (see n 19), 76.
[83] Habermas (see n 19), 76.
[84] M Poiares Maduro, 'Contrapunctual Law: Europe's Constitutional Pluralism in Action', in N Walker (ed) *Sovereignty in Transition* (Oxford: Hart Publishing, 2003), 521.

unexpected. Pluralism acknowledges that we live in a complex world, a complex legal world, and justice presents itself as every bit as conflicting, multi-dimensional, and paradoxical in nature as law. However, the discussion of justice so far raises a quandary for legal theory, and more particularly, for a theory of justice for the EU. What direction should legal and political theory of the EU take if it is, on the one hand, aware of the past problems caused by reasoning on justice, reasoning which during Modernity tended to take on a universalistic, homogenizing, even oppressive nature, but on the other hand, wants to avoid the pessimistic, aporetic reasoning of a postmodern jurisprudence? How to avoid these undesirable conclusions? On the one hand, too uniform and constricting an account of justice; on the other, a recognition of a plurality of justices which seems almost unworkable in its fixity with the ideal, and in its pessimism about the actual legal world.

With these concerns in mind, I start from the premise that it is unrealistic (at least at present) to offer an overarching, substantive, redistributionist theory of justice for the EU. The EU's own redistributive policies, such as the European Regional Development Fund and European Social Fund remain very limited in nature. The circumstances of the EU (namely a lack of consensus among its Member States as to the desirability of EU redistributive social welfare policies—a situation underlined by the rapidity with which austerity measures have been imposed under the Eurozone crisis) render achievement of a substantive justice particularly difficult—a state of affairs which inevitably results in continued injustice in the EU, of imbalances of rich and poor, in the absence of every Member State implementing equivalent redistributive policies of its own.[85] This is a regrettable state of affairs. Nor am I denying the desirability of social justice. It remains an important aspiration. I merely assert the unlikelihood of its realization within the EU at present and focus instead on what is possible and too often ignored. However, even if this assertion is not accepted, it should be noted that the rest of my argument still stands and can work in tandem with attempts for a substantive, redistributive theory of social justice.

The core of my argument is that, in addition to prioritizing the fulfilment of human rights, and at least *aspiring* to social justice, the EU should seek to achieve *legal* justice through the rule of law, and it is on this latter priority that the rest of this chapter focuses. It is just this type of justice, that assured by the rule of law, which has been notably absent in EU activities (and not only in the EU, but in many other legal environments, given the current attachment to flexibility and reflexivity in law-making, and a turn toward pluralism overall). However, this seemingly more limited aspiration for a 'legal' justice should by no means be taken as a counsel of despair. A great deal may be still be achieved by working with a more formal concept of justice which is still very ambitious in nature, given the problems of the EU.

Many of the most glaring injustices within the EU derive from its failure to observe some basic fundamental requirements and procedures; for example, lack of access to

---

[85] Perhaps one outcome of the Eurozone crisis will be an eventual fiscal union and greater harmonization of other policies, including social policy. But this would be immeasurably complex and beyond the scope of this chapter.

justice in certain areas (such as EU third pillar pre-Lisbon, or the inflexible standing requirements for judicial review under the pre-Lisbon Article 230 EC); overuse of broad, vague principles, and standards engendering unpredictability; less than transparent law-making slanted towards executive law-making (for example, a large amount of delegated law-making by the Commission, excessive use of confusing comitology procedures). EMU is a prime example of this lack of transparency—as one author recently commented: 'the EU's economic governance rules fail the test of transparency, because of their near-total complexity and unreadability, scattered across a dozen primary, secondary and soft-law sources, with more to come. This might be justifiable if the subject matter of these rules were a technical issue like chemicals regulation, but it is hardly acceptable that the basic rules on the EU's coordination and control of fundamental national economic decisions are essentially unintelligible.'[86] Part of the problem has been too great a reliance on 'output' legitimacy—that is, on efficient and effective results, irrespective of the means used to achieve them. Yet notably, the failure of EMU has also been a failure of output legitimacy. Remedying these situations requires no overarching substantive theory of justice for the EU, but rather recourse to a more formal, legal justice through the means of observance of the rule of law.[87]

An immediate objection, however, might be to question whether the rule of law can be characterized in any sense as justice at all, but rather as a mechanism for securing order and predictability in law, and society more generally. Such a concept of justice for the EU may seem to some to be too modest, to others unfashionable and too liberal in inclination. Considering my plea for justice to be taken seriously as a value for the EU, does this simply not reinforce the absence of justice in Article 2 TEU, by replacing it with the rule of law, which of course is listed as a value for the EU in Article 2, but which might be seen as either too minimal a form of justice or as not a form of justice at all? So this theory might seem to be lessening its sights, cleaving to a formal, anodyne value for the EU, rather than the more impassioning call of justice.

Yet I believe such criticisms are misplaced. For although the rule of law may not help us achieve perfectly just outcomes, nor deliver an impressive theory of ideal justice, it can help us to deter injustice.[88] Also, to stress—it is to be applied in conjunction with a rigorous application of human rights and a quest for social justice. It is not a complete vision of justice. The remainder of this chapter will argue strongly that the rule of law, understood and recast as *Critical Legal Justice*—taking it beyond the bland and empty assertion of the rule of law in Article 2 TEU—is a powerful form of justice, not an emaciated, second-class form of it. I also draw support from the fact that many critical theorists previously antagonistic to the rule of law now strongly

---

[86] Per S Peers, 'Analysis: Draft Agreement on Reinforced Economic Union (REU Treaty)' *Statewatch*, 21 December 2011.

[87] See eg S Douglas-Scott, 'The Rule of Law in the European Union—putting the security into the "Area of Freedom, Security and Justice"' [2004] 29 ELR 219.

[88] See A Sen *The Idea of Justice* (London: Allen Lane, 2009) who states that his overall project is not to deliver a perfect theory of justice but 'to clarify how we can proceed to address questions of enhancing justice and removing injustice'. (*Preface* at ix).

support its values,[89] and it has always received support from others who might have been supposed to be critical of it.[90] This theory of legal justice concentrates on what EU law *can do*, and I believe should do. It seeks what is possible, the achievement of some sort of justice in the here and now, while recognizing Derrida's point that justice can never fully be done, is always deferred in some way, is always still to come.

Indeed, the concept of critical legal justice is not modest at all. It aims to provide a theory of justice for the EU, but ultimately commits itself to an attempt for global justice, and thus is cosmopolitan in outlook. In combination with this, it asserts the crucial importance of the rule of law both nationally and internationally, in conjunction with an accountability for the creation, promulgation, and impact of all laws, public or private. It takes seriously the contemporary dilemma posed by complex pluralism, in terms of its under-provision of accountability and justice, a problem which seems to have been under-researched in legal theory. As a form of *legal* justice, it provides a distinctly legal solution to the problems of pluralism. The rule of law (and sometimes even human rights law) is apt to be derided as too liberal, imperialistic even; the tool of an oppressive use of law by Western capitalistic culture, a particular problem in a market-driven EU. This approach seeks to reclaim it from this derision, and in so doing to recast the rule of law in the particular form of critical legal justice— as a concept of justice rather than an anodyne formal concept.

6 A Common Conception of Justice? Critical Legal Justice

(A) The Rule of Law

The rule of law is what is very often understood by the concept of 'legal justice', importantly acknowledging it as a form of justice. For many it is also seen as playing a key role in the legitimacy of law—such legitimacy itself being somewhat of a holy grail of modern jurisprudence as well as of EU constitutional theory. There exists a strong intuition that power, position, and status should not corrupt, or 'maim' justice, and the rule of law functions to constrain and control the abuse of power. The rule of law has traditionally been seen to require laws to rest on legal norms that are general in character, relatively clear, certain, public, prospective, and stable, as well as recognizing the equality of subjects before the law.[91] It stresses the fixed and stable enforcement of general principles—legitimate expectations, formal rights of access to the courts,

---

[89] eg A Hutchinson, 'The Rule of Law Revisited: Democracy and Courts' in D Dyzenhaus (ed) *Recrafting the Rule of Law: The Limits of Legal Order* (Oxford: Hart Publishing, 1999); R West, *Reimagining Justice* (Burlington, VT: Ashgate, 2003).

[90] eg EP Thompson, *Whigs and Hunters* (London: Penguin Books, 1977); F Neumann, *The Rule of Law: Political Theory and the Legal System in Modern Society* (Leamington Spa: Berg, 1986).

[91] See both J Raz, 'The Rule of Law and its Virtue' (1977) 93 LQR 195 at 196, and L Fuller, *The Morality of Law* (New Haven: Yale University Press, 1965) who both give similar but not identical accounts to this.

equality before the law. Its benefits can be stated simply. Observance of the rule of law enhances certainty, predictability, and security both among individuals, and between citizens and government, as well as restricting governmental discretion. It restricts the abuse of power. Thus it has both private and public law functions—an attraction in the world of growing legal pluralism. Citizens are able to interact together, knowing in advance what rules will regulate conflicts, should there be any.

The rule of law is often seen as anathema to postmodern and critical theory because of the belief in the possibility of a justice of neutrality and of general application—and therefore derided as an ideology, a 'totalizing theory', of which we should be suspicious, or else as a useless bromide, a salve to cover a multitude of sins. As Beatty writes, 'Where the rule of law is endorsed by Abdul Rashid—an Afghan warlord, Mohammed Khatami when he was President of Iran, Robert Mugabe and George Bush, something cannot be right'.[92]

On the other hand, in contrast to supposedly 'thin' theories, some theorists take these qualities further, to include elements of a more substantive morality. 'Thick' theories of the rule of law tend to incorporate substantive notions of justice.[93] They conceive the rule of law more broadly as a set of ideals, whether understood in terms of protection of substantive human rights, specific forms of organized government, or particular economic arrangements such as free market capitalism. Philip Selznick characterizes these theories as 'more affirmative, more demanding, and in some ways a more risky point of view'.[94] These theories go beyond the abuse of power, to include values that need affirmative protection by law. Examples of those modern jurists who have advocated explicitly substantive rule of law theories include Ronald Dworkin, TRS Allan, Sir John Laws, and John Finnis. For Finnis, the rule of law, properly understood, comprises more than a *minima moralia*, indeed it can be seen as an element helping ensure the goodness of law, it is part of a holistic theory of law's place in society.

These further aspirations for the rule of law listed above highlight a range of benefits extending beyond legality and avoidance of arbitrariness to a richer notion of law. Yet the benefits of a 'thin' theory of the rule of law are often seen to lie in its very bareness, in its lack of prescriptions as to the substance of law. In its pared-down form, the rule of law is of use to a very broad range of systems and societies. It makes no stipulation as to content, sets no necessary requirements as to democratic government, or even human rights protection. Raz perceives a fundamental problem with thick theories: 'If the rule of law is the rule of the good law then to explain its nature is to propound a complete social philosophy. But if so the term lacks any useful function. We have no

[92] D Beatty, 'Law's Golden Rule' in G Palombella and N Walker (eds), *Relocating the Rule of Law* (Oxford: Hart Publishing, 2009), 100.

[93] See P Craig, 'Formal and Substantive Conceptions of the Rule of Law: An Analytical Framework' (1997) PL 467.

[94] P Selznick, 'Legal Cultures and the Rule of Law', in M Krygier, A Czarnota, and W Sadurski (eds), *The Rule of Law after Communism* (Aldershot: Ashgate, 2003), 21–38.

need to be converted to the rule of law just in order to discover that to believe in it is to believe that good should triumph.'[95]

(B) Critical Legal Justice

However, in proposing the theory of critical legal justice, I attempt to escape from the binary either/or, thick/thin categorizations which beset the rule of law and indeed modern conceptions of law more generally. Such juxtapositions and oppositions fail to capture the complexities of contemporary law.

The key to this recasting of the rule of law as critical legal justice, and to reconciling of the rule of law with complex or even chaotic legal pluralism, lies, I suggest, in adhering strongly to the *values* that the rule of law protects—namely in looking to its spirit, rather than overly focusing on the forms which it has taken in various contexts. I assert that a belief in the rule of law does not commit one to a consequent belief in law as rules, nor in law as a strongly bounded, autonomous discipline. It does not commit one to the legal theory of legal positivism—nor to any other legal theory for that matter. Further, I also argue that the rule of law does not violate substantive equality, nor is it blind to difference, because of its apparent focus on a philosophy of neutral, formal equality. To do all of this (naturally no small order) it is necessary to reclaim the rule of law and to re-imagine it. That is why I prefer to recast this concept as Critical Legal Justice, in order to distinguish it in perception from discredited,[96] understandings of the rule of law. I also wish to identify it more clearly with *justice*, rather than with the bland identification of the rule of law as a value in Article 2 TEU, whose content is empty and undefined.[97]

There exists no single model for the rule of law.[98] Yet this should not mean that its value is lessened, nor that it may be dismissed as incoherent or essentially contested. Rather, I believe it suggests that we should acknowledge that there exist different ways of furthering the values it serves. What are these values? Surely at its base lies the opposition to unrestrained, despotic power, to be achieved through the accountability of power, and correlative emphasis on freedom and equality which are enhanced by restraining power. In order to reclaim the rule of law, it is necessary to focus on these values rather than on specific, contingent, historical practices which have sometimes been used to further these values, otherwise there is a danger of believing that

---

[95] Raz (see n 91), 196.

[96] Namely, those understandings of the rule of law which have been perceived as overly formalist and blind to difference.

[97] Notably the rule of law is nowhere defined in the EU Treaties and different Member States have different understandings of it, according to their diverse legal traditions—ie *Etat de Droit* in France, *Rechtstaat* in Germany, and so on. See also L Pech, '"A Union Founded on the Rule of Law": Meaning and Reality of the Rule of Law as a Constitutional Principle of EU Law' (2010) 6 *European Constitutional Law Review* 359, for further elucidation.

[98] Selznick makes this point, see M Krygier, 'Philip Selznick: Incipient Law, State Law and the Rule of Law', in J van Schooten and JM Verschuuren (eds), *International Governance and Law: State Regulation and Non-State Law* (Cheltenham: EE Elgar, 2008), 31–55.

contingent practices are in fact the essence of the rule of law—a fault which Dicey might be said to have committed by identifying the rule of law with its rather singular form under Victorian constitutional law.[99] In this way, the danger of 'goal displace-ment'[100] may be avoided, whereby practices introduced as a means to serve as a way of achieving the goals of the rule of law—for example, identifying it with a system of law as rules, or with thick or thin versions of it—become identified with the rule of law itself. So, for example, although principles of legality, in their capacity to aid the calculability and transparency of the law, and enable people to plan their lives, may serve the aims of the rule of law at certain times, they will not always be the best means to ensure the constraint of power. An overemphasis on predictability, rule-bound behaviour, and calculability may itself become oppressive.

With its associations of order, regularity, proportionality, and equality there is something geometric or architectonic about the rule of law—a contrast with the 'chaos of surfaces' and 'rhetorical fronts'[101] of postmodernity—and seemingly the reverse of the chaotic trajectories and vortices of much contemporary law. The rule of law requires that law consist of standards, sometimes even described as 'rules'. This may seem difficult in a legal world where 'the model of rules' may no longer clearly be applicable. And yet, the very fact of complex trajectories and perspectives might suggest a reason why this structural component is needed more than ever—as a bulwark against, a counterpoint to, injustice, a means of containing the chaos of the legal universe. It does not require that actual, substantive laws form rule-like systems, but rather that certain structural components be applied to shore up laws, or even eject them where necessary.

It is also particularly needed in the EU. The rule of law and proceduralism in the EU have been attacked as insisting on 'integration through law', and overwhelmingly through the actions of the Court of Justice, and the pressing of free-movement principles which ignore policy and social-market interests. Yet the *lack* of the rule of law has been glaring and damaging in areas of EU affairs. For example in the lack of access to courts in the criminal law pillar of EU (at least until the Lisbon Treaty), or in the lack of institutional balance which has granted too much power to unelected unaccountable agencies such as Eurojust and Europol; in less than transparent, almost secretive law-making;[102] and in the non-transparent measures of the ESM and 'six pack' which result in the inability of Eurozone Member States to predict whether and what disciplinary action may be taken against them—this suggests a *dearth* rather than the presence of the rule of law. The experience of actions taken in the course of the 'war on terror', such as the willingness of some EU states to accept landing of US flights in

---

[99] AV Dicey, *The Law of the Constitution*, 10th edn (London: Macmillan, 1961).

[100] M Krygier, 'False Dichotomies, Real Perplexities and the Rule of Law', in A Sajó (ed), *Human Rights with Modesty: The Problem of Universalism*, (Leiden/Boston: Martinus Nijhoff, 2004) 251–77.

[101] See Goodrich (see n 65).

[102] See eg Case C-345/06 *Gottfried Heinrich* [2009] ECR 000.

the course of 'extraordinary rendition',[103] and the unwillingness of the EU to take any action against those states under Article 7 TEU, also suggests that the rule of law, along with human rights, is likely to be lost in a search for 'expedient' measures.

Yet before I complete my proposal of Critical Legal Justice for the EU, I must first engage more closely with its critique—in particular, that it is an impoverished theory of justice, and that it is too closely linked to capitalism.

7 Addressing the Critiques

(A) An Impoverished Theory of Justice?

This critique derides formal justice and formal or thin versions of the rule of law as 'morally impoverished', 'the shabby remnant of the sum total of virtues that was once called justice' where now 'only a *minima moralia* remains'.[104] This critique is salient, given that my call for the absent value of justice for the EU to be filled by a recasting of the present value of the rule of law in Article 2 may be seen as carrying a risk of downgrading justice to something lesser. Naturally, as I do not wish to be associated with a 'morally impoverished' theory of justice for the EU, this critique must be addressed.

Lon Fuller did not believe the rule of law to be morally impoverished. Fuller stressed the link of the rule of law with freedom, describing his eight canons or principles of legality as 'the inner morality of law'[105]—and argued for their intimate association with a moral view of the relation between citizen and authorities, and with their ability to support normative grounds for believing that citizens have a moral obligation to obey the law. He believed that they indicated and mandated an element of reciprocity between government and citizen, established by the observation of certain types of rules. The building of such reciprocity is very important if the EU is to work toward establishing a European identity and the growth of solidarity necessary for developing social justice. Although, in the context of the Hart-Fuller debate, Hart famously suggested that Fuller's 'internal morality of law' consisted of no more than principles of efficiency, which could be 'compatible with very great iniquity',[106] Fuller vehemently denied Hart's critique. Fuller believed that compliance with the principles of legality increased the capacity of law to become *good* law, and that it was extremely difficult, if not impossible, for a regime bent on immoral or unsavoury ends to achieve them through the rule of law.[107] He gave Nazi Germany as an example, which, he felt, far from using formally viable laws to

---

[103] For which now see the application lodged against Poland, *Al Nashiri v Poland,* in the European Court of Human Rights on 6 May 2011, in which it is alleged that Poland hosted a secret CIA prison at a military intelligence training base in Stare Kiejkuty where the applicant was held incommunicado and tortured.

[104] A Heller *Beyond Justice* (New York: Blackwell, 1987).

[105] Fuller's 'internal morality of law' basically follows the key tenets of the rule of law.

[106] See eg HLA Hart, *Essays in Jurisprudence and Philosophy* (Oxford: Oxford University Press, 1983), 207.

[107] L Fuller, 'Positivism and Fidelity to Law—A Reply to Professor Hart' (1958) 71 *Harvard Law Review* 630.

achieve substantively immoral ends, had actually failed to produce 'law' at all,[108] due to its near complete lack of consistency, publicity, clarity, and coherence.

Further, Nonet and Selznick, writing in *The Moral Commonwealth*,[109] suggested that the guarantee of the rule of law was in some sort of way *a vehicle or conduit for more substantive justice*, in that it nurtures a greater commitment to respect for persons, and self-restraint in the use of power—that is, the belief that the rule of law contains the germ of substantive justice, that consistency, treating like cases alike, are not just empty, barren propositions but necessary components in the quest for substantive justice.

Note that I am not here committing to critical legal justice as either thick or thin, formal or substantive justice. However, I believe these responses to the impoverishment critique are persuasive indications that even thin versions of the rule of law are not productive of only an impoverished, diminished justice. It suggests that the values that the rule of law serves are variegated or levelled—on the one hand, a 'cynical' aspect requiring the simple function of constraining power and its abuse, on the other, a more aspirational one of enabling individuals to plan their lives productively and securely in the context of a transparent, reciprocal administration of law.

(B) A Critique of Liberalism

An important series of critiques attack the rule of law not so much for an impoverished formalism and legalism, but rather for its association with the broader doctrine of liberalism and associated notions. In particular, these critiques assault the rule of law for its connection with the perceived 'totalizing' and universalizing doctrine of liberalism and its lack of attention to the Other. These may be linked to the arguments made by those who promote radical pluralist theories of justice such as those discussed in earlier sections.

However, these critiques rest on mistaken assumptions about the rule of law and a naivety about the kinds of social relations which might be possible in its absence. First, surely the rule of law does recognize otherness and singularity because the requirements that it sets, that law be predictable, open, impartial, etc, are set as requirements precisely in order to ensure that each individual's very different qualities are respected, that each is treated as an individual, able to pursue their different agendas within the structures set by law. Mary Wollstonecraft's *A Vindication of the Rights of Women*[110] very forcefully makes the point that the rights of women must be protected just as much as the rights of man—justice must have a universal reach, *precisely in order to*

---

[108] An opinion which was shared by Franz Neumann in *Behemoth: The Structure And Practice Of National Socialism* (New York and Evanston: Harper Torchbooks, 1966); also H Arendt, *The Origins of Totalitarianism* (Cleveland, 1958).

[109] P Nonet and P Selznick, *The Moral Commonwealth: Social Theory and the Promise of Community* (Berkeley, California: University of California Press, 1992).

[110] M Wollstonecraft, *A Vindication of the Rights of Men and A Vindication of the Rights of Woman* (Cambridge: Cambridge University Press, 1995).

recognize and give the Other their due. All too often categorization of difference and otherness have been used to *defeat* claims for recognition of identity, as in the US Supreme Court decision in *Plessy v Ferguson* in 1896,[111] in which it held that the US Federal Constitution's 14th Amendment requirement of equal protection of black people under the law could be construed as 'separate but equal'—'separate' treatment being different from that of white people, and in reality not equal at all—thus justifying racial segregation for a further sixty years until its subsequent decision in *Brown v Board of Education.*[112] Indeed, the undeniable disadvantage which has been suffered by women and by members of cultural minorities in modern society should be seen not as a failure of the rule of law itself but rather as a failure of society to respect and realize the values of the rule of law.

On the contrary, the alternatives proposed to the rule of law—such as a politics of recognition, or an ethics of care—may actually function to the detriment of disadvantaged groups. They are often advocated on the basis of some sort of face-to-face relationship, or at least a direct, caring community, somehow perceived as possible in the absence of the more formal requirements of equality imposed by the rule of law. Yet surely they may work to the further disadvantage of those already treated unequally? These critiques fail to capture the sense in which law operates in the public sphere, a sphere not overly characterized by care and consideration and recognition of the other (least of all in the EU!) regardless of how desirable such an ethic of consideration for strangers may be. As Patricia Williams has written, those who are discriminated against and disadvantaged seek not intimacy but the status of 'bargainers of separate worth, distinct power, sufficient rights'.[113]

Nor does the rule of law *prevent* a more substantive justice, on account of embedded circumstances, from application. It sets a necessary minimum. Different regimes may then go further. This is important in the context of social justice in the EU, where it may not be possible for the EU to pursue its own, fully developed, redistributive policies of social justice, but this should not mean that EU law should interfere with those states that do pursue such policies.

It is also, however, undeniable that the rule of law has a connection with a certain type of liberalism, which serves as a basis for some criticism of it. A trajectory may be mapped out from John Locke through Karl Marx and Max Weber to Friedrich von Hayek, which posits an 'elective affinity' between the rule of law and capitalism.[114] And capitalism of course has its dark side. The rule of law has sometimes played a historical role in protecting private property, especially when it was interpreted as supporting a right to accumulate private wealth.

---

[111] *Plessy v Ferguson* 163 US 537 (1896).

[112] *Brown v Board of Education of Topeka*, 347 US 483 (1954).

[113] P Williams, *The Alchemy of Race and Rights* (Cambridge MA: Harvard University Press, 1991).

[114] See eg W Scheuerman, *Liberal Democracy And The Social Acceleration Of Time* (Baltimore: Johns Hopkins Press, 2004).

Both liberal and critical accounts highlight certain features as indicative of this connection between capitalism and the rule of law. For example, capitalism and economic development require certainty, predictability, and security in order to flourish. By securing these measures, it is possible to ensure the stability of contract law and predict the costs and benefits of particular transactions. The origins of the EU may be partly explained in this way. Both neo- and ordo-liberals justified the creation and existence of the EU by its capacity to support free market rights, guaranteeing private property, and exchange of goods, based around the economic nexus, or even 'constitution', of the Treaty of Rome.[115] The rule of law offers protective functions for business, sheltering trade against political arbitrariness, or expropriation of property rights.[116] Thus capitalism is able to focus on commerce rather than on shielding its existing efforts from capricious conduct.[117]

Later critical theorists (for example, those of the Frankfurt School) and radical theorists of the 1960s and 70s, also derided the rule of law, believing it unable to deliver on its promises, as well as creating a 'false consciousness'.[118] In focusing on its close ties with capitalism, Marxist and critical theory insists that this supposed universal, formal, neutral rule of law is in fact a concept inseparable from a particular kind of social and political order. Later critiques share with Marx the assertion that the perception of a formal equality in entities of vastly different power undermines the rule of law itself.[119] Thus it is possible for corporations to exploit their great financial resources to vigorously protect certain rights, such as property or business confidentiality in anti-trust cases, to the detriment of 'just' outcomes. The alternative for most such critics is to turn to an account that focusses on substantive social justice, to be brought about by political means instead.

However, there are two ways in which these all of these supposed 'anti-liberal' critiques fail to give credit to the rule of law as a means for assessing legitimacy and justice. The first is that they fail to account sufficiently for the fact that many of the situations they describe are ones in which the rule of law and its principles have been *abused* and usurped, and its features and components distorted, or substantive features imported (such as overemphasis on property rights) which do not necessarily belong to it. These might be characterized as what Habermas has called 'distorted

---

[115] See eg HP Ipsen, 'Europaische Verfassung—Nationale Verfassung' (1987) *Europarecht*, 195.

[116] However, this does not necessarily give rise to an excessively formalistic or codified law. The English common law courts have had a long tradition of protecting property. The willingness of the common law courts to protect freedom of enterprise, and the development of the rule of law in this way, was characterized by Max Weber as the 'England problem', namely an example of legal justice achieved through laws that were not formal and codified.

[117] W Scheuermann, *Frankfurt School Perspectives on Globalization, Democracy, and the Law* (New York: Routledge, 2008), and B Tamanaha, *On the Rule of Law: History, Politics, Theory* (Cambridge: Cambridge University Press, 2004); B Tamanaha, 'The "Dark Side" of the Relationship Between the Rule of Law and Liberalism', (2008) 33 *NYU Journal of Law and Liberty* 1.

[118] An accusation made by Critical Legal Studies scholars.

[119] Indeed even Hayek stated that 'It cannot be denied that the rule of law produces economic inequality'; F Hayek, *The Road to Serfdom*, (Chicago: University of Chicago Press, 2007), 117.

communication', as well as by instrumental reason—the use of the 'language' of human rights and the rule of law with the ulterior aim of market colonization, rather than human rights and justice as ends in themselves.[120] Few of the situations they critique are actually ones in which morally obnoxious, substantive laws have been enforced and imposed in ways compliant with the rule of law; that is, clearly, unambiguously, and transparently. For example, Mansell *et al.*[121] critique the shift in contractual arrangements for money lending to developing countries since the end of the Second World War, as illustrating the pernicious effects of the rule of law because it has involved a move from formerly clear terms and conditions and fixed-term interest rates, to a situation where it is now much easier for one (more powerful) party to unilaterally alter the contract, especially interest rates. This shift has aided the transfer of wealth from poor to rich, and, in this way, it has been possible for scarce resources to be taken from those in abject poverty to enrich those who already enjoy massive material wealth. Such a shift with such consequences is clearly hugely unjust, but hardly the result of transparent, unambiguous rule-of-law conditions—rather of their opposite. Is contract law to blame for this, as the critique of liberalism suggests? In this context, the relevant 'contracts' may simply be managerial orders written up in legalese but lacking the party autonomy (at least for the less powerful party) and formal attributes of contract law. Similar critiques might be made of Eurozone measures such as Greek bailout, the ESM, or the enforcement rules under the 2011 'six-pack legislation'. The move from clear contractual terms to those favouring the dominant party is not an example of the rule of law in action, but rather of the thwarting of its principles. The remedy for this type of abuse or bad faith is surely not to dispense with some sort of rule of law altogether but to ensure that it is not corrupted.

Secondly, and relatedly, these critiques fail to take into account a change in business practices—a preference for more flexible regulation, rather than predictability and stability—the sorts of changes noted by Teubner in his *Global Bukowina*,[122] or characterized in the EU by the growing reliance on flexibility and soft law. Many of the practices so castigated rely not on formal rule of law, but anti-formalist practices designed with very specific interests of business in mind, indeed, on highly complex financial trading rules akin to gambling. Here, a short reflection on, and diversion into the work of Franz Neumann is instructive and valuable.

Franz Neumann, an anti-Nazi legal theorist working in the conditions of Weimar Germany,[123] might not appear the most obvious ally of the rule of law against the Marxist critique of global capitalism (especially as he himself was a member of the Frankfurt critical theory school), but in fact in his work, he sought to rehabilitate

---

[120] Habermas, (see n 42 59), 57.

[121] See also L Nader and U Mattei, *Plunder: When the Rule of Law is Illegal* (Wiley-Blackwell, 2008).

[122] See Teubner (see n 66).

[123] The post-Great War Weimar Constitution had attempted to reconcile economic liberties and social rights—indeed it was unique at the time for doing this.

the rule of law and ascribe an ethical function to it. In his writings on Weimar Germany, Neumann crucially noted growing anti-formalist trends in business law, which appeared to reduce capitalism's traditional reliance on stable, predictable laws, its traditional 'elective affinity' with formal law. Large monopolistic enterprises were able to manipulate law creation and application, and by their economic power produce measures that suited their needs rather than general laws applicable to all.

Neumann acknowledged, along with many others, that in Weimar Germany there existed a crisis of the rule of law but, unlike many of his contemporaries, such as Carl Schmitt, he thought that the solution to this crisis could be found in the rule of law itself, which he believed had unfulfilled potential to support democracy. Neumann acknowledged that in situations of social and political inequality the 'neutral' rule of law could serve to maintain existing inequalities, but he believed that the 'social rule of law' (which Neumann also considered could be found in the Weimar Constitution) could be used to rectify these relations of inequality and dominance. Neumann asserted that the answer to the crisis was not to undermine the rule of law but to transform society in a democratic and anti-capitalist direction.[124] For him, the troublesome, undemocratic aspect of the rule of law lay in the way it had been manipulated by capitalism. Indeed Neumann believed that, and described in his 1944 work, *Behemoth*,[125] how Nazi Germany's subsequent annihilation of rational, formal law could be traced to capitalist abuses denying equal application of the rule of law. To counter this, there could be departure from the formal rule of law to redistribute private property—a shifting of the understanding of the rule of law from one dominated by economic liberalism to one rooted in social democratic formulations. He believed that the rule of law could actually be enhanced by social and political relations of equality. If property were to be more equally divided, there would be less danger of social crises and panics, and of crime committed against property, and all the unpredictability that follow from these. Further, he considered that access to justice and to good lawyers could and should be more fairly distributed, in keeping with general principles of equality that would apply (in Lockean terminology) to 'the favourite at court', as much as to 'the countryman at plough'.[126]

Admittedly, some of Neumann's proposed recasting of the rule of law would be difficult to achieve in the EU as a polity overall. It would be hard to transform the EU in anti-capitalist ways through the redistribution of private property when capitalist free-market principles lie at its very centre, and when such a move would be vetoed by

---

[124] F Neumann, 'The Change in the Function of Law in Modern Society' in W Scheuerman (ed) *The Rule of Law Under Siege: Selected Essays of Franz L. Neumann and Otto Kirchheimer* (Berkeley: University of California Press, 1996) and 'The Social Significance of the Basic Laws in the Weimar Constitution' in K Tribe (ed) *Social Democracy and the Rule of Law: Otto Kirchheimer and Franz Neumann*, (London: Allen and Unwin, 1987); see also R Cotterrell, 'The Rule of Law in Transition: Revisiting Franz Neumann's sociology of legality' (1996) *Social and Legal Studies* 456.

[125] F Neumann, *Behemoth: The Structure And Practice Of National Socialism* (New York and Evanston: Harper Torchbooks, 1966).

[126] J Locke, *Second Treatise on Civil Government* (Oxford: Basil Blackwell, 1982), ch 11.

many of its Member States. But this does not mean that there should not be greater equality within the EU, nor that we should fail to recognize, where present, the seeds of a social rule of law in EU law, and attempt to work with it where possible. At present, it is all too easy for certain business interests to capture the EU agenda, and to manipulate its less than transparent processes. In any case, in order for EMU to survive, the EU may have either to adopt a fiscal union and a greater embrace of the presently (unsatisfactory) flanking policies, or drastically cut back in its ambition.

But most crucially, Neumann also asserted (and here his thinking was very much in line with traditional liberal theorists, Locke and Bentham) that ambiguous laws presented a danger to democracy, because they could be used to advance the needs of social elites. Therefore for Neumann, it was essential to preserve formal law as an element of the liberal democratic heritage, even in a post-capitalist legal order. In this way, Neumann's approach provided a more optimistic prognosis for rescuing, reinventing, and rendering more robust the rule of law, and may be contrasted to the pessimism of other members of the Frankfurt School, such as the melancholy of Adorno and Horkheimer's *Dialectic of Enlightenment*, or Marcuse's revolutionary approach.

Contemporary EU law possesses similar anti-formal trends to those noted by Neumann—often being flexible and discretionary with vague clauses and general principles (the 'fundamental freedoms' in the EU Treaty are prime examples of this). Cases such as *Viking Line* and *Laval*, for all that they have been vaunted as examples of an over-strenuous 'integration through law', of relentless application of the rule of law as rule of free trade, are not examples of the application of the rule of law. For they present an unpredictable, slanted application of a principle (that is, free movement of goods) in favour of business. What will constitute a 'restriction' on trade, what restrictions will be proportionate, becomes ever more uncertain, except in its favouring of business over anything else. The classification of a fundamental right as a restriction on trade is surely the example of the unfortunate cohabitation of EU law with capitalism rather than the predictable application of clear law? The failure to take Article 7 TEU seriously and to suspend membership of those states which do not take fundamental rights seriously as it requires, or the proliferation of a comitology so Byzantine as to lack transparency, are other examples.[127] A further glaring example is provided by the failure of the EU Council to enforce the Stability Pact rules against its earlier infringers, Germany and France, in 2003, illustrating a willingness to be 'flexible' and not proceed against more powerful countries, and thus not treat all parties equally (a clear breach of the rule of law).[128] What we see are ad hoc,

---

[127] The proposed REU treaty envisages new legislative procedures, whereby action will go ahead unless there is a reverse Qualified Majority Vote against it, but as the legislative provisions in the EU Treaties themselves may not be altered, it seems that this would only be applicable by way of a 'gentleman's agreement'—see 'The Eurozone's Treaties—That Clever Mr Legal' *The Economist* 18/12/2011.

[128] See on this eg G Majone, 'Monetary Union and the Politicization of Europe' at 16, Keynote speech at the Euroacademia International Conference, Vienna, 8–10 December 2011, paper accessible at: <http://euroacademia. eu/wordpress/wp-content/uploads/papers/december/Giandomenico_Majone-Monetary_Union_and_the_Politici-zation_of_Europe.pdf>.

discretionary trends rather than traditional virtues associated with the rule of law. Neumann's analysis illustrates how dissatisfaction with law's links with capitalism, as well as concern over legal indeterminacy, need not lead to rejection of the rule of law, deconstruction, nor the trashing of law.

8 Reclaiming the Rule of Law as Critical Legal Justice

I conclude with a reminder of EP Thompson's defence of the rule of law. EP Thompson famously described the rule of law as an 'unqualified human good',[129] 'a cultural achievement of universal significance', adding that to deny this good 'in this dangerous century when the resources and pretensions of power continue to enlarge, a desperate error of intellectual abstraction ... a self fulfilling error ... which encourages us to disarm ourselves before power'.[130] EP Thompson rejected the orthodox Marxist position that the rule of law creates a false consciousness which enables the powerful to manipulate its forms to their own advantage. Instead, he understood the rule of law as an ideology requiring ruling classes to accept a degree of self-limitation to govern effectively. Thompson also rejected the nihilism of the Marxist critique, expressing his opinion thus: 'law surely *is* an instrument of class power, but that is not all it is'.[131] Thompson believed that law could and should function as a form of mediation, to impose 'effective inhibitions on power'.[132]

Therefore EP Thompson provides us with an account of law that acknowledges both law's ability to function as ideology, to aid those in power, and one that recognizes law's ability to do the reverse—to constrain the powerful. This is because law itself is complex and contradictory, and incapable of being captured by straightjacket modern theories of law, such as those that conceive of law as a system of rules. The subtlety and sensitivity of EP Thompson's approach lies in his recognition of this fact.

The rule of law has its contradictions, its opposites, its 'both/ands'.[133] Its nature may shift, using different means to fulfil its values in different contexts. The rule of law may be seen as providing accommodation between some sort of yin and yang, or between an idealist, aspirational Apollonian rule-like order for law and a Dionysian undisciplined fury of politics,[134] between formalism and chaos, the contradictory and contrarian impulses noted by Thompson, an almost Hegelian dialectic, in the interplay of law and power, as evidenced by, for example, the seventeenth-century battles between the monarchy and Lord Chief Justice Coke over the royal prerogative, or in the law suits in

---

[129] EP Thompson, *Whigs and Hunters* (London: Penguin Books, 1977), 266.

[130] EP Thompson, 266.

[131] EP Thompson, 266.

[132] EP Thompson, 267.

[133] For some, its takes the form of the principle of proportionality—see D Beatty (see n 92), 100.

[134] Per Robin West, *Re-Imagining Justice: Progressive Interpretations of Formal Equality, Rights, and the Rule of Law* (Ashgate, 1993), at 5.

the UK and US over indefinite detention in the war on terror.[135] Ruti Teitel has also suggested that there exists 'a tension between the rule of law as backward looking and forward looking, as settled versus dynamic'.[136] It also *restrains*—that is, places inhibitions on power as well as *enables*—by making a space for a realm of aspiration through law. As Selznick recognized, it is a blend of scepticism and confidence. And it will fulfil these functions in different ways in different times. In this way it can protect the various forms of pluralism. As already stressed, it is a minimum. It is necessary—there can be no fair and just system without it, yet it will not always be sufficient to ensure such a system.

This may sound vague. There is no detailed blueprint for institutional design, no formula for its realization. Yet there are crucial requirements, although these may be achieved in different ways over different time periods. They relate to the key values that the rule of law serves. It must be possible to constrain power. Nor must law be administered and implemented in ways that are arbitrary. Law must also be sufficiently intelligible and public so that people may be able to comply with it and use it to guide and plan their lives. Finally, it is very important to acknowledge that, for it to exist, it is necessary that people *believe* in and be committed to the rule of law. Trust and belief in law must be nurtured and earned, which is not very likely if only elites have access to law creation and enforcement. This is of particular concern in the EU, whose citizens do not identify with, nor are truly committed to it. And why should they? They observe debacles such as that of the Santer Commission resignation due to mismanagement and fraud, the crisis of the Eurozone, through which the EU, intended to foster prosperity, imposes ever greater austerity, and find EU law-making impenetrable, its laws unreadable, its results undesirable. Fuller stressed the reciprocity between citizens and authorities nurtured by the rule of law. Evidence suggests that compliance with, for example, tax laws will be greatly increased if people believe they are being treated with respect and procedural fairness by revenue authorities, in addition to believing that tax laws are substantively, distributively fair.[137] If people neither expect the rule of law nor insist on it when officials move to compromise its application, it is soon corrupted and replaced by rule of power. Scepticism, the absence of a conception of justice, wreaks its own havoc. Solzhenitsyn highlighted the absence of such a tradition of law as the basic explanation for the failure of the Russian people to resist the Bolshevik takeover through its nocturnal arrests and ad hoc political trials and executions.[138] This is why it is important that crimes committed by those in government, such as in the context of extraordinary rendition, be accounted for, so that a firm and progressive tradition of, and belief in, the rule of law be maintained.

---

[135] See eg *A v Secretary of State for the Home Department* [2004] AC 56.

[136] R Teitel 'Transitional Rule of Law' in A M Krygier, A Czarnota, and W Sadurski (eds), *The Rule of Law after Communism* (Aldershot: Ashgate, 2003).

[137] J Braithwaite, *Restorative Justice and Responsive Regulation* (Oxford: Oxford University Press, 2001).

[138] A Solzhenitsyn, *The Gulag Archipelago*. Vol 3. trans H Willetts (New York: Harper and Row, 1978).

The EU presents extraordinary obstacles to the accomplishment of a transnational theory of justice. At present, its problems seem almost insurmountable, the EU itself facing the prospect of either disintegration[139] or the imposition of a fiscal union which its citizens would not wish for it. Neither of these prospects seems palatable. The Byzantine complexity of its operations both renders injustice and lack of accountability all the more likely, and justice all the more difficult to achieve. A monist, universalizing type of justice risks deadening the vibrancy of its many legal cultures, of failing to do justice in many singular instant cases. An alternative embrace of plural justices risks the creation of a neo-medieval feudal world of private, self-serving justices, or of failing to meet some very real needs for an overarching transnational justice.

And yet it is imperative that the EU values justice, that it takes justice seriously, in a way which it has not done to date. In this situation, one cannot be overambitious for the EU, nor yet inactive. The way forward, I suggest, lies in reimagining the rule of law in a critical, dynamic way, in rejecting pessimism, yet also realizing and acknowledging that flexible, reflexive legal pluralism brings its own problems that may find their solutions only through the reimagining and reworking of some rather old ideas of classical legal thought.

---

[139] See comments by Joschka Fischer, 'Europe and the "new German question"' Eurozine, 6 April 2011.

INDEX